HF5549.5.J63 H64 2006
0134109687274
Hosie, Peter,

Happy-p
manage
c2

Happy-Performing Managers

NEW HORIZONS IN MANAGEMENT

Series Editor: Cary L. Cooper, CBE, *Professor of Organisational Psychology and Health*, Lancaster University Management School, Lancaster University, UK.

This important series makes a significant contribution to the development of management thought. This field has expanded dramatically in recent years and the series provides an invaluable forum for the publication of high quality work in management science, human resource management, organisational behaviour, marketing, management information systems, operations management, business ethics, strategic management and international management.

The main emphasis of the series is on the development and application of new, original ideas. International in its approach, it will include some of the best theoretical and empirical work from both well-established researchers and the new generation of scholars.

Titles in the series include:

Human Nature and Organisation Theory
On the Economic Approach to Institutional Organisation
Sigmund Wagner-Tsukamoto

Organisational Relationships in the Networking Age
The Dynamics of Identity Formation and Bonding
Edited by Willem Koot, Peter Leisink and Paul Verweel

Islamic Perspectives on Management and Organisation
Abbas J. Ali

Supporting Women's Career Advancement
Challenges and Opportunities
Edited by Ronald J. Burke and Mary C. Mattis

Research Companion to Organisational Health Psychology
Edited by Alexander-Stamatios G. Antoniou and Cary L. Cooper

Innovation and Knowledge Management
The Cancer Information Service Research Consortium
J. David Johnson

Managing Emotions in Mergers and Acquisitions
Verena Kusstatscher and Cary L. Cooper

Employment of Women in Chinese Cultures
Half the Sky
Cherlyn Granrose

Competing Values Leadership
Creating Value in Organisations
Kim S. Cameron, Robert E. Quinn, Jeff DeGraff and Anjan V. Thakor

Happy-Performing Managers

The Impact of Affective Wellbeing and Intrinsic Job Satisfaction in the Workplace

Dr Peter J. Hosie
Curtin Business School, Curtin University of Technology, Australia

Dr Peter P. Sevastos
School of Psychology, Curtin University of Technology, Australia

Professor Cary L. Cooper
Lancaster University Management School, Lancaster University, England

NEW HORIZONS IN MANAGEMENT

Edward Elgar
Cheltenham, UK • Northhampton, MA, USA

© Peter J. Hosie, Peter P. Sevastos, Cary L. Cooper 2006

All rights reserved. No part of this publication may be reproduced, stored in a retrieval system or transmitted in any form or by any means, electronic, mechanical or photocopying, recording, or otherwise without the prior permission of the publisher.

Published by
Edward Elgar Publishing Limited
Glensanda House
Montpellier Parade
Cheltenham
Glos GL50 1UA
UK

Edward Elgar Publishing, Inc.
136 West Street
Suite 202
Northampton
Massachusetts 01060
USA

A catalogue record for this book
is available from the British Library

Library of Congress Cataloguing in Publication Data
Hosie, Peter, 1957–
  Happy performing managers : the impact of affective wellbeing and intrinsic job satisfaction in the workplace / Peter Hosie, Peter Sevastos, Cary Cooper.
      p. cm. — (New horizons in management)
  Includes bibliographical references and index.
  1. Job satisfaction. 2. Performance. 3. Management. I. Sevastos, Peter, 1938– II. Cooper, Cary L. III. Title. IV. Series.

  HF5549.5.J63H64 2006
  658.4'0714—dc22   2006002695

ISBN-13: 978 1 84542 148 9
ISBN-10: 1 84542 148 5

Printed and bound in Great Britain by MPG Books Ltd, Bodmin, Cornwall

Contents

Acknowledgements	*vi*
About the Authors	*ix*
Foreword	*x*
Preface: Putting the head back on the body	*xiii*
PART 1: THE 'HAPPY-PRODUCTIVE WORKER' THESIS	**1**
1. Introduction: Exploring the links between happiness, job satisfaction and job performance	3
2. Job-related affective wellbeing and intrinsic job satisfaction	27
3. Managers' job performance	73
4. Links between affective wellbeing, intrinsic job satisfaction and managers' job performance	107
PART 2: METHODOLOGY, MEASUREMENT AND RESULTS	**119**
5. Research methodology and data analysis techniques	121
6. Measuring managers' performance	159
7. Analysing the relationship between affective wellbeing, intrinsic job satisfaction and performance	211
PART 3: FINDINGS, IMPLICATIONS AND CONTRIBUTION TO ORGANISATIONAL THEORY AND MANAGEMENT PRACTICE	**233**
8. Conclusion: Surviving and thriving in the age of surprises	235
Appendices	*329*
References	*355*
Index	*431*

Acknowledgements

Completing the research that forms the basis of this book has been made possible by the inspiration and encouragement of many people. Dr Peter Sevastos, from the School of Psychology, Curtin University of Technology, gave exceptional conceptual guidance, methodological advice for the development of the survey, the analysis and interpretation of the data. Professor Nick Forster, the supervisor of this research, from The University of Western Australia's Graduate School of Management, provided exemplary intellectual guidance, enduring patience and encouragement throughout this demanding process.

I wish to express my gratitude to my initial research supervisor Rob Donovan, Professor School of Marketing, Curtin University of Technology, who undertook the initial methodological supervision of the research, including extensive input into the questionnaire design and preliminary analysis of the data. Expert medical advice about affective wellbeing was generously provided by Dr Ken Orr and Dr Hans Stampfer. My close friends, Mr Keith Saggers, Ms Samantha Jacobs, Mr Jolyon Forsyth, Dr Linda Herkenhoff, Professor Tony Travaglione, Dr Robert Brown, Mr Anthony Penney, and my father Mr John Hosie provided inspiration and valuable feedback on drafts of the thesis that kept me grounded to the realities of organisational life throughout the process.

Key Western Australian and international organisations and managers supported this study. All are thanked for their ongoing support throughout the many vicissitudes of this complex and challenging process. This book was made possible by the time and effort that managers and executives took in completing the questionnaire.

Financial support for this study was provided in the form of an Australian Postgraduate Stipend, scholarship and grants from The University of Western Australia. The Curtin Business School provided timely funding to assist with the completion of the book. Long may the Australian Government and Universities invest in the intellectual development of Australian postgraduates.

Last, a heartfelt thank you to my wife, Ying Li, family and friends for their constant patience and support.

Peter J. Hosie

Acknowledgements

The publishers wish to thank the following who have kindly given permission for the use of copyright material.

Peter Sevastos for Figure 2.2 'Principal axes of affective wellbeing space' and Figure 2.4 'Attitudinal and affective outcomes of complexity on work pressure'. *Job-related affective wellbeing and its relation to intrinsic job satisfaction.* Unpublished PhD Thesis. Curtin University.

Cornell University, The Johnson School for Figure 2.3 'Demand control model' by Karasek, R.A. 1979, Job demands, job decision latitude, and mental strain: Implications for job redesign, *Administrative Science Quarterly, 24*(2), 285-308.

Oxford University Press for Figure 2.6 'Vitamin model' and Table 2.1 'Affective wellbeing axes of measurement and levels of specificity' by Warr, P. 1987, *Work, unemployment and mental health.* Oxford University Press, Oxford. By permission of Oxford University Press.

Taylor and Francis for Table 2.2 'Vitamin Model' by Warr, P. 1994, A conceptual framework for the study of work and mental health, *Work & Stress, 8,*(2), 84-97.

Pearson Education, Inc for Figure 3.1 'Managerial roles' by from Mintzberg, Henry: *THE NATURE OF MANAGERIAL WORK,* © 1980. Adapted with the permission of Pearson Education, Inc., Upper Saddle River, NJ.

John Wiley & Sons, Inc. for Figure 3.2 'Competing values framework' by Quinn, R.E., Faerman, S.R., Thompson, M.P. & McGrath, M.R. 1996, *Becoming a Master Manager,* John Wiley & Sons, Inc

John Wiley & Sons, Inc. for Figure 3.3 'Model of effective performance' and Figure 3.4 'Integrated Model of Effective Job Performance and Skills Typology' by Boyatzis, R.E. 1982, *The competent manager: A model for effective performance,* John Wiley & Sons, Inc.

Blackwell Publishing for Table 3.2 'A lay model of least and most effective managers' by Cammock, P., Nilakant, V., & Dakin, S. 1995, Developing a lay model of managerial effectiveness: A social constructionist perspective, *Journal of Management Studies, 32*(4), 443-474.

Lawrence Erlbaum Associates, Publishers for Figure 3.5 'Theory of individual differences in contextual and task performance' by Motowidlo, S.J., Borman, W.C. & Schmit, M.J. 1979, A theory of individual differences in task and contextual performance, *Human Performance, 10*(2), 71-83

Sage Publications Ltd. for Figure 3.6 'Antecedents, determinants and components of performance' reproduced with permission from Neal, A. & Griffin, M.A. 1999, Developing a model of individual performance, *Asia Pacific Journal of Human Resources, 37*(2) 44-59. © Australasian Human

Resources Institute, 1999, by permission of Sage Publications Ltd.

Pearson Education, Inc. for Figure 8.3 'Job characteristics model' From Hackman, J. Richard and Oldham, Greg R.: *WORK REDESIGN* © 1980 by Addison-Wesley Publishing Co., inc. Adapted with the permission of Pearson Education, Inc., Upper Saddle River, NJ.

American Psychological Association and Frank L Schmidt for f 'Determinants of job performance' by Schmidt, F.L., Hunter, J.E. & Outerbridge, A.N., Impact of job experience and ability on job knowledge, work sample performance, and supervisory ratings of job performance, *Journal of Applied Psychology*, *71*, 432-439. American Psychological Association. Adapted with permission.

Blackwell Publishing for Figure 8.6 'Measures of work performance' by Quinones, M.A., Ford, K.J., & Teachout, M.S. 1995, The relationship between work experience and job performance: A conceptual and meta-analytic review, *Personnel Psychology*, *48*, 887-910.

Every effort has been made to trace all the copyright holders but if any have been inadvertently overlooked the publishers will be pleased to make the necessary arrangements at the first opportunity.

About the Authors

Dr Peter J. Hosie is the CBS Post Doctoral Research Fellow at Curtin Business School, Curtin University of Technology, Perth, Western Australia. Peter has published over 50 articles and reports which have been widely cited in international articles, papers and reports. His primary research interests include the relationships between managers' job-related affective wellbeing, intrinsic job satisfaction and performance, crisis and security management, and Technologically-Mediated Learning.

Dr Peter P. Sevastos is a lecturer in the School of Psychology at Curtin University of Technology, where he specialises in organisational psychology and human resource management. His current research involves job-related affective wellbeing and job satisfaction, work-family conflict, job insecurity, emotional labour, organisational commitment and contextual performance.

Professor Cary L. Cooper CBE is currently Professor of Organisational Psychology and Health at the Lancaster University Management School, Lancaster University, UK and Pro Vice Chancellor (External Relations) of the university. He is the immediate past President of the British Academy of Management and the author of numerous books and articles and a Fellow of the Royal Society of Medicine, Royal Society of Arts, Royal Society of Health, the British Psychological Society and the American Academy of Management. In 2001, he was awarded the Commander of the British Empire (CBE) for his contributions to organisational health. Professor Cooper also leads a prominent new UK government think tank The Sunningdale Institute, in the National School of Government in the Cabinet Office.

Foreword

Organisations today are facing an increasingly turbulent and challenging environment. Several factors have emerged to raise the performance and competitiveness bar. These include globalisation, increased use of technology, more demanding customers and clients, a more diverse workforce, competition from low cost developing countries, and changing employee attitudes towards the role of work in one's life. As this was being written, several organisations with long histories such as the Big 3 automakers, were making dramatic workforce reductions in efforts to remain viable. What can organisations do to increase their performance?

This volume convincingly argues for paying more attention to increasing the positive emotions of employees. It builds on the common assumption that happy workers are productive workers, what researchers referred to as the 'happy-productive worker' hypothesis. There has been considerable debate on the validity of this assumption, first expressed over 70 years ago. Happy employees were productive employees, spurring the Human Relations movement in the 1960s. In the 1970s, however some researchers offered up the notion that performance led to job satisfaction or happiness, reversing the order of causation. During the past decade, the research pendulum has swung back in support of the 'happy-productive worker' hypothesis.

Happy-Performing Managers makes a strong case for this position. Peter J. Hosie, Peter P. Sevastos and Cary L. Cooper CBE report the results of a study of Australian managers and their supervisors, collecting data from each pair separately. They show, using sophisticated data analyses, that managers reporting higher levels of affective wellbeing and higher levels of intrinsic job satisfaction perform at higher levels of both task and contextual job performance, the latter measured using both self and supervisor ratings.

These findings fit in well with three broader trends in our understanding of managerial behaviour and peak performing organisations. The first trend is reflected in greater attention now being paid to the role of emotions in the workplace (Boyatzis & McKee, 2005). The second is the emphasis on positive organisational behaviour concepts (Cameron, Dutton, & Quinn, 2003). Managerial research for too long has been concerned with negative work experiences and outcomes such as anxiety and depression, job insecurity, burnout, cynicism, absenteeism, turnover, and disengagement from one's work. This volume places the critical role of positive emotions front and centre as factors in job performance. This includes concepts such as flow, optimism, hope, community and citizenship.

The next question becomes one of identifying the levers available to managers to unleash positive emotions, the practical implications that follow from their findings. Their suggestions here are consistent with a third emerging trend gaining prominence over the past decade - that of Strategic Human Resource Management. These include job design, providing challenging and supportive work environments, attending to the attraction, selection and retention of capable managers, providing performance feedback, rewarding high levels of contribution, offering training and development opportunities, addressing health and safety concerns and reducing workplace stressors (Burke & Cooper, 2006). It goes without saying that enlightened organisational leadership is critical to the implementation of these Strategic Human Resource Management practices.

This volume lays out the links between organisational conditions shown to increase both affective wellbeing and intrinsic job satisfaction, and between these two positive emotional states and job performance, in a clear and compelling way. We know a lot about developing high performing organisations that satisfy the needs of their employees and employers (Lawler, 2003). This volume offers such a roadmap. It's time we got on with it.

Ronald J. Burke PhD
Professor of Organisational Behaviour
Schulich School of Business
York University
Toronto, Ontario, Canada

Preface: Putting the head back on the body

Squeezing the pips - 1/2 x 2 x 3 - whereby half as many people are being paid twice as much, to produce three times more.
(Handy, 1996)

INTRODUCTION

In the new millennium happiness in the workplace is well and truly back in vogue. There has been an explosion of research into happiness, optimism and positive character traits. In the 21st century, effective managers' performance is even more central to the success of organisations. So what is driving the surge of interest into employees' and managers' job happiness and performance?

The 'happy-productive worker' thesis

Few conundrums have captured and held the imagination of organisational researchers and practitioners as has the 'happy-productive worker' thesis. Proponents of this idea are convinced 'a happy worker is a good worker'. Support for this 'commonsense theory' is based on the belief that happy workers are believed to perform better than their unhappy co-workers.

A variation on the enduring debate of this happiness-productivity theme, the 'happy-performing managers' proposition, is tackled in this book. Specifically, a thorough investigation is undertaken into the impact of two important aspects of job happiness - affective wellbeing and intrinsic job satisfaction - on managers' contextual and task performance.

Notwithstanding the general support for the 'happy-productive worker' idea, decades of research have been unable to establish a strong link between employees' happiness and their performance. Perhaps the 'happy-productive worker' thesis is a self-sustaining 'urban myth', founded in opinion but lacking empirical support. Evidence presented in this book definitely suggests otherwise. An important shift in addressing this age old conundrum is evolving the 'productive worker' thesis into the 'performing managers' proposition.

The 'happy-performing managers' proposition

The metamorphosis of the 'happy-productive worker' thesis into the 'happy-performing managers' proposition is determined by the need to focus on managers' performance in the workplace. As a butterfly is not simply a better caterpillar, the construct 'managers' performance' is likewise different to 'workers' productivity'. As such, a manager is not simply an improved worker but is differentiated by a more complex array of roles and responsibilities informed by the function of contextual and task performance. The findings and observations in this book explain the 'happy-performing managers' proposition and how this intersects with the needs of organisations. The challenge is to reorientate our thinking to utilise modes of managers' performance which are relevant and realistic for organisational success.

This book establishes the veracity of the 'happy-performing managers' proposition. From a broader perspective this discourse is also intended to contribute to the debate over what underpins human performance at work. Findings about employees' affective wellbeing, intrinsic job satisfaction and performance also apply to managers who are invariably employees in some form. Whether the affect/satisfaction-performance relationship applies to managers is answered in a study by the principal author (Hosie, 2003).

Comprehensive and robust evidence was found to support the existence of a definite relationship between managers' job-related affective wellbeing, intrinsic job satisfaction and performance. Specific indicators of affective wellbeing and intrinsic job satisfaction were found to be reliable predictors of certain dimensions of managers' contextual and task performance. Insights are supplied into how positive affective wellbeing and intrinsic job satisfaction are related to enhanced managerial performance, whereas conversely, poor affective wellbeing indicates diminished performance. In addition, the structure and substance of managers' contextual and task performance is established to a standard previously unachievable. Evidence to support these assertions is provided in the proceeding chapters.

SOMEONE KEEPS MOVING THE GOAL POSTS

Pressures to manage within increasingly complex local, national and global workplace dynamics are greater than ever before. Restructuring, deregulation, tariff reductions, outsourcing, rapid uptake of technology, and internationalisation are just some of the competitive forces that continue to drive organisations to intensify workplace productivity. Long working hours, necessitated by 'downshifting' as organisations move from 'lean to mean', are impacting on individual performance and organisational productivity from the 'shop floor to the top floor'. The consequence of these pressures is that fewer managers are doing considerably more work in an effort to maintain and improve organisational output.

Seismic shifts across all sectors of the workplace have led to a more insecure work environment where managers are expected to efficiently perform a wider range of complex functions. Increasingly, knowledge creation and the management of knowledge workers are a particularly challenging aspect of the ever expanding roles expected of managers. These unsettling and relentless changes to the work environment are having a major impact on managers at all levels in the workplace which are in turn flowing through to the employees.

In combination, pressures for change and the propensity of organisations to maximise short term financial and capital gain are impacting on the wellbeing of managers. Not surprisingly, this scenario is a potential source of considerable anguish for managers as well as for the organisations who rely on their performance. So, how do these developments relate to the emergence of the 'happy-performing managers' proposition?

Successful organisations are dependent on managers who are capable of achieving and fully maintaining high levels of individual job performance. Individual and collective levels of managers' performance are therefore critical to the survival and prosperity of small and large scale organisations alike. In this ultra competitive marketplace, the capacity of organisations to be productive and profitable is highly reliant on managers creating a work environment where employees are fully engaged, contributing and committed.

OTHERWISE ENGAGED

A negative outcome of ignoring managers' affective wellbeing and intrinsic job satisfaction is the alarming and counterproductive increase in actively disengaged and demotivated employees. Diminished performance resulting from disengaged employees is very costly to organisations. Attaining and sustaining the optimal individual and collective performance of employees in this dynamic environment is impacting on the happiness and performance of managers.

Increased pressures to lift individual performance in organisations have reached critical mass. Managers are now expected to produce higher quality goods and services with fewer resources. The result of economic rationalisation and globalisation is directly attributable to the high incidence of stress, burnout and depression amongst employees and managers. These dramatic and ongoing changes to the macro economic environment have driven substantial changes in managers' roles and their performance.

Managers are now expected to perform in a business context where significantly increased performance is demanded. These circumstances have given rise to a generation of managers who are both 'time poor' and 'wellbeing poor'. Eventually, declines in managers' performance will hamper the capacity of organisations and national economies to create wealth. In short, these changes in the workplace emphasise the need to understand how managers can retain their positive affective wellbeing by working smarter and faster, rather than harder and longer.

HAPPINESS IS BACK IN TOWN

In January 2005, Time magazine published an entire issue on the 'New Science of Happiness'. Philosophers, neuroscientists, pharmacologists, political scientists, geneticists, linguists and all manner of 'new age' gurus are contributing to this timely dialogue on happiness in the workplace. Seldom has an academic quest come into play so quickly and deliberately.

Curiously, most interest about happiness is being generated at the edges of the two 'dismal sciences' of economics and psychology. The worlds of this 'dreary duo' converged in 2002, when the Nobel Prize for Economics was awarded for the first time to a psychologist. Princeton Professor Daniel Kahneman received the laurel for investigating a phenomenon known as the 'hedonic treadmill' which explains why money can buy happiness but does not continue to keep people happy (Bagnall, 2004). Economists of various persuasions are now furiously devising equations for putting a dollar value on the stuff that relates to happiness.

London School of Economics Professor Lord Layard (2005), author of *Happiness: Lessons from a New Science*, provides evidence of the relationship between increasing wealth and decreasing happiness in the developed world. Layard contends that economic growth does not automatically increase social harmony. Instead, Layard argues for the unpopular position that increased taxes can improve the work-life balance of citizens and increase overall wellbeing in a society. Likewise, Paul Martin's (2005) book *Making Happy People: the Nature of Happiness and its Origins in Childhood* argues that people are not always motivated by financial incentives, and in some cases, financial incentives can actually reduce motivation instead of increasing it.

Layard and Martin both pay homage to Jeremy Bentham, the great 18th century utilitarian philosopher. Bentham (1776) argued that the purpose of public policy should be to maximise the sum of happiness in society, as expressed by the famous utilitarian doctrine of 'the greatest happiness for the greatest number'. This assertion led economists to focus on the utility of happiness which was assumed to be measurable and comparable across people. Noted economists of the late 20th century, such as Paul Samuelson in the USA, and John Hicks from the UK, spawned the movement to transform economics into a 'hard science'.

An unfortunate consequence of this fundamental shift in direction of thinking was that it encouraged economists to abandon the 'pursuit of happiness' for the more narrow 'pursuit of wealth'. Increased personal wealth was naively assumed to lead to enhanced individual happiness. In the process, a mythical rational being, the 'economic man (sic)' was created in an attempt to help economists deal with their dark quantitative condition of 'physics envy'. In a *History of Happiness in Economics*, Luigino Bruni (2005) alerts us to the economists' long held misunderstanding that all humans are rational beings who find happiness in maximising their personal utility. Clearly, happiness is back on the public policy agenda. Some devilish elements in popular media have also picked up on the interest in wellbeing in the workplace.

STRESS IS NO LAUGHING MATTER

Interest in employee affective wellbeing has reached the level of public recognition where parodies are beginning to emerge. An amusing but somewhat disturbing example is Edwards's (2004) satirical book, *Stress in the Workplace: How to Cause it*. In the foreword Edwards posits that 'mental anguish is the precursor of productivity and claims to have exploded the myth that a 'happy company is a productive one'. Inventive and imaginative ways are provided in his book to ensure that employees will reach their full potential in a work environment that is 'bereft of comfort and languor'. Fierce competition between employees is argued to be a great motivator, and those who feel good are berated for being too placid. Edwards's tongue in cheek position reverses contemporary advice about the preference and desirability of harmonious workplaces.

In David Williamson's play *Influence* (2005), Ziggy Blasko, a 'shock-jock' radio announcer poses the question, 'Stress - we all have stress in our lives. So what's new?' Ziggy is enraged by this 'stress is bad talk', angrily proclaiming that, 'All this rubbish about stress and depression is just a way to keep thousands of so-called mental health gurus making a good living'.

Another pertinent example comes from the television series *The Office* (BBC, 2005; Gervais & Merchant, 1995). The central character is David Brent, the 'boss from hell' who is a 'legend in his own lunchbox' who is portrayed as an overtly happy manager who specialises in facilitating a cheerful working environment by being an 'entertaining manager'. He delights in telling gratuitous off-colour jokes and is blissfully unaware of the effect of this obnoxious behaviour on those around him. Despite the obvious misery wreaked on his hapless employees, Brent is convinced he is performing exceptionally well as a manager by using a self-professed skill as 'professional entertainer' to create a happy working environment.

Maybe the unpalatable reality for workers is the realisation that miserable managers, who adopt oppressive work practices, are just as effective as happy ones! But this position flies in the face of the evidence that overbearing attitudes, appalling communications and toxic personalities all have a major negative effect on employee motivation. Certainly, evidence in this book provides a clear positive link between managers' happiness and their performance.

MAGNITUDE OF MENTAL HEALTH PROBLEMS IN THE WORKPLACE

Organisations that do not take care of workplace happiness ultimately experience diminished individual performance. Over the last decade, mental health problems in the workplace have increased substantially for both industry and government. Approximately one in ten employees is estimated to be suffering from depression, anxiety, stress or burnout in Australia, the European Union, USA and Canada. Some 3–4% of GNP worldwide is estimated to be expended on mental health problems in the workplace, which are rapidly becoming the most common reasons for allocating disability pensions and for people opting to retire early.

By 2020, it is estimated that depression will be the most common health problem in the workplace. In addition to workers' compensation claims, employers who fail to address workplace mental illness can expect to pay increased higher compensation and insurance premiums. Other problems in the workplace resulting from neglecting to look after managers' affective wellbeing are: disengagement, absenteeism, higher staff turnover, higher accident rates, reduced productivity and morale.

International estimates of the cost of depleted mental health show a consistent and disturbing trend. The incidence of mental health problems in the workplace is an issue that has reached alarming proportions. The resultant cost to organisations and nation-states is unacceptably high and is increasing exponentially. This has led governments in developed countries to begin to legislate to force organisations to accept the consequence of inappropriate management decisions on employee health. Deteriorations in managers' affective wellbeing and intrinsic job satisfaction can lead to disillusionment and burnout, which is likely to result in severe reductions in individual job performance.

All this bad news about diminished mental health in the workplace needs to be countervailed by good news. Evidence of this can be found in a new movement rapidly taking hold - Positive Organisational Scholarship (POS).

POS - PUTTING THE HEAD BACK ON THE BODY

The last decade has seen a growing movement in psychology to abandon the exclusive focus on the dark side of human existence with a preference to explore a more positive view of the mind. This book contributes to the emerging movement of POS; a health model based on the premise that understanding and enabling human potential will create a positive path to human and organisational wellbeing.

There are sound social and economic reasons for promoting happiness through healthy workplace practices. Numerous studies have shown that happy people are successful in many aspects of life, including friendship, marriage, income, health and job performance. A link between happiness-success is evident where positive affect engenders success (Lyubomirsky, King, & Diener, 2005). In essence, the POS movement is metaphorically reattaching the head on to the body of Organisational and Occupational Psychology. Likewise, this book confronts the challenge to explore new models, theories and ideas about managers' that contribute to enhancing affective wellbeing and performance in the workplace.

HOW TO GET THE BEST FROM THIS BOOK

In writing this book, the authors have attempted to strike a delicate balance between retaining the integrity of the original research process, while making the commentary accessible. As with any scholarly contribution, there are certain conventions required to satisfy academic standards and practices. These protocols have been kept to a minimum to ensure that an informed reader can participate in the reasoning and research process, albeit given the convoluted and contradictory nature of the past 70 years of research in the area.

This book will appeal to academics, postgraduate students, human resource practitioners, executives and managers who are interested in gaining a deeper understanding of the factors that underpin human performance in the workplace. The material is valuable reference reading for postgraduate and honours level undergraduate students in the fields of Management, Human Resource Management, Organisational Behaviour,

Organisational and Occupational and Industrial Psychology. Academic researchers and postgraduate students should find the methodology useful to scrutinise, critique and replicate.

Informed and inquisitive practitioners who are seeking advanced professional development will benefit in terms of their increased understanding of what determines human performance in the workplace. Management consultants will find this book a useful desk reference of the latest thinking and evidence of 'optimal practice' in human performance in the workplace. Equally, executives will find compelling information on how to effectively develop the affective wellbeing and performance of the managers with whom they work. Others will be drawn to the substance of the findings and may therefore elect to skim the details of the methodology. These readers may not necessarily find the detail about the research process to be essential reading but will find throughout many useful suggestions for managing. In particular, useful advice can be found in the concluding chapter on how to improve the work environment and performance of managers and employees.

FINDINGS

A *Partial Model of Managers' Affective Wellbeing, Intrinsic Job Satisfaction and Performance* ('Partial Model') was developed from the literature to investigate the research questions and test the hypotheses.

Of particular importance was the development and testing of the Measurement Model of managers' job performance. An 8-Dimensional Measurement Model of managers' performance, derived from the contemporary literature, was tested to differentiate the structure of managers' contextual and task performance. The job performance construct was found to consist of four contextual dimensions (Endorsing, supporting and defending organisational objectives; Helping and cooperating with others; Persisting with enthusiasm and extra effort to complete task activities successfully; Following organisational rules and procedures) and four task dimensions (Monitoring and controlling resources; Technical proficiency; Influencing others; and Delegating to others).

Managers' self-report of affective wellbeing and intrinsic job satisfaction was related to superiors' ratings of managers' performance to ensure the independence of the measures. Specific indicators of affective wellbeing and intrinsic job satisfaction were found to be reliable predictors of certain dimensions of managers' performance. Affective wellbeing (Positive Affect, Intrinsic Job Satisfaction) was found to be positively associated with a dimension of superiors' report on task performance

(Influencing).

Positive Affect is a personality trait characteristic associated with extraversion, a personality characteristic that is central to managerial jobs in dealing with peers, superiors, subordinates and external constituents. Positive Affect is an 'activation based' affect which enables managers to influence decisions from which they derive considerable Intrinsic Job Satisfaction, which has a substantial cognitive component. Possibly, the opportunity to influence decisions within an organisation may also result in enhanced Intrinsic Job Satisfaction and heightened affective wellbeing. Thus, managers who have elevated Positive Affect and Intrinsic Job Satisfaction are more likely to influence decisions.

A more complex relationship was found between affective wellbeing, intrinsic job satisfaction and performance. Positive associations between dimensions of self-report for affective wellbeing (Positive Affect, Anxiety and Relaxation) were found to be negatively associated with dimensions of superiors' reports (i.e., downward) on managers' task performance (Monitoring) and contextual performance (Following). Positive Affect, Anxiety and Relaxation were positively associated with the contextual performance variable, Following, and the task performance variable Monitoring.

Negative Affect and Enthusiasm were negatively associated with the performance variable Technical but positively associated with Monitoring and Following. This indicated that high arousal (Positive Affect with Negative Affect) was present, but these administrative job tasks were not found to be particularly motivating, as indicated by negative Enthusiasm but positive Relaxation. This finding indicates that managers will experience a degree of arousal but low distress when undertaking administrative or transactional roles. Managers with high Positive Affect are likely to experience elevated anxiety but have opportunities for relaxation that lead to acceptable levels of affective wellbeing when undertaking work involving Monitoring and Following.

An alternative explanation for these associations may be that aspects of managers' jobs requiring essentially transactional or administrative roles (negative Technical, with positive Monitoring and Following) may lead to high arousal with Positive Affect and Anxiety, but provide opportunities for Relaxation in conjunction with negative Enthusiasm and Negative Affect. A positive association with Monitoring and Following indicated that these performance characteristics require vigilance and consequently high arousal (Anxiety and Positive Affect with the attendant Negative Affect), but do not lead to a motivating environment (negative Enthusiasm).

Notably, managers reported Positive Affect, a personality trait, to be the only variable common to both dimensions of contextual and task performance, indicating that it is a prerequisite for managerial jobs. From this finding it could be inferred that successful managers will have a positive disposition to work.

METHODOLOGY

This book is intended to fill the niche between methodology textbooks, which are sometimes too general for students undertaking advanced field research, and academic articles which often address rather specific techniques. An empirical case study is used in this book to explain how to apply advanced statistical techniques for field research. A cross-sectional questionnaire was administered to managers from a range of private, public, and third sector occupational groupings in 19 Western Australian organisations. An empirical methodology was used to test the hypotheses to enable the research questions to be answered and to develop the Partial Model.

Items for the questionnaire were derived from established affective wellbeing and intrinsic job satisfaction scales. Managers' contextual and task performance scales were devised from the literature. Self-report data were used to measure affective wellbeing and intrinsic job satisfaction, while superiors' ratings (by the person to whom managers report) provided an evaluation of managers' contextual and task performance. The statistical techniques employed are explained in enough detail to permit critique and replication.

Of particular interest to Occupational and Organisational Psychology researchers is the methodology used to develop the Measurement Model of managers' performance. Testing of the Measurement Model of managers' performance is described in detail, including Exploratory and Confirmatory Factor Analysis, multigroup analyses, and accounting for the biasing effect of method.

Advanced statistical techniques are used to analyse these important managerial issues by measuring the substance and structure of job performance to a standard previously unachievable. Another distinctive contribution to the field is the use of Canonical Correlation and Standard Multiple Regression to analyse the multifarious relationships between managers' affective wellbeing, intrinsic job satisfaction and their contextual and task performance.

STRUCTURE OF THIS BOOK

This book is divided into three parts and eight chapters:

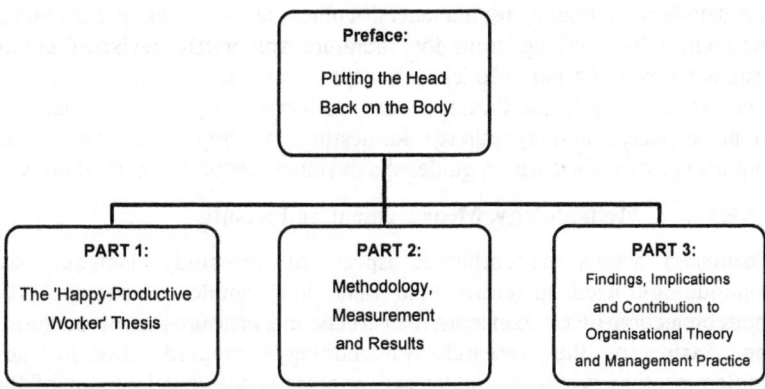

PART 1: The 'Happy-Productive Worker' Thesis

Chapter 1 begins the review of the existing literature on managers' affective wellbeing, intrinsic job satisfaction and performance. Chapters 2–4 cover the relevant and influential literature that forms the theoretical foundations of the research reported in this book. The extensive literature in these areas is then evaluated and transformed into a cohesive form suitable for interpretation. Chronological and theoretical developments are traced and connections are made between these conceptual bases. Theoretical and research issues pertinent to these domains are identified.

Chapter 2 evaluates the existing affective wellbeing and job satisfaction literature. Various disciplines, theories, models and schools of thought on affective wellbeing and intrinsic job satisfaction theories are synthesised. Dispositional, Activity and Telic categories are used to contextualise the Vitamin Model, the Demand-Control Model, and the dispositional approach to job satisfaction. Affective wellbeing and intrinsic job satisfaction were used to measure workplace happiness. The popular notion of 'Emotional Intelligence' emerges as a potential contender for integrating these theories and for guiding practice in the workplace.

Chapter 3 traces the clusters of literature relating to theoretical frameworks of job performance in order to demonstrate how managers' performance is conceptualised and measured. Managers' jobs are defined, followed by a contemporary description of the roles and responsibilities that they typically undertake. Clusters of literature relating to theoretical frameworks of job performance are reviewed, including the distinction between managers' contextual and task performance. Contemporary theories of managers' performance are conceived of within the framework of the different schools of performance appraisal. Important links between organisational effectiveness and managers' performance are explored.

Chapter 4 links the extant literature on affective wellbeing and intrinsic job satisfaction related to managers' contextual and task performance. Pertinent issues arising from the literature are briefly revisited before proposing the Partial Model. Concepts, constructs, dimensions and measures relating to the Partial Model are formed into research questions to be answered and hypotheses for testing. An important new line of inquiry is established which guides the development of the methodology.

PART 2: Methodology, Measurement and Results

Chapter 5 details the empirical aspects of this study, including the methodology used to collect the data and sample parameters. The interconnection of the concepts, constructs and measures involved forms the basis of the research methodology adopted. Design and implementation issues are addressed, especially the development of the measurement instruments. The statistical techniques used to analyse the data to test the hypotheses and answer the research questions are described in detail.

Chapter 6 articulates the testing and calibration of the Partial Model. Descriptive statistics on the sample are provided. Existing affective wellbeing and intrinsic job satisfaction instruments are verified. A unique statistical model was developed to measure managers' performance. An instrument is developed by testing methodological hypotheses on managers' performance.

Chapter 7 provides the results of the analyses of the relationships between managers' affective wellbeing, intrinsic job satisfaction and performance. Canonical Correlation and the Standard Multiple Regression used for the analysis was based on multivariate analysis of variance. The results of the analysis of the hypotheses are discussed in detail, as are the methodological issues influencing the study.

PART 3: Findings, Implications and Contributions to Organisational Theory and Management Practice

Chapter 8 explains the distinct contribution made by this book to our understanding of the relationship between managers' affective wellbeing, intrinsic job satisfaction and performance. The main findings and limitations are summarised and contextualised. The results are examined in relation to the research questions and accompanying hypotheses. Finally, the implications of these findings are discussed, and the organisational practice and policy implications are analysed. Potential new research directions are suggested. The connections between management theory and practice are explored and the implications for practitioners made. A comprehensive review is undertaken of the many and varied international, national and organisational initiatives to foster affective wellbeing in the workplace.

Implications for research and practice

Findings in this book are intended to progress the debate as to how work might be structured to improve managers' affective wellbeing and performance. Managerial and practitioner recommendations are provided, followed by a close examination of the implications for Strategic Human Resource Management. A better understanding of how affective wellbeing and intrinsic job satisfaction influence managers' behaviour has the potential to enhance aspects of their performance.

Pressures, strains and stresses on managers in the workplace have been identified as an important determinant of a person's mental health. Individual levels of affective wellbeing, intrinsic job satisfaction and performance have the potential to eventually impact on organisations' productivity. More importantly the personal cost of the demise in affective wellbeing to an individual's life is immense. An improved understanding of the way in which changes in affective wellbeing and intrinsic job satisfaction impact on performance will assist in identifying what can be done to promote a healthier and more productive work environment for managers.

Managers are in the front lines of ever shifting, difficult and dynamic business landscapes. Increased calls for efficiency gains, cost cutting, and improved employee performance, including their own, require managers to simultaneously cope with workplace stress, fatigue, and burnout. Managers seem to be unaware of the factors that influence individual performance which results in organisational productivity. A better understanding of 'performance levers' that managers should be pulling, and encouraging others to pull, to improve workplaces are provided in this book.

Workplace problems attributed to 'stress' may actually be symptoms of depression and anxiety. Job stress can lead to poor mental health. The terms stress, mental health and burnout are often used interchangeably in the literature. Stress and burnout are mainly used to describe work-related outcomes, while mental health may be context free. As a result, research on the construct of stress informs our understanding of affective wellbeing. Job satisfaction has also been found to be an important contributor to psychological health in the workplace.

Providing more rigorous measures of performance has the potential to guide the implementation of human resource development initiatives to improve individual managers' performance. Timely feedback about affective wellbeing and intrinsic job satisfaction may assist organisations to monitor and implement changes to managers' jobs in order to sustain and improve their performance. More refined assessments of performance may facilitate managers' self-development, as they indicate what managers need to do in order to enhance their potential and to perform with sustainable effectives.

Insights in this book will make it possible to predict how deterioration, or an improvement, in affective wellbeing and intrinsic job satisfaction impacts on managers' performance. Management practices that increase managers' affective wellbeing and intrinsic job satisfaction may result in corresponding reductions in workplace tension and improved efficiency. Evidence is disclosed on how affective wellbeing and intrinsic job satisfaction interact with managers' performance will be valuable for determining job designs and organisational level interventions. Changes to the design of jobs can be enacted and embedded to enhance, or to avoid a decline in affective wellbeing, intrinsic job satisfaction and performance. Such an understanding has the potential to translate into improved managerial practices, which can impact on the performance of managers.

Conversely, this book also shows how the individual consequences of diminished affective wellbeing and intrinsic job satisfaction can be disastrous. Diminished affective wellbeing will ultimately translate into the bottom line of organisational effectiveness, productivity, profitability and share prices. Such information may be used to develop interventions for promoting healthier and more supportive work environments. These findings are also intended to progress the debate as to how work might be structured to improve all employees' performance.

CONCLUSION

This book emanates from an enduring stream of research into individual performance and organisational productivity. Contemporary and classic theories and models and research are employed to inform an age-old mystery in management - do happy workers, or in these cases managers, perform better, or worse, or does their affective state make no difference? Extrapolations are made from the interrelationships between the various interconnected disciplines, theories and models in the field. Implications of the research are of relevance to the body of management theory and practice.

Despite the mixed research findings of over half a century, there is support in the literature but scant empirical evidence to suggest that a link exists between happiness and job performance. A thorough re-assessment of the 'happy-productive worker' thesis, and its development into the 'happy-performing managers' proposition, is undertaken by investigating the relationship between managers' affective wellbeing, intrinsic job satisfaction and performance.

Managers' performance was found to be multi-dimensional and consist of two components: contextual and task performance. Certain indicators of affective wellbeing and intrinsic job satisfaction were found to reliably predict dimensions of managers' contextual and task performance. A more sophisticated understanding of how the relationships between affective wellbeing and intrinsic job satisfaction interact with managers' performance has resulted in a better understanding of the 'happy-performing managers' proposition.

There are many advantages to improving managerial practices in relation to affective wellbeing. Circumstances that might otherwise lead to a managers' dismissal or burnout may be less likely to arise if there is a means to identify managers 'at risk'. Such information can be used to assist in identifying defective organisational practices that have the potential to damage managerial affective wellbeing and intrinsic job satisfaction.

Interest in the 'happy-performing managers' proposition can be seen within the broader context of the trend to POS. Insights from POS movement give cause for great optimism. POS has an affirmative bias towards the health model's capacity to discover and maintain ways that organisations can improve people's working lives. From this perspective, employee health and wellbeing are seen in terms of the presence of the potential for growth, optimism, contentment and actualisation - not simply as the absence of dysfunctional behaviour. The time has come to move away from the negative forms of psychology (based on a 'deficit model') and affirm managers' future by embracing the 'happy-performing managers' proposition.

Peter J. Hosie, Peter P. Sevastos, and Cary L. Cooper CBE

PART 1:

The 'Happy-Productive Worker' Thesis

1. Introduction: Exploring the links between happiness, job satisfaction and job performance

> When you feel good about yourself, you perform better. And when you perform well, you feel good about yourself. Neither can endure without the other.
> (Tracey, 1993: 69)

INTRODUCTION

The origins of the 'happy-productive worker' thesis can be traced to the seminal Hawthorne studies (Roethlisberger & Dickson, 1939), where higher levels of job related performance were attributed to happy employees, compared to their unhappy counterparts. Research into emotions and affect in the workplace were initiated and peaked in the 1930s (Fisher & Hanna, 1931; Kornhauser & Sharp, 1932; Hoppock, 1935; Roethlisberger & Dickson, 1939; Fisher, 1980).

Hersey's (1932) research represented a seminal work on emotions and performance in the workplace which coincided with the Hawthorne studies and Hoppock's (1935) investigations into job satisfaction. Hersey was arguably the first researcher to demonstrate a definite relationship between emotional state and productivity in the workplace (Weiss & Cropanzano, 1996). He maintained that the primary causes of satisfaction and dissatisfaction were specific work events. Research into the links between affective states and performance has evolved over decades as the definitions, measures and dimensions of interest and terminology have been refined.

Studies from the 1930s onwards had found only modest support for the link between worker satisfaction and improved job performance (Organ & Paine, 1999). Belief in the 'happy-productive worker' thesis also has its roots in the Human Behaviour School of the 1950s (Coyle-Shapiro, 2004). Improving employee morale was believed to result in higher productivity. Proponents of the 1970s Human Relations Movement had a significant influence on job redesign and quality-of-life initiatives through Herzberg, Mausner, and Snyderman's classic work (1959), which was credited with specifying the original satisfaction-performance relationship (Strauss,

1968; Perrow, 1986; King & Peter, 1993; Coyle-Shapiro, 2004).

In the 1970s, the perceived direction of the causal relationship was reversed; employees who performed better were expected to be more satisfied because they received greater rewards (Lawler & Porter, 1967). Tenets of the Human Behaviour School and Human Relations Movement now coexist with the productivity doctrines espoused by economic rationalists in the late 1980s and early 1990s (King & Peter, 1993). Interest in the 'happy-productive worker' thesis then plateaued in the intervening decades, until being revived in the mid-1980s and 1990s (Brief & Weiss, 2002). From the 1990s onwards there has been a veritable avalanche of research into emotions and affect in organisations (Ashkanasy, 2004). Barsade, Brief and Spataro (2003) were even moved to announce that an 'affective revolution' had occurred in Industrial and Organisational Psychology of similar proportions to the cognitive shift depicted a decade earlier by Ilgen, Major and Tower (1994).

From a broader perspective, research into affective wellbeing has consistently shown that the 'characteristics and resources' valued by society correlate with happiness' (Lyubomirsky et al., 2005: 925). High happiness levels have been found to covary with marriage (Mastekaasa, 1994), a comfortable income (Diener & Biswas-Diener, 2003), superior mental health (Koivumaa-Honkanen et al., 2004), a long life (Danner, Snowdon, & Friesen, 2001), and have the capacity to handle managerial jobs better (Lyubomirsky et al., 2005) as 'happy people are likely to acquire favourable life circumstances' (Lyubomirsky et al., 2005: 803). By rigorously testing the happiness-success link, Lyubomirsky and colleagues demonstrated that happy people tend to be successful and flourish. Positive emotions and chronic happiness were found to be 'often associated with resources and characteristics that parallel success and thriving - that is, desirable behaviors and cognitions such as sociability, optimism, energy, originality, and altruism'(Lyubomirsky et al., 2005: 846). Considerable evidence was presented by Lyubomirsky and colleagues to challenge the belief that successful outcomes and desirable characteristics are primarily the causes, not the consequences, of happiness.

Notwithstanding this renewed interest, evidence to support the proposition that happy employees perform better was still not compelling as subsequent studies had only found modest support for this predicted relationship. Despite the lack of empirical evidence, the notion that happy workers are more productive is firmly entrenched in management ideology (Cropanzano & Wright, 1999; Ledford, 1999; Wright & Staw, 1999a; 1999b; Wright & Cropanzano, 2000; Cropanzano & Wright, 2001; Wright, Cropanzano, Denney, & Moline, 2002). Research reported in this book articulates and expands on the debate into how indicators of affective wellbeing and intrinsic job satisfaction are predictors of managers' contextual and task performance.

ARE HAPPY WORKERS GOOD WORKERS?

Half a century of active research has been unable to establish a strong link between job satisfaction and performance. Wright and Staw (1999a; 1999b) reopened the general debate as to whether happy workers are more productive after decades of research had found inadequate evidence to fully support the 'happy-productive worker' thesis (Staw, 1986: 41), or the proposition that 'a happy worker is a good worker' (1995: 111). Conversely though, 'lay' people are thought to believe in the 'happy-productive' worker thesis despite the indifferent evidence supporting this supposed relationship (Fisher, 2003). Research has also been unable to establish a close link between job satisfaction and performance (c.f. Brayfield & Crockett, 1955; Porter, 1963; Vroom, 1964; Locke, 1976; Iaffaldano & Muchinsky, 1985).

Authors critical of the veracity of the 'happy-productive worker' thesis, such as Wright, Cropanzano, Denney and Moline (2002: 146) concluded that 'despite decades of study, support for this hypothesis remains equivocal ... these inconsistent findings may also be a consequence of the disparate manner in which happiness has been operationalized'. Happiness has invariably been conceived and measured as satisfaction, when a more accurate operationalisation of happiness is 'job-related affect' and 'intrinsic job satisfaction'. Actually, job satisfaction in general is probably closer to a state of 'bovine contentment' than an actual state of happiness (Wright & Staw, 1999a; 1999b).

Researchers have erroneously conceived and operationalised job satisfaction as being synonymous with affective wellbeing (Cropanzano, James, & Konovsky, 1993; Wright & Cropanzano, 2000; Cropanzano & Wright, 2001). Also, this could be a consequence of 'happiness' being mistakenly operationalised as job satisfaction in organisational research. Job (un)happiness has been equated with job (dis)satisfaction when these are actually discrete constructs. In addition, the word job 'satisfaction' is more relativistic in character than the word 'happy'. Furthermore, job-related affect (i.e., feelings relating to specific tasks undertaken by individuals in a particular work setting) has rarely been used as a predictor of managers' job performance outcomes.

Refocus on this debate occurred with evidence to indicate that affective states and the disposition to experience affective states (state personality) influence the way people perform their jobs (George & Zhou, 2002).

Organisational researchers have found that affect correlates with employee job performance but the associations found were weak and showed ambiguous relationships (Barrick & Mount, 1991; Gardner & Koslowski, 1993; Saks, 1996). There are also other potential moderators or mediators of the relationship between affect and job performance. An investigation into the under researched short term and long term state-trait models of affect was recommended.

More recent meta-analyses have indicated that there is a stronger relationship between job satisfaction and job performance than was previously evident (Judge, Thoresen, Bono, & Patton, 2001; Harter, Schmidt, & Hays, 2002). However, overall the average observed relationship between job satisfaction and performance is positive but relatively weak, ranging from .14 to .25 (Judge et al., 2001). A strong association ($r = .57$) between momentary task satisfaction and momentary task performance, using within-person analysis (i.e., the same person rating both satisfaction and performance) has been reported by Fisher (2003). Satisfaction-performance correlations are usually stronger in high-complexity jobs, such as those undertaken by managers. Since managers undertake high complexity tasks an association is likely to exist between satisfaction-performance.

Researchers have mainly ceased investigating whether satisfied employees are more productive, possibly as a consequence of using undifferentiated job satisfaction as the predictor variable, instead of more appropriate measures, such as 'happiness' (Wright & Staw, 1999a; 1999b), or using a close proxy, affective wellbeing (Sevastos, 1996). The research in this book posits that affective wellbeing and intrinsic job satisfaction may be a more accurate predictor of managers' job performance when compared to undifferentiated job satisfaction. Furthermore, the construct, 'managers' job performance' previously has not been robustly measured, making associations between these constructs problematic, partly due to conceptual misspecification and the use of inadequate research methodologies. Rather than being an aberrant stream of investigation these findings result from poorly specified and measured constructs.

HAPPIER-AND-SMARTER OR SADDER-BUT-WISER?

In 1993, Staw and Barsade (1993) conducted a trial simulation to test whether people with a positive disposition performed better or worse on decisional and interpersonal tasks. A positive relationship between dispositional affect and performance was found which supported the 'happier-and-smarter' as opposed to the 'sadder-but-wiser' hypothesis. However, as Staw and Barsade noted, the literature does not consistently support the view that Positive Affect (PA) always has beneficial consequences. Research into the 'depression-realism' effect indicates depressed people may actually be more inclined, in certain circumstances, to make accurate judgements compared to their less depressed counterparts.

Subsequent to this study Weiss and Cropanzano (1996: 55) posed a question seminal to this book, by asking 'How are the behaviors in the emotion domain related to the behaviours in the job domain?'. They argued that behaviours in the emotional domain have the potential to facilitate, interfere or are simply unrelated with behaviours in the job domain. Weiss and Cropanzano contended that emotional responses tend to produce decrements in performance. These decrements are argued to be the outcome of both positive and negative emotions (affects) which are incompatible with job demands as they consume cognitive resources required to perform the job tasks. The debate over whether emotional responses by managers are 'happier-and-smarter' or 'sadder-but-wiser' is continued in Chapters 2 and 7.

Organ (1977: 46) has attributed the acceptance of the conventional wisdom that 'satisfaction causes performance' to the broader conceptualisation of the construct 'performance'. Apart from studies by Wright and Straw, (1999a; 1999b) affective wellbeing has seldom been investigated in the field as a predictor of favourable work outcomes for managers. Wright and Staw (1999b: 2) found a 'plausible link' between employees' affective states and work behaviour that justified 're-opening the question as to whether happy workers are also more productive'. Nevertheless, despite these mixed and often contradictory findings, a viable stream of research may be found in the 'happy-productive workers' thesis that is both 'important and worthy' of investigation (West, Arnold, Corbett, & Fletcher, 1992: 1), as it 'begins to make a claim on our attention' (Christensen, Andrews, & Porter, 1982: 6).

Expanding the construct space for both affect and performance in the workplace makes it possible to test potential new linkages between these variables. A more sophisticated understanding of how affective wellbeing and intrinsic job satisfaction interacts with managers' performance is posited in this book to contribute to a better understanding of aspects of the relationships underlying these constructs. There is a case for extending the happy-productive worker thesis into an examination of the extent to which managers' affective wellbeing influences performance using a more robust methodology to measure these constructs. Re-invigorating this debate may also inform the more general, but unproven proposition that happy employees, or in this case managers, perform more effectively, which is the prime motivator behind this book.

In fact, Warr (1987: 293) suggested over a decade ago that researchers should explore 'what is known about the relationship between rated work performance and the components of mental health'. A range of organisational variables have been found to predict 20% of the unique variance in job satisfaction, and an additional 5% of unique variance in affective wellbeing (Sevastos, 1996). As noted earlier, research has mainly focused on job satisfaction when affective wellbeing and intrinsic job satisfaction have been shown to relate differently to important job features (Sevastos, 1996).

The main goal of the research reported in this book was to explore the impact of job-related affective wellbeing ('affective wellbeing') and intrinsic job satisfaction on managers' contextual and task performance ('managers' performance'). A series of ancillary research questions, underscoring the main goal of the research, were developed from the gaps identified in the literature to establish if there was an association between managers' affective wellbeing, intrinsic job satisfaction and their contextual and task performance:

- To what extent does affective wellbeing and intrinsic job satisfaction determine different dimensions of managers' contextual and task performance?
- Does the construct of managers' performance consist of the two dimensions, contextual and task performance?
- Does positive affective wellbeing result in enhanced managers' performance, and is poor affective wellbeing detrimental to managers' performance?

In addition, two further questions about practical outcomes are addressed:

- How might managers' jobs be changed to enhance, or prevent a decline in affective wellbeing?
- How might these findings be integrated with workplace initiatives to improve the quality of managers' life and job performance?

These research questions were developed into a series of hypotheses for testing (see Chapter 4). Answers to these questions and the implications of findings are addressed in Chapter 7. Simultaneous analysis of affective wellbeing and intrinsic job satisfaction has the potential to improve predictions about managers' job performance. A *Partial Model of Managers' Affective Wellbeing, Intrinsic Job Satisfaction and Performance* ('Partial Model') was developed from the literature. When tested these have predictive power, as illustrated in Chapter 4, Figure 4.1.

'COMMONSENSE' THEORY ON THE 'HAPPY-PRODUCTIVE WORKER' THESIS

As indicated in the preface, lay people are thought to believe that happy people exhibit better job performance despite indifferent evidence from the literature to corroborate this link. Fisher (2003: 771) has documented the 'widespread existence of a strong commonsense theory; that happy workers are more productive workers, or that employees who are satisfied with their jobs are likely to be better performers on those jobs'. Fisher (2003: 773) contended that:

> Individuals may believe that satisfied employees are good performers because of their own highly accessible experiences of being more satisfied at moments that they are performing work tasks more efficiently, and less satisfied when they are performing less well.

Students, managers and supervisors from a diversity of national and cultural backgrounds have considered their positive feelings (mood, happiness or job satisfaction) were related to better performance (Fisher, 2003). With regard to the satisfaction-performance relationship the momentary mood and task satisfaction may seem to lay people to covary between persons, when compared with more stable measures of job satisfaction and job performance. Fisher argued that this belief may stem from the 'lay' people's belief that feeling more than usually satisfied at work translates into better job performance. Possibly this may lead lay people to erroneously attribute their experiences of this perceived covariation between satisfaction-performance and then somehow generalising this idea into the notion that satisfied workers perform better.

Kluger and Tikochinsky (2001) have identified the reasons why the lay belief or 'commonsense theory' may identify a strong relationship between two variables such as the satisfaction/happiness-performance. According to them, using alternative definitions of constructs and units of analysis may result from lay people using different operationalisations to those used by researchers, of identical or similar constructs (such as happiness or performance) based on loose definitions of the constructs involved. For example, productivity usually refers to assessments undertaken at the organisational level, whereas performance is defined and measured at the individual level. Both satisfaction, happiness and performance may be given different meanings by researchers and lay people and this could account for the perceived magnitude of differences in the relationship between the satisfaction/happiness-performance constructs (Fisher, 1980; Judge et al., 2001; Fisher, 2002).

SIGNIFICANCE OF THE HAPPY-PRODUCTIVE WORKER THESIS

> Nevertheless, I still suspect a consistent, significant job satisfaction/task performance relationship is out there to be found.
> (Brief, 1998: 43)

Competitive advantage through managers

A central point in the debate over the importance of managers to organisations and the competitiveness of nation-states, is the assertion that 'good managers are the key to a more competitive economy and higher performing enterprises' (Karpin, 1995a: 1). Managers are pivotal to an organisation's productivity and effectiveness as they have ultimate responsibility for maximising the resources available for organisations to create value (Jones, 1995). The resource-based view of the firm recognised the value added by human capital (Wernefelt, 1984; Hamel & Prahalad, 1994).

Regardless of the industry or country concerned, managers represent the human capital that is critical to an organisation's success (Williams, 1991). Any decline in managers' performance inevitably results in revenue forgone, opportunities lost, and increased costs. In turn, this hampers the capacity of organisations and ultimately, national economies to create wealth. Ascertaining the factors that determine managers' performance has the potential to assist in initiatives to improve organisational competitiveness. Findings in this book may be applicable to managers in a variety of working situations because, as many studies have demonstrated managers are critical to the success, or failure, of companies and organisations (Hanson, 1986).

Relationship to organisational productivity and effectiveness

Managers are increasingly being required to demonstrate the effectiveness of human resource interventions at the organisational level, and to integrate these functions with the strategic direction of the organisation. An organisation's human resources can be a source of competitive advantage when the policies and practices for managing people are integrated with strategic business planning and organisational culture (Beer, Spector, Lawrence, Mills, & Walton, 1984; Beer, Spector, Lawrence, Quinn Mills, & Walton, 1985). This approach emphasises the importance of congruence between human resource policies and organisational objectives (Guest, 2002; Guest, Michie, Conway, & Sheehan, 2003; Guest, Conway, & Dewe, 2004). Human resource practices targeted at individual performance have been found to be associated with perceptual and financial measures of organisational effectiveness (Terpstra & Rozell, 1993; Huselid, 1995; Snell & Youndt, 1995; Becker & Gerhart, 1996; Delaney & Huselid, 1996; Youndt, Snell, Dean, & Lepak, 1996; Huselid, Jackson, & Randall, 1997). A strong link has been indicated between people management and business performance (Ichniowski, Shaw, & Prennushi, 1997; Patterson, West, Lawthom, & Nickell, 1997; O'Reilly & Pfeffer, 2000; Purcell, 2004). In a groundbreaking study, Huselid (1995) determined a set of human resource practices (high performance work systems) were related to turnover, accounting profits, and firm market value.

Compared to other management practices (e.g., strategy, quality focus, investment in research and development), human resource practices explained 18% of the variation in productivity and 19% in profitability of companies in the UK (Patterson et al., 1997). Two clusters of skills, acquisition and development of employee skills (including the use of appraisals) and job design was shown to be particularly important. Patterson and colleagues have established an empirically strong argument supporting the relationship between people management practices and commercial performance. A longitudinal study by Ichniowski and colleagues (1990; 1997) found that clusters of innovative human resource management systems had large effects on workers' performance but changes in individual employment practices had minimal effect.

An optimal bundle or combination of properly applied human resource policies was found by Purcell (2004) to be necessary for the achievement of high performance. Consistent with Ichniowski et al.'s (1990; 1997) findings the 'human resource bundle' requirements were found to be different for different occupations. Eleven human resource policy areas were associated with achieving the desired ability, motivation and opportunity to achieve higher levels of organisation commitment, job satisfaction and ultimately performance. Integrated 'bundles' or 'clusters' of human resource practices are likely to produce greater improvement in organisational effectiveness than isolated interventions (Ichniowski, 1990; Huselid, 1995; Huselid et al., 1997; Ichniowski et al., 1997; Purcell, 2004).

Way (2002: 765) boldly stated in the same vein that 'Theoretical and empirical HRM research has led to a general consensus that the method used by a firm to manage its workforce can have a positive impact on firm performance.' Positive workplace perceptions and feeling were found by Harter, Schmidt and Hays (2002) to be associated with higher business unit customer loyalty, higher profitability, higher productivity and lower rates of turnover. A review of the literature by Spector (1997) indicated that more satisfied employees are more cooperative towards co-workers, punctual, time efficient, have fewer days off work, and remain with organisations longer than their colleagues who had lower levels of job satisfaction. Employee psychological wellbeing has been found to be in the best interests of employers (Harter, Schmidt, & Hays, 2002). A meta-analysis by Harter and colleagues (2002) of the relationship between employee workplace perceptions and business unit outcomes found a positive relationship between job satisfaction and employee performance, especially aspects of satisfaction with supervisors and satisfaction with work.

According to Nankervis (2004) the mutual contribution of 'soft' (people-driven human resource features, such as motivation and leadership), and 'hard' (market-driven forces such as strategy formulation and programme evaluation), aspects of management have yet to be established. A subsequent review of the published literature on human resource practices and organisational performance from 1994 by Wall and Wood (2005) takes a more sobering position. They claimed that existing studies have opened up a promising line of inquiry, but methodological limitations preclude making a definitive conclusion about causal relationship human resource practices to performance. Wright, Gardner, Moynihan and Allen (2005) argued that claims by Huselid and Becker (1997) that existing research suggesting a positive link between human resource practices and organisational performance lacked sufficient methodological rigor to demonstrate a causal relationship. Wright et al (2005) found human resource practices were strongly related to future performance but they were also strongly related to past performance.

Controlling for past or concurrent performance eliminated the correlation of human resource practice with future performance negating proof that these practices 'cause' that high organisational performance. Both reviews by Wall and Wood and Wright et al. excluded large amounts of accumulated evidence reported in books and reports supporting the human resource management-productivity link (Ichniowski, 1990; Lawler, Mohrman, & Ledford, 1995; Lawler, Mohrman, & Ledford, 1998; Appelbaum, Bailey, Berg, & Kalleberg, 2000; Harter, Schmidt, & Keyes, 2002). However, evidence is emerging to indicate that management practices designed to humanise the workplace are being reciprocated by improved productivity (Maister, 2001). The importance of soft aspects to managerial performance is further developed in Chapter 7.

Trend towards 'squeezing the pips'

Organisations are under increasing pressure to improve productivity while simultaneously reducing costs. This situation has resulted in an epidemic of 'corporate anorexia' (Hamel, 1996). An enterprise formula has emerged - '1/2 x 2 x 3' - whereby half as many people are being paid twice as much, to produce three times more (Handy, 1996). This trend towards 'squeezing the pips' is particularly evident for managers, where the incidence of stress and burnout is increasingly common (Quinn, Faerman, Thompson, & McGrath, 1996; Reinhold, 1997). An incessant drive by organisations to cut costs and downsize has resulted in fewer people undertaking more work. There is also a pervasive sense of unease about the lack of job tenure.

The rapid adoption of information technology has also accelerated the pace of work and increased role expectations. Ease of access to the Internet has exacerbated the demand for a '24/7' (24 hours, 7 days a week) work culture that requires immediacy of responses to management and customers' demands (Kenny & Cooper, 2003). This development needs to be seen as a part of the movement to team-based work becoming more widespread, downsizing forcing employees to exert more effort, pressures to deliver results in shorter time frames, customer service being emphasised and 'fields of work' replacing specific 'jobs' (Borman & Motowidlo, 1997). In all, a number of countervailing forces are apparent as 'Organizations are becoming more flexible, participative and simultaneously tougher and more humane' (Stone, 2002: 330). These rapid changes to the working environment will eventually impact on the levels of affective wellbeing experienced by managers and this is likely to be deleterious to long term performance.

RELATIONSHIP TO CONTEMPORARY MANAGERIAL ISSUES

Impact of globalisation on managers

Enormous changes in society generally, and workplaces particularly have been experienced in the past several decades (Dive, 2002). Globalisation and market deregulation have dramatically altered the competitive landscape facing managers in the 21st century. Globalisation may be described as the expanse of economic interdependence through international trade and investments (Lebel, 2005). Commercial indicators are emerging to suggest that a global economic revolution is occurring (Ployhart, Wiechmann, Schmitt, Sacco, & Rogg, 2003). Economic growth in developed nations has been fuelled in response to deregulation in the 1980s and 1990s, and this has opened these economies to increased competition (Cascio, 1993).

Structural micro and macro economic reforms implemented by governments have forced many nation-states to become more competitive. With increased global competition, managers are being forced to adapt to the liberalisation of world trade and investment regimes such as the deregulation of financial markets (Brooks & Faff, 1997). Following the example of the UK in the 1980s, successive governments throughout the world have also deregulated their economies, notably the finance and manufacturing sectors, while simultaneously reducing tariffs across industries (Brooks & Faff, 1997). These events were preceded by the reduction in prominence of nation-states and deregulation of the global economy (Porter, 1990; Guehenno, 1995; Ohmae, 1995).

Since the 1980s, downsizing and delayering has emerged as a pervasive international trend affecting economies (Kitney, 1996; Palmer & Dunford, 1996). Downsizing has a serious impact on surviving managers, including the necessity to work longer hours (Brammall, 1999) and decreased job security (IAER, 1998). If no change is made to the way work is done then the 'same amount of work as before downsizing is simply loaded onto the backs of fewer workers' (Cascio, 1993: 103). This is particularly the case for managers who are experiencing greater role complexity and significant increase in the sheer volume of work demanded.

The capacity of managers to make decisions may also be impeded by increasingly complex working environments (Keating, 1988; Karpin, 1995a; 1995b). In 1976, Livingston identified decision making as the capacity to 'find the problems that need to be solved, to plan for the attainment of desired results, or to carry out operating plans once they are made' (Livingston cited in Mintzberg, 2003: 38). In this environment, managers are driven by results (Karpin, 1995a; 1995b). Some managers make good decisions in such complex and demanding environments, others do not. Hence, there is an unmet need to discover the reasons for exemplary and deficient performance.

As indicated, since the 1980s many developed enterprises have faced rapid technological advances coupled with globalisation accompanied by dramatic changes to organisational structures (Simons, 1998). Flatter organisational structures have emerged from the 1990s onwards. This is a result of significant downsizing along with the uptake of new, flexible and lean technologies together with non-traditional work practices (Sauter & Murphy, 2003). These changes have compelled a shift in the pace and direction of managerial practices (Hammer & Champy, 1993; Limerick & Cunnington, 1993; Quinn et al., 1996). Managers were formerly required to achieve results directly through people, using a centralised and narrow span of control. Several levels have been eliminated from many organisational hierarchies thus resulting in managers having a more dispersed span of control (Beittenhausen & Fedor, 1997).

Relinquishing this direct supervisory role means that managers now perform different roles, such as empowering employees and facilitating team-based work. Managers are expected to plan and prioritise their own work as well as for those reporting to them. This trend has led to increased work intensity and complexity, and mounting deadlines to produce high quality outcomes. At the same time, managers' jobs also require specialised tasks be performed to increasingly higher levels of efficiency. Outsourcing imperatives, the loss of in-house expertise, and demands for contract management have also created a general trend to increase the role complexity for managers (Breusch, 2000). Employees are working more flexible hours and teleworking which have further complicated managers' responsibilities.

In the 21st century, managers are also expected to produce more with less. Better services, quicker response times, more products to market, shorter product cycles, increased sales, and better value for money are demanded. As a direct consequence of globalisation, and other developments identified in this chapter, the roles and performance expectations of managers have changed substantially. Managers are operating in a 'just in time' mode, where they are teetering on the brink of not having adequate time to complete their work. Such changes to the workplace highlight the need to understand how managers can work smarter and faster, rather than harder and longer, and still retain their affective wellbeing.

Strategically integrated human resource initiatives are likely to contribute to an organisation's success (Guest, 1990). As noted earlier, human resource practices have emerged as a key competitive advantage for countries and organisations (Schuler & Macmillan, 1984; O'Reilly & Pfeffer, 2000; Collins, 2001). Decisions about the direction human resource management practices take will ultimately be largely dependent on the world economy. Likewise, managers are dependent on the financial prosperity of the organisations they work for. As such, the financial viability of organisations and nation-states will be in large measure determined by their managers' capacity to contribute to the generation of wealth. In this environment, strategic human resource initiatives that enhance managers' affective wellbeing and intrinsic job satisfaction is one way of contributing to managers' performance (O'Reilly & Pfeffer, 2000; Collins, 2001; Forster, 2005). In this dynamic and competitive environment an important aspect of Strategic Human Resource Management is rigorous selection, performance appraisal and the adoption of appropriate reward systems.

Organisations seeking to create and maintain a healthy working environment for the benefit of the physical, mental and social wellbeing of their employees must implement strategies that promote workplace health and safety (Cooper & Cartwright, 1994). Consistent patterns of association have been found between PA and markers of physical health (Pressman & Cohen, 2005). Evidence of the process of how affective wellbeing and intrinsic job satisfaction interact with managers' performance will be invaluable in determining job designs and organisational level interventions. Such an understanding has the potential to translate into improved managerial practices.

This book has the potential to improve the quality of managers' working lives and their performance by resonating and building on insights into human resource management practices that have large effects on organisational productivity as described by Ichniowski, Shaw and Prennushi (1997) and Patterson et al. (1997). In combination, these benefits may result in more effective organisational outcomes including increased productivity, reduced organisational costs, reduced staff-turnover and avoidance of protracted legal actions arising from claims of unfair dismissal, breach of contract, or 'stress'. In all, failure to address affective wellbeing issues in the workplace potentially retards an organisation's capacity to maximise efficiency and effectiveness (Staw & Barsade, 1993).

PSYCHOLOGICAL DISORDERS IN THE WORKPLACE

As noted earlier in this chapter, developed societies are increasingly aware of the incidence of psychological disorders in the workplace (Levi, 1990; Millar, 1990; Ganster & Schaubroeck, 1991), prompting occupational and organisational psychologists to scrutinise levels of psychological health amongst employees (Gebhardt & Crump, 1990; Theorell, 1993; Cooper & Cartwright, 1994; Cartwright & Cooper, 1997). In addition, organisational theorists have long recognised the considerable financial and human costs attributable to employee psychological dysfunction (Wright, Cropanzano et al., 2002). Mental health concerns in the workplace are now regarded as an international problem of considerable magnitude (World Health Organization, 2005b).

Much earlier, Weick (1979) had urged researchers to focus on the emotional dimensions of work-life. Despite his advice, much of the research into management issues is predicated on the assumption that people's behaviour is rational, cognitive and stable. Yet, emotions have also been found to comprise aspects of reason, action and feelings, including decision-making and the disposition to act (James, Milton, & Gibb, 2000). Rather than interfering with employee rationality, emotions may be seen as assisting in wise decision-making. Conversely, a lack of emotional expression has been shown to result in irrational behaviour (Damasio, 1994). Research on emotions indicates that people do indeed reason with emotion (Lane, 2000).

Academic and lay interest in affect and emotions has intensified in the

1990s and beyond (Izard, 2002). Until now investigations into affect and emotions in organisational settings have been avoided due to difficulties of empirically investigating the phenomena (Turnball, 1999). Researchers continue to show renewed interest in the impact of emotions in organisational contexts (Ashkanasy, 1998; Fisher & Ashkanasy, 2000). Emotional states are no longer regarded as illogical responses to events in the workplace (Nicholson, 2000). A dispositional proclivity to cope with and manage emotional experiences has been popularised as 'emotional intelligence' (Salovey & Mayer, 1990; Goleman, 1995; Mayer & Salovey, 1997; 1999; Mayer, Salovey, & Caruso, 2000). Emotional intelligence is evident when a person uses their capabilities to determine the ways to deals with their life and the workplace. Salovey and Mayer originally conceived of the emotional intelligence construct in terms of an individual's ability to perceive emotion in self and others, to understand emotion, and then to manage emotion in self and others. Goleman refers to about two dozen social and emotional characteristics that are linked to successful performance in the workplace, such as: self-awareness; self-confidence, self-control, commitment, integrity, the ability to communicate and influence, and to initiate and accept change-skills are vital to managers.

As discussed earlier in this chapter, this book focuses on one aspect of emotional and mental health; job-related affective wellbeing. Although extensive research has been conducted into workplace affective wellbeing and job satisfaction (Warr, 1990a; 1990b; Kelloway & Barling, 1991; Kahn & Cooper, 1993; Warr, 1996b; 1996a) there has been no specific empirical research into the impact of affective wellbeing and intrinsic job satisfaction on managers' performance. A research opportunity exists for using affective wellbeing as the predictor variable of managers' performance, in conjunction with intrinsic job satisfaction. Chapter 7 relates the findings of this book to these theoretical and practical aspects of managers' affective wellbeing and intrinsic job satisfaction on performance.

MAGNITUDE AND COST OF DIMINISHED AFFECTIVE WELLBEING IN THE WORKPLACE

The accumulated evidence from epidemiological, survey and clinical studies from Europe and elsewhere indicates that work and mental health are related (Gabriel & Liimatainen, 2000; The Institute for Employment Studies, 2001). An International Labour Organization (2000) analysis of mental health policies and programmes in Finland, Germany, Poland, United Kingdom and United States showed that the incidence of mental health problems affecting these workforces is increasing (Gabriel & Liimatainen, 2000).

In the order of one in ten employees were estimated to be suffering from depression, anxiety, stress or burnout. Somewhere between approximately 3–4% of GNP was spent on mental health problems in the European Union. Early retirement that is attributed to mental health problems has become the most common reason for allocating disability pensions (Gabriel & Liimatainen, 2000).

In addition to workers' compensation claims, employers who fail to address workplace mental illness face increased absenteeism, higher staff turnover, higher accident rates, reduced productivity and lowered morale (Gabriel & Liimatainen, 2000; The US National Institute of Occupational Safety, 2005). The *WHO European Ministerial Conference on Mental Health* (World Health Organization, 2005a) estimated that depression will be the most common health problem by 2020. In terms of the overall organisation, all of this translates into reduced productivity and reduced output, which can significantly affect organisations' bottom line. A number of common threads link to the high incidence of stress, burnout and depression to a volatile labour market resulting from the effects of economic globalisation.

In all, the cost of mental health problems to industry and government has increased significantly over the last decade. Dealing with anxiety, depression and stress in the workplace has become an important issue for many organisations. Specific data is emerging to support the thrust of the International Labour Organization's concerns. These concerns are echoed in the *WHO Mental Health Action Plan for Europe* (World Health Organization, 2005b) which urged national governments, agencies and employers to undertake measures to improve work-related mental health.

STRESS IN THE WORKPLACE

In this book, affective reactions are conceptualised as precursors to stress in the workplace. The Health and Safety Executive (1995) in the UK have defined stress as 'the adverse reaction people have to excessive pressures or other types of demand placed on them'. The US National Institute of Occupational Safety (2005) defined stress generically as, 'the harmful physical and emotional responses that occur when the requirements of the job do not match the capabilities, resources, or needs of the worker' adding that 'Job stress can lead to poor mental health and even injury'. Affective wellbeing is treated in this book as a first order concept which underpins stress as a second order concept.

As noted earlier, job stress can lead to poor mental health. The terms 'stress', 'mental health' and 'burnout' tend to be used inconsistently and interchangeably in the literature (Pressman & Cohen, 2005). At times the terms 'stress' and 'burnout' are used predominantly to describe work-related outcomes, while mental health may be context free. Accurately measuring mental ill health, and conditions such as stress has proven difficult. Some people may indicate that they are suffering from stress rather than disclose that they actually feel depressed.

What one person believes to be stress, anxiety or depression may differ from what another understands as the terminology for the identical condition. Thus, different surveys may indicate similar levels for the cost of mental ill health to industry. Evidence is emerging to suggest that mental illness may be identified in measures of stress. One example is the ASSET (An Organizational Stress Screening Tool), which demonstrated good convergent validity with the General Health Questionnaire 12, an existing measure of minor psychiatric disorders (Johnson & Cooper, 2003).

Stress is not a medical condition but depression and anxiety are (Cooper, 2005). Frequently, workplace problems attributed to stress may actually be symptoms of depression and anxiety. Emotional reactions, resulting from intrinsic and extrinsic stimuli determine a person's reactions to stressful situations. As such, much of the research on the construct of stress informs the study of the construct of affective wellbeing, and vice versa. Job satisfaction has also been strongly associated with mental and psychological health problems, particularly burnout in the workplace (Faragher, Cass, & Cooper, 2005).

Lay people tend to have a common belief that all work stress or pressure is harmful, when in moderation it is actually beneficial. There is a positive aspect to pressure which has been found to stimulate motivation and vigilance in order to respond appropriately to challenging situations (Giga, Cooper, & Faragher, 2003). Stress is either the stimulus (cause) or response (symptoms) of workers to their environment. These have been separated into positive (eustress) and negative (distress) effects on individuals (Nankervis, 2004). Eustress represents the positive stress associated with achievement and exhilaration, such as meeting challenges (Selye, 1974). Distress refers to the negative aspects of stress such as feelings of inadequacy, insecurity, helplessness or desperation that result from too much or not enough pressure or tension (Selye, 1974). Two more forms of stress have been identified by Forster (2005: 60); hypostress ('rust out'), the absence of adequate stress and hyperstress ('burnout'), reduced personal health over an extended period of time leading to diminished affective wellbeing and performance.

Advocates of the person-environmental fit stress perspective (French,

Caplan, & Van Harrison, 1982) consider that employees' wellbeing and performance is hindered by strain (i.e., excessive challenge) or boredom (i.e., inadequate challenge). Demands that exceed or fall below employees' capacity to cope result in experiences of undesirable states (strain and boredom) that hamper wellbeing and performance. A healthy workplace from a stress standpoint is characterised by the absence of strain or boredom (Edwards, Caplan, & Van Harrison, 1998). Stressors have also been found to have a positive effect on personal initiatives, an aspect of contextual performance (Fay & Sonnentag, 2002).

When pressure becomes extreme, persistent and unrelieved it can lead to feelings of anger, fear and frustration which cause a range of illnesses that harm a person's mental and physical wellbeing (Giga, 2001). Empirical findings from longitudinal studies support the view that the work environment exerts an influence on mental and physical health, including both short and long term outcomes and health impairment, particularly cardio-vascular disease (Karasek, 1979; Wall, Kemp, Jackson, & Clegg, 1986; Karasek, 1989), as discussed in Chapter 2.

Organisational dynamics experienced by Australian managers, who comprised the dataset for this study, are similar to those facing managers in many other nation-states. Australian managers are under increasing pressure to produce superior results in shorter time-frames, with fewer resources (Forster & Still, 2001). Handy (1996) considered the '1/2 x 2 x 3' formula 'about right' for the work environment in Australia, New Zealand, the United Kingdom and North America. These findings are likely to apply to many managers in developed capitalist countries. To reach and sustain heightened levels of performance and to avoid burnout in this environment, it is desirable that organisations develop strategies for maintaining managers' affective wellbeing and intrinsic job satisfaction. Of the three psychological aspects of burnout (emotional exhaustion, depersonalisation, diminished sense of personal accomplishment), emotional exhaustion is becoming increasingly prevalent in workplaces (Lee & Ashforth, 1996).

Stress and the law

Stress related affective disorders are the newest form of 'social inflation' that organisations are increasingly being forced to deal with. This is symptomatic of the epidemic of overwork and pressures being experienced in contemporary workplaces. Work-related stress and associated medical ailments are amongst the costliest hazards of modern society (Smith, 1998). The incidence of stress in the developed world is approaching epidemic proportions, such that as long ago as 1993 'social commentators have been struck by the rising level of anxiety over the last 20 years by the extent to which people report stress as a central feature of their lives' (Mackay, 1993: 7). However, it is important to distinguish between the increased proclivity of employees to report stress as important to their wellbeing and the actual incidence of the disorder.

Managers who suffer physical or psychological injury are increasingly seeking legal compensation from their employers. In the USA, employees have been suing for stress related and job induced illness for over 30 years. A similar trend can now be seen in Australia's workplaces (Forster & Still, 2001). Occupational health and safety litigation by employees against their employer is increasing. Employees are now successfully suing for stress related illnesses, when they have suffered stress caused by their normal work and not by a physical accident as was previously the case (e.g. Walker vs. Northumberland County Council (Earnshaw & Cooper, 2003).

Previously, any injured person could claim damages where they suffered stress as a result of a negligent accident. These claims are based on the employer's duty to provide the employee with a safe working environment. As in the USA, this duty of care has been extended in many countries to include all aspects of work and foreseeable injury, including stress related clinical conditions. For a summary of the UK and USA cases where employees have successfully litigated on workplace stress refer to Earnshaw and Cooper (2003). Employers who fail to identify and act to reduce unreasonable work pressure may be liable for financial sanctions because organisations have a legal duty of care to protect their employees (Cooper & Cartwright, 1994).

MANAGERIAL THEORY

Theoretical foundations for this book

Theories about affective wellbeing and intrinsic job satisfaction have emerged mainly from Occupational Psychology, with a tangential influence from Organisational Behaviour. Research into managers' performance has been studied from a number of theoretical perspectives, including Industrial, Organisational and Occupational Psychology, Organisational Behaviour and Strategic Human Resource Management.

Industrial and Organisational Psychology research considers the influence that the affective wellbeing and intrinsic job satisfaction of individuals or groups has on organisational outcomes. Organisational psychologists typically investigate factors exogenous to individuals in the workplace. Organisational Behaviour research concentrates on the performance of individuals and work groups within organisations. This focus on organisational outputs has been criticised for over-emphasising managerial perspectives to the exclusion of individual affective wellbeing and job satisfaction (Staw, 1984).

In contrast, this book represents a departure from the conventional approaches to studies in this area by investigating endogenous factors related to managers. It is primarily located in the disciplines of Industrial and Occupational Psychology. Insights are also drawn from the interrelationships between a number of disciplines, theories and models related to the field of Management.

These disciplines, theories and models have been developed into a composite framework, as illustrated in Figure 1.1.

Figure 1.1 Theories, disciplines and schools

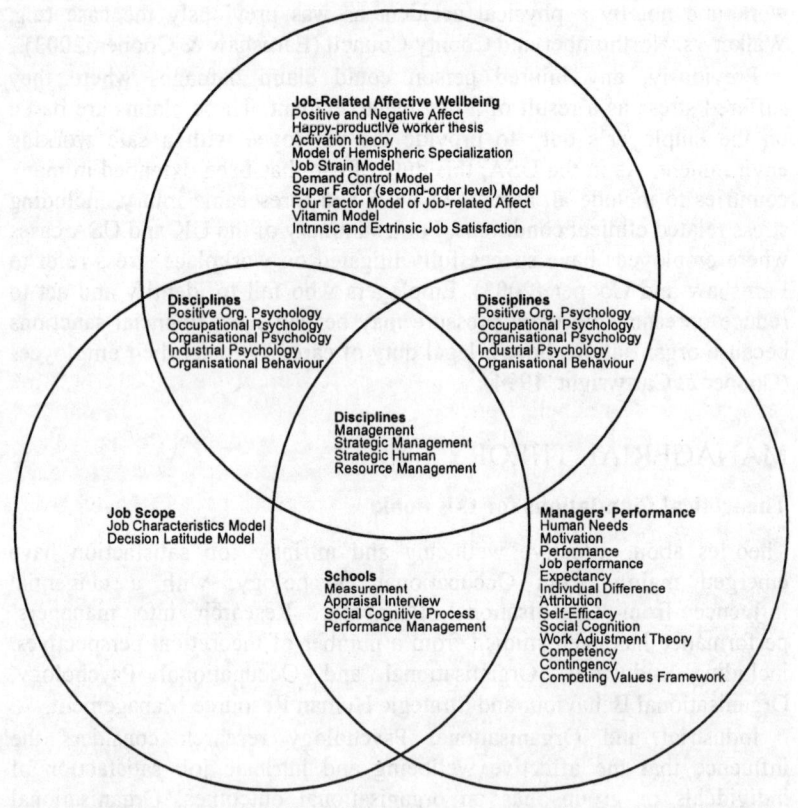

Job-Related Affective Wellbeing
Positive and Negative Affect
Happy-productive worker thesis
Activation theory
Model of Hemispheric Specialization
Job Strain Model
Demand Control Model
Super Factor (second-order level) Model
Four Factor Model of Job-related Affect
Vitamin Model
Intrinsic and Extrinsic Job Satisfaction

Disciplines
Positive Org. Psychology
Occupational Psychology
Organisational Psychology
Industrial Psychology
Organisational Behaviour

Disciplines
Positive Org. Psychology
Occupational Psychology
Organisational Psychology
Industrial Psychology
Organisational Behaviour

Disciplines
Management
Strategic Management
Strategic Human Resource Management

Job Scope
Job Characteristics Model
Decision Latitude Model

Schools
Measurement
Appraisal Interview
Social Cognitive Process
Performance Management

Managers' Performance
Human Needs
Motivation
Performance
Job performance
Expectancy
Individual Difference
Attribution
Self-Efficacy
Social Cognition
Work Adjustment Theory
Competency
Contingency
Competing Values Framework

None of these nominated disciplines are comprehensive in determining the nature of the relationship between managers' affective wellbeing, intrinsic job satisfaction and their performance. Therefore, a book on these phenomena is appropriately situated in an Industrial, Organisational and Occupational Psychology framework, complemented by elements of

Organisational Behaviour and Strategic Human Resource Management. Research in this book may be conceived of as part of the emerging movement to Positive Organisational Scholarship, a health model based on the premise that understanding and enabling human potential will create a positive path to human and organisational welfare (Cameron et al., 2003).

Human resource systems have the potential to facilitate or inhibit the development of organisational competencies (Lado & Wilson, 1994). Strategic Human Resource Management adopts a considered approach to managing an organisation's employees, consistent with the resource-based view of the firm (Schuler & Jackson, 1987). Strategic Management focuses initially on the environment, organisational sub units within organisations, work groups and finally individuals, as a means of bringing the organisations into alignment with its external environment. As such, Strategic Human Resource Management is concerned with aligning and integrating workplace practices that contribute to organisation's effectiveness. Theories about Organisational Behaviour and Strategic Management are interdependent because managers invariably implement an organisation's competitive strategy.

MANAGERS' PERFORMANCE

Job performance is arguably the most important dependent variable in Occupational, Industrial and Organisational Psychology. However, there is a lack of shared understanding in the literature about the construct 'job performance' (Campbell, Dunnette, Lawler, & Weick, 1970). Despite the large body of research and theoretical models, the concept of managers' performance is empirically underdeveloped. Research into managers' performance has not developed a comprehensive perspective of what constitutes a robust measure of managers' performance.

Managers' self-report was used by Befort and Kattrup (2003) to examine variations in the rating of the importance of contextual and task performance. Task performance proved to be important to all managers, and experience was positively correlated with rating of the importance of two contextual performance dimensions (Compliance and Extra Effort). But studies by Befort and Kattrup (2003) and Scullen, Mount and Judge (2003) yielded inconclusive results on the structure of employees' contextual and task performance.

Studies are emerging on the substance and structure of contextual and task performance managers. A 360° managerial development instrument used by Scullen, Mount and Judge (2003), employed a Confirmatory Factor Analysis of four lower order factors (Technical Skills, Administrative Skills, Human Skills and Citizenship Behaviours). They found that four rater perspectives (boss, peer, subordinate, and self) were generalizable across rater perspectives. Higher order factors (Contextual and Task Performance) were determined to be problematic using the same raters, indicating the structure of these rating was not generalizable.

Previous studies have conceived managers' job performance as a construct that comprises mainly task performance. To date, no research has explicitly and simultaneously measured both managers' contextual and task performance (Borman & Brush, 1993; Motowidlo & Schmit, 1999) in the field using onsite ratings by the superiors. Thus, a more sophisticated understanding of the concepts that underlie managers' performance needs to be developed before it can be related to affective wellbeing and intrinsic job satisfaction.

The approach adopted in this book contrasts with previous investigations into these concepts, as they have tended to focus on either isolated individual, or organisational factors of managers' performance. Indications are emerging from the literature to suggest that managers' contextual performance is an important contributor to organisational effectiveness. When aggregated over time and people, organisational citizenship behaviour (OCB), a subset of contextual performance, is postulated to enhance organisational effectiveness (Organ, 1988; Karambayya, 1990). Organisations are increasingly depending on behaviour that is outside managers' formal job descriptions (e.g., perseverance and conscientiousness). Reviews into the construct of performance (Isen & Baron, 1991; George & Brief, 1992) have indicated that positive affective wellbeing may be related to antecedents of contextual performance (e.g., persistence on uncertain tasks). Contextual performance is therefore poised to become increasingly important to organisations as global competition demands more of employees.

METHODOLOGY

A cross-sectional questionnaire was administered to managers from a range of private, public, and third sector occupational groupings in 19 Western Australian organisations to test establish research questions and test hypotheses questions derived from Partial Model to explain the link between affective states, traits and performance. Third Sector refers to private incorporated organisations receiving private, Commonwealth and/or State Government funding. Data was collected using self-report measures of affective wellbeing and intrinsic job satisfaction, and downward appraisal of managers' performance (by the person to whom managers report). A composite selection of private, public and third sector organisations were surveyed, representing managers from a range of occupational groups. A total of 400 questionnaires were returned from the 1,552 distributed, representing a 26% useable response rate.

Items for the questionnaire were derived from established affective wellbeing and intrinsic job satisfaction scales. Managers' contextual and task performance scales were sourced from the literature. Self-report data were used to measure affective wellbeing and intrinsic job satisfaction, while superiors' ratings provided an evaluation of managers' contextual and task performance. An empirical methodology was used to test the hypotheses to enable the research questions to be answered and to develop a Partial Model.

SUMMARY AND CONCLUSION

This book revisits a seminal question in management theory and practice - the 'happy-productive worker' thesis. There has long been an adherence to the intuitively appealing notion that happy employees perform better. The conceptualisation and analysis in this book has made substantial progress towards supporting the 'happy-productive worker' thesis as it has evolved into the 'happy-performing managers' proposition. The main goal was to establish which indicators of managers' affective wellbeing and intrinsic job satisfaction predict dimensions of their performance. In the process a substantial research question is revisited; what is the impact of affective wellbeing and intrinsic job satisfaction on managers' performance?

Answering this question required the development of a new instrument for measuring managers' performance, and also the differentiation of the constructs of affective wellbeing from intrinsic job satisfaction. Managers' job performance is arguably the most important dependent variable in Organisational Behaviour, Occupational, Industrial and Organisational Psychology but the construct is conceptually and empirically underdeveloped. A more refined understanding of what constitutes managers' performance needs to be undertaken before it can be related to affective wellbeing and intrinsic job satisfaction. There has been no prior explicit measurement of both managers' contextual and task performance using field ratings by the superiors.

Insights in this book are derived from the interrelationships between a number of disciplines, theories and models related to the field of management. The study of affective wellbeing, intrinsic job satisfaction and managers' performance is primarily situated in an Industrial, Organisational and Occupational Psychology framework which is complemented by elements of Organisational Behaviour and Strategic Human Resource Management. This research is situated in the emerging movement to Positive Organisational Scholarship which has begun investigating the link between happy employees and productive organisations.

Recent decades have witnessed two related major structural changes in developed economies - the intensification of global competition and the pervasive dispersal of computer-based technologies. Structural changes in state policies, resulting from the emergence of significant competitors in manufacturing industries from low-wage economies, has had important consequences for labour markets, particularly pay and working conditions. Radical alterations in work organisation have been reinforced by widespread and systematic changes in the workplace. Rising effort requirements of jobs, the changing extent of task discretion and other forms of employee involvement could be expected to affect managers' affective wellbeing. A further major change with implications for intrinsic job satisfaction is the rising level of competencies required in jobs resulting from the adoption of skill biased technological change.

Work is a pervasive and influential aspect of individual and organisational life. The incidence of work-related affective disorders in the developed world is approaching epidemic proportions. Individuals and organisations are increasingly being forced to acknowledge that this emerging form of social inflation may be attributed to overwork and pressure. The incidence of mental health problems affecting these workforces is increasing. Work-related stress and associated medical ailments are amongst the costly hazards for modern society. Mental health problems in the workplace are now regarded as an international problem of considerable magnitude. The 'happy-performing managers' proposition confronts a wider vista to contemplate how managers' 'private troubles' have become structural influences on 'public concerns'.

Changes to the design of managers' jobs have the potential to either improve or worsen managers' affective wellbeing and intrinsic job satisfaction and consequently, their performance. Identifying factors that either positively or negatively impact on managers' affective wellbeing and intrinsic job satisfaction will enable recommendations to be made for designing jobs and altering work environments that will then assist managers to achieve optimal performance. Such information may permit the identification of the relevant job characteristics that can be adjusted to assist in promoting positive affective wellbeing and intrinsic job satisfaction. This can be seen as preventative 'managerial medicine'.

2. Job-related affective wellbeing and intrinsic job satisfaction

INTRODUCTION

> Man is the only animal that laughs and weeps, for he is the only animal that is struck with the difference between what things are, and what they ought to be.
> (Hazlitt, cited in Pearsall, 1988: 118)

This chapter critiques the substantial literature on how affective wellbeing and intrinsic job satisfaction are conceived and measured. The nature of happiness is explored, beginning with the philosophical roots and ending with contemporary understandings of the phenomenon. Insights gained from this exploration form the basis for an understanding of affective wellbeing, and how it is differentiated from intrinsic job satisfaction. The relative importance of the cognitive and affective aspects to intrinsic job satisfaction is debated.

Various disciplines, theories, models and schools of thought are detailed which contextualise affective wellbeing and intrinsic job satisfaction. A tripartite heuristic framework comprising: Dispositional, Activity and Telic categories are used to organise the affective wellbeing literature. Each category of the framework explains the tenets of the most influential theories and debates their veracity.

Key theoretical developments are integrated to provide linkages between the conceptual bases of these constructs. These categories are used to contextualise the Vitamin Model, the Demand-Control Model, and the dispositional approach to job satisfaction. Models of affective wellbeing are identified, and issues involved in developing an integrated model of affective wellbeing are given. In particular, Warr's Vitamin Model was identified as the most comprehensive synthesis of research and theories into affective wellbeing. 'Emotional Intelligence' also emerged as a way of integrating these theories in the workplace.

DIFFERENTIATING THE FORMS OF AFFECTIVE WELLBEING

Affective wellbeing (Warr, 1990b) refers to feelings about either life in general (i.e. 'context-free'), or affect in relation to a specific domain (i.e., 'job-related' and 'facet-specific'). In relation to affective wellbeing, the term 'job' refers to the specific tasks undertaken by individuals in a particular setting, whereas, work, refers to jobs in general (Warr, Cook, & Wall, 1979: 1179).

Table 2.1 and Figure 2.1 also illustrate how aspects of job-related, context-free and facet-specific affective wellbeing and intrinsic job satisfaction relate to the affect axes of Discontented-Contented, Anxious-Comfortable and Depressed-Actively Pleased. A host of context-free and facet-specific factors impact on affective wellbeing. Differences between job-related, facet-specific and context-free affective wellbeing are schematically represented in Figure 2.1.

Figure 2.1 Differentiating job-related affective wellbeing from facet-specific and context-free affective wellbeing

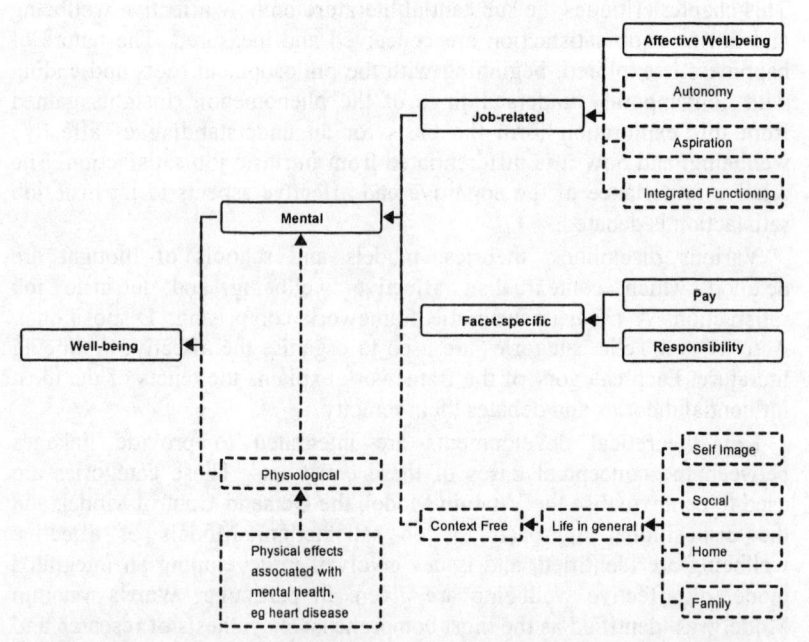

Context-free and facet-specific affective wellbeing have different predictors. Facet-specific affective wellbeing includes factors such as pay, responsibility, colleagues, supervisors, working conditions, promotional prospects, security of employment, the organisation as a whole, and the kind of work undertaken. Different facet-specific satisfactions tend to be inter-correlated.

Context-free affective wellbeing includes factors such as satisfaction with self image, physical health, and social and home life which are known to contribute to affective wellbeing, but are outside the scope of the this investigation (Warr, 1987), and although there is ample research evidence of interactions between managers' work and their life in general, these have not been included as they have already been thoroughly dealt with in other studies (e.g., Warr, 1990a; Cooper, 1996).

Table 2.1 provides details of the differences between job-related, facet-specific and context-free affective wellbeing.

Table 2.1 *Affective wellbeing axes of measurement and levels of specificity*

Bipolar Axes	Context-free	Job-related	Facet-specific
	Affective wellbeing		
Discontented-Contented	Happiness Life satisfaction General distress Negative affect	Job satisfaction Job attachment Organisational commitment Alienation from work	Specific satisfaction (with pay, amount of responsibility, etc)
Anxious-Comfortable	Anxiety Neuroticism	Job-related tension Job-related pressure Resigned satisfaction	Specific feelings of job strain
Depressed-Actively Pleased	Positive affect Depression Tedium Self-denigration	High morale Job involvement Job boredom Job-related depression Job-related burnout	Specific aspects of job boredom, and learned helplessness

Source: Warr (1987: 47).

ORIGINS OF RESEARCH INTO AFFECTIVE WELLBEING AND EMOTIONS

Emotions, happiness and affective wellbeing

> Striving toward pleasure or happiness is the basic motivation for all human behaviour.
> (Tracey, 1993: 73)

Psychologists now recognise the critical influence of affect in human experience. Affective wellbeing has its philosophical and theoretical foundations in the concept of happiness. Happiness is one of the most obscure expressions in the English language (Haybron, 2003). The word happy is 'characterised by or indicative of pleasure, content, or gladness' (Delbridge, Bernard, Blair, Peters, & Butler, 1996: 801). Classical philosophers have contemplated the authentic nature of happiness for centuries. To this day, numerous journal articles and books continue to pursue this most fundamental and elusive of human meaning. Some contend that 'the secret of happiness is the holy grail of the new millennium' (Bagnall, 2004).

The Greek philosopher Epicurus proffered a hedonistic perspective of happiness which he reasoned to be a natural condition 'guided by our innate instincts for pleasure and penchant for avoiding pain' (cited in Waterfield, 1993: 11). According to the ancient philosophers, humankind is destined never to attain happiness, as only the Gods are permitted to recognise the sensation or experience this feeling. As with beauty, Plato reasoned that happiness cannot be described, but only experienced. Aristotle, an early proponent of 'activity theory', maintained that happiness is achieved through virtuous activity performed well. In the *Categoria*, Aristotle (cited in Ackrill, 1963) approached the concept of happiness in a more temperate way, as one of the eight metaphysical dimensions of life that humans are destined to struggle to attain.

The type of flourishing described by the philosophers Aristotle and Plato was called eudaimonia ('having a good guardian spirit'), a valuable kind of wellbeing that is more than a state of mind (Haybron, 2003). Aristotle proposed that the pursuit of happiness is the ultimate human undertaking; 'something final and self-sufficient, and is the end of action' (Aristotle, translated by Ross, 1952: 343). He concluded: 'Therefore, we call final without qualification that which is always desirable in itself and never for the sake of something else. Such a thing is happiness, above all else, is held to be; for this we choose always for itself and never for the sake of something else' (p. 342).

In a similar vein, Pascal asserted that 'man wishes to be happy, and only wishes to be happy, and cannot wish not to be so' (Pascal cited in Hutchins, 1952: 203). More recently, Existentialists argued that humankind is forced to choose between freedom and happiness, because they cannot both be experienced simultaneously (Adolphs, Tranel, Damasio, & Damasio, 1995). Happiness is fundamental to the human condition, and is the natural state for a human being (Domeyko, 1996). Debate continues amongst psychologists over whether happiness is a state, a fleeting occurrence due to some positive event, or simply the accumulation over time of individual happy feelings Veenhoven (1995b; 1995a) reasoned that happy people are those most able to control their environment.

A contemporary metaphysical perspective as to what constitutes happiness is, according to Domeyko, 'essentially an energy flow that occurs when you remove the negativities and blocks from your mind and so open yourself to more of the life force' (1996: 10). Thus, a clear sense of direction seems to be an important aspect of making a valuable contribution to life through 'the progressive realization of a worthy ideal' (Frankl, cited in Tracey, 1993: 29). This immutable 'striving toward pleasure or happiness is the basic motivation for all human behaviour' (Tracey, 1993: 73). More globally, the Dalai Lama (1999: 62, 263) concluded, 'the purpose of life is happiness', and that:

> Ultimate happiness depends on eliminating our negative behaviours and mental states - things like anger, hatred, greed, and so on, since excessive levels of worry and anxiety serve no useful purpose and do nothing but undermine ... happiness and interfere with [the] ability to accomplish goals.

Defining the fundamental nature of happiness and measuring its essence is bound to be difficult. Damasio argued that 'The essence of sadness or happiness is the combined perception of certain body states with whatever thoughts they are juxtaposed to, complemented by a modification in the style and efficiency of the thought process' (1994: 146-147).

Paradoxically, according to others, our experience of happiness must also include a measure of darkness; as its opposing force loses its meaning if not balanced by sadness (Jung, 1933). Marcel Proust believed that 'Happiness serves hardly any other purpose than to make unhappiness possible' in conjunction with Mark Twain, who in 1909 observed that 'happiness ain't a thing in itself - it's only a contrast with something that ain't pleasant'. Happiness is essentially a feeling, a state of mind that is an individualistic experience, since 'what brings happiness to one person ill fits another' (Epicurus, cited in Waterfield, 1993: 9).

Reasoning and research into the construct of happiness preceded research into affective wellbeing. Emotions and happiness are arguably the 'primitive' (or first order) conceptual bases of affective wellbeing. According to George and Brief (1996: 145) affect is 'a broad generic term that covers both the intense feelings and reactions people have, which are commonly referred to as emotions, and the less intense, but no less important, feelings often called moods'. While emotions and happiness are closely related, they are not identical to the construct of affective wellbeing. Happiness is related to emotional states like hopefulness, optimism and contentment. Job-related affective wellbeing is the closest expression of happiness available at present.

There are substantial differences between emotions and affect or mood. Emotions are of short duration, while affect or mood persists over a longer period of time. Managers who are happy would be expected to display these rather stable characteristics over time. Because emotion or affect encompasses a broad class of events to fall into a single scientific category, Russell and Feldman Barrett (1999) offered the following illustration to differentiate emotion from affect or mood. They made an important distinction between *prototypical emotional episodes* and *core affect to* draw attention to the practice of using qualitatively different kinds of events to describe the more generic term *emotion*. A prototypical emotional episode is described by Russell and Feldman Barrett (1999: 806) 'as a complex set of interrelated sub events concerned with a specific object ... that the emotional episode is about'. We are, for example, fearful off, surprised at, or angry with someone or about something. Core effect, on the other hand, was referred to by Russell and Feldman Barrett (1999: 806) as 'the most elementary consciously accessible affective feeling (and their neurophysiological counterparts) that need not be directed at anything ... and can be free floating as in moods'. Although core affect and prototypical emotional episodes are related, they are distinguishable, with core effect forming part of a prototypical emotional episode.

Core effect can be described in terms of two orthogonal dimensions - degree of pleasantness and degree of activation. A combination of these two independent dimensions provides a descriptive map that can be used to collate core affect at any particular point in time. Russell (1980) argued that affect descriptors in this map are organised in a circular arrangement forming an affect circumplex, where affects at a 90° angle are independent of each other (e.g., elated vs stressed), while those 180° apart are semantic opposites (e.g., tense vs relaxed), as illustrated in Figure 2.2. Although the even spacing of the affect descriptors around the circumference is not a necessary condition for the model, the requirement that the affects are equidistant from the centre of the circle is essential (Russell & Feldman Barrett, 1999).

THE MEASUREMENT OF AFFECTIVE WELLBEING

Although there may be some ambiguity as to whether happiness is an emotion (i.e., joy), a cognitive evaluation (i.e., satisfaction), or a combination of both (Argyle & Martin, 1991), the majority of studies have treated 'happiness' as an emotional state. The empirical nature of contemporary definitions of happiness (many have lamented the atheoretical nature of research in the area) originated with Bradburn's (1969) and his colleague's research. They investigated how certain macro level societal changes (e.g., educational level, urbanisation, etc.) impacted the life of the individual, and influenced psychological wellbeing which was measured through the development of an affect scale intended to measure emotional wellbeing. These researchers found that the scale items formed two clusters that were relatively independent of each other.

This chance finding emanating from a study of social change was counter-intuitive, because it meant that people who reported high positive affect were neither more nor less likely than others to report high negative affect. Up to that time it had been assumed that experiencing one type of affect (either positive or negative) would act against experiencing the other. These two dimensions were also found to be related differentially to sets of variables. For example, positive affect (PA) was related to active participation in social activities, while negative affect (NA) was found to be associated with anxiety, marital and sexual problems, and symptoms of ill-health. In Bradburn's terms happiness has been operationalised as the balance between positive and negative affect.

There is now a large body of research confirming Bradburn's results. When these ratings of adjectives describing affects are factor analysed, two dimensions usually account for the major portion of variance. The usual finding from the unrotated solution has been a pleasantness-unpleasantness dimension defined by such terms as *satisfied, pleased* vs. *unhappy, sad,* and an activation or arousal dimension defined by *aroused, surprised* vs. *still, quiet,* and so forth (Russell, 1980). If the axes of the unrotated solution are subjected to a Varimax (orthogonal) rotation, a two-factor structure of affect emerges (Watson & Tellegen, 1985). Watson and Tellegen (1985) concluded that 'in our own studies and in virtually all published self-report studies that we have subsequently reanalysed, we have encountered the same two large, bipolar dimensions'. These were labelled Positive Affect (PA) and Negative Affect (NA).

POSITIVE AND NEGATIVE AFFECT SCHEDULE (PANAS)

Scales capturing the two high poles of these affects have been developed by Watson, Clark and Tellegen (1988). The Positive and Negative Affect Schedule (PANAS) defines PA with such items as *enthusiastic, interested, determined,* etc., and NA with items such as *scared, afraid, upset,* etc. A more comprehensive scale, the Job Affect Scale (Brief, Burke, George, Robinson, & Webster, 1988), captures the entire PA and NA space (i.e., both high and low poles of PA and NA), as does Warr's (1990b). conceptualisation of affect. According to this definition the opposite of high PA (*enthusiastic, elated,* etc.) is low PA (*sluggish, sleepy,* etc.), while the opposite of high NA (*hostile, scornful,* etc.) is low NA (*calm, relaxed,* etc.). In this bipolar conceptualisation of affect only the high poles represent the experience of affect per se, while the low poles represent states that are relatively free of emotional involvement (Watson, 1988).

The labelling of Positive Affect (PA) and Negative Affect (NA) has been criticised in the literature because it misrepresents the valence of these two affect dimensions (Watson, Vaidya, & Tellegen, 1999). PA, for example, may imply fluctuations in positive mood states throughout the length of the dimension, although it actually contains adjectives that are negatively-valenced in its low pole. The reverse is also the case with the NA dimension; that is, adjectives describing its low pole are positively-valenced. For this reason, and in order to eliminate any ambiguity, it is important that researchers make explicit whether they are considering either the bipolar or the high poles of the dimensions only. This prescription, however, is not evident in the literature and has led to the misrepresentation and measurement of affect dimensions (e.g., Green, Goldman, & Salovey, 1993). As recently as 2003, Huelsman, Furr, and Nemanick (2003) mislabelled the bipolar dimensions describing the low NA pole of Watson et al's model PA, and the low PA pole NA, adding to the confusion.

Other researchers have proposed similar affective structures, albeit using different labels to explain the equivalent constructs. For example, Watson's (1988) high PA is Thayer's (1978) 'high energetic arousal', and Mackay, Cox, Burrows and Lazzarini's (1978) 'high arousal'. Watson's low PA is Thayer's 'low energetic arousal', and Mackay's et al. 'low arousal'. Also, Watson's high NA is Thayer's 'high tense arousal', and Mackay's et al. 'high stress', while Watson's low NA is Thayer's 'low tense arousal', and Mackay's et al. 'low stress'.

Consistent with this conceptualisation is Warr's (1990a; 1994d) description of affective wellbeing in the occupational setting through two principal axes. These two axes are labelled anxiety-comfort (high and low NA respectively) and depression-enthusiasm (low and high PA respectively). These two axes parallel those of Watson and his colleagues, and are measured through scales that capture similar affects to those captured by Brief et al. (1988). The dimensions from the Brief et al. scales have been re-labelled nervousness-relaxation, and enthusiasm-fatigue by Burke, Brief, George, Roberson and Webster (1989).

Diener and Emmons (1985), however, have proposed a somewhat different affect structure from the one proposed by Watson and his colleagues. Diener and his colleagues used for PA such items as *happy*, *pleased*, and *satisfied*, while NA was defined by *unhappy*, *blue*, and *lonely*, etc. PA, therefore, captures the 'pleasantness' sector of Watson and Tellegen's (1985) affective space (shown in Figure 2.2, sectors 2 and 3), and NA captures the 'unpleasantness' and 'high negative affect' space (sectors 6, 7 and part of sector 8).

An issue that has emerged from research on affect is whether it is useful to distinguish between the frequency and intensity of affective reactions. The distinction is important, because the popular view would suggest that wellbeing is at its maximum when positive affect is both frequent and intense, while negative affect is infrequent and in low intensity (Diener, Sandvik, & Pavot, 1991). A number of studies were carried out to test this common sense view. Diener, Larsen, Levine and Emmons (1985) reported research suggesting that positive and negative affect are strongly inversely correlated. However, work on subjective wellbeing indicated that over time, positive and negative affect were independent across persons.

Figure 2.2 represents the affective space in wellbeing research by integrating Russell's (1980), Warr's (1990a; 1994d), and Watson's and Tellegen's (1985) conceptualisations of affect.

Figure 2.2 Principal Axes of Affective Wellbeing Space

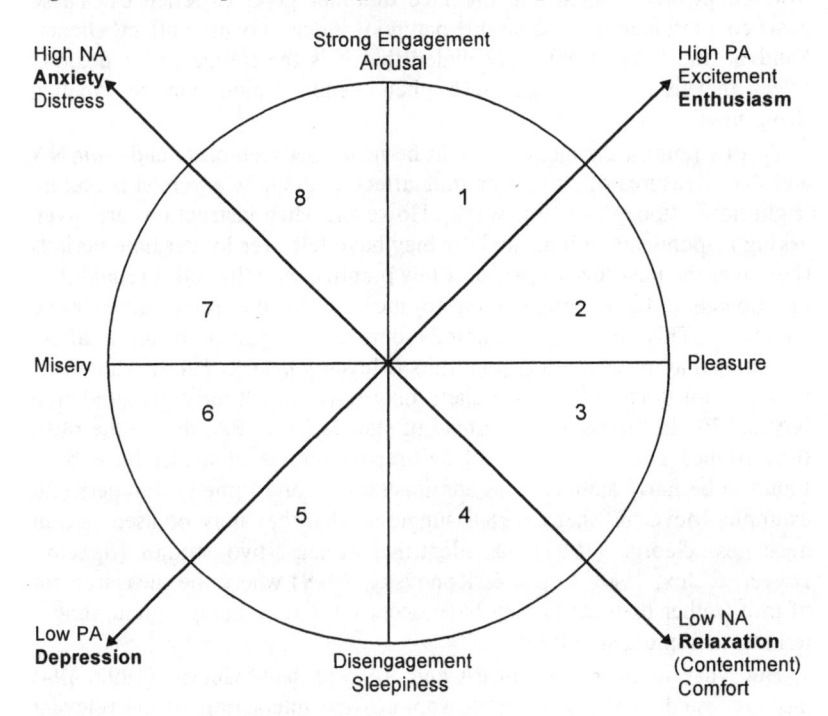

Source: Sevastos (1996: 12).

To reconcile this inconsistency, Diener et al. (1985) proposed a two-dimensional affective structure: the frequency of PA vs NA, and the intensity of affect. Across three studies designed to explore this inconsistency they found that the frequency and intensity of affect varied independently. Although average levels of PA and NA showed low correlations, this relationship became strongly inverse when intensity was partialled out. In this way, the intensity dimension helped explain the relative independence of PA and NA.

Diener, Sandvik and Pavot (1991) also addressed the question whether frequency of PA, intensity of PA, or both are necessary and sufficient for happiness. Their results suggested that happiness or affective wellbeing is related primarily to the frequency and not to the intensity of PA. But why do intense positive experiences (although desirable at the time of experience) not contribute greatly to subjective wellbeing in the long run? This question was answered by Diener, Colvin, Pavot, and Allman (1991) who in a series of five studies concluded that intense positive experiences may sometimes have costs in the form of increased negative affect, and lowered positive valence in the face of other good experiences. These costs counterbalance the desirable nature of intense positive affect. Diener, Sandvik and Pavot (1991) concluded that it is the frequency of positive affect that is the 'essence of a phenomenon which can be labelled 'happiness'.

At this point a distinction should be made between *state* and *trait* NA and PA. Measures of current or *state* affect assess how a person is feeling 'right now', 'today', or 'this week'. However, when instructions are given asking respondents to indicate how they have felt over longer time periods (i.e., over the past few weeks, past few months, etc.) the retest reliabilities of subjects' affect ratings tend to increase as the rated time frame increases. This stability prompted some to suggest that these affect measures may in fact be tapping traits (Meyer & Shack, 1989). Therefore, it is possible that some researchers may have unwittingly captured trait NA and PA in their studies, instead of state NA and PA, due to the rated time frame. The coefficients of self-report ratings of affect have been found to be fairly stable across administrations, and some researchers (for example, Meyer & Shack, 1989) suggested that they may be used as trait measures. George (1991) has identified at least two studies (Spector, Dwyer, & Jex, 1988; Organ & Konovsky, 1989) where the measurement of trait (rather than state) may have occurred, due to inappropriate longer term time frame instructions.

But what do state and trait PA and NA represent? George (1992: 194) has suggested 'that a given state captures the interaction of the relevant personality or dispositional and situational factors'. State affect is, therefore, a function of the person and the situation. On the other hand trait PA and NA reflect individual differences in positive and negative emotionality (also referred to in the literature as positive and negative affectivity) that are maintained under all conditions, even in the absence of external stimuli. High NA individuals are, therefore, more likely to report distress, discomfort, and dissatisfaction over time regardless of the situation (Watson & Pennebaker, 1989), whereas high PA individuals have a sense of excitement and enthusiasm (Watson, Pennebaker, & Folger, 1987), a generalised sense of wellbeing, and a zest for life, independent of the influences of NA (Costa & McCrae, 1980).

Measurement issues in PA and NA research

A number of studies investigated the possibility that PA and NA will show different associations depending on the response format. Warr, Barter, and Brownbridge (1983), for example, found that their PA and NA scales correlated only -.01 when the customary dichotomous (yes–no) Bradburn (1969) response format was used, but the correlation increased to -.54 when a 7-point frequency mode was used, in which subjects rated the proportion of a given time period they had experienced each affective state. A replication study by Watson (1988) confirmed the Warr et al. results; that is, the PA and NA scales were more highly negatively correlated using the frequency format. However, Watson also found that this relationship was dependent on the choice of descriptors. For example, pleasantness-unpleasantness descriptors making up the scales were affected more by the frequency format than *pure* PA and NA markers. Scales which were made up with pure PA and NA markers, such as the PANAS scales, remained largely independent.

The choice of descriptors has also resulted in some contradictory findings in the literature of self-rated affect. Although orthogonal PA and NA factors emerged from ratings based on short time periods (Watson & Tellegen, 1985), others (e.g., Emmons & Diener, 1985) reported strong negative correlations using the same time instructions. This anomaly was attributed to the complexity of some descriptors (those reflecting happiness, contentment, and sociability), which captured in addition to PA low NA. Conversely, descriptors that loaded high on NA captured also low PA (items reflecting depression and loneliness). Watson (1988) argued that, because these terms are part of the pleasantness and unpleasantness dimensions, they will produce NA and PA scales that are negatively correlated with each other.

Inappropriate mood descriptors were also used by Green, Goldman, and Salovey (1993) who questioned the consistent results reported in the literature confirming the independence of PA and NA. When they investigated the independence of happiness and sadness using confirmatory factor analytic techniques, the observed correlation of -.27 was estimated at -.85 after controlling for random and systematic measurement error. They concluded that pleasant and unpleasant affect are in fact opposites, but this relationship is masked by measurement error. However, in two out of three reported studies, their adjective list of mood items clearly captured the high PA and low PA affective space (i.e., segments 1, 2 and 5, 6 respectively in Figure 2.2), and not PA and NA (i.e., segments 1, 2 and 7, 8 respectively in Figure 2.2). When the mood adjective list was correctly modified to capture affect operating in a state of arousal (an operationalisation consistent with findings of orthogonal dimensionality), the estimated inter-factor correlation after controlling for random error was -.57, and -.58 with non-random error controlled. These results are rendered inconclusive on bipolarity as Green et al.'s (1993: 1037) comment in a footnote states that in 'none of our studies does a nested χ^2 difference test enable us to accept the null hypothesis that one rather than two factors generated the data'.

Based on this data Sevastos (1996) argued that PA and NA are neither bipolar nor orthogonal but correlated and distinguishable affects. More recently, Feldman Barrett and Russell (1998) have made recommendations for the use of mood descriptors to test the bipolarity versus independence of affect by selecting affect adjectives that were 180° apart in the affect circumplex, and were opposite in both the arousal and valence dimensions. The circumplex model may assist in the identification of such semantic opposites, as the affect descriptors are arranged in a continuous fashion around the perimeter of the affective space defined by the orthogonal dimensions of arousal and pleasure (Russell, 1980). However, Haslam (1995b; 1995a) argued for a simple structure where the circumplex may be better represented by a number of category boundaries that identify discrete segments of the affective space, with low levels of discriminability within segments and stronger levels in adjacent segments, analogous to the colour spectrum.

A decision confronting the researcher often is whether to measure affect at the discrete level or at the second order level. For example, Watson and Tellegen's (1985) hierarchical model of self-rated affect has two broad general dimensions (NA and PA) each composed of several correlated yet ultimately distinguishable sub-dimensions. Diener, Smith and Fujita (1995) found in their study that despite strong correlations between discrete emotions of the same hedonic tone (shame, fear, sadness, anger, and love and joy), these could not be conflated into two global positive and negative groupings.

When competing models of affect were tested (through structural equations modelling), the model that included the discrete affects fitted the data significantly better than a second order model. Diener et al. concluded that although the same individuals tended to experience as many pleasant as unpleasant affects, individual differences in the discrete affects could not be completely reduced to the two global categories of PA and NA. Their results demonstrate the importance of assessing both levels of the hierarchical structure in studies of self-rated affect.

Watson and Clark (1992b) recognised the importance of specificity versus non-specificity in studies of self-rated affect, but view these two levels of analysis as complementary rather than mutually exclusive. They argue that since these phenomena exist in tension with each other, it is a scientifically important task to disentangle their unique contributions to affect-related phenomena as much as possible. In a more recent reformulation of their model Watson and his colleagues (Watson et al., 1999) proposed a modified three level hierarchical structure that consists of a bipolar Pleasantness-Unpleasantness dimension at the highest level in the hierarchy, the two largely orthogonal Positive and Negative Affect dimensions at the intermediate level, and at the lowest level in the hierarchy the discrete effects (i.e., enthusiastic, depressed, anxious, and comfortable to borrow Warr's marker variables).

MEASURING JOB-RELATED AFFECTIVE WELLBEING

Given the difficulty of defining and identifying the essence of happiness, when specifying affective wellbeing, it is not surprising that centuries passed before psychometrically robust measures of the concepts were developed. The quandary remains; how can a subjective feeling like happiness be adequately measured?

Research into the relationships between context-free psychological wellbeing and organisational outcomes has a long tradition of theoretical development and empirical testing (Mayo, 1933). For example, Bradburn and Caplovitz (1965) attempted to assess a person's sense of overall affective wellbeing using a global measure based on a single item; 'Taking all things together, how would you say things are these days - would you say you are very happy, pretty happy, or not too happy these days?' (Bradburn, 1969: 55). Watson and Tellegen (1985) noted that a substantial body of studies have confirmed Bradburn and Caplovitz's results as being strong predictors of overall life satisfaction.

A large amount of research in Organisational Behaviour and Occupational Psychology has focused on affective wellbeing as one aspect of mental health. Typically, in the workplace affective wellbeing has been measured in an undifferentiated way, by referring to 'feeling good', or 'feeling bad', or 'being satisfied' in your job or 'unsatisfied' (Warr, 1990b). A number of researchers have identified two separate dimensions, 'pleasure' and 'arousal', and they have been usefully incorporated in more sophisticated forms of measurement of affect (Mackay et al., 1978; Russell, 1980; Watson & Tellegen, 1985; Matthews, Davies, Westerman, & Stammers, 2000) Thayer (1989).

Many inventories have been developed by researchers based on Beeham's (1981) measure of 'general psychological wellbeing' and particular self-report aspects of job-related affect such as distress, life satisfaction, anxiety and depression. Diener (1984) reviewed a plethora of single and multi-item measures of general affect. Originally, affective wellbeing was measured by scales designed to measure context-free wellbeing. Two independent clusters of items emerged from these scales, indicating that people who report high PA were not predisposed to report high NA. PA was found to be related to active participation in social activities, and NA was associated with anxiety and symptoms of ill-health. Thus, a differential relationship was established between these two dimensions, a finding that overturned the prevailing assumption that experiencing either PA or NA mitigate against experiencing the other.

Based on a similar conceptualization, Warr (1990a; 1990b) developed two-dimensional bipolar measures to capture the high and low affective poles. These have been labelled Enthusiasm-Depression, and Anxiety-Comfort. Because Warr's measures are intended to measure 'state' affect (i.e., 'how have you been feeling over the last few days?'), while the PANAS capture temperament (i.e., 'how do you normally feel?'), it is customary in affect studies to use the PANAS as control variables when assessing state affect, so that the impact of situational factors may be assessed more accurately.

Costa and McCrae (1980: 1062) proposed a 'model of happiness', asserting that differences among individuals in PA and NA are a direct consequence of differences in the personality variables of extraversion and neuroticism. Thus, PA is not simply the opposite of NA but represents a distinct dimension of personality. Watson, Clark and Carey (1988: 1062) explained:

> Positive Affect (PA) reflects the extent to which a person feels enthusiastic, active and alert. High PA is a state of high energy, full concentration and pleasurable engagement, whereas low PA is characterized by sadness and lethargy. In contrast, Negative Affect is a general dimension of subjective distress and unpleasurable engagement that subsumes a variety of adverse mood states, including anger, contempt, disgust, guilt, fear, and nervousness, with low NA being a state of calmness and serenity.

Trait PA and NA are also reflected in individual differences that are maintained by people under all conditions, even in the absence of external stimuli. Consequently, low-NA people are more likely to report distress, discomfort, and dissatisfaction over time, regardless of the situation (Watson & Pennebaker, 1989). By contrast, high-PA individuals possess a sense of exuberance and enthusiasm (Watson et al., 1987), a generalised sense of affective wellbeing, and a zest for life independent of the situation

(Costa & McCrae, 1980).

A subsequent longitudinal study by Costa and McCrae (1988) reported high test-retest correlations, supporting the stability of the PA and NA constructs (Watson & Tellegen, 1985; Watson, 1988; Watson, Clark, & Tellegen, 1988). PA and NA have also been shown by other researchers to be related to the personality constructs of extraversion and neuroticism respectively (Eysenck & Eysenck, 1985; Larsen & Ketelaar, 1989; Meyer & Shack, 1989; Williams, 1989).

SUMMARY

Many attempts to measure affect in occupational settings began with context-free affect, prior to measuring this phenomenon in occupational settings. Robust methods, based on Confirmatory Factor Analysis (CFA), have been developed to determine the dimensionality of context-free affect. Empirical research in the occupational literature suggests that antecedents of affective wellbeing constructs can be accurately measured.

THE PHYSIOLOGICAL BASIS OF EMOTION

> From the brain and the brain alone arise our pleasures, joys, laughter and jests, as well as our sorrows, pains and griefs.
> (Hippocrates translated by Jones, 1923, 1981).

Watson and his colleagues (1999) have argued that the accumulating evidence suggests that fluctuations in self-reports of PA and NA reflect the subjective components of two broad bio-behavioural systems involving the left and the right frontal cortex, whose operations have been linked to frontal asymmetry (Tomarken & Keener, 1998). These systems have evolved to handle key adaptive tasks associated with goal-directed approach and withdrawal behaviours, respectively (Davidson, Ekman, Saron, Senulis, & Friesen, 1990).

Self-report NA is associated with the withdrawal-oriented Behavioural Inhibition System (BIS), while PA has been associated with the approach system known as the behavioural engagement system (BES). The function of the BIS is to facilitate the withdrawal of the individual from sources of aversive stimulation (Irwin, Rebert, McAdam, & Knott, 1966). It has also an anticipatory function, which inhibits behaviour that could potentially create dangerous situations for the organism, by scanning the environment to detect stimuli that are emotionally laden.

Information from any aversive stimulus travels from the sensory thalamus to the amygdala and the cortex. The cortex feeds back to the amygdala this information and initiates the release of the stress hormone, activates the autonomic system, triggers emotion, suppresses pain, and evokes attention. The amygdala therefore, as a substrate for aversion, is critically involved in the withdrawal system (LeDoux, 1995), and the experience of negative affect (Adolphs et al., 1995).

Self-report PA on the other hand is associated with the operation of the BES, an appetitive system of behavioural approach, which directs the organisms toward experiences that are potentially pleasurable and rewarding (Wise, 1996). A major convergence zone for motivationally relevant information is the nucleus accumbens, particularly the cudomedial shell region of this centre, which forms part of the mesolimpic dopamine system (Cacioppo, Gardner, & Berntson, 1999). Cells in this region increase their firing rate during reward expectancy, and this stimulation triggers release of dopamine (Hoebel, Rada, Mark, & Pothos, 1999), which is behaviourally expressed in terms of enthusiasm and confidence as the organism moves towards the attainment of the desired goal.

Another form of PA is associated with post-goal attainment when cells in the nucleus accumbens tend to decrease their firing rate, and this is experienced as contentment (Davidson, 1998). These positive feelings increase the likelihood that goal-directed activities are performed in future. In contrast, low levels of PA are associated with depressed effect (Mineka, Watson, & Clark, 1998) expressed as loss of pleasure due to failure to receive sufficient rewards for one's efforts leading to a reduction in goal-directed behaviour (Tomarken & Keener, 1998).

A model that focuses on the underlying physiological processes that are linked to the experience of positive and negative affect is the Evaluative Space Model (ESM) (Cacioppo & Berntson, 1994; Cacioppo et al., 1999; 2001). This model posits that just because PA is linked to the approach system and NA to the withdrawal system this does not imply that they must be reciprocally activated. In fact the neurophysiological evidence suggests that the left and right cortical hemispheres are differentially involved in affective processing, with the right and left frontal cortex involved in withdrawal and approach affective reactions, respectively.

Activation may occur, for example, when changes in one system are not associated with changes in the other; or when changes in one system are accompanied by parallel or opposite changes in the other system. This model of affect, therefore, is inconsistent with Russell's bipolar model, which treats affects that are semantically opposites as mutually exclusive (i.e., happiness and sadness), although Russell and Feldman Barrett (1999) made a distinction between evaluative reactions to a stimulus, and 'core affect' as pointed out earlier.

Larsen, McGraw, and Cacioppo (2001) have reviewed the evidence on

Russell and Carroll's (1999) circumplex model, Watson and Tellegen's (1985) PA and NA model (i.e., high arousal PA and NA as measured with the PANAS), and compared these models with the ESM. They found convergent evidence from neurophysiology and subjective experience that evaluative reactions are more easily accommodated within a bivariate rather than a bipolar space. By arguing that positive and negative affect are separable, the ESM predicts that the concurrent experience of mixed feelings, such as feeling happy and sad, is possible.

In a series of studies designed to test this possibility the researchers found that the majority of participants when surveyed under typical conditions indicated that they felt either sad or happy (consistent with core affect reactions). However, when participants responded after watching a movie with an emotionally complex theme, when undergraduates moved out of their dormitories at the end of their academic year; or when a group of students graduated from university; over 50% of participants reported feeling both sad and happy. Watson and Tellegen (1985: 695) concluded that 'In our view, bipolarity represents the stable endpoint of processes that are organized in a bivariate space rather than a bipolar continuum' and that 'Though the circumplex and similar models provide valuable descriptive models of emotion as it is typically experienced, a more complete understanding can only be obtained by also focusing on the underlying affective processes'.

Other researchers have also argued for the organisation of affect in a bivariate space. Diener and Iran-Nejad (1986) observed that people rarely experience intense pleasure or displeasure, but are more likely to report mixed feelings at low to moderate levels of intensity. Schimmack (2001), for example, provided evidence to support the coexistence of a model of reciprocally activated affect. Based on a MIN (i.e. minimum) values test, which relied on the level of intensity of the weaker of the two affects, he tested whether pleasure and displeasure ratings conformed to the L-shaped pattern predicted by the one-dimensional bipolar model. The L-shaped pattern is produced when pleasure has values greater than zero, while values on displeasure are zero.

His results demonstrated the absence of an L-shaped pattern when Schimmack plotted his data, and he concluded that pleasure and displeasure are best represented by two distinct feelings, or monopolar dimensions that are sometimes experienced concurrently as mixed feelings. The observation that people may experience mixed feelings concurrently is not new and Schimmack, for example, cites McDougal (1905) who remarked more than a 100 years ago:

> It is, I think, indisputable that a man may be unhappy while he actually experiences pleasure, and that he might make it more difficult to find pleasure

and might make his pleasure thin in quality, but the two modes of experience, are though antagonistic, not absolutely incompatible and mutually exclusive.

A test on bipolarity versus independence model of affective wellbeing was undertaken by Sevastos (1996), using confirmatory factor analysis with two large datasets. The discrete affects (enthusiasm, depression, anxiety and relaxation) were found to fit the data significantly better than a two-dimensional bipolar model (Enthusiasm–Depression and Anxiety–Comfort) proposed by Warr (1990a). The appropriateness of using the four monopolar model (Sevastos, 1996) in this book is based on the evidence presented earlier, that affects are organised in a bivariate space, and that in managerial positions affective feelings of different hedonic tone coexist within a context of daily hassles and uplifts (Kanner, Coyne, Schaefer, & Lazarus, 1981) that has become the norm in such occupations.

Understanding the neurobiological substrates underlying temperament is potentially the key to understanding the biological basis of core affective traits. There is evidence to suggest that the specific areas of the prefrontal cortex (including the dorsolateral prefrontal, anterior cingulate, and orbitofrontal cortices) and limbic structures (including the amygdala, hippocampus and nucleus accumbens) are the most important regions of the brain associated with fundamental dimensions of temperament (Whittle, Allen, Lubman, & Yucel, 2005). A model has been proposed by Whittle and colleagues detailing how these structures might comprise neural networks whose functioning underlies the three temperaments: NA, PA, and Constraint and their relationship with specific neural networks.

Consistent with recent models of neural circuitry Whittle and colleagues found these networks determine different behavioural functions which connect to specific areas of the prefrontal cortex (responsible for conscious behavioural and affective regulation) to subcortical-limbic structures (responsible for automatic affective processing and production of affective states). NA has been linked with a network of regions linking the hippocampus, dorsolateral prefrontal cortex (right side specifically) and dorsal anterior cingulate cortex to limbic and subcortical regions including the ventral anterior cingulate cortex and amygdala. PA has been linked with a similar network of regions linking the dorsolateral prefrontal cortex (left side specifically) and dorsal cingulate cortex to limbic and subcortical regions including the ventral anterior cingulate cortex to subcortical structures including the amygdala and nucleus accumbens.

A strong association has also been established between emotions and the heart, to suggest that there is a 'systematic relationship between psychiatric status and heart rate in which core physiological differences between certain states are reflected in distinctly different circadian patterns of activity' (Stampfer, 1998: 197). Evidence from over 5000 recordings has consistently shown a diagnostic relationship between certain classified psychiatric disorders and the 24 hour circadian heart rate (Iverson, Stampfer, & Gaetz, 2002; Stampfer, 2005). For example generalised anxiety and melancholic depression were found to be associated with distinctly different circadian patterns, particularly during sleep, when confounding influences are largely absent.

The distinctly different patterns during sleep suggest distinctly different regulatory abnormalities, since heart rate during sleep is largely an expression of physiological or 'visceral' regulation not influenced by conscious activity or environmental stimuli. Stampfer (1998: 189) had earlier contended that 'the visceral aspects of anxiety and depression are unlikely to have changed in eons, and a nosology based on visceral functioning as indicated by circadian pattern of heart rate is likely to prove more reliable'. Recording and analysis of a person's circadian heart rate was found by Stampfer to provide indications of a patient's 'core' psychiatric status. This finding suggests a fundamental shift in the conceptualisation and diagnosis of anxiety and depression. Stampfer's work has provided biological and physiological evidence for the existence of both anxiety and depression.

JOB SATISFACTION

Several decades of research have informed the conceptualisation of job satisfaction as a person's cognitive appraisal of the working environment (Organ & Near, 1985). Organisational Behaviour theorists have extensively researched motivational aspects of intrinsic work attitudes such as job satisfaction. Job satisfaction is a multi dimensional construct that is strongly influenced by disposition and mood. Hoppock (1935) initially conceived of job satisfaction as the aggregate of dispositional and situational influences. Job satisfaction has been established as an important contributor to mental and psychological health problems in the workplace (Faragher et al., 2005).

Others have suggested that job satisfaction is the positive emotional reaction and cognition a person has towards the job (Oshagbemi, 1991). Consistent with this view is Locke's (1976: 1299) definition of job satisfaction as 'a pleasurable or positive emotional state resulting from the appraisal of one's job or job experience'. A more balanced treatment of the self-report of job satisfaction was made by Motowidlo, Packard and Manning (1986: 176), who defined it as 'judgements about the favorability of the work environment'. Job satisfaction may be divided into two elements: intrinsic and extrinsic. Intrinsic Job Satisfaction refers to the internal state associated with characteristics inherent in a job, such as utilisation of skills, amount of job complexity and opportunities for control, amount of responsibility, and challenges (Brayfield & Rothe, 1951; Warr et al., 1979; Clegg, Wall, & Kemp, 1987; Koestner, Zuckerman, & Koestner, 1987; Clark, Oswald, & Warr, 1996).

Extrinsic Job Satisfaction refers to an external state contingent upon aspects of a job, such as pay, working conditions, industrial relations, conditions of employment, hours of work, and job security (Brayfield & Rothe, 1951; Brayfield & Crockett, 1955; Warr et al., 1979). Intrinsic and extrinsic job satisfaction are invariably positively intercorrelated, but they do not indicate a conceptual duality (Herzberg, 1959). In addition, measures of job satisfaction are highly correlated in the range of .50 to .60 with measures of life satisfaction (Judge & Watanabe, 1993).

Some support exists for the view that certain aspects of job satisfaction may be genetically determined (Staw, Bell, & Clausen, 1986; Arvey, Bouchard, Segal, & Abraham, 1989). While it seems unlikely that job satisfaction (i.e., the attitude) is inherited, it may be possible that some personality characteristics associated with job satisfaction are partially determined by genetic factors (Arvey et al., 1989). If this is the case, there is a prospect that some genetic sources of job satisfaction operate through NA, PA, or both. For people with a predisposition to negatively construe life events (i.e., trait NA), this tendency may be partially inherited and would register as part of a job satisfaction score (Chen & Spector, 1991).

Other findings suggest that both NA and PA exert influence on a variety of variables, like job satisfaction that are, for the most part, situationally determined (Watson & Clark, 1984). Cropanzano, James, and Konovsky (1993), for example, found that both PA and NA were related to a global measure of job satisfaction, while a recent meta-analytic study reported a mean correlation of $r = .49$ between PA and job satisfaction (Connolly & Viswesvaran, 2000). PA and NA of course are significantly related to Extraversion and Neuroticism, respectively. Watson et al. (1999) using a large sample (N = 4,457) found that trait NA was related to Neuroticism ($r = .58$) and Extraversion ($r = -.25$); trait PA was related to Neuroticism ($r = -.33$) and Extraversion ($r = .51$); while the correlation between trait PA and NA was $r = -.19$, and between Extraversion and Neuroticism $r = -.31$. However, Ilies and Judge (2003) concluded that PA and NA has a stronger genetic mediating effect on job satisfaction (about 45%) than the Five-Factor personality model that mediated only 24% of these genetic influences.

Although the debate has not been settled in the literature as to whether job satisfaction is inherited, as the studies reported above would suggest, or influenced by situational determinants as others have argued (Davis-Blake & Pfeffer, 1989), there are those who have recently advocated that since 'control of 'all' exogenous variables can never be achieved in field research .... it is time for dispositional researchers to move from their defensive posture ... to a more ambitious agenda for understanding the role of personality in organizational settings' (Staw & Cohen-Charash, 2005: 73). This requires a new way of approaching job satisfaction and affect.

DISPOSITIONAL AFFECT AND PERFORMANCE

The dispositional approach to affect can be traced back to the writings of Münsterberg (1913) who described the goal of applied psychology as 'the selection of those personalities which by their mental qualities are especially fit for a particular kind of economic work'. As noted in Chapter 1, Wright and Staw (Wright & Staw, 1999a; 1999b) and others such as Harter et al. (2002) have rekindled the debate over whether happy workers are also more productive. Wright and Staw (1999a: 11) found mixed support for the happy-productive worker thesis but concluded that 'the dispositional measure of affect is a more successful predictor of rated performance'. In the process of reviving this debate, Wright and Staw (1999a: 3) have highlighted an important methodological consideration, stating that 'dispositional rather than state affect may be a stronger operationalisation of the happy-productive worker thesis'. Assessments of dispositional affect provided a closer fit for individual-based measures of performance than did measures of affective state or mood (Cropanzano et al., 1993; Cropanzano & Wright, 1999; Wright & Staw, 1999a; 1999b; Cropanzano & Wright, 2001).

This view found support in a study by Staw and Barsade (1993). After controlling for the effects of general mental ability, age, gender, and years of work experience, dispositional PA predicted managerial performance (decision-making and interpersonal behaviour), and overall managerial potential, supporting the hypothesis of the happier-and-smarter worker. In the same vein Ilies and Judge (2003) consider trait affectivity a more important predictor of organisational performance than job satisfaction, because of its stability over time, as opposed to the situational determinants of job satisfaction. However, as Weiss and Cropanzano (1996) have argued in their Affective Events Theory (AET), affective states fluctuate over time and current satisfaction levels may reflect recent events and personal affect histories. Suh, Diener, and Fujita (1996) found, for example, that although an individual's level of extraversion and neuroticism predicted wellbeing over a period of years, recent events did also matter.

These events associated with daily living may not be major in one's life. Kanner (1981) recommended the consideration of such 'irritating, frustrating, distressing demands that to some degree characterize everyday transactions with the environment'. They have argued that the sum total of these events (coined hassles and uplifts) may temporarily affect psychological health. Such typical life events, however, may lose their psychological potency after three to six months (Suh, Diener, & Fujita, 1996). Although the concept of these discrete events was introduced to the stress literature to differentiate them from stressful major life events, their consideration in the organisational setting, especially through the AET framework, has been a welcome development (Teuchmann, Totterdell, & Parker, 1999; Zohar, 1999).

Research into antecedents to job satisfaction has focused on broadening the theoretical base of causal factors, including dispositional effects (Agho, Mueller, & Price, 1993; Judge, 1993; Judge, Locke, Durham, & Kluger, 1998), perceptual mediators (Carlopio & Gardner, 1995), and organisational obstacles (Brown & Mitchell, 1993). Despite such extensive investigation, causal relationships concerning antecedents to, and consequences of, job satisfaction are still not settled (Cranny, Smith, & Stone, 1992). There is mixed empirical support for the relationship between job satisfaction and performance. A meta-analysis by Judge et al. (2001) concluded that a re-conceptualisation of the satisfaction-performance relationship was warranted.

Warr (1991) has suggested that it may be possible to test certain predictions within the framework of the work adjustment theory. In the context of the results reported in this book, it is worth investigating the assertion that 'it seems likely that job performance will, in certain circumstances, be more strongly associated with one axis of wellbeing than with the other' (Warr, 1991: 163). This is highly relevant to the consideration of managers' growth needs in relation to affective wellbeing, since 'the satisfaction of growth needs implies a continuous increase in aspirations, while deficiency needs are satisfied at a given saturation level' (Heylighten & Bernheim, 2000: 232).

Thus, it is worthwhile testing whether managers' optimal performance is associated with a particular aspect of affective wellbeing (i.e., enthusiasm, depression, anxiety or comfort). Confounding trait variables related to affect, such as PA and NA, should be included in studies that use only one source of data (i.e., self-report). There still remains a need to explain how job-related affective wellbeing relates to intrinsic job satisfaction.

RELATIONSHIP BETWEEN INTRINSIC JOB SATISFACTION AND AFFECTIVE WELLBEING

Some researchers, such as Agho, Mueller and Price (1992) considered that job satisfaction indicated the extent to which an individual likes a job. Other researchers (e.g., Evans, 1986; Clegg et al., 1987) found that job satisfaction represents a positive affective orientation towards a job, or to intrinsic and extrinsic facets of a job. These findings led many researchers to operationalise affective wellbeing as job satisfaction (Brayfield & Rothe, 1951; Iaffaldano & Muchinsky, 1985). Satisfaction with the type of work undertaken has been found to be closely associated with other specific satisfactions and with overall job satisfaction (Cook, 1981). As stated, Warr (1987; 1992) has argued that affective wellbeing is more than job satisfaction, while Judge et al. (2001) concluded from a meta-analysis that job satisfaction does not equate to affect.

Within Warr's conceptual framework of affective wellbeing, job satisfaction is located in the horizontal axis in a space defined by the orthogonal axes of arousal and pleasure as shown in Figure 2.2 Warr argued that when measuring job satisfaction 'no consideration is taken of level of arousal' (Warr, 1986: 163). This implies that job satisfaction, shown on the horizontal axis as 'pleasure-misery' in Figure 2.2 captures mainly cognitions, while anxiety-contentment and depression-enthusiasm capture affect. This view is inconsistent with findings by Brief, Burke, George, Robinson and Webster (1988), who developed a Job Affect Scale that permitted job satisfaction to be partitioned into affect and cognitions. However, if job satisfaction is conceptualised as an attitude then it is necessary to include both cognitions and affect.

Sevastos (1996) has demonstrated that there is a substantial overlap between intrinsic job satisfaction scales and affect scales, indicating they are not exclusively cognitive evaluations of a person's working environment. Based on a weighting procedure following Canonical Correlation analysis, between a composite consisting of job features (e.g., autonomy, skill utilisation, role ambiguity, etc.) and organisational variables (e.g., tenure, organisational level, etc.), and a second composite made up of intrinsic job satisfaction and affective wellbeing, 28% of the variance among the wellbeing measures was shared. However, intrinsic job satisfaction uniquely contributed 22% while affective wellbeing contributed only 5% of the variance. The results are consistent with those of Brief and Roberson (1989) who have demonstrated the relative contribution of cognition and affect to measures of job satisfaction. In all, cognitions account for the largest percentage of unique variance of job characteristics in the literature.

There are sound theoretical reasons for hypothesising that job satisfaction is causally linked to mental health. A large scale meta-analysis by Faragher, Cass and Cooper (2005) based on 500 studies with a combined N = 267,995, showed a substantial relationship ($r = .312$, or .370 after Schmidt-Hunter adjustment) between job satisfaction and both subjective physical and mental health. In this context correlations exceeding .3 are unusual and suggest that job satisfaction has an important influence on the health of workers.

Specifically, job satisfaction was most strongly associated with mental/psychological problems, with the strongest correlations being found for burnout (corrected $r = .478$); self esteem ($r = .429$); depression ($r = .428$); anxiety ($r = .420$) but a modest correlation with subjective physical health ($r = .287$). Thus, employees experiencing low levels of job satisfaction are most likely to experience burnout, reduced levels of self esteem, and to have elevated levels of anxiety and depression.

SUMMARY ON AFFECTIVE WELLBEING AND EXTRINSIC JOB SATISFACTION

A differentiation has been established between affective wellbeing and extrinsic job satisfaction, which is in large part concerned with cognitions and is better conceived separately from intrinsic job satisfaction. Intrinsic job satisfaction is related to affective wellbeing, but is a distinct construct, which also has a cognitive element. The degree to which individuals feel intrinsically satisfied with their work is an important mental health concern.

TYPOLOGIES OF AFFECTIVE WELLBEING

As noted earlier in this chapter, affective wellbeing may be categorised into three general clusters of theories; Dispositional, Activity and Telic (Diener, 1984). The notion of happiness is related to these affective wellbeing categories. These typologies feature in contemporary occupational psychology literature; Warr's (1986; 1987; 1994d) Vitamin Model, Karasek and Theorell's (1990) Demand Control Model, and Staw and Ross' (1985) dispositional approach to job satisfaction. These theoretical typologies were derived from the occupational and organisational psychology literature and provide a useful theoretical framework for conceiving of theories about affective wellbeing. Each typology makes predictions that explain affective wellbeing and the models represent well-conceived and thoroughly investigated conceptualisations of affective wellbeing.

Dispositional theories

Ledford defined disposition as an 'enduring personal attribute' (1999: 30). Trait affect is more closely equated with the notion of disposition described by Wright and Staw (1999a; 1999b), and may be described as a constellation of inherited and enduring behaviours that in some instances, may be modified over long periods of time (Ledford, 1999). Dispositional theories treat affective wellbeing as an integral part of a person's make-up, whereas situational factors are only considered to contribute a small amount of variance to a person's affective wellbeing.

There is considerable debate taking place among psychologists on the nature of happiness or wellbeing. The question being asked is whether happiness is a state - simply the accumulation of individual happy feelings - or the predisposition to react in a happy way (Diener, 1984). Lewinsohn and Amenson (1978) contend that lack of pleasant events lead to depression. In contrast, dispositional theorists argue that depression prevents an individual from feeling pleasure in circumstances that are normally pleasant (Sweeney, Schaeffer, & Golin, 1982).

Great proponents of the dispositional approach are Costa and McCrae (1980) who proposed a 'model of happiness'. Costa and McCrae asserted that differences among individuals in PA and NA over time are a direct result of differences in extroversion and neuroticism, respectively. This view was strengthened by the research of Meyer and Shack (1989) based on factor analytic techniques to examine the degree of convergence between the two-dimensional model of affect and personality structure. It was shown that extroversion and PA share a common dimension in the combined affect and personality space, while neuroticism and NA together defined the second dimension of this space. This finding persisted whether affect was evaluated as a state or a trait.

Findings showing convergence of affect and personality structure were reported by a host of other researchers (see for example, Watson & Clark, 1984; Emmons & Diener, 1985; Costa & McCrae, 1987; Larsen & Ketelaar, 1989; Meyer, Paunonen, Gellatly, Goffin, & Jackson, 1989; Williams & Podsakoff, 1989; Brown & Mitchell, 1993). Costa and McCrae (1987) concluded that 'over time, the small but persistent effects of traits emerge as a systematic source of variation in happiness, whereas situational determinants that vary more or less randomly tend to cancel each other out'. Research on this 'systematic source of variation' was carried out with trait NA as a control variable examining the relationships between self-report stressors and self-report strain outcomes. Brief, Burke, George, Robinson, and Webster (1988), and Cooper and Payne (Cooper & Payne, 1988) who controlled neuroticism rather than NA, as in this study, found that the stressor-strain relationship was attenuated, when trait NA or neuroticism was controlled.

In a study by Schaubroeck, Ganster and Fox (1992), using Confirmatory Factor Analysis, the results showed that, although NA did not share a common factor space with measures of subjective strain, it attenuated the effects of self-report work stressors. These findings, however, are in disagreement with those of Chen and Spector (1991) who found little evidence of attenuation when they partialled NA and trait anxiety respectively from correlations between self-report of work stressors and self-report strain outcomes. More consistent results have been reported, however, when the examination focuses on trait PA. Studies by Schaubroeck et al. found little evidence to suggest that this trait is substantially related to either stressors or strains.

Individual differences in trait PA and NA are likely to persist over time. Research has found that personality differences in extroversion and neuroticism were found to antedate and predict differences in happiness over a period of years (Costa & McCrae, 1980; Warr et al., 1983). This finding is presented by some as evidence to rule out the rival hypothesis that temporary affective states account for any observed relations.

Additional evidence suggests that affective wellbeing exhibits correlational stability with age. Costa, Zonderman, McCrae, Cornoni-Huntley, Locke and Barbano (1987) examined maturational changes and cohort differences on subjective wellbeing. The results indicated that older participants tended to be lower in both PA and NA, but longitudinal changes in overall wellbeing were not found. Stacey & Gatz (1991) reported similar cross-sectional findings, with older cohorts reporting lower levels of both PA and NA. However, longitudinal analyses indicated small but significant changes toward decreased PA and NA, with NA registering the strongest effect size.

Are PA and NA related to anxiety and depressive disorders? Research by Watson, Clark and Carey (1988) has shown that NA is broadly associated with symptoms and diagnoses of both anxiety and depression (and as such is a predictor of psychiatric disorder), while PA is inversely related only to symptoms and diagnoses of depression. Tellegen (1985) carried out a factor analysis of a number of self-report measures of anxiety, depression, and state NA and PA, and found a high correlation between depression and anxiety. However, after plotting the factor structure the depression measures loaded closer to low PA, whereas the anxiety measures loaded closer to high NA. This prompted Tellegen to conclude that anxiety and depression might be better differentiated if the depression measures included more items tapping low PA, and anxiety measures had more items reflecting high NA. Tellegen's findings, therefore, are in agreement with the description and location of the anxiety and depression dimensions in Warr's (1990a) wellbeing model (see Figure 2.2).

Because NA is treated by many researchers as a pervasive predisposition to experience negative emotions and cognitions (Watson & Clark, 1984), it has been linked also to perceptions of the working environment. There is support for the view that job satisfaction is genetically determined (Staw et al., 1986; Arvey et al., 1989), and as Chen and Spector (1991) observe, this genetic source of job satisfaction may operate through NA. Many have reasoned that since NA permeates job satisfaction and other job affect measures NA may operate as a nuisance factor in self-report data.

To the extent that various self-report measures all tap the same underlying NA construct, presumed 'independent variables' and 'dependent variables' may actually represent little more than different measures of the same thing' (Watson et al., 1987: 155). If this is the case, then widely-used work attitude measures do not discriminate between positive and negative affects and cognitions (Organ & Near, 1985). Responses on job satisfaction scales may, therefore, be subject to the influences of NA and PA depending on the affective content of the scale. There are, however, certain job satisfaction scales (such as the satisfaction scale in the Job Diagnostic Survey), which were shown to provide results that are less affected by dispositional characteristics (Schaubroeck et al., 1992).

Activity theories

Feelings offer us a glimpse of what goes on in our flesh.
(Damasio, 1994: 159)

Activity theorists consider that happiness is a by-product of certain types of human activity. Happy people are those who are immersed in interesting activities. Aristotle was a major proponent of one of the earliest and most important activity theories. He maintained that happiness comes about through virtuous activity, that is, from activity that is performed well. The emphasis here is on the behaviour itself (the activity) rather than the achievement of some end point (i.e., a goal).

In a somewhat similar vein Gardner and Cummings (1988) have proposed an activation theory to predict wellbeing in the occupational setting. This theory maintains that humans have an idiosyncratic or 'characteristic level' of activation. Activation has been defined by Gardner and Cummings (1988: 83) as the 'state of neural excitation in the reticular activation system (RAS) of the central nervous system (the brain and spinal cord)'. Within this context, arousal is treated by the proponents of this theory as a manifestation of activation levels. A characteristic level of activation is one that allows the central nervous system to operate more effectively. The psychological benefits from operating at or close to one's characteristic level of activation are reflected in enhanced wellbeing or positive affect. Deviations from this characteristic level (either positive or negative) result in diminished central nervous system efficiency, with accompanying deterioration of motor responses and thought processes.

Activation theory further posits that individuals are motivated to maintain their characteristic level of activation through appropriate behaviours. However, in many situations the application of impact modifying behaviours is thwarted, for example, through machine pacing, rules and regulations, or supervisory directives. The theory, therefore, predicts that positive psychological outcomes would only result when the individual's ability to modify the situation is not constrained. Although activation theory makes similar predictions to those made by Hackman and Oldham's (1975) job characteristics model, or Karasek's (1979) job-strain model, it represents a very different interpretation of how certain job characteristics (e.g., task novelty, complexity, etc.) lead to certain outcomes.

Unlike Hackman and Oldham's and Karasek's models, which are based on cognitive approaches, activation theory has relied more on the work of physiologists, physiological psychologists, and psychophysiologists (Gardner & Cummings, 1988). Although activation theory presents a viable alternative to the other job design and job stress models, it has been largely ignored as a research topic in occupational and organisational psychology, due mainly to measurement difficulties. By contrast, the work of Karasek (1979), which makes similar predictions to those made by the activation theorists, has generated considerable research output in the last fifteen years.

The research based on the work of Karasek (1979) and his associates has focused on the relationship between perceptions of stressful jobs and job related wellbeing and mental health (Caplan, Cobb, French, Harrison, & Pinneau, 1975; Cooper & Marshall, 1978; Landsbergis, 1988; Warr, 1990b). The model posits that there is a synergistic relationship between job demands and control or job decision latitude; that is, the interactive effects of high job demands and lack of control produce a strain effect greater than the simple additive effect of these two variables. In his original formulation of the model Karasek (1979: 341) defined job decision latitude as a composite of 'decision authority' and 'intellectual discretion', and job demands as a measure of 'the psychological stressors involved in accomplishing the work load, stressors related to unexpected tasks and stressors of job-related personal conflict'.

In a revision of the job strain model Karasek and Theorell (1990: 58) re-defined the combination of intellectual discretion and job decision authority as 'control', because 'in our opinion a high level of skill gives the worker control over which specific skills to use to accomplish the task'. The key prediction from this model is that when job demands are very high and control is low, wellbeing suffers disproportionately. The revised model has also been expanded by the inclusion of a third variable that has been identified by other researchers in the literature as a 'buffer'. This variable is social support, and incorporates the constructs of supervisory and peer support. These three broad constructs (i.e., control, demands, and support) act interactively to determine the quality of the psychosocial work experiences of workers.

Figure 2.3 describes a typology of jobs resulting from different combinations of job demands and job control. 'High strain' jobs are those with a combination of high job demands and low levels of control. 'Low strain' jobs have low levels of job demands and high levels of job control. 'Passive jobs' are those characterised by low job demands and low job control, resulting in learned helplessness as a way of coping. When job demands and job control are simultaneously high these jobs would not be associated with strain because they are 'active jobs'. These jobs allow the individual to develop new behaviour patterns to mitigate the effects of high demands. The psychological strains are not great under these circumstances, because the energy generated by the job's many challenges is translated into action through effective problem solving (Karasek & Theorell, 1990). Furthermore, research has shown that people with active jobs enjoy the highest material and psychological rewards (Karasek, 1979).

Although low strain jobs, shown in the high control low demand quadrant in Figure 2.2, characteristic of self-paced occupations, may be considered 'a relative psychosocial paradise with low levels of psychological strain' (Karasek & Theorell, 1990: 42), they are not considered desirable from a wellbeing and mental health perspective. Warr (1994d: 86) in particular has adopted a value-laden position on this issue by suggesting that this 'passive contentment' view of mental health ought to be rejected in preference to the active involvement in the pursuit of challenging goals. A problem arises, however, if the strain is particularly severe or becomes chronic.

Employees occupying high status managerial or professional jobs with exceptionally high levels of control, for example, may experience this control as a significant demand in itself (Karasek & Theorell, 1990). This may give rise to unacceptable levels of job-related anxiety (Warr, 1990a; Birdi, Warr, & Oswald, 1995), and general psychological distress. A curvilinear relationship between certain job characteristics and wellbeing has also been proposed by (Champoux, 1980). This suggests that Warr's Vitamin Model may be considered a viable alternative to Karasek's model, because it addresses some of the anomalies found when the Karasek model is tested empirically.

Warr (1990b); Landsbergis (1988); Spector (1987); and Payne and Fletcher (1983) were all unable to replicate the interactive effect of job demands and decision latitude of Karasek's (1979) Job Strain Model.

Figure 2.3 Demand Control Model

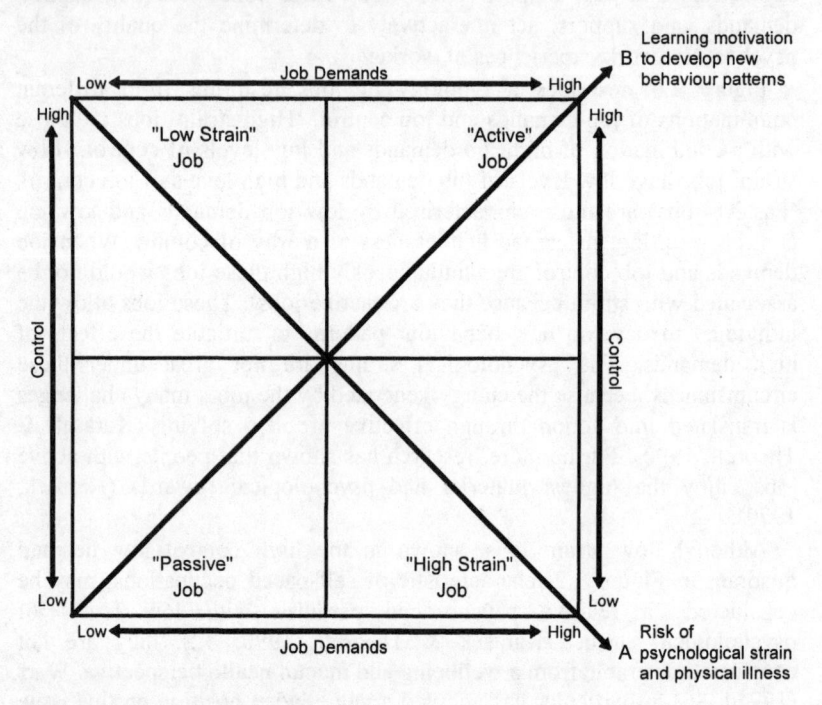

[Figure: Demand Control Model showing a square divided into four quadrants: "Low Strain" Job (high control, low demands), "Active" Job (high control, high demands), "Passive" Job (low control, low demands), "High Strain" Job (low control, high demands). Diagonal arrows indicate: A - Risk of psychological strain and physical illness; B - Learning motivation to develop new behaviour patterns.]

Source: Adapted from Karasek (1979: 288).

Researchers who have attempted to replicate Karasek's findings have invariably neglected to account for the interation between job demands and decision latitude, since both appear to have only 'main effects' on job satisfaction (Hurrell & McLaney, 1989; Kasl, 1989). Kauppinen-Toropainen et al. found 'relatively low total explanatory power of the [Job Strain] model' (1983: 201) but questioned why only two job factors were posited to underpin job strain. Fletcher (1991) argued that a more appropriate model should include a wider range of job features, such as social support. This perspective is consistent with the findings of Parkes,

Mendham and von Rabenau (1994); Johnson (1991), and Parkes (1990; 1991). Ganster (1989) has suggested that Karasek's findings exaggerated the role of control because it may be that job complexity (or challenge) is the more important predictor of psychological health outcomes.

A model that used an expanded number of job characteristics was proposed by Sevastos (1996). Using two large samples of employees to reflect different levels of job complexity, the first from the clerical and supervisory occupational categories (n = 1,667), and the second from the managerial categories (n = 1,418), Sevastos demonstrated through a multivariate analysis based on Canonical Correlation that the relationship between the cluster of IVs (ten job characteristics and five demographic variables) and DVs (intrinsic job satisfaction, enthusiasm, depression, anxiety, and comfort or relaxation) could be explained by two orthogonal dimensions.

The first dimension was labelled task complexity and consisted of supervisory support, skill utilisation, role clarity and feedback, which were related primarily to intrinsic job satisfaction (i.e., cognitive evaluations), and to a lesser extent enthusiasm, anxiety, and depression (inverse association); while the second dimension was defined by low work pressure and role ambiguity, which were related to anxiety (inversely), relaxation, enthusiasm (inversely), and depression (i.e., all the affective states). When combined, these dimensions provided a job typology that is consistent with Karasek's passive-active jobs, represented in Figure 2.4 diagonally from quadrant 1 to quadrant 4, and low strain-high strain, shown diagonally from quadrant 3 to quadrant 2 jobs respectively.

Outcomes depicted in Figure 2.4 are associated with 'passive' jobs (Low Skill Variety, Lack of Autonomy, Feedback, Skill Utilisation, Supervisory Support, High Role Ambiguity and Low Work Pressure), 'high strain' jobs (Low Skill Variety, Autonomy, Feedback, Skill Utilisation, Supervisory Support and High Work Pressure), 'low strain' jobs (High Skill Variety, Autonomy, Feedback, Skill Utilisation, Supervisory Support and Low Work Pressure), and 'active' jobs (High Skill Variety, Autonomy, Feedback, Skill Utilisation, Supervisory Support, Clear Role Definition and High Work Pressure) respectively.

'Passive jobs' (see quadrant 1) are characterised by outcomes, such as dissatisfaction, lack of enthusiasm, lack of relaxation, depression and low anxiety. The outcomes for 'high strain' jobs outcomes are described in quadrant 4 comprise dissatisfaction, lack of enthusiasm and relaxation, depression and anxiety. For 'low strain' jobs, the outcomes are indicated by satisfaction, enthusiasm, relaxation, and low depression and anxiety, as shown in quadrant 3. Outcomes for 'active jobs' are satisfaction, enthusiasm, relaxation, anxiety and low depression and intrinsic job satisfaction (quadrant 4).

These jobs have the potential to provide a worker with 'flow' experiences (Csikszentmihalyi, 1990) due to the challenging nature of the work, but only if the complexity of the task is matched with self-efficacy to meet these challenges. In this instance, anxious apprehension (Heller & Nitschke, 1998) characterised by approach tendencies would be associated with positive valence and experienced as pleasant affect (i.e., eustress) consistent with the overall hedonic tone of satisfaction, enthusiasm, and relaxation. A differential source for depression and anxiety, therefore, is evident in Sevastos's (1996) model (see Figure 2.2).

Figure 2.4 Attitudinal and affective outcomes of complexity on work pressure

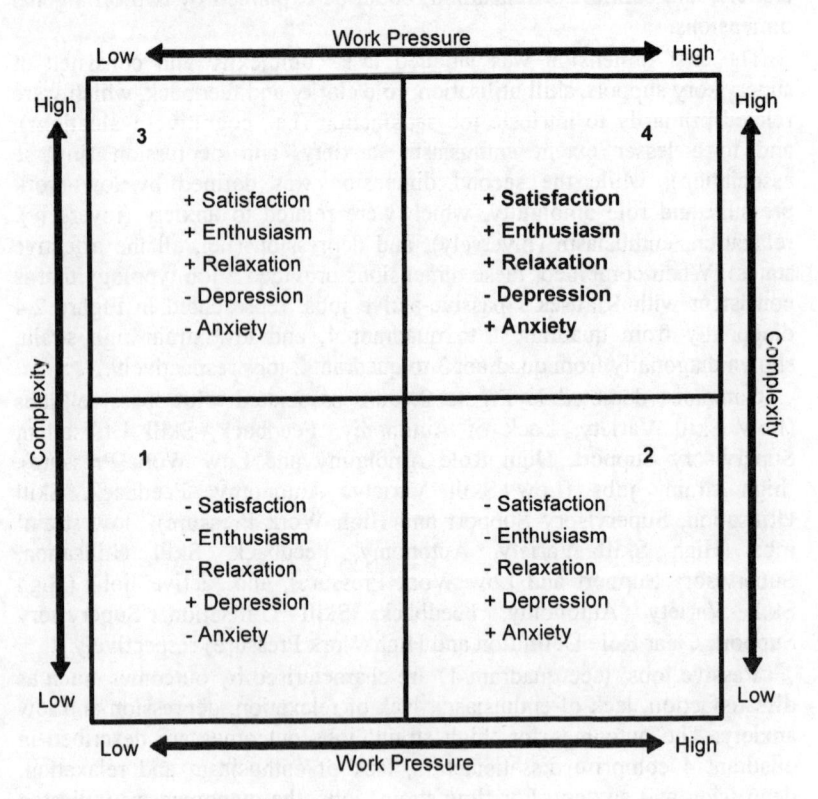

	Work Pressure Low	Work Pressure High
High Complexity	**3** + Satisfaction + Enthusiasm + Relaxation − Depression − Anxiety	**4** + Satisfaction + Enthusiasm + Relaxation − Depression + Anxiety
Low Complexity	**1** − Satisfaction − Enthusiasm − Relaxation + Depression − Anxiety	**2** − Satisfaction − Enthusiasm − Relaxation + Depression + Anxiety

Source: Sevastos (1996: 78).

This analysis provides evidence that job features are differentially related to psychological outcomes, an observation also made by Warr (1990a).

Sevastos (1996) concluded that the additive combination of the independent variable set (i.e., the job features), when related to the intrinsic job satisfaction and wellbeing set, impacted differentially on the workers, creating either psychological distress or affective wellbeing depending on the level of task complexity and job pressure. This generalised psychological distress or wellbeing may be attributed to a cognitive mechanism that can either amplify or dampen affect of similar hedonic tone (Diener, Colvin et al., 1991).

For example, there is evidence from the clinical literature (e.g., Clark, Beck, & Stewart, 1990), that the comorbidity of anxiety and depression is qualitatively different from either of these conditions considered separately, and is indicative of 'a more severe form of psychological distress' (Clark et al., 1990: 153). The psychological impact on the worker, therefore, would be consistent with a 'synergistic approach', even though the two sets of independent variables may act additively. These conditions are present in quadrant 2 of Figure 2.4, where anxiety and depression co-occur. The longstanding argument related to Karasek's demand-control model, therefore, whether the influence of the independent variables on wellbeing is additive or synergistic, appears to be a moot point (Sevastos, 1996: 95).

The Demand Control Model predicted that enriched job characteristics are associated with job satisfaction and low depression, and impoverished jobs are normally associated with job dissatisfaction and depression. As such, high work pressure is normally associated with high anxiety, while low pressure is associated with low anxiety. Thus, effective managers are predicted to report positive satisfaction, enthusiasm, relaxation, eustress, and low depression, as evidenced and tested by Sevastos's (1996) proposed Four Factor Model of Affective Wellbeing. Consistent with the Demand Control Model, Iverson and Erwin (1997) have predicted that the greater sense of self-efficacy may be reflected in jobs with a higher degree of task engagement, such as managers.

However, managers experiencing a persistent high level of anxiety (i.e., eustress) may not experience depression and job dissatisfaction, because important job content variables, such as skill utilisation; feedback; role clarity; and superior support, are available at high levels. Stress is either stimulus (cause), or response (symptoms), of worker reactions to their environment that has been separated into positive (eustress) and negative (distress) effects on individuals (Nankervis, Compton, & McCarthy, 1996). Eustress represents the positive stress associated with achievement and exhilaration, like meeting challenges (Selye, 1974). Distress refers to the negative aspects of stress, like feelings of inadequacy, insecurity, helplessness or desperation that result from too much or not enough pressure or tension (Selye, 1974).

Telic theories (End State theories)

The central proposition of Telic or End State theories is that affective wellbeing is attained when certain inherent human needs are satisfied, such as competence or aspiration (Diener, 1984). Warr's (1994d), and Ryff and Keyes's (1995) models fall into telic or endpoint theories of wellbeing. The main characteristic of a telic or end state theory, is that wellbeing is achieved when some needs (e.g., competence, aspiration, etc.), either inborn or learned, are fulfilled. The argument is being made that if these needs are truly universal, their fulfilment should be associated with happiness in all cultures. However, it is unlikely that consensus among researchers will be achieved in identifying universal components of mental health (Warr, 1994d).

A consolidated theory of employee mental health is overdue, given the confused and desegregated nature of research in the area. Warr's (1986; 1987; 1994b) Vitamin Model synthesised the bulk of research and theorising about job-related mental health. By integrating the existing knowledge, Warr (1987) constructed a comprehensive model of mental health and jobs (see Ross, 1989; Kelloway & Barling, 1991; Hosie, 1994). Warr's Vitamin Model provided a cohesive schematic framework that incorporated complex and interrelated variables that influence employee mental health. Warr (1987; 1994d) departed from the dominant mental health paradigm that considered job satisfaction to be axiomatic to affective wellbeing in the workplace. Long before 'affect' and 'emotions' research made its appearance in the occupational literature, Warr (1986: 163-167) stated that:

> We must move away from the conventional narrow focus upon 'job satisfaction'. This orthodoxy and its associated from of measurement has greatly hampered the development of occupational psychology. We must of course work to understand job-related well-being and the factors influencing it, but we need a shift in perspective away from job satisfaction. It now seems desirable to focus upon three dimensions of measurement, including arousal as well as pleasure in our theories and measuring instruments.

Ten features of jobs and environmental categories applicable to job settings are argued by Warr (1986; 1990a; 1994b) to underlie affective wellbeing: opportunity for control; opportunity for skill use; externally generated goals; variety; environmental clarity; availability of money; physical security; opportunity for interpersonal contact; valued social position, and supportive supervision (a later addition to his original list of work features). The third part of Warr's framework examined the differences between people.

Table 2.2   Vitamin Model

1)	Opportunity for control: discretion, decision latitude, independence, autonomy, job control, self-determination, personal control, absence of close supervision, participation in decision-making, absence of routinisation.
2)	Opportunity for skill use: skill utilisation, utilisation of valued abilities, application of skills and abilities, required skills.
3)	Externally generated goals: job demands, task demands, quantitative or qualitative workload, environmental demands, structural imperatives in a job, time structure, time demands, role responsibility, time pressure at work, required concentration, conflicting demands, role conflict, job-induced goals, normative requirements.
4)	Variety: variation in job content and location, non-repetitive work, varied roles and responsibilities, skill variety, number of different job operations.
5)	Environmental clarity: (a) information about the consequences of behaviour, availability of feedback, task feedback; (b) information about the future, absence of job future ambiguity, absence of job insecurity, low uncertainty about the future; (c) information about required behaviour, low role ambiguity, clarity of role requirements.
6)	Availability of money: income level, amount of pay, moderate/high standard of living, absence of poverty, material resources.
7)	Physical security: absence of danger, low physical risk, good working conditions, ergonomically adequate equipment, adequate health and safety conditions, safe levels of temperature and noise, absence of continuous heavy-lifting.
8)	Opportunity for interpersonal contact: (a) quantity of interaction, absence of isolation, friendship opportunities, contact with others, social density, adequate privacy; (b) quality of interaction, good relationships with others, social support, co-worker support, emotional support, instrumental support, good communications.
9)	Valued social position: (a) cultural evaluations of status, social rank, occupational prestige, or social stratification; (b) more localised social evaluations of in-company status or job importance; (c) personal evaluations of task significance, valued role incumbency, meaningfulness of job, or self-respect from the job.
10)	Supportive supervision: social support from one's supervisor and management, effective leadership based on consideration.

Source: Warr, P. (1994d), A conceptual framework for the study of work and mental health, Work & Stress 8(2), 84-97. By permission of Taylor & Francis Ltd. http://www.tandf.co.uk/journals.

While the overall model is intended to be 'situational', it is also 'enabling' and assumes that people are able to shape their environment and influence its possible impact on them. Aspects of the environment have the potential to impair or promote affective wellbeing, when present at critical levels. The enabling contribution of affective wellbeing to managers' job performance is likely to be most noticeable at high or low critical levels.

Figure 2.5   A conceptual representation of person and situations within the Vitamin Model

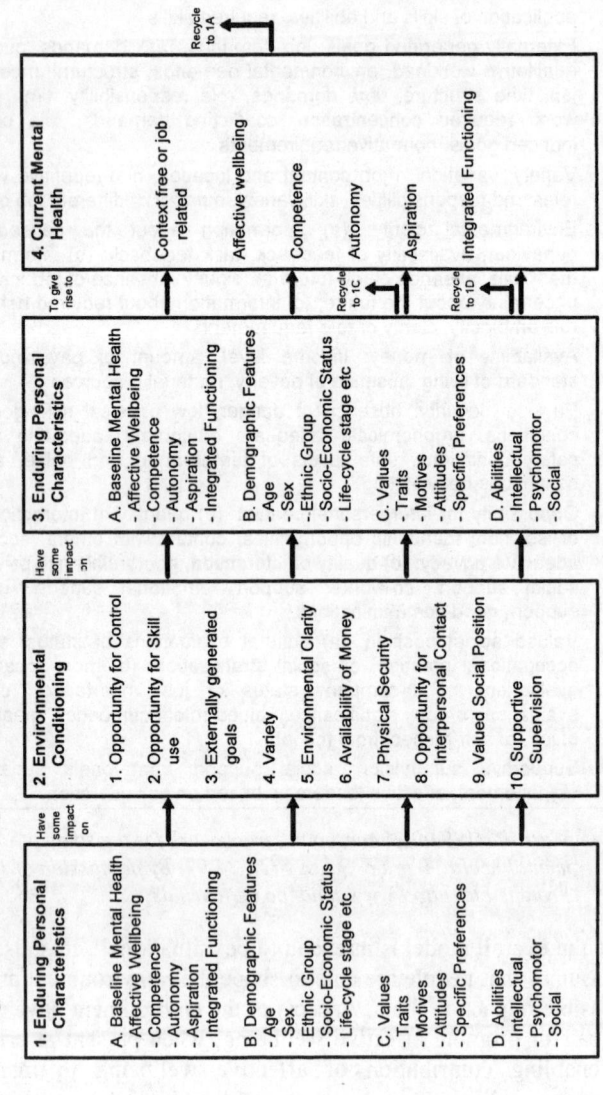

1. Enduring Personal Characteristics

A. Baseline Mental Health
- Affective Wellbeing
- Competence
- Autonomy
- Aspiration
- Integrated Functioning

B. Demographic Features
- Age
- Sex
- Ethnic Group
- Socio-Economic Status
- Life-cycle stage etc

C. Values
- Traits
- Motives
- Attitudes
- Specific Preferences

D. Abilities
- Intellectual
- Psychomotor
- Social

Have some impact on

2. Environmental Conditioning

1. Opportunity for Control
2. Opportunity for Skill use
3. Externally generated goals
4. Variety
5. Environmental Clarity
6. Availability of Money
7. Physical Security
8. Opportunity for Interpersonal Contact
9. Valued Social Position
10. Supportive Supervision

Have some impact on

3. Enduring Personal Characteristics

A. Baseline Mental Health
- Affective Wellbeing
- Competence
- Autonomy
- Aspiration
- Integrated Functioning

B. Demographic Features
- Age
- Sex
- Ethnic Group
- Socio-Economic Status
- Life-cycle stage etc

C. Values
- Traits
- Motives
- Attitudes
- Specific Preferences

D. Abilities
- Intellectual
- Psychomotor
- Social

To give rise to

4. Current Mental Health

Context free or job related

Affective wellbeing

Competence

Autonomy

Aspiration

Integrated Functioning

Recycle to 1A
Recycle to 1C
Recycle to 1D

Source: Adapted from Warr (1987).

62

This assertion leads to speculation that high performing managers are likely to experience periods of heightened anxiety followed by periods of relaxation, while maintaining an overall sense of positive affective wellbeing. Highly motivated managers who desire challenges may react to risks in ways that raise their anxiety level without negatively impacting on their affective wellbeing.

Table 2.3   Components of mental health

1) Affective wellbeing Two separate dimensions of affective wellbeing are considered important - 'pleasure' and 'arousal' - which can be treated as independent of each other ... A strong interconnection between affective wellbeing in general and self-esteem in particular is posited. At different times people desire different combinations of arousal and pleasure, and people sometimes switch rapidly between modes. Specific affects derive from pleasure and arousal. Feelings can be concentrated upon the environment or aspects of the self, which is concerned with the notion of self-esteem.
2) Competence Environmental mastery in terms of success in interpersonal relations, problem-solving and paid employment correlates with good mental health. Competent people possess the psychological resources necessary to cope with pressures. Objective and subjective levels of competence are usually positively inter-correlated. Low levels of competence are not necessarily an indication of low mental health. Autonomy and aspiration have a positive cause of impact upon affective wellbeing.
3) Autonomy Successful interdependence, rather than extreme interdependence or, counter independence, is an indicator of positive mental health. There are two features to autonomy; one reflects the extent a person acts as an independent agent and the other the extent to which a person is interdependent with others.
4) Aspiration Mentally healthy people engage the environment and have established goals and make concerted efforts to achieve them, resulting in motivated behaviour, alertness to new opportunities and effecting challenges of personal significance. Exposing oneself to situations that are unfamiliar is a feature of psychological growth.
5) Integrated functioning Integrated functioning refers to the person as a whole in regard to the above relationships. Several forms of balance, harmony and interrelationships are exhibited by psychologically healthy people. A balance between social role functioning (love, work, play) is important. Other general issues important to mental health are cultural norms, the time distribution of different levels of health, and occasional divergences between components.

Source: Adapted from Hosie (1994: 50-51).

Therefore, it seems worthwhile to extend Warr's model to test whether job-related anxiety, when linked to aspirations, leads to altered managerial performance. Warr (1990b); Landsbergis (1988); Spector (1987); and Payne and Fletcher (1983) were all unable to replicate the interactive effect of job demands and decision latitude of Karasek's (1979) Job Strain Model.

Features of jobs and other environments that Warr (1987; 1990b; 1992; 1994d; 1996b) assumed to underlie 'positive' mental health are represented in Figure 2.5. These categories are further deconstructed to create a 'differentiated treatment of the environment' (Warr, 1987: 9). Terms used in these sub-categories in Figure 2.5 representing specific explications from the literature are detailed in Table 2.3.

Figure 2.3 highlights how Warr's dimensions are interrelated in the work context. Warr's (1994b) model comprised five components: affective wellbeing; competence; aspiration; autonomy; and integrated functioning. Warr's Vitamin Model posits that environmental features of jobs impact on affective wellbeing. As with the physical effects of vitamins, the model is conceived as being analogous to aspects of the work environment. Collectively, vitamins have a beneficial effect (when taken in moderation), or a detrimental effect (if taken in excessive doses), on affective wellbeing. Moreover, environmental features can promote or decrease mental health, as illustrated in Figure 2.6. These job features impact adversely on affective wellbeing in a way similar to the toxic effect of ingesting vitamins A and D in large quantities.

Figure 2.6   Vitamin Model

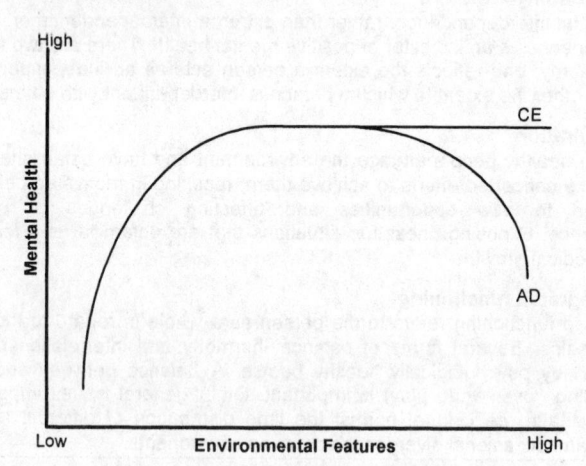

Source: Warr, P. (1987: 10). Work, unemployment and mental health. Oxford University Press, Oxford. By permission of Oxford University Press.

Conversely, taking large doses of vitamins C and E has no known adverse effects. Thus, the availability of associated environmental features, like money, physical security, and valued social position is analogous to the effect of vitamins C and E on human physiology. These features increase affective wellbeing up to a critical point, then level off, maintaining what Warr (1986) terms a 'constant effect', as represented by the CE curve in Figure 2.6.

Warr (1986) argued that the Vitamin Model predicts those opportunities for control and skill use (or job decision latitude) that result in a curvilinear relationship with affective wellbeing. However, while a subsequent test of the model by Warr (1990b) supported this prediction, there was no evidence for the moderating effect of job decision latitude on job demands as predicted by Karasek's (1979) Job Strain Model. As such, Warr's Vitamin Model may be considered a viable alternative to Karasek's Job Strain Model by virtue of providing a plausible explanation of the anomalies encountered when Karasek's model is empirically tested.

Super Factor (Second-Order Level) Model

Published models of affective wellbeing converge on three components, but differ in their conception of the constituent parts (Diener, 1984). Ryff and Keyes's (1995) Super Factor (Second-Order Level) Model of affective wellbeing is theoretically underpinned by the convergence of a number of approaches from developmental psychology (Erikson, 1959), from clinical psychology (Jung, 1933; Allport, 1961; Rogers, 1961; Maslow, 1968), and from affective wellbeing (Birren & Renner, 1980). Six dimensions of context-free psychological wellness were derived from 'multiple theoretical accounts of positive functioning' (Ryff & Keyes, 1995: 4) to form the Super Factor Model.

Ryff and Keyes's (1995) research used confirmatory analytic procedures to create a second-order factor model of affective wellbeing. The data fitted the proposed hierarchical structure of affective wellbeing better, although not adequately for acceptable criteria of fit, compared to alternative models of affective wellbeing, included first-order factors. A two-factor model of positive and negative affectivity and a six-factor model emerged from the analysis, after subtracting the higher order factor latent structure.

The Super Factor Model includes six distinct components of psychological wellness: self-acceptance; environmental mastery; purpose in life; positive relations with others; personal growth; and autonomy. The Super Factor Model subsumed a number of the dimensions identified in Warr's (1994c) wellbeing and mental health model, including: self-acceptance (positive evaluations of oneself); environmental mastery (the ability to deal successfully with the environment); purpose in life (a sense of purpose and meaning in one's life); positive relations with others (the existence of quality interpersonal relations); personal growth (a sense of continued growth and development as a person); and autonomy (self-determination).

There is overlap between the Super Factor Model and Warr's Model. Warr's notion of autonomy corresponds to Ryff and Keyes's (1995) conceptualisation of autonomy. Likewise, Warr's aspiration dimension, the extent to which a person strives to achieve goals through purposeful activity, corresponds closely to Ryff and Keyes's (1995) personal growth dimension: the tendency to strive for independence and self-regulation in one's life. Moreover, the dimension of Warr's competence, an ability to deal effectively with life's problems, closely resembled Ryff and Keyes's (1995) dimension of environmental mastery.

In the absence of a universally applicable definition of wellbeing or mental health, both Warr's (1994c) and Ryff and Keyes's (1995) models adopted a relativist position, imbued by Western values. In addition, these models are derived from both categorical and process theories that converged on three affective wellbeing or mental health dimensions. When the Super Factor Model dimensions are considered in combination they represent a comprehensive perspective of wellbeing or mental health. Despite these similarities, the models are not identical and different conceptualisations of the components of wellbeing and mental health are evident.

EMOTIONAL INTELLIGENCE

> Reason may not be as pure as most of us think it is or wish it were, that emotion and feelings may not be intruders in the bastion of reason at all: they may be enmeshed in its network.
> (Damasio, 1994: Introduction)

Emotions are the fundamental drivers of human endeavour (Tracey, 1993). People's emotions have a critical role in thought, decision-making and individual success. Emotional intelligence is best defined in terms of abilities concerning the recognition and regulation of emotion in the self and others (Ashkanasy & Daus, 2005). Debate and controversy rages about the definition and nature, measurement, and application of emotional intelligence (Spector, 2005). 'Emotional intelligence' has emerged as a potential new construct for explaining behavioural variance not accounted for by measures of general intelligence or personality. Emotional intelligence was conceived of by Mayer (2000) as essentially about emotion, founded in modern understanding of the role of emotional circuits ('hot intelligences') in the brain (see Chapter 2 for a detailed discussion on physiological-psychological links in affect.

Emotional intelligence's heritage can be traced to definition in a doctoral dissertation by Payne (1986). Emotional intelligence was initially defined by (Salovey & Mayer, 1990: 189) as a 'subset of social intelligence that involves the ability to monitor one's own and others' feelings and emotions, to discriminate among them and to use this information to guide one's thinking and actions'. Reference to 'social intelligence' (Thorndike, 1921) in this definition in this seminal article by Salovey and Mayer was unfortunate as this has been used by detractors (cf. Conte, 2005; Landy, 2005; Locke, 2005) to discredit the concept and measurement of emotional intelligence. Mayer and Salovey (1997) have since carefully distinguished emotional intelligence from the notion of social intelligence. Mayer and Salovey (1997) further refined their conceptualisation of emotional intelligence into four branches: (1) perception of emotion (in self and others); (2) assimilation of emotion to facilitate thought; (3) understanding of emotion; and (4) managing and regulating emotion in self and others (Ashkanasy & Daus, 2005).

Boyatzis, Goleman and Rhee (2000) have argued that a particular type of human competencies, called emotional intelligence/competencies (i.e., self-awareness, self-discipline, persistence and empathy) is of greater consequence to performance than intelligence and training. Debate continues on the definition, nature of measurement and application of emotional intelligence. Those antagonistic to the idea of emotional intelligence, such as Locke (2005: 425) went so far as to proclaim that emotional intelligence is an 'invalid concept' because it is not a form of intelligence, a position strongly rebuked by Ashkanasy and Daus (2005).

Emotional intelligence has emerged as an important construct in relation to job performance (Lopes, Côté, & Salovey, 2005). The emotion-performance link has been explored in general by Bar-On, Handley and Fund (2005) and specifically in relation to managers by Caruso and Salovey (2004). Goleman (1995; 1998; 1999; 2000; Goleman, Boyatzis, & McKee, 2002) has argued vigorously that emotional skills are twice as important as cognitive and technical skills in the workplace. Boyatzis and Sala's (2004) definition of emotional intelligence is useful when considering the potential link to job performance *'an emotional intelligence competency is an ability to recognize, understand, and use emotional information about oneself or others that leads to or causes effective or superior performance.'* Studies operationalising emotions using a variety of methods have also shown a positive relationship between forms of emotions and performance (Cropanzano et al., 1993; Staw & Barsade, 1993; Wright & Staw, 1999a; 1999b; Wright & Cropanzano, 2000; Cropanzano & Wright, 2001).

A positive relationship between emotional intelligence and job performance is noticeable for jobs that would be expected to require high levels of emotional intelligence (Cage, Daus, & Saul, 2004; Daus, Rubin, Smith, & Cage, 2004). Aspects of emotional intelligence have been shown by qualitative and qualitative investigations to be critical for effective job performance and the prevention of negative job stress (Daus et al., 2004; Offermann, Bailey, Vasilopoulos, Seal, & Sass, 2004). Intellectual intelligence has also been shown to be a strong predictor of individual job performance but group performance has been shown to be more a function of emotional than intellectual intelligence (Jordan & Troth, 2004; Offermann et al., 2004)

Leaders of organisations are increasingly understanding how valuable emotional intelligence is to an enterprise. Mayer and Salovey (1993) have stressed the value of emotional self-management. Sometimes the way a person manages emotions involves not expressing negative emotions. For example, the accurate communication of negative emotion can be damaging to group morale and effectiveness (Elfenbein & Ambady, 2003). There is support in the literature for the assertion that emotional intelligence leads to measurable business outcomes (Spencer, McClelland, & Keiner, 1997).'

An intriguing tension is noticeable between academic researchers (e.g. Salovey, Caruso & Mayer) and more commercially orientated researchers (e.g., Goleman). For example, Münsterberg's (1913) and Mayer's (1999: 50) approach typifies the cautious approach, 'the popular literature's implication - that highly emotionally intelligent people possess an unqualified advantage in life - appears overly enthusiastic at present and unsubstantiated by reasonable scientific standards'. In contrast those supporting the commercial approach make expansive claims typified by Goleman on the applied value of emotional intelligence. Those using a more academic approach are typically more conservative in the claims about the benefit of emotional intelligence. As Landy (2005) observed, there is strong and continuing support for the emotional intelligence idea, instruments and interventions in the lay business community.

Landy (2005) considered it would be intriguing to examine emotional intelligence as a predictor of the constructs worker personality, performance, satisfaction, affect, and disposition. Also, Landy recommended further investigating how emotional intelligence relates to measures of mental health and organisational citizenship or contextual behaviour. In the broader arena of dependent variables, associations between contextual performance and emotional intelligence would be expected. In all research extensions, Landy recommended always including measures of personality attributes (e.g., the Big-Five) and measures of emotional intelligence. Testing these relationships is predicated on the assumption that emotional intelligence can be coherently defined and consistently measured.

Table 2.4 Conceptual relationships between affective wellbeing theories, models, schools and streams of research

Models/Schools/Streams of Research	Typologies of Affective Wellbeing		
	Dispositional	Activity	Telic
Positive and Negative Affect (Bradburn, 1969)	√		
Dispositional Approach to Job Satisfaction (Staw & Ross, 1985)	√		
Happy-productive worker thesis (Staw, 1986; Wright & Cropanzano, 1997; Cropanzano & Wright, 1999; Wright & Staw, 1999a; 1999b; Wright & Cropanzano, 2000; Cropanzano & Wright, 2001; Wright, Cropanzano et al., 2002)	√	√	
Activation theory (Gardner & Cummings, 1988)		√	
Positive and Negative Affect (Brief et al., 1988)		√	√
Model of Hemispheric Specialisation (Tucker & Williamson, 1984)		√	
Job Strain Model (Karasek, 1979)		√	√
Demand Control Model (Karasek & Theorell, 1990)		√	√
Super Factor Model (Ryff & Keyes, 1995)			√
Four Factor Model of Affective Wellbeing (Sevastos, 1996)			√
Vitamin Model (Warr, 1987; 1990b; 1992; 1994d; 1996b)		√	√
Emotional Intelligence (Salovey & Mayer, 1990; Mayer & Salovey, 1993; Salovey, Hsee, & Mayer, 1993; Goleman, 1995; 1997; 1998; 1999; Mayer, 1999; 2000; Mayer, Salovey, & Caruso, 2004a)	√	√	√

Emotional intelligence is a broad concept that can be related to many of the elements of the composite framework of the theories, disciplines and schools illustrated in Table 3.1 and detailed in Chapter 2. Table 2.4

provides a conceptual overview of the relationships between affective wellbeing typologies of theories, models, schools and streams of research.

SUMMARY AND CONCLUSIONS

This chapter examined the philosophical roots and contemporary understandings of happiness, the most fundamental aspect of affective wellbeing. The nature of happiness was explored, beginning with the philosophical roots and ending with contemporary understandings of the phenomenon. Happiness is conceived as an emotional state, and affective wellbeing as an antecedent of happiness.

Work-related affective wellbeing was categorised as Dispositional, Activity or Telic. These typologies provide a useful framework for conceiving theories about affective wellbeing. Warr's (1986; 1994c) Vitamin Model, Karasek and Theorell's (1990) Job Strain Model, and Staw and Ross's (1985) dispositional approach to job satisfaction are theoretical frameworks that make useful predictions about affective wellbeing.

Dispositional theories consider affective wellbeing to be an integral part of a person's psychological make-up. Exogenous work circumstances are largely discounted as contributing to a person's happiness, so situational factors are not considered to contribute a great deal to an individual's affective wellbeing. Activity theorists expound an alternative 'process' view of the world that focuses on a person's behaviour. Happiness is considered to be a by-product of human activity; happy people immerse themselves in interesting activities.

Positive affective outcomes are predicted to result when a person's capacity to modify a situation is unconstrained. Proponents of Telic theory believe affective wellbeing is attained when some inherent or learned needs are satisfied, such as the need for competence or aspiration. They also believe consensus among researchers will eventually result in the identification of universal components of mental health. Warr's Vitamin Model represents the most comprehensive synthesis of research and theories into occupationally related affective wellbeing. The Vitamin Model of mental health is far more inclusive, comprehensive and supported by empirical evidence than competing models.

Evidence supporting a monopolar model of affective wellbeing structure is theoretically and empirically robust. A monopolar construction is more stable over time, is appropriate for measuring state affect and is therefore suitable for use in this study. Dispositional affect is most appropriately measured in conjunction with individual managers' performance. Sevastos (1996) has argued that it is possible for an individual to experience jobs with high arousal and relaxation at separate times. This finding is highly relevant for managers, who are likely to experience periods of high arousal (characterised by anxiety) followed by periods of relaxation. People are motivated to maintain their characteristic level of activation through appropriate behaviours. Four dimensions have been linked to the brain's major cortical regulatory systems (activation and arousal): negative activation (anxiety), low activation (relaxation), positive arousal (enthusiasm) and low arousal (depression).

Depending on the time-frame instructions, these dimensions may also be measured as state or trait PA and NA. State affect represents a person's mood, while trait PA and NA represent enduring aspects of a person's personality. Measures of personality per se are unlikely to explain enough variance to warrant inclusion in this study that is restricted to measuring two dispositional aspects of personality, NA and PA. From this it may be possible to establish whether or not affective wellbeing is acquired through changing behaviours. This has important implications for managerial practice.

Job satisfaction has been found to be an important influence on mental/psychological wellbeing, particularly in relation to burnout, self esteem, depression and anxiety. A differentiation was established between affective wellbeing and extrinsic job satisfaction, which is mainly concerned with cognitions. Intrinsic job satisfaction is related to affective wellbeing but is a distinct construct. Intrinsic job satisfaction should be incorporated in research that accounts for cognition's potential to contribute to job-related affective wellbeing.

Enriched or complex jobs, such as those undertaken by managers, are generally associated with increased job satisfaction, motivation, and work performance. Job-related affect has exhibited acceptable levels of discriminant validity with intrinsic job satisfaction. Enthusiasm and depression are more strongly related to intrinsic job satisfaction than are anxiety and relaxation. While intrinsic job satisfaction measures are presumed to reflect cognitive evaluations of the working environment, they also capture substantial levels of job-related affect.

This chapter critiqued the substantial literature on how affective wellbeing and intrinsic job satisfaction are conceived and measured. Established and empirically robust measures of affective wellbeing and intrinsic job satisfaction were identified. These self-report instruments were suitable for measuring managers' affective wellbeing and intrinsic job satisfaction in relation to their contextual and task performance. In particular, the scales were more theoretically congruent with the notion of happiness.

The next chapter deals with issues about managers' job performance before identifying the potential links between affective wellbeing and intrinsic job satisfaction.

NOTE

[1] Those who wish to pursue the nature of happiness in general may wish to begin this journey by reading Bertrand Russell's classic *The Conquest of Happiness* (1930), Michael Argyle's (2001) *The Psychology of Happiness*, Martin Seligman's (2002) *Using the New Positive Psychology to Realize Your Potential for Lasting Fulfilment*, Richard Layard's (2005) *Happiness: Lessons from a New Science*, Paul Martin's (Martin, 2005), *Making Happy People: The Nature of Happiness and its Origins in Childhood*, along with Luigino Bruni's (Bruni, 2005) *History of Happiness in Economics*, the Dalai Lama and Howard Cutler's (1999) *The Art of Happiness: A Handbook for Living*.

Other sources of data on social, economic and psychological factors on the general nature of happiness include the *Journal of Happiness Studies*, the *World Database of Happiness* (Veenhoven, 1995b) and the Australian Unity Wellbeing Index (International Wellbeing Group, http://acqol.deakin.edu.au/index.htm). However, none of these sources of information explicitly address the link between managers' happiness and their performance.

3. Managers' job performance

> Because job performance is the most widely studied criterion variable in the organizational behaviour and human resource management literatures (cf. Heneman, 1986; Campbell, 1990; Schmidt & Hunter, 1992) the construct validity of performance measures is critical.
> (Bommer, Johnson, Rich, Podsakoff, & McKenzie, 1995: 587)

INTRODUCTION

This chapter describes how managers' performance is conceived and measured. Before managers' job performance can be thoroughly analysed, it is necessary to decide what managers do, the diversity of their responsibilities and roles undertaken. Exploring the multi-dimensional nature of the managers' responsibilities and roles assists in guiding decisions about what should be incorporated into measures of their performance. Definitions of managers' performance have evolved from a fragmented literature.

Not surprisingly, there is considerable debate about the diverse performance expectations of managers. Contemporary theories of managers' performance are related to the framework of the schools of performance appraisal. Links between organisational effectiveness and managers are explored in depth because this connection is vital to an understanding of what constitutes their performance. The theoretical foundation of managers' contextual and task performance is followed by a summary of the main findings and general conclusions.

MANAGERS' DEFINITION, RESPONSIBILITIES, ROLES

Definition of a manager

Manage was first used in English writings in the 16th century, and had Latin origins with influence from Italian and French. *Manaeggio* originally referred to a horse riding school, handled by the Latin *manum*, or from the *manus* or hand (Carlopio, Andrewartha, & Armstrong, 2005). *Menage* meant the control or mastery of horses; to handle or train a horse in the exercises of *manege* (Delbridge et al., 1996). Over time, the meaning of the word *manage* was extended from horses to all animals, to things, and finally to people and commercial enterprises (manufacturers in the 19th century).

In 1980, Mintzberg considered that there was no universally accepted definition of a manager. By 2004 (p. 11), Mintzberg went on to observe that 'After almost a century of trying, by any reasonable assessment management has become neither a science nor a profession' but a blend of craft (experience), art (insight), and science (analysis), so that 'Effective management therefore happens where art, craft, and science meet' (Mintzberg, 2004: 10). Management is now considered by Mintzberg to be a professional fusion of science and an art form resulting in a craft steeped in what managers *actually do*.

In this conceptualisation, managing is seen as 'largely a facilitating activity' where contemporary exponents 'have to lead better, so that others can know better and therefore act better ... so as to bring out the best in other people' (Mintzberg, 2004). Contemporary research and practice renders these definitions arbitrary, since 'most managers show some leadership skills, while most leaders find themselves managing at times' (Karpin, 1995a: 1210). Mintzberg also considered management was replete with ambiguity and characterised by intractable problems.

Karpin's (1995a) definition of managers was intended to reflect the widening responsibilities for the 'development, maintenance and promotion of flexible management competencies for use in all industries, including small businesses, by managers operating at all levels' (Karpin, 1995a p. 35). Karpin (1995a: 14, 63) devised a definition of a manager based on the work of Quinn (1992) and Boyatzis (1982):

> An individual who achieves enterprise goals through the work of others ... Managers are responsible for the control or direction of people, a department or an organization.

Measures of managers' performance need to reflect the value of the work undertaken. In this context, performance is conceived of as an assessment of managers' recent performance. Murphy (1990: 162) further develops this logic;'[the] performance domain is defined as the set of behaviours that are relevant to the goals of the organisation or the organisational unit in which the person works'.

Performance must be measurable in relation to the level of individual contribution to organisational goals. Motowidlo, Borman and Schmit (1997: 72) defined job performance as the 'aggregated value to the organisation of the discrete behavioral episodes that an individual performs over a standard interval of time'. As state, Campbell, Gasser and Oswald (1996: 40) 'Performance is not the consequence or result of action, it is the action itself'. Assessing the cumulative information about a person's behavioural episodes permits an individual performance construct to be scaled to form a common metric, the 'contribution value', a construct that contributes to 'organisational effectiveness'.

Macro-organisational effectiveness is generally beyond the control of an individual manager. Thus, the scope of measures of managers' performance needs to be constrained so that 'performance consists of goal-relevant actions that are under the control of the individual, regardless of whether they are cognitive, motor, psychomotor or interpersonal' (Campbell et al., 1996: 40). Performance can be distinguished from effectiveness, which is conceived of as the value of those behaviours for the organisation (Campbell, McCloy, Oppler, & Sager, 1993).

This does not mean that measures of effectiveness lack utility for assessing managers' performance. Ensuring valid assessments requires that only sources of variation in performance and effectiveness under managers' control should be assessed (Campbell et al., 1970). Thus, evaluations of managers' performance should only include elements that are within their sphere of influence to control.

Management occurs within the context of organisation. Therefore, to be effective, there needs to be a fit between managers' performance and organisational goals (Hart & Quinn, 1993). As such, managers' net contributions represent their total value to an organisation. A consolidated definition of managers' performance, derived from the literature is *the recent net contribution value to organisational effectiveness and goals, attained in conjunction with people, determined by events under managers' control, in a particular environment.*

Managers' responsibilities and roles

A clear idea of the responsibilities and roles undertaken by managers is needed before attempting to define them. Management has also been described as 'a strategic thoughtful influence through goal setting and motivation to ensure achievement of the organization's objectives' (Whetton & Cameron, 1991). The outcomes-orientated approaches focus on managers' measurable contribution to organisations' effectiveness (Nankervis, 2004). Cammock, Nilakant, Dakin (1995) conceived of effectiveness as a socially constructed phenomenon, resulting from managers' efforts to achieve results through people, as detailed in Table 3.2. Therefore, a critical responsibility of managers is to maintain and improve the performance of the people reporting to them. Hence, managers' performance is related to the level of achievement of enterprise goals in conjunction with people. A more contemporary perspective of managers' jobs also includes the practice of empowering by enabling employees.

Fayol's (1916) view of managers' roles has dominated management theory since early in the 20th century. Broad descriptions of managers' roles prompted management researchers, such as Quinn (1988), Mintzberg (1980), and Argyris and Schon (1978) to specify the competencies required to effectively execute managerial responsibilities and roles. When conditions are stable, managers undertake a central role in organisations by formulating policy, developing strategies, and in directing, facilitating and monitoring the performance of others (Carlopio et al., 2005). Managers' roles have been consolidated into the organisational functions of 'planning, organising, leading and controlling' (cited in Robbins, Millett, Cacioppe, & Waters-Marsh, 2001: 5). These roles have been refined by Cammock and colleagues (1995: 455) into the managerial behaviours of 'direction setter, problem solver and decision maker'.

Scott also distinguished managers' behaviour from that of non-managers: 'Managers decide, performers implement; managers command, performers obey; managers coordinate, performers carry out specialised tasks' (1992: 278). From a rationalist perspective, these distinctions control, shape and influence participants' behaviour to deliver and service the organisation's objectives. Such tasks are undertaken to meet the organisation's goals; cope with environment complexity; manage its productive system; improve its productive capacity; acquire resources to service its objectives; direct its internal affairs, and to assemble and mobilise the components necessary to service its objectives (Scott, 1992).

Mintzberg (1973; 1980) took a neutral view of the managerial role which ignores matters of ownership and power and suggests that contingency factors explain variations in the content/characteristics of managerial work. Contingent factors include:

- Environmental matters (the location, community, industry, weather);
- Job factors (hierarchical level, functions and degree of supervision);
- Person variables (personality and style);
- Situational variables (including technological and time-related factors).

These roles justify and legitimise managerial purposes in terms of contingency theory by: designing and maintaining stable and reliable systems for efficient operations: in a changing environment, ensuring that the organisation satisfies those that own and control it; and boundary management to maintain information links between the organisation and players in the environment. Turbulence caused by competition, rate of change, growth, pressure to produce, forces managers to spend more time in informal and verbal communication that is varied and fragmented with a bias towards action being an imperative.

A job role is an organised set of behaviours. Managers assume multiple roles in order to meet the many demands of performing their functions. Mintzberg (1973) has identified 10 roles common to the work of all managers which are divided into three groups: interpersonal, informational, and decisional as illustrated in Figure 3.1.

Figure 3.1   Managerial roles

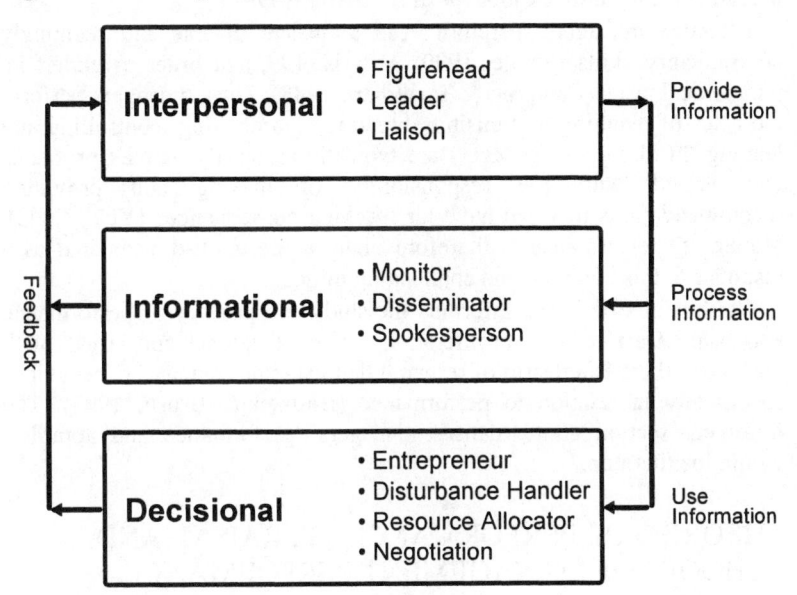

```
                    ┌─────────────────────────────────────┐
                ┌──▶│ Interpersonal   • Figurehead        │──▶ Provide
                │   │                 • Leader            │    Information
                │   │                 • Liaison           │
                │   └─────────────────────────────────────┘
                │   ┌─────────────────────────────────────┐
         F      │   │                 • Monitor           │
         e      │◀──│ Informational   • Disseminator      │◀── Process
         e      │   │                 • Spokesperson      │    Information
         d      │   └─────────────────────────────────────┘
         b      │   ┌─────────────────────────────────────┐
         a      │   │                 • Entrepreneur      │
         c      │   │                 • Disturbance Handler│
         k      │◀──│ Decisional      • Resource Allocator│──▶ Use
                    │                 • Negotiation       │    Information
                    └─────────────────────────────────────┘
```

Source: Mintzberg, Henry: *THE NATURE OF MANAGERIAL WORK*, © *(1973: 92-93). Adapted with the permission of Pearson Education, Inc., Upper Saddle River, NJ.*

These managerial roles are described individually by Mintzberg but actually form an integrated whole. Informational roles link all managerial work together, interpersonal roles ensure that information is provided, and decisional roles make significant use of the information. Depending on the level and function of management, the performance of managerial roles and the requirements of these roles can be undertaken at different times by the same manager to different degrees. As a manager enacts a role, these will come together as a gestalt (integrated whole) reflecting the competencies associated with the roles.

Managers inhabit organisational situations replete with behavioural complexity (Hooijberg & Quinn, 1992; Mintzberg, 2004). As Andrews observed in 1976, managers work in 'calculated chaos' and 'controlled disorder', rather than a neatly ordered environment often portrayed in academic literature. As such, managers are required to assume multiple highly integrated and complementary roles and, sometimes, competing roles, to implement cognitively elaborate strategies (Quinn, Spreitzer, &

Hart, 1992). Successfully performing these competing roles results in superior firm performance (Hart & Quinn, 1993). Situation awareness, planning, and problem-solving are important cognitive components of performance in complex jobs (Neal & Griffin, 1999).

Effective managers therefore need to master diverse and seemingly contradictory skills (Senge, 1990; Argyris, 1992) in order to undertake paradoxical tasks (Cameron & Tschirhart, 1988). Thus, managers perform the roles of planning, organising, directing, coordinating, controlling and leading. In doing so, managers are typically assigned complex problems and vested with the responsibility of making and providing recommendations that can have far reaching consequences (Yukl, 2002). Managers' performance is therefore likely to be multi-dimensional as a response to this complex and challenging milieu.

Various theories have informed the study and practice of performance appraisal. Despite the proliferation of publications concerned with managers, there is a dearth of research that examines managers' behaviour specifically in relation to performance (Borman & Brush, 1993). The following section contextualises managers' performance and appraisal within the literature.

THEORIES OF PERFORMANCE APPRAISAL AND SCHOOLS OF MANAGEMENT PERFORMANCE

> From its earliest days as a distinct area within the behavioural and social sciences, industrial/organizational psychology has recognized 'performance' as perhaps its ultimate variable, if not its raison d'etre.
> (Organ & Paine, 1999: 337)

Two streams of research into the nature of managerial work, the unitarist and the functionalist, have emerged since the 1960s (Morse & Wagner, 1978; Boyatzis, 1982; Luthans, Rosenkrantz, & Hennessey, 1985; Luthans, Welsh, & Lewis, 1988; Martinko & Gardner, 1990). From the unitarist standpoint, managers are viewed from a growth perspective by the functions, behaviours, roles, and decisions they make (Borman & Brush, 1993). Most of the research into managers' work has focused on managerial activities and behaviours, not on the relationship 'between what managers do and what they achieve' (Stewart, 1989: 2).

The functionalist perspective emphasised measurement of managers' objective output as an indicator of effectiveness. Quinn et al. (1996) identified productivity, profit, stability, continuity, commitment, cohesion, morale, adaptability and external support as criteria for organisational effectiveness. Using this approach, appraisal is conceived as an integral part of a broader performance management system. Functionalism is a view of managers' performance located within an interpretative paradigm (Burrell & Morgan, 1979). Functionalism has been criticised for failing to provide a comprehensive perspective of organisational phenomena (Morgan & Smircich, 1980; Rao & Pasmore, 1989; Gioia & Pitre, 1990). Many studies of social phenomena subscribe to a positivist perspective of organisations (Burrell & Morgan, 1979; Gioia & Pitre, 1990). Functionalism assumes that managerial effectiveness is quantifiable, a social constructivist perspective, based on the assumption that organisational phenomena are socially constructed (Cammock et al., 1995). Integrating the functionalist (task performance) and social constructivist (contextual performance) perspectives offers a more holistic conceptualisation of managers' performance.

In order to clarify the managers' job performance construct, theories relating to managers' job performance need to be considered within the schools of performance appraisal. Table 3.1 encapsulates the relationships between the schools of performance appraisal and theories of management performance. How these schools and theories relate to the theoretical and practical aspects of managers' performance is further developed in Chapter 7.

Table 3.1 *Conceptual relationships between schools and theories of management performance*

THEORY	Measurement	Appraisal Interview	Social Cognitive Process	Performance Management
Attribution	YES	YES	YES	PARTIAL
Competence	YES	PARTIAL	YES	PARTIAL
Competing Values		YES		PARTIAL
Contingency		PARTIAL		YES
Emotional Intelligence		YES	PARTIAL	PARTIAL
Expectancy			PARTIAL	YES
Human Needs			PARTIAL	YES
Individual Differences			PARTIAL	YES
Job Performance	YES		YES	
Motivation	PARTIAL	PARTIAL	PARTIAL	YES
Performance	YES	PARTIAL		PARTIAL
Self-Efficacy		PARTIAL	PARTIAL	YES
Social Cognition			YES	YES
Work Adjustment			PARTIAL	YES

The social constructivist perspective of managers' performance is underpinned by theories of: motivation (McClelland, 1985); human needs (Johnston, 1979); expectancy (Vroom, 1964); job performance (Motowidlo et al., 1997); individual differences (Borman & Motowidlo, 1993; Motowidlo et al., 1997); attribution (De Vader, Bateson, & Lord, 1986); self-efficacy (Bandura, 1977); social cognition (Bandura, 1986); work adjustment (Dawis & Lofquist, 1984; 1993); contingency (Pfeffer, 1982; Jones, 1995); competence (Guion, 1991; Goleman, 1999), and emotional intelligence (Salovey & Mayer, 1990; 1993; Goleman, 1995; 1996; Mayer & Salovey, 1997; 1999). These theories provide a comprehensive social constructivist perspective of managers' performance.

The Competing Values Framework developed by Quinn, Faerman, Thompson and McGrath (1996) is informed by, and complements attribution, work adjustment theory and self-efficacy theory (based on social cognition theory) and competency theory (McClelland, 1973; Spencer & Spencer, 1993). Each of these theories impacts in some way on the conceptualisation and operationalisation of managers' performance, affective wellbeing and intrinsic job satisfaction. The conceptualisation of performance appraisal is integral to measuring managers' performance.

The following section critiques contemporary theories of managers' performance appraisal in order to contextualise the concept of managers' performance.

COMPONENTS OF PERFORMANCE APPRAISAL

There have been many investigations into performance and appraisal issues, measurement instruments, and cognitive and behavioural processes. As would be expected there have also been as many attempts to identify the attributes of managers' performance. In 1993, Wood and Marshal (p. 17) alerted us to the need to 'design performance appraisal systems which properly align organisational purposes and goals of individual managers in performance appraisals'. For this to occur, managers' performance needs to be accurately measured. An optimal mix of the key findings of research needs to be incorporated into any measurement of managers' performance. For this to occur it is necessary to review the major research findings about job performance before moving on to those aspects of managers' performance that are described and measured in Chapter 6.

Researchers have been attempting to construct accurate appraisal devices of job performance since the turn of the 20th century. The classical theory of performance has predominated (Campbell et al., 1996). The earliest reference to the systematic measurement of work activity was introduced in the 1930s through Taylor's (1947) concept of 'scientific management', followed by Thorndike's (1949) seminal work on selection. Thorndike believed there was one general performance factor, or 'ultimate' criterion to be measured. Thus, performance was considered a unitary construct, with one general 'objective' factor that could account for most of the true-score-covariance measures. Job performance appraisals at this time centred on using the best available 'objective' indicator of an individual's achievements. Contrary to these views, Scott (1992) argued that any attempt to find objective measures of managers' performance is futile because the 'Criteria for evaluating organizational effectiveness cannot be produced by some objective, apolitical process. These are always normative and often controversial' (Scott, 1992: 361). Politicisation of the performance appraisal system is an inevitable by-product of organisational existence.

During the first half of the 20th century, performance appraisal researchers were preoccupied with identifying the personality traits of successful leaders (Fiedler, 1967; Bennis, 1997; Conger, 1998; Goleman, 1999; Yukl, 2002). Industrial psychologists in the USA began studying performance appraisal immediately preceding World War II (Scott, Clothier & Spriegal, 1941, cited in Murphy & Cleveland, 1991: 3). Early performance appraisal instruments focused on evaluating how congruent managers' behaviours were with the personality characteristics of successful managers. This approach did not prove to be a valid or predictive measure of managers' performance. Personality only explains a small percentage of the variance in job performance and is therefore an unreliable indicator of managers' performance.

Four schools of performance appraisal - Measurement, Appraisal Interview, Social Cognitive Process and Performance Management - have been identified by Wood and Marshall (1993). These schools have informed the issues studied and assumptions made about the practice of performance appraisal (De Vries, Morrison, Shullman, & Gerlach, 1986). Aspects of each of these schools are incorporated into the measurement instrument devised to measure managers' performance as shown in Table 3.1. In the following section, a description of the four schools of performance is given as originally reported by Wood and Marshall (1993).

Measurement School

Until the 1950s, researchers mostly investigated 'what successful employees are' (in some intrinsic sense), rather than 'what successful employees do'. Performance appraisal instruments were designed to provide valid data of a person's performance. Performance assessment methodologies developed during this period were intended to provide objective measures of outcomes. Earlier research treated performance appraisal as essentially a measurement issue to be solved by the development of valid rating scales, which minimised sources of potential error (Murphy & Cleveland, 1991). The majority of the research into rating scales has focused on the development of criterion-referenced formats that involved comparing an individual's performance on a rating scale against pre-determined standards.

In practice, it is extremely difficult to obtain reliable and valid indicators to assess multiple outcomes of performance. Research comparing the merits of various rating formats has found that no one approach is consistently superior to another for accurately rating performance (Landy & Farr, 1980; Bernardin & Beatty, 1984; Murphy & Cleveland, 1991; Carroll, Yik, Russell, & Barrett, 1999). As with most performance appraisal systems, the main output of the Measurement School is the rating of one person by another. Regardless of the ratings approach used, the main weakness of performance assessment is the presence of systematic error variance that is unrelated to the performance of the person being assessed (Campbell, 1996).

Appraisal Interview School

In the 1970s and 1980s, the Appraisal Interview School's research interests expanded to include the role of performance appraisals in employee counselling and feedback. Also, during this period, the performance appraisal process became an extension of corporate planning and budgeting, resulting in the Management by Objectives School (MBO), a precursor to the Performance Management School. Personal development was seen as the central purpose of the performance appraisal, with managers' roles progressing from that of a judge in the Measurement School to a coach, or counsellor in the Appraisal School. Following Maier's (1958) investigations into managerial dynamics, particularly communication processes, the focus of studies of appraisal interviews has shifted to a facilitative approach of goal setting and feedback in the appraisal process (Ilgen, Fisher, & Taylor, 1979).

Trust was established by the Appraisal Interview School as a critical intervening factor resulting from managers' actions, which influences the effectiveness of a performance appraisal. For example, open communications, clear expectations and a supportive management style have been found to result in more accurate performance appraisals (Wood & Marshall, 1993). However, the Appraisal Interview School model is limited by its assumption of an apolitical model of management.

Social Cognitive Process School

In the early 1980s, there was a substantial movement away from instrument design and training to measure managers' performance, towards ways of achieving rater agreement. This entailed conceiving of the rater as a decision-maker capable of processing a range of social cues when judging people. Concerns about rating accuracy remained but have been extended beyond achieving outcomes through rating formats to examining the rater's ability and motivation to rate accurately. A considerable amount of the variance in measuring managers' performance may be accounted for by a rater's response to multiple and competing pressures impinging on the appraisal process (Murphy & Cleveland, 1991).

The Social Cognitive School extended the work of the Measurement School to show that, regardless of the scale used, raters do not just report observations, but actively evaluate appraisal information in relation to their personal motivations and goals (Ilgen, Barnes-Farrell, & McKellin, 1993). People are known to vary in their capacity and desire to make accurate appraisal judgements. Irrespective of the technical qualities, simple-to-use rating formats, with a clear purpose and accountability, are likely to result in more accurate appraisals.

Delays in the observation of data and the recording of ratings, have not been found to significantly influence the recall of behaviours, and subsequently influence the accuracy of performance ratings and rankings (Murphy & Balzer, 1986). Other advances in thinking have progressed the Measurement School's preoccupation with error correction to frame of reference instructions, which give managers greater knowledge of the specific standards assigned to appraisal performance criteria (Wood & Marshall, 1993).

Performance Management School

Two assumptions are central to the Performance Management School's position: appraising employees' performance can enhance productivity, and performance appraisal is critical to achieving performance management (Bartz, Schwandt, & Hillman, 1989; Gioia & Longnecker, 1994). Substantial improvements in organisational productivity have been reported using goal setting and work planning systems when performance management features are used, particularly when supported by senior management (Latham & Wexley, 1994).

There is considerable evidence to suggest that organisations which utilise performance management systems strategically perform more effectively in financial terms than those which invest less in this aspect of the human resource management process (Rheem, 1996; Glendenning,

2002). Generally organisations who effectively manage the employees' performance are more likely to outperform their competitors than those who fail to do so (McDonald & Smith, 1995). Despite the profusion of literature expounding the importance of the benefits of performance management these findings have not been connected with a widespread adoption of effective performance management systems (Compton, 2005). Consensus has emerged to support the potential of these techniques together to motivate individual employees, work groups, to evaluate the efficacy of all human resource management functions, and to provide organisations with a strategic advantage in achieving competitive goals and imperatives (Compton, 2005).

The Performance Management School assesses an individual's contribution to organisational effectiveness. Of all the management practices investigated, goal setting and feedback have consistently been associated with significant gains in individual performance (Locke & Latham, 1990). With this approach, performance-rating accuracy becomes critical when related to the attainment of organisational goals. Achievements are assessed against perceived contributions to organisational goals, often described as 'value-adding'.

The Performance Management School assesses an individual's contribution to organisational effectiveness. Of all the management practices investigated, goal setting and feedback have consistently been associated with significant gains in individual performance (Locke & Latham, 1990). With this approach, performance-rating accuracy becomes critical when related to the attainment of organisational goals. Achievements are assessed against perceived contributions to organisational goals, often described as 'value-adding'.

Competing Values Framework

This theme is echoed in Quinn et al.'s (1994) suggestion that 'organisational effectiveness' is the key construct to be evaluated in the context of the 'competing values' environment that managers inhabit. The complexities of organisations within which managers work prompted Quinn et al. (1996) and Quinn, Kahn and Mandl (1994) to integrate the seemingly opposing human relations, open systems, internal process, and rational goal perspectives of managers into a Competing Values Framework (Quinn, 1988). The Competing Values Framework posits that managers are inevitably judged by the same conflicting criteria experienced by organisations. Managers' contributions are considered to determine organisational effectiveness and support the proposition that the supposedly different perspectives of managers' roles are actually closely related (Jones, 1995; Quinn et al., 1996). The Competing Values

Framework represents an integration of managers' performance that accounts for the non-routine cognitive complexity associated with all managerial jobs, as illustrated in Figure 3.2..

Figure 3.2 Competing Values Framework

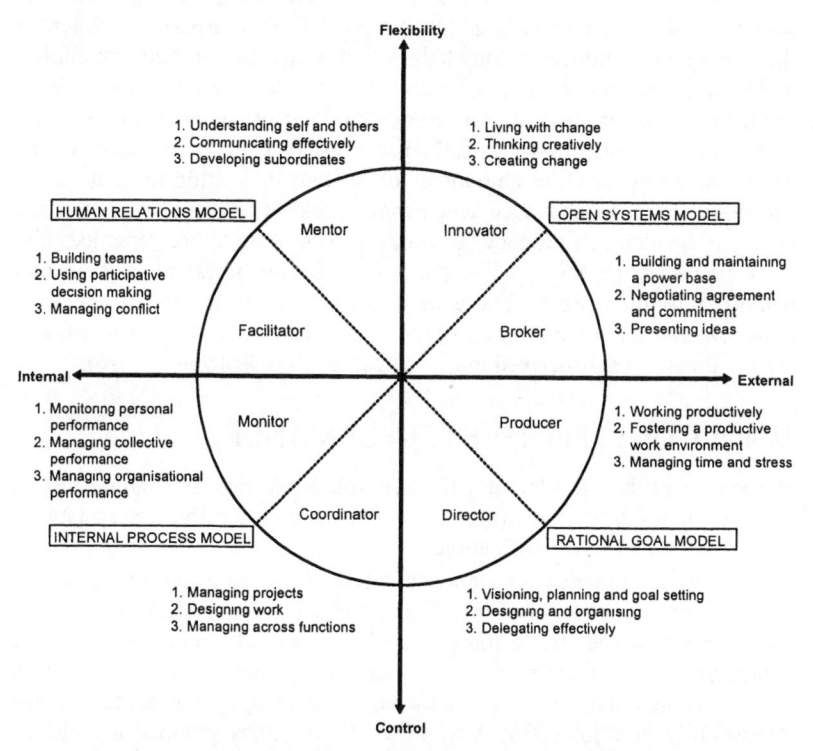

```
                              Flexibility
                                  ↑
        1. Understanding self and others    1. Living with change
        2. Communicating effectively        2. Thinking creatively
        3. Developing subordinates          3. Creating change

   ┌─────────────────────┐                      ┌──────────────────┐
   │ HUMAN RELATIONS MODEL│   Mentor  Innovator │ OPEN SYSTEMS MODEL│
   └─────────────────────┘                      └──────────────────┘
   1. Building teams                             1. Building and maintaining
   2. Using participative                           a power base
      decision making                            2. Negotiating agreement
   3. Managing conflict                             and commitment
                        Facilitator    Broker    3. Presenting ideas

Internal ←────────────────────────────────────────────────→ External

   1. Monitoring personal                        1. Working productively
      performance         Monitor    Producer    2. Fostering a productive
   2. Managing collective                           work environment
      performance                                3. Managing time and stress
   3. Managing organisational
      performance
                        Coordinator   Director
   ┌─────────────────────┐                      ┌──────────────────┐
   │INTERNAL PROCESS MODEL│                     │ RATIONAL GOAL MODEL│
   └─────────────────────┘                      └──────────────────┘
        1. Managing projects              1. Visioning, planning and goal setting
        2. Designing work                 2. Designing and organising
        3. Managing across functions      3. Delegating effectively
                                  ↓
                              Control
```

Source: *Adapted from Quinn, Faerman, Thompson and McGrath (1996: 16).*

Like so many instruments described in the literature that purport to measure managers' performance, Quinn's (1988) Competency Framework measurement instruments have essentially been developed for selecting or developing managers, rather than appraising their performance.

Summary on performance appraisal

Performance appraisal research is integral to human resource management systems and practices (Wood & Marshall, 1993). Contemporary performance appraisal approaches recognise that performance appraisal is a useful method of predicting future performance, not merely a way of judging past performance. This approach views performance appraisal as an integral aspect of managers' jobs that permits resources to be allocated, expectations shaped, employees motivated and problems to be identified and solved (Wood & Marshall, 1993).

Recently, several theoretical developments have resulted in the integration of the three main schools of motivation theory (content, process and reinforcement) in the context of work behaviour. Each of these integrated models acknowledges that motivation affects the choice, action and performance of employees (Weiner, 1974). Motivation is likely to have stronger impact on contextual performance than on task performance. Motivation can influence individual's performance if they have discretion over the amount of effort that they allocate to the task. Motivation can be enhanced when individuals achieve mastery over the task and develop self efficacy (Hesketh, 1997). Motivational practices aim to increase a person's willingness to allocate physical and mental resources to their work. These motivational practices are evaluated as either facilitating, or inhibiting opportunities for increased self-worth and for fulfilment of self-derived motives (Campbell & Pritchard, 1976).

MODEL OF EFFECTIVE PERFORMANCE

Boyatzis's (1982) Model of Effective Job Performance (Figure 3.3) is seminal to models of management competencies for the assessment of performance and role clarification.

For Boyatzis, competencies were characteristics that are causally related to superior performance in a job. Competencies were broadly conceived, going beyond specific technical skills to include motives, traits or characteristics of the superior manager. A managerial competency was defined as 'any characteristic of a manager that enables him/her to perform successfully in a job' (Boyatzis, 1982: 5). Boyatzis grouped a range of competencies, exhibited by high performing 'superior managers', under broader groupings such as 'leadership', 'goal' and 'action clusters'.

Boyatzis has provided a description of some important competencies of managers, rather than simply detailing how managers actually manage. Furthermore, potentially, tasks can exist solely as a dominant factor, without necessarily being part of the organisational environment. According to Boyatzis, effective action, and therefore performance, occurs when the critical components (job demands, individual competencies and the organisational environment) of the model are consistent. If any of these aspects of the Model of Effective Performance are not congruent, ineffective behaviour or inaction is predicted to be evident. For example, the outer circle indicates the importance of the 'Organisation environment in which the job exists'. These conditions may sometimes be incompatible, resulting in inconsistent managerial performance.

Figure 3.3   Model of Effective Performance

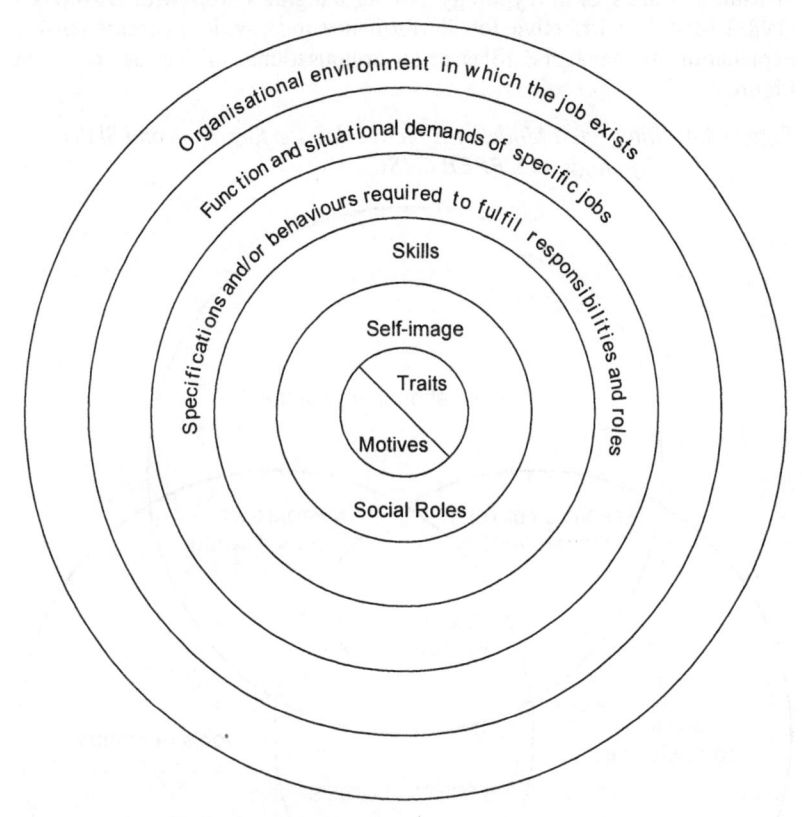

[Concentric circles diagram, from innermost to outermost:
- Traits / Motives
- Self-image
- Social Roles
- Skills
- Specifications and/or behaviours required to fulfil responsibilities and roles
- Function and situational demands of specific jobs
- Organisational environment in which the job exists]

Source: Adapted from Boyatzis (1982).

Boyatzis's model ignored an important element of managers' work by not including the complex interactions between the individuals being managed. In addition, the interfaces between the variables in the model are not as clearly delineated as the model suggests, since, depending on circumstances all these factors are likely to have a varying effect on each other. Also, Boyatzis's model does not make it clear how traits and motives are related to self-image, and how they are linked to social roles.

Managers possess a variety of important values and attitudes that influence their behaviour (e.g., integrity, responsibility and selflessness), that are not authentic traits or values. Also, the 'social roles' and 'self-image' managers perform and possess are important elements for managing or leading. Thus, there remained a need to refine the concept of what constitutes effective managers' performance before it can be reliably measured. Katz's Skill Typology (1974) integrates well with Boyatzis's (1982) Model of Effective Job Performance to provide a comprehensive explanation of managers' roles in an organisational milieu, as shown in Figure 3.4.

Figure 3.4 Integrated Model of Effective Job Performance and Skills Typology (in UPPER CASE)

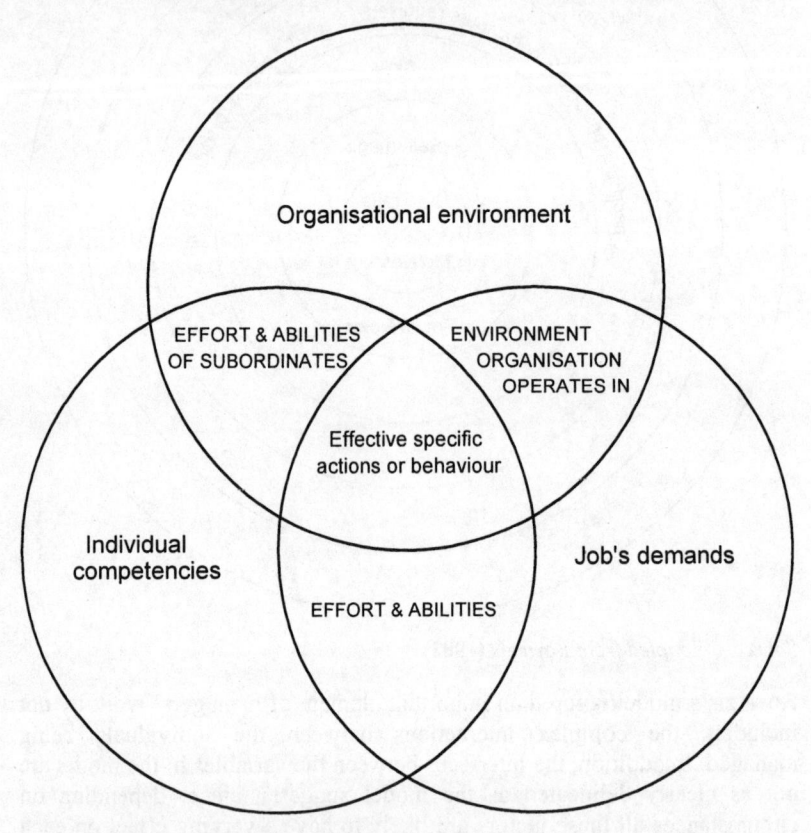

Source: Adapted from Boyatzis (1982) and Katz (1974)

A conceptual deficiency is evident in Katz's inclusion of the 'Environment the organisation operates in', which corresponds to Boyatzis's 'Functions and situational demands'; both are exogenous, and therefore out of the control of the individual.

MANAGERS ORGANISATIONAL EFFECTIVENESS

There is broad agreement in the literature about the desirability of measuring outcomes of managers' effectiveness. To recap, managers undertake highly integrated complementary roles that are sometimes competing and diverse, which may require contradictory skills to undertake paradoxical tasks. Managerial performance in the functional areas of planning, supervising, delegating and coordinating has been linked to organisational effectiveness (Borman & Motowidlo, 1993). Fenwick and De Cieri (1995: 81) have argued that 'Effective performance management begins with an effective manager'. Subsequent reviews have 'deplored the lack of attention to effectiveness' (Stewart, 1989: 2) that has been given to managers' jobs. How managers create value for an organisation may be dealt with by operationalising and measuring the construct of organisational effectiveness, in relation to managers' performance (Quinn et al., 1996).

Notwithstanding the difficulties of measuring outputs, organisations constantly attempt to assess managers' performance. Luthans et al. (1988) have identified specific managerial activities related to organisational effectiveness and the behaviours that reportedly contribute to organisational effectiveness. Jansen and Stoop (1997) replicated and extended Luthan's study. These results provide a way of identifying the managerial competencies that may contribute to organisational effectiveness. Managers' output is an acceptable substitute for managers' performance, when embedded in a broader context of organisational dynamics. As Barraclough (cited in Karpin) argued, the profile of an 'ideal manager' (at middle and senior level) is likely to be generic across a range of situations (1995a: 534). Thus, measures of public and private sector managers should include aspects of generic performance for them to be comparable.

Cammock and colleagues (1995) concluded that 'managerial effectiveness may have some content which is similar across diverse settings' (1995: 463). A number of similarities between managers are argued to be dependent on situation-specific descriptions but the 'constructs underpinning managerial effectiveness may be more generic than is normally assumed' (Cammock et al., 1995: 463). These research findings need to be empirically validated to establish whether managerial effectiveness is more generic than has previously been assumed. Further research is required to establish if managers' effectiveness, in different and similar contexts, is underpinned by a set of comparative, enduring and transferable dimensions (Stewart, 1989; Cammock et al., 1995).

As noted earlier in this chapter, effectiveness is an important aspect of managers' job performance. Ten behavioural characteristics of effective managers were identified by Whetton and Cameron (1991) from interviews with peers and supervisors of senior officers in business, healthcare, education and state government. The characteristics were verbal communication, managing time and stress, managing individual decisions, recognising, defining and solving problems, motivating and influencing others, delegating, setting goals and articulating a vision, self-awareness, team building and managing conflict. Effective managers were found by Whetton and Cameron (1991) to exhibit 'paradoxical skills', a finding akin to Quinn et al.'s (1996) notion of 'competing values'.

Significant differences have been found in the activities, behaviours, skills and qualities of effective (i.e., successful), as opposed to less effective, managers (Boyatzis, 1982; Luthans et al., 1985; Martinko & Gardner, 1985; Hales, 1986; Stewart, 1989; Martinko & Gardner, 1990). The assumption is that the possession of particular competencies distinguishes a 'superior' from an 'average' performing manager. Cammock et al. (1995) extended Boyatzis's cluster into descriptions of Most Effective (superior) and Least Effective (average) managers.

A social constructivist approach was used by Cammock et al. (1995) to develop a Lay Model of Least and Most Effective Managers. Common sense or 'lay' theories were used to explain the shared understandings of these social actors. Proponents of this approach argued that lay theories provide powerful contextual understandings of managers' effectiveness. The differences between most effective and least effective managers is axiomatic to considering what constitutes effective managers and needs to be integrated into a measure of managers' performance. These differences are summarised in Table 3.2.

Table 3.2 A Lay Model of Least and Most Effective Managers

The least effective manager:	The most effective manager:
Conceptual Abilities/Direction Setting	
Needs to have direction set for him/her. Their units have no sense of purpose.	Able to set their own direction and instill a clear sense of purpose onto their units.
Innovation	
Satisfied with the status quo, avoids change.	Constantly looking for new approaches thrives on change.
Future orientation	
Thinks short term and cannot visualise the future.	Future-oriented and can think in the long term.
Overview	
Gets bogged down in detail and loses the big picture.	Avoids getting bogged down in detail and maintains the big picture.

Managing/Operating	
Too involved in detailed work. Leaves little time to manage.	Doesn't get involved in detailed work. Leaves time to manage.
Drive	
Lacks drive and ambition. Limited capacity for work.	High levels of drive and ambition. Great enthusiasm and drive for work.
Decisiveness	
Indecisive. Lacks confidence and backs away from tough decisions.	Decisive. Will tackle unpleasant tasks and confident can make tough decisions.
Prioritising	
Has little sense of priorities and is easily sidetracked from bottom line concerns.	Has a good sense of priorities and keeps sight of the bottom line.
Problem-solving	
Doesn't allocate time well. Poor at planning, organising and scheduling work.	Allocates time well. Good at planning, organising and scheduling work.
Interpersonal Abilities/Delegation and training	
Tries to do too much and doesn't train successors.	Delegates well, involves others, and grooms successors.
Consultation	
Imposes change without consulting and is rigid and unwilling to learn.	Consults the staff before introducing change and is flexible and willing to learn.
Feedback	
Highlights the negative and doesn't give sufficient recognition for good performance.	Highlights the positive and recognises good performance.
Contact	
Seen infrequently and is out of touch with his/her unit.	Highly visible and on top of critical issues.
Support	
Unapproachable and reluctant to help.	Approachable, friendly and supportive.
Personality	
Negative outlook and has difficulty relating to others.	Positive outlook and relates well to others.
Integrity	
Devious and goes behind people's back.	Straightforward and honest.

Source: Adapted from Cammock, Nilakant and Dakin (1995: 456).

Cammock et al.(1995) have summarised the issues related to A Lay Model of Least and Most Effective Managers:

> Most effective managers avoid getting bogged down in detail and maintain the big picture. They stand back, from their work, to get an objective view and have a broad vision of the different areas of the organization and their needs. They maintain contact with other managers and are concerned about the whole organization, not just their own patch. They are flexible and are willing to bend the rules, if it means getting the job done better. They are concerned with the overall work effectiveness of staff rather than minor aspects of staff behaviour, that have little effect on work performance.
>
> In contrast, ineffective managers get bogged down in detail and lose the big picture. They are too close to the work to be objective and lack a broad vision of the organisation. They spend too much time on one area under their administration, to the detriment of others. They have a narrow view of the organization and are concerned only about their patch. They are inflexible and won't bend the rules, even if following them rigidly causes inefficiency. Rather than concentrating on the overall work effectiveness of staff, they nitpick on minor things, which have little impact on work performance.
>
> (Cammock et al., 1995: 455)

There are noticeable consistencies between A Lay Model of Least and Most Effective Managers (Cammock et al., 1995) and other studies of effectiveness (Quinn, 1988) and competency studies (Boyatzis, 1982; Dulewicz, 1989; Page, Wilson, & Kolb, 1994). Cammock et al. (1995) claimed that there are a number of similarities between the Lay Model of Least and Most Effective Managers and the competencies identified by Boyatzis. Consistent with Kaplan and Norton (1992; 1993; 1996b; 1996a), Cammock et al. (1995) found an orientation to the future of an organisation was also a factor that needed to be included in assessments of managers' performance.

Summary of job performance and effectiveness

Organisations are social structures created by individuals to continuously support the collaborative pursuit of specific goals. Organisational effectiveness refers to the alignment of managers' contributions to an organisation's purpose and goals (Quinn et al., 1996). Productivity is the ratio of effectiveness to the cost of achieving that level of effectiveness (Mahoney, 1988). Output is the contribution to an organisation's effectiveness.

Performance can be distinguished from effectiveness (the evaluation of the results of performance), productivity (the ratio of effectiveness to the cost of achieving that level of effectiveness) and utility (the value of a particular level of performance, effectiveness or productivity). Performance consists of the actions and behaviour under an individual's control that contribute to organisation's goals.

Job performance represents the extent to which an individual contributes to achieving goals that enhance the aggregated value of an organisation. An aggregated contribution represents an individual's net value to an organisation. A complete understanding of job performance depends on the contribution of managers to organisational goals. To be meaningful, assessments of managers' performance should be relevant to the external environment. Measuring the tasks (inputs) undertaken by managers is difficult, since tasks do not necessarily equate to a direct measure of output. This realisation has prompted considerable debate about the notion of organisational effectiveness, job-related competencies, and performance.

The following sections review the emergent literature relating to managers' contextual and task performance.

CONTEXTUAL AND TASK PERFORMANCE

A considerable amount of research has focussed on identifying predictors of superior job performance. However, to reiterate, performance is difficult to define as a construct, making predictive studies of it challenging. Recent findings have distinguished two types of performance: contextual and task (Borman & Motowidlo, 1993; Motowidlo et al., 1997; Motowidlo & Schmit, 1999). Both of these domains of performance contribute to accomplishing organisational goals, but through different mechanisms. As noted earlier, managers plan, organise, coordinate and supervise, functions that indirectly contribute to the efficient and effective operation and output of an organisation.

Task and contextual performance may be differentiated by three assumptions: (1) Activities associated with contextual performance are relatively similar across jobs, whereas activities associated with task performance will vary between jobs; (2) Contextual performance is related to personality and motivation; whereas task performance is related to ability; (3) Contextual performance is discretionary and extra role, whereas task performance is prescribed and comprised of in-role behaviour (Borman & Motowidlo, 1997; Motowidlo & Schmit, 1999).

Managers' performance is conceived in the literature as mainly constituting task performance which is defined as the 'effectiveness with which job incumbents perform activities that contribute to its technical core either by directly implementing a part of its technological process, or by providing it with needed materials or services' (Borman & Motowidlo, 1993). Organ and Paine (1999: 357) considered task performance to be 'part and parcel of the workflow that transforms inputs of energy, information and materials into outputs in the form of goods and services to the external constituency'.

On the other hand, contextual performance deals with the psychological linkages between people, and is represented by discretionary forms of contributions to the organisation that have uncertain or indirect rewards compared to task performance (Organ & Paine, 1999). Contextual performance acts to reinforce the linkages amongst employees, and thereby sustain and enhance the collective character of the organisation (Organ & Paine, 1999). In contrast, task activities are role prescribed; incumbents must demonstrate proficiency in performing tasks in exchange for rewards. Conversely, contextual activities require discretionary behaviours, which have interpersonal and motivational implications. In all, contextual acts are what managers may perform beyond what is expected of them. Sometimes these behaviours are rewarded, but they are unlikely to be explicitly incorporated into formal job requirements with the notable exception of leading edge employers of choice.

Moreover, task performance varies across jobs and differentiates jobs, whereas contextual performance is common to most jobs. Task performance is about the proficiency with which task activities are accomplished. Thus, variability across employees on task performance is logically attributable to differences in individual knowledge, skills, and ability, while contextual performance 'has the effect of maintaining the broader organisational, social and psychological environment in which the technical core must function' (Motowidlo et al., 1997: 75). Contextual performance is a multi-dimensional concept, rather than a single set of uniform behaviours (Van Dyne & LePine, 1998). Contextual performance is less a function of managers' levels of proficiency than volition, and is therefore related more to differences in individual dispositions and personalities.

Employers have defined performance more broadly than the proficiency within which employees perform duties in sales contexts (Podsakoff & MacKenzie, 1994), the defence force (Motowidlo & Van Scotter, 1994) and manufacturing settings (Podsakoff, Ahearne, & MacKenzie, 1997). Contributions for overall performance were evident from the performance of both contextual and task activities which have been found to make independent contributions to job performance (MacKenzie, Podsakoff, & Fetter, 1991; Borman & Motowidlo, 1993; Motowidlo & Van Scotter, 1994). In multitrait-multimethod matrices, 55% of performance was reliably identified as task dimensions and 30% of managers' work as contextual dimensions, with disagreement over the remaining 15% of variance (Borman & Brush, 1993: 87). A correlation of .20 was found between contextual and task performance, with contextual performance explaining 12–34% of the total variance in performance (Motowidlo & Van Scotter, 1994).

Contextual performance and organisational effectiveness

Scholars from the different traditions agree that patterns of behaviour outside formal job task requirements are important for human performance, organisational effectiveness and profitability (Borman & Motowidlo, 1997). Contextual behaviours are claimed by Organ (1997) to contribute towards maintenance and enhancement of the social and psychological climate that supports the technical production system. There is evidence to suggest that contextual performance does improve the effectiveness of work groups and organisations as a whole (Podsakoff et al., 1997; Podsakoff & MacKenzie, 1997).

A tentative link between Organisational Citizenship Behaviour (OCB) and organisational effectiveness has been established by Podsakoff and MacKenzie (1997). This association adds empirical evidence to the logical and conceptual connections described by Quinn et al. (1996) and Jones (1995). Thus, it was worth including a measure of the contribution of managers to an organisation's effectiveness when measuring managers' performance. Contextual aspects of managers' jobs are potentially substantial and critical to an organisation's productivity (Organ & Paine, 1999). Further, evidence is emerging to establish a link between individual managers' performance on contextual dimensions to organisational effectiveness.

Operationalising managers' performance

An accurate index of managers' job performance was critical to this study. Research into managers' performance has been limited by the absence of a common metric to assess performance. There are widely divergent opinions in the literature in, and practice about, what constitutes valid measures of managers' performance in an organisational context. Measuring managers' performance in order to make comparisons between managers from different domains and firms is methodologically difficult (Murphy, 1990), as managerial work is highly complex and contingent (Hales, 1986; Stewart, 1989; Pettigrew & Whipp, 1991). Appendix 2 summarises the studies consulted for conceiving and measuring managers' competency and performance.

Links between managers' contextual and task performance

Motowidlo, Borman and Schmit's (1997) distinction between contextual and task performance is illustrated in Figure 3.5.

Figure 3.5 Theory of individual differences in contextual and task performance

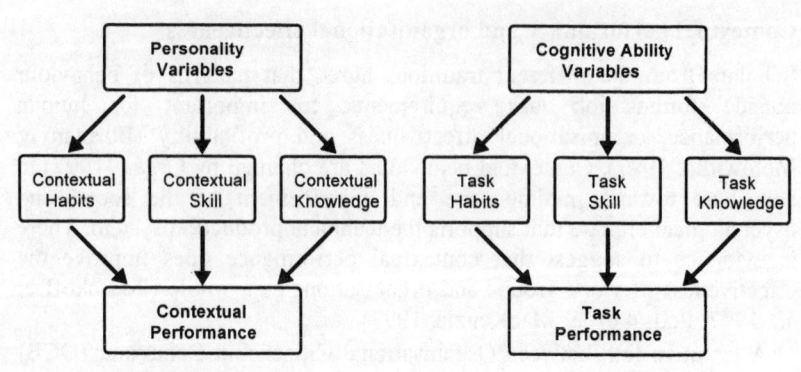

```
   Personality                              Cognitive Ability
    Variables                                   Variables
   ↙   ↓   ↘                                 ↙   ↓   ↘
Contextual Contextual Contextual        Task    Task    Task
 Habits     Skill   Knowledge          Habits   Skill Knowledge
   ↘   ↓   ↙                                 ↘   ↓   ↙
    Contextual                                   Task
   Performance                               Performance
```

Source: Motowidlo, S.J., Borman, W.C., and Schmit, M.J. (1997: 79). A theory of individual differences in task and contextual performance, Human Performance, 10(2), 71-83.

A taxonomy of contextual and task performance was identified from the literature that was suitable for developing a measurement instrument. Motowidlo, Borman and Schmit (1997) separated managers' performance into contextual and task categories to identify dimensions that constitute performance. Contextual behaviours may contribute to organisational effectiveness, if maintained consistently over time and across individuals (Borman & Brush, 1993; Podsakoff & MacKenzie, 1997).Contextual performance has been associated with personality, whilst task was associated with cognitive ability (Motowidlo et al., 1997). Motowidlo and Van Scotter (1994) confirmed MacKenzie et al.'s (1991) findings that contextual and task performance are determined by different predictors. Motowidlo, Borman and Schmit (1997) argued that cognitive ability and personality are mediated by knowledge, skills and work habits.

All classifications emphasise behaviours that involve cooperation and helping others in the organisation, and behaviours that ultimately contribute to organisational effectiveness. For this reason, researchers have recently begun investigating the antecedents for these cooperative behaviours. These contextual work activities were derived from conceptual frameworks that describe the organisational behaviour domains considered necessary for attaining organisational effectiveness. Neal and Griffin (1999) drew on Borman and Motowidlo's (1993) conceptualisation of task and contextual performance.

A Model of Individual Performance for Human Resource

A model of the antecedents, determinants and components of performance is provided in Figure 3.6. The Model of Performance (Neal & Griffin, 1999) to synchronise interventions to existing mechanisms and thereby identify and remove key situational constraints in the workplace. The components of performance represent the behaviours that individual managers perform at work.

Figure 3.6   Antecedents, Determinants and Components of Performance

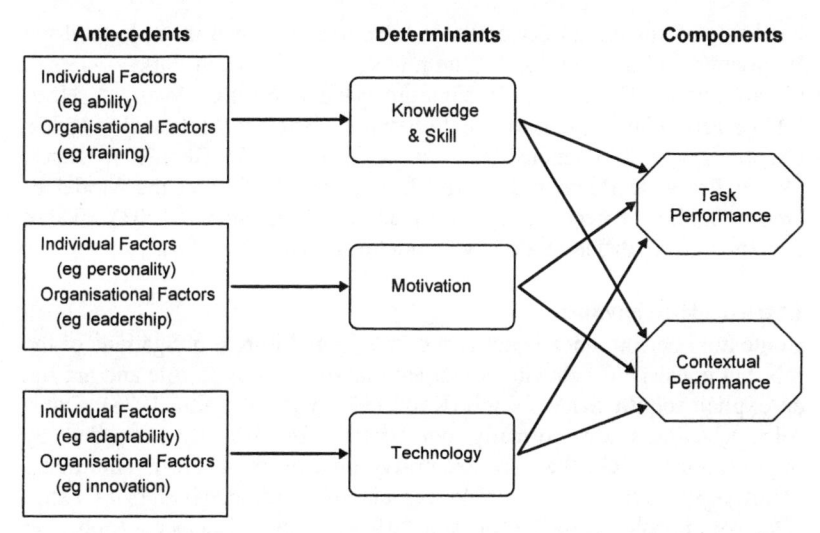

Antecedents	Determinants	Components
Individual Factors (eg ability) / Organisational Factors (eg training)	Knowledge & Skill	Task Performance
Individual Factors (eg personality) / Organisational Factors (eg leadership)	Motivation	Contextual Performance
Individual Factors (eg adaptability) / Organisational Factors (eg innovation)	Technology	

Source: Reproduced with permission from Neal, A. and Griffin, M.A. (1999: 48), Developing a model of individual performance, *Asia Pacific Journal of Human Resources*, 37(2), 44-59. © Australasian Human Resources Institute, 1999, by permission of Sage Publications Ltd.

Research has yet to confirm whether managers' contextual and task performance constructs are conceptually or empirically distinct, or linked. Overall performance is a function of both perceptions of contextual actions, and the performance of task activities. Task activities normally vary across different jobs but contextual activities are reported to be common to many jobs(Borman & Motowidlo, 1993; Motowidlo & Schmit, 1999). Task activities are role-prescribed, whereas contextual behaviours are not usually explicitly stated as a formal organisational obligation.

A convergence of theoretical and empirical findings is emerging amongst scholars from different research traditions to suggest that other patterns of behaviour, besides formal job requirements, are critical for organisational effectiveness (Borman & Motowidlo, 1993). Managers' contributions to organisational effectiveness may exceed the role-specific tasks they perform, and either assist or impede the achievement of organisational goals. These findings encourage further exploration of the construct 'contextual performance'.

Antecedents of contextual performance

> Individuals contribute to organizational effectiveness in ways that go beyond the activities that comprise their 'job'.
>
> (Borman & Motowidlo, 1993: 71)

Elements of contextual performance have been deduced from: Extra-Role Behaviour (Van Dyne, Cummings, & McLean-Parks, 1995); Organisational Citizenship Behaviours (OCB) (Smith, Organ, & Near, 1983), Prosocial Organisational Behaviour (Brief & Motowidlo, 1986); Organisational Spontaneity (George & Brief, 1992; George & Jones, 1997); Pro-Role Behaviour (Parks & Kidder, 1994); and the Model of Good Soldier Effectiveness (Borman & Motowidlo, 1993). These constructs were differentiated by Dunnette and Hough (1994).

Extra-Role Behaviour

Contextual performance is not part of the formal in-role obligations of the job, but consists of behaviours that are classified as extra-role and are not an explicit requirement of a job (Katz, 1974; Katz & Kahn, 1978). Extra-role behaviours are normally not directly or formally rewarded by organisations unless they are exemplary employers. There is continuing controversy over whether employees classify such behaviours as extra-role, or in-role (Wolfe-Morrison, 1994; Pond, Nacoste, Mohr, & Rodriguez, 1997).

Research conducted on contextual performance is predicated on the assumption that employees are clear about the boundary between in-role and extra-role behaviour (Organ, 1988; Podsakoff, 1990; Williams & Anderson, 1991). Wolfe-Morrison (1994), challenged this assumption by observing that role requirements evolve over time and that roles in organisations are rarely fixed. Variations exist between how broadly employees define their job, and specifically where they make the distinction between in-role and extra-role behaviour.

Organisational Citizenship Behaviour

The beginnings of OCB can be traced to the argument proposed by the Human Relations School that a 'happy worker is a productive worker' (Coyle-Shapiro, 2004). Contextual performance is closely aligned with, and an extension of, the construct of OCB (Podsakoff & MacKenzie, 1997). Organ and Paine have noted that contextual performance 'sounds much like the enumerated categories of OCB' (1999: 357). Organ (1988: 4) defined OCB as 'behaviour(s) of a discretionary nature that are not part of the employee's formal requirements, but nevertheless promote the effective functioning of the organization'.

OCB refers to extra-role, discretionary behaviour that assists organisational participants to do their jobs or exhibit support for conscientiousness towards an organisation (Bateman & Organ, 1983; Smith et al., 1983; Borman & Brush, 1993). OCB has important consequences for an organisational functioning both at the individual and group level (Coyle-Shapiro, 2004). This extends Barnard's (1938) notion of combining efforts amongst organisational members, and Katz and Kahn's (1978) 'spontaneous behaviour', such as cooperative gestures and actions to protect the organisation, that go beyond prescribed role behaviour. Discretionary behaviours are unenforceable requirements of the job role description that cannot be specified in terms of a person's employment contract with an organisation. Organ (1988) considered such behaviour to be a matter of personal choice, whose omission is not normally punishable.

Long term goal seeking behaviour is related to OCB because it is 'beneficial for an organisation but falls outside of formal requirements such that it is difficult to formally specify or reward' (Morrison, 1996) and is 'extra-role discretionary behaviour intended to help others in the organisation or demonstrate conscientiousness in support of the organisation' (Borman & Motowidlo, 1997: 100). OCB improves an organisation's overall efficiency, in particular, helping behaviour may enhance managerial performance and may be positively related to the quantity and quality of managers' performance (Walz, 1995; Walz & Niehoff, 1996; Organ & Paine, 1999).

A number of studies have been conducted into the relationship of OCB to leadership style and supportiveness, including the Leader-Member Exchange Relationship (Wayne & Green, 1993; Deluga, 1994), leadership trust (Konovsky & Pugh, 1994; Robinson & Wolfe-Morrison, 1995), leadership style (Schnake, Dumler, & Cochran, 1993), leadership monitoring techniques (Niehoff & Moorman, 1993), and how training in organisational justice was received by leaders (Skarlicki & Latham, 1996).

OCB stems from two motivational bases in the literature: cognitive job attitude determinants (Organ & Near, 1985; Organ & Konovsky, 1989; Moorman, 1993; Organ, 1994a; Organ & Ryan, 1995), and affective/dispositional determinants (Organ & Lingl, 1995). These studies are based on the social exchange theory of motivation (Organ, 1990; Konovsky & Pugh, 1994). Employers who are perceived to treat employees fairly are likely to invoke social exchange and the norm of reciprocity (Organ, 1990), commonly in the form of employee OCB (contextual performance).

Research into using cognitive factors as predictors of OCB derives from work by Smith, Organ and Near (1983), who found contextual attitudes to be antecedents of OCB. Empirical support for the construct of OCB is derived from studies by Karambayya (1989) and Podsakoff and MacKenzie (1994; 1997). Karambayya (1989) found that members of work units displaying high levels of OCB were rated as having superior levels of performance. Podsakoff and MacKenzie (1994; 1997) found that OCB accounted for 17% of variance in performance. Notwithstanding promising findings, these studies had methodological limitations, such as the use of subjective self-ratings by key informants, and the use of different measurement metrics. Nevertheless, a large proportion of performance is attributed to OCB as managers' advance up organisational hierarchies. OCB was found to contribute 43% of managerial evaluations and was found to be 15 times more important than 'quantifiable' performance (Organ & Paine, 1999).

However, research linking OCB to performance has produced mixed results (Organ & Paine, 1999). Empirical evidence supporting the relationship between OCB and performance is lacking, and is 'typically logical and conceptual rather than empirical' (Borman & Motowidlo, 1993: 88) and 'rests more on its plausibility than direct empirical support' (Organ & Konovsky, 1989: 157). In addition, none of these studies into OCB have directly observed its impact on managers' performance. Nevertheless, there is a broad-based rationale for a deeper investigation into 'dispositional predictors' that suggest affective job states (Organ & Paine, 1999). Also, links between OCB and job satisfaction have been found to be stronger than those between job satisfaction and task performance (Organ & Paine, 1999). This book develops the empirical evidence to confirm or refute these assertions.

Prosocial Organisational Behaviour
Prosocial Organisational Behaviour is a similar construct to OCB. Prosocial Organisational Behaviour is defined as 'a behaviour performed with the intention of promoting the welfare of individuals or groups to whom the behaviour is directed' (Brief & Motowidlo, 1986, as cited in Borman & Motowidlo, 1997), and is behaviour that is 'not contractually nor practically enforceable by supervision or job description' and is 'extra role and not contractually rewarded' (Konovsky & Organ, 1996: 254). Prosocial behaviour is a positive orientation for individuals that is characterised by the absence of certain behaviours, such as complaining (Organ, 1988). Differences between the two constructs centre on prosocial behaviour not being contractual and therefore outside role-prescribed behaviour, whereas OCB is extra-role behaviour (Organ, 1988).

Model of Good Soldier Effectiveness

The Model of Good Soldier Effectiveness was based on the performance constructs of soldiers who were considered important for unit effectiveness, but were outside standard performance requirements (Borman, White, & Dorsey, 1995). A conceptual model of soldier effectiveness, common to all soldiering jobs, was developed by Borman et al. (1993). Soldier performance is closely tied to constructs of organisational commitment, the 'strength of a person's identification with and involvement in the organisation' (Borman & Motowidlo, 1993: 78).

Affective commitment has been defined by Travaglione (1998: 3) as an 'employee's emotional attachment to, identification with, and involvement in, the organization'. Wiener and Vardi (1980) distinguished commitment from motivation, and suggested that work behaviour was a function of both motivation and commitment. Motivation was found to be driven by a collective focus, while commitment was driven by the normative, value-based concept. Wiener and Vardi argued that commitment is a normative and therefore 'independent of direct, 'selfish' interests, and of immediate and temporary situational concerns' (Wiener & Vardi, 1980: 84).

Summary on conceiving of contextual performance

When combined, Extra-Role Behaviour, OCB, Prosocial Organisational Behaviour and a Model of Good Soldier Effectiveness are essentially aspects of contextual performance that represent domains of behaviours that are relevant to organisational effectiveness. OCB was originally conceived as a way of improving overall organisational effectiveness and performance (Organ, 1977). This trend is encapsulated by Organ and Paine (1999: 364) who stated that 'the cumulative record of contributions in this area indicates that industrial and organisational psychology cannot do without some constructs akin to what is now called Organisational Citizenship Behaviour or contextual performance'.

Objective measures of individual job output were argued by Organ (1977) to have minimal effect on individual job output because of constraints imposed by technology, work design and aptitude. Instead, Organ (1977) called for attention to be given to voluntary behaviour that contributes to 'the maintenance and enhancement of the social and psychological context that supports task performance'. Given the challenge of measuring managers' global contribution to an organisation's effectiveness, there is a case for also using more generic measures of managers' performance, such as contextual performance to complement task performance (Organ, 1994a).

Measuring contextual performance

Borman and Motowidlo (1997) have developed the most recent and robust taxonomy of contextual performance from a meta-analysis of the literature. Though this taxonomy was specifically developed for managers, it provided a framework suitable for incorporating elements of: Extra Role behaviour; OCB; Prosocial Organisational Behaviour and the Model of Good Soldier Effectiveness. This structure permitted suitable items to be incorporated into a framework that was derived from studies by Konovsky and Organ (1996), and Podsakoff et al. (1990).

Factors identified by Konovsky and Organ's (1996) work inform elements of the evaluation of contextual performance: Agreeableness (friendliness, likeability and the capacity for getting along with others in pleasant and harmonious relationships); Altruism (helping specific people in face-to-face interactions at work); Courtesy (gestures that people exhibit at work to help prevent work problems for others); Sportsmanship (inclination to absorb minor inconveniences and impositions without complaints and excessive demands for relief and redress); Civic Virtue (responsible and constructive involvement and participation in issues confronting the organisation), and Generalised Compliance (contributions in the form of exemplary adherence to rules regarding attendance, punctuality, use of time while at work and respect for organisational property and resources).

Factor analyses of contextual performance studies have not consistently yielded the intended factor loadings. As far as factor structure is concerned, Podsakoff et al.'s (1990) 5–factor version has produced the intended factor loadings, making it the most reliable version. Konovsky and Organ (1996) have developed contemporary items to measure the same factors as Podsakoff et al. (1990). Borman and Motowidlo (1997) have further refined some of the constructs developed by Konovsky and Organ (1996) for incorporation into a taxonomy of contextual performance. Appendix 3 details the taxonomy of contextual performance and the items derived from the literature to measure these constructs.

Summary on conceiving managers' contextual and task performance

Managerial performance is a multi-dimensional construct composed of contextual and task performance. Task performance consists of behaviours that contribute to the core transformational and maintenance activities of organisation, such as producing products, delivering services, selling merchandise and managing subordinates (Motowidlo & Schmit, 1999). In contrast, contextual performance is concerned with behaviours that contribute to the culture and climate of organisations, which contribute to the transformation and maintenance activities, such as helping and cooperating with others, following rules and procedures, supporting and defending the organisation, and volunteering for extra work (Motowidlo & Schmit, 1999).

Determining the 'mega-dimensions' of managers' performance

Borman and Brush (1993) identified managers' performance dimensions, which included most of the major studies of managers' dimensions (Flanagan, 1951; 1954; Williams, 1956; Hemphill, 1959; Steers, 1975; Tornow & Pinto, 1976; Yukl, 1998). These dimensions are behaviourally based, resulting from many critical incident and job activity statements, and thus reflect what managers actually do, as opposed to what they, or others, believe they do. Some of these dimensions are cognitive and five represent interpersonal skills All meta-analysis of major investigations into managers' performance dimensions refer to, or are dependent on, Boyatzis's (1982) seminal work discussed earlier in this chapter.

Borman and Brush (1993) developed a method for determining the 'mega-dimensions' of managers' performance. Appendices 3 and 4 provide more information on these mega-dimensions of contextual and task performance. Not all of Borman and Brush's dimensions were solely based on theoretical formulations, or highly specific aspects of managers' jobs, but actual job performance requirements. These dimensions are representative samples of the domain of managers' performance. By integrating multiple dimensions, Borman and Brush's, and Borman and Motowidlo's (1997) taxonomies have provided a more comprehensive view of the dimensionality underlying managerial performance. As noted earlier, there is a lack of contemporary and robust measurement instruments of managerial performance. This is partly a function of the methodologies employed to study managers. Managerial performance dimensions are mostly derived from questionnaires and focus groups.

In contrast, critical incident studies are useful for differentiating between behaviourally effective and ineffective managers and identifying performance-related dimensions. Borman and Brush's (1993) study builds on Hemphill's (1959) work, which incorporated data from numerous managerial jobs. Consistent with other prominent researchers in the area (cf. Murphy, 1990), Borman and Brush (1993) viewed the 'bandwidth of all job performance measures to be broad and advocate multiple and complex predictors to map the criterion space'.

Borman and Brush's (1993) meta-analysis of managers' performance was derived from behaviourally based critical incidents and job activity statements. Researchers analysed 13 different organisations to discern 19 empirically derived dimension sets from published and unpublished research into managerial jobs. Information was also gathered from 7 published studies from 26 sets of dimensions for a total of 246 dimensions (Borman & Brush, 1993). The remaining pool of 187 individual dimensions was sorted into categories based on the similarity of their content by experienced and PhD qualified industrial and organisational psychologists.

An indirect similarity index (Rosenberg & Sedlak, 1972) was generated from the 187 x 187 similarity index by pooling information about similarity dimensions information across participants. The matrix of pooled indirect dimensions was factor analysed using the principal factors method and an 18–factor solution was chosen based on the psychological meaningfulness of the solution, as well as the uninterperability of additional factors. Factor analysis of pooled similarity correlations resulted in 18 groupings of dimensions (Borman & Brush, 1993).

Not all of the 18 mega-dimensions Borman and Brush (1993) identified were found to be statistically independent. The percentage of common variance was accounted for in each mega-dimension. From comparisons of the 18 mega-dimension set with other managerial performance taxonomies it was apparent that there was not a corresponding dimension with one of the mega-dimensions (organisational commitment) in 3 of the taxonomies, and 7 of the mega-dimensions were not apparent in 2 of the 6 taxonomies. Conversely, only 3 dimensions (exercise of broad power and authority, personal demands and interfacing) from other category systems in the literature were not content matched to one or more of the mega-dimensions.

By summarising the behavioural performance requirements of managers' jobs, Borman and Brush (1993) satisfied Campbell's (1991) challenge to use a broad sample of managerial jobs in order to identify core dimensions and to compare different managerial jobs. This suggests the mega-dimensions represent a consensus of many of the behavioural dimensions representing managers' jobs in a wide range of organisations. These dimensions equate to task performance. Borman and Brush's mega-dimensions were derived from data in a range of management jobs, providing a useful benchmark of categories to compare the dimensions from studies of managers' performance in other organisations.

In all, Borman and Brush's (1993) meta-analysis and Borman and Motowidlo's (1997) taxonomies represent the most comprehensive and rigorous taxonomy of the tasks that managers perform. This taxonomy represented the best contemporary consolidation of what is known about the domains influencing managers' performance. In addition, this meta-analysis was in a form suitable for developing into an instrument to measure managers' performance.

SUMMARY AND CONCLUSIONS

This chapter has provided a bridge, linking empirical research with the theoretical conceptualisation of managers' performance. Affective wellbeing researchers have not explicitly identified or measured managers' performance. A theory-derived approach was used to describe and assess the multifarious roles managers occupy. Measurement, Appraisal Interview, Social Cognitive Process and Performance Management schools of performance appraisal were integrated with social constructivist perspectives of managers' performance, including theories of: Attribution; Competence, Competing Values, Contingency; Emotional Intelligence, Expectancy; Human Needs; Individual Differences, Job Performance; Motivation; Performance; Self-Efficacy; Social Cognition; and Work Adjustment. When combined with the measurement of generic job tasks undertaken by managers, these theories explicate managers' performance and permit an integrated approach to conceiving the link between performance and roles. In Chapter 7 these theories are further reviewed and the relevance of them is considered in view of the findings in this book.

Despite extensive investigations into the construct of job performance there is still no common framework for considering the underlying performance dimension requirements of jobs. Indeed, the 'search for reliable, uncontaminated, objective indicators that significantly reflect the ultimate criterion has been a failure' (Campbell et al., 1996: 11). Likewise, attempts to identify the one general factor (i.e., critical deficiency model) to assess managers' performance have been fruitless. A strong case exists for avoiding the use of traditional 'objective' measure of managers' performance, as typified by functionalist perspective (Quinn et al., 1996), in preference to more generic measures favoured by the unitarist standpoint (Borman & Brush, 1993). There is a wealth of evidence to substantiate the multi-dimensional and dynamic nature of managers' performance (Campbell, 1996; Ployhart et al., 2003). Proponents of the critical deficiency model, such as Viswesvaran, Ones and Schmidt (1996), have agreed that there are likely to be subfactors underlying a general factor of performance. Managerial effectiveness may be more generic than has previously been assumed.

There has been a trend away from a rationalist view (i.e. what managers do and achieve) of organisations to an interpretivist perspective (i.e., functions, behaviours, roles, and decisions) of managers' performance. Despite this trend there is an increased emphasis on outputs, rather than simply behaviours, which should be included in measures of managers' performance that link to organisational outcomes. Therefore, managers' generic competencies need to be measured, since the way that managers use these competencies represents their individual performance. Managers' competence has the potential to ultimately lead to organisational effectiveness.

Managers' job performance is conceived and explained in the literature as being comprised of both contextual and task performance, although they are not mutually exclusive. Managers' contextual performance is an aspect of job behaviour, besides formal job requirements, that contributes to organisational effectiveness. Managers' task performance refers to the activities that result in the implementation of processes that contribute, either directly to an organisation's technical core, or indirectly by providing required materials or services. Given global trends, contextual performance is likely to become increasingly recognised as important to organisations. Therefore, any instrument designed to rate managers' performance should incorporate items designed to measure both contextual and task performance. Borman and Brush's 18 mega-dimension taxonomy of managers' contextual and task performance, provided a basis for the development of an instrument to measure managers' performance that is supported by the literature.

Conceptual indicators, and emerging empirical evidence, suggest that the contextual performance and task performance domains are distinct. There was a strong case for developing an instrument to measure both managers' contextual and task performance based on Borman and Brush, and Borman and Motowidlo's taxonomy. Notably, contextual performance also contributes to organisations' effectiveness, and is of particular relevance to these domains of managers' performance, and should therefore be incorporated into appraisals of their performance.

In the next chapter, the linkages between managers' performance and intrinsic job satisfaction and affective wellbeing are refined. Research hypotheses and questions to be pursued are proposed.

4. Links between affective wellbeing, intrinsic job satisfaction and managers' job performance

> Few topics in the history of industrial-organizational psychology have captured the attention of researchers more than the relationship between job satisfaction and job performance.
> (Judge et al., 2001: 388)

INTRODUCTION

Chapters 2 and 3 reviewed the relevant literature on affective wellbeing, intrinsic job satisfaction, and managers' performance. This chapter explores the potential linkages between managers' affective wellbeing, intrinsic job satisfaction and their performance. Potential interrelationships are proposed between these constructs. This process begins by briefly reiterating the main issues arising from the literature. The main research questions emanating from the literature that are suitable for testing were identified. A Partial Model is proposed. This is followed by an explanation of the ways in which the concepts, constructs, dimensions and measures identified in the literature relate to the model. Research questions and hypotheses are then developed from the proposed linkages between affective wellbeing and managers' performance. Finally, a point of departure from the extant literature is established and a new line of inquiry identified to guide the conceptual development of the methodology.

THE 'HAPPY-PRODUCTIVE WORKER' THESIS

To recapitulate on the substance of Chapters 1–3, there is substantial literature pertaining to managers' affective wellbeing, intrinsic job satisfaction and performance. There has long been intuitive appeal of the 'happy-productive' thesis notwithstanding an absence of results to support the idea. The quest to find a relationship between job satisfaction and job performance is revered as the 'holy grail' of organisational behavioural research (Weiss & Cropanzano, 1996).

Decades of research have been unable to establish a credible link between job satisfaction and performance. Affect has rarely been used exclusively as a predictor of managers' job performance outcomes. Typically, job (un)happiness has been equated to job (dis)satisfaction which has mainly been operationalised as job satisfaction rather than affect. There is widespread support in the literature (e.g., Katzell & Thompson, 1995; 1999a; Wright & Staw, 1999b), despite scant empirical evidence, to suggest that a causal relationship exists between affective wellbeing and managers' performance. Proponents of the affective wellbeing perspective argue that positive emotional states within the workplace accentuate employees' performance and quality of life (Isen, 1987; Warr, 1999). Research to date has not used robust measures to empirically measure the relationship between managers' affective wellbeing or intrinsic job satisfaction as they relate to aspects of their performance (c.f. Judge et al., 2001).

There is considerable evidence in the theoretical and empirical psychological literature to suggest that certain levels of dissatisfaction actually increase motivation and, ultimately, performance. Faragher, Cass and Cooper (2005) found that when individual mental health is compromised at work this may result in high levels of dissatisfaction. Conversely, they also argued that providing inadequate personal job satisfaction is likely to lead to feelings of unhappiness which could eventually lead to emotional exhaustion. These potential links are worth further exploration in relation to managers' performance.

Generally, the literature indicates that happy people are believed to be more productive, creative, generous and physically healthier than those who are unhappy. Possibly, happiness provides the motivation to continue to perform complex tasks well and ensures high performance. Managers with good mental health would be expected to report making active progress towards goals as well as to have high intrinsic motivation, integrated functioning as evidenced by balance, harmony and interrelatedness (Warr, 1987; Warr, 1992).

Managers with the highest levels of reported mental health would also be expected to have high self-efficacy, be risk-takers, have a healthy sense of self and a positive belief in the future (Warr, 1987). A drive to achieve may bring purpose to managers' working lives. Succeeding at performing difficult job tasks may also provide the meaning and motivation essential for effective job performance. Conversely, evidence from the literature suggested that impoverished affective wellbeing or intrinsic job satisfaction might have a negative impact on performance (Judge et al., 2001).

There have been many studies into separate aspects of managers' and affective wellbeing, intrinsic job satisfaction and performance, but few have empirically tested the relationship between these constructs.

Insufficient evidence was found by Staw (1986) to fully support the 'happy-productive worker' thesis or the proposition that 'a happy worker is a good worker' (Katzell & Thompson, 1995: 111). Also, a number of studies have been unable to establish a close link between the hypothesised relationship between job satisfaction and performance (c.f. Brayfield & Crockett, 1955; Porter, 1963; Vroom, 1964; Locke, 1976; Iaffaldano & Muchinsky, 1985) (1999a; 1999b).

Modest support has been found for a link between worker satisfaction and improved job performance (Organ & Paine, 1999). Measures of job satisfaction are argued to reflect a respondent's cognitive assessment of the work context rather than their affective mood state (Organ, 1988; 1990; Organ & Moorman, 1993). In another study, Wright and Staw (1999a) found a plausible link between various predictors of affect and rated performance. Dispositional affect was found to be a stronger operationalisation of happiness and 'may be a more useful predictor of managers' performance than satisfaction because it is more stable and enduring over time allowing continual as opposed to fleeting attitudinal influences on behavior' (Staw & Barsade, 1993: 323). The constant nature of dispositional affect makes it particularly valuable in predicting performance over time. Psychological wellbeing has been found to predict job performance, but a relationship was not evident between job satisfaction, dispositional affect and predictors of job performance (Wright, Cropanzano et al., 2002).

Cropanzano and Wright (1999) found that when happiness is operationalised as affective wellbeing it was positively related to measures of objective indices and subjective ratings of performance. Various predictors of affect were also found by Cropanzano and Wright (2001), Wright and Cropanzano (2000) and Wright and Staw (1999a; 1999b) to predict rated performance. This supported the proposition that happy workers are more productive. Meta-analyses by Judge et al. (2001) and Harter, Schmidt and Hays (2002) indicated that a possible relationship existed between job satisfaction and job performance. All these studies did not exclusively focus on managers or include contextual and task aspects of performance. Job performance has been measured primarily with reference to the general dimensions of self-reported job satisfaction and performance from non-managerial samples.

Scholars from different traditions are converging on the idea that contextual performance is an important aspect of human performance. Domains of managers' contextual performance and task performance are posited to be theoretically discrete, but this distinction has yet to be empirically established. The measurement model in Chapter 6 differentiate between contextual and task performance.

LINKS BETWEEN AFFECTIVE WELLBEING, INTRINSIC JOB SATISFACTION AND PERFORMANCE

George and Brief (1996) hypothesised how Positive Affect (PA) might facilitate employees' achievement or performance. Using well established models of motivation, such as expectancy theory (Vroom, 1964), George and Brief (1996) argued that PA may enhance a person's expectations of achieving effective performance. This finding suggested that a path from affective wellbeing and intrinsic job satisfaction to performance may exist. This causal path is believed to result in positive outcomes, which may eventually lead to improved performance. From this standpoint, managers with PA are predicted to develop an expectancy that their efforts will lead to high performance and that this performance will lead to positive outcomes (Wright, Cropanzano et al., 2002). These predictions were based on findings that demonstrated PA might lead to enhanced self-efficacy (Forgas, Bower, & Moylan, 1990) and optimistic attitudes about future circumstances (Wright & Bower, 1992).

Similar propositions could also be derived from a goal-setting perspective of motivation (Locke & Latham, 1990). Employees with an optimistic predisposition tend to set challenging goals, or welcome challenging goals that contribute to higher performance (Locke & Latham, 1990). Attribution models of motivation (Weiner, 1985) posit that affective wellbeing will have a facilitative influence on individual task perseverance (George & Brief, 1996). Individuals high in dispositional PA, or who have optimistic tendencies with a high locus of control, perceive failure as a transitory impediment caused by the external environment (Forgas, 1992). Such people are more likely to persevere in the face of negative feedback, compared with those with Negative Affect (NA) or a pessimistic attitude (Burke, Brief, & George, 1993).

Affect may determine more than just the motivational aspects of task performance. In particular, the link between job satisfaction and contextual performance is likely to be stronger than the link between job satisfaction and task performance (Organ & Paine, 1999). PA has been found to influence helping behaviour and interpersonal cooperation, and may therefore also predict contextual behaviour in organisations (Organ, 1988; George & Brief, 1992; Motowidlo et al., 1997). Links are also apparent between contextual performance and organisational effectiveness (Podsakoff & MacKenzie, 1997). Discretionary work behaviours may be conceived as contextual performance, an aspect of which is the freedom to act according to one's judgement. Before the research questions in this book can be addressed it is necessary to relate the specific aspects of the A *Partial Model of Managers' Affective Wellbeing, Intrinsic Job Satisfaction and Performance* ('Partial Model') to the research question and hypotheses.

Partial Model of Managers' Affective Wellbeing, Intrinsic Job Satisfaction and Performance

A flow model of managerial affective wellbeing, intrinsic job satisfaction and performance is presented in Figure 4.1.

Figure 4.1   Partial Model of Managers' Affective Wellbeing, Intrinsic Job Satisfaction and Performance

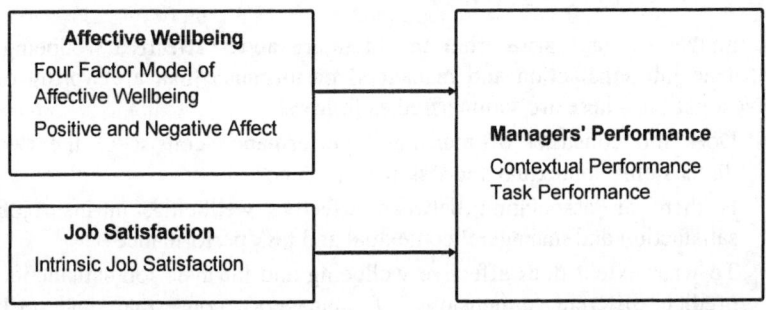

```
┌─────────────────────────┐
│  Affective Wellbeing    │
│  Four Factor Model of   │
│  Affective Wellbeing    │
│  Positive and Negative Affect │──────┐   ┌─────────────────────────┐
└─────────────────────────┘      │   │  Managers' Performance  │
                                 ├──▶│  Contextual Performance │
┌─────────────────────────┐      │   │  Task Performance       │
│  Job Satisfaction       │──────┘   └─────────────────────────┘
│  Intrinsic Job Satisfaction │
└─────────────────────────┘
```

The Partial Model was informed by the literature on affective wellbeing, intrinsic job satisfaction and managers' contextual and task performance. Questionnaire items were derived from established affective wellbeing and job satisfaction scales that provide psychometrically robust measures of dispositional and state affect that are suitable for predicting managers performance: the Four Factor Model of Job-related Wellbeing (Sevastos, 1996); PANAS (Watson & Clark, 1984), and Job Satisfaction (Cook, 1981).

Managers' contextual performance scales were devised by the principal author based on Borman and Motowidlo's (1997) 5–dimension taxonomy. Borman and Brush's (1993) 18–dimension taxonomy of managerial performance was used to develop and test the task performance scales.

The Partial Model is also methodologically well grounded in the literature. Generally, the research indicates that:

> greater employee wellbeing is significantly associated with better job performance, lower absenteeism, reduced probability of leaving an employer, and the occurrence of more discretionary work behaviours.
> (Warr in Kahneman, Diener, & Schwarz, 1999: 593)

Both the theoretical literature and empirical evidence indicate that PA and intrinsic job satisfaction lead to favourable job performance (Judge et al., 2001). The direction of the relationship between the variables, reported in the literature, is from affective wellbeing and intrinsic job satisfaction to performance (Warr in Kahneman et al., 1999: 593). Therefore, the direction of the relationship to be tested in the Partial Model will be from affective wellbeing and intrinsic job satisfaction, to managers' contextual and task performance, but this does not infer causality. Other commentators (e.g., Côté, 1999) have concluded that there is a bidirectional causal relation between pleasant affect and strong job performance.

RESEARCH QUESTIONS

A number of gaps arise from the literature about affective wellbeing, intrinsic job satisfaction and managers' performance that are worthy of investigation. These are summarised as follows:

- Does the construct of managers' performance consist of the two dimensions, contextual and task performance?
- Is there an association between affective wellbeing, intrinsic job satisfaction and managers' contextual and task performance?
- To what extent does affective wellbeing and intrinsic job satisfaction predict different dimensions of managers' contextual and task performance?
- Does positive affective wellbeing result in enhanced managers' performance, and is poor affective wellbeing detrimental to managers' performance?

In addition, two further questions about practical outcomes are addressed:

- How might managers' jobs be changed to enhance, or prevent a decline in affective wellbeing?
- How might these findings be integrated with workplace initiatives to improve the quality of managers' life and job performance?
- These research questions were developed into a series of hypotheses which are described below.

HYPOTHESES

Hypothesis 1:

> Affective wellbeing, as rated by their superiors, is associated with managers' contextual and task performance

Ability aside, managers with high affective wellbeing would be expected to perform better than those with less affective wellbeing (Campbell, 1991). People in higher-level jobs report significantly less job-related depression-enthusiasm than workers in lower-level jobs, but also significantly more job-related anxiety-contentment (Warr et al., 1979; Warr, 1990b; 1994d; Birdi et al., 1995). Affective states are posited to translate into behavioural outcomes that would affect employees performance (Staw & Barsade, 1993).

Highly motivated managers who desire challenges may react to risks in a way that raises anxiety but does not negatively impact on their affective wellbeing. High-performing managers are likely to experience periods of heightened anxiety, followed by periods of relaxation, yet maintain an overall sense of positive affective wellbeing.

In relation to work adjustment theory, Warr concluded other than Westman; 'it seems probable that the contribution of job-related affective wellbeing to performance will arise primarily at low levels of affective wellbeing' (Warr in Hesketh, 1993: 151). Wright and his colleagues were unable to establish a relationship between dispositional affect (PA) as a predictor of supervisor-rated job performance (Wright & Staw, 1999b; Wright, Cropanzano et al., 2002; Wright, Larwood, & Denney, 2002).

Hypothesis 2:

> Components of affective wellbeing are differentially associated with contextual performance and task performance.

Both theory (George & Brief, 1996) and empirical evidence (Isen & Baron, 1991) indicate that PA is related to employee motivation. A positive disposition may result in successful performance involving helping behaviours. People tend to be more attracted to those who have a positive rather than a negative demeanour, and are therefore more likely to receive higher performance ratings. Individuals exhibiting PA are also more likely to receive social support (McGovern, Jones, & Morris, 1978; Caplan, Cobb, French, Harrison, & Pinneau, 1980), be invited to join supervisory cliques (Graen, 1976), be selected for prestigious positions (McGovern et al., 1978; Rasmussen, 1984), appear more energised (Staw & Barsade, 1993), and be positively assessed by others (Cardy & Dobbins, 1986; Krzystofiak, Cardy, & Newman, 1988). Managers demonstrating PA may also be more successful in organisations because of adept interpersonal skills (Wright & Staw, 1999a; 1999b).

Managerial work involves decision-making, often with ambiguous and incomplete information, which would be expected to influence affective states (Mintzberg, 1973). Managers perform multifarious roles requiring working with employees, supervising others, participating in meetings and liaising with external constituents. These aspects of managerial work were shown by Staw and Barsade (1993) to impact on the performance of interpersonal responsibilities and decision-making.

Sevastos's (1996) Four Factor Model of Job-related Wellbeing indicated that employees can experience high arousal and relaxation at separate times. When the duration and frequency of managers' performance are punctuated by intermittent experiences of low affective wellbeing, this may increase tension and anxiety. In such situations, impairment of managers' affective wellbeing may be experienced over a period of time.

This line of reasoning can possibly be extended to establish whether high performing managers, who constantly experience periods of high anxiety, will also experience depression. In these circumstances, extended periods of anxiety may not lead to a demise in affective wellbeing. As such, it is worth testing whether experiencing anxiety leads to depression, when intrinsic job satisfaction is high. Enthusiastic behaviour (high levels of arousal) is posited to be associated with superior performance, while depression (low levels of arousal and hence boredom) is likely to be associated with poor performance. This highlights a research proposition suitable for further examination, that is, people in managerial level jobs will report significantly less job-related depression than anxiety (Birdi; Warr & Oswald, 1995; Warr, 1990a).

Hypothesis 3:

> There is a positive association between managers' enthusiasm and contextual performance, as rated by their superior.

Managers must interact with others to get policies approved and implemented and procure resources to achieve organisational goals. Individuals with positive affective wellbeing are likely to be more effective in circumstances requiring interpersonal persuasion and negotiation (Staw & Barsade, 1993). Contextual and task performance are determined by different predictors (Motowidlo & Van Scotter, 1994).

Affective wellbeing may be more conceptually aligned with contextual rather than task performance. Affective variables, such as job satisfaction and mood have been found to be causally related to contextual performance behaviours, involving cooperating and helping others (Bateman & Organ, 1983; Motowidlo et al., 1986; Organ & Konovsky, 1989; Organ & Lingl, 1995). A link is yet to be established between managers' affective wellbeing and contextual performance. Managers reporting elevated levels of enthusiasm may receive higher contextual performance ratings from the person to whom they report.

Hypothesis 4:

> There is a negative association between managers' anxiety and task performance, as rated by their superior.

Perceived workload has been associated with anxiety (Warr, 1990b). Consistent with Warr's (1992) findings, those in higher-level jobs (e.g., managers) would be expected to report elevated anxiety. Even if experienced for extended periods, this may not indicate NA or low PA. For example, managers with high levels of motivation and risk-taking behaviour may experience raised anxiety and high performance. Managers may be psychologically healthy and also experience consistently high levels of anxiety as a response to a hostile environment. In this circumstance, lowered affective wellbeing is unlikely to occur. However, when the duration and frequency of anxiety is experienced over a period of time, it may lead to impairment in managers' task performance. This leads to a question requiring further examination: does constantly experiencing anxiety impact on managers' task performance?

Hypothesis 5:

> Enthusiasm and relaxation (pleasantness based affect) are stronger predictors of rated contextual performance than anxiety and depression (activation based affect), as rated by their superior.

Performance implications for negative emotions have been suggested to be more pronounced than for positive emotions and to 'predict greater decrements in performance for negative emotional states than for positive states' (Weiss & Cropanzano, 1996: 55). Wright and Staw (1999a: 17) found that 'Pleasantness-based dispositional affect was strongly predictive of performance evaluations ... whereas activation-based affect did not predict rated performance'. Wright and Staw (1999a: 19) suggested that, 'research should now examine whether a syndrome exists in which dispositional affective wellbeing and performance are associated'. Sevastos also categorised anxiety as a 'strong arousal' (activation affect) affect but depression with 'disengagement' (see Figure 2.1). This was at odds with Wright and Staw's predictions. Thus, the 'happy-productive worker' thesis may hold when happiness is operationalised by a pleasantness-based measure of affect.

Hypothesis 6:

> There is a positive association between managers' overall intrinsic job satisfaction and their rated contextual and task performance, as rated by their superior.

Lawler and Porter (1967) and Locke (1976) claimed that high performance results in job satisfaction rather than the converse. There is some empirical evidence to suggest that 'links between overall satisfaction and rated performance are stronger among professional and managerial samples than among blue-collar workers' (Warr, 1987: 293). However, these differences 'seem likely to arise from different performance-reward contingencies in the two types of jobs', and this required further clarification (Warr, 1987: 293). Moreover, it is yet to be confirmed whether these findings can be applied to a discrete population of employees, such as managers.

The failure to establish a relationship between job satisfaction and performance may be a result of a narrow definition and operationalisation of job performance (Organ, 1988). A broader conceptualisation of job performance that includes contextual and task performance may lead to an increased correlation with the construct.

More recent research into the antecedents of job satisfaction has focused on broadening the theoretical base of causal factors affecting job satisfaction, including dispositional effects (Agho et al., 1993; Judge & Hulin, 1993; Judge et al., 1998). Also, it was more appropriate to use a more affective orientated (i.e., intrinsic) measure of job satisfaction. Judge et al. (2001) have also argued that reconsideration of a satisfaction-performance relationship was justified.

Hypothesis 7:

> **Managers' affective wellbeing is positively associated with contextual performance, while managers' cognitions are positively associated with task performance, as rated by their superior.**

The bulk of recent research has found personality to be associated with contextual performance (Borman & Motowidlo, 1997; Motowidlo et al., 1997). There have been a number of studies into the effects of disposition and personality as predictors of Organisational Citizenship Behaviour (OCB) and contextual performance that are predicated on the belief that mood stems from an individual's disposition; (Watson & Clark, 1984; Watson & Tellegen, 1985; Organ, 1994b; Penner, Midili, & Kegelmeyer, 1997).

Focused personality constructs, which measured prosocial personality, also predicted enduring levels of Organisational Citizenship Behaviour (Penner et al., 1997). Motowidlo, Borman and Schmit (1997) predicted that contextual performance will be associated with personality variables, whereas task performance is associated with cognitive ability. Furthermore, they argue that task proficiency varies with the tasks being executed, and that knowledge, skills and abilities covary with task proficiency.

Hypothesis 8:

> **Managers who report intrinsic job satisfaction and enthusiasm will have elevated relaxation, anxiety and low depression.**

Sevastos (1996) found elevated enthusiasm and low depression to be more strongly related to intrinsic job satisfaction when compared to anxiety and relaxation. Also, job-related affect was strongly related to work pressure or job demands. In the Job Demand Model, positive outcomes from an 'active' job may potentially change into negative outcomes consistent with a 'high strain' job (i.e., job dissatisfaction) without any concomitant changes in the job features. According to the Job Strain Model, enriched jobs are associated with job satisfaction and low depression.

Conversely, impoverished jobs will normally be associated with job dissatisfaction and depression. Higher job performance is predicted to be associated with high anxiety, while low job performance will ordinarily be associated with low anxiety. The contribution of affective wellbeing to job performance is likely to be most noticeable at very high or very low levels.

To be consistent with the Job Strain Model, managers experiencing high levels of challenges in a job are predicted to have a positive experience in relation to satisfaction, enthusiasm, relaxation and anxiety, but low depression. Managers with less enriched jobs will exhibit lower performance, accompanied by the experience of low pressure, dissatisfaction and low anxiety, but increased depression. Managers are predicted to occupy the fourth quadrant (positive satisfaction, enthusiasm, relaxation, anxiety and low depression) of the Demand Control Model (see Figure 2.3).

CONCLUSION

This chapter presented the main issues that were derived from the literature to suggest research directions. An explanation is given for the way in which the concepts, constructs, and dimensions are measured, as identified in the literature, relating to the Partial Model. Linkages were explored from the literature about the potential relationships between managers' affective wellbeing, intrinsic job satisfaction and their performance. A Partial Model was proposed for testing in order to establish the possible relationship between managers' affective wellbeing and intrinsic job satisfaction and contextual and task performance. Specific research questions were then developed from the confluence of the literature. Hypotheses that are suitable for testing were developed to establish the potential linkages between the main constructs.

The end of this chapter signifies the beginning of the research component of this book. Details about how the constructs relating to hypotheses developed in this chapter are operationalised and measured are given in the methodology, measurement and results sections in Chapters 5 and 6.

PART 2:

Methodology, Measurement and Results

5. Research methodology and data analysis techniques

> Care must be taken not to put 'the methodological cart before the conceptual horse'.
> (Harter, 1990: 292)

INTRODUCTION

This chapter details the research methodology adopted, beginning with an explanation of the interconnection of the concepts, constructs and measures involved. The choice of research methodology is justified as is the process used to collect the sample data given. Design and implementation issues are addressed, in particular the development of the measurement instrument. Details of the sample, including units of analysis and recruitment of participants, are given. This is followed by a description of the statistical techniques used to analyse the data, test the hypotheses and answer the research questions described in Chapter 4. Methodological issues are identified and discussed, including relevant ethical issues and considerations.

CHOICE OF RESEARCH METHODOLOGY

To advance understanding of management theory and practice, research designs involving single sample, self-report studies need to be based on existing theory, and incorporate new types of measures or validate existing self-report questionnaire data (West et al., 1992). Qualitative information also has the potential to provide a valuable source of verification and elucidation to explain relationship findings that are not readily accessible to quantitative methods. These criteria are addressed by the research design used in this book.

One contribution of this book to the field of Organisational Behaviour in particular, and management in general, is a function of the qualities of the samples used and the robustness of the methodology and analyses. The study reported in this book is a departure from previous research, which concentrated largely on non-managerial samples of managers' affective wellbeing and performance. There have not been any explicit investigations undertaken of managers' contextual performance, affective wellbeing and intrinsic job satisfaction, using an Australian sample.

Figure 5.1 summarises the research methodology that guided this study. Where appropriate, the sequence of this methodology was modified to suit the circumstances encountered, as many of the steps were undertaken simultaneously. Methodological considerations are integrated with the relevant cognate issues, since form ultimately determines the content of research (Foucault, 1980). As such, the methodologies employed have, in some ways, determined the findings.

Figure 5.1   Summary of research methodology

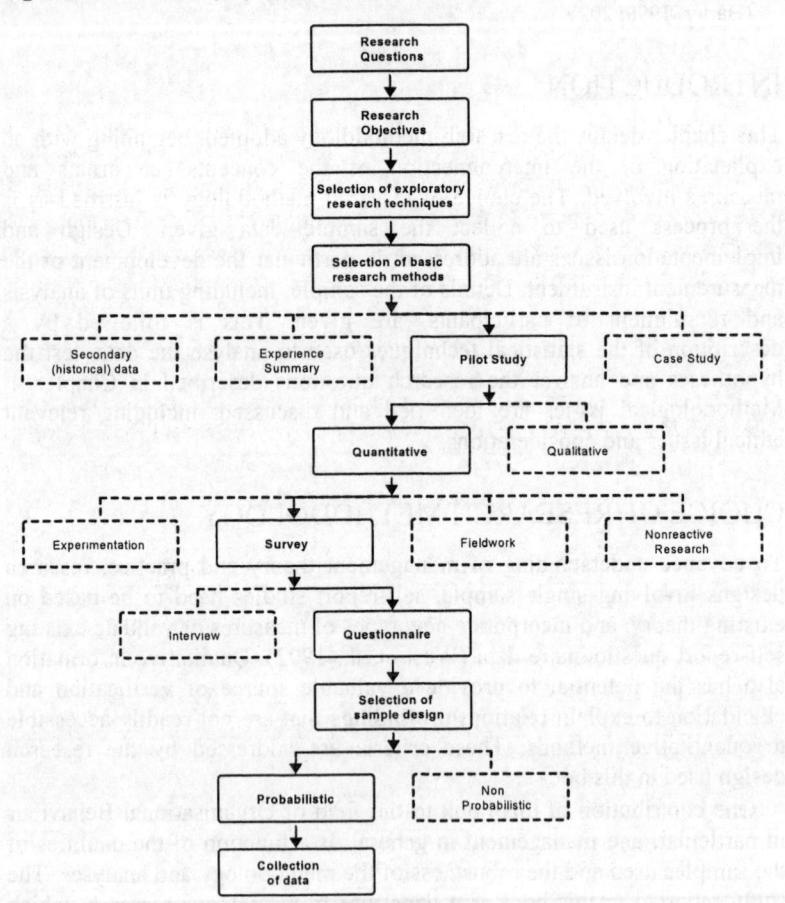

```
                    Research
                    Questions
                        ↓
                    Research
                    Objectives
                        ↓
              Selection of exploratory
               research techniques
                        ↓
                Selection of basic
                research methods
                        ↓
   ┌──────────┬──────────────┬──────────┬──────────┐
 Secondary   Experience    Pilot Study           Case Study
(historical   Summary
   data)
                              ↓
                        Quantitative      Qualitative
                              ↓
   ┌──────────┬──────────────┬──────────┬──────────┐
Experimentation  Survey     Fieldwork          Nonreactive
                                                 Research
                              ↓
                     Interview       Questionnaire
                              ↓
                       Selection of
                       sample design
                              ↓
                    Probabilistic         Non
                                       Probabilistic
                              ↓
                       Collection
                         of data
```

Source: Adapted from Brewer and Hunter (1989) and Zikmund (2002).

CONTEXTUAL AND TASK PERFORMANCE

Expert review and pilot

An expert review and pilot was undertaken in order to refine the measurement instrument. The expert review and pilot study aimed to:

- refine the instructions for completing the questionnaire;
- improve the quality of items included in the measurement instrument;
- reduce the number of managers' contextual and task performance items; and ensure all the necessary biodata was requested.

Even with the limited sample size of a pilot survey, it was advisable to ensure that the instruments used in the pilot questionnaire were reliable (Zikmund, 2002). The validity of affective wellbeing scales used in this study had already been well established. Therefore, only the managers' performance items were scrutinised for face validity, and content reliability, to verify that the instrument measured the relevant content and to ensure the method of measurement matched the expected outcome (Zikmund, 2002). See Table 5.1 for details of the samples used for the expert review and pilot.

Table 5.1   Samples used for expert review and pilot

SAMPLE	TOTAL	RESPONDENTS REPRESENTATIVENESS and PURPOSE
Expert Review	18	Experts in area Clarification and consistency with the literature Improvements to items and instructions Face validity and content reliability
Pilot	31	Convenience sample Variable and factor reduction Face validity and content reliability

At least one, and preferably two rounds of data collection of draft versions are recommended for new instrument development (Sackett & Larson, 1991). During this process items need to be added, deleted and modified to achieve conceptual consistency and appropriate psychometric characteristics. Questionnaires were issued in a declarative mode (i.e., by already stating a position or direction of attitude) and reviewers were informed that the items were under development (Converse & Presser, 1986). Data and feedback from the expert review and pilot were analysed. In consequence, the PANAS scale was added to control for dispositional affect.

Multirater and multisource assessment v self-assessment

Empirical evidence was sought to ensure that the instruments measured the constructs they purported to measure. Evidence of construct validity is required when instruments that comprise several subscales exhibit a well-defined factor structure consistent with the underlying theory (Byrne, 1996). Beer, Spector, Lawrence, Mills and Walton (1985) has documented the difficulties involved with achieving scale construct validity when attempting to measure managers' performance.

There is a tendency, in the literature and practice, to use multiple perspectives of performance. Moreover, as managers' performance is contextual, it was desirable to have subjective (self-report) and normative (organisational specific) measures of performance. Potential gains in accuracy from using multisource ratings of managers' performance needed to be balanced against the pragmatic considerations of implementing this methodology in organisations that are inexperienced in the process. In these circumstances, multisource ratings may have resulted in less consistent ratings of managers' performance than with traditional superior appraisal, and/or self-report.

METHODS

The 'matched pairs' subsamples 1 and 2 (n = 200) refers to managers' self-report with corresponding superiors' ratings of managers' performance. The 'pair congruence' subsample 2 (n = 125) refers to a one-to-one correspondence of ratings, where only one superior's (i.e. person to whom the manager reports) rating was congruent with one manager's self-rating of their performance, affective wellbeing and intrinsic job satisfaction.

Subsample 1 was used to report the demographics of the data and Exploratory Factor Analysis (EFA) for variable and factor reduction. Subsample 2 was used for the Confirmatory Factor Analysis (CFA) to establish, validate and cross-validate the Measurement Model of managers' performance. Data from subsample 2 was used to establish whether the construct *managers' performance* could be generalised across groups.

Combining managers' and superiors' performance ratings in Subsample 2 involved double the number of responses being available for the CFA of the Measurement Model. Methodological hypotheses were tested and the Measurement Model was refined to establish the structure, the most reliable indicators, and the shared meanings attributable to dimensions of managers' contextual and task performance.

For subsample 2, managers' self-report performance indicators were congruent with a superior's rating of their performance for the Multitrait-Multimethod Method (MTMM) of analysis. Also, superiors' ratings of managers' performance indicators were linked to the corresponding self-report of managers' affective wellbeing and intrinsic job satisfaction for the Canonical Correlation and Standard Multiple Regression analyses.

Table 5.2 describes the subsamples used for interpretation and analysis.

Table 5.2   Samples used for interpretation and analysis

N	Sample	Description	Analysis
281(M)	1	Managers' self-rated affective wellbeing	EFA
			Descriptive statistics
		Managers' self-rated performance	Variable and factor reduction
200(M)	2	Managers' self-rated performance (independent)	CFA
			Establish
125 (S)		Superiors' rated performance (independent)	Measurement Model Validation sample
			Cross validation sample
125(M)	3	IVs managers' self-rated affective wellbeing	MTMM
			Purification of measures Canonical Correlation
125 (S)			
		DVs superiors' rated performance	Standard Multiple Regression

Note: M = Managers; S = Superiors. IVs = Independent Variables. DVs = Dependent Variables. Total responses N = 400 (n = 281 managers and superiors = 125 superiors).

The pair congruence subsample 2 (where one superior rated one manager's performance) was used in preference to the matched pairs subsample 1 (where one superior rated many managers' performances), to avoid introducing systematic rating error into the Measurement Model. Superiors' ratings and self-ratings of performance from subsample 2 were used to establish the most reliable measure of managers' objective performance using MTMM analysis. The last recorded multiple ratings superiors' ratings of managers' performance were selected to randomise the pair congruence subsample. Listwise deletion of variables resulted in managers' self-report cases being removed if they were not matched by superiors' ratings, reducing the sample to 125 cases.

Concepts, constructs, dimensions and measures

Measures used in this book were consistent with the established theory base in this stream of research, and were closely aligned to the constructs being investigated. During the literature review it became apparent that there were a considerable number of well-validated instruments for measuring affective wellbeing and intrinsic job satisfaction, but few that were suitable for collecting data on variables identified as determining behavioural outcomes of managers' performance.

Table 5.3 Constructs, dimensions, and measures

CONSTRUCTS	DIMENSIONS	MEASURES
Positive Affect. Negative Affect.	Interested, Distressed, Excited, Upset, Strong, Guilty, Scared, Hostile, Enthusiastic, Proud, Irritable, Alert, Ashamed, Inspired, Nervous, Determined, Attentive, Jittery, Active, Afraid.	20–item Positive and Negative Affect Schedule (PANAS) (Watson & Clark, 1984).
Enthusiasm, Depression, Anxiety, Relaxation.	Gloomy, Calm, Anxious, Enthusiastic, Motivated, Worried, Restful, Tense, Depressed, Optimistic, Relaxed, Miserable.	12–item Four Factor Model of Affective Wellbeing (Warr, 1990b; Sevastos, 1996).
Intrinsic Job Satisfaction.	Utilisation of skills, amount of job complexity and opportunities for control, amount of responsibility and challenges.	7–item subscale (Cook, 1981).
Managers' Contextual Performance.	Persisting, Volunteering, Helping, Following, Endorsing.	Author devised 22–item scale of managers' contextual performance developed from Borman & Motowidlo's (1997) 5–dimension taxonomy. Items from Konovsky & Organ (1996), Organ & Lingl (1995), Brush (1993), Podsakoff et al.(1990).
Managers' Task Performance.	Planning, Guiding, Training, Communicating, Representing, Technical, Administrating, Maintaining, Coordinating, Deciding, Staffing, Persisting, Stressing, Committing, Monitoring, Delegating, Influencing, Interpreting, Organisational Effectiveness.	Author devised 75–item scale of managers' task performance developed from Borman & Brush (1993) 18–dimension taxonomy. Subscale items developed to measure 'Judgement' (Mintzberg, 1980; Cialdini, 1993; Mintzberg, 2004) and 'Organisational Effectiveness' (Quinn et al., 1996).

Affective wellbeing items were drawn from published and validated scales. Managers' performance items, developed for the measurement instrument used, were closely tied to the literature. Separate scales were designed and piloted to measure contextual and task performance dimensions. Linkages between the relevant concepts, constructs, dimensions and measures established in previous studies are given in Table 5.3

As indicated in Chapter 1, this book extends upon Wright and Staw's (1999a; 1999b) research by more reliably measuring state affect (mood) and managers' performance. Ledford (1999: 30) also determined that the 'most important problem to address in research on the happiness-productivity connection is the operationalisation of the two key constructs'. Wright and Staw (1999a: 11) considered that their 'data might have been stronger had there been better calibration in the measurement of mood and rated performance'.

Acceptable alpha test-retest reliability coefficients (Price & Mueller, 1986; Cronbach, 1984) of $\alpha = .74$ (study 1) and $\alpha = .77$ (study 2) were reported for Berkman's index (Wright & Staw, 1999a; 1999b). These reliability coefficients for the Berkman index were one standard deviation ($\alpha = .74$ and $\alpha = .77$) less than the PANAS test-retest reliability alphas of $\alpha = .91$ (T1) and $\alpha = .86$ (T2) for PA $\alpha = .93$ (T1) and $\alpha = .90$ (T2) for NA (Wright & Staw, 1999a; 1999b). This result indicated that the PANAS scale had superior psychometric thresholds when compared to Berkman's index. Alpha coefficients for Berkman's index were also lower than those reported for published bipolar affect instruments with superior psychometric properties.

Alphas reported for bipolar affect (Depression–Enthusiasm/Anxiety–Contentment) scales by Sevastos (1992) and Warr (1990b) are given in Table 5.4.

Table 5.4   Alphas for bipolar affect scales

	α Enthusiasm–Depression	α Anxiety–Contentment
Sevastos (1992)	.85	.82
Warr (1990b)	.80	.76

Unit of analysis

Of particular concern was the methodological problem of the lack of conceptual congruence between the units of analysis The terms productivity and performance were undefined by Wright and Staw (1999a; 1999b) and used interchangeably (see Chapter 3 for definitions). Generally, productivity is associated with assessments undertaken at the organisational level, rather than at the individual level which is performance. In this book, the notion of performance is defined and measured at the individual level to be consistent with the literature and intent of this book.

Maintaining a consistent unit of analysis is important for occupational psychological studies (Cooksey & Gates, 1996). Crossing unit of analysis boundaries, from psychological to organisational levels, had the potential to threaten the internal consistency of this study. Herein was a critical methodological challenge, as noted in Chapter 4 managers' performance is determined at both the individual and organisational level. Hence, rather than begin at the organisation's aggregate level (the nomothetic approach), this study integrated managers' performance at the individual level because it is 'critical to study and understand human behaviour and experience at the idiographic level [in terms of individual behaviour] before we aggregate what is learned to make nomothetic statements' (Cooksey & Gates, 1996: 20, citing Brunswick, 1956).

An organisation's competitive productivity is generally accepted as the fundamental strategic unit of analysis for strategic theorists (Hamel & Prahalad, 1989). However, not much is known about how the mechanisms link individual performance to organisational effectiveness (Neal & Griffin, 1999). Ideally, managers' performance should be linked to organisational productivity to gain and sustain competitive advantage (Porter, 1990; Pfeffer, 1994). In contrast, research into affective wellbeing is focused on the individual unit of analysis. Therefore, relating managers' affective wellbeing, intrinsic job satisfaction and performance to organisational productivity is an extremely difficult association to measure, which is normally not undertaken in studies of Organisational Behaviour or Occupational Psychology.

Within levels of analysis there are important issues to address including clearly defining the construct of interest and ensuring congruency between the conceptualisation, operationalisation, and interpretation of results (Ostroff & Ford, 1989). To avoid introducing confounding variables into the study, the units of analysis adopted were kept comparable to assist in resolving the conflict between the upper (organisational) and lower (individual) boundaries of this book. Individual-level measures of managers' performance were developed because directly measuring the impact of managers' performance at the organisational level, such as contribution to Return on investment, was not possible. This ensured that the associations between individual managers' affective wellbeing and performance could be reliably measured. Items incorporated into the final instrument served to indirectly indicate managers' contributions to organisational productivity.

Measures of affective wellbeing

As discussed in Chapter 2, Warr's Vitamin Model formed the theoretical foundation for this book. Instruments with high construct validity were used or developed to measure affective wellbeing and intrinsic job satisfaction. Several previously published scales for affective wellbeing and intrinsic job satisfaction were incorporated in the questionnaire, and questions were specifically developed to measure managers' performance. This approach was used to increase the convergent validity to establish when the results from the measurements were highly correlated, thereby indicating that they were measuring similar constructs (Burns & Grove, 1997).

Two scales assessing the affective wellbeing were used: Positive And Negative Affect Schedule (PANAS), and the Four Factor Model of Affective Wellbeing.

PANAS

PANAS, a dispositional measure of affect, was incorporated into this questionnaire as a control variable as detailed in Chapter 2. Using a multiformat measurement and CFA, Feldman Barrett and Russell (1999) resolved the paradox of bipolarity and independence of PANAS. Barrett and Russell (1999: 969) concluded that 'Valence was found to be independent of activation, positive affect the bipolar opposite of negative affect, and deactivation the bipolar opposite of activation'. Valence and activation measures were accounted for by the dimensions underlying Watson et al.'s (1988) PANAS.

In combination, a person and situation are known to determine state affect. Trait PA and NA were also reflected in individual differences (also referred to as emotionality in the literature) that are maintained under all conditions, even in the absence of external stimuli. Consequently, high-NA people are more likely to report distress, discomfort, and dissatisfaction over time, regardless of the situation, than high-PA individuals (Watson & Pennebaker, 1989). High PA individuals, who possess a sense of excitement and enthusiasm (Watson et al., 1987), a generalised sense of affective wellbeing, and a zest for life, were found to be independent of these situational influences (Costa & McCrae, 1980).

There are a number of alternatives for operationalising PA and NA. PANAS scales capture the high poles of PA (*enthusiasm*) and NA (*anxiety*) but not the low poles (*low activation*) that define depression and fatigue. PA is correctly operationalised (Russell & Carroll, 1999), when it captures PA motivational and emotional states that are approach-related (i.e., moving towards a goal), while NA is associated with forms of NA that are withdrawal-related (i.e., withdrawal from sources of aversive stimulation). Cortical mechanisms have been proposed by Davidson and colleagues (1990) to support these relationships. Chapter 2 details the physiological basis of affect.

Depending on the time instructions used, PANAS may be used to measure dispositional affect (Watson, Clark, & Tellegen, 1988). Respondents rated the extent to which each item best indicated how much they generally felt each different affect, on a 5-point Likert scale ranging from 1 (Not At All or Slightly) to 5 (Extremely). Correlations of NA and PA are unaffected by rated time frames, and 'stability coefficients of the general ratings are high enough to suggest that they may in fact be used as trait measures of affect' (Watson, Clark, & Tellegen, 1988: 1065). Reliability of the PA and NA scales were shown by Watson, Clark and Tellegen (1988) to be unaffected by the time instructions.

State and trait affective wellbeing are distinguished when respondents indicate how anxious they were over longer time periods, such as the past months, or generally, as opposed to how they feel right now, today, or this week. Short term instructions, like 'right now', capture mood. Negative affect measures show trait like stability when long term instructions, such as 'in general', are given (Clark & Watson, 1991) that are related to self-reports of job stressors, such as role overload (Brief et al., 1988; Burke et al., 1993).

Two Factor Bipolar and Four Factor Models of Affective Wellbeing

Affective wellbeing constructs of the Two Factor Bipolar or Four Factor Models of Affective Wellbeing are derived from a recognised theory base that closely aligns with Warr's (1987; 1994d) Vitamin Model and incorporates other research relevant to the affective wellbeing of employees. Previously developed instruments, with high construct validity, have been used in the Australian context to measure managers' affective wellbeing (Sevastos et al., 1992). De Jonge et al. (1994) and Sevastos, Smith and Cordery (1992) have established the reliability and construct validity of Warr's (1990b) affective wellbeing measures. Although not specifically developed for managers, these instruments are well regarded for collecting data across employment categories. Given the quality of research into these constructs, it was reasonable to accept that the Two Factor Bipolar or alternatively Four Factor Models of Affective Wellbeing would reliably measure managers' affective wellbeing.

Scales developed by Warr (1990a) are work-based, rather than clinically oriented, and are capable of measuring bipolar affective wellbeing (Enthusiasm-Depression and Anxiety-Contentment). These scales are sufficiently developed and validated to serve as a framework for conceiving and assessing affective wellbeing constructs in relation to the model being tested. Affective wellbeing was measured using four factoral independent scales (Enthusiasm, Depression, Anxiety and Relaxation) to tap the entire affective space originally developed by Warr (1990a), and later refined by Sevastos (1996).

Both the Two Factor Bipolar and Four Factor Models of Affective Wellbeing tap low activation and the arousal affect space (see Figure 2.2). Measures of hedonic tone may be improved by using existing validated scales. The Four Factor Model of Affective Wellbeing scale taps hedonic tone using the Enthusiasm factor (i.e., 'enthusiastic', 'motivated', 'optimistic' items) and the Relaxation factor (i.e., 'calm', 'restful' and 'relaxed' items). This addressed Wright and Staw's (1999a) criticism of PANAS, by providing a state measure of affect, which denotes hedonic tone in addition to activation, suitable for predicting employee performance.

Participants were asked to reflect on the 'last few weeks' (state affect) to indicate 'how much of the time their job made them feel each of the following?' In contrast to the other scales, a 6–point Likert scale was used for this scale, with options ranging from 1 (Never), 2 (Occasionally) 3, (Some of the Time), 4 (Much of the Time), 5 (Most of the Time) to 6 (All the Time).

Intrinsic job satisfaction

Job satisfaction was assessed using a 15–item global index originally developed by Brayfield and Rothe (1951) and refined by Cook et al. (1981). This scale is often used in management studies and has acceptable psychometric properties (Jamal, 1997a; 1997b). A Likert-type scale is used with a 1–to–5 response option, ranging from Strong Disagreement to Strong Agreement. The intrinsic job satisfaction subscale has well-established construct validity (Cook, 1981; Sevastos, 1996).

Intrinsic job satisfaction is used to emphasise job characteristics that involve personal achievements and task success, as opposed to extrinsic job satisfaction characteristics, that focus on pay or working conditions (Warr et al., 1979). The intrinsic job satisfaction subscale has been used in the Australian context in conjunction with measuring affective wellbeing by Sevastos (1996), and Sevastos, Smith and Cordery (1992).

Summary of the 'happy-productive workers' thesis

There are specific methodological issues impacting on the conceptualisation and measurement of the 'happy-productive worker' thesis. Items for the questionnaire used in this study were derived from established affective wellbeing and job satisfaction scales: the Four Factor Model of Job-related Wellbeing (Sevastos, 1996); PANAS (Watson & Clark, 1984), and job satisfaction (Cook, 1981). Intrinsic job satisfaction, PANAS and The Four Factor Model of Affective Wellbeing were used in conjunction to provide psychometrically robust measures of dispositional and state affect that also denoted hedonic tone suitable for predicting employee performance.

Managers' contextual performance scales were devised from Borman and Motowidlo's (1997) 5–dimension taxonomy. The task performance scales used Borman and Brush's (1993) 18–dimension taxonomy of managerial performance. Subscale items were also developed to measure constructs of 'Organisational Effectiveness' and 'Judgement'.

DEVELOPMENT OF THE MEASUREMENT INSTRUMENT

Managers' performance

Despite the extensive research into the construct 'performance', there 'appears to be no instrument available to tap job-related competence ... for both shop-floor and managerial employees' (Warr, 1992: 11). Managers' performance was conceived of in terms of observed behaviour to ensure that the appraisal process was simple and obviated the need for psychological tests of underlying skills and traits. In addition, the performance ratings based on observed behaviour are less controversial and more robust. As indicated in Chapter 3, attempts to identify a unidimensional general factor that reflects managers' performance generally have failed due to lack of a common framework for considering the underlying dimensions of the performance requirements of managers' jobs. There is merit in distinguishing between managers' contextual and task performance, when conceiving of and measuring job performance.

Given the inadequacy of instruments available to measure managers' performance, there was a compelling case for developing an instrument based on Borman and Motowidlo's (1997) contextual taxonomy and Borman and Brush's (1993) task taxonomy. Thus, managers' performance items were developed by the researcher from the literature, and incorporated items designed to measure both contextual and task performance domains. Managers and their superiors were presented with 19 subscales designed to assess achievements on a range of job tasks. Additional items were adapted from OCB measures for the five contextual performance subscales (Podsakoff, 1990; Organ & Ryan, 1995; Konovsky & Organ, 1996). See Chapter 3 for details.

Two new dimensions were incorporated into the Managers' Performance Questionnaire task subscale, to measure the constructs, 'Contribution to Organisational Effectiveness' (Quinn, 1992), and 'Judgement'. One of the variables fundamental to successful soft and hard management is the capacity for 'judgement' as identified by Mintzberg

(2004), Cialdini (1993), and Vickers (1965). Managers must be able to make judgement calls by identifying the issues diagnosing their character, conceiving of and locating choices, and seeing the solution through to its logical conclusion. These various stages of the decision-making process are seen by Mintzberg as essentially soft in nature. Authorities in the field (e.g., James, Mulaik, & Brett, 1982), recommended that at least three, and preferably four indicators (items), should be used to ensure the construct validity of each new factor.

The 'bandwidth versus fidelity' trade-off is relevant to this analysis (Cronbach, 1984). This instrument was developed to be consistent with Hogan and Robert's contention that 'prominent researchers in I/O consider the bandwidth of all job performance measures to be broad and advocate multiple and complex predictors to map the criterion space'. When measuring job performance, relatively narrow bands produce unreliable tests while reliable tests have resulted from broad bands (Murphy, 1994).

Internal consistency (or fidelity) can be increased for a scale by narrowing the scope of the measure (bandwidth). What is traded off in 'bandwidth fidelity' is gained in useability (Hogan & Roberts, 1996). However, a narrow bandwidth measure is as useful as a broadband measure with greater measurement error (Cronbach, 1984). In these circumstances, a slightly lower reliability may be acceptable when using a broadband measure (Cronbach, 1984).

Managers' performance rating scale

Simple to use instructions, with a clear frame of reference, were given in the questionnaire. Respondents were asked to, 'Select the option that best describes each behaviour or task described using a 6–point Likert scale' (1 –Poor, 2–Acceptable, 3–Very Good, 4–Excellent, 5–Outstanding, 6–Not Applicable). Both the contextual and task performance subscales used the same scale and provided the same instructions to participants.

Operationalising the definition of managers' performance made it necessary to assess behaviours that discriminated the performance of managers who were judged as excellent performers (effective managers) from those who were judged as average, or poor performers (less effective managers) as described in Chapter 3. To reduce the halo effect, questionnaire instructions were consistent with Cammock et al.'s (1995: 464) recommendation that raters be directed to 'avoid giving generalised high or low ratings but to focus on the specific behaviours or characteristics described by the statement and 'to focus on the specific behaviours or characteristics described by the statement'. With this in mind, respondents were also asked to 'Please avoid giving generalised high or low ratings. Focus on the specific behaviours or characteristics described by the statement' (see Appendix 5).

SUMMARY ON MEASUREMENT INSTRUMENTS

The scales used in the final questionnaire, except for managers' performance, are available in the source documents and have been used previously in occupational psychology research. Affective wellbeing scales are psychometrically robust and some (e.g., Two Factor Bipolar and Four Factor Models of Affective Wellbeing, Job Satisfaction) have been used with Western Australian samples, though not explicitly with managers. The items were consistent with instruments administered by Sevastos (1996), Warr (1990a; 1994d), Sevastos, Smith and Cordery (1992), and Kelloway, and Barling (1991) to ensure comparability with previous studies.

The final questionnaire was designed to collect information to test the hypotheses and the Partial Model. The Managers' Performance Questionnaire (for superiors' to rate managers' performance) and the Managers' Performance and Wellbeing Questionnaire (for managers to rate their affective wellbeing, intrinsic job satisfaction and performance) on contextual and task subscales were both designed and developed to produce the measurement instrument (see Chapter 6), based on the applicable literature. Performance items were identical for both questionnaires.

THE SAMPLE

Categorisation of managers' jobs

The Australian Standard Classification of Occupations (McLennan, 1997) is appropriate for determining the tasks allied with managers' job-families, since this study investigated Australian managers. ASCO (ABS, 1996) provided descriptions of the tasks performed by Australian managers. These job dimensions are statistically robust and have been field-tested with industry training bodies, unions, employer and professional organisations, to verify the construct validity (Pithers, Athanasou, & Cornford, 1996; McLennan, 1997). ASCO is concordant with the Australian and international occupational statistical classifications, such as International Standard Classification of Occupations (International Labor Organization, 2004).

There was considerable utility in focusing on the managerial category of middle managers as a target group to investigate. Peterson, Smith, Akande, Ayestaran, Bochner and Callan (1995: 436) have noted that, 'Studying middle managers reduces the occupational and organisational effects found to influence work values, norms, and beliefs'. Upper middle and middle managers are located between executives and first-level superiors, indicating there is minimal variance between job profiles of both groups (Spencer & Spencer, 1993), a debatable proposition.

Table 5.5 defines and details the categories of Australian managers used in this study.

Managers were logically clustered into four levels: top, upper-middle, middle and frontline. Managers were classified into job families based on ASCO's 11 functional categories to identify respondents undertaking specialist managerial jobs, such as those with a technical or creative role. In addition, Karpin (1995a) provided a useful framework for differentiating managers' jobs consistent with ASCO.

Table 5.5   Categories of Australian Managers

LEVEL	DESCRIPTOR (ABS, 1996)	SPECIALIST MANAGER DEFINITIONS (Karpin, 1995a)
Top	Chief Executive Officer Executive Director President Vice-President	Strategic position at or above general managers' level, controlling substantial resources and personnel.
Upper middle	Senior Manager Managing Director	Major responsibility at a senior level for implementation, which may require control of resources and/or personnel.
Middle	Superintendent	Above direct supervision of employees and below department, function or area responsibility.
Frontline	Co-ordinators Firstline manager Forepersons Leading hands Supervisors Team leaders	Responsible for a number of work-groups or teams.

Demographics

Demographic variables were included in the final version of the questionnaire to obtain information about gender, education, marital status, seniority, length of service, hours of work, employment type, managerial category and career stage (Zikmund, 2002). These questions were used to determine if significant individual demographic differences existed between the participants. The second question required respondents to indicate how many years in total they had worked as managers, in this or other organisations. Ages were calculated from birthdates.

Recruitment of participants

Several methods were used to recruit participants for the study. Proximity and the willingness of organisations to be involved in the study was a practical consideration. Large and medium-sized businesses and government agencies located in Western Australia were selected. Agencies selected for inclusion in this study had participated in management education conducted by the Australian Institute of Management and the former Management Development Institute of The University of Western Australia (now the Graduate School of Management). The largest private companies in Western Australia were identified by the Western Australian Department of Commerce and Trade.

Organisations were selected by distributing a letter of invitation to be involved in this study. The letter of invitation was usually received by, or referred to, each organisation's Human Resource Department, or the equivalent. In most cases, the Manager or Director of the respective Human Resources Department conferred with the head of the organisation before agreeing or declining to become involved. After agreeing to participate in the study, the designated Human Resources contact, and sometimes the head of the organisation, arranged for the letter of invitation, or a version of it, to be distributed by hard copy or email to managers.

Human Resource personnel within each participating organisation acted as organisational 'gatekeepers'. They were also largely responsible for promoting, and sometimes defending, the value of the research with internal management. Concern was expressed about the intrusion of the questionnaire into managers' work time. In some cases, Human Resource Managers were keen to be involved (e.g., two large private sector organisations), but senior management declined the offer, attributing the reluctance to competing priorities on their time. Indeed, every organisation the researcher contacted indicated that they were inundated with requests from universities to be involved in survey research.

Cross-sectional data

Hypotheses detailed in Chapter 4 permitted testing of the model using a cross-sectional methodology. Cross-sectional designs are the dominant method for studies involving managerial behavioural outcomes and are sufficient to suggest research propositions that deserve further attention (Martin & Wall, 1989; Zikmund, 2002). Research designs based on single samples, with self-reported variables, are able to produce worthwhile statistical patterns between variables. A limitation of previous studies in this area has been the reliance on cross-sectional information that relies on one source of data. Similarly, single-source methods may not necessarily generate causal inferences that extend our understanding about organisational behaviour. See Chapter 6 for a critique of these methodologies.

An inherent weakness in the Wright and Staw (1999a; 1999b) study was the reliance on a single source of report of performance. Only ratings from two superiors were used for an entire sample of a single public sector social welfare department. This cohort may have been pre-disposed to reporting affect due to the emotionally charged nature of the work undertaken. Supervisory performance evaluations used in the Wright and Staw (1999a; 1999b) study were developed in conjunction with management, without input from the employees being rated, resulting in a lack of congruence between self and other rated performance. A one-on-one congruence (pair congruence) was used in this study for managers' rating of performance, where one superior rated the performance of only one manager.

Summary on methodology

Self-administered questionnaires were used to collect the data for this study, a common method for collecting survey data for reaching a geographically dispersed sample at a relatively low cost (Zikmund, 2002). Questionnaires containing variables with theoretical significance were administered to a purposive sample of managers. Managers' affective wellbeing, intrinsic job satisfaction and performance were measured using self-report. Superiors' appraisal was used to simultaneously assess managers' individual performance.

The population for this study was defined as middle managers in Australia and the sampling frame was managers' within Western Australian organisations who responded to the invitation to be involved in the study. Nineteen major organisations participated in the study. These organisations were selected from a variety of industries to ensure that the sample was representative of different Australian managerial positions in private, public, and third sector organisations. This method of collecting data is compatible with the intent of this study.

ADMINISTERING THE QUESTIONNAIRE

The questionnaire was administered with assistance from senior management and Human Resource managers. The questionnaire, a pre-addressed return envelope, and a covering letter signed by the researcher and a senior manager in the organisation concerned, were sent to all managers of participating organisations via the internal mail system. Confidential coding of responses was used so that no respondent could be identified. Questionnaires were sent directly to individual participants from mailing lists provided by each organisation.

Managers' individual performances were simultaneously measured by self-ratings for affective wellbeing, intrinsic job satisfaction and performance. Superiors rated managers' performance on identical contextual and task performance items, using a separate questionnaire. The covering letter explained the purpose of the study and stressed that all responses were confidential. Completed questionnaires were returned directly to the researcher by mail to ensure confidentiality.

Questionnaire return rates varied widely across organisations from 7%–88%. The bulk of the questionnaires were received from seven organisations. Higher response rates were obtained from smaller organisations. The modest overall return rate of questionnaires (26%) may be attributed to a combination of internal and external factors:

- the sensitive nature of the questions asked;
- the length of the questionnaire and complexity of the questions;
- voluntary participation;
- managers' workload;
- survey fatigue;
- internal communications of the participating organisations;
- the adverse impact of economic circumstances;
- organisational dynamics of the private sector.

Prevailing external organisational dynamics, such as downsizing and restructuring, combined with the adverse economic environment at the time. may also have contributed to a lower rate of returns of the questionnaire than anticipated. Organisational restructuring at the time of the survey was indicative of the uncertain career prospects of managers in the Western Australian public as well as private sector organisations. Private sector managers also commented on the constant pressure to 'do more with less', and their susceptibility to stochastic economic upheavals. Obtaining superior appraisals of managers' performance was also very difficult due to heavy workloads.

Summary on data collection

The strategies used resulted in a reasonably ordered, though somewhat discontinuous, collection of data. A key tactic was to ensure that senior management's support for the study was conveyed to managers in order to maintain the confidentiality of individual responses. The modest questionnaire response rate may be attributed to the sensitive nature of the information being collected; organisational dynamics; economic circumstances; time of administration; and the length of the questionnaire.

A reliable and valid measure of managers' performance was important for this study. Performance measures are notoriously value-laden, especially when self-assessed. The questionnaire addressed issues for which the participants were likely to have strong feelings. Managers were unlikely to be indifferent about their affective wellbeing, intrinsic job satisfaction or their performance. Hostile responses to the questionnaire had the potential to contaminate the results and lead to a loss of support from participating organisations. Given these dynamics, the researcher limited follow-up letters and emails for non-replies (i.e., n = 1,271).

DATA ANALYSIS TECHNIQUES

In order to test hypotheses without ambiguity it was essential to establish the structural congruence between managers' perception of performance ratings and superiors' rating of their performance. There were four aspects to the analysis of managers' performance:

- EFA was used to determine the items that formed the factors of superiors' perceptions of managers' performance.
- CFA was used to test the invariance analysis of the items and factors.
- MTMM analysis was used to evaluate the accuracy of self- and other-ratings of job performance.
- The major analysis of both the affective wellbeing and managers' performance variables was undertaken using Canonical Correlation and Standard Multiple Regression.

The following decision rules were used to determine the appropriate clusters of variables on the basis of a correlation matrix: a factor analysis was conducted using eigenvalues for determining the number of factors. In addition, a scree test was undertaken to help decide the eventual factor solution. This approach is recommended for detecting structures with manifest intercorrelations between variables (Schweizer, 1992).

Measurement Model

Exploratory Factor Analysis (EFA)
A factor analysis was conducted before modifying or deleting redundant performance items. Factor analyses were used to re-define and compose the managers' performance scales. The value of factor analysis for theory development depends on the manner in which it is implemented (Cattell, 1978; Comrey, 1978). The following methodological issues were

incorporated into the factor analysis (Fabrigar, Wegener, MacCallum, & Strahan, 1999: 273).

- The size and nature of the indicator variables that are included in the study and the nature of the sample used. Indicator variables were included in the instrument devised by the researcher.
- EFA is the appropriate form of the analysis for the goals of the research; the specific procedure to fit the model to be tested.
- How many factors to include in the model and the method for rotating the initial factors?

Fabrigar, Wegener, MacCallum, and Strahan (1999: 273) noted that such 'decisions have important consequences for the results obtained'. A priori, 5 contextual and 19 task performance factors were predicted from the data.

Factor analysis

Each scale, subscale and item was separately analysed for communality, eigenvalue, percentage of variance, and cumulative variance. Before conducting the Maximum Likelihood Estimation (MLE), the distributions for each of the variables were examined for general normality, for the presence of outliers and errors in coding, and for missing data.

Maximum Likelihood Estimation (MLE)

Factor analysis is appropriate for deriving dimensions for theoretical purposes that are uncontaminated by unique or error variance (Tabachnick & Fidell, 2001). Therefore, factor analysis was used to identify latent variables (common factors) that account for correlations among measured variables. MLE was used to compare the managers' self-report and superiors' report data. Hair et al. (1995: 605) stated:

> Maximum likelihood estimation (MLE), the most common estimation procedure, has been found to provide valid results with a sample size as small as 50, but a sample size this small is not recommended. It is generally accepted that the minimum sample size to ensure appropriate use of MLE is 100 to 150.

MLE is a more effective factor analysis for using only eigenvalues ≥ 1. Maximum Likelihood (ML) assumes that the data being analysed are multivariate normal. ML represents and separately estimates the unique portion of each variable measured. ML has more restricted assumptions and only analyses shared variance (latent dimensions). The ML begins with the input of Pearson product-moment correlation using squared multiple correlations to make initial estimates of communality. Theoretically based solutions, uncontaminated by unique and error variance, are produced by ML (Hair et al., 1995).

Factor Rotation

An oblimin rotation was used because of the hypothesised intercorrelation among constructs (Cordery & Sevastos, 1993). An oblique or oblimin (as opposed to an orthogonal) rotation more realistically portrays correlated data and is suitable for interpreting the rotated solution, since it 'provides a more accurate representation of how constructs are likely to be related to one another' (Fabrigar et al., 1999: 282). Oblique rotations more accurately represent the clustering of variables, because they are theoretically related to the underlying dimensions and show the magnitude of factor interrelations (Hair et al., 1995).

An oblimin solution provided a more meaningful result for this data because differences between high and low loadings are more readily interpretable in the pattern matrix. Factors may correlate with one another when an oblique rotation is used, so oblique rotations tend to produce items with lower loadings due to the lower communalities of the variable. Thus, item loadings for oblique solutions may be interpreted at lower levels than for those using orthogonal rotations.

Factors were rotated until each item was clearly loaded onto a construct. A factor was deemed to reflect a particular construct, when three or more items had loadings of ≥ .30 on a factor, and no loadings ≥ .30 on any other factor (Tabachnick & Fidell, 2001). Moreover, non-complex variables load ≥ .30 or higher on only one factor, whereas complex variables have loadings ≥ .30 on more than one factor. Factors with eigenvalues greater than one were retained, except when the scree plot indicated more factors were present. Items that did not meet these criteria were deleted.

Scree test

Depending on the circumstances, the scree test sometimes provides a better indication of underlying factors than other methods (Cattell, 1966). Scree tests also assist in identifying the optimum number of factors that could be extracted before the amount of unique variance begins to dominate the common variance structure. Scree tests are an appropriate adjunct to eigenvalue analysis for selecting the number of factors (Cattell, 1966; Holmes-Smith, 1998). Eigenvalues were compared with Catell's scree plot to determine the numbers of factors to retain. Extracting components with eigenvalues > 1.0 overestimates or underestimates the appropriate number of factors to retain (Tucker, Koopman, & Linn, 1969; Hakstian, Rogers, & Cattell, 1982).

Internal reliability

Cronbach's alpha coefficient is the most common way of calculating internal scale reliability (Cronbach, 1984; Price & Mueller, 1986). Alpha coefficients were calculated for each scale and subscale in the questionnaire, to decide which items to delete, modify, and check for congruence with the underlying dimensions. An internal reliability ≥ .7 is acceptable for most psychological scales, which may be reduced to .6 in factor analysis (Hair et al., 1995). However, a value of < .5 is usually considered unacceptable (Cronbach, 1984).

Statistical power and factor loadings

Criteria for judging the significance of factor loadings are provided by Hair et al. (1995: 12):

> (1) the larger the sample size, the smaller the loading to be considered significant; (2) the larger the number of variables being analyzed, the smaller the loading to be considered significant; (3) the larger the number of factors, the larger the size of the loading on later factors to be considered significant for interpretation.

Sample size, alpha and effect size were all analysed concurrently to achieve a threshold of 80% statistical power. However, factor analysis is particularly susceptible to sample size effects (Hinkin, 1995). Over 200 responses of managers' performance were used to maximise statistical reliability and power. Clearly, the number of indicators (97) relative to the subsample size (200) was going to result in an 'overfitting' of the data, a good fit to the sample that is not generalizable to the population (Tabachnick & Fidell, 2001). Therefore, the subsample for the EFA was split into those variables predicted to load separately onto the contextual and task dimensions, which were evaluated separately. This was clearly a less desirable procedure, due to the overall small sample size.

Factor loadings usually have considerably larger standard errors than typical correlations and should therefore be assessed at stricter levels (Bentler & Chou, 1987). Guadagnoli and Velicer (1988) considered that a sample size of 150 is sufficient for an accurate solution in factor analysis, provided the items are strongly correlated. Comrey and Lee (1992) considered that solutions with high loading markers, or pure variables (≥ .80), require samples of above 150 to be suitable for factor analysis.

Variable loadings of .50 are recommended by Hair et al. (1995) for a sample of 120 (.4 for 200) to maintain a statistical power level of 80% based on a .05 significance level (α). According to Hair et al., 'a .30 loading translates to approximately a 10% explanation, and .50 loading denotes that 25% of the variance is accounted for by one factor [and a] loading must exceed .70 for the factor to account for 50% of the variance' (1995: 111). Factor loadings of 50% are considered by Hair et al. (1995) as being practically significant, 40% to be important and 30% to meet minimum requirements for samples of over 100.

These recommendations are consistent with Comrey and Lee (1992), who calculated more precise cut-off values, and argued that a loading exceeding ± .71 (representing 50% of overlapping variance) is excellent, ±.63 (40% of overlapping variance) is very good, ± .55 (30% of overlapping variance), ±.45 (20% of overlapping variance) fair, and ±.32 (10% of overlapping variance) is poor. For newly devised performance scales, it was considered acceptable to retain items that loaded ≥ .30, and did not cross-load ±.30 on other factors.

Confirmatory Factor Analysis power

To determine whether a hypothesis about a model is acceptable, adequate power needs to be demonstrated. Power analysis for tests of model fit requires the specification of null and alternative hypotheses that translate into an effect size (i.e., the extent to which the null hypothesis is incorrect). MacCallum et al. (1996) have developed calculations for power and determination of sample size. Power of .80 is achieved when the null hypothesis is ≤ .05, and the alternative hypothesis is ≥ .08, with an alpha level of .05. All model fit evaluations were based on the MacCallum et al. (1996) guidelines to demonstrate adequate power and sample size influencing the root mean squared error of approximation (RMSEA), an index of model fit.

Confirmatory Factor Analysis

CFA is growing in importance in the social sciences because confirmatory methods 'provide researchers with a comprehensive means for assessing and modifying theoretical models' (Anderson & Gerbing, 1988: 411). Bentler and Chou (1987) have observed that larger sample sizes (N ≥ 400) are required for accurate CFA parameter estimates. However, Boomsma and Molenaar (1986) and Hoetler (1983) recommended that a minimum of 200 subjects (critical N) is a satisfactory sample size for CFA.

The main focus of CFA analysis was to establish the extent that the hypothesised model 'fits' or adequately describes the sample data. A number of criteria are necessary to assess the adequacy of the fit of the model overall and on an individual basis. CFA allows the modelling of covariation among constructs. Widaman's (1985) guidelines were used to test for evidence of construct validity of managers' performance using a CFA framework.

Analytical methods used to conduct CFA are provided, including a general coverage of the fit indices applicable to this study. EFA may be used for model specification prior to cross-validation with CFA, 'particularly with varimax rotation of principal axes factors' (Gerbing &

Hamilton, 1996: 72). ML with oblimin rotation was used in preference to varimax rotation because it is more rigorous for this particular type of study.

CFA may be used for theory testing and development of application and prediction models. Theory testing and development 'emphasizes the transition from exploratory to confirmatory analysis' (Jöreskog & Wold, 1982: 270), while application and prediction 'is primarily intended for causal-predictive analysis in situations of high complexity but low theoretical information' (1982: 270). The distinction between EFA and CFA is an important methodological consideration. Gerbing and Hamilton (1996: 71) argued that these distinctions are somewhat arbitrary.

> Most uses of 'confirmatory' factor analysis are, in actuality, partly exploratory and partly confirmatory in that the resultant model is derived in part from theory and in part from a respecification based on the analysis of model fit.

An EFA results when the number of factors is not specified a priori. A factor analysis is essentially exploratory because individual items are not forced onto an appropriate factor. EFA is appropriate in the early stages of scale development because CFA does not indicate how well items load on non-hypothesised factors (Kelloway, 1995). EFA was therefore appropriate for developing the managers' contextual and task performance subscales prior to CFA for testing.

In contrast, CFA occurs when the number of factors is specified a priori, such that the number of factors is known and individual items are attached to each factor. CFA is preferred when there is a well developed underlying theory for hypothesised factor loadings (Hurley et al., 1997). A substantial theory base underlying a Measurement Model, as with the managers' performance model, is required before analysing data using CFA (Williams, 1995). This technique is used to confirm that the factors that have been adequately constructed to fit the data.

The independence of the dimensions of the subscales was tested through CFA, using the EQS computer program, which permits parameter estimates to be restricted to remain within reasonable bounds (Harris & Bladen, 1994; Bentler & Wu, 1995), and deals effectively with negative error variance (Rindskopf, 1984; Harris & Schaubroeck, 1988). EQS does not allow error variances to become negative and adjusts the offending parameters. Also, EQS adjusts the non-multivariate normality of the data through the Satorra-Bentler chi-square (S-Bχ^2) using the ML method of estimation.

Byrne (1994b: 293) considered that the S-Bχ^2 performs 'as well, or better than the usual asymptotically distribution-free methods generally recommended for non-normal multivariate data'. Byrne (1995: 293) also observed that:

EQS uses an estimation method that assumes the data are multivariate normal but bases evaluation of model fit on a test statistic that has been corrected to take nonnormality into account.

Satorra and Bentler's (1988) S-Bχ^2 statistic therefore incorporates a scaling statistic if distributional assumptions are violated. Such a computation accounts for the model being tested, the estimation method, and the sample kurtosis values. The S-Bχ^2 is a reliable test statistic for evaluating covariance structure models under various distributions and sample sizes.

EQS was used to establish the Measurement Model of managers' performance, and to determine the structural relations among the factors (Anderson & Gerbing, 1988). An appropriate covariance matrix was used to obtain maximum likelihood parameter estimates. The Measurement Model represents the confirmatory measurement or factor analysis which 'specifies the relations of the observed measures to their posited underlying constructs', according to Anderson and Gerbing (1988: 411). Bollen and Long (1993) also recommended using multiple measures of fit to evaluate models.

Calibration and cross-calibration of the performance construct

In this study, it was important to empirically demonstrate the validity of managers' ratings of their contextual and task performance. In particular, it was necessary to establish whether managers rated their contextual and task performance differently compared with their superiors, in terms of convergent validity, methods effects and discriminant validity. Methodological hypotheses on managers' performance are developed and tested in Chapter 6 to establish the structure, the most reliable indicators and the shared meaning attributable to dimensions of managers' contextual and task performance.

The factoral validity of managers' performance was tested using analysis of covariance structures within a CFA framework (Byrne, 1994b). Contemporary restricted models, which use confirmatory analysis, offer a useful way of approaching the latent structure of the managers' performance domain. CFA procedures are used to test the validity of hypotheses and factoral structures across groups, using rigorous statistical procedures, to provide evidence of convergent and discriminant validity within the framework of a MTMM model (Byrne, 1994b).

When instruments comprise several subscales, construct validity is evident when the scales demonstrate a well-defined factor structure consistent with the underlying theory (Byrne, 1994b). To establish the independence of responses, all observations must also be independent (Hair et al., 1995). As such, it was necessary to establish congruence between focal persons' (managers) and superiors' rating of performance. The structure of the CFA indicates which of the factors are measuring the same construct (see Chapter 7 for details).

A parsimonious number of factors, particularly for task performance, were required, to include in the model to be tested. Specific procedures to fit the structured model of managers' performance were applied. These dimensions were confirmed through multi-sample analysis and cross-validation techniques of managers' self-ratings and superiors' ratings. The factor structure of the measurement instrument was examined using EFA and CFA analyses on data obtained from subsamples 1 and 2. CFA tests of the Measurement Models and invariance analysis involved double the number of responses when managers' and superiors' responses were analysed.

A CFA was conducted to test if the Measurement Model for managers' performance represents independent factors. These analyses were applied to different subsamples, to evaluate the generalisability of the Measurement Model. The invariance of the Measurement Model was examined, across managers, and superiors groups, to establish whether the factorial structure of the performance constructs was equivalent. An instrument was designed to measure 8–dimensions of managers' performance. The focus on factoral validity aimed to test hypotheses related to the factoral structure being studied. Specifically, each CFA seeks to determine the extent that items actually measure the predicted factors. Subscales of the measuring instrument are intended to represent factors, so that all items comprising a particular factor load on the related factor. The viability of the CFA procedure depends on the accuracy of the factors specified.

Multitrait-Multimethod Method (MTMM)

A CFA framework was used to model multiple traits that were assessed by multiple methods. MTMM tests hypotheses arising from complex model structures provided a means of testing the construct validity of hypotheses (Byrne, Goffin, & Jackson, 1993). Several approaches to MTMM have evolved (c.f. Schmitt & Stults, 1986). Of these approaches, those based on covariance structures have gained considerable support, particularly the general CFA approach to MTMM (Byrne, 1994b).

The present application of MTMM was based on the work by Byrne (1994b), and Byrne, Goffin and Jackson (1993), designed to assess the concordance of multiple prominent covariance structures. A CFA approach that assumes trait and rater variance combine additively was adopted, in preference to the Composite Direct Model, which assumes that a multiplicative approach. Goffin and Jackson (1992) found support for the Composite Direct Model, but acknowledged that the technique provides only a proportion of true score variance.

Canonical Correlation

Canonical Correlation is a 'multivariate statistical model that facilitates the study of interrelationships among sets of multiple dependent variables and multiple independent variables' (Hair et al., 1995: 444). For studies with multiple DVs and IVs, Canonical Correlation is the 'most appropriate and powerful technique' (Hair et al., 1995: 444). Canonical Correlation is suitable for assessing the relationship between metric IVs and multiple dependent measures to ascertain the strength and the nature of the defined relationship (Hair et al., 1995).

Canonical Correlation answers two related research questions. First, what is the degree of the relationship between the sets of variables (e.g., predictors and criteria), and second, what is the nature of the relationship between these sets of variables? The latter attempts to establish the number of dimensions and the underlying dimensions that explain these relationships. Optimal dimensionality is identified by a Canonical Correlation to maximise the relationship between each set of IVs and DVs. Measures of the relative contribution of each variable to canonical functions are then extracted.

Canonical Correlation extends multiple linear regression from a single criterion variable to multiple criteria variables. To be effective, each set of variables must have theoretical meaning. This technique is well suited to predicting multivariate criterion measures, such as job performance (Bobko, 1990), and for omnibus testing, where a set of continuous predictor variables, such as affective wellbeing, are related to criterion variables, like multi-dimensional measures of job performance (Larzelere & Muliak, 1977).

Sets of DVs and IVs were regressed to maximise the correlation between linear composites. In the process, a number of pairs of canonical variates (functions) were generated. Canonical variates are based on the correlation between canonical variates. One variate is for IVs and the other for DVs. These variates are derived to maximise the correlation. Variable weights are selected by simultaneously forming two sets of weights that accentuate the correlation between the two resultant composites between the IVs and the DVs. If residual variance between the two sets of variables still exists after the extraction of the first canonical variate, the process continues until all variance is extracted. However, only statistically significant pairs of variates are interpreted and those contributed to $\geq 10\%$ of explained variance.

All linear composites are a differential weighting of all variables. Each linear composite of the IVs is a reduction of the set of IVs to a single independent composite variable. Similarly, each linear composite of the DVs is a composite of the DVs to a single composite DV. The correlation coefficient between the two linear composites is the measure of the degree of association between the two sets of IVs and DVs, for the given weightings.

The canonical variates are the particular linear combinations of a set of weightings that maximise the degree of association between the two sets of variables (equivalent to multiple R from regression analysis). Statistical significance conventions apply for testing the number of canonical variate pairs. For the purposes of the study, only statistically significant canonical variates were considered for further inclusion. Data gathered from the questionnaires were combined into unweighted composite scores and used when the two sets of variables had equivalent status, so that no clear-cut distinction was made between DVs and IVs (Cliff, 1987).

The interpretation of the canonical variates may be difficult because they are calculated to maximise the relationship, and there are no aids for interpretation, such as rotation of variates, seen in factor analysis. It is difficult to identify meaningful relationships between subsets of independent and dependent variables because precise statistics have not yet been developed to interpret canonical analysis, and we must rely on inadequate measures such as loadings and cross loadings. Tabachnick and Fidell (1996: 196) concluded that 'In its present stage of development, Canonical Correlation is best considered a descriptive technique or a screening procedure rather than a hypothesis testing procedure'. One way of overcoming the limitations of Canonical Correlation is to use the statistically significant variates as DVs in subsequent analyses, for example, a multiple linear regression, where hypotheses can be tested.

Standard Multiple Regression

Multiple regression analysis is a statistical technique for analysing the relationships between a single dependent (criterion variable) and several predictor variables (Hair et al., 1995). The regression analysis procedure ensures the maximum prediction from the set of IVs by weighting each IV. A Standard Multiple Regression was used on the predictor variables to test the specified hypotheses. Standard Multiple Regression analysis is used to predict DVs from the knowledge of one or more IVs (Tabachnick & Fidell, 2001). Affective wellbeing and intrinsic job satisfaction were designated as the IVs, and contextual and task managers' performance as the DVs. As established earlier, managers' performance was predicted to be multi-dimensional, so the issue of how to combine factor scores for assessing their performance needs to be addressed. For this to be achieved, composite variables must be combined linearly to calculate a comparative assessment of performance.

In a Standard Multiple Regression all the IVs are entered into the regression equation at once. Standard Multiple Regression makes it possible, through squared semi-partial correlations, to assess regression with each IV as though each had been entered into the regression after all the other IVs had been entered into the computation. Each IV is evaluated separately to ascertain how it adds to predicting the DVs. The linear combination of IVs that best predicts the DVs is formed into the regression variate by the set of weighted IVs (Hair et al., 1995). Thus, both the full correlation and the unique contribution of IVs need to be interpreted for Standard Multiple Regression (Tabachnick & Fidell, 2001).

Normally, the research strategy for exploring the predictive power of sets of IVs is conducted within a DV's context (e.g., affective wellbeing, intrinsic job satisfaction, etc). This procedure is expected to identify how well each DV may be predicted from a set of IVs. Such an approach is unsatisfactory, because when a large number of analyses are involved, with each DV the prevalence of Type I errors is likely to rise (Tabachnick & Fidell, 2001). Invariably, the majority of IVs in studies of this nature are intercorrelated (e.g., PANAS and other conceptually related affective wellbeing measures), and would therefore show considerable shared variance. With the weighting of the performance variables into two statistically significant composite DVs, orthogonal to each other, through Canonical Correlation only two Standard Multiple Regressions are necessary rather than eight separate analyses.

Summary on the statistical methods

The statistical analytic methods included: EFA; CFA; Canonical Correlation; and Standard Multiple Regression. Differences between EFA and CFA analysis were explained, including why the latter was used to ensure the independence of the measures. CFA was used to ensure the independence of the measures of managers' performance. This included a justification for the analytical methods used to conduct the CFA. Appropriate fit indices for this study were considered. A general coverage of the fit indices that are appropriate when reporting the results of CFA was included.

The next section scrutinises the methodological constraints of this study.

METHODOLOGICAL CONSIDERATIONS

Choice of research methodology

Quantitative social science research has well documented limitations. This section identifies the methodological constraints inherent in the design of this study, which relied primarily on cross-sectional, questionnaire data, based on a correlational methodology, as often is the case in studies of this nature (Mathieu & Zajac, 1990).

Constrained sampling frame

The sampling frame was constrained to managers from organisations based in Western Australia. A larger, more diverse sample would have improved the statistical power of the study. Behavioural research data is generally not normally distributed (Micceri, 1989). Data collected for this study were therefore expected to be non-normal. Obtaining random samples of a broadly defined target population and universe such as managers is extremely difficult (Sackett & Larson, 1991). As a consequence, most organisational research is conducted with non-representative samples (cf. Dipboye & Flanagan, 1979). However, the variety of organisations and industries sampled operates in favour of generalisability and representativeness.

Cross-sectional and longitudinal designs

There are substantial difficulties in monitoring the work output of employees so that affect and performance can be precisely linked. As Wright and Staw noted, (1999b: 16) 'performance in most work settings was not easily delimited in time'. Accurately measuring performance, in an organisational context, would require data to be collected over many years and at several time intervals. Individual and organisational level variables of managers' performance have typically been measured simultaneously, making it difficult to discern a psychologically meaningful period within which this construct may be measured. Typically, performance ratings are infrequent events intended to reflect many months, or even years, of work.

Longitudinal studies have been suggested as a way of reducing the limitations inherent in cross-sectional studies, such as the empirical validation of causal inferences (Frese & Zapf in Cooper & Payne, 1988). Generally, longitudinal designs are preferred to cross-sectional research designs, because they are believed to have the capacity to examine causal relationships between work outcomes (Randall, 1990). However, longitudinal research designs do not necessarily ensure the establishment of causal relationships (Meyer & Allen, 1997), an empirical causal sequencing of effects (Kelloway & Barling, 1991), or add greatly to an understanding of how behavioural causes originate (Cooper & Payne, 1988). A cross-sectional approach is acceptable for exploratory studies. Longitudinal studies are likewise prone to contamination by measurement error. Longitudinal designs do not assist in accounting for the phenomenon of ratees (superiors) rating participants (managers) higher on contextual performance, simply because they like the ratees (Organ & Paine, 1999). Factors such as the likeability of ratees, introduces another distortion when rating contextual performance.

The majority of empirical research on stressors and health is cross-sectional. Applying longitudinal designs does not necessarily solve the problems inherent in cross-sectional designs (Williams & Podsakoff, 1989). Frese and Zapf (1988) concluded, from a review of the literature on longitudinal studies in organisational stress, that reverse causation and third party variables (e.g., social desirability, acquiescence, and NA) do not automatically reject third party variable explanations. Moreover, Frese and Zapf (1988) argued that the exaggerated influences of mood in cross-sectional designs have a two-fold effect in longitudinal studies.

Longitudinal information is required to establish if the flow of relationship runs from affective wellbeing, intrinsic job satisfaction to performance as predicted by the A *Partial Model of Managers' Affective Wellbeing, Intrinsic Job Satisfaction and Performance* ('Partial Model'). There were practical impediments to collecting longitudinal data in this study. Organisations were experiencing volatile dynamics, as detailed in Chapter 1. In consequence, managers involved in this study may not be performing the same job for the duration of a longitudinal study. Also, some of the organisations were in the process of being restructured or, in one case, ceased to exist before the study was completed.

Collecting longitudinal data was beyond the scope of this study because it was an exploratory investigation. The desire for additional data had to be balanced with the possibility that more data collection had the potential to antagonise some managers, which could have jeopardised the validity of the data collected. A longitudinal design may not have contributed enough to the plausibility of the affect-performance phenomena to justify further interruption of the organisations involved in the study. In all, there was no clear advantage to justify further intrusion into managers' time.

Multirater and multisource assessment v self-assessment

As indicated in Chapter 4, reliable and objective measures of managers' performance were important for this study. Performance measures are notoriously value-laden, especially when self-assessment is used. This has resulted in a growing preference, in the literature and practice, for the use of multiple perspectives of performance.

There are potential gains in accuracy when using multisource ratings of managers' performance. Multirater, multisource assessment (e.g., 360° appraisal) has recently become a popular, but poorly understood, management and organisational intervention (Church & Bracken, 1997). Multisource performance feedback is based on the assumption, derived from measurement theory, that observations of individuals, made from multiple sources, will result in more accurate assessments of individual performance (Church & Bracken, 1997). This preference for multisource assessment needs to be balanced against the pragmatics of implementing such methodology with organisations that are inexperienced with the process.

A comprehensive meta-analysis of the literature by Kluger and De Nisi (1996) revealed that performance was not always improved by multisource feedback interventions. Also, the literature indicates that people perceive that upward appraisal systems have many negative consequences (De Nisi & Mitchell, 1978; Kane & Lawler, 1978). As London, Smither and Adsit (1997: 163) argued, multisource feedback essentially depends on the extent that raters and ratees are 'accountable for applying the process in a serious and meaningful way'. Given the exigencies of this study, this outcome could not have been achieved within a reasonable time span with the participating organisations.

Practitioners (Antonioni, 1996) and researchers (Church & Bracken, 1997) have advised against the overzealous application of multisource appraisal. Tsui and Ohlott (1988) have warned of the problem of poor inter-rater reliability or equivalence (entailing two observers measuring the same event) amongst multiple assessments of managerial performance. Raters who agreed to be given multisource feedback, have been found to be more positively disposed to upward appraisal, and felt more confident in the accuracy of their performance (Westerman & Rosse, 1997). Multisource assessment is also subject to attribution error.

Multiple source assessment of performance is resource intensive and requires commitment of executive management to be implemented. Given the highly sensitive nature of this study, and the inexperience of some of the participating organisations in using multisource feedback, there were serious methodological impediments to this approach. In this scenario, multisource ratings have the potential to result in less accurate ratings of managers' performance, than would traditional downward appraisal, or self-report.

Attempting to use multisource assessments of managers' performance using a wide range of data points (e.g., peer, subordinates, external and internal stakeholders) had the potential to increase resistance to completing the questionnaire. Again, this would have involved considerable disruption to the participating organisations and would potentially have resulted in less veracity in the data collected.

There is substantial existing literature about the two dimensions (contextual and task) of managers' performance. Studies that have investigated the impact of affect (feelings of liking or disliking) and contextual performance on superiors and peer ratings of task performance have indicated that when superiors rate staff members' overall performance, they weight contextual performance as highly as task performance (MacKenzie et al., 1991; Motowidlo & Van Scotter, 1994; Borman et al., 1995).

Summary on methodological considerations

Multisource feedback of performance is being used more frequently in organisations but the empirical research to support its use is limited, when compared to traditional methods. There were ethical concerns in the present study, organisational resistance and methodological impediments to implementing a multisource assessment of managers' performance. As discussed, the situational dynamics did not predispose the use of multi-rater, multisource assessments of managers' performance.

Self-report

This study relied heavily on self-report questionnaires of affective wellbeing and intrinsic job-satisfaction, a method used in more than half of published studies in Organisational Behaviour and Industrial and Organisational Psychology (Sackett & Larson, 1991). Self-report is ubiquitous in published research in Organisational Behaviour and management (cf. Dipboye & Flanagan, 1979; Sims, 1979; Gupta & Beehr, 1982; Mitchell, 1985). A cross-sectional, self-report study was developed using the population to investigate the most significant components of performance outcomes related to affective wellbeing factors that influence managers' performance.

Behavioural ratings scales are the method of choice for measuring performance in organisations (Murphy & Cleveland, 1995). The inadequacies associated with the self-report assessment of performance are well known (cf. Campbell, 1998). Common method variance was an inevitable methodological problem for this study. Issues related to common method variance (where everything comes from one source) have long been a concern for psychologists (cf. Campbell & Fiske, 1959; Fiske, 1982). Using same-source data was a problem for Fisher's (2002) study of the satisfaction/happiness-performance constructs. Sackett and Larson (1991: 473) warned that:

When two variables intended to represent different constructs are assessed using the same method (e.g., self-report) a question that must be addressed is the extent to which any observed relationship between the variables is attributable to a true relationship between the constructs or to bias resulting from the use of a common data collection method.

Self-report is an established and appropriate way for measuring affective wellbeing and intrinsic job satisfaction constructs. After reviewing the literature about methodological issues relating to interpreting self-report data in job design studies, Fried and Ferris (1987: 299) concluded, 'problems potentially associated with self-rated data are less serious than initially believed'. As such, 'when we obtain self-report measures from a person at one sitting for several variables, there certainly was the risk that the transient mood state will contribute a consistent but artifactual bias across the measures' (Podsakoff & Organ, 1986: 515).

In contrast, Dunnette and Hough (1991: 197) were less concerned with these artefacts of measurement, concluding that 'subjective reports from focal persons are appropriate for measuring constructs that are themselves subjective states of the focal person's belief systems, the two are best measured directly using self-report'. However, self-report data is known to result in respondents giving socially desirable responses (Randall, 1990).

Social desirability

The tendency to give socially desirable responses is well known in social research (Moorman & Podsakoff, 1982). Socially desirable responses from this heterogeneous sample of managers had the potential to increase the potential bias of the sample provided this trend was uniform. There was unlikely to be a problem interpreting the correlations involving the scale, unless the correlations were attenuated due to the restricted variance in scale scores (Podsakoff & Organ, 1986). Social desirability goes beyond merely adding bias to responses (Podsakoff & Organ, 1986). Nevertheless, the responses received indicated a spread of opinions that were forthright, as indicated by written comments about the questionnaires returned. As mentioned earlier, participation in the study was voluntary; organisations, then managers, self-selected into the study.

Performance rating errors

Common performance rating errors (e.g., central tendency, halo effect, harshness, extreme bias and leniency error) were minimised in the design of the questionnaire and administration of the instrument, as recommended by Noe et al. (1994). As Wright and Staw (1999a: 18) noted 'seldom is behaviour objectively measured, and even when it is, the measures may not tap what actually contributes to organisational effectiveness'. Overall performance ratings are likely to be influenced by ratees' perceptions (i.e., supervisor ratings) of their contextual performance. Generally, people tend to like positive people. More positive evaluations may be given to happy managers who exhibit PA because they are more pleasant to be around. The basic thesis of this study would be negated if halo effects were the means by which happy managers receive higher ratings. A more constrained definition of halo effects may explain how interpersonal attraction may influence performance assessments.

Possibly, the contextual performance antecedent is indicative of superiors' appreciation of 'lack of complaining'. In a laboratory study of the relationship between effect and performance, Staw and Barsade (1993) excluded a halo explanation. A covariation of affect and ratings of performance was also not found in a field study by Wright and Staw (1999a: 18), whose 'results did not show uniform relationships between all forms of affect and rated performance, a highly idiosyncratic halo effect would be necessary to account for the findings'.

Qualitative research

This study relied exclusively on quantitative research methodology. Qualitative information would have provided a valuable source of additional information for verifying findings from the data collected. This would have assisted in explaining relationships that are not readily accessible to quantitative methods. Subtle determinants of managers' performance and affective wellbeing and intrinsic job satisfaction are documented when compared to the quantitative data.

Qualitative research techniques, such as focus groups and structured interviews, are well suited for the purpose of gaining a deeper understanding of affective wellbeing and intrinsic job satisfaction. In-depth interviews would confirm and explain the causality of the link between affective wellbeing and performance, as exhibited by high levels of competence and aspiration.

Summary on methodological limitations

This section identified the limitations in the methodology used in this study. Alternative methodologies that could have been used in the study but were impractical due to organisation constraints.

ETHICAL CONSIDERATIONS

The study complied with all requirements for conducting ethical research, as stipulated by The University of Western Australia's Human Rights Committee. Participation in the study by managers was voluntary. All organisations involved were aware of the sensitive nature of the research. Each participating organisation agreed to be involved in the study, some of them on the condition that they would not be explicitly identified in published material related to the study. The University of Western Australia's Human Rights Committee only permits information gathered about managers to be released to a third party if the express written permission is obtained from the managers participating in the study. Such permission was not a condition of managers being involved in the study. Individual level reports of managers' affective wellbeing, intrinsic job satisfaction or performance were not made available to any third party.

Forthright responses to the questionnaires were achieved by establishing a data collection process that was shown to treat all responses in the strictest confidence. Only the researchers had access to the completed questionnaires. Queries or concerns regarding the study were directed to the researchers via telephone or email. Results were only reported to the organisations at the aggregate level to ensure the privacy and integrity of the data collected.

An Information Sheet and Consent Form were distributed to all participants in the study, as required by The University of Western Australia's Human Rights Committee. This accountability extended to ensuring the data was accurately keyed and anomalies (such as missing data) were appropriately dealt with. None of the organisations involved in the study requested information about individuals at any time during or after the study. An Interim Industry Report on the Job Scope, Psychological Wellbeing and Performance of Managers (Hosie, 2000) was distributed to organisations that participated in the study. Again, it was only reported at the aggregate level so no individual could be identified.

SUMMARY AND CONCLUSION

This chapter explained the methodology used by justifying the choice of research methodology, including a rationale for the methods employed to collect and analyse the data related to the research questions and hypotheses posed. Procedures used for data collection were outlined. Details of the instruments used were given. An Expert Review and Pilot of the instrument were undertaken. An identical questionnaire was used by all respondents involved in the study.

Data were collected once through cross-sectional questionnaires, the predominant methodological approach used to investigate the links between affective wellbeing, intrinsic job satisfaction and managers' performance. The properties of the instruments used met acceptable standards for measuring state and trait affective wellbeing and managers' performance. Self-report data from the sample was used to measure managers' affective wellbeing and intrinsic job satisfaction. Self and superiors' appraisals were used to gauge managers' performance.

Job-related affective wellbeing and intrinsic job satisfaction items were obtained from published scales. There were no validated measures of managers' performance identified that were suitable for use in this study. Managers' contextual and task performance items were developed from the literature. Methods used to analyse the data were detailed. Methodological issues were examined, such as using multisource, self-report ratings and the presence of common method variance. Details were given of the techniques used to analyse the data in order to test the hypotheses and Partial Model was used to reduce response bias as described.

Uniqueness of this study was assured by using a newly developed measure of managers' performance in a range of organisations. A systematic and statistically robust methodology, using EFA and CFA will be adopted in this study to validate the managers' performance Measurement Model. Another distinctive contribution to the field is the use of Canonical Correlation and Standard Multiple Regression to analyse the multifarious relationships between managers' affective wellbeing, intrinsic job satisfaction and their contextual and task performance.

The next chapter describes the results obtained from the analyses of the data used to test the hypotheses for the Measurement Model.

6. Measuring managers' performance

> Because job performance is the most widely studied criterion variable in the organizational behaviour and human resource management literatures ... the construct validity of performance measures is critical.
> (Bommer et al., 1995: 587)

INTRODUCTION

This chapter begins with a description of the statistics on the sample and verifies the reliability of existing affective wellbeing and intrinsic job satisfaction instruments. Evidence is provided to reconfirm the reliability of the affective wellbeing and intrinsic job satisfaction instruments on this sample. A Measurement Model was developed from measures of managers' performance using the data collected. The model was calibrated before testing. A detailed explanation of the development of the managers' performance instrument is then given. Methodological hypotheses for managers' performance are developed and tested. Factor analyses on the process associated with managers' performance is specified. Testing of the Measurement Model is described in detail, including Confirmatory Factor Analysis (CFA), multigroup analyses, and the biasing effect of method.

SAMPLE CHARACTERISTICS

This section provides statistical details of the sample. Figure 6.1 shows the response rate by organisational type. In total, 502 questionnaires were returned of the 1,552 distributed. The total response rate (32%) consisted of a total of 400 useable questionnaires which included 200 'matched pairs'.

Matched pair refer to returned questionnaires with managers' self-reports and the corresponding superiors' assessment on managers' performance (i.e., n = 200 managers and n = 200 superiors).

Pair congruence consisted of a subset of 125 corresponding pairs, where superiors contributed only *one* performance rating to the study. This random elimination of multiple ratings by superiors, to control for systematic error in our main analysis, resulted in a reduction of 75 matched pair questionnaires of the total superiors' ratings made available to the study.

Unmatched (n = 81) refers to managers' self-report without the corresponding assessment from their superiors. A further 21 questionnaires were also discarded due to missing data.

Analysis of data was undertaken using the Statistical Package for Social Sciences (SPSS) program, version 10.1 and the EQS program, version 5.5. EQS is a Structural Equation Modelling software package that handles non-normally distributed data (Ullman, 1996).

Multisample

The multisample (all responses for the questionnaire) was formed by merging the responses from the 19 primary organisations involved in the study. Responses from each organisation's managers were combined to avoid the statistical problems inherent when analysing small samples, as indicated in Chapter 5. There are methodological problems in cross validating samples using small individual organisational samples. Empirical studies about affective wellbeing, intrinsic job satisfaction and performance to date have tended to be conducted with samples drawn from a similar population.

In contrast, the 19 organisations involved in this study were demographically diverse, including managers from a variety of job classifications. This diverse source of respondents assisted in establishing the generalizability of the measurement instrument, and contributed to the existing empirical base of what constitutes managers' performance. Large and independent samples are required when testing for invariance. This requirement was especially relevant in this study, because the model had a large number of variables. Inevitably, combining similar constructs with too many manifest variables often results in the failure to identify a good-fitting model (Bentler & Chou, 1987).

Representativeness

The entire sample (N = 481), including 'unmatched' questionnaires ('deleted pairs'), refers to managers' self-report without the corresponding assessment from their superiors. Variables that had no matched ratings from superiors were not analysed.

As mentioned in Chapter 5, subsample 1 (matched pairs, n = 200) was used to report the demographics of the data, for the EFA and the CFA. Subsample 1 was also used to validate and cross validate the sample to purify managers' performance measures.

Subsample 2 (pair congruence, n = 125) was used for the MTMM analysis of superiors' and managers' self-ratings on performance. Subsample 2 was also used to link superiors' ratings of managers' performance with the corresponding self-report of managers' affective wellbeing and intrinsic job satisfaction, for the Canonical Correlations and Standard Multiple Regression analysis (see Tables 7.1–7.5).

Some superiors made multiple ratings of managers' performance, typically rating two or three managers, and sometimes up to five. Basing the statistical analysis only on subsample 1 (i.e., superiors' ratings on more than one manager) would have increased the possibility of systematic rating bias. Cases with multiple ratings by superiors of managers' performance were not included in the CFA, Canonical Correlation, and Standard Multiple Regression analysis. For the following analyses variables were deleted that had no matched ratings from superiors, or when there were multiple ratings by superiors of managers' performance. When superiors provided multiple ratings on managers' performance their ratings were not used. A one-to-one congruence (one superior rating one manager) resulted in the pair congruence subsample 2 being reduced to 125 cases.

Nominal information

Table 6.1 indicates the representatives of the cohort of Western Australian and Australian managers and administrators.

Table 6.1   Comparison of the distribution of managers in Western Australia and Australia population with the sample

Population managers	25–34 age bracket Males	25–34 age bracket Females	35–54 age bracket Males	35–54 age bracket Females	55+ age bracket Males	55+ age bracket Females	Total by gender Males	Total by gender Females
WA [1]	9,406	3,896	31,361	11,463	9,104	3,158	49,871	18,517
WA %	13.75%	5.70%	45.86%	16.76%	13.31%	4.62%	72.92%	27.08%
Aust. [1]	93,657	43,109	306,539	109,977	94,554	31,283	494,750	184,369
Aust. %	13.79%	6.35%	45.14%	16.19%	13.92%	4.61%	72.85%	27.15%
Sample [2]	21	12	181	45	19	3	221	60
Sample % [2]	7.47%	4.27%	64.41%	16.01%	6.76%	1.07%	78.65%	21.35%
Sample % WA	0.223%	0.308%	0.577%	0.393%	0.209%	0.095%	0.443%	0.324%
Sample % Aust.	0.022%	0.028%	0.059%	0.041%	0.020%	0.010%	0.045%	0.033%

Note: Based on total sample of managers' self-report ($N = 281$).

---

[1] 'WA' (Western Australia) and 'Aust' (Australia) uses the Australian Bureau of Statistics (1996) data.
[2] 'Sample' and 'Sample %' refer to the useable questionnaires.

Australian managers constituted the population for this study. Western Australian private, public and third sector managers were the target population. Consistent with the sample, the respondents resembled a purposive sample (Zikmund, 2002). The sample represented .39% of the estimated 71,383 managers in Western Australia and .04% of Australian managers (Australian Bureau of Statistics, 1996). These figures may overestimate the number of Australian managers because 'administrators' are categorised with 'managers', though they may not necessarily perform managerial roles.

Table 6.1 provides a comparison on the research sample of managers used with the total population of managers in Western Australia (WA) and Australia (Aust.). These figures are based on Australian Bureau of Statistics (1996) data grouped by age bracket. The data presented covers the total number of people in each category, by gender and age bracket as well as totals for gender. These statistics were converted into percentages of the WA, Australia and research sample to permit comparison of the proportions represented in each category.

There were some differences between the research sample and the WA and Australian populations of managers. In the research group there were a larger percentage of respondents in the male, 35–54 age bracket (64% compared to 45% for both WA and Australia). There is a corresponding lower male representation in the other two age brackets. The research sample, compared to WA and Australia, has a lower percentage of females overall and specifically for the 25–34 and 55+ age brackets. However, in the 35–54 bracket females are similar to the WA and Australian populations. The age bracket 35–54 is by far the largest with 80% of the total research sample in this bracket, compare to 62% for the WA and Australian population.

Biographical and demographic information

Minimal differences were found in the demographics of managers across the subsamples. Each had very similar proportions of managers within each biodata category. Table 6.3 provides the demographics relating to gender and level of seniority of the congruence sample. The mean age of 44.69 years overall and the proportion of male (79%) to female (21%) managers reflected the gender ratios (4:1) of the managerial workforce in Australia and Western Australia.

Tenure and age criteria indicates that the profile of managers was mid-career, with a mean of 9.57 years of managerial work experience and 6.03 years with a particular organisation, including 11.60 years working for this organisation. Reichers (1986) conceived of career stages as being less than 5 years experience for early career, to 15 years experience for mid career, and more than 15 years experience as late career. According to Reichers (1986), these managers may be categorised as mid career, which explained bias of the age distribution of respondents as shown in Table 6.1.

Figure 6.1   Organisation type participating in the study

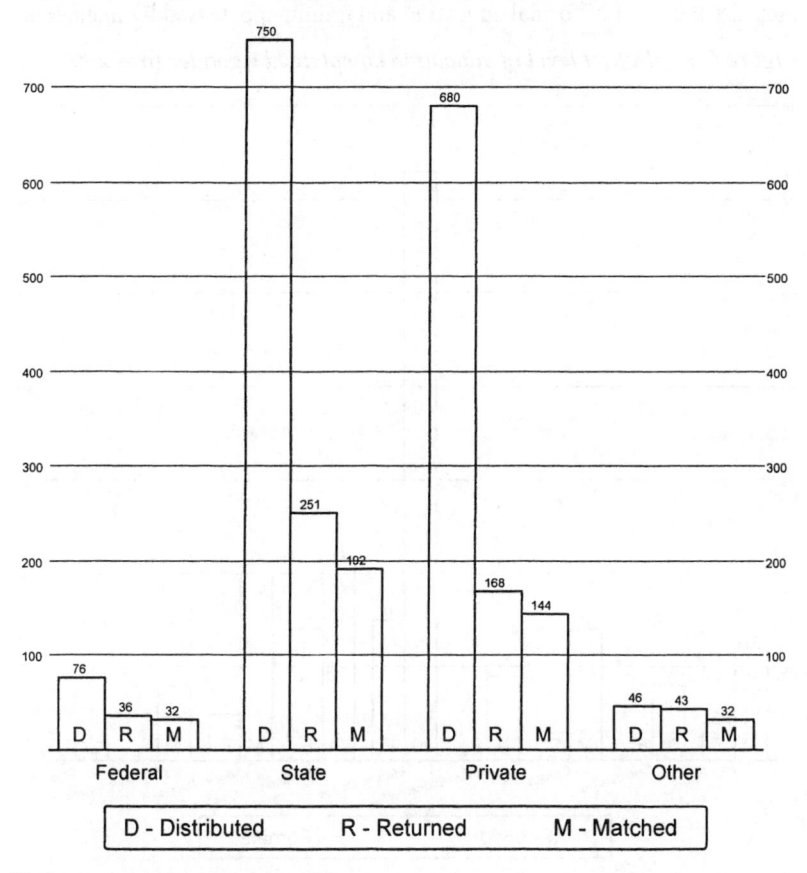

Sector	D - Distributed	R - Returned	M - Matched
Federal	76	36	32
State	750	251	192
Private	680	168	144
Other	46	43	32

Tenure, experience and sector

Organisations were selected to participate in this study from a variety of industries to ensure representation from a range of managerial jobs. The subsample 1 included 56.7% of responses from the public sector, 41.3% from the private sector and 2.0% from the third sector. Average hours worked per week were reported as 47.26, which is just slightly lower than the 50 hours or more per week Australian middle managers reported regularly working over the past 10 years (The West Australian, 2001: 8).

Educational qualifications

Standardised nomenclature was used to describe the training and education of those managers participating in the study. Australian Statistical Classification of Occupations (McLennan, 1997) terminology was used to measure the level of formal education and training possessed by managers.

Figure 6.2 Highest level of education completed by gender (n = 200)

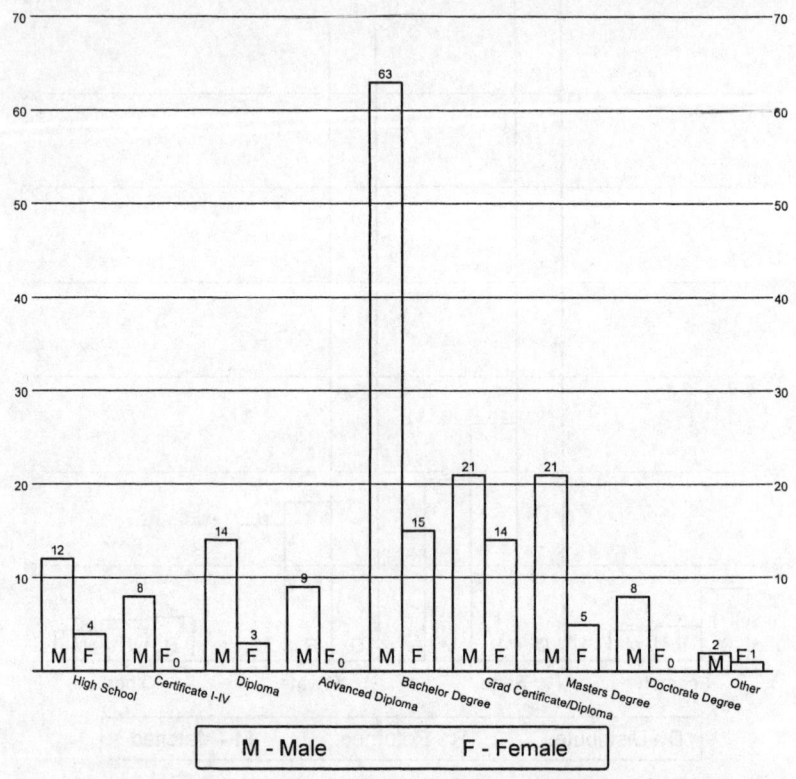

From Figure 6.3 it will be apparent that the 'highest educational level attained' ranged from: 'High school' (8.0%); 'Certificate 1–1V' (4.0%); 'Diploma' (8.5%); 'Advanced Diploma' (4.5%); 'Bachelor Degree' (39.3%); 'Graduate Certificate/Diploma' (17.4%); 'Masters Degree' (12.9%); to 'Doctorate Degree' (4.0%) and 'Other' (1.5%). The modal qualification was a Bachelor degree. A substantial percentage of managers (34.5%) reported possessing a postgraduate qualification (Graduate Certificate, Graduate Diploma, Masters/Doctorate) indicating the cohort had undertaken considerable formal education.

Seniority

Figure 6.3 shows the sectors managers were employed in and their current level of responsibility. It is apparent that females were under-represented at executive and senior levels of management, as reflected in Australian and Western Australian ABS statistics (see Table 6.1).

Figure 6.3 Gender and position demographics (n = 200)

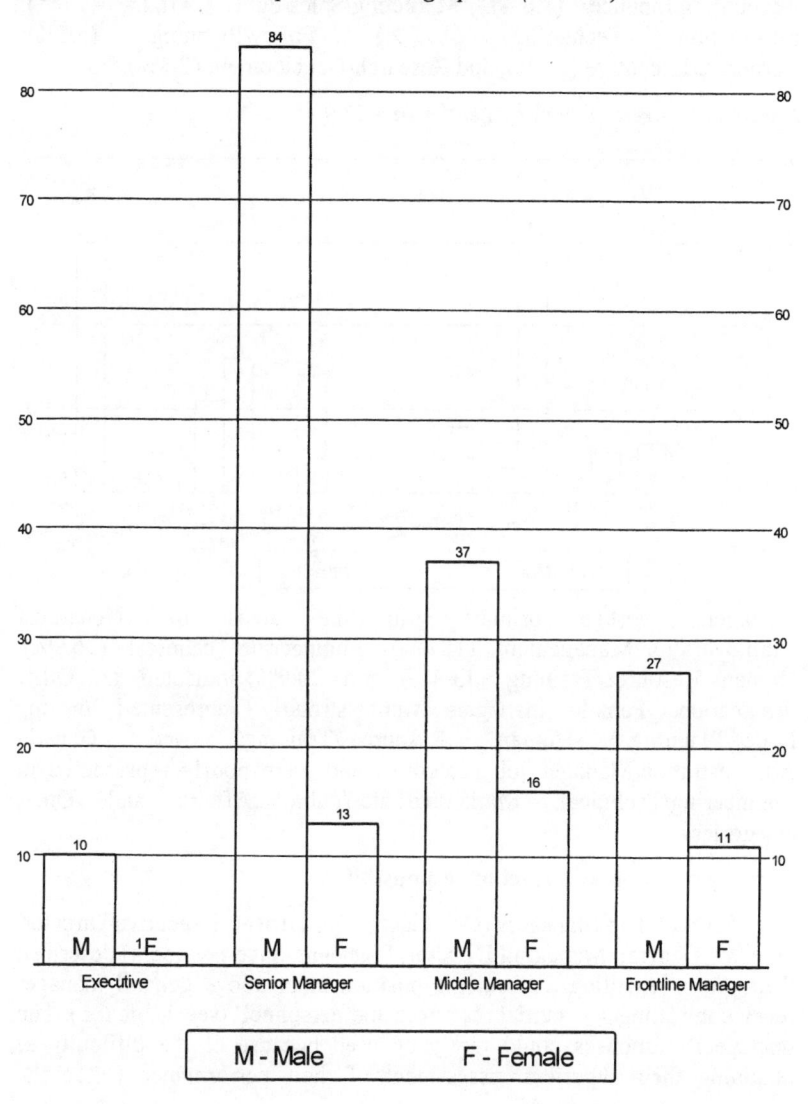

	Executive	Senior Manager	Middle Manager	Frontline Manager
M	10	84	37	27
F	1	13	16	11

M - Male   F - Female

Areas of work

Figure 6.4 shows that managers responding to the survey worked primarily in the four areas of: General Administration/Manager (18.4%), Engineering/Technical (16.9%); and Human Resources/Training (13.4%), while Other (20.9%) accounted for 69% of the job categories. The remaining 31% of jobs were represented by the categories of: Accounting/Finance (8.0%), Marketing/Sales/Pubic Affairs (7.0%); Information Technology (5.0%); Policy/Planning (5.5%); Corporate/Executive (2.0%); and Research/Development (2.5%).

Figure 6.4   Area of work by gender (n = 200)

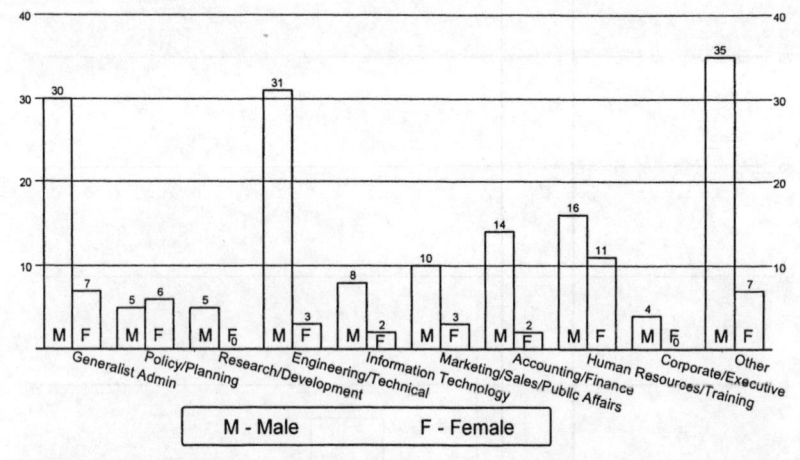

Managers worked primarily in the areas of: Generalist Administration/Management (18.4%), Engineering/Technical (16.9%), Human Resource/Training (13.4%) and 20.9% indicated an Other designation. Female managers were strongly represented in the Policy/Planning, Human Resources/Training, and General Administration/Manager job categories and were poorly represented in Engineering/Technical, Marketing/Sales/Pubic Affairs and Other categories.

Sector worked in and level of responsibility

Only 5.5% of Top Managers (Chief Executive Officer, Executive Director, Director-General, Managing Director, President, Vice-President) described their job as entailing a 'Strategic position at or above general manager level, controlling substantial resources and personnel' (see Table 6.5). Top managers' responses could rarely be used because of the difficulty of obtaining their superiors' assessment of their performance (often the

Chairperson or Government Minister).

A large proportion of managers (48.78%) reported being in the Senior Manager (Upper Middle Manager) category, described in the questionnaire as having a 'Major responsibility at a senior level for implementation, which may require control of resources and/or personnel'. A much smaller percentage (26.64%) of respondents reported being Middle Managers (Superintendent), described in the questionnaire as being 'Above direct supervision of employees and below department, function or area responsibility'. Senior and Middle Manager categories more realistically represented by the profile a 'Middle Manager' (ABS, 1996). When combined, these groups accounted for 75.20% of the sample as indicated in figure 6.5.

Figure 6.5   Employment sector and level of responsibility (n = 200)

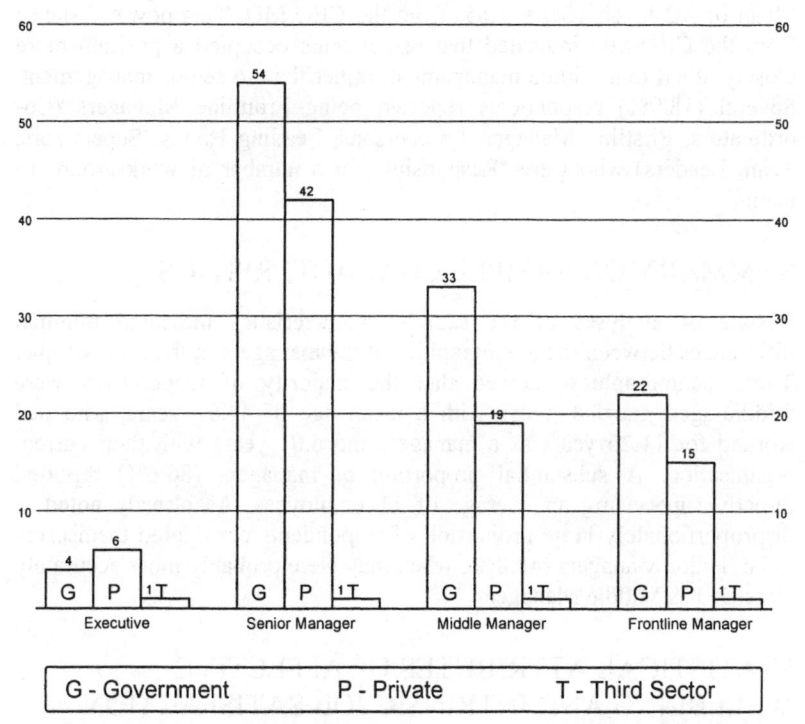

	Executive	Senior Manager	Middle Manager	Frontline Manager
G - Government	4	54	33	22
P - Private	6	42	19	15
T - Third Sector	1	1	1	1

An unexpectedly high percentage of managers (48.80%) indicated they undertook a Senior Manager's level of job responsibility. Most managers (88.6%) reported directly supervising the work of, on average, 11.39 employees, with a minority (11.4%) indicating they did not directly supervise the work of others.

This may be partly attributed to the use of the ASCO (ABS, 1996) that defined Superintendent as a subset of the Middle Manager category, contributing to a disproportionate number of managers rating themselves as Senior Managers, when their work titles and respective levels indicated they belonged to the Middle Manager category. Superintendent is a job title commonly used to describe Frontline Managers. Respondents may have considered this an inappropriate way of describing their position ('title inflation') within their organisation and, as a consequence, self-selected up into the Senior Manager category.

Another possible explanation may be that respondents over-estimated their level of seniority within their respective organisations. This view was reinforced by reference to the organisational classification levels reported; 'How many levels are you from the CEO/MD of your organisation?' Respondents who reported being Senior Managers indicated they were a Mean of 3.2 levels (SD = 1.65) from the CEO/MD. This power distance from the CEO/MD indicated that respondents occupied a position more closely allied to a middle management, rather than to senior management. Several (18.9%) respondents reported being Frontline Managers (Co-ordinators, Firstline Manager, Forepersons, Leading Hands, Supervisors, Team Leaders) who were 'Responsible for a number of work-groups or teams'.

SUMMARY ON SAMPLE CHARACTERISTICS

Results of analyses of the sample characteristics indicated minimal differences between the demographics of the managers in the multisample. These demographics showed that the majority of respondents were middle-aged married males with a mean age of 44.67 years, who had worked for 11.26 years as a manager, and 6.01 years with their current organisation. A substantial proportion of managers (86.6%) reported directly supervising an average of 11 employees. As already noted, a disproportionately large proportion of respondents considered themselves to be Senior Managers (48.8%), when they were probably more accurately classified as Middle Managers.

STATISTICAL ATTRIBUTES OF AFFECTIVE WELLBEING AND INTRINSIC JOB SATISFACTION SCALES

As discussed in the previous Methodology Chapter 5, two affective wellbeing and intrinsic job satisfaction scales were compared and evaluated before selecting those suitable for multivariate analysis. Both of these scales were suitable for measuring managers' affective wellbeing in relation to their contextual and task performance. In particular, the scales were more theoretically congruent with the notion of happiness.

The following scales were used to measure and analyse managers' affective wellbeing:

- 12–item Four Factor Model of Job-related Affective Wellbeing (Sevastos, 1996); and
- 20–item PANAS (Watson & Clark, 1984).

The IV (independent variable) scales (affective wellbeing and intrinsic job satisfaction) used were robust as they have been developed and replicated with large samples and are widely published. The affective wellbeing scales were not altered because the properties of these scales had already been established. Nevertheless, the psychometric properties of the scales were still pertinent. Properties of the scales are reported to ensure that the measures are within statistically acceptable criteria.

Table 6.2 provides a summary of affective wellbeing and intrinsic job satisfaction data, including alpha coefficients.

Table 6.2   Alpha coefficients and items for wellbeing scales and subscales (n = 200)

Construct	Subscales	Items	Variable Code	α
Trait Affectivity	Positive Affect	10	1,3,5,9,10,12,14,16,17,19	.89
	Negative Affect	10	2,4,6,7,8,11,13,15,18,20	.87
Job-related Affective Wellbeing	Enthusiasm	3	25,25,30	.90
	Depression	3	21,29,32	.83
	Anxiety	3	23,26,28	.80
	Relaxation	3	22,27,31	.84
Job Satisfaction	Intrinsic Job Satisfaction	7	33–39	.85

In Table 6.2 all the alpha coefficients for affective wellbeing and intrinsic job satisfaction were well above the recommended threshold of .70 (Nunnally, 1978), ranging from .80– 90.

Means, standard deviations and correlations

Table 6.3 provides the abbreviations used for affective wellbeing and intrinsic job satisfaction variables.

Table 6.3 Affective wellbeing and intrinsic job satisfaction abbreviations

Abbreviation	Trait Affectivity, Wellbeing, & Intrinsic Job Satisfaction
PA	Positive Affect
NA	Negative Affect
DEPRESS	Depression
ENTHUS	Enthusiasm
ANXIETY	Anxiety
RELAX	Relaxation
INTJS	Intrinsic Job Satisfaction

Table 6.4 gives the managers' self-report on range, means and standard deviations for affective wellbeing and intrinsic job satisfaction variables for subsample 1 (n = 200).

Table 6.4 Managers' self-report on means and standard deviations for affective wellbeing and intrinsic job satisfaction variables (Subsample 1, n = 200)

Variable	N	Minimum	Maximum	Mean	Std. Deviation
PA	200	1.18	4.91	3.3186	.6953
NA	200	1.00	3.92	1.6660	.4775
DEPRESS	200	1.00	5.33	1.7550	.7911
ENTHUS	200	1.67	6.00	4.0633	1.0887
ANXIETY	200	1.00	5.33	2.6183	.8410
RELAX	200	1.00	5.33	2.6983	1.1453
INTJS	200	1.43	5.00	3.9021	.6802

Table 6.5 gives the managers' self-report on range, means and standard deviations for affective wellbeing and intrinsic job satisfaction variables for subsample 2 (n = 125). The possible range of responses for Table 6.5 was: 1–5 for PA and NA, 1–6 for Depression, Enthusiasm, Anxiety and Relaxation, and 1–5 for Intrinsic Job Satisfaction.

The discrepancy between the subsamples in Table 6.4 and Table 6.5 is attributable to the completeness of the superiors' ratings of managers' performance. For subsample 1 (n = 200), some superiors' rated the performance of more than one manager, which potentially biased the data. For subsample 2 (n = 125), only one rating by superiors of a manager's performance was congruent with managers' self-ratings of affective wellbeing and intrinsic job satisfaction.

Table 6.5 Managers' self-report on means and standard deviations for affective wellbeing and intrinsic job satisfaction variables (Subsample 2, n = 125)

	N	Minimum	Maximum	Mean	Std. Deviation
PA	125	1.18	4.73	3.3047	.6782
NA	125	1.00	3.92	1.6782	.5128
DEPRESS	125	1.00	5.33	1.7600	.8377
ENTHUS	125	1.67	6.00	4.0427	1.0438
ANXIETY	125	1.00	5.33	2.6107	.8282
RELAX	125	1.00	5.33	2.7600	1.1790
INTJS	125	1.43	5.00	3.9131	.6783

Subsample 2 data was included in the Canonical Correlation and Standard Multiple Regression analysis (see Chapter 4). Table 6.6 provides the means, standard deviations and Pearson intercorrelations for the affective wellbeing and intrinsic job satisfaction variables for subsample 2.

Table 6.6 Pearson intercorrelations for affective wellbeing and intrinsic job satisfaction items (n = 125)

Variable	Mean	SD	1	2	3	4	5	6	7
1. PA	3.30	.68	.89						
2. NA	1.68	.51	-.36	.88					
3. Depress	1.76	.84	-.53	.60	.85				
4. Enthus	4.04	1.04	.71	-.28	-.57	.90			
5. Anxiety	2.61	.83	-.41	.54	.56	-.37	.80		
6. Relax	2.76	1.18	.30	-.31	-.39	.51	-.44	.86	
7. IntJs	3.91	.68	.43	-.20	-.57	.50	-.19	.11	.85

Notes: n = 125 (listwise deletion of cases). Correlations ≥ .18 are statistically significant (two-tailed tests). Coefficients in the diagonal are alpha reliabilities.

As expected, the Four Factor Model of Affective Wellbeing and PANAS were moderately correlated, and therefore contained overlapping variance. Enthusiasm was positively correlated with PA ($r = .71$), Relaxation ($r = .51$), and Intrinsic Job Satisfaction ($r = .50$), and inversely related to NA ($r = -.28$), Anxiety ($r = -.37$), and Depression ($r = -.57$). Intrinsic Job Satisfaction was positively correlated with PA ($r = .43$), and inversely associated with Depression ($r = -.57$), Anxiety ($r = -.19$), and NA ($r =

-.20). The factorial structure of Intrinsic Job Satisfaction and PANAS scales have already been established in the literature with large samples. Factor loadings are provided to verify the item loadings for PANAS scales on subsample 1 (see Table 6.7).

PANAS

Table 6.7   PANAS (n = 200)

Pattern Matrix

	Factor 1 PA	Factor 2 NA
Indicators		
1) Interested.	.78	
3) Excited.	.59	
5) Strong.	.60	
9) Enthusiastic.	.81	
10) Proud.	.63	
12) Alert.	.61	
14) Inspired.	.77	
16) Determined.	.76	
17) Attentive.	.67	
19) Active.	.53	
2) Distressed.		.53
4) Upset.		.57
6) Guilty.		.46
7) Scared.		.81
8) Hostile.		.41
11) Irritable.		.44
13) Ashamed.		.52
15) Nervous.		.71
18) Jittery.		.72
20) Afraid.		.91

Rotation converged in 7 iterations.

PANAS was used as a dispositional (personality) control of affect. PANAS has two factors that contained positive and negatively worded items. Consistent with Watson, Clark, and Tellegen's (1988) intention, all the PANAS variables had strong primary loadings on their target factors, indicating relatively pure markers of PA and NA. Table 6.7 gives the item loadings for the maximum likelihood (ML) procedure with oblimin pattern matrix loadings for PANAS. Total variance explained for PANAS was 50.61%. Loadings < .3 are not shown.

Table 6.8 gives the ML with oblimin pattern matrix loadings for the Four Factor Model of Job-related Affective Wellbeing.

Table 6.8   Four Factor Model of Job-related Affective Wellbeing (n = 200)

Pattern Matrix

	Factors			
Indicators	1 Enthusiasm	2 Anxiety	3 Depression	4 Relaxation
24) Enthusiastic.	1.026			
25) Motivated.	.873			
30) Optimistic.	.598			
26) Worried.		.772		
23) Anxious.		.764		
28) Tense.		.628		
29) Depressed.			.905	
32) Miserable.			.849	
21) Gloomy.			.389	
31) Relaxed.				.882
27) Restful.				.811
22) Calm.				.612

Rotation converged in 9 iterations.

The Four Factor Model of Job-related Affective Wellbeing scale taps the entire affect space (see Figure 2.2). The amount of variance explained was 77.91%. All items exhibited substantial loadings ≥ .5, except Gloomy (.389). Six of the 12 items loaded ≥ .80, indicating the presence of a large number of marker variables in the solution. This result further supports the four factor unipolar model of affective wellbeing.

An examination of the loading indicates that the manifest variable Enthusiastic loaded 1.026 on its target dimension (i.e., Enthusiasm). Although this result may appear anomalous, pattern matrix values slightly greater than 1.00 may be obtained when structure matrix values are very high. This happens occasionally with empirical data, since loadings are not correlations, and consequently are not limited to values of less than 1.00 (Child, 1990).

Intrinsic job satisfaction

Intrinsic job satisfaction variables were predicted to be closely aligned with affective wellbeing. As anticipated, the Intrinsic Job Satisfaction indicators exhibited a very high internal reliability ($\alpha = .85$), and loaded strongly on their target factor (see Table 6.9). Total variance accounted was 54.416%.

Table 6.9   Intrinsic Job Satisfaction (n = 200)

Factor Matrix

Indicators	Factor IntJS
33) The amount of variety in your job?	.535
34) The recognition you get for good work?	.702
35) Your chances of promotion?	.566
36) The opportunity to use your abilities?	.793
37) The attention paid to suggestions you make?	.797
38) The amount of responsibility you are given?	.757
39) The freedom to choose your own method of working?	.624

1 factor extracted. 5 iterations required.

DEVELOPMENT OF MANAGERS' PERFORMANCE MEASUREMENT INSTRUMENT

Before addressing the potential links arising from the literature between managers' affective wellbeing, intrinsic job satisfaction and job performance, it was critical to establish the structure of managers' performance. Defining and measuring managers' performance in order to devise a model that could be operationalised in other organisations was a major aim of this study. To achieve this outcome it was necessary to test the measurement properties of the managers' performance scales in different contexts.

Managers' self-reported items from the matched pairs subsample 1 (n = 200) were used to develop the EFA structure of managers' performance. Both subsamples of managers' self-report and superiors' ratings were used to confirm the Measurement Model. See Figure 6.10 for a schematic representation of managers' performance using MTMM to represent the evaluation relationships.

The factor structure of the measurement instrument was examined using EFA and CFA on data obtained from the samples. A CFA was conducted to test hypotheses in order to establish the Measurement Model for managers' performance. Applying these analyses to different samples was done to evaluate the robustness of the Measurement Model. Testing the invariance of the Measurement Model was examined using CFA to establish that the dimensionality of the performance construct was equivalent across manager and superior groups.

HYPOTHESES RELATING TO THE CONSTRUCT OF MANAGERS' PERFORMANCE

This section deals with how the methodological hypotheses, in addition to the hypotheses described in Chapter 3, were derived from the literature relating to managers' performance. These hypotheses were developed and tested in order to establish the structure, the most reliable indicators, and the shared meaning attributable to dimensions of managers' contextual and task performance. Factors need to be established to indicate the dimensions of performance. These hypotheses also tested whether the construct 'managers' performance' can be generalised across groups.

Hypothesis 1:

> Task performance and contextual performance are:
> a) distinct measures;
> b) generalizable across different groups;
>
> that is, managers' and superiors' contextual and task performance will remain invariant when compared across groups.

Superiors are likely to consider both in-role (task) and extra-role (contextual) behaviours when rating managers' performance. Contextual performance may enhance managerial performance and be positively related to the quantity and quality of managers' performance. Borman and Motowidlo (1997) have argued that the contextual performance domain is conceptually distinct from components of task performance, and so may be measured separately. Conway (1996) found support for the existence of contextual and task performance dimensions using CFA and a multitrait-multirater database. Task performance is role prescribed, while contextual performance is typically discretionary (Katz & Kahn, 1978). However, the distinction between them has yet to be directly empirically tested for managers (Motowidlo & Van Scotter, 1994). The independence of contextual and task performance needs to be distinguished to establish if both contribute independently to managers' performance. This leads to the first hypothesis of the managers' Measurement Model:

Hypothesis 2.1:

> Managers and their superiors will perceive the same dimensions of performance, in terms of:
> a) Pattern relationships;
> b) Loadings; and
> c) Covariances.

Studies of the job activities of managers by Luthans et al. (1988), revealed that traditional activities - planning, coordinating, decision-making, controlling, and monitoring performance - were rated as most important by managers. Jansen and Stoop (1997) confirmed and extended these findings. Additionally, planning and coordinating activities, as well as the non-traditional network of activities, were correlated with managerial success (Jansen & Stoop, 1997). Both studies relied solely on managers' self-report of their job activities. Perceptions of other actors, such as superiors, are important in constructing accurate ratings of managers' performance.

Bommer et al. (1995) recommended that future research address the appropriate dimensionality of employee performance. Borman and Motowidlo (1993) found superiors consistently weigh the contextual performance of subordinates approximately the same as task performance. For this proposition to hold, managers' superiors should assess managers' contextual performance as contributing the equivalent amount of variance to overall job performance as task performance. Contextual performance may be positively related to the quantity and quality of managers' performance. An association across managers' and their superiors' perceptions, on the same dimensions of contextual and task performance, needs to be established, leading to the next hypothesis.

Hypothesis 2.2:

> A multi-dimensional construct of performance will fit the data better than either a unidimenisonal construct of performance, or a two dimensional construct (contextual and task performance).

Managers' rated performance has traditionally been conceived as a unidimensional construct. Conceptualisation of the job performance domain is being expanded (Arvey & Murphy, 1998). It remains to be established if managers' performance is a multivariate construct as stated in hypothesis 2.2.

Hypothesis 3:

> Managers will rate their contextual and task performance less accurately compared to the person to whom they report (superiors).

Fundamentally, attribution error is the tendency to over-attribute behaviour to internal rather than to external causes (Heider, 1958; George & Jones, 1996). Managers are likely to attribute the behaviour of others to internal causes and their own behaviour to external causes (Jones & Nisbett, 1972; De Vader et al., 1986). In these circumstances, managers' superiors are likely to attribute good performance to environmental factors and poor performance to a person's character (George & Jones, 1996). Conversely, supervisors and peers attribute others' good performance to environmental factors and poor performance to a person's disposition (Jones & Nisbett, 1972; De Vader et al., 1986).

Warr reminded us that 'most studies of work performance have been based upon ratings by superiors or peers. These ratings tend to be rather crude, and may be subject to a number of biases' (Warr, 1987: 293). Studies that have used self-ratings of contextual performance, in conjunction with self-reports of dispositional and attitudinal variables, generally result in spuriously high correlations amongst performance variables that are confounded by common method variance (Organ & Ryan, 1995). Supervisory ratings of job performance neglect to report correlations among self-raters (e.g., Barrick & Mount, 1991; Judge et al., 2001).

Crampton and Wagner (1994) have argued that inflated ratings caused by self-report varies according to the domain of research - an issue that warrants empirical testing and verification in the case of managers' contextual performance. The veracity of managers' ratings of contextual and task performance have yet to be empirically demonstrated. It is still to be established if contextual performance is best measured by other or self-ratings (Organ & Ryan, 1995). A meta-analysis by Bommer et al. (1995) concluded that objective and subjective measures of employees' performance should not be used interchangeably.

Based on this evidence a multitrait-multimethod (MTMM) analysis will test hypothesis 3, and will help establish whether there is evidence of methods effects and response bias. MTMM is a technique for testing the construct validity of hypotheses using multiple traits and multiple methods (Byrne, 1994b). Construct validity of managers' ratings on contextual and task performance are established by MTMM on the evidence of convergent validity, methods effects, and discriminant validity (Campbell & Fiske, 1959; Byrne, 1994b).

EXPLORATORY FACTOR ANALYSES OF MANAGERS' PERFORMANCE

This section reports on the results obtained from a series of exploratory factor analyses (EFA) undertaken to determine the acceptable measures for the hypothesised model of managers' performance. EFA was used to indicate the most important dimensions of managers' performance. Rated performance has previously been conceived of as a unidimensional construct. This section tests whether there were more dimensions to performance. Contextual and task dimensions were assumed to constitute managers' performance. The initial factor structure was determined by the managers' self-report on performance using the total sample (n = 200).

Multiple and redundant scales in multivariate analysis increases the potential for error in the data, especially when using a small sample. There was a need to undertake theoretical exclusion and empirical data reduction of selected scales. Raghunathan's (1995: 975) advice was adopted as the guiding principle for examining the scale properties, so the 'Rationale for the retention and deletion of variables was clearly linked both theoretically and empirically'. The most appropriate scales are both theoretically and empirically comparable. Only the scales and variables needed to test the model were retained.

Variables with factor loadings $\leq .40$ were eliminated to ensure each particular variable was a pure representation of the construct underlying each factor, unless there was a compelling theoretical reason for retaining the variable. There is a tendency to over interpret factor loadings below .40 (Nunnally, 1978). The newly developed contextual and task performance scales were deemed to be significant if the items loaded $\geq .50$, did not cross load $\geq .30$, and had a communality of .45. These criteria were used as guidelines for eliminating variables that did not contribute adequate variance to the solution, unless they were theoretically congruent with the study. Indicators that met all of these criteria were retained.

Statistical assumptions for performance measurement scales

Different statistical assumptions were applied to contextual and task performance scales, due to the theoretical structure of the factors, the source of variables, and the ratio of variables-to-cases. Pure measures were essential to test whether contextual and task performance factors were distinct dimensions. A first-order factor analysis was used to explain the majority of variance. An a priori 5–factor model was predicted for the 22–

indicators comprising the contextual performance scale, and 75–indicators were predicted for the task performance scale. Abbreviated phrases for each dimension are given in Appendix 1.

An EFA was also used to explain and test the logical and statistical properties of the managers' performance data. This established the independence of the managers' performance measures, which contained overlapping and redundant variables. The factor analysis established which variables loaded strongly on single factors and the reliability of observed variables was confirmed, using measures such as communalities and loadings. Indicators with the highest loading were retained. Variables that cross-loaded with measures intended to be distinctive were removed.

Tabachnick and Fidell (2001) and Hair et al. (1995) both considered that a ratio of 10 cases per factor was acceptable. As noted earlier, at least three variables are needed per dimension to define a construct (although Bollen, 1989b has suggested that two indicators were sufficient for this purpose) to be retained for CFA analysis. The most parsimonious solution, consistent with the theoretical taxonomy, was sought for contextual and task performance.

Maximum Likelihood (ML) with oblimin rotation was used to establish the factor structure and to decide which variables to eliminate. 'Scale trimming' was used judiciously to reduce the number of factors that were intended to be distinct. An oblique rotation was considered appropriate because the factor correlation matrix indicated a moderate correlation between the first five factors. Over 50% of total variance is usually accounted for by the first four components of a factor solution (Hair et al., 1995; Tabachnick & Fidell, 2001). EFA has a tendency to produce too many dimensions for a clear congruence with predicted definitions and constructs. Invariably, the last factors extracted do not explain enough variance to be useful. These variables are the least representative of the domain(s) of interest. To identify whether variables cross-loaded on other factors, a $\geq .30$ cut-off was used for the correlation matrix to produce relatively pure indicators. Variables that significantly cross-loaded ($\leq .30$) on other factors were eliminated. For this type of study, Hair et al. (1995) recommended the construct reliability of variables loading should exceed .70 to extract a total value of variance .50 for each construct.

Bartlett's test of sphericity was used to determine whether the correlation matrix differed from the identity matrix (Bartlett, 1950). All significant values were $> .05$. Bartlett's test of sphericity is recommended at the lower bound of a matrix because it is sensitive and highly dependent on sample size (Tabachnick & Fidell, 2001). A more sophisticated test of factorability, the Kaiser-Meyer-Olkin measure, was used to determine sampling adequacy (Tabachnick & Fidell, 1996). A Kaiser-Meyer-Olkin measure of > .6 ensured factorability. Both contextual and task performance scales met this value requirement.

Communalities were calculated to measure how much variation in one variable could be explained by variation in all other variables included in the analysis. Variables with communalities < .5 usually do not provide sufficient explanation of the variance, and were mostly excluded from further analysis. Low communalities (≤ .30) suggest that a variable may not have enough in common with any of the other variables and should be deleted from the analysis (Tabachnick & Fidell, 1996; Holmes-Smith, 1998). All variables exceeded a communality of .30, suggesting that none of the variables should be eliminated using this technique.

After the number of factors and associated loadings were identified, it was determined whether the scales were related to each other in order to establish the factorability of the correlation matrix. The correlation matrix exceeded correlation coefficients of .32 (Kim & Mueller, 1978b; 1978a; Kline, 1994) in both correlation matrices, which suggested that some of the variables may be useable in a factor analysis (Tabachnick & Fidell, 2001). Subsequent analyses and composite scores were calculated from the variables for each factor (Hair et al., 1995).

Contextual performance (EFA)

Using eigenvalues for establishing the number of factors is most reliable with the number of items between 2–50 (Hair et al., 1995). With 22–indicators, the contextual performance scale was expected to produce a reliable number of factors. When developing new univariate subscales, Hair et al. (1995) recommended using a minimum of two indicators for established scales and 3–5 indicators for untested scales. Contextual performance had 22–indicators to 281 cases for a ratio of approximately 1:13, exceeding the recommended 1:10 ratio (Hair et al., 1995). Contextual performance variables were predicted to indicate accurate eigenvalues, because these indicators were within the range of 20–55 indicators, and had already been used in published studies. In this situation, removing too many indicators from the factor matrix would have resulted in a reduction in the alpha coefficient of the scale.

A small sample is best analysed by reducing the number of indicators. Items were compared to establish those indicators that contributed to parsimony, possessed a simple structure, and were consistent with the predictions from which the scale was developed (Borman & Motowidlo, 1997). Factor loadings of ≥.5 were acceptable for contextual performance, as they were based on indicators derived from previous studies.

Inspection of the scree plot (Figure 6.7) and pattern matrix (Table 6.10) indicated the a priori five factor structure from the initial iteration of the variables consistent with literature on contextual performance. Five factors were indicated in the initial factor matrix rotation. Twelve of the indicators loaded unidimensionally on the predicted subscales. Ten of the 22 indicators exhibited low or complex loadings on the predicted factors. Indicators were progressively deleted until the most parsimonious solution was achieved that explained the most amount of variance consistent with the predicted structure.

Competing factor structures were examined, but none accounted for more variance, or resulted in higher subscale alphas or loadings of indicator on factors, than the solution given in Table 6.10. Grouping suggested by Borman and Motowidlo's (1997) taxonomy was maintained, with the exception of the Volunteering factor (not formally part of own job) which failed to form a distinct factor.

Four indicators that loaded on the Volunteering factor and two on the Helping factor were deleted, because their factor loadings failed to attain the $\geq .30$ loading required for practical significance. The slope of the plot line falls dramatically after the fourth factor and before the fifth factor is extracted, indicating the presence of four factors. A commensurate drop in total variance of initial eigenvalues (from 1.431 to .754) was evident between factors 4–5 (see Figure 6.7).

Figure 6.6 Contextual performance: Scree plot (n = 200)

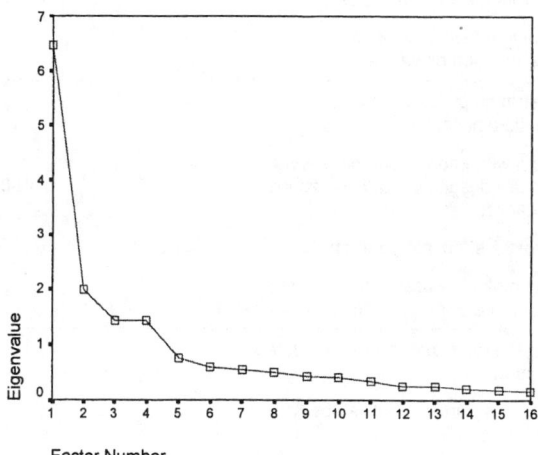

A maximum of four factors was used to avoid introducing noise into the solution. As stated earlier, each variable needed to load $\geq .5$ on each factor and with communalities of the same magnitude. All loadings exceeded .50 on each indicator (see Table 6.10), except items 50 (-.481), 55 (.489) and

256 (.384). Indicators that failed to achieve the .50 benchmark were retained for further analysis if they were theoretically closely aligned with the other items in the subscale. Refer to Table 6.10 for the ranked factor loading for indicators on contextual performance.

Table 6.10 Ranked factor loading for indicators on managers' self-ratings contextual performance (n = 200)

Indicators	1 Endorse	2 Help	3 Persist	4 Follow
58) Exhibiting a concern for organisational objectives.	.859			
57) Showing loyalty to the organisation.	.838			
60) Representing the organisation favourably to outsiders.	.755			
61) Demonstrating concern about the image of the organisation.	.698			
59) Working within the organisation to effect change.	.537			
49) Helping others who have been absent.		-.968		
48) Helping with heavy work-loads.		-.794		
50) Maintaining effective working relationships with co-workers.		-.481		
40) Demonstrating perseverance and conscientiousness.			.889	
41) Persisting with effort to complete work successfully despite difficult conditions and setbacks.			.868	
42) Putting extra effort into your job.			.588	
43) Trying to make the best of the situation, even when there are problems.			.534	
54) Obeying the rules and regulations of the organisation.				.942
53) Adhering to organisational values & policies.				.888
55) Treating organisational property with care.				.489
56) Paying attention to announcements, messages, or printed material about the organisation.				.384

Rotation converged in 11 iterations.

Table 6.11 provides a factor correlation matrix of the indicators for contextual performance.

Table 6.11 Contextual performance: Factor correlation matrix (n = 200)

Factor	1	2	3	4
1	1.000			
2	-.401	1.000		
3	.408	-.416	1.000	
4	.454	-.280	.274	1.000

Table 6.12 provides the contextual performance EFA variables and alpha coefficients.

Table 6.12 Managers' self-report contextual performance EFA data reduction by variables (n = 200)

Construct	Original Subscales	λ	α	Retained Subscales	λ	α
Persisting	40–43	4	.84	40–43	4	.84
Volunteering	44–47	4	.79	–	–	–
Helping	48–52	5	.79	48–50	3	.79
Following	53–56	4	.83	53–56	4	.83
Endorsing	57–61	5	.88	57–61	5	.88
CONTEXTUAL PERFORMANCE	40–61	22	15	40–3, 48–50, 53–56, 57–61	16	–

Note: $n = 281$. λ = number of indicators; α = alpha reliabilities.

Task performance EFA

A scale from a 75–item pool of managers' task performance was devised by the researcher from Borman and Brush's (1993) 18–dimension taxonomy of managerial performance, including subscale variables developed to measure Organisational Effectiveness and Judgement dimensions. Too many factors are invariably extracted when there is a pool of over 50 items. An initial rotation indicated there were 16 factors present in the pattern matrix. The final iteration of the Kaiser-Meyer-Olkin measure of sampling adequacy was .861, and the Bartlett test of sphericity was significant, indicating that the data were suitable for further analysis.

Modest-sized subsamples are prone to error. Comrey and Lee (1992) consider 150 cases to be adequate for solutions with high loading marker indicators. When developing new scales, it is important to obtain the 'purest' manifest variables possible. Given the large number of variables in the task performance scales, it was necessary to ascertain how the variables could be reduced to smaller underlying dimensions. Thus, only indicators with loadings of ≥ .60 were retained for further EFA item and factor reduction, unless there was a strong theoretical reason for retaining them. For the final structure, a target of .70 was the predetermined loading for each item to ensure reliable scales and a reduction of noise in data.

An iterative process was used to refine the factor structure of task performance. Considerable culling and combining of indicators was therefore necessary to achieve a postulate of parsimony (Kim & Mueller, 1978a; Burke et al., 1989). Culling improved the factor structure and loadings of indicators on factors. Only clean, high loading items that did not cross-load were retained. A scree plot indicated the existence of four factors for task performance as shown in Figure 6.8.

Figure 6.7 Scree plot indicators on the managers' self-ratings on task performance (n = 200)

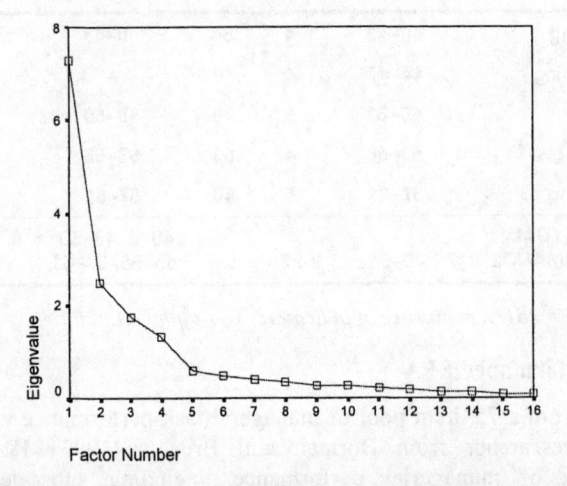

A large drop off in the scree plot line was evident after the extraction of the fourth factor. There was a commensurate drop in total variance for the initial eigenvalues (1.332% to .573%) from factor 4–5. Subsequent iterations refined the solution into four meaningful factors represented by 16 high loading indicators. These indicators were intended to be formed into composite scores which exceeded an average of .70. Five task performance items were slightly below the .70 target but they did not reduce the composite scores below the benchmark for each factor. Four factors emerged from the final iteration: Monitoring (4–indicators); Technical (4–indicators); Influencing (4–indicators); and Delegating (4–indicators).

Table 6.13 *Ranked factor loading for indicators on managers' self-ratings on task performance (n = 200)*

Indicators	Factor 1 Monitor	Factor 2 Tech	Factor 3 Influence	Factor 4 Delegate
118) Monitoring and overseeing appropriate use of funds within existing constraints and guidelines.	.994			
119) Monitoring and overseeing utilisation of funds.	.961			
117) Controlling budgets by allocating funds internally.	.910			
120) Controlling personnel resources.	.557			
84) Solving technical problems.		.975		
85) Applying technical expertise.		.898		
83) Providing technical advice to others in organisation.		.882		
82) Keeping technically up-to-date.		.678		
126) Persuading others in the organisation to accept your ideas and position.			.985	
127) Convincing those holding opposing or neutral opinions and promoting own positions or ideas.			.891	
125) Influencing others inside and outside of the organisation.			.803	
128) Presenting own position clearly and decisively.			.672	
122) Effectively delegating responsibility and authority.				.942
124) Delegating authority and responsibility to assist staff's professional development.				.811
121) Assigning staff duties and responsibilities consistent with their abilities as well as the organisation's needs.				.666
123) Avoiding interfering with areas of responsibility delegated to others.				.644

Rotation converged in 8 iterations.

In all, the final structure for task performance was reduced from the predicted 19 factors comprising 75–items, to a 4–factor structure with 16–indicators. Fifty-nine indicators were discarded because they failed to achieve loadings necessary to form meaningful factors. Throughout the data reduction process, each subscale was monitored to ensure optimum internal consistency.

Several high loading indicators were evident in both the contextual and task performance subsamples. There were seven high loading 'marker' variables ($\geq .80$) for contextual performance, and 11 task performance factors representing 18 high-loading indicators. This indicated that the limits to parsimony for this matrix had been reached. See Table 6.14 showing the intercorrelations among the four factors, and Table 6.13 for the ranked magnitude of loadings.

Table 6.14 Task performance: Factor correlation matrix (n = 200)

Factor	1	2	3	4
1	1.000			
2	.307	1.000		
3	.309	.554	1.000	
4	.439	.403	.513	1.000

Task performance indicators and alpha coefficients are presented in Table 6.15.

Summary on the EFA of managers' performance scales

EFA was used to empirically establish the dimensionality of the variables. Factorial independence was established as each indicator loaded highly on a single factor. Four factors and 16 indicators fitted four of the dimensions of Borman and Motowidlo's (1997) taxonomy of managers' contextual performance. Likewise, 4–factors and 16–indicators fitted 4 of the dimensions of Borman and Brush's (1993) taxonomy of managers' task performance.

Byrne (1994a: 309) concluded that all 'exploratory factor analyses (EFAs) have been technically incapable of determining and evaluating error, and were unable to suggest alternative model specifications'. Therefore, it was necessary to confirm the structure of contextual and task performance dimensions.

The next section describes the CFA process used to establish the precise structure of the contextual and task performance subscales.

Table 6.15 Managers' self-ratings on task performance: EFA data reduction by variable (n = 200)

Construct	Original Subscales	λ	α	Retained Subscales	λ	α
Planning	62–66	5	.75			
Guiding	67–69	3	.80			
Training	70–73	4	.87			
Communicating	74–77	4	.84			
Representing	78–81	4	.74			
Technical	82–85	4	.91	82–85	4	.91
Administrating	86–88	3	.84			
Maintaining	89–92	3	.84			
Coordinating	93–96	4	.80			
Deciding	97–101	5	.86			
Staffing	102–105	4	.80			
Persisting	106–108	3	.82			
Handling	109–112	4	.87			
Committing	113–116	4	.81			
Monitoring	117–120	4	.93	117–120	4	.93
Delegating	121–124	4	.84	121–124	4	.84
Influencing	125–128	4	.90	125–128	4	.90
Data	129–132	4	.90			
Contributing	133–137	5	.88			
TASK PERFORMANCE	2.23–98	75			16	

Note: n = 200, λ = number of indicators, λ = alpha reliabilities.

MODEL TESTING STRATEGY

Before the relationship between affective wellbeing, intrinsic job satisfaction and managers' performance could be tested, it was necessary to develop reliable measures of managers' performance. A multi-stage approach was used for the data analysis to permit the model fit to be evaluated from different perspectives. Byrne (1994a; 1994b) recommended using multiple criteria to account for substantive, statistical, practical and parsimonious fit of the model. A correlation between constructs must be less than one to indicate the discriminant validity of a scale (Bagozzi & Heatherton, 1994).

Assumption Testing

Outliers

Tests of univariate normal distributions were restricted to contextual and task performance variables. Multivariate outliers are cases with an unusual combination of scores on two or more variables (Hair et al., 1995; Tabachnick & Fidell, 2001). There was no evidence of outlying cases, based on the observation that all estimates for outlying cases fall approximately within the same range.

Dentrended normal plots graph the deviations of the points from a straight line. Normal probability plots and dentrended normal plots were generated for the data. Observed values were then paired with their expected values based on a normal distribution assumption in the normal probability plots. Examination of the linearity of the distribution revealed that most of the cases did not assemble around a horizontal line through zero, so a non-normal distribution was assumed (Tabachnick & Fidell, 2001).

The Lilliefors statistic was calculated (Revesz, 1979), but not the Shapiro-Wilks statistic, as the sample size exceeded 50 (Hair et al., 1995). The Lilliefors test statistic calculates the level of significance for the differences from a normal distribution and is identical to the two-sided Kolmogorov-Smirnov one-sample test (Daniel, 1990; Tabachnick & Fidell, 2001). When the level of significance is > .05, normality is assured.

Kurtosis and skewness

Managers' contextual and task performance variables were checked for unusual distribution by examining the skewness and kurtosis. Kurtosis indexes associated with the scales were evaluated to check for multivariate normality. Mardia's standardised coefficient, a multivariate kurtosis measure, was used to test for the multivariate non-normality of the performance data (Mardia, 1974). Values obtained from Mardia's standardised coefficient, 20.206 for the managers' sample and 15.959 for the superiors' sample, indicated that the data were not normally distributed. Multivariate non-normality of the data was adjusted using the Satorra-Bentler adjustment S-Bχ^2 (Satorra & Bentler, 1988). The S-Bχ^2 'incorporates a scaling correction for the χ^2 statistic when distributional assumptions are violated' (Byrne, 1994b: 293).

Satorra and Bentler's (1988) modifications to the standard goodness-of-fit T-test provided a function of distribution behaviour that more closely approximates χ^2. The scaled test statistic available in EQS, uses a simple multiplier to yield a new statistic with a mean closer to that of the reference χ^2 distribution. The S-Bχ^2 statistic provides a χ^2 distribution with associated degrees-of-freedom. Chou, Bentler, and Satorra (1991) considered that the S-Bχ^2 statistic approximates more closely the usual test statistic and performs as well as, or better than, asymptotically distribution-free methods, generally recommended for non-normal multivariate data. Sample kurtosis values are also included (Hu, Bentler, & Kano, 1992).

Multicollinearity and singularity

Contextual and task performance indicators contained similar elements, so it was important to test for multicollinearity. A high degree of multicollinearity may produce imprecision and instability in the estimation of regression coefficients (Pedhazur, 1982). Correlations exceeding .80 indicate high multicollinearity (Asher, 1983; Berry & Feldman, 1985). The variables did not highly correlate with each other and the correlation coefficients did not exceed .80, suggesting the existence of multicollinearity (Bryman & Cramer, 1994). Singularity exists when two indicators are exactly the same, or when one variable is a composite of other variables in the analysis. With singularity, the correlation matrix cannot be inverted in factor analysis, because the next operation in inversion involves a division by zero.

Confirmatory Factor Analysis

EQS was used to conduct these analyses because the data were multivariate non-normal (Ullman, 1996). Bentler and Wu (1995) recommended that non-normal data, when analysed by the Maximum Likelihood Estimation (MLE) method, should use robust statistics (Maximum Likelihood robust). Both the ML robust and the S-Bχ^2 are available in EQS (Satorra & Bentler, 1988). A robust chi-square statistic (χ^2) and robust standard errors are provided in EQS (Bentler & Dijkstra, 1985; Satorra & Bentler, 1988). Both of these have been corrected for non-normality in large samples. Model fitting is evaluated in terms of χ^2 statistics and associated degrees-of-freedom. However, Hackett, Bycio, and Hausdorf (1994: 17) considered that when there are only small differences between the actual and estimated matrices:

> this test is not very useful because it has the power to detect non-substantive differences between the matrices.

Therefore, relying on the χ^2 statistic alone for non-nested model evaluation is not recommended, because the statistic depends on sample size and is prone to generate a significant result even when cases have a relatively poor fit to the data (Bentler & Bonett, 1980).

For model evaluation, the Comparative Fit Index (CFI) represents a more realistic value (Byrne, 1994b). Dunham, Grube and Castaneda (1994) used the CFI (Bentler, 1990) because this fit measure is less influenced by sample size than the χ^2 index (Anderson & Gerbing, 1988; Bollen, 1989a; Marsh, 1989; Bentler & Wu, 1995). A CFI value > .90 (with a range 0–1) usually indicates a good fitting model (Ullman, 1996). While the lower limit of acceptable CFI values is .80, 'a value of at least .93 is expected for models considered to be well-fitting' (Byrne, 1994b: 24), although Hu and Bentler (1999), in their 2–index presentation strategy, recommended a .95 cut-off criterion for this index.

Both the CFI and Robust CFI (for single-group analyses) are reported. The CFI was adopted because of its capacity to deal with the variance in individual sample sizes (Byrne, 1994b). Robust CFI is not yet available for multigroup analysis in the EQS version 5.5, although this facility is available in the new version of EQS (6.1).

Bentler and Bonett's (1980) Non-Normed Fit Index (NNFI) is equivalent to the Tucker-Lewis index. The NNFI incorporates the degrees-of-freedom in the model (Ullman, 1996). For small subsamples, like this study, Bentler cautioned that the NNFI indicates 'a terrible fit when other indexes suggest an acceptable model fit' (1990: 240). Anderson and Gerbing (1984) found the NNFI underestimated model fit in small subsamples. The NNFI was included because this fit index was more accurate for larger organisations involved in the study samples. Values of > .90 are indicative of a good-fitting model for the NNFI.

The Root Mean Square Error of Approximation (RMSEA) (Steiger, 1990) was also reported. The RMSEA is comparatively independent of sample size and exhibits known distributional properties. RMSEA values of < .05 suggest a close fit (Steiger, 1989). Values between .05–.08 indicate a fair fit (Browne & Cudeck, 1993), and those in the range of .08 to .10 indicate a mediocre fit (MacCallum et al., 1996).

Steiger (1990) recommended that Confidence Intervals CI be used to assess the precision of RMSEA values. MacCallum, Browne, and Sugawara (1996) considered that narrow CI indicates the RMSEA value was a precise indicator of fit, so this permitted the model to be tested on the basis of CIs. MacCallum, Browne, and Sugawara (1996) have developed a framework for evaluating model fit based on CI that recommended rejecting models where the entire CI of the RMSEA is below .05 for hypothesised 'not-close fit' but not for 'close fit'.

When the entire CI interval is above .05, the hypothesis of a 'close fit' is rejected but not that of 'not-close fit'. For CI that 'straddle' .05 the decision is ambiguous to interpret, as a hypothesis of 'close fit 'and 'not-close fit' cannot be rejected because both are plausible.

However, Hair et al. (1995) recommended going beyond the fit indices when determining the construct reliability and variance extracted. In terms of modification indices, both the Lagrange Multiplier (LM) univariate and multivariate tests were used. EQS can be used to conduct both univariate and multivariate LM tests. Parameters that may be added to improve the fit of a model are identified by the LM test to indicate if the model can be improved by estimating fixed parameters.

Summary on the model testing strategy

Because the χ^2 statistic is sensitive to sample size, it was necessary to introduce additional fit indices. Five fit indices were used to conduct the CFA and structural relationship testing the:

- Comparative Fit Index (CFI);
- Satorra-Bentler scaled statistic (S-Bχ^2);
- Bentler-Bonett Non-Normed fit Index (NNFI);
- Robust Comparative Fit Index (RCFI); and
- Root Mean Square Error of Approximation (RMSEA).

DEVELOPING CFA OF MANAGERS' CONTEXTUAL AND TASK PERFORMANCE MEASURES

This section describes the steps taken to refine the Measurement Model for managers' performance using CFA. These steps are a response to questions emanating from the literature and are part of the process of refining the methodological verification of the Measurement Model variables. This analysis was based on Byrne (1994a; 1994b). These steps are proposed as a related sequence of questions.

These research questions are developed into steps in the next section and they are subsequently tested for verification:

- Does managers' performance consist of distinct constructs that are dimensions of contextual and task performance?
- What are the most reliable indicators of managers' contextual and task performance?
- Can shared meaning be attributed to dimensions of managers' contextual and task performance across managers and their superiors?
- Is the construct 'managers' performance' generalizable across different occupational groups?

TEST OF THE MEASUREMENT MODEL

Four models of managers' job performance

All analyses were based on the maximum likelihood (ML) method. The input for the analyses was the covariance matrices for the managers' self-report and superiors' ratings on performance indicator sub-samples. The variance for each of the eight constructs was fixed at 1 and respective covariances were freely calculated.

To test the hypothesised models only random error was analysed, which assumed absence of systematic error in the data. The CFA used data from both managers' (n = 200, calibration sample) and superiors' ratings (cross-validation sample, n = 125) of performance to ensure independence. Four models of managers' performance were tested:

- 'Null' Model, a baseline model with no hypothesized structure. Simplest theoretically justified model used for comparison with incremental fit indices. Each item is uncorrelated with all other indicators.
- 1–Dimensional Model, to ascertain if managers' performance is a global unidimensional construct.
- 2–Dimensional Model, to ascertain if managers' performance has two distinct dimensions: contextual and task performance.
- 8–Dimensional Model based on the a priori model of managers' four factors of contextual performance and four factors of task performance.

A best fitting model was sought that separately fitted these datasets (see Table 6.16). A preliminary analysis showed that two task indicators were complex and were eliminated from further analysis: 'controlling personnel resources' (Monitoring) and 'keeping technically up-to-date' (Technical), leaving 30–indicators for the cross-validation of the model. Ideally, the EFA should have been performed on the sample independent from the calibration and cross validation samples. However, this was not possible due to the sample size.

A comparison of the Null, 1, 2 and 8–Dimensional Models of performance was undertaken separately on each subsample to evaluate each model for fit or non-fit criteria. To base the evaluations of model fit on the RMSEA index, a sample and power analysis was undertaken. The minimum sample size required for the use of the index was N = 55, while power analysis, based on N and degrees of freedom for the least restricted model, showed a value of 1.00 for Subsample 1, and a value of .999 for Subsample 2, ensuring that the index could be applied with confidence to evaluate model fit.

Subsample 1

Table 6.16 provides a comparison of the Null, 1, 2 and 8–Dimensional Models of Performance to evaluate each model for fit or non-fit criteria.

Table 6.16 Comparison of Null, 1, 2 and 8–Dimensional Models of Performance

Models	$\Delta\chi^2$	df	S-Bχ^2	NNFI	RCFI	RMSEA (CI)
Subsample 1	n = 200 (M)					
Null	4530.776	.435	–	–	–	–
1–Dimensional	3143.140	.405	2617.032	.282	.359	.191 (.184, .197)
2–Dimensional	2872.240	.404	2412.246	.351	.418	.182 (.175, .187)
8–Dimensional	633.420	.377	586.296	.928	.939	.061 (.052, .069)
Subsample 2	n = 125 (S)					
Null	3202.009	.435	–	–	–	–
1–Dimensional	1957.375	.405	1543.242	.397	.524	.180 (.171, .187)
2–Dimensional	1849.730	.404	1501.279	.437	.541	.174 (.165, .181)
8–Dimensional	574.285	.377	520.291	.918	.940	.067 (.055, .077)

Null Model

As expected, the χ^2 value for the Null Model (4530.776, df = .435, p = < .001) was very high indicating a poor fit. Fit follows from p values rather than χ^2 values. Large χ^2 values relative to the degrees-of-freedom for the Null Model indicated that the model would have to be substantially modified to better fit the data (Jöreskog & Sorbom, 1993).

1–Dimensional Model

The 1–Dimensional Model was also not a very good fitting model because the indices for the NNFI (.282) and RCFI (.359) were far below .9, and the RMSEA value was > 1.0 (.191), while the CI represented a high error of approximation (.184, .197), indicating a poor fit to the data.

2–Dimensional Model

The 2–Dimensional Model hypothesized that there were two distinct dimensions: one for task and one for contextual performance. The 2–Dimensional Model was also not a good fitting model, because the indices for the NNFI (.351) and RCFI (.418) were below .9, while the RMSEA value was > 1.0 (.182), and the CI represented a high error of approximation (.175, .187), indicating a poor fit to the data.

8–Dimensional Model

For the 8–Dimensional Model, χ^2 dropped substantially (633.420) relative to the chi-square for the competing models, the NNFI was .928, while the RCFI value was .939. The RMSEA was .061 with a narrow CI that ranged from .052 to .069, indicating a reasonable fit to the data.

Subsample 2

Null Model

The χ^2 value for the Null Model (3202.009, df = 435) was very high, indicating a poor fit to the data for a model with no structure. Large χ^2 values relative to the degrees-of-freedom for this model required substantial modification to better fit the data (Jöreskog & Sorbom, 1993).

1–Dimensional Model

The 1–Dimensional Model was also not a very good fitting model because the indices for the NNFI (.397) and RCFI (.524) were substantially below .9, while the RMSEA value was > 1.0 (.180), and the CI represented a high error of approximation (.171, .187), indicating a poor fit to the data.

2–Dimensional Model

The 2–Dimensional Model tested a one task and one contextual performance dimension. This was also not a very good fitting model, because the indices for the NNFI (.437) and RCFI (.541) were below .9, while the RMSEA value was > 1.0 (.174), and the CI represented a high error of approximation (.165, .181), indicating a poor fit to the data.

8–Dimensional Model

For the 8–Dimensional Model the χ^2 dropped substantially (574.285), the NNFI was close to the recommended threshold (.918), and with a RCFI value of .940 it was close to the recommended cut-off criterion of .950. The RMSEA was .067 with a narrow CI (.055, .077), indicating an adequate fit to the data.

Summary on the Measurement Model of managers' performance

Indices in both samples for the 8–Dimensional Model indicated a reasonably well-fitting model, with comparable values for the RMSEA and associated confidence intervals in both groups. These results suggest that the 8–Dimensional Model of performance adequately fits both data sets.

Superiors' and self-ratings on managers' performance

Refer to Table 6.17 for the Pearson inter-correlations among variables of superiors' ratings on performance and managers' self-report on performance related to trait affectivity, affective wellbeing, and intrinsic job satisfaction. Of particular interest is the association between performance rated by superiors and managers' self-reports.

The results show that ratings of performance by superiors are associated with self-reports on wellbeing. There is a statistically significant inverse association between all the performance dimensions and Depression, and a positive association between seven of the performance dimensions (excluding Following) and Intrinsic Job Satisfaction. Five of the eight dimensions of superiors' ratings of performance are also statistically significant and positively associated with Enthusiasm (excluding Monitoring, Delegating, Following) and PA (excluding Technical, Delegating, Helping).

Neither NA nor Relaxation was related to the performance dimensions, while Anxiety was inversely related to only one performance dimension (Influencing). An examination of the sign of correlations, and the statistical significance of the coefficients, indicates that there is a 68% agreement between wellbeing and performance, when performance is rated either by *self* or *other*.

Statistically significant correlations between performance indicators (self-ratings and superiors' ratings) and indices of affective wellbeing and intrinsic job satisfaction were compared using Fisher's Z transformation to test the significance of the difference between two correlation coefficients for independent samples. Sixteen pairs of statistically significant correlations were compared, but no statistically significant difference between self-ratings and superiors' ratings on these correlations was detected ($p > .05$).

Specifically, Technical was related to Enthusiasm ($r = .25$, and $r = .21$, for superior and self respectively, $Z = .333$).

Similar results were obtained for the association between Monitoring and PA ($r = .21$, and $r = .19$, $Z = .165$); Influencing and PA ($r = .36$, and $r = .31$, $Z = .447$); Influencing and Depression ($r = -.27$, and $r = -.23$, $Z = -.341$); Influencing and Enthusiasm ($r = .27$, and $r = .26$, $Z = .085$); Influencing and Anxiety ($r = .28$, and $r = .22$, $Z = .508$); Influencing and Intrinsic Job Satisfaction ($r = .31$, and $r = .47$, $Z = -1.504$); Influencing and Anxiety ($r = -.28$, and $r = -.22$, $Z = .500$); Persisting and PA ($r = .39$, and $r = .26$, $Z = 1.156$); Persisting and Depression ($r = -.22$, and $r = -.23$, $Z = .084$); Persisting and Enthusiasm ($r = .35$, and $r = .23$, $Z = 1.042$); Persisting and Intrinsic Job Satisfaction ($r = .29$, and $r = .40$, $Z = -.992$); Following and PA ($r = .25$, and $r = .23$, $Z = .168$); Endorsing and PA ($r =$

Table 6.17 *Pearson intercorrelations of variable of managers' self-report on affective wellbeing and intrinsic job satisfaction and performance and superiors' ratings on performance (n = 125)*

Variable	Mean (SD)	1	2	3	4	5	6	7	8	9	10	11	12	13	14	15	16	PA	NA	DE	EN	AN	RE	JS
1. Technical (M)	3.23 (.78)	86																						
2. Monitor (M)	3.26 (.71)	38	95																					
3. Delegate (M)	3.22 (.67)	44	36	85																				
4. Influence (M)	3.10 (.78)	46	24	54	91																			
5. Persist (M)	3.57 (.62)	53	45	39	54	82																		
6. Help (M)	3.22 (.70)	35	37	48	36	51	81																	
7. Follow (M)	3.36 (.77)	23	27	29	28	34	40	82																
8. Endorse (M)	3.64 (.76)	29	36	26	41	50	41	49	87															
9. Technical (S)	3.50 (.72)	40	11	08	22	24	05	01	08	85														
10. Monitor (S)	3.33 (.75)	-02	12	-04	14	17	11	06	12	18	95													
11. Delegate (S)	3.19 (.68)	-01	-12	13	24	17	11	-07	08	22	26	88												
12. Influence (S)	3.26 (.81)	07	04	13	36	31	14	08	12	42	37	58	90											
13. Persist (S)	3.76 (.70)	04	01	05	25	29	12	02	18	34	35	39	62	85										
14. Help (S)	3.16 (.66)	02	-04	06	17	17	18	-01	17	32	30	56	57	51	78									
15. Follow (S)	3.56 (.75)	01	03	07	17	09	08	24	23	30	43	20	33	37	41	82								
16. Endorse (S)	3.72 (.70)	07	-06	04	30	21	-02	-03	17	33	37	50	61	57	62	56	86							
17. PA(M)	3.30 (.68)	21	21	12	36	39	19	25	33	14	19	03	31	26	14	23	26	89						
18. NA(M)	1.68 (.51)	-11	09	-02	-17	-03	04	-21	-02	-02	-16	-06	-10	05	-11	-13	-08	-36	88					
19. Dep(M)	1.76 (.84)	-17	-04	-02	-27	-22	00	-15	-16	-20	-23	-25	-32	-23	-27	-19	-28	-53	60	85				
20. Enth (M)	4.04 (1.04)	25	24	14	27	35	17	20	31	21	-02	08	26	23	18	07	18	71	-28	-57	90			
21. Anx (M)	2.61 (.83)	-11	04	-15	-28	-08	04	-11	01	-12	-04	-12	-22	-02	-16	-09	-14	-41	54	56	-37	80		
22. Relax (M)	2.76 (1.18)	03	05	07	16	04	07	20	03	-02	-05	-02	08	00	14	11	04	30	-31	-39	51	-44	86	
23. Int. JS (M)	3.91 (.68)	14	-08	-01	31	29	03	09	26	18	25	32	47	40	36	16	40	43	-20	-57	50	-19	11	85

Note: n = 125 (listwise deletion of cases). Decimal points for coefficients are not shown. Correlations ≥ .18 are statistically significant (two-tailed tests). Coefficients in the diagonal are alpha reliabilities; underlined coefficients are scale validities. (M) = self-report ratings of performance; (S) = superiors' ratings of performance.

.33, and $r = .26 = .609$); Endorsing and Enthusiasm ($r = .31$, and $r = .18$, $Z = 1.099$), and Endorsing and Intrinsic Job Satisfaction ($r = .26$, and $r = .40$, $Z = -1.254$).

Validities for task and contextual performance (i.e., between self-ratings and superiors' ratings) were mainly statistically significant. Those dimensions that showed acceptable levels of convergence were: Technical ($r = .40$), Influencing ($r = .36$), Persisting $r = .29$), Helping ($r = .18$), and Following ($r = .24$). Three dimensions of performance (two contextual and one task) were not statistically significant: Monitoring ($r = .12$), Delegating ($r = .13$) and Endorsing ($r = .17$).

A correlation matrix of the study variables shows in Figure 6.17 that trait affectivity, affective wellbeing, and intrinsic job satisfaction were associated with dimensions of managers' performance, irrespective of whether the performance scores were from self-report or superiors' ratings.

Multisample procedure

This section deals with invariance across samples. The cross-validation sample (i.e., superiors' rating of managers' performance) was independent of the CFA calibration sample. Invariance means that the model parameters in one dataset (managers' self-report) is replicated in another dataset (superiors' ratings), starting with a baseline model that specifies the same Measurement Model in both samples.

Initially, the models were used to assess the factorial structure of the construct. The best-fitting model was then compared for equivalence across subsamples 1 and 2. Evidence of equivalence was based on tests of invariance of parameters in the two subsamples by estimating the constrained parameters in subsample 2 to be equal to the unconstrained values in subsample 1. A series of χ^2 difference tests between two nested models was performed (Bollen, 1989b).

Tests of invariance between the two subsamples were undertaken, after separately establishing the best baseline model for each group as reported above (Byrne, Shavelson, & Muthen, 1989). Invariance was initially sought between the baseline model, and a model that had item-factor loadings constrained in the replication subsample. Following this step the analysis, in addition, constrained the covariances among the performance constructs to be equal across the two groups.

Tests of hypotheses relating to group invariance began by scrutinising the Measurement Model, particularly the equivalence of factor loadings across groups (Byrne, 1994b). There were:

- four EFA dimensions for contextual performance (Endorsing, Helping, Persisting, Following); and

- four EFA dimensions for task performance (Monitoring, Technical, Influencing, Delegating).

Figure 6.8 provides a schematic representation of the CFA of managers' performance indicators and constructs.

Figure 6.8: CFA of variables and factors

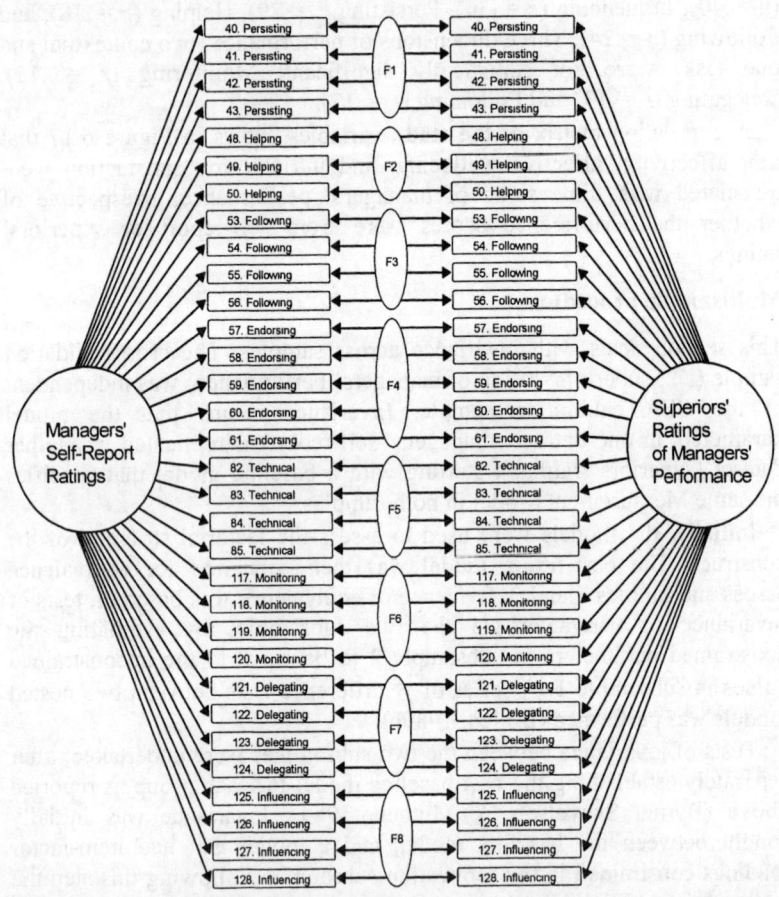

Results from the invariance analysis on the data are shown in Table 6.18. For assessing the extent to which a respecified model exhibits improvement, the difference in χ^2 between the models was examined (Byrne, 1994b). EQS provides a χ^2 value that reflects a weighted combination of fit for all groups used to perform multigroup analyses. Multigroup analyses confirmed the consistency of the 8–Dimensional Model for the two combined subsamples.

Invariance Analysis

Table 6.18 provides a comparison of the Null, 1, 2 and 8–Dimensional invariance analysis on the data to test the Models of Performance.

Table 6.18 Invariance Analysis

Models	χ^2	$\Delta\chi^2$	df	Δdf	NNFI	CFI	RMSEA (CI)
I. Null	8070.625	–	756	–	–	–	–
II. Baseline	1084.984	–	644	–	.929	.940	.044 (.039, .048)
III. Baseline + Loadings	1122.049	37.065	672	28	.931	.938	.043 (.039, .048)
IV. Baseline + Loadings + Covariances	1159.119	37.070	700	28	.932	.937	.043 (.038, .047)

Note: To test the RMSEA for the 8–Dimensional Model the required subsample for the degrees-of-freedom in the model was n = 63; the Power to test the model based on the RMSEA (with 322 degrees-of-freedom and an n = 180). Power = .999.

Model I. Null

As expected, the Null Model (a model without structure) had an extremely large χ^2 (8070.625) with 756 degrees-of-freedom, indicating a poor fit to the data.

Model II. Baseline

The χ^2 from Model II was 1084.984 with a reduction of 112 degrees-of-freedom. NNFI was .929, CFI .940 and the RMSEA was .044 (CI = .039, .048 respectively), indicative of a very good fit to the data. This Measurement Model assumed an 8–Dimensional Model of performance (4 dimensions of task performance, and 4 dimensions of contextual performance).

Model III. Baseline + Loadings

Model III had a χ^2 of 1122.049 (with df = 672), while the NNFI was .931, CFI .938 and the RMSEA was .043 (CI = .039, .048 respectively). The results were not statistically significant ($\Delta\chi^2$ = 37.065, Δ28 df, p > .05), indicating equivalence between the free parameters in the calibration sample, and the constraint parameters in the validation sample. Acceptability of the loadings on the indicators as invariant across groups was established, using stringent criteria. The difference in the χ^2 ($\Delta\chi^2$) was used as the benchmark to judge the differences between competing models. Changes in χ^2 with 28 df, indicated that these loadings were invariant across groups.

Model IV. Baseline + Loadings + Covariances

Model IV (χ^2 1159.119, df = 700) - the most restrictive model - was tested, which included in addition to invariant loadings, invariant factor covariances. The results were not statistically significant ($\Delta\chi^2 = 37.070$, $\Delta df = 28$, $p > .05$). Fit indices improved slightly from Model III, the CFI from .938 to .937, while the RMSEA remained constant at .043, and the CI were slightly narrower (.038, .047).

These results may be taken as evidence indicating equivalence between all the parameters tested in the calibration and validation samples. The 8–Dimensional Model of managers' performance was thus successfully cross-validated, and these results add weight to the hypothesis that managers and their superiors conceptualise performance similarly. Specifically, the Measurement Model hypotheses 1–3 yielded the following results.

Hypothesis 1:

> **Task performance and contextual performance are:**
> a) **distinct measures;**
> b) **generalizable across different groups;**
>
> **that is, managers' and superiors' contextual and task performance will remain invariant when compared across groups.**

Hypothesis 1 tested whether performance was a multi-dimensional construct. Table 6.16 provides a comparison of the Null, 1, 2 and 8–Dimensional Models of managers' performance. Also, Table 6.18 tested the equivalence of parameters across two samples (managers and their superiors). Thus, hypothesis 1 was confirmed by the data.

Hypothesis 2.1:

> **Managers and their superiors will perceive the same dimensions of performance, in terms of:**
> a) **Pattern relationships;**
> b) **Loadings; and**
> c) **Covariances.**

Hypothesis 2.1, dealt specifically with the second part of hypothesis 1, was therefore confirmed on the basis of: a) Pattern relationships; b) Loadings; and c) Covariances.

Hypothesis 2.2:

> A multi-dimensional construct of performance will fit the data better than either a unidimenisonal construct of performance, or a two dimensional construct (contextual and task performance).

Managers' rated performance has traditionally been conceived as a unidimensional construct. Conceptualisation of the job performance domain is being expanded (Arvey & Murphy, 1998). It remains to be established if managers' performance is a multivariate construct as stated in hypothesis 2.2.

BIASING EFFECT OF THE METHOD

Multitrait-multimethod (MTMM)

This section assessed the extent that two prominent structure MTMM Models were concordant (Byrne et al., 1993). The model examined was composed of performance domains and methods, which included self-rating and superiors' rating on the pair congruence subsample (n = 125). A schematic of the MTMM being tested is given in Figure 6.9.

Figure 6.9 Schematic of managers' performance MTMM evaluation of relationships (n = 125)

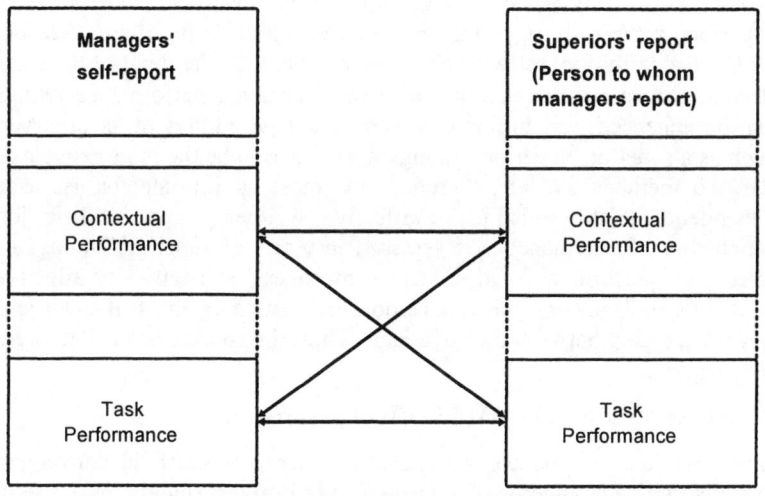

After testing the equivalence of the performance constructs across the two groups, it was necessary to establish if they were equally valid in terms of representing the performance from managers' self-reports and superiors' ratings. Factors underlying self-rating of performance have been found to diverge from those of peer and superiors' ratings, to suggest the presence of rater bias (Goffin & Jackson, 1992). Consistent with the literature on self-report techniques the term 'bias' is not used in the strict statistical sense but in reference to the context of the ratings. The reliability of the focal persons' ratings may be enhanced, and in this case supplanted, by ratings from another person, such as a superior.

Correlations were arranged by a MTMM matrix (see Table 6.19). MTMM analysis was undertaken to determine whether there was bias in the self-reporting of these performance indicators. Testing for evidence of validity using CFA is typically undertaken at both the matrix (model) and individual (parameter) levels. Byrne (1994b) recommended testing for the methods effects, construct and discriminant validity of research conducted within the MTMM framework.

Table 6.19 shows the dimensions of performance that were confirmed by managers' self-report and superiors' ratings. This MTMM matrix permitted the analysis to be extended further to establish the convergent and discriminant validity at a general (i.e., matrix), and individual parameter level. The matrix compared the correlations between managers' self-reported and superiors' ratings. Perceptions of superiors' and managers' rating were congruent for five (Technical, Influencing, Persisting, Helping, and Following) of the eight traits. The traits Monitoring, Delegating, and Endorsing were not significant.

Factors underlying self-rating have been found to diverge from superiors' ratings, to suggest the presence of rater bias (Goffin & Jackson, 1992). By definition, self-ratings are based solely on the input of the focal person. However, the reliability of a focal person's performance ratings can be enhanced, and in this case substituted, by ratings of an observer, such as a superior. Superiors' ratings were found to be the more reliable of the two methods and are, therefore, the most appropriate for use as a dependent variable relating to affective wellbeing and intrinsic job satisfaction. Performance was assessed in terms of superiors' ratings of managers' performance and related to managers' self-report of affective wellbeing and intrinsic job satisfaction in order to establish if there was any relationship between the covariates. Thus, the sources of the data were independent.

Goodness-of-fit for MTMM Models of performance

In this section, four models were tested in order to establish the convergent and discriminant validity of managers' performance measure. A useful baseline model for comparing alternative models to evaluate improvements in fit was based on a model with freely correlated traits and methods (i.e., no restrictions were imposed on the models).

Table 6.19 MTMM matrix (n = 125)

Indicators	1	2	3	4	5	6	7	8	9	10	11	12	13	14	15	16
Managers' ratings																
1. Technical																
2. Monitoring	.377															
3. Delegating	.444	.365														
4. Influencing	.458	.244	.537													
5. Persisting	.531	.449	.394	.545												
6. Helping	.346	.370	.482	.356	.507											
7. Following	.235	.269	.289	.281	.343	.395										
8. Endorsing	.293	.359	.262	.407	.502	.405	.490									
Superiors' ratings																
1. Technical	**.401*****	.105	.076	.223	.239	.048	.006	.076								
2. Monitoring	-.019	.124ns	-.044	.139	.167	.108	.058	.122	.183							
3. Delegating	-.013	-.122	.125ns	.242	.166	.108	-.074	.079	.223	.264						
4. Influencing	.065	.043	.131	**.365*****	.311	.138	.078	.122	.421	.374	.583					
5. Persisting	.045	.007	.055	.254	**.294****	.119	.025	.179	.341	.348	.389	.618				
6. Helping	.017	-.036	.056	.171	.167	**.179***	-.010	.170	.320	.304	.557	.569	.507			
7. Following	.008	.030	.069	.174	.094	.075	**.240***	.234	.296	.432	.202	.326	.367	.408		
8. Endorsing	.071	-.065	.042	.295	.214	-.019	-.025	.172ns	.328	.367	.499	.606	.568	.615	.556	

Note: *p = <.01; *** p = <.001. Statistical significance was only reported for validities (the underlined coefficients); ns = not statistically significant (two-tailed tests). Statistically significant traits are indicated in **bold**.

General and individual level testing of parameters of construct validity

MTMM analysis was undertaken at both the general (model) (e.g., Table 6.20) and the individual (parameter) level (e.g., Table 6.22). However, interpretation of MTMM is more informative at the individual level of analysis that examined individual parameters. The test for evidence of construct validity related to the eight facets of performance, as measured by self-ratings and superiors' ratings. Data comprised scores on the 16 variables (8 for each rating method) that served as indicators for the MTMM analysis (Byrne, 1994b). Results of the analysis are shown in Table 6.20.

Table 6.20 Summary of goodness-of-fit indices for MTMM Models of performance (n = 125)

Model	χ^2	$\Delta\chi^2$	df	Δdf	CFI	RMSEA (CI)
Model I Freely correlated traits. Freely correlated.	79.847	–	64	–	.978	.045 (.000, .073)
Model II No traits. Freely correlated.	214.968	135.121	103	39	.846	.094 (.076, .111)
Model III Perfectly correlated trait. Freely correlated.	157.029	77.182	88	24	.905	.080 (.059, .099)
Model IV Freely correlated traits. Perfectly correlated.	90.386	10.539	61	3	.960	.063 (.032, .088)

Notes: Increments in χ^2 and dfs are based on the baseline Model I. All χ^2 differences between Model I and the alternative models are statistically significant. When evaluating parameters, increases in the number of degrees-of-freedom in some of the analyses are due to fixing the error variances at lower bound to prevent them from becoming negative.

Model I: Freely correlated traits. Freely correlated methods

The first hypothesised model was the baseline for comparing alternative MTMM Models. Typically, the first model is the least restrictive of those compared because it allows for correlation amongst trait, methods and traits, and methods factors. These serve as a standard against which to compare competing models to determine their construct validity (Byrne, 1994b). For this model the $\Delta\chi^2$ was 79.847 with a CFI of .978 and a RMSEA of .045, indicating a very good fit to the data, as expected.

Model II: No traits. Freely correlated methods
With an increase in degrees-of-freedom, through a restriction of the correlations amongst the performance traits, there was a substantial increment in chi-square over the baseline model (χ^2 = 214.968, df = 103) as well as a deterioration of the RMSEA (.094) and CFI (.846) indexes. These values for Model II suggested a poor fit to the data.

Model III: Perfectly correlated trait. Freely correlated methods
As with the hypothesised Model I, each observed variable loaded on both a trait and a method factor. Correlations among the trait factors were fixed to 1.0 (i.e., perfect correlation). Fit for this model showed a marked improvement when compared with Model II (χ^2 = 157.029; CFI = .905; RMSEA = .80, and the CI ranged from .059 to .099), although the fit to the data was mediocre.

Model IV: Freely correlated traits. Perfectly correlated methods
For this model the correlation between the two rating methods was fixed at 1, suggesting perfect correlation, while the performance traits were freely calculated. Goodness-of-fit for Model IV was substantially improved the χ^2 = 90.386 and the CFI = .960. The RMSEA was .063 with an acceptable CI (.032, .088) that indicated an acceptable fit to the data.

Evidence for convergent and discriminant validity at the general level
The extent that independent measures of the same traits are correlated (i.e., managers' self-rating and superiors' ratings) is one criterion of construct validity. These variables need to be substantial and statistically significant (Campbell & Fiske, 1959). A model that specified correlation amongst the traits (Model I) with a model that has not specified such a relationship (Model II) provides evidence of convergent validity.

The difference in χ^2 between the nested models provided the basis for either supporting or rejecting the existence of convergent validity. Table 6.21 clearly shows that the difference in χ^2 was statistically significant (p < .001), while the difference in practical fit was substantial, based on the CFI (.132) as suggested by Byrne, Jackson and Goffin (1993), supporting the existence of convergent validity at the general level.

Discriminant validity was evaluated for both traits and methods. Testing for evidence of discriminant validity among traits was undertaken by comparing the model that had traits correlated freely (Model I) with a model that had perfectly correlated traits (Model III). Model III suggested a differentiation existed amongst the traits.

Table 6.21 *Differential goodness-of-fit indices for MTMM Models comparisons (n = 125)*

Model Comparisons	$\Delta\chi^2$	Δdf	ΔCFI
Test of Convergent Validity			
Model I vs. Model II (traits)	135.121	39	.132
Test of Discriminant Validity			
Model I vs. Model III (traits)	77.182	24	.073
Model I vs. Model IV (methods)	10.539	3	.018

Strong evidence for discriminant validity was indicated by the large increment in χ^2 ($\Delta\chi^2 = 77.182$, df = 24, p = < .001). These results indicated a substantial difference between nested models, and therefore provided strong evidence of discriminant validity. The freely correlated methods model (Model I) was compared with the perfectly correlated ($r = 1.00$) model (Model IV). A statistically significant increment in χ^2 ($\Delta\chi^2 = 10.539$, df = 3, p < .025) indicated discriminant validity, and evidence of lack of common bias across the methods of measurement.

Individual level testing of parameters

Convergent and discriminant validity

As was suggested earlier, a more thorough assessment of construct validity may be undertaken at the individual parameter level of analysis. The focus here is on the factor loadings and factor correlations of the baseline model (Model I). Table 6.23 shows that 15 out of the 16 trait loadings were statistically significant. However, when the factor loadings are scrutinised across traits and methods, it is clear that, in every case, the method variance, based on self-ratings, exceeds that of the trait variance. For example, for managers' self-ratings on performance the trait rating coefficient for Delegating (.232) was lower than the method coefficient (.642).

By contrast, comparing the trait and method loadings for superiors indicated that trait variance always exceeds that of the method variance. To illustrate the point, the coefficient for the superiors' method ratings for Delegating (.117) is far smaller than the coefficient to the trait (.829). This is strong evidence that method effects tend to attenuate trait effects at the individual parameter level, thus putting into doubt the evidence gathered from the previous MTMM analysis at the matrix level. See Table 6.19 for evidence of convergent validity at the matrix level.

Dimensions of job performance

Evidence of discriminant validity may be assessed by examining the correlations among traits. In order to support discriminant validities, these correlations need to be very low. However, validity correlations were greater than .80 between: Influencing and Delegating ($r = .819$); Endorsing and Influencing ($r = .879$); Endorsing and Persisting ($r = .901$); and Persisting and Influencing ($r = .878$). Influencing correlated $\geq .8$ with three of the factors. Further evidence of discriminant validities was obtained by comparing the upper and lower confidence intervals for these correlations for the .95 confidence limit. These intervals did not contain $r = 1.00$. This suggests that although the association between the pair of constructs is substantial, the constructs were nevertheless distinct. Table 6.22 gives the trait and method correlations for the MTMM Models of performance.

Table 6.22 *Trait and method correlations of MTMM Models of performance (n = 125)*

Variables	1	2	3	4	5	6	7	8
1. Technical	1.00							
2. Monitor	.086ns	1.00						
3. Delegate	.239 ns	.282	1.00					
4. Influence	.362	.367	.819	1.00				
5. Persist	.361	.409	.609	.878	1.00			
6. Help	.226 ns	.260	.661	.597	.602	1.00		
7. Follow	.135 ns	.383	.216 ns	.264 ns	.322	.343	1.00	
8. Endorse	.484	.437	.654	.879	.901	.726	.709	1.00

Note: * $p = < .05$; ** $p = < .01$; *** $p = < .001$, ns = not significant.

The next examination of discriminant validity concentrates on the correlation between two sources of data: self and superiors. Correlations between these sources of report on managers' performance were predicted to be low and not statistically significant; although the correlation between these sources ($r = .250$) was modest, it was statistically significant. At first examination this may appear surprising, (i.e., the first and other-ratings are similar), but the items in the questionnaires were identical for both managers and superiors, and this may account for the result. Byrne (1994b) encountered an analogous circumstance, when correlations obtained were as high as .60 between student self-ratings and parents' ratings.

Table 6.23 *Trait and method loadings for the MTMM Model of contextual and task performance (n = 125)*

Ratings	Traits								Methods	
	Technical	Monitoring	Delegating	Influencing	Persisting	Helping	Following	Endorsing	Self-ratings	Superiors' ratings
Self										
Technical	.442								.642	
Monitoring		.137ns							.578	
Delegating			.232						.642	
Influencing				.459					.616	
Persisting					.432				.745	
Helping						.230			.691	
Following							.218		.553	
Endorsing								.288	.589	
Superiors										
Technical	.881									.517
Monitoring		.974								.225
Delegating			.829							.117
Influencing				.803						.384
Persisting					.709					.321
Helping						.957				.269
Following							.921			.377
Endorsing								.952		-.159

Potential systematic error of superiors' ratings was minimised by including in the analysis ratings of superiors that were independent of other ratings; that is, only one randomly selected rating from individual superiors was included in the analysis, and this rating was matched with the focal (manager) person's rating. In research of this type this potential error is not controlled, by allowing a superior to rate more than one subordinate (see for example, Wright & Cropanzano, 2000).

Therefore, hypothesis 3 was confirmed.

Hypothesis 3:

> Managers will rate their contextual and task performance less accurately compared to the person to whom they report (superiors).

Table 6.23 provides the trait and method loadings for the MTMM Model of contextual and task performance. The MTMM analysis indicates that there is bias in the self-report of these performance indicators. Self-report on managers' performance was shown to be contaminated as opposed to superiors' ratings of managers' performance, which was found to be more reliable.

CFA OF MANAGERS' PERFORMANCE

This section investigated whether the hypotheses related to managers' performance presented earlier were supported by the data collected from the sample. Accurately measuring managers' performance was a necessary precursor to answering the main research questions posed in this book. The CFA explored the construct of managers' performance in detail. Results of the various CFA were conducted to test the Measurement Model.

Summary on CFA findings

The Measurement Model clarified the construct of managers' performance and was found to be generalizable across groups. The CFA findings indicated that the construct of managers' performance was multi-dimensional. However, as shown through the MTMM at the individual parameter level of analysis, managers' self-reports on their performance were contaminated by considerable systematic error through a tendency of the self-rated performance method to inflate the performance effects. By contrast, the superiors' ratings of managers' performance had only a modest method variance and were therefore a reliable measure of managers' objective performance.

SUMMARY AND CONCLUSION

This chapter provided descriptive statistics on the sample, subsamples and details of the development of the Measurement Model. Theoretical and statistical attributes were provided for the managers' performance subscales used in this sample. Evidence is given to support the validity and reliability of the instruments used to measure the constructs embedded in the model. The psychometric properties of the 12–item Four Factor Model of Job-related Affective Wellbeing (Sevastos, 1996), the 20–item PANAS (Watson & Clark, 1984) and the 7–item Intrinsic Job Satisfaction scale (Cook, 1981; Sevastos, 1996) scales remained statistically robust with this cohort.

A major contribution of this book was to define and measure the construct of managers' performance. This was made on the assumption that managers' performance consists of two multi-dimensional components: contextual performance and task performance. Contextual performance scales were sourced from existing items in the literature, whereas the researcher developed the task performance variables. A thorough and statistically robust methodology was adopted for the validation and cross-validation of the managers' performance Measurement Model. This analysis ensured there was a congruence of perceptions, for managers and their superiors, on what were the most important elements of managers' performance.

A Measurement Model of managers' performance dimensions was confirmed to be multivariate and to consist of eight distinct dimensions. Four contextual performance dimensions (Endorsing, Helping, Persisting, Following) and four task performance dimensions (Monitoring, Technical, Influencing, Delegating) formed the scales for the managerial activities. Indicators forming these scales were of most consequence to managers and their superiors.

Contextual and task performance scales shared convergent and discriminant validity at the matrix level but at the individual parameter level the results were less encouraging. At the individual parameter level, self-report was less reliable, because method obscured the true nature of managers' ratings. On the other hand, superiors' ratings were found to be the more reliable of the two methods and were clearly independent of affective wellbeing and intrinsic job satisfaction. Thus, the potential for common method variance was controlled. The next chapter describes the results obtained from the analyses of the relationship between managers' affective wellbeing, intrinsic job satisfaction and performance.

7. Analysing the relationship between affective wellbeing, intrinsic job satisfaction and performance

> it is better to imperfectly measure relevant dimensions than to perfectly measure irrelevant ones.
> (Bommer et al., 1995: 602)

This chapter examines the results obtained from testing the hypotheses concerning the relationships between managers' affective wellbeing, intrinsic job satisfaction and performance. Reports of the Canonical Correlation results are given, including a canonical analysis estimation of the sample and the Standard Multiple Regressions which were used to complement the Canonical Correlation analysis. Reports of the Canonical Correlation results are given, including canonical analysis estimation of the sample and results of Standard Multiple Regressions. An explanation is given as to why Standard Multiple Regressions were used to complement the Canonical Correlation analysis. Results of the hypotheses are discussed in detail, as are the methodological issues impacting on the study.

INTRODUCTION

Canonical Correlation analysis was used as the method for combining the individual performance dimensions into weighted components of performance, so that these could then be used in a series of Standard Multiple Regressions with independent variables (IVs) for the affective wellbeing and intrinsic job satisfaction scales. All the information relevant to the hypotheses and the Partial Model are contained in this analysis, including statistically significant results, plus unique variance. As was shown in Table 6.21, the performance dimensions overlapped (i.e., exhibited high intercorrelations) making it necessary to evaluate the multi-dimensional performance construct through a weighted linear combination of the individual performance dimensions.

A decision to evaluate each performance dimension separately by relating it to the intrinsic job satisfaction and affective wellbeing dimensions would have been misplaced, due to the overlapping variance among the performance dimensions. In summary, the superiors' ratings of managers' performance are the most valid, and this information is presented as the focus of this study. The Pair Congruence (superiors' ratings) Subsample 2 (n = 125) was used for the Canonical Correlation and Standard Multiple Regression analysis.

CANONICAL CORRELATION

As discussed in Chapter 5, research strategies for exploring the predictive power of sets of variables are normally conducted between IVs (in this case affective wellbeing and intrinsic job satisfaction) and dependent variables (DVs) (contextual and task performance). In Chapter 6, it was shown that managers' performance dimensions (i.e., the DVs) were confirmed to be multi-dimensional and to consist of eight distinct constructs. Four contextual performance dimensions (Endorsing, Helping, Persisting, Following) and four task performance dimensions (Monitoring, Technical, Influencing, Delegating) formed the scales for the managerial activities that were rated as being of most consequence by the managers of the organisations who were involved in this study. The IVs consisted of the Four Factor Model of Job-related Affective Wellbeing (Sevastos, 1996), the Positive And Negative Affect Schedule (PANAS) (Watson, Clark, & Tellegen, 1988), and Job Satisfaction (Cook, 1981), and represented previously established and valid measures of wellness.

Canonical Correlation procedures are intended to identify how well each DV, individually or as a set, can be predicted from a set of IVs. A framework with the kind of research questions posed in this book, involved identifying the maximum correlation between the set of IVs and the set of DVs; or preferably, the identification of a number of different dimensions of association between the two sets, and the major variables accounting for each set. These types of research questions may be answered through the statistical procedure of Canonical Correlation, and then supplemented through the use of more extensive analysis based on multiple regression.

The rationale for using Canonical Correlation analysis is that, with a large number of analyses for each DV there is no protection level for accepting validation in the hypotheses due to Type I errors when the null is evident. Because most of the variables in studies of this kind are intercorrelated (i.e., intrinsic job satisfaction and other conceptually related job affect measures are likely to have considerable shared variance) it is advisable to consider all variables (DVs and IVs) simultaneously in a single multivariate analysis, and Canonical Correlation 'represents the only technique available for examining the relationship with multiple dependent variables' (Hair et al., 1995: 445).

Canonical Correlation analysis may be applied when the two sets of variables have equivalent status, and where no clear-cut distinction can be made between dependent and independent sets (Cliff, 1987); that is, either set may be treated as criterion or predictor. A Canonical Correlation is intended to produce a linear combination from each set of variables so that the correlation between them is maximised. Linear combinations from each set of variables are known as canonical variates, and are analogous to principal components derived from a principal component analysis (Nie, Hull, Jenkins, Steinbrenner, & Bent, 1975). To account for all the variance in the dataset, additional variates are extracted in order of magnitude and all are orthogonal to one another.

Dillon and Goldstein (1984) have suggested the use of cross-loadings instead of simple loadings. These are considered to be a preferable base for interpretation because they are less inflated than within-set loadings. Dillon and Goldstein (1984) emphasised the relationship of each variable separately with the canonical variate from the other set. Cross-loadings are calculated by multiplying each loading separately in a set with the Canonical Correlation coefficient of the set. When interpreting these results, Tatsuoka (1970) has suggested a standardised weight coefficient equal to or greater than half the size of the largest coefficient in the set as a more acceptable base for interpretation.

In this study, the focus of the multivariate analysis is on the relationship between the composite performance criteria and the set of DVs. Because Canonical Correlation analysis does not evaluate the statistical significance of individual predictors, the results of the Standard Multiple Regressions will be relied upon for interpretation. Both analyses are closely related, and Canonical Correlation is equivalent to multiple R (linear combination of one dependent and several IVs) from regression analysis.

Canonical significance

In this study, canonical dimensions were determined to be statistically significant for interpretation if significance of the F values were above the established convention of .05 (or .01 where appropriate). Rao's V approximation (F statistic) was used to test for lower levels of significance (Tabachnick & Fidell, 2001); (Hair et al., 1995). For Canonical Correlation, Wilk's lambda is a more appropriate statistic because it is a multivariate test, capable of evaluating the significance of the discriminatory power of discriminate functions on all canonical roots (Tabachnick & Fidell, 2001). Wilk's lambda indicates the amount of separation between the variable components. In essence, the lower the

Wilk's number, the better the separation between components. A canonical regression with a Wilk's lambda of < .6 is necessary to adequately discriminate between variables (Hair et al., 1995). Variables with a canonical weight ≥ .6 were not considered suitable for canonical regression.

The significance of the F roots was checked to determine how many factors were significant at .05, after the normality of the data distribution was established. Having established significance, it was critical to establish the amount of variance accounted for by the significant factors. Three assessments of variance are important to the two sets of variables. First, only variance overlap between each set of variate pairs above .30 was interpreted. Second, the different amount of variance extracted was related to each respective set of variables. Third, these were also calculated and interpreted identically to the method used for factor analysis, except that canonical variates are always orthogonal and therefore independent of each other.

A minimum ratio of observations to IVs for multiple regression of 1:5 is recommended to avoid *overfitting* data and to maintain a statistical power of 80% (Hair et al., 1995). This study had 125 cases for 16 IVs, a ratio of 7.8:1, above the recommended minimum.

Last, redundancies for pairs of canonical variates are usually not equal. Redundancies for a set of variables are added between canonical variates to calculate the total of DVs relative to IVs. Redundancy is the percentage of variance a canonical variate extracts from one set of variables in the other set. Variance is the overlap between a variate and the other related variables. Singularity did not exist in either matrix as the DVs were not perfectly correlated (Hair et al., 1995; Tabachnick & Fidell, 2001). Normality was assessed using both graphical and statistical tests as recommended by the American Psychological Society (Smithson, 1999).

CANONICAL ANALYSIS

Estimation sample

Results of the Canonical Correlation analysis for the first matched sample (n = 125) are shown in Table 7.1. This table shows the Canonical Correlations, cross-loadings, the standard canonical variate coefficients or weights, the percent of variance extracted from within its own set of variables, and redundancies (the percent of variance extracted from the opposing set of variables). Redundancies are analogous to R^2 and are the products of the squared Canonical Correlation and the proportion of that set's variance accounted for by the canonical variate (Dillon & Goldstein, 1984). Canonical variates are orthogonal to each other, and the percent of variance and redundancies are additive, as shown in the 'total' column in Table 7.1.

Table 7.1 Canonical Correlation with DV based on superiors' rated performance (n = 125)

Variables	First Canonical Variate Cross-Loadings	First Canonical Variate Standardised Coefficients	Second Canonical Variate Cross-Loadings	Second Canonical Variate Standardised Coefficients
Performance Variable Set (DV)				
Technical	.177	-.091	-.208	-.563
Monitoring	.306	.202	.252	.616
Delegating	.264	-.142	-.131	-.321
Influencing	.510	.642	-.090	-.067
Persisting	.423	.214	-.081	-.259
Helping	.245	.039	-.011	.054
Following	.221	-.070	.217	.549
Endorsing	.432	.322	.008	.013
Percent variance		37.129		10.978 Total = 48.107
Redundancy		11.602		2.323 Total = 13.925
Affective Wellbeing Variable Set (IV)				
PA	.389	.591	.067	.976
NA	-.096	.221	-.152	-.478
Depression	-.328	-.083	.012	-.058
Enthusiasm	.278	-.375	-.187	-1.337
Anxiety	-.179	-.117	.071	.619
Relaxation	.076	.046	.046	.595
Intrinsic Job Satisfaction	.503	.803	-.085	-.014
Percent variance		29.046		5.201 Total = 34.248
Redundancy		9.076		1.101 Total = 10.177
Canonical Correlation	.559***		.460*	

Note: *$p = < .05$; **$p = < .01$; ***$p = < .001$, ns = not significant.

Canonical Correlations for the two variates of superiors' ratings were .559 ($p < .001$) and .460 ($p < .05$), indicating they were suitable for interpretation. For superiors' ratings, the first canonical variate extracted 37.129% of variance from the criterion set and 29.04% of variance from the predictor set. For redundancies, the first criterion-set variate accounted for 11.602% of variance in the predictor set, and the first predictor set variate accounted for 9.067% of variance in the criterion-set for a total of 13.925%.

The second canonical variate extracted 10.978% of variance from the criterion-set, and 5.201% of variance from the predictor set. For redundancies, the second criterion-set variate accounted for 2.323% of variance in the predictor set, and the second predictor set variate accounts for 1.101% of variance in the criterion set for a total 10.177%.

Both canonical variates accounted for a total of 48.107% of the criterion-set variability, and 34.248% of the predictor set variability. As was mentioned earlier, in order to interpret the results from a Canonical Correlation, either the cross-loading and/or the standardised coefficients may be used. However, because the Canonical Correlation analysis here was used only as a method of creating composite DVs through weighting, and not for testing of hypotheses, cross-loadings were not evaluated.

As an exploratory preliminary step, an examination of the loadings and the weights for each variable may be carried out to detect any instability in the standardised weights. Instability in the standardised weights (e.g., a small weight relative to a loading, or a negative algebraic sign where a positive sign was expected) may be due to either multicollinearity, or to the variance in a variable having already been accounted for by some of the other variables (Dillon & Goldstein, 1984). The problem of multicollinearity was already addressed earlier in this chapter. Squared Canonical Correlation represents the variance shared by the linear composites of sets of DVs and IVs but not the variance extracted from the sets of variables. Variates are derived to maximise the correlation and identify the optimum structure or dimensionality of each IV and DV set.

A strong Canonical Correlation may be evident between two linear composites (canonical variates), even though these canonical variates may not extract significant amounts of variance from either set of variables. This accounts for the maximum amount of the relationship between two sets of variables but does not ensure a substantial relationship of practical and conceptual significance. Practical significance of canonical functions is represented by size of Canonical Correlations but there are no generally established guidelines regarding suitable sizes for Canonical Correlations (Hair et al., 1995). Further analysis, using a Standard Multiple Regression, is required to determine the amount of the composite DV variance accounted for, or shared with the original IVs.

STANDARD MULTIPLE REGRESSION

Canonical Correlation is a preliminary step for establishing the relationship between the sets of IVs and DVs. As noted earlier, a Canonical Correlation does not provide the significance levels for individual variables. In this case, statistical significance of the predictor variables was determined more precisely through multiple linear regression using the information gained from the Canonical Correlation.

Significance testing is possible using Standard Multiple Regression to establish how sensitive to unique variance an IV's contribution is to the R2. This permitted explicit hypotheses to be tested on the variances attributable to some of the IVs in the equation to answer two fundamental questions: what is the size of the overall relationship between affective wellbeing and performance; and how much of the relationship is contributed uniquely by each IV?

In a single step, Standard Multiple Regression assesses the influence of a set of IVs on individual DVs. In this instance, the weighted linear combination of the performance dimensions is defined by the first and second canonical variates as shown in Tables 7.2–7.5. An assessment of the relative importance of an IV may be based on such an analysis where the unique variance explained by a particular variable could be obtained through the squared semi-partial (part) correlations. However, it should be noted that the results of these analyses are specific to the compound DVs. These were linearly combined (i.e., the variates), and not with the original variables.

A Standard Multiple Regression was conducted separately on each of the predictor variables (affective wellbeing and intrinsic job satisfaction) against each criterion variable (the two orthogonal compound variables from the Canonical Correlation).

RESULTS OF MULTIPLE REGRESSION & DISCUSSION

Tables 7.2–7.5 show four separate Standard Multiple Regressions performed on the matched sample explanation (n = 125). DVs for Tables 7.2 and 7.3 are the composite performance dimensions from the first and second canonical variates from superiors' ratings of managers' performance. For Tables 7.4 and 6.5, the DVs are the composite affective wellbeing and intrinsic job satisfaction dimensions from the first and second canonical variates obtained from managers' ratings. That is, in Tables 7.2 and 7.3, predictions are made about performance using the predictors' intrinsic job satisfaction and affective wellbeing variables, while in Tables 7.4 and 7.5 reversing the order, predictions are made about intrinsic job satisfaction and affective wellbeing variables from the performance dimensions.

Due to the weighting procedure derived from the Canonical Correlation, the multiple R's for the Standard Multiple Regression analyses are exactly the same as that obtained from the Canonical Correlation analysis (i.e., .559 and .460 for the first and second canonical variate, respectively) indicating that all the information in the Canonical Correlation has been successfully contained in the Standard Multiple Regression analysis.

Table 7.2 Predicating performance with DV the 1st canonical variate from superiors' ratings, and IVs self-ratings of PA, NA, wellbeing, and satisfaction (n = 125).

Variables	Self-ratings of affective wellbeing and satisfaction	% Unique variance
PA	.330**	4.757
NA	.127	.880
Enthusiasm	-.210	1.481
Depression	-.046	.073
Anxiety	-.065	.234
Relaxation	.026	.041
Intrinsic Job Satisfaction	.449***	11.233
Total Unique Variance		18.699
R	.559	
R^2	.312	
Adjusted R^2	.271	
F	7.596***	

Note: $*p = < .05; **p = < .01; ***p = < .001$.

Semi-partial correlations from Standard Multiple Regressions were squared to calculate the amount of unique variance contributed by each variable. Results from the first variate (with DV of the first canonical variate consisting of the composite of contextual and task performance) showed that the two variables contributed 1% or more of unique variance for superiors' ratings: Intrinsic Job Satisfaction (11.23%) and PA (4.75%). Collectively, these two variables contributed 15.99% of total unique variance. Enthusiasm only accounted for an additional 1.48% of unique variance and this is not statistically significant. The other variables contributed the remaining 1.22% of total unique variance. As with the Canonical Correlation analysis, Intrinsic Job Satisfaction was the most important variable.

When the order of the first canonical variate was reversed (i.e., the composite DV was now based on affective wellbeing and job satisfaction), the only statistically significant association was with Influencing (5.93% of unique variance) while the other variables contributed the remaining 3.94% of variance. Endorsing only accounted for an additional 1.50% of unique variance, and this is not statistically significant. All the other variables collectively contributed an additional 2.43% of unique variance. As with the Canonical Correlation analysis, Influencing was the most important variable. Results of this analysis are shown in Table 7.3.

Table 7.3   *Predicting performance with DV the 2nd canonical variate from superiors' ratings, and IVs self-ratings of PA, NA, affective wellbeing, and intrinsic job satisfaction (n = 125).*

Variables	Self-ratings of affective wellbeing and satisfaction	% Unique variance
PA	.449***	8.788
NA	-.220*	2.651
Enthusiasm	-.615***	12.738
Depression	-.052	.025
Anxiety	.285*	4.424
Relaxation	.274**	4.578
Intrinsic Job Satisfaction	-.006	.002
Total Unique Variance		33.206
R	.460	
R^2	.212	
Adjusted R^2	.164	
F	4.487***	

Note: * $p = < .05$; ** $p = < .01$; *** $p = < .001$.

Table 7.3 shows the results of the second Standard Multiple Regression, with DV the performance dimensions from the second canonical variate, and IVs the intrinsic job satisfaction and affective wellbeing measures. In order of importance, most of the unique variance was contributed first by Enthusiasm (12.738%); PA (8.788%); followed by Relaxation (4.578%);

Anxiety (4.424%); and NA (2.651%) for a total of 33.179%. All the other variables collectively contributed only an additional .027% of unique variance.

When the association between the set from the second variate was reversed (i.e., the composite of affective wellbeing and intrinsic job satisfaction became the DV, and the original performance variables the IVs), this resulted in two variables contributing unique variance greater than 1% of superiors' ratings.

Table 7.4 Predicting wellbeing and satisfaction from self-ratings with DV the 1st canonical variate, and IVs from superiors' ratings of performance dimensions (n = 125).

Variables	Superiors' ratings of performance	% Unique variance
Technical	-.051	.204
Monitoring	.113	.953
Delegating	-.079	.392
Influencing	.359***	5.935
Persisting	.120	.761
Helping	.022	.033
Following	-.039	.094
Endorsing	.180	1.507
Total Unique Variance		9.879
R	.559	
R^2	.312	
Adjusted R^2	.265	
F	6.590***	

Note: * $p = < .05$; ** $p = < .01$; *** $p = < .001$.

Summary of results from the multiple linear regressions

Three statistically significant performance variables contributed the following percentages of unique variance: Monitoring (6.010%); Technical (5.359%); and Following (3.950%) for a total of 15.31%. Delegating only accounted for an additional 1.370% of variance although this was not statistically significant. All the other variables collectively contributed an additional .84% of unique variance. Refer to Table 7.4 for the results.

The results from the Canonical Correlation analysis supported by multiple regressions, indicate that managers' performance is related to managers' affective wellbeing and intrinsic job satisfaction. Although this association has been suggested previously in the published literature, this study provided clear evidence of this relationship. Therefore, Hypothesis 1 was supported.

Table 7.5 Predicting wellbeing and satisfaction from self-ratings with DV the 2nd canonical variate, and IVs from superiors' ratings of task and contextual performance dimensions (n = 125).

Variables	Superior's ratings of performance	% Unique variance
Technical	-.259**	5.359
Monitoring	.283**	6.010
Delegating	-.148	1.370
Influencing	-.031	.044
Persisting	-.119	.754
Helping	.025	.044
Following	.252*	3.950
Endorsing	.006	.002
Total Unique Variance		17.533
R	.460	
R^2	.212	
Adjusted R^2	.157	
F	3.892***	

Note: $*p = < .05$; $**p = < .01$; $***p = < .001$.

Hypothesis 2 was also confirmed. Affective wellbeing was found to predict both contextual and task dimensions of performance. PA, Anxiety, and Relaxation were positively associated, and NA and Enthusiasm were inversely associated with aspects of managers' task (Monitoring, and Technical), and contextual performance (Following). PA and Intrinsic Job Satisfaction were also related to task performance (Influencing).

A number of methodological improvements have been introduced in this study. For example, performance was assessed in terms of superiors' ratings, while managers' affective wellbeing and intrinsic job satisfaction were based on self-reports. Thus, the sources of the data were independent. In addition, as a distinct improvement over previous studies (e.g., Wright

& Cropanzano, 2000), each superior contributed only one randomly selected rating to the study, even though many superiors provided more than one.

Although this procedure resulted in the reduction of cases available for the analyses, it did control for systematic error in ratings. Also, responses were collected from different organisations rather than a single organisation as is normally the case.

Finally, and more importantly, the performance measure constructs were based on heterogeneous samples and which were validated and cross-validated across managerial and supervisory classifications. These findings need to be related to the original A *Partial Model of Managers' Affective Wellbeing, Intrinsic Job Satisfaction and Performance* ('Partial Model') proposed for testing in Chapter 3, as shown again in Figure 7.1.

Figure 7.1 Partial Model of Managers' Affective Wellbeing, Intrinsic Job Satisfaction and Performance

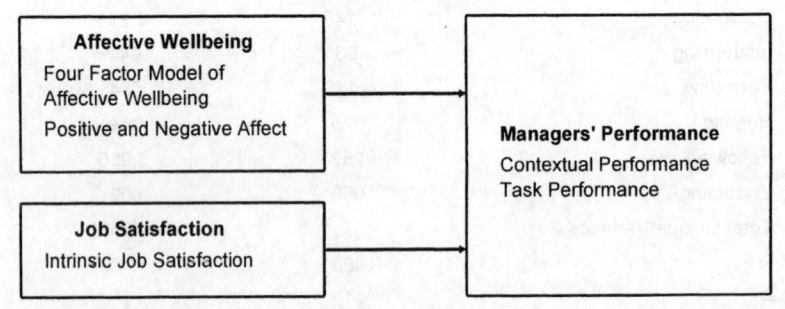

Affective Wellbeing
Four Factor Model of Affective Wellbeing
Positive and Negative Affect

Job Satisfaction
Intrinsic Job Satisfaction

Managers' Performance
Contextual Performance
Task Performance

The association between managers' wellbeing and performance is shown in Figure 7.2 and this is summarised by two orthogonal dimensions.

HYPOTHESES RESULTS

Evidence from the Standard Multiple Regressions indicated that dimensions of affective wellbeing and intrinsic job satisfaction predicted dimensions of managers' contextual and task performance. Two orthogonal variates explained the association between these dimensions. Indicators of affective wellbeing and intrinsic job satisfaction predicted dimensions of managers' performance, irrespective of whether the performance scores were from superiors' ratings or self-report.

Consistent with the literature was the independence of PA and NA. The most important variables identified through the two regression analyses (i.e., those that contributed more than 1% of unique variance) are discussed in more detail later. Tables 7.2–7.5 and 6.17 provide evidence to support or disconfirm the hypotheses.

The first canonical variate explained 31.25% (multiple R = .559) of the variance of performance and the second canonical variate explained 21.16% (multiple R = .460) of the variance of performance. Superiors' ratings of performance were related to *trait affectivity* (PA, β = .330, 4.76% unique variance) and Intrinsic Job Satisfaction (β = .449, 11.23% unique variance), were statistically significant ($p < .01$, and $p < .001$ respectively), and accounted for substantial unique variance. When the DVs were the composite of managers' self-ratings of job satisfaction and wellbeing and IVs the performance dimensions, Influencing was the only statistically significant predictor (Influencing, β = .359, 5.94% unique variance).

Figure 7.2   Two orthogonal variates of managers' affective wellbeing, Intrinsic Job Satisfaction and performance (n = 125)

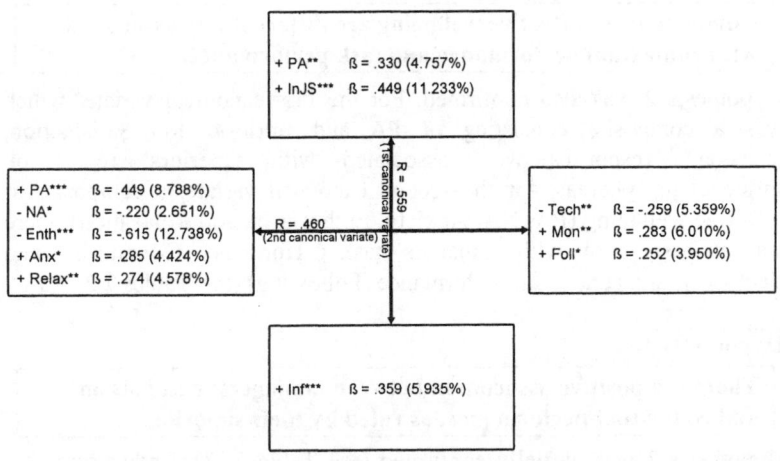

```
                        ┌─────────────────────────────────┐
                        │ + PA**    ß = .330 (4.757%)     │
                        │ + InJS*** ß = .449 (11.233%)    │
                        └─────────────────────────────────┘
                                      │ (1st canonical variate)
                                      │ R = .559
┌──────────────────────────────┐      │      ┌──────────────────────────────┐
│ + PA***   ß = .449 (8.788%)  │      │      │ - Tech**  ß = -.259 (5.359%) │
│ - NA*     ß = -.220 (2.651%) │  R = .460   │ + Mon**   ß = .283 (6.010%)  │
│ - Enth*** ß = -.615 (12.738%)│◄────────────│ + Foll*   ß = .252 (3.950%)  │
│ + Anx*    ß = .285 (4.424%)  │ (2nd canonical variate) │                  │
│ + Relax** ß = .274 (4.578%)  │      │      │                              │
└──────────────────────────────┘      │      └──────────────────────────────┘
                                      │
                        ┌─────────────────────────────────┐
                        │ + Inf***  ß = .359 (5.935%)     │
                        └─────────────────────────────────┘
```

Note: $* p = < .05;$ $** p = < .01;$ $*** p = < .001.$

For the second variate, superiors' ratings of performance were related to affective wellbeing (PA, β= .449, 8.788%; NA, β = -.220, 2.651%; Enthusiasm, β = -.615, 12.738%; Anxiety β = .285, 4.424%; and Relaxation β = .274, 4.578%). When the DV was the composite of managers' self-ratings of intrinsic job satisfaction and affective wellbeing and IVs the performance dimensions, the only statistically significant contextual performance variable was Following (β =.252, 3.950%). From the task performance variables only Monitoring (β = .283, 6.010%) and Technical (β = -.259, 5.359%) reached statistical significance. PA was the only variable to be highly significant (PA, β = .449; 8.788%; PA, β = .330,

4.757%) for the first and second performance canonical variates, respectively.

Hypothesis 1:

> Affective wellbeing is associated with managers' contextual and task performance (as rated by their superiors).

As predicted, affective wellbeing was related to enhanced managerial performance, whereas poor affective wellbeing indicated diminished performance, as specified in the previous paragraph. Since the relationship between wellbeing and performance is positive and linear, high performance is expected to be associated with elevated wellbeing, and low performance with low wellbeing. Thus, hypothesis 1 was confirmed.

Hypothesis 2:

> Components of affective wellbeing are differentially associated with contextual performance and task performance.

Hypothesis 2 was also confirmed. For the first canonical variate, which was a composite consisting of PA and Intrinsic Job Satisfaction, managers' responses were associated with superiors' report on Influencing. Whereas, for the second canonical variate, a composite of affective wellbeing (PA, NA, Anxiety, Enthusiasm, and Relaxation), there was an association with managers' task performance (Monitoring and Technical) and contextual performance (Following) (see Tables 7.2–7.5).

Hypothesis 3:

> There is a positive association between managers' enthusiasm and contextual performance, as rated by their superior.

Hypothesis 3 was partially confirmed (see Table 6.18). Enthusiasm was positively and significantly related to Following, Endorsing, Helping Persisting. However, Following, a contextual variable although positively related to Enthusiasm, was not statistically significant.

Hypothesis 4:

> There is a negative association between managers' anxiety and task performance, as rated by their superior.

Hypothesis 4 was also partially confirmed (see Table 6.18). Although Technical, Monitoring, and Delegating were negatively associated with Anxiety, the relationship was not statistically significant. Influencing was the only task performance variable that reached statistical significance ($r =$

-.22, p < .05).

Hypothesis 5:

> Enthusiasm and relaxation (pleasantness based affect) are stronger predictors of rated contextual performance than anxiety and depression (activation based affect), as rated by their superior.

Hypothesis 5 was not confirmed (see Table 6.18). None of the contextual variables were significantly related to either Anxiety or Relaxation. However, all contextual performance variables were inversely and significantly related to Depression (Persisting, Helping, Following and Endorsing), while only two task variables were significantly and positively related to Enthusiasm (Technical and Influencing).

Hypothesis 6:

> There is a positive association between managers' overall intrinsic job satisfaction and their rated contextual and task performance, as rated by their superior.

Hypothesis 6 was generally supported. All task performance variables (Technical, Monitoring, Delegating, Influencing) were significantly and positively related to intrinsic job satisfaction with all but one of the four contextual performance variables (Following) reaching statistical significance (see Table 6.18).

Hypothesis 7:

> Managers' affective wellbeing is positively associated with contextual performance, while managers' cognitions are positively associated with task performance, as rated by their superior.

Hypothesis 7 was not confirmed. Table 6.18 shows that both Intrinsic Job Satisfaction (cognitive evaluations) and Depression (affective responses) showed statistically significant associations (the first positive and the second negative) with the task and contextual performance variables.

Hypothesis 8:

> Managers who report high levels of intrinsic job satisfaction and enthusiasm will have elevated relaxation, anxiety and low depression.

Hypothesis 8 was substantially confirmed, based on the multivariate results. Positive values were predicted for Intrinsic Job Satisfaction, Enthusiasm, Relaxation, Anxiety and negative values for Depression, attitudinal and affective outcomes of complexity on work pressure model, as depicted in Figure 2.3. The Partial Model predicted that enriched job characteristics were associated with job satisfaction and low depression, while impoverished jobs were associated with job dissatisfaction and Depression. High work pressure will be associated with high anxiety, while low pressure was associated with low anxiety. For 'low strain' jobs the outcomes are Intrinsic Job Satisfaction, Enthusiasm, Relaxation, and low Depression and Anxiety (Quadrant 3). For 'active jobs' the outcomes were Satisfaction, Enthusiasm, Relaxation, Anxiety and low Depression (quadrant 4).

In the first canonical variate, where the stronger wellbeing component was Intrinsic Job Satisfaction ($p < .001$), there was a positive and strong association with the task performance variable Influencing ($\beta = .359^{***}$, 5.94% unique variance). For the second canonical variate, the wellbeing components were PA ($p < .001$), NA ($p < .05$), and negative Enthusiasm ($p < .001$), Relaxation ($p < .01$), and Anxiety ($p < .05$).

For the second canonical variate, all variables except Depression (an affective wellbeing variable associated with low activation) were significant and contributed considerable unique variance in the relationship with the task performance variables Technical ($\beta = -.259^{**}$, 5.36% unique variance), Monitoring ($\beta = .283^{**}$, 6.01% unique variance) and the contextual performance variable Following ($\beta = .252^{*}$, 3.95% unique variance). The negative association of the performance second canonical variate with Enthusiasm may be explained with reference to the low motivating potential of the work components of the performance dimension (i.e., work performance requiring auditing tasks, following of rules and procedures, and low levels of technical expertise).

METHODOLOGICAL DISCUSSION

The relationships between affective reactions and managers' performance were consistent with the literature. Indicators of affective wellbeing and intrinsic job satisfaction predicted dimensions of managers' performance, irrespective of whether the performance scores were from self-report or superiors' ratings. Managers' self-report of performance was contaminated by common method variance and halo effect. Superiors' ratings of managers' performance were deemed to be more reliable indicators of managers' performance.

A possible methodological problem was the use of self-report data and the possibility that the relationships between the set of DVs (contextual and task performance) and the set of IVs (PA and NA, enthusiasm, depression, anxiety and relaxation, intrinsic job satisfaction) were a result of the influence of positive and negative affectivity (Watson et al., 1987; Brief et al., 1988). As Burke, Brief and George (1993: 410) observed, 'self reports of negative features of the work situation and negative affective reactions may both be influenced by NA, whereas self-reports of positive aspects of the work situation (e.g., social interaction on the job) and positive affective reactions may both be influenced by PA'. Evidence of the influences of PA and NA on work was also found by Williams and Anderson (1994). However, these effects 'were shown to have little impact on the parameter estimates representing the relationships among substantive constructs' (1994: 325). Chen and Spector (1991) came to a similar conclusion.

The results from the Canonical Correlation indicated that when a set of job-performance variables was analysed simultaneously with a set of affective wellbeing and intrinsic job satisfaction variables, two orthogonal canonical variates emerged. The composite of the first canonical variate on superior-rated dimensions was mainly made up of PA, and Intrinsic Job Satisfaction. This dimension was related to the performance variable of Influencing.

The second canonical variate was a composite of Enthusiasm, PA, NA, and Anxiety. This dimension was related to the performance variables Technical, Following and Monitoring.

In the present study, the influence of dispositional variables (i.e., PA and NA) could only have impacted on the intrinsic job satisfaction and affective wellbeing variables, since the performance ratings were obtained from a different source. With reference to the wellbeing variables, an examination of the explanatory contribution of the wellbeing variables relative to the two dispositional variables, indicated that they have contributed by far the greater percentage of unique variance to the solution. This suggested that the situational variables (i.e., intrinsic job satisfaction and affective wellbeing) also play an important role in the relationship between wellbeing and job performance, beyond dispositional influences.

Canonical Correlation

As mentioned in an earlier section, Canonical Correlation is the most generalised of multivariate methods. This technique was suitable for analysing variables without strict assumptions of normality, but this was constrained to distinguishing linear relationships. Canonical Correlations are essentially a descriptive technique (Tabachnick & Fidell, 1996). Empirical evidence indicates that canonical weights and canonical loadings are unstable unless sample sizes are large (Bobko, 1990). However, the wellbeing dimensions that emerged from the present study are consistent with those reported by Sevastos (1996), who used two large samples (n = 1,667, and n = 1,418) to replicate these results.

Some deficiencies are evident in significance testing for Canonical Correlations. Significance largely depends on the sample size. Currently, there is no available significance test for each individual variate pair. In certain situations, the first canonical variate pair may not be significant alone, but will achieve significance when combined with the accompanying canonical variate pairs (Tabachnick & Fidell, 2001). Also, SPSS MANOVA does not calculate canonical variant scores, or produce multivariate plots and this further constrains the interpretability of the analysis.

There are also a number of limitations to interpreting the results of Canonical Correlations. Canonical weights are subject to considerable instability and do not extract the variance, but they do maximise the correlation between linear composites. Precise statistics are unavailable for interpreting a canonical analysis, making it difficult to identify meaningful relationships between subsets of IVs and DVs (Hair et al., 1995). Some of these limitations have been addressed through the use of multiple regression analysis.

Methodological Constraints of Self-report Instruments

> I do not regard a measurement as a meaning.
> (Murphy, 1982)

Earlier, a detailed discussion was made of the methodological limitations anticipated for this study. Unconscious misrepresentation of managers' ratings may result in four types of bias: acquiescence; extremity; auspices; and social desirability (Zikmund, 2002). Acquiescence bias is due to the respondents' tendency to concur with a particular position. As the subject matter pertains to individual level performance, affective wellbeing and intrinsic job satisfaction, the acquiescent response set was considered by checking if contradictory questions (e.g., Depression/Enthusiasm, PA/NA) were answered in a logically consistent manner. In terms of methodological limitations, the potential errors associated with random and systematic processes as demonstrated, were minimal. Similarly, both sample selection error and respondent error were not major issues. Acquiescence, extremity, auspices, and social desirability biases were deemed negligible.

To avoid the problems associated with self-report data some researchers have used superiors' ratings (downward appraisal). Superiors' ratings may overcome the problem of social desirability that may occur in self-report data, but this creates the problem of 'subjective favouritism' where superiors give biased performance reports. These reasons may range from simply not accurately knowing the level of performance of an employee, through to personal conflict that results in an intentional underestimation of performance reporting. The variability of managers involved in this study, in terms of occupational category, level of seniority and organisational type, should have minimised this problem.

Relationships between perceptions of the work environment and self-report of mental and physical health are widely documented in the literature (Parkes, 1990). Self-attribution findings (cf. (Mitchell, Green, & Wood, 1981) indicated that managers reporting stressors may be more predisposed to implicate exogenous factors such as poor job design or organisational policies, rather than their own shortcomings. Presumably, those who became involved in this study were intrinsically interested in the perceived value of the study to spend the time to fill in the questionnaire. Self-report of affective wellbeing and intrinsic job satisfaction were consistent with the intent of this investigation, as to the focus on endogenous factors that influence managers' behaviour.

Organisations were initially approached by the researcher and agreed to become involved in this study. Individuals from these participating organisations self-selected into the study. This approach was used because of the sensitive nature of the data being collected. Sample bias was possible at both stages of this process. Ergo, it was tempting to attribute the participation of managers in the study to social acquiescence. Given the considerable workloads reported (Mean = 47.27 hours per week, SD = 9.72) and voluntary involvement, it seems unlikely that managers would have expended the energy required to complete the questionnaire unless they perceived some benefit in the study.

Participation in the study was voluntary but potentially subject to acquiescence. High performing managers may have self-selected into the study and possibly biased the sample. Equally, managers who do not perform well may have been reluctant to be identified and may have opted not to participate in this study. Non-participation of managers from organisations who agreed to be involved in the study could also be attributed to the perennial concerns of fear and indifference, or lack of encouragement (Lange, 1984).

Perhaps managers with high workloads opted to be involved with the study because of strong opinions they had about affective wellbeing and intrinsic job satisfaction. The majority of managers from the participating organisations consistently indicated they were extremely busy and over exposed to questionnaires. No attempt was made to ascertain the underlying reasons for managers' participation in the study, other than to assume that their willingness to be involved was a result of the perceived benefits outlined in the original letter of invitation. Presumably, organisations that agreed to be involved in the study did so because of a concern or interest in the relative and absolute state of affective wellbeing, intrinsic job satisfaction and performance of their managers. Nevertheless, there is further scope for speculation about the motivation, at both the organisational and individual level, as to the reasons managers agreed to be involved in the study.

The incidence of common method variance and bias was anticipated. To overcome this bias, another rating source from managers' superiors was also used because of the potential bias in managers' self-ratings of their performance. Managers' self-reports were also used to measure affective wellbeing, intrinsic job satisfaction, performance and biodata. This eliminated the problem of common method variance as the sources of report were independent to ensure the reliability of managers' ratings on contextual and task performance subscales.

Missing data

Organisations and individuals who responded to the survey are subject to the typical criticism made of this form of methodology - nonresponse bias. This arises when 'persons who respond differ from those who do not. The results do not directly allow one to say how the entire sample would have responded' (Armstrong & Overton, 1977: 396). The missing data problem was quite severe. Respondents either left items blank, or more commonly, selected the 'Not Applicable' option. This resulted in a loss of data when listwise deletion was used. The 'Not Applicable' response option was inserted in the questionnaire because it was assumed that there would be some information superiors would not have known about the managers they were rating. Also, this indicated that managers were not undertaking specific tasks. This may have resulted in more accurate observations regarding the applicable indicators for the majority of managers.

SUMMARY AND CONCLUSION

Robust evidence was found to suggest that relationships existed between managers' affective wellbeing, intrinsic job satisfaction and job performance. This was found by relating superiors' ratings of managers' performance with self-report of their affective wellbeing and intrinsic job satisfaction. Managers' performance was explained by affective wellbeing and intrinsic job satisfaction, without common method variance.

Canonical Correlation and Standard Multiple Regression were used to analyse the relationship between affective wellbeing, intrinsic job satisfaction and managers' performance. Two orthogonal canonical variates were extracted from the Canonical Correlation analysis for both the superiors' rated and self-rated performance datasets. Only significantly correlated variables were reported. PA and Intrinsic Job Satisfaction variables were associated with Influencing. PA, NA, Enthusiasm, Anxiety and Relaxation were associated with Technical, Monitoring and Following.

Managers' self-report of affective wellbeing and intrinsic job satisfaction was related to superiors' ratings of managers' performance to ensure the independence of the measures. Indicators of affective wellbeing and intrinsic job satisfaction were found to predict dimensions of managers' performance, irrespective of whether the performance scores were from self-report or superiors' ratings. In the first canonical variate, affective wellbeing self-report (Affect, Intrinsic Job Satisfaction) was found to be positively associated with a dimension of superiors' evaluations on task performance (Influencing).

A more complex relationship was found in the second canonical variate between affective wellbeing, intrinsic job satisfaction and performance. Positive associations for dimensions of self-report for affective wellbeing (Positive Affect, Anxiety and Relaxation) were found to be negatively associated with dimensions of superiors' reports on managers' task performance (Monitoring) and contextual performance (Following). Negative Affect and Enthusiasm were negatively associated with performance the variable Technical but positively associated with Monitoring and Following. Managers with Positive Affect are likely to experience elevated anxiety but have opportunities for relaxation when undertaking Monitoring and Following work. Positive Affect, Anxiety and Relaxation were positively associated with the contextual performance variable, Following, and the task performance variables Monitoring and Technical.

An alternative explanation for these associations may be that aspects of managers' jobs requiring essentially transactional or administrative roles (negative Technical, with positive Monitoring and Following) may lead to high arousal with PA and Anxiety, but provide opportunities for Relaxation in conjunction with negative Enthusiasm and Negative Affect. A positive association with Monitoring and Following indicated high arousal (Anxiety and Positive Affect with the attendant Negative Affect), but do not lead to a motivating environment (negative Enthusiasm). Managers reported PA, a personality trait, to be the only variable common to both dimensions of contextual and task performance, indicating that it is a prerequisite for managerial jobs. From this finding it could be inferred that managers have a positive disposition to work.

The next part provides the findings, implications and contribution made by this book to organisational theory and management practice.

PART 3:

Findings, Implications and Contribution to Organisational Theory and Management Practice

8. Conclusion: Surviving and thriving in the age of surprises

> A growing body of research is demonstrating that happy workers [are] not only are happier in life but are also crucial to the health of a company.
> (Park, 2005: 621)

INTRODUCTION

As detailed in Chapters 1 and 2, the 'happy-productive worker' thesis has intrigued organisational researchers and practitioners since the 1930s. In this book a close derivation of this theme, the 'happy-performing managers' proposition was thoroughly re-examined by investigating the relationship between managers' affective wellbeing, intrinsic job satisfaction and their performance. The aims and methods employed in revisiting this seminal issue in management have been detailed in the preceding chapters.

This chapter brings together the findings, and links them to an overview and discussion of their contribution to occupational theory and managerial practice. It begins by summarising the study and then analysing the *Partial Model of Managers' Affective Wellbeing, Intrinsic Job Satisfaction and Performance* ('Partial Model'). Conclusions are then given on the major research questions posed and the distinct contribution made to the pool of knowledge in the field. Recommendations for Strategic Human Resource Management are given followed by an exploration of the implications for management theory. Potential new research directions are considered, including a more complete Model of Managers' Performance. Finally, conclusions are made about how to cultivate conditions for happy-performing managers.

OVERVIEW OF THE STUDY

A Partial Model was proposed that linked indicators of affective wellbeing and intrinsic job satisfaction to a number of the dimensions of managers' performance. In the process, a new instrument was developed and refined to establish the structure of the dimensions of managers' contextual and task performance.

The extensive literature on affective wellbeing, intrinsic job satisfaction and managers' performance was critiqued in Chapters 1–4. At the time of writing, this critique represented the most comprehensive, up-to-date review of these concepts and constructs. Key theoretical developments were integrated into the relevant conceptual bases. In Chapter 2, Warr's Vitamin Model was identified as the most inclusive synthesis of research and theories into affective wellbeing. Emotional Intelligence has emerged as a credible contender for integrating these theories in the workplace.

Various theory bases related to managers' performance have informed the issues considered, and assumptions made about job performance in Chapter 3. The literature indicated that managers' job performance is multi-dimensional, comprising the domains of contextual and task performance. Chapter 4 linked the conceptual bases of affective wellbeing, intrinsic job satisfaction and managers' performance to form the Partial Model, and proposed research questions for consideration, and the hypotheses for testing. A series of ancillary research questions, related to the main thrust of this study, was developed from the gaps identified in the literature.

An empirical methodology was used to test the hypotheses to enable the research questions to be answered. Chapter 5 dealt with this phase, including the methodology used to collect the data, sample parameters, and the methods used to develop the measurement instrument. Self-report data were used to measure affective wellbeing and intrinsic job satisfaction, while superiors' ratings was found to be the most accurate way to evaluate managers' contextual and task performance.

An account of how the managers' performance Measurement Model was developed and how the Partial Model was specified is given in Chapter 6. Questionnaire items were sourced from the literature to establish the affective wellbeing and intrinsic job satisfaction scales. Managers' contextual and task dimension and performance scales were devised from the literature. In Chapter 7, the hypotheses and the Partial Model were tested and calibrated. Insights are presented into the inter-relationships among the affective wellbeing, intrinsic job satisfaction and managers' contextual and task performance through a correlational methodology of Canonical Correlation and Standard Multiple Regression.

Finally, this chapter summarises and contextualises the distinct contribution made by this book to our understanding of the managers' happy-performance relationship. Implications of these findings are discussed, and the organisational policy suggestions are considered in detail.

ANALYSIS OF THE PARTIAL MODEL

The Partial Model was developed from the literature (see Figure 4.1) and testing to demonstrate how affective wellbeing and intrinsic job satisfaction impact on managers' performance variables, and The Partial Model was summarised into two orthogonal dimensions for illustration in Figure 8.1.

Figure 8.1 Partial Model of Managers' Affective Wellbeing, Intrinsic Job Satisfaction and Performance (n = 125)

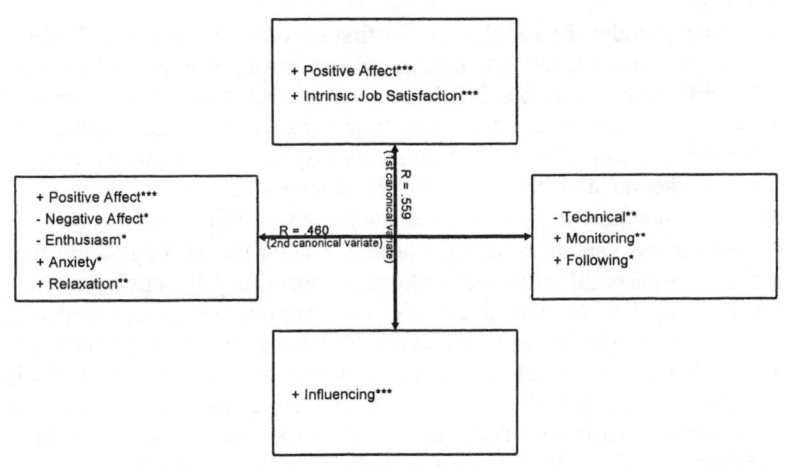

```
                    ┌─────────────────────────────┐
                    │  + Positive Affect***        │
                    │  + Intrinsic Job Satisfaction***│
                    └─────────────────────────────┘
                                 ▲
                                 │ R = .559
                                 │ (1st canonical variate)
┌──────────────────┐             │             ┌──────────────────┐
│ + Positive Affect***│         │             │ - Technical**    │
│ - Negative Affect* │  R = .460 │             │ + Monitoring**   │
│ - Enthusiasm*     │◄──(2nd canonical variate)──►│ + Following*  │
│ + Anxiety*        │           │             │                  │
│ + Relaxation**    │           │             └──────────────────┘
└──────────────────┘             │
                                 ▼
                    ┌─────────────────────────────┐
                    │  + Influencing***           │
                    └─────────────────────────────┘
```

Note: $*p = < .05$; $**p = < .01$; $***p = < .001$.

Unless otherwise stated, it is assumed, as reported in the literature, that the direction of the relationship between the variables is from affective wellbeing, intrinsic job satisfaction to performance (Warr in Kahneman et al., 1999). However, this should not be taken to infer causality between these dimensions. Affective wellbeing and job performance are assumed to be linked in a reciprocal framework of relationships, with each set of factors influencing the other across time (Warr, 1987). Partial model clearly suggests that happiness leads to performance although proposition was not fully tested. However, Lyubomirsky et al. (2005, p. 842) concluded happiness-as-cause is a viable model, rather than the opposite 'In summary, taken together, a variety of different sources of evidence suggest that positive affect leads to certain outcomes rather than simply being caused by them.

Findings on the Partial Model

The managers task performance variables indicated: Monitoring (being vigilant to check the accuracy of information such as budgets); Technical (the applications of technical skills and knowledge); and Influencing (decision making power and leadership); and the contextual performance variable Following (instructions and procedures). The distinction between disposition al and state affect need to be differentiated to assist in interpreting the findings. PA and NA are characteristics of a person irrespective of the work situation. On the other hand state affect (Enthusiasm–Depression and Anxiety–Relaxation), although related to dispositional affect, emerge in interaction with the environment (i.e., job features)

The Partial Model showed that for the first canonical variate, PA (Positive Affect) and Intrinsic Job Satisfaction are very strongly associated with the task performance variable Influencing suggesting that PA also enables managers to influence decisions. Conversely, the opportunities to influence decisions within an organisation may result in enhanced Intrinsic Job Satisfaction and contribute to heightened PA. Managers may also derive considerable Intrinsic Job Satisfaction from Influencing decisions.

The second canonical variate showed a complex set of relationships between aspects of affective wellbeing, intrinsic job satisfaction and performance. PA, Anxiety and Relaxation were positively associated with the contextual performance variables Following and task performance Monitoring but negatively associated with the task performance variable Technical. NA and Enthusiasm were negatively associated with the task performance variable Technical, and task performance variable Monitoring and contextual variable Following. This indicated that high arousal (positive PA with negative NA) was present, but job features were not particularly motivating (as indicated by negative Enthusiasm but positive Relaxation). This finding indicates that managers will experience arousal from Monitoring tasks but low distress when undertaking administrative or transactional roles.

Another explanation for the second canonical variate may be that aspects of managers' jobs requiring essentially transactional or administrative roles (negative Technical, with positive Monitoring and Following) may lead to arousal with PA and Anxiety, but provide opportunities for Relaxation in conjunction with negative Enthusiasm and NA. A positive association with Monitoring and Following indicated that these performance characteristics require vigilance and consequently elevated arousal (Anxiety and PA with the attendant NA), but do not lead to a motivating work environment, as indicated by negative Enthusiasm.

Performing Monitoring and Following roles were shown to provide opportunities for Relaxation that lead to acceptable levels of affective wellbeing. From this finding it could also be inferred that managers with a positive disposition, who also experience some Anxiety and Relaxation, are likely to be successful when performing Monitoring and Following roles. PA, Anxiety and Relaxation were positively associated with the task performance variable Monitoring, and the contextual performance variable Following, but negatively associated with the task performance variable Technical.

PA is a personality trait characteristic associated with extraversion; a personality characteristic that research has shown is central to managerial jobs in dealing with peers, superiors, subordinates and external constituents. Managers reported the personality trait PA to be highly significant and the only affect variable common to both dimensions of contextual and task performance, indicating that may this be a prerequisite for managerial jobs. Possibly, it may be inferred from this that an engaging personality is the reason that individuals are promoted, or self-select into managerial positions.

CONCLUSIONS ABOUT THE RESEARCH QUESTIONS

This section summarises the conclusions reached on the major findings relating to the research questions as posed in Chapter 4. Inferences on the data leading to these findings are given in the sections on the theoretical and practical implications. Four main research questions were investigated that were derived from the extant literature.

Does the construct of managers' performance consist of the two dimensions, contextual and task performance?

Managers' rated performance, previously conceived as a unidimensional construct, was found to consist of two performance dimensions: contextual and task. A multivariate and multi cross-validation of self and superiors' ratings confirmed that managers' performance was multi-dimensional, consisting of eight distinct dimensions - four contextual performance dimensions (Endorsing, Helping, Persisting, Following) and four task performance dimensions (Monitoring, Technical, Influencing, Delegating). Indicators contributing to these dimensions were found to be of most consequence to managers and their superiors in these organisations.

Is there an association between affective wellbeing, intrinsic job satisfaction and managers' contextual and task performance?

PA was found to be a highly significant predictor for both dimensions of contextual and task performance. As anticipated by Judge et al. (2001), Intrinsic Job Satisfaction was found to be associated with performance. Affective wellbeing self-report (PA, Intrinsic Job Satisfaction) was positively associated with a dimension of superiors' report on task performance (Influencing). Positive associations for dimensions of affective wellbeing (PA, Anxiety and Relaxation) were associated with the task performance dimensions (Monitoring) and contextual performance (Following). Of note was the finding that PA, Anxiety and Relaxation were negatively associated with a task performance dimension (Technical). This inverse relationships suggest that technical expertise is not required for routine, programmable tasks (such as Following and Monitoring. Programmable tasks are not motivating but the utilisation of technical skills and knowledge is. Hence, the positive relationships between Enthusiasm and Technical tasks.

To what extent does affective wellbeing and intrinsic job satisfaction predict different dimensions of managers' contextual and task performance?

A large amount of this variance of performance was explained by affective wellbeing and intrinsic job satisfaction and this enhanced the predictive power of the Partial Model. The first canonical variate explained 31.25% of the variance of performance and the second canonical variate explained 21.16% of the variance of performance. Each of the canonical variates separately accounted for substantial amounts of managers' performance in relation to affective wellbeing and intrinsic job satisfaction. This is counter to Wright et al.'s (2002) finding which did not establish a relationship between job satisfaction and dispositional affect as a predictor of job performance. Certain aspects of managers' affective wellbeing and intrinsic job satisfaction (PA, Intrinsic Job Satisfaction, Enthusiasm, and to a lesser extent, Anxiety) were found to be most influential for managers' contextual performance (Following) and task performance (Monitoring, Influencing, Technical).

Does positive affective wellbeing result in enhanced managers' performance, and is poor affective wellbeing detrimental to managers' performance?

As predicted, positive affective wellbeing was related to enhanced managerial performance, whereas diminished affective wellbeing indicated poorer performance. In common with Warr's Vitamin Model, a link between managers' affective wellbeing, intrinsic job satisfaction and performance was evident. Consistent with the literature, Intrinsic Job Satisfaction was positively correlated with PA and negatively correlated with NA (Agho et al., 1992; Watson & Slack, 1993; Judge, Heller, & Mount, 2002). Also, consistent with Warr's (1992) findings, those in higher-level jobs (e.g., managers) reported less job-related depression, but significantly more job-related anxiety. PA was found to be a significant predictor of dimensions of both task and contextual performance, supporting George and Brief's (1996) argument that positive affects (one of the indicators of extraversion) is related to distal and proximal indicators of motivation. PA was positively associated with Influencing and Monitoring, dimensions of task performance, and Following a dimension of contextual performance.

NA and Enthusiasm were negatively associated with Monitoring and Following, possibly indicating some disengagement amongst managers. Although NA and Anxiety are variables with negative hedonic tone, they indicate 'arousal' not 'disengagement' (see Figure 2.1). PA is an 'activation-based' affect that was positively associated with the task performance variable, Influencing. Managers with PA are likely to experience elevated Anxiety, but have opportunities for Relaxation when undertaking Monitoring and Following work. Thus, managers who have high PA and intrinsic job satisfaction are more likely to influence decisions.

In addition, two further questions about practical outcomes are addressed.

- How might managers' jobs be changed to enhance, or avoid a decline in affective wellbeing?
- How might these findings be integrated with workplace initiatives to improve the quality of managers' life and job performance?

The next section extends on how the knowledge emanating from this book may be useful for practitioners and organisations.

MANAGERIAL AND PRACTITIONER IMPLICATIONS

> In theory there is no difference between theory and practice. But, in practice, there is.
> (Van de Snepscheut, 1993)

The Partial Model identified some of the factors that indicate how managers attain and sustain heightened levels of performance. This book lends qualified support to the proposition that happy managers perform better. In turn, this helps to explain the process of upward and downward spirals of managerial effectiveness, whereby positive or negative affective wellbeing and intrinsic job satisfaction lead to increased or reduced performance. These in turn either enhance positive, or exacerbate negative affective wellbeing and intrinsic job satisfaction. These issues need to be addressed if organisations are to operate effectively in an integrative manner. Inappropriate and uncoordinated initiatives to improve managers' affective wellbeing, intrinsic job satisfaction and performance may result in costly and ineffectual outcomes for organisations.

As noted in Chapter 1, managers' jobs are likely to increase in complexity in the future, and as a consequence become far more demanding. A deregulated global marketplace is likely to result in increased outsourcing. In this scenario, managers' roles are likely to evolve more into managing the outsourcing of organisations' needs rather than just managing people. Technological developments and movements to deregulation are exacerbating the speed and spread of this trend. These trends in the marketplace are likely to have a significant impact on managers' personal operating styles, making contextual performance an area warranting particular attention.

Successful initiatives to improve managers' affective wellbeing and intrinsic job satisfaction depend on individual and situational contingencies. Therefore, the normal human resource policies focusing on trying to enforce control, conformity and standardisation across an organisation are in conflict with these findings. Contingency theory indicates that one general intervention is unlikely to be effective for all managers in all situations, whereas combinations of approaches are likely to result in longer term benefits.

'Soft' and 'hard' forces

According to Legge (1995), the normative approached to human resource management suggests a distinction between 'hard' and 'soft' models. These diametrically opposed approaches to managing people are differentiated by the emphasis given to aspects of 'human' or 'resource' to increase the competitive advantage of organisations. Hard approaches emphasise the quantitative, strategic aspects of managing people as organisational assets. Hard approaches are based on tight calculative strategic control based on an economic model driven by utilitarian-instrumentalist principles (Storey, 1989; 1992; Legge, 1995). Human resources are largely viewed as a factor of production, a variable expense of doing business whose value depends on market demand (Tichy, Fombrun, & Devanna, 1982; Fombrun, Tichy, & Devanna, 1984; Hendry & Pettigrew, 1986).

In contrast, soft approaches emanates from the human-relations school and focuses on the importance of communication, motivation, leadership and the mutual commitment of employees and employers (Nankervis, 2004). The soft approach focuses on having a highly competent, flexible and committed work force. People are led rather than managed (Beer, Spector, Lawrence, Quinn Mills et al., 1985; Guest, 1987). Both soft and hard approaches are involved in determining and realising organisation's strategic objectives (Storey, 1989). Organisations rarely adopt a pure hard of soft approach but rather emphasise even when the tenets of the soft version are embraced at the rhetorical level (Truss, Gratton, Hope-Hailey, McGovern, & Stiles, 1997). Inevitably, an organisation's hard underlying rationale for improving bottom line imperatives will prevail over individual interests.

Many studies have confirmed that so-called soft skills are critical for a vital economy (Boyatzis, 1982; Carnevale, 1988; U.S. Department of Labor, 1991; Spencer et al., 1997). Management occurs within the complex milieu of organisations, entities riddled with messy challenges. Dealing with these intractable problems requires a fundamentally soft approach that is dependent on the imprecise, but fundamental notions, of intuition, wisdom and judgement (Mintzberg, 2004). In this situation, affective wellbeing and contextual performance may be seen as conceptually aligned and mutually reinforcing. Management may be characterised as 'mostly soft stuff - working with people, doing deals, processing vague information, and so forth' (Mintzberg, 2004: 41).

Individual task performance only captures a portion of what managers contribute to organisations. This portion of managers' performance is mainly attributed to the knowledge, skills, abilities and experiences of managers. In addition, performance is part of this iterative system. Performance is not simply an outcome but is also an input into other variables. As such, performance is not independent, as all dependent variables impact iteratively on each other. Contributions beyond contextual and task performance may be more accurately termed as discretionary behaviour. These behaviours contribute to organisational effectiveness and go beyond 'soft' psychology, or 'humanistic' concerns to become a critical part of the managers' contribution. As Cohen (2005: 44) says, 'We need to rethink the whole area of corporate education and become more humanistic'. Unfortunately, as Barnard (1938: 5) observed, 'successful cooperation in, or by formal organisations, is the abnormal, not normal condition', so:

> perhaps the reason for the dearth of explanatory power of the 'softer' side of I/O psychology in the study of performance has not been because it is too soft, but that our dependent variable, 'performance', has been too hard.
> (Organ & Paine, 1999: 338)

Incorporating the hard aspects of organisational existence with the less tangible soft dimensions has the potential to improve the interconnections between managers and employees. Hard control in management can be augmented with soft control as well as self-discipline emanating from individual empowerment and individual autonomy. Soft skills, such as inspiring employees and generating commitment, are more difficult to master and sustain than the hard skills associated with strategic and operational business planning (Ulrich, 1997). Also, using soft skills does not come naturally to some managers.

By integrating soft aspects of managers' performance, with hard aspects of management, this book explored how affective wellbeing and intrinsic job satisfaction of managers are relevant to the attainment of personal and organisational performance outcomes. Hence, the soft aspects of managers' performance may be associated with hard organisational outcomes, such that these:

> two apparently disparate approaches are not necessarily mutually exclusive. They can be reconciled through a contingency framework, which provides guidance on the positioning of an organization's human resource strategies as part of the organization's overall change strategy and ultimately its business strategy.
> (Dunphy & Stace, 1990: 87)

The statistical analyses described in Chapters 6 and 7 demonstrated that, when considered holistically, the use of separate job-related affects in organisational research can enhance our understanding of the relationships between affective outcomes (soft) and aspects of managers' performance (hard) variables. This provides support for a differential application of human resources, rather than a uniform application and management policies and procedures. Such an approach requires changes to some organisations' policies and *modus operandi* away from command control and conformity to a contingency approach to human resource policies and practices.

Job design

In context, job enrichment is a potentially powerful way of encouraging enhanced performance. Social needs (the desire for significant social relationships) and growth needs (the desire for personal accomplishment, learning and development) can most effectively influence work designs (Cummings & Huse, 1989). When combined with recent advances in management theory and practice, these findings have the potential to enhance managers' affective wellbeing, intrinsic job satisfaction and performance. The degree of social needs of individual managers should inform how work is designed. For example, managers with low requirements for social relationships are likely to be more content working on individualised jobs than being involved with groups. Those who have high social needs will probably be more attracted to group work rather than individualised situations.

Further, Mitchell (1979: 246) reported that 'people who are high in achievement needs or growth needs respond more favourably (are more satisfied, happier and perform better) when faced with enhanced, challenging jobs than do people low in these needs'. In isolation, job enrichment may only enhance motivation for those managers who desire autonomy and challenge at work and in organisations where executives support participative decision-making. Challenges and responsibility have been found to be the most important drivers of satisfaction in the contemporary workplace (Florida, 2003).

An important contribution to managers' affective wellbeing and intrinsic job satisfaction will be through job design analysis, with particular attention to locating specific and real data. Socio-technical, quality of work, work design and initiatives are established methods of maintaining and improving the affective wellbeing and intrinsic job satisfaction of the employees (Cummings & Huse, 1989). All of these are intended to improve human fulfilment and organisational effectiveness. These are established techniques that should already be embedded in organisational human resource practice. However, it is essential that any human resource practices must fit with the business objectives of the organisations to have any chance of being implemented and ultimately being successful. There are other ways of effectively motivating people to perform. One of these is through attention to the built working environment.

Work environment

Organisations providing pleasant work environments that are challenging and supportive are likely to attract managers who are more creative, energised and productive. Workplace climate has been shown to have a direct impact on productivity and efficiency, accounting for up to 25% of performance (HayGroup, 1999). Google is an interesting example of a company that combines an attractively built environment with an outstanding stock price. The 'Googleplex' is described by Maney (2002):

> Scooters lean against walls. Big exercise balls are everywhere. Walk around and you'll see piles of roller hockey equipment, random toys, a bin offering 13 kinds of cereal including Lucky Charms, a wall mural of the company's history done in crayon, a spalike room marked by a sign that says 'Googlers massaged here' and a cafeteria where gourmet meals are served by the former chef for the Grateful Dead.

Organisations could increase the efficacy of managers and employees by creating built environments that are in sympathy with their psyche. This sense of *joie de vire* can also significantly enhance the work culture of an organisation. For example Southwest Airlines has, for three decades, demonstrated the capacity to create a superior winning culture when compared to any other airline. Southwest's performance is based on total staff involvement, assisted by profit sharing and a particularly generous staff stock option bonus system. Apparently, getting a job at Southwest is reportedly more difficult than being accepted into the Harvard Business School (Thomas, 2004).

The establishment of a work environment that is conducive to optimal performance has the potential to ameliorate debilitating pressures on managers arising from unrealistic demands for performance. This may be achieved by reducing the complexity of organisational practices and increasing job security. Watson and Clark (1984) explicitly identified negative emotions as aspects of negative affectivity (i.e., low challenge), pessimism, that leads to a tendency to perceive the environment as threatening. Similarly, Costa and McCrae (1987) identified self-esteem, negative affectivity, social anxiety, and perceived ability to cope (i.e., low challenge) as aspects of neuroticism. Long term exposure to work pressure associated with more complex jobs can lead to either negative or positive affectivity (Schmitt, 1994).

Assessments of affective wellbeing and intrinsic job satisfaction need to closely match the work environment that a manager is located in, a general consideration frequently overlooked according to Warr (1987). Competence, autonomy and aspiration are three behavioural components of mental health usually connected with positive levels of affective wellbeing and intrinsic job satisfaction (see Table 2.3). Managers who are supposed to be high performers are likely to be the recipients of interesting and challenging job assignments (e.g., Graen & Uhl-Bien, 1995).

Managers who spend long periods in jobs that lack opportunities for control and skill use are likely to experience an adverse impact on job-related competence. However, in some cases job-related anxiety, when linked to aspirations, is not necessarily linked to diminished affective wellbeing and intrinsic job satisfaction. For example, highly motivated managers who desire challenges may react to risks in a way that raises their anxiety level but it does not negatively impact their affective wellbeing and intrinsic job satisfaction.

Managers are liable to have elevated anxiety but not the concomitant depression, when considered in relation to the rest of the general population because of the nature of their work. Extended periods of work anxiety need to be followed by opportunities for managers to have commensurate periods of relaxation. Therefore, organisations that intersperse periods and aspects of work that invoke acceptable levels of anxiety with opportunities for relaxation are likely to have managers who perform well on administrative roles (such as Monitoring and Following).

One important way of promoting affective wellbeing among managers is to encourage them to take recreational leave after demanding work assignments. Individual affective wellbeing and intrinsic job satisfaction could be assessed and reported to managers at regular intervals. These measures can be compared with industry and organisations' norms to indicate levels of affective wellbeing and intrinsic job satisfaction. For example, the ASSET (An Organizational Stress Screening Tool), showed good convergent validity with existing indicators of mental illness (Johnson & Cooper, 2003). ASSET is normed with 80,000 international organisations.

Stressors in the workplace

In this book, affective reactions were conceived as a precursor to stress in the workplace. Affective wellbeing was treated as a first order concept that underpinned stress, which is conceived of as a second order concept. Emotional reactions, resulting from intrinsic and extrinsic stimuli, have been shown to determine a person's reactions to stressful situations. A credible variant of Warr's Vitamin Model based on monopolar dimensions of affective wellbeing (i.e., the Four Factor Model of Affective Wellbeing) (Sevastos, 1996) was used here to assess psychological wellbeing (i.e., the co-occurrence of Intrinsic Job Satisfaction, Enthusiasm and Relaxation) and distress (i.e., a combination of Anxiety and Depression), rather than the more elusive construct of 'stress', which is beset with conceptual, and methodological problems (Kenny & Cooper, 2003).

As Osipow and Davis (1988: 2) state 'high occupational stress does not itself predict strain. Only by including the degree to which coping resources exist was an adequate prediction of strain possible'. Job-related stress is related but distinct from the concept of affective wellbeing and intrinsic job satisfaction. Stress forms but one facet of affective wellbeing and intrinsic job satisfaction in jobs. Thus, it should not be conceived of separately, but in the context of the working milieu. Stressors may have a physical or psychosocial origin which may interact with each other and affect a person's physical or psychological health (Cox, Griffiths, & Rial-Gonzalez, 2000). The European Council of Ministers (European Union, 2001, November) concluded that:

> stress and depression related problems ... are of major importance ... and significant contributors to the burden of disease and the loss of quality of life within the European Union.

Further, stress and depression were considered to be:

> common, cause human suffering and disability, increase the risk of social exclusion, increase mortality, and have negative implications for national economies.
> (cited in Levi, 2002: iii)

Thus, the affective wellbeing of the workforce in general, and for managers in particular, is an important public policy issue. Carlopio (2005) reported on a study which showed that on average, managers engage in 237–1073 separate incidents demanding their daily attention. More than a third of managers indicated that they could not achieve what they set out to do each day. Pervasive feelings of pressure, being overloaded, and out of control are likely to worsen. At the individual level, stress and time pressure may be symptomatic of a deficient personal management problem resulting from a lack of self-awareness and unbalanced work priorities (Carlopio et al., 2005).

Unlocking employee potential through leadership

Since leadership permeates all organisational activities it is arguably the most critical role assumed at every level of management. Leadership has traditionally been associated with the kind of things that top executives do (e.g., goal setting, articulating a vision) to ensure organisations are dynamically transformed. Contemporary research and practice renders such definitions arbitrary, since 'most managers show some leadership skills, while most leaders find themselves managing at times' (Karpin, 1995a: 1210). Put another way, 'managers have to lead and leaders have to manage' (Mintzberg, 2004: 6). As with management, leadership is also about 'releasing the positive energy that resides within people' (Mintzberg, 2004: 143). Management has been characterised as 'doing things right', while leadership involves 'doing the right things' (see Bennis & Nanus, 1985: 21). There is evidence suggesting that leadership influences individual motivation and performance at the organisational level (Seltzer & Bass, 1990; Brown & Leigh, 1996; Griffin & Mathieu, 1997).

There is a vital human element to managing people. As Livingston (1971) concluded, managing successfully is not just about managers' success but also about fostering success in others. Therefore, leadership should be considered a vital aspect of managers' repertoire of competences. Truman (1976) considered leadership to be the 'ability to get people to do what they don't want to do and like it.' Management competence subsumes leadership, such that leadership and management have become virtually indistinguishable and 'managers cannot be successful without being good leaders, and leaders cannot be successful without being good managers' (Carlopio et al., 2005: 12).

As with managers, the 'leader's task was to get work done through other people, and social skill makes that possible' (Goleman, 1999: 102). Emotional intelligence has been promoted as the *sine qua non* of leadership Goleman and others (e.g., George, 2000; Prati, Douglas, Ferris, Ammeter, & Buckley, 2003; Boyatzis & McKee, 2005). Goleman (1999:

3) went so far as to assert that 'most effective leaders are alike in one crucial way: they all have a high degree of what has come to be known as emotional intelligence. George (2000) proposed a intuitive link between emotional intelligence and leadership which was extended to incorporate a connection between emotional management of transformational leadership. Transformational leadership has been associated with emotional intelligence (Daus & Harris, 2003; Coetzee & Schaap, 2004). Empirical evidence is emerging to substantiate a link between leadership ability and transformation leadership in particular and the ability model of emotional intelligence (Daus & Harris, 2003).

All managers also need to undertake leadership roles when it comes to orchestrating collaborative workplaces. Organisational leaders and managers need to know how to influence others to get things done by collaborating and engaging the emotions of employees to achieve the bottom line (Cullen cited in Barker & Coy, 2005). The process of influencing is central to such a notion of leadership, to ensure the 'followers' in organisations are committed to the leader's goals and have a genuine desire to work together to achieve organisational outcomes.

A new dynamic is evident in contemporary organisations: 'Being articulate, being able to sell ideas, and engage the minds and hearts of employees are the new bottom line issues for managers' (Hatcher, 2005: 62). How managers promote engagement varies widely within and between organisations. Findings from this study are consistent with the aforementioned views: Influencing was found to be strongly associated with dispositional PA and Intrinsic Job Satisfaction. Thus, manager-leaders are likely to possess high PA and report intrinsic job satisfaction. This positive disposition of managers needs to be transmitted into a feeling of hope amongst employees (Simmons, Nelson, & Quick, 2003).

Generating hope in the workplace

Hope is an attitude that is responsive to change (Simmons et al., 2003). Its constituent parts are positive affect that reflects the degree of expected benefit that will be derived from an evaluation of a particular situation. Hope is an attribute and is therefore made up of a cognitive set based on a sense of self-efficacy through successful goal-directed determination, and planning to meet goals (Snyder et al., 1996). Better health has been found to result when a hopeful and optimistic psychological view is combined with flexible and strong behaviour, complemented by a hopeful interpretive style (Simmons et al., 2003).

Hope is proposed as an attribute of emotional intelligence, a conceptualisation wedded to the belief that an individual possesses both the will and the wherewithal to accomplish goals (Huy, 2003). Managers' success in this mindset depends on them making astute evaluations of situations and allocating the resources necessary for employees to achieve organisational goals. This conceptualisation of hope led Luthans (2002) to declare that hope was the most unique positive organisational capacity, a construct capable of being developed by individuals.

Managers are in a unique position in terms of their ascribed organisational and legitimate authority, to promote affectively healthy high performing work environments. Managers need to accept and act on the responsibility of engendering a sense of hope in the people who work with them. The goal-directed behaviour of hope has been found to represent an active engagement in work (Simmons et al., 2003). Managers can help to generate an attitude of hope amongst employees by establishing meaningful goals and allocating the resources necessary for individuals to achieve these goals (Smith, Haynes, Lazarus, & Pope, 1993). A positive frame of mind reflected in managers' attitude, when reinforced by actions, goes a long way towards engendering a feeling of hope in employees. As active role models for employees, managers and executives should be active participants in any initiatives to develop positive individual wellbeing and performance within an organisational context. Managers can engender hope by harnessing intrinsic motivation through employees through good, clear, and persuasive communications.

Results reported in this book provided strong support for the contention that executives and senior managers define performance more broadly than simply assessing whether managers are proficient at completing and performing task activities. It was also found that additional factors such as contextual performance should be taken into account when forming an evaluation of managers' performance. Perhaps, as Organ (1977) argued, people would be more inclined to exhibit gestures of organisational cooperation as a way of reciprocating satisfying work experiences to ensure 'successful cooperation in or by formal organisations is the abnormal, not the normal condition' (Organ & Paine, 1999: 400).

Emotional Intelligence

As discussed in Chapter 1, emotions are important aspects of affective wellbeing in the workplace. Goleman (1995) has argued vigorously that IQ and technical skill are perennial 'threshold capabilities' required for entry to management positions. Emotional intelligence is potentially relevant to contextual performance constructs, specifically leadership and to management in general. Goleman (1999: 21) observed 'As more companies put a premium on people who can lead, the ability to *influence* [emphasis added] is one of the competencies at a premium'. Thus, managers' emotional intelligence should be incorporated into assessments of managers' affective wellbeing and performance. Goleman (1999) has argued that the further managers' progress in organisations, the more vital all aspects of emotional intelligence become. Managers with well developed emotional intelligence are likely to be more effective, particularly in jobs requiring extensive contextual performance.

Technical expertise is not considered to be an important aspect of managers' task repertoire. As Goleman (1999: 21) noted, 'outstanding supervisors in technical fields are not technical but rather relate to handling people'. Goleman (1999:38) has asserted that 'the higher the level of the job, the less important technical skills and cognitive abilities were, and the more important competence in emotional intelligence became'. This result is consistent with the HayGroup (1999) finding that less than 10% of Fortune 500 companies believed an overemphasis on managers' technical ability had resulted in the careers of high potential managers and leaders becoming 'derailed'. This result was confirmed by this study, where NA and Enthusiasm were negatively associated with the task performance variable Technical.

Managers now need to produce tangible outcomes (task actions), as well as be competitive in the way they (contextual actions) achieve organisational goals. In a study of the managers of scientists and engineers, Dreyfuss (1990) found the distinguishing abilities of successful managers in this environment were the capacity for group building or team building. The ascendancy of work teams in large organisations has put a new premium on team skills. Organisations whose core business is technically orientated should consider selecting and developing managers with team building experience, or with the capacity to develop these competencies.

Organisational researchers investigating emotions have neglected to include employee job performance where 'behaviours or actions that are relevant to the goals of the organization in question' (McCoy, Campbell, & Cudeck, 1994: 493). How well employees handle themselves and each other emotionally, is seen by Goleman (1995; 1999; Goleman et al., 2002) to be as important as the intelligence or expertise possessed. Apart from intelligence, the single most important factor distinguishing 'star performers' from the 'also rans' is considered by Goleman to be emotional intelligence. Goleman (1998: 5) boldly proposed that 'IQ takes second position to emotional intelligence in determining outstanding job performance'. Emotions are considered by Goleman (1995) to play an important role in business decision making - the more important the decision, the stronger the influence.

Managers who aspire to be stellar performers should be encouraged to master their own emotions, as well as those around them. Management training should focus on developing a set of emotional intelligence skills, including: control of one's impulses, self-motivation, empathy and social competence in interpersonal relationships (Goleman, 1998). Additionally, training that involves the development of emotional competence may be more effective than those based on traditional cognitive based initiatives. Promotable managers are those most likely to benefit from training and development in emotional intelligence. General support was found in this book for enhancing affective wellbeing as a way of improving self-efficacy to motivate managers with the competence to perform. This can be achieved by managers enhancing self-awareness, self-management, social awareness and social skills (Salovey & Mayer, 1990; Mayer & Salovey, 1993; Mayer & Salovey, 1997; Goleman, 1998; HayGroup, 1999).

Fortunately, managers and their employees can learn how to become better equipped and empowered to deal with their own and co-workers' affective health. Mintzberg (2004) and Goleman (1999) have suggested ways in which managers can improve their personal competencies with soft skills, acquired through training and development. In managing people to make the great transition from potential to practice, Buckingham and Coffman (2005) argued that it is necessary to know three things about a person: their strengths, the triggers that activate those strengths, and how a person learns. Buckingham and Coffman (2005) believed this leap is made by asking the right questions, pressing the right triggers, and becoming aware of one's employees' learning styles. This is considered by them to be the best way to discover what motivates each person to excel. However, before knowledge of another person can be gained, managers must first know themselves very well.

Know thyself and others

For thousands of years, knowledge of self has been known to be at the core of human behaviour. Managers may therefore consider heeding the advice of the ancients and undertaking some form of personal development to fully 'know thyself'. An ancient Chinese expression attributed to Lao Tzsu explained the nature of true awareness this way: 'knowing others is intelligence; knowing yourself is true wisdom'. Invariably, such self-knowledge, and other-empathy should entail a close examination of personal and interpersonal communication style to discover the authentic self through active reflection.

As Emerson (1965) so eloquently expressed, we cannot help giving off who we are because, 'What you are shouts so loud in my ears I cannot hear what you say'. Exposing managers to different ways of thinking in order to inform their behaviour, is important for increasing self-and-other awareness (Mintzberg, 2004). A spirit of reflection is a way of encouraging consciousness raising by managers about the competencies needed to permit ongoing learning (Lee, 1989; McKnight, 1991: 205; Conger, 1998; Mintzberg, 2004). All this may sound like 'warm and fluffy' advice but it has served to guide the philosophy and actions of leaders throughout the ages and thus deserves active consideration. As with POS, this approach is about discovering one's strengths and building on them for improved self-reliance and self-improvement. For example, Salovey, Rothman, Detweller and Steward's (2000) work suggests that positive emotions generate psychological resources by promoting resilience and optimism.

In some part, managers' affective reaction to their environment determines the interplay between the organisational dynamics encountered and external environment forces. Managers with positive affective wellbeing and intrinsic job satisfaction were found in this study to perform better on certain dimensions than those with poor affective wellbeing and low intrinsic job satisfaction. Such an outcome can also result from the circumstances of managers' working environments. Creating a work environment that provides managers with the opportunities to realise their needs through personal development may result in a greater contribution to organisational outcomes. Individual needs can be fostered through high degrees of autonomy, and regular and meaningful feedback by encouraging a reasonable amount of risk taking to achieve work goals (McClelland, 1985).

A wealth of literature exists to support the position that managers who are capable of more accurate self-ratings are likely to be successful and effective on the job (Atwater & Yammarino, 1997). A growing body of research on the psychological contract, and more especially on Organisation Citizenship Behaviour (OCB), is indicating how discretionary behaviour is triggered (see Coyle-Shapiro, 2004). High levels of OCB have been shown to influence performance. Also, OCB outcomes emanate from people with high levels of affective organisational commitment and job satisfaction (Purcell, 2004).

Leaders whose self-ratings concur with their direct reports, particularly those whose ratings can be described as 'good' as opposed to 'poor' on the target criterion, have a high potential to secure psychological contracts for role behaviour. This may be due to the direct reports to leaders believing them to be both trustworthy and altruistic. By achieving such psychological contracts, such managers are well positioned to create social capital that allows them then to contribute to the goals and objectives of the organisation in ways that exceed the normal expectations of their ascribed positions (Boyatzis & McKee, 2005).

The importance of contextual performance

Organisations now need employees who will willingly exceed formal job requirements in order to improve organisational productivity. Human resource practices should strive to create an environment that overtly encourages desirable behaviours, such as establishing a social exchange relationship in preference to purely economic exchange relationships within organisations (Witt, 1991; Konovsky & Pugh, 1994; Robinson & Wolfe-Morrison, 1995). A careful balance needs to be sought to create an environment where employees identify with and share the organisation's values, goals and objectives (Organ, 1990), that allows employees to feel empowered (Organ, 1990), and provides leadership training to executives and managers (Koh, Steers, & Terborg, 1995; Latham & Skarlicki, 1997).

In an era where more effectiveness is expected from organisations, managers' adaptability and flexibility is essential for sustaining organisational competitiveness, and cooperation from employees, using team based structures. Feelings and emotions, stemming from mood and affective disposition, have also been found to play an important role in increasing organisational productivity (George & Brief, 1992). This knowledge provides organisations with a more sophisticated explanation and assessment of performance by explaining and explicitly monitoring contextual performance, as distinct from task performance.

Adopting an affective determinant perspective has resulted in mood significantly contributing to helping and prosocial behaviour (George, 1991). This relationship demonstrated that people in positive moods have a more optimistic outlook on life, and as a result think more about the rewards received from helping others rather than the cost of offering assistance (Isen & Baron, 1991). Such gestures may be altruistic or in expectation of a social reward. Regardless of the motivation, these actions lubricate the critical informal social mechanisms of organisations (Scott, 1992).

However, employers should exercise caution when requiring employees to slavishly follow rules and regulations. If these guidelines about behavioural expectations are presented and perceived by managers as immutable, there is a risk of creating circumstances where there is inadequate room for healthy dissent or for expression of new ideas that are counter to the prevailing organisational views. On the other hand, neglecting to recognise the contextual dimension of managers' performance may reduce intrinsic motivation to exhibit such behaviour. As a consequence, this has the potential to reduce managers' inclination to effectively deal with unforeseen contingencies (Smith et al., 1983).

People in positive moods have been found to desire to maintain these moods and choose to help others, as this serves to sustain their mood

(Carlson, Charlin, & Miller, 1988). Engaging in contextual performance activities may serve a similar function, as it increases the possibility that a person will be working in a positive and healthy environment (George & Brief, 1992). It is worth speculating, as Organ and Paine (1999: 344) have, that 'people consciously and deliberately use OCB (contextual performance) to reciprocate their employees for positive work experiences'. This form of reciprocation has been shown to lead to better work performance. Organisations that encourage and reward contextual performance for managers are likely to be recompensed in subtle but important ways. This kind of recognition is more likely to occur with employees of choice.

IMPLICATIONS FOR STRATEGIC HUMAN RESOURCE MANAGEMENT PRACTICES

> The proper management of one's feelings clearly lies along a complex (and therefore not simple or easy) balanced middle path, requiring constant judgement and continuing adjustment.
> (Peck, 1978: 169)

An important aspect of human resource management in practice or organisational behavioural research concerns optimising an organisation's less tangible assets through constant vigilance and calibration. This commitment is likely to be reciprocated as part of the social contract inherent in contextual performance and has the potential to become a self-perpetuating relationship. A large proportion of human resource initiatives are intended to improve organisation effectiveness through individual performance (Neal & Griffin, 1999). Organisations should give serious consideration to investing initiatives that provide managers with a sense that their organisation cares and is seriously prepared to look after their wellbeing.

A clear reward system would need to involve a measurable demonstration of desired behaviours that lead to defined performance outcomes. For such reinforcement to occur, the levels of job performance would be expected to increase, commensurate with improvements in affective wellbeing and intrinsic job satisfaction. High levels of affective wellbeing and intrinsic job satisfaction may in turn lead to elevated levels of performance. These findings have implications for managerial effectiveness. The main premise is that actively promoting the affective wellbeing and intrinsic job satisfaction of managers has the potential to improve certain aspects of their performance.

Employee respect and financial success

The Gallup Organisation (2005) has conducted periodic large-scale random polls of 5.4 million workers in 474 organisations. A strong relationship with co-workers and a supportive boss indicate a strong sense of belonging in the workplace. Employees have basic human needs that transcend organisational and industry boundaries. Attending to these basic human needs has been found by The Gallup Organisation to be a powerful predictor for engagement at work and is connected with customers' satisfaction and profitability.

The most financially successful business operations have been found to share a number of characteristics (Maister, 2001). Such businesses are not only more profitable but they do better than their competitors in virtually every aspect of employee attitudes. The attitudes of employees were found to drive the financial results of businesses. Most importantly, specific skills and behaviours of the manager have been found to predict this success (Maister, 2001). In such organisations the management was perceived by employees as operating in accordance with the organisations' overall philosophy and values.

These managers were found to be trusted by those they manage (Maister, 2001). Individual managers were seen as working for the interests of their groups, and not just to advance their personal welfare. In this environment, people's personal potential was being realised in accordance with their underlying needs. The quality of people in these businesses was seen as high, which is partly attributable to the uncompromising adherence professional hiring standards. Compensation systems were also managed equitably in these organisations.

Those employers who are perceived to treat employees fairly invoke social exchange and the norm of reciprocity (Organ, 1990), commonly in the form of employee OCB. Many studies have been conducted on the relationship of OCB to leadership style and supportiveness. These include such notions as: the Leader-Member Exchange Relationship (Wayne & Green, 1993; Deluga, 1994), leadership trust (Konovsky & Pugh, 1994; Robinson & Wolfe-Morrison, 1995), leadership style (Schnake et al., 1993), leadership monitoring techniques (Niehoff & Moorman, 1993), and how training in organisational justice was received by leaders (Skarlicki & Latham, 1996; Latham & Skarlicki, 1997). These studies are informed by the social exchange theory of motivation (Organ, 1990; Konovsky & Pugh, 1994).

The top factors predicting profitability in Maister's (2001) work were the soft issues of trust and respect. When trust and respect between management and employees is high, then financial performance is more likely to increase. The top 20% of offices on the financial performance index showed distinctive responses to seven items of the 'top twenty things that the most successful offices do' better than the rest (Maister, 2001). This list includes a management that listens, values input, can be trusted and by supervisors who are effective coaches. The behaviour of individual supervisors matters more than considerations of corporate strategy or policy. Employees were found to believe that in order to win their trust it is necessary for managers to listen, communicate well and treat people with respect by valuing their input.

Implications for recruitment, selection and retention of managers

By inference, managerial competencies should be incorporated into organisation's selection, development and succession planning processes. Collins (2001: 64) argued that the old adage 'People are our greatest asset' is wrong. People are not your most important asset. The right people are'. Collins (2001: 64) goes on to assert that 'Whether someone is the right 'person' has more to do with character traits and innate capabilities than with specific knowledge, background, or skills'. This is congruent with the finding here that PA, a dispositional characteristic is closely linked to aspects of both contextual and task performance.

Person-environment fit is important to ensure that an individual's proclivity is congruent with the environment the manager will be expected to perform in. Selecting the right person for a particular job is critical. Emphasis also needs to be placed on cultural 'fit' and adaptability (Forster, 2005). Realistic job previews have been shown to reduce uncertainty by providing reasonable expectations that allow a transition into a new work environment (Schweiger & De Nisi, 1991).

As a minimum, high performing managers and new recruits would be expected to have the following emotional intelligence competencies: self-awareness, impulse control, persistence, zeal and motivation, empathy and social deftness (Goleman, 1998). As Rozell, Pettijohn and Parker (2002: 287) observed, a 'potential manager's understanding of management techniques dealing with interpersonal interaction and intrapersonal emotions may have a fundamental place in the overall success of that individual in the workplace'. In consequence, a modicum of emotional intelligence may well qualify as a core competency of aspiring managers.

Recruitment and selection of high performing managers

Employee job performance variability for managers is large enough to be important to the viability of organisations. The most important practical value of a personnel assessment is the ability to accurately predict future job performance and amount of job-related learning. Predictive validity has been found to be directly proportional to the economic utility of the selection method (Brogden, 1949; Schmidt, Hunter, McKenzie, & Muldrow, 1979). Adopting selection methods with high predictive validity is likely to lead to considerable increases in employee performance when measured as increases in output, increased value of output and increased learning of job-related skills (Hunter, Schmidt, & Judiesch, 1990). Also, the importance of making accurate selection decisions becomes even more critical when anticipating the long term value of building a pool of managerial talent for succession planning and future promotions.

In a highly competitive world, these organisations who fail to use valid selection methods are unnecessarily creating a competitive disadvantage for themselves (Schmidt, 1993). The well established principle that the best predictor of future performance is past performance is consistent with the behavioural consistency method of evaluating previous training and experience (Schmidt et al., 1979; McDaniel, Schmidt, & Hunter, 1988). By adopting more valid hiring procedures, organisations can turn this into a competitive advantage.

The practical utility of valid selection methods is considerable. The validity of selection measures for predicting job performance has been determined by Schmidt and Hunter (1998). Research conducted over the last 15 years has shown that the variability of performance varies greatly among employees (Schmidt et al., 1979; Hunter & Schmidt, 1983; Schmidt & Hunter, 1983; Hunter & Schmidt, 1990; Schmidt & Hunter, 1998). When performance variability is very large, as with managerial and professional jobs, it is even more critical to select applicants with best potential to perform. For managerial and professional jobs the standard deviation of output as a percentage of average output is 48% (Hunter & Schmidt, 1990). A high performing manager or professional will produce in the order of 48% output above or below the average. Given this large variation, mistakes in hiring managers can be extremely costly for organisations. Conversely, the payoff from using valid hiring methods to predict later job performance of managers is equally large.

The most valid personnel predictor of future performance and learning for managerial applicants is general mental alibility (GMA). More than any other measure, GMA can increase the odds of successful managerial performance (Schmidt & Hunter, 1998). Job experience remains an important factor in predicting performance. GMA and an integrity measure (composite validity of .65); and the combination of a GMA test and a structured interview (composite validity of .63) are both practical to use for most hiring decisions because they have high composite validity (Schmidt & Hunter, 1998). Personnel assessment methods can also predict future job performance and future learning. Many of the selection methods also predict job related learning, the acquisition of job knowledge with experience on the job, and the amount learned by training and development. When used to select employees who will have a high level of job performance, GMA has also been found to predict those who will learn the most from job training and will acquire job knowledge more quickly from job experience (Hunter & Hunter, 1984).

Many other measures can also contribute to the overall validity of the selection process, for example, measures of conscientiousness and personal integrity, structured employment interviews, and job knowledge and work sample tests. A combination of personnel measures used in hiring is directly proportional to the practical value of the method used, as measured by a dollar value of increased output or percentage of increase in output. In economic terms, the gains from increasing the validity of hiring methods can amount over time to literally millions of dollars.

In this study, PA and Intrinsic Job Satisfaction were strongly associated with Influencing. PA is a trait personality characteristic associated with extraversion, a personality characteristic that is central to managerial jobs in dealing with peers, superiors, subordinates and external constituents. This indicates that managers who exhibit high levels of PA and Intrinsic Job Satisfaction may be effective at influencing others within and outside organisations. Executives with assignments that require extensive influencing may look to managers who exhibit or report high levels of PA and Intrinsic Job Satisfaction which indicates they are highly engaged at work. PA incorporates a personality trait (extraversion) that may also be a more useful indicator of a competency for selection purposes than the literature currently indicates. However, this finding should be tempered with the caveat that competencies represent managers' potential to perform rather than actual observed performance. This reality needs to be tempered with the realisation that a person's affective tendencies can influence their likeability, likelihood of being hired and the evaluation of their performance (Cook, Vance, & Spector, 2000).

An engaging personality may be a reason individuals are promoted or self-select into managerial positions. PA may enable managers to influence decisions from which they derive considerable Intrinsic Job Satisfaction, which incorporates a substantial cognitive component. A positive outlook is indicated by a personal belief in the future which is a trait associated with greater resilience (Park, 2005). Possibly the opportunity to influence decisions within an organisation may result in enhanced Intrinsic Job Satisfaction in addition to heightened PA. Also, it was shown that PA was the *only* variable common to both dimensions of contextual and task performance, indicating that it could be a useful prerequisite for managerial jobs.

Collins et al.'s (2001; 2004) work underscores the importance to organisations of selecting the best managers. Collins likens the selection process to making sure that the right people are 'on the bus' before determining where you want them to sit (i.e., what you want them to do). Selecting staff is argued by Collins and colleagues to be about locating the best player for the team, as opposed to selecting the best player on the team (Collins, 2001; Collins & Porras, 2004). As noted earlier, high performance organisations and employers of choice will 'thick screen' potential recruits to identify dispositional (contextual) behaviour and attitudes above and beyond task skills. This needs to involve the competencies required by employees of choice. To assist in the process of deciding who should be on or off the bus it is worth relating the implications of the finding in this book to the recruitment and selection of high performing managers. Forster (2005: 539) has identified a cluster of seven core skills, competencies and qualities of leaders-managers which all normal people wish to follow:

- Honesty and integrity,
- Competence and credibility,
- Ability to motivate and inspire people,
- Good two-way communications skills,
- Equity/parity and fairness,
- Sense of humour.

These time honoured elements are argued by Forster to be essential for successful leadership and people management both now and in the future. The capabilities are necessary for leaders-managers to lead, inspire, motivate, mentor and empower people to effectively create a sustainable advantage for organisations. Other aspects of this 'virtuous circle' of attributes to include are: an optimistic outlook, being outgoing, and a capacity and willingness to work in teams. Further, the personal values held by managers is increasingly being shown to influence their behaviour and performance and ultimately to impact on organisational effectiveness (Westwood & Posner, 1997).

Consistently successful companies in the USA expend a considerable amount of resources on recruitment and selection procedures than their less successful counterparts (O'Reilly & Pfeffer, 2000; Collins, 2001; Collins & Porras, 2004). A large part of making the transition from mediocre to an excellent organisation is the discipline in selecting the right people through rigorous selection choices incorporating 'thick screening' to select and recruit the right managers. Thick screening includes: written aptitude tests, psychometric testing, group problem solving and leadership exercises, extensive reference checks combined with several rounds of interviews with senior management, peers and those who might be working with the potential new recruit.

Importantly, managers reported PA, a personality trait, to be the only variable common to both dimensions of contextual and task performance. From this it may be inferred that a positive disposition is a useful requirement for managerial jobs that require a high level of influencing. Conversely, high NA individuals may be more suited to jobs that require attention to detail and minimal contact with employees. This finding has implications for the recruitment, selection and development of managers. Part of a 'thick selection' process then should require candidates to take psychometric tests to measure positive and negative state and disposition. Instruments suitable for making these measures are featured in this book. These are the PANAS and the Four Factor Model of Affective Wellbeing. Other validated psychometric tests are available to test a wide range of candidate attributes, such as GMA and conscientiousness. However, a *carte blanche* adoption of selection psychometric state and dispositional tests of affect is not premature. Findings from this study are indicative and need to be replicated with a more diverse international sample before more specific recommendations can be made about the selecting managers using state and trait affect.

Expending time and energy trying to motivate people is argued by Collins (2001) to be a waste of organisations' resources. Essentially, Collins believes that the right people for a job are already self-motivated. Resources are therefore better deployed in identifying and selecting the people with the required technical competencies who have realistic job expectations of the organisation they intend to join. This includes a complete picture of work experience, attitudes and fit with the prospective organisation's culture.

Performance appraisal

Research into performance appraisal continues to be criticised for being irrelevant to practice, and thereby reducing the advancement of practice (Organ & Paine, 1999). Research in this context is seen to be taking place in rarefied academic atmosphere which is seem to be out of touch with what happens in the workplace. In part, this was a result of studies conducted in laboratory settings that focus on psychometric issues and cognitive processes with neither being congruent with practitioner interests (Wood & Marshall, 1993). Well developed performance appraisal initiatives have the potential to effectively link managers' performance to business strategies (Carlopio et al., 2005).

Such an alignment is more likely to contribute to an organisation's effectiveness when human resource practices related to managers are congruent with organisational strategies. More sophisticated and comparable measures of managers' performance in situ are required in order to ascertain individual contributions to organisational effectiveness. Managers tend not to receive timely feedback about their current level of skill competency (Forster, 2005). Performance assessments are invariably narrow in scope and neglect to fully acknowledge some of the most critical aspects of managerial work such as discretionary actions. On a more positive note, there is a noticeable trend from employees of choice to recognise and reward discretionary job effort (Martin, 2005).

As noted earlier in this chapter, a new instrument was developed as part of this study to measure and establish the multi-dimensional structure of managers' contextual and task performance. Superiors' ratings were found in this study to be the more reliable measure of managers' performance, while self-report was found to be a less reliable measure. When selecting and rating managers' performance it is important to recognise that their performance is multi-dimensional and consists of contextual and task performance dimensions. The 8–Dimensional Measurement Model of managers' performance was tested to differentiate the structure of managers' contextual and task performance domains. Performance construct was found to consist of four contextual dimensions (Endorsing, Helping, Persisting, Following) and four task dimensions (Monitoring, Technical, Influencing, Delegating). This 8–Dimensional Model of managers' performance could be incorporated into performance appraisals. Thus, performance appraisals of managers should include a multifaceted array of contextual and task work activities.

Contextual performance is based on the belief that these behaviours are likely to enhance organisational effectiveness and efficiency (Podsakoff & MacKenzie, 1997). Since contextual performance improves organisational effectiveness, it is in an organisation's interest to recognise and reward this aspect of managers' performance. Managers' contextual performance also has the potential to enhance the performance and success of the people to whom managers report. Consistent with other research, this book has demonstrated that managers, as well as their superiors, do consider contextual performance important when evaluating job performance. Thus, it is worth including contextual contributions to organisational effectiveness when rating managers' performance. Therefore, it would seem reasonable to embrace a domain of performance broader than just task activities by incorporating contextual activities into human resource practices such as selection, performance management, rewards, and training and development, in order to improve organisational productivity.

As suggested in Chapter 5, contextual performance, which may be better conceptualised and measured as 'discretionary effort', is important for shaping the organisational, social, and psychological context that serve as a critical catalyst for task activities and processes. Unlike task activities that are made explicit in documents, such as job descriptions, contextual activities are not normally explicitly included in performance appraisals for managers. As a consequence, contextual performance is an important aspect of managers' performance that is not usually explicitly included as criteria when assessing managers' performance. Contextual performance may well be a psychological construct rather than purely a performance construct and therefore should be measured and treated as such. Performance appraisal systems for managers need to more clearly disentangle contextual performance from task performance. The instrument developed for this study provides a robust measure of both contextual performance and task performance for managers.

The incorporation of contextual components into performance management systems needs to be carefully implemented. Expecting managers to volunteer for additional duties outside the realms of the job, requesting that they work above and beyond the call of duty, and requiring assistance for co-workers and superiors, has the potential to impact on managers' performance in ways that are not formally recognised. Applying sanctions to managers for not doing more than what is required, may have unanticipated consequences. Making expectations about these requirements explicit will serve to shift the original idea of classifying these behaviours as extra-role. This has the potential to reduce the likelihood of the spontaneous occurrence, or unplanned incidence of such behaviour in organisations.

Encouraging high levels of task performance may be detrimental to contextual performance (Organ & Paine, 1999). This may result to some extent, from contextual and task performance constructs being mutually exclusive. In this situation, the notion of Following may be incompatible with Influencing. This is possibly a function of those managers who are content to perform transactional roles, as opposed to those who seek to influence decisions. However, formally specifying or rewarding contextual performance is difficult to achieve because it involves behaviour that is often difficult to measure effectively.

Feedback to managers

Providing timely feedback to managers may assist them to self-monitor their affective wellbeing, intrinsic job satisfaction and performance by providing a yardstick against which to measure and compare themselves. Positive and negative affective wellbeing factors identified as having an impact on managers' performance may also be used to construct guidelines for the design of managers' jobs and work environments conducive to optimal performance. Initiatives which adopt positive workplace management systems can complete existing management systems by documenting, measuring, implementing, managing and training managers and their teams in building a positive workplace that is similar and compatible with quality and occupational health and safety systems (Manion, 2005).

A heightened sense of self-awareness, when combined with the capacity to develop rapport with a range of people, is valuable for motivating others. Psychometrically robust measures of performance, when combined with multisource feedback, would permit managers to see themselves as others do, both within their organisations and in relation to those in other organisations. Masked and unconscious behaviours would be apparent. Increased self-awareness would assist managers to identify shortcomings and areas of performance needing improvement. Self and other awareness can be developed by targeted training and coaching. An important aspect of self awareness is the development of the facility for empathy, an aspect of emotional intelligence.

In an increasingly complex legal framework governing employment, it is also prudent for organisations to implement performance appraisal practices that are legally sound and defensible. Adopting valid measures of affective wellbeing and management performance appraisal practices, including documentation of actions taken to alleviate any problems, has the potential to reduce an organisation's exposure to employment related litigation. Concentrating on managers' behaviour, what they *do*, rather than attempting to address the more contentious question of what managers *are* in some intrinsic psychological sense, allows performance assessment to be viewed in a more positive light. As such, performance appraisal instruments were designed here to provide valid data of a manager's performance. Performance assessments that are more rational, focusing on behaviour alone, may help to make claims arising from a dismissal potentially more difficult to establish, and easier for employers to defend. Organisations may eventually benefit from adopting a regime of performance and affective wellbeing measurement through reductions in costs associated with employment litigation.

Managers and executives invariably find discussions about performance appraisal with employees to be awkward and as such often avoid addressing difficult issues. Performance appraisal is one aspect of organisational life that has largely defied scrutiny at a time when organisations are engaged in constantly seeking ways to improve their operations and reduce costs (Nickols, 2000). Possibly this is because performance appraisals are taken for granted in most large organisations. Regarding this aspect of organisational life, Nickols (2000: 2) contended that 'As with most unquestioned facts, a critical examination can prove beneficial'. Formal performance appraisal systems annually consume billions of dollars in large organisations' hard operating costs. The associated soft costs may well be even higher. The primary offsets to these costs are the purported benefits of performance appraisal systems.

There are a variety of political, structural, and systemic reasons why performance appraisal systems cannot function as intended. Of more concern is the negative impact on the employees of performance appraisal systems that are supposed to assist them. Given this scenario Nickols argued that the net benefit of these performance appraisal systems range from non-existent to minimal and could be eliminated without causing great economic and emotional fallout. An extreme end of this debate about performance appraisal is for change-focused executives to ignore pleas to redesign an organisation's performance appraisal system but instead give serious thought to scrapping it entirely (Nickols, 2000).

There are good reasons for re-engineering an ineffective performance appraisal system. One change is worth considering to the way performance appraisal is undertaken which is unrelated to the actual performance appraisal system. The usefulness of individual performance management is heavily dependent on the competence of the manager conducting the performance review. Of particular importance is the capacity of managers to clearly communicate feedback to employees during the appraisal review. As with everyday managing there is a need to focus on behaviours that will facilitate desired outcomes and discourage the ones not wanted.

Training and development issues

Executive management development is increasingly being seen as involving personal development related to the way in which the individual deals with work/life issues, stress, and health (Hall, 1995). By their very nature, developing self-awareness, self-insight and self-understanding are within an individual managers' capacity for development. Training and development efforts have not always distinguished between cognitive learning and emotional learning. Nevertheless, such a distinction is important. A shift in attitude and emphasis is needed for this to occur, beginning with recognition of the importance of affective wellbeing in the workplace and the contribution of intrinsic job satisfaction to managers' performance. Developing these competencies is one way of ameliorating the debilitating effects of stressors on individual managers.

Since behaviour is something that can be changed and developed, the emphasis in this investigation was on developing an aspect of human potential to enhance managerial performance. Creating ingrained patterns of thoughts, feeling and behaviour may require an extensive development effort over several months, and may require a further 3–5 years to fully develop (Chernis & Goleman, 2001). An 'emotional competence is a learned capability based on emotional intelligence that results in improved job performance' (Goleman, 1999: 25). Emotional competence requires that emotional learning be recognised and given the same prominence as cognitive learning. Developing emotional intelligence takes time and most of all, commitment from organisations and individuals. Benefits that flow from a well developed emotional intelligence for both the individual and the organisation, are likely to make the effort and cost worthwhile (Goleman, 1999).

Traditionally, task relevant improvements (e.g., job design) or motivational techniques (e.g., goal setting and reinforcement) or improvements in ability (e.g., training and development) have been used to improve performance. Essentially, these interventions concentrate on the cognitive aspects of managers' jobs. Organisations that are most successful at developing managers provide extensive development and coaching, and measurement of progress that is coupled to an appropriate reward system (HayGroup, 1999). Certain affective wellbeing states (e.g., Enthusiasm, Anxiety and Relaxation) were found, in this study, to influence managers' likelihood of achieving optimal performance. Finding ways of improving self-efficacy is important to furthering our understanding of how motivation influences performance that may translate into increased organisational productivity. This can be achieved by changing work environments to be more flexible and intrinsically rewarding.

A growing body of research on emotional learning and behaviour change suggests that it is possible to help people of any age to become more emotionally intelligent at work. However, many programmes designed to do so fail to recognise the difference between cognitive and emotional learning. According to Goleman (1998: 317), 'Companies are naive in how they spend their development dollars in training for people skills - they can get a far better return on their investment if they do it right ... The rules of work are changing. We're being judged by a new yardstick: not just how smart we are, or our expertise, but also how well we handle ourselves and each other'. This book reinforces the need to rethink how we approach developing soft skills in the workplace.

Cognitive learning involves fitting new data and insights into existing frameworks of association and understanding, extending and enriching the corresponding neural circuitry. Emotional learning involves more than this, it requires managers to also engage their neural circuitry which stores the repertoire of social and emotional habit. Changing habits, such as learning to approach people positively instead of avoiding them, to listen better or to give feedback skilfully are more challenging tasks than simply adding new information to old. Individual motivational factors also make social and emotional learning more difficult and complex than purely cognitive learning.

Emotional learning often involves ways of thinking and acting that are more central to a person's identity. Goleman (1998) has specifically linked the ability to influence others to a person's emotional intelligence. However the importance of emotional intelligence needs to be kept in perspective, 'Emotional intelligence skills are synergistic with cognitive ones: top performers have both' (Goleman, 1998: 21). Developing managers' emotional competencies requires a broad and sophisticated array of development tools. Traditional training needs to be blended with a variety of ongoing planned developments such as career assignments and individual coaching. A period of months involving ongoing coaching, encouragement, peer support, modelling and on-the-job practice is necessary (HayGroup, 1999). Such initiatives have important resource implications for organisations and therefore demand careful consideration.

Retention of key employees

Gaining and retaining talented managers is crucial to an organisation's survival and prosperity. Over the last 20 years The Gallup Organisation has extensively researched the workplace by surveying over 20 million people. One of the most compelling findings, over three decades, is the realisation that people consistently tend to join organisations, but whether they choose to stay or leave depends on the enabling attributes of managers. People may join organisations because of an organisation's reputation but how long they stay and how productive they are depends on the relationship with their supervisor (Brown, 2005).

By logical extension this finding would also be more relevant to executives. This applies to the quality of the relationship between executives as well as that between managers, and also between managers and employees. Moreover, turnover at managerial level is very damaging to organisations - typically three times a person's annual salary (Chynoweth, 1998).

Socially responsible companies generally have a happier workforce and will retain better and more capable staff. This will also be important to the future as Generation Y starts to make career decisions based on companies' position on social ethics. Such recommendations may also impact on the employees that managers' work with, particularly influencing retention. The future generation of employees have clearly indicated a desire for greater meaning and personal development in their work. These employees look for intrinsic satisfaction from aspects of work that are enjoyable, fulfilling and socially useful (Avolio & Sosik, 1999).

Since the best employees invariably leave their managers, not organisations (Buckingham & Coffman, 2005) companies can best support their employees by ensuring they have competent managers. Managers make the difference when employees decide to stay at a job or leave. From interviews with in excess of a million employees, the Gallup Organisation established that when top employees decide to continue working for their current organisations, their foremost consideration is the quality of the management. Clearly, employees will not tolerate dysfunctional relationships with their managers or the executives they work with.

This phenomenon is likely to apply when talented managers are faced with the decision to continue or depart from organisations. Managers who are set clear expectations by executives who know, trust and invest in them, are more likely to forgive a lack of development opportunities, profit-sharing programmes or gain sharing opportunities. In order to get employees to make a great deal of money for an organisation, Maister (2001) believes that it is necessary to first set high standards and to give employees goals to energise towards. Further, it is necessary to be managed by people who are genuine, have integrity and who care about their co-workers as much as the business.

Remuneration has traditionally been used as the main way to motivate people to perform. However, not all people are motivated purely by financial incentives. Actually, in some cases, financial incentives can reduce motivation instead of increasing it (Faragher et al., 2005; Martin, 2005). Remuneration only motivates people to a certain point of performance beyond which affective wellbeing and job satisfaction are more likely to assist in achieving goals. Consistent with other studies in the field the Gallup Organisation polls have shown that beyond a certain minimum level (i.e., $AUD50,000 in the USA) pay or benefits do not make people any happier at work (Easterbrook, 2005). Warr (1986) refers to this phenomenon in the Vitamin Model as the 'constant effect'. Beyond a certain threshold, feelings of intrinsic job satisfaction can be as important as money for persuading people to increase productivity (Herzberg, 1966; Kahneman et al., 1999). But how can employees, who are not fully motivated by financial incentive, be encouraged to exhibit desirable discretionary behaviour?

Promoting and rewarding discretionary effort

Discretionary performance reward schemes are used by over 40 of Australia's top 200 companies to recognise traditional work tasks that are well executed, or for helping colleagues (Carruthers, 2005). Employees are able to nominate their colleagues for four categories: helping others, leadership, sustainability and leadership, and achievement (Carruthers,

2005). This mode of reward is potentially more transparent and accountable than traditional ways of recognising discretionary performance (Finlayson cited in Carruthers, 2005).

A feature of these schemes is that employees can nominate their colleagues for exceptional work, which may have gone unnoticed by their superiors. Intranet reward programmes use a points system to select goods or holidays. However, a danger of such scheme is that they should not be used to replace pay rises or other performance incentives (Williams cited in Carruthers, 2005). Well designed reward and recognition programmes can take many forms. The most successful schemes will be those that are closely aligned with the strategic directions and value of an organisation. Performance reward schemes are initiatives organisations can promote to reward discretionary behaviours by employees.

From the literature it is apparent that organisations expect more of managers than defined in-role performance as a means to increasing organisational productivity. Increased organisational effectiveness is dependent on contextual performance (Werner, 1994). This expectation should be made explicit to managers and those involved in rating their performance. In particular, managers who take their in-role performance literally may be unfairly disadvantaged unless all criteria for judging their performance are pre-specified. Evaluations of higher-level managers are likely to be even more dependent on contextual performance (Borman & Motowidlo, 1997). In-role expectations of senior managers and executives are likely to be even more diffuse (Organ, 1988). Contextual performance may well contribute similar amounts of variance as does task performance (Podsakoff et al., 1997; Podsakoff & MacKenzie, 1997).

Mintzberg on management education

Mintzberg's (2004) book *Managers not MBAs*, makes a scathing criticism of the state of management education and management itself, claiming that both are in trouble and need a radical overhaul. A Master of Business Administration (MBA) is traditionally the academic qualification of choice for managers. According to Mintzberg, this is the basis of an extensive problem as the MBA degree fails to develop managers and breeds a dysfunctional style of managing that is undermining organisations and societies. He goes on to argue that leaders of organisations are needed with human skills, not just professionals with an academic qualification. MBA courses, it is argued admit the wrong people, teach them in the wrong way and deliver the wrong results.

In the process of obtaining an MBA, a distorted impression seems to be created of the practice of management. The trouble with 'management education', Mintzberg contends, is that it is actually 'business education'.

According to Mintzberg, conventional MBA classrooms ignore the art and denigrate the craft of management, while overemphasising the scientific aspect. Existing MBA programmes are intended for people without managerial experience and so overvaluing analysis to the detriment of experience. This leaves a distorted impression of management which has resulted in a corrupting influence in its practice.

Mintzberg has called for a more engaging approach to managing and to management education. An alternative scenario is provided as a means for practising managers to increase the effectiveness of their management skills without doing a traditional MBA. Consequently, a very different approach to management education is proposed whereby practising managers learn from their own experience. Mintzberg proposes putting the art and the craft back into management education, and into management itself, because managing is primarily about working with people. An important aspect of this approach revolves around using 'reflective learning' based on experience to inform practice which is in keeping with the POS approach of developing the best self approach for managers to learn to be more aware.

Mintzberg's approach goes well beyond the analytical focus of most graduate business schools by proposing that gaining self-knowledge and empathy with others, is essential to management education and training. Hill (1992: 275) concluded that 'the education many business schools provide do little to prepare managers for their day to day realities'. It is argued that MBA graduates need to learn more about soft skills. As discussed in Chapters 1 and 2, and in the emotional intelligence section of this chapter, these calls for the development of soft skills by managers are well founded. Mintzberg proposed a radical re-think of management education as a way of getting back to a more engaging style of management in an effort to breed better organisations rather than inflated share prices.

Bennis and O'Toole (2005) are two leading US academics who also believe that many business schools have lost their way. They argued that MBA programmes are failing to impart useful skills to prepare managers for corporate life. While some business schools may be conducting excellent research, not enough is grounded in actual business practices. A considerable amount of work published in academic management journals is irrelevant to the practitioners and commercial interests it should serve (Hosie, Smith, & Gunningham, 2003). Much of basic and applied research conducted in management academia research is bereft of social benefit. Research is needed into the complex social and human factor issues actually facing practising managers. Issues surrounding judgement, communications and ethics are some of the soft skills needed by contemporary managers. Many graduate business schools are becoming increasingly constrained and less relevant to practitioners.

However, it is worth bearing in mind that many of these criticisms are based on observation of USA full-time MBA programmes. These criticisms are not as relevant to UK and Australian MBA programmes, as these are mainly undertaken by part-time students with considerable work experience. These courses are more focused on people-based subjects and are not case driven.

Influencing through communications

Influencing change is at the heart of effective management.
(2005: 198)

In some capacity everyone is trying to influence people to get them to do something. Eales and Spence (2005: 198) defined 'Influence is the effect that all our actions, both conscious and unconscious, have on our surroundings'. Barker and Coy (2005), the editors of the book *Understanding Influence for Leaders at all Levels*, recognised the importance of the subtle art of influencing others, especially employees, as being important in leadership roles that managers undertake. Managers need to be particularly adept at 'persuasive communications' (Hatcher, 2005). The problem is that managers, like *'most people are not as good at communicating as they like to believe they are'* (Forster, 2005: 95). Boyatzis (1982) (see Chapter 3) identified the 'art of influencing' as being a fundamental aspect of managers jobs, which is a demonstrated behaviour resulting from the interaction between managers and their environments. These findings are reinforced by results reported in this book in relation to the task performance dimension: Influencing.

Influencing is a rapidly expanding field of psychological inquiry dedicated to establishing the principles that determine beliefs, create attitudes, and move people to agreement and action. Research into influencing has examined the judgement and decision-making processes that motive people to efficiently change in positive directions. Cialdini's (1993) book *Influence: The Psychology of Persuasion* provides reasons why people are convinced to negotiate and comply with requests in business settings. Research into persuasion has demonstrated how sensitively selected influence strategies have the power to convince others in the workplace (Varghese, 2004). Choices made about the use of expressions, content and placement of ideas contribute to persuading others.

When trying to identify high performance managers it is important to make holistic measures that align with the stated aspirations and values of the organisation (Varghese, 2004). As Hatcher (2005: 62) concluded

'Being articulate, being able to sell ideas and engage the minds and hearts of employees are the new bottom line for managers. One very important path to influencing others is through persuasive communications'. Subtle forms of control help employees become 'connected, committed and inspired' to do their best not just for managers but the whole organisation. Effective communication is paramount to the success of initiatives in organisational affective wellbeing and performance. Giga et al. (2003) considered the 'viability and success of an intervention to be dependent on senior managers sending clear signals demonstrating their intent and long term support'. This goes to the very heart of organisational existence - the dominant culture. From a resource based view of the firm Barney (1986: 656) asserted that:

> firms with sustained superior performances typically are characterized by a strong set of core managerial values that define the ways they conduct business. It is these core values (about how to treat employees, customers, suppliers and others), that foster innovativeness and flexibility in firms. When they are linked with managerial control they are thought to lead to sustained superior financial performance.

Developing a corporate culture where employees are willing to communicate, analyse and revise plans is essential to create initiatives to promote affective wellbeing and performance (Giga et al., 2003: 291). This goes beyond gaining the support of senior management, to a cultural shift directed to embedding a recognition and desire to create and maintain positive affective wellbeing and performance within existing organisational dynamics. These actions permit organisations to meet future challenges through ongoing processes based on communications, culture, participation and negotiation (Nytrö, Saksvik, Mikkelsen, Bohle, & Quinlan, 2000).

The high cost of employee disengagement

Disengagement and demotivated employees, including managers, are very expensive for organisations and countries. Actively disengaged employees are reported to be costing US businesses some $US300 billion a year in productivity losses (Crabtree, 2004). The Gallup Management Journal's semi-annual Employee Engagement Index (Crabtree, 2004) found that 17% of employees are actively disengaged, the equivalent of about 22.5 million US workers. The majority of workers (54%) report being 'not engaged'. Only 29% of employees felt 'engaged', as defined by Gallup employees that 'work with passion and who feel a profound connection to their company.' Gallup Australia (Donaldson, 2005) estimates that the 20% of employees who are 'actively disengaged' at work costs Australia about $AUD31.5 billion a year in lost productivity, profitability and a customer service. Similarly, disengaged employees in New Zealand cost around $NZ3.6 billion a year through being less loyal and more disruptive at work.

Actively disengaged employees may be physically present but more importantly they are psychologically absent. From Figure 2.2 it is apparent that 'strong engagement' (indicating arousal) and 'disengagement' (indicating lethargy) occupy space at opposite poles of the axes of affective wellbeing circumplex. Employees who are unhappy with their work are often intent on sharing that discontent with their otherwise engaged coworkers which undermines their performance. A low level of commitment or achievement can be very disruptive in the workplace. Engaged employees have consistent levels of high performance and are more likely to stay with an organisation. Even employees of choice will harbour pockets of disengaged employees within their organisation.

Curiously, on the whole the employee disengagement crisis has gone unnoticed despite the obsession with productivity improvement that dominates so much of corporate management's attention. Few organisations seem aware of the costs of employee disengagement, possibly because it is hard to observe, and even more difficult to measure. Engaged employees are customer-focused, less likely to leave, and more likely to care about gaining and retaining customers. Motivating employees is a crucial role of managers. Re-motivating disengaged employees is therefore a vital aspect of managers' work.

ORGANISATIONAL IMPLICATIONS

> It's clear that we can change our happiness levels widely - up and down.
> (Lykken cited in Wallis, 2005: 17)

Global dynamics and Australian managers

Pressures to manage the increasingly complex and varied contingencies impacting on organisational performance are greater than ever (Patterson et al., 1997). In this environment, managers' performance is central to the success of organisations. Achieving and sustaining high individual performance and organisational productivity in this intensely competitive economic environment has the potential to impact on the affective wellbeing of managers worldwide (Kinicki, McKee, & Wade, 1996). In dynamic, competitive markets, successful organisations are likely to be staffed with managers capable of adapting to constantly evolving roles, with the capacity to achieve and sustain optimal levels of performance. Individual and collective levels of affective wellbeing, and intrinsic job satisfaction of managers are therefore critical to an organisation's survival and prosperity.

Chapter 1 highlighted the realisation that managers have entered an era that demands for competencies with global relevance, where managers are expected to efficiently perform a wider range of complex functions. For organisations with international responsibilities and aspirations, some managers are now required to perform highly complex tasks, such as coaching employees for overseas assignments and developing skills that are transportable to international settings. Managers now operate within these global dynamics. In the wider context the nexus between these 'personal troubles' and 'public concerns' needs to be considered (Bernardin & Beatty, 1984).

When 'personal trouble' becomes 'public concern'

Estimates of the cost of depleted mental health show a consistent and disturbing pattern. Clearly, mental health in the workplace is an international problem of considerable magnitude. The cost to organisations and nation-states is unacceptably high and appears to be increasing unabated. As a consequence, governments in developed countries are legislating to ensure organisations accept more liability for the consequences of work practices on employees' health (Kenny & McIntyre, 2004b; 2004a). Of more concern is the debilitating effect on the individual of diminished mental health. The personal cost of reduced affective wellbeing to an individual's life is incalculable. In these circumstances, personal trouble related to personality characteristics must also become a public concern and this is closely related to work characteristics and the epidemiology of occupational health. Progressing the 'happy-performing managers' proposition has implications as to how managers' 'private troubles' have become 'public concerns' (Wright Mills, 1959).

Promoting employee affective wellbeing

There is still an overwhelming tendency to target affective wellbeing strategies and evaluations at individual employees (Giga et al., 2003). Such interventions attempt to empower workers to deal with difficult work situations by developing their own coping skills and abilities. Some examples include relaxation, meditation, biofeedback cognitive behaviour therapy, exercise, time management and employee assistance programmes (Giga et al., 2003). Individual level initiatives are usually the prerogative of management involving limited employee consultation over the time and minimal resources required to ensure success.

This individually focused approach usually involves psychologists who concentrate on subjective and individual differences. Inaccurate conclusions about the effectiveness of such programmes are often made, bringing into doubt the long term effectiveness of such initiatives (Bellarosa & Chen, 1997). Person-directed attempts to develop coping skills and abilities are invariably rendered ineffective by organisational situational contingencies, such as the allocation of inadequate time and resources. Individual coping strategies have exerted minimal influence on the occupational psychology literature (Giga et al., 2003). There is a point at which even the most resilient manager will break down (Kenny & Cooper, 2003). Individual programmes that empower employees to deal with difficult work circumstances are intended to develop personal coping skills and abilities and seem unlikely to result in sustained health and affective wellbeing.

Employers could do more to structure the work environment in a positive way. Organisational policies to develop and sustain employee affective wellbeing should stem from strategies to comprehensively address health and safety issues (Giga et al., 2003). Three levels of stress management - Individual, Individual/Organisational, and Organisational - have been identified by DeFrank and Cooper (1987) which may be productively applied to initiatives to promote and avoid decline in employees' affective wellbeing and performance. Primarily, secondary and tertiary prevention is most productively targeted at all levels of organisations, groups or individuals. Organisational level initiatives to promote affective wellbeing and performance have the most chance of long term success (Giga et al., 2003). Comprehensive organisational policies and practices are necessary to promote positive affective wellbeing (Cartwright & Cooper, 1997; Van der Klink, Blonk, Schene, & Van Dijk, 2001). There are a number of useful sources of advice available to managers, such as the book *Tackling work-related stress: A managers' guide to improving and maintaining employee health and wellbeing* (Health and Safety Executive, 2001). A comprehensive analysis of stress that managers experience and ways of dealing with the problem is provided by Forster (2005).

Organisational level initiatives face major logistical difficulties as the interventions inevitably concentrate on reducing the effects of stress on individuals without addressing the root cause of workplace dissonance. Unfortunately, senior managers may fail to recognise or may choose not to acknowledge the existence of organisational level wellbeing and performance problems. There is a disturbing propensity amongst senior managers to blame employees' personality and lifestyle for these difficulties instead of accepting responsibility for work environment problems (Giga et al., 2003). Vigorous support and tangible commitment from top and senior management is critical for such initiatives to succeed.

Senior managers are likely to be persuaded to support interventions if issues pertaining to expected outcomes, resources, cost and cost effectiveness are clearly addressed at the outset. Finally, the quality of the relationship between line managers and employees determines the levels of organisational commitment and job satisfaction that are crucial for triggering discretionary behaviour (Coyle-Shapiro, 2004; Purcell, 2004).

Work Outcomes and Cost Benefits (WORC) is a joint research project, being conducted by the University of Queensland and Harvard University to evaluate the costs and benefits of proactive screening and treatment of depression in the Australian workforce (Bennett, 2004). The WORC project is intended to demonstrate why it is advisable for organisations to deal with depression in the workplace. Successful prevention and management of workplace conditions is imperative to promote individual affective wellbeing and performance in organisations and consequently improve organisational efficiencies and achievements (Hilton, 2006).

Competitive advantage

Creating an environment capable of liberating human potential is widely acknowledged as the key source of competitive advantage available to organisations. Encouraging and developing human potential is a means of creating a competitive edge capable of increasing an organisation's potential to create value. When employees discern an opportunity to meet their affective needs, they are more likely to engage in maximisation of an organisation's operation, to assist in achieving its goals (Pfeffer, 1994; O'Reilly & Pfeffer, 2000; Collins, 2001; Collins & Porras, 2004). Such commitment from managers has the potential to result in superior organisational productivity and competitiveness. Evidence for this assertion has long been established, and continues to emerge, confirming that psychologically meaningful work is positively related to effort expended in a job, which in turn leads to enhanced job performance (Brown & Leigh, 1996). A general work environment, and specific job characteristics that managers find psychologically supportive, are conducive to improvements in their performance

Implicit in the drive for international competitiveness is the recognition that the only sustainable competitive advantage is the quality of an organisation's workforce (Collins, 1988). Competitive advantage is achieved through people (Pfeffer, 1994). As Sanchez and Heene (1996: 13) asserted, 'managers' cognitive processes are at the head of a chain of causality that can eventually reshape the nature of competition in an industry'; a proposition extended here by determining the contribution managers' affective wellbeing and intrinsic job satisfaction make to this process. However, Hampson and Morgan (1997: 405) alert us to the other contingencies affecting managers' performance, 'managerial expertise is a necessary but not sufficient condition for international competitiveness', noting that 'it is one of a cluster of key factors that determine national success.' Organisations can potentially gain a competitive advantage through improved human resource practices, such as performance appraisal, when these initiatives are derived from and integrated with organisational strategies. Ensuring individual affective wellbeing and intrinsic job satisfaction are aspects of this process.

Managers' ever-expanding role

Implicit in the expanded roles that managers are now expected to perform is the responsibility to ensure employees' ongoing affective wellbeing. Part of the expanded repertoire of skills required of managers is the need to fully understand the role they need to undertake in supporting employees' wellbeing and performance (Stansfield, Head, & Marmont, 2000). There are some individual and organisational level initiatives that managers can take which have the potential to improve and sustain the affective wellbeing of employees.

A process of continuous improvement in the work environment is needed to ensure a healthy work climate. Frequent evaluation, analysis and reporting of the state of affective wellbeing and performance of employees are essential aspects of promoting healthy workplaces. Standardised instruments with established psychometric properties, such as those reported here, may be used to ensure valid measurements are made of affective wellbeing and performance. Data on employees' affective wellbeing can be accurately and rapidly collected using the Internet. Planned interventions to improve the affective wellbeing and performance of employees need to be tracked and realigned to be kept consistent with organisational goals. Programmes should also be developed and modified to meet the specific needs of organisations and to be continually evaluated against these requirements to ensure effective strategies are developed to protect employees and assist in guarding against potential future litigation. Ensuring effective and consistent communication about the state of wellbeing of employees is an important aspect of the expanded role of managers.

As mentioned, managers have a crucial role in ensuring the individual and organisational affective wellbeing of employees. Ironically, this additional role is likely to impact on the affective wellbeing of managers! The added responsibility of promoting and maintaining the affective wellbeing of employees is considerable. Moreover, managers are not always particularly well equipped to undertake this role by virtue of their training, experience and socialisation. This is not to suggest that managers should attempt to perform the role of an occupational or clinical psychologist in the workplace. This role should only be undertaken by those trained and equipped for such a complex undertaking. Managers have a major role to play in engaging the services of an occupational or clinical psychologist to promote the affective wellbeing of employees.

Within an organisation, only a minority of managerial jobs are likely to have psychological health deficiencies; attention should be expended on improving these jobs. Local environmental factors, such as a lack of autonomy in decision making can be manipulated to improve job performance for managers with poor affective wellbeing. However, before attempting to change the design of managers' jobs, it is important to identify, measure and analyse the cause of the poor affective wellbeing and intrinsic job satisfaction. The Partial Model developed and methodology used in this book will assist in such a process.

Job stress

As noted in Chapter 1, job stress can lead to poor mental and physical health. Job satisfaction has been strongly associated with mental and psychological health problems, particularly burnout. To reiterate, job stress, mental health, burnout and affective wellbeing are related but distinct constructs. The terms, stress, mental health, affective wellbeing and burnout tend to be used interchangeably in some of the literature, although the terms stress and burnout are used predominantly to describe work-related outcomes, while mental health may be context free. Also people may find it socially more acceptable to refer to a condition as 'stress' in preference to 'anxiety' or 'depression' for what may be the identical condition.

A range of other factors is also influencing the relationship between managers' affective wellbeing and their performance. Depression and anxiety are aspects of affective wellbeing and mental health in the workplace. As suggested, mental illness may be identified as a function of stress. As a result, different indicators may actually be measuring similar levels for the cost of mental ill health to organisations.

Researchers have shown that stress causes physical illness. Garvan Institute (Wheway et al., 2005) medical scientists have discovered a hormone, neuropeptide Y is released into the body during periods of stress. Neuropeptide Y is released from neurones in stressful situations and regulates blood pressure and the heart rate and can also affect the immune system. This hormone can stop the immune system from functioning properly. A direct link has been made by Garvin researchers to show how stress can weaken the immune system and make people more vulnerable to colds or flu and in more serious circumstance to cancer. Employees who are constantly stressed and under pressure are more likely to get sick.

Garvin scientists have warned people to minimise stress in the workplace before it becomes a serious problem.

Given the increasingly complex legal framework governing employment and Duty of Care provisions, it is also prudent for organisations to implement legal performance appraisal practices. Accurate monitoring of affective wellbeing through management appraisal practices has the potential to reduce an organisation's exposure to employment related litigation. Managers are likely to experience considerable stress due to the nature of the work, and as a consequence be more disposed to seek redress for work-related affective illness.

Managers who are dismissed for perceived poor performance may potentially bring legal actions for breach of contract, unfair dismissal or discrimination. Adopting defensible performance management approaches, which also incorporate measures of affective wellbeing, may reduce an organisation's exposure to expensive employment-related litigation (McKenna, 1994). This is possible to achieve when organisations provide valid measures of managers' affective wellbeing and document actions taken to alleviate any problems. Laws intended to prevent industrial accidents in countries with legal systems similar to the UK, can also be applied to psychological stress (World Health Organization, 2005a). Organisations instituting wellness programmes may eventually benefit from initiatives designed to improve affective wellbeing in the workplace through a reduction in costs associated with employment litigation. Such initiatives should indicate whether reported increases of stress are attributable to more effective monitoring, or to changes in job-strain (i.e., affective reaction to jobs).

INTERNATIONAL TRENDS

WHO Mental Health Action Plan for Europe

The WHO European Ministerial Conference on Mental Health (World Health Organization, 2005b) intends to improve job-related mental health. WHO plans to achieve these reforms through national governments, agencies and employers undertaking measures to improve the access to work and the social inclusion of people with mental health problems. There is a focus on the capacity of interventions at the workplace to improve mental health. Corporate management strategies will be used to incorporate mental health aspects into national policies, legislation, and programmes dealing with occupational health and safety.

Under this plan, all employees, especially those at high risk, will have access to occupational health services that can develop effective measures to assist in protecting mental health. Recommendations are made to monitor job-related mental health through the development of appropriate indicators and instruments. Training of personnel, and awareness raising, are proposed to improve capacities for protection and promotion of mental health at work through risk assessment and management of stress and psychosocial factors. Increasingly, insurance companies are offering substantial reductions in premiums to organisations prepared to be actively involved in reducing occupational work injuries.

Of particular note is the WHO initiative to make reforms to workplace mental health through national governments, agencies and employers to improve the access to work and the social inclusion of people with mental health problems. The focus is on using interventions in the workplace to improve mental health. Corporate management strategies will be used to incorporate mental health aspects into national policies, legislation, and programmes. All employees deserve reasonable access to occupational health services. Effective measures are to be developed to assist in protecting employees' mental health. Workplace mental health can be monitored through the development of appropriate indicators and instruments to make risk assessments and aid in the management of stress and psychosocial factors. Awareness raising and training personnel are also proposed as ways to improve capacities for protection and promotion of mental health.

The next section addresses the theoretical implication of the finding made in this book.

CONTRIBUTION TO MANAGEMENT THEORY

> That's all very well in practice, but how does it work in theory?
> (Groucho Marx, n.d.)

This book was intended to meet West et al.'s (1992: 2) challenge to advance knowledge about behaviour at work, in an 'attempt to derive ... research designs directly from existing theory' by 'incorporating other types of measures ... or using multiple methodologies, particularly those involving validating reports or observing self-report questionnaire data.' A number of theories were invoked (see Chapters 2–4), since the 'most productive studies have often drawn on methodologies which have different underlying philosophical bases' (West et al., 1992: 2). Drawing on related theory bases provided a more complete explanation of how affective wellbeing and intrinsic job satisfaction were linked to managers' performance (see Figure 4.1).

Settling on a general agreement about the dimensions of managers' job performance is problematic, due to the diversity of organisational goals in different contexts. However, there are sufficient broad similarities in organisational goals and job demands to justify a framework for defining performance for many classes of managers' jobs. These performance behaviour domain clusters are linked to managers' jobs. Organisational functions undertaken by managers were refined beyond planning, organising, leading and controlling. Managers' performance was shown in this study to be a construct that is multi-dimensional and generalizable. As posited, managers and their superiors were shown to have the same perceptions of what constitutes job performance across different organisations, which allows robust comparisons to be made of the construct. This permitted the equivalence of managers' performance to be measured between various organisations and levels within organisations.

In Chapters 1–4, theories and models with the potential to impact on managers' affective wellbeing, intrinsic job satisfaction and performance were explained. Refer to Table 3.1 for a summary of the relationships between the schools of performance appraisal and theories of management performance. Theories informing managers' performance that were found to be the most directly applicable to this study, included: attribution; competence, competing values, contingency; emotional intelligence, expectancy; human needs; individual differences, job performance; motivation; performance; self-efficacy; social cognition; and work adjustment.

Motivation and human needs theory

Motivation theory is seminal to any consideration of individual job performance (McClelland, 1985). A considerable amount of research has demonstrated that motivation is an important factor in determining job performance (Campbell et al., 1996; Sonnentag & Frese, 2002). Motivation theory posits that the need for achievement and intelligence are the two most important factors determining human performance (McClelland, 1985). Campbell and Pritchard (1976: 65) defined motivation as 'a psychological force that affects (a) the choice to initiate effort on a certain task, (b) choice to expend a certain amount of effort and (c) propensity to persist in expending effort over a period of time.' This definition explained the direction, amplitude and persistence of an individual's work behaviour on a given task, while holding constant the effects of aptitude, skill, job knowledge and situational constraints operating in the immediate work environment.

From a wider perspective, motivation to work forms the basis of the theory of human needs (McClelland, 1985). Constructs related to motivation may be partially subsumed under theories of individual differences (e.g., need for achievement), situational perspectives (e.g., extrinsic rewards), and performance regulation perspectives (e.g., goal setting). Individual differences seek to identify the underlying factors between individuals. Three determinants of individual differences were identified by Campbell (1990) as: declarative knowledge, procedural knowledge and skills and motivation. Motivation is considered by Campbell to comprise the choice to perform, level of effort, and persistence of effort. Motowidlo et al. (1997) extended upon Campbell's work to infer that task performance is a function of cognitive ability, and contextual performance is mainly a function of personality and motivation (see Figure 3.5). Need for achievement is also related to job performance (Vinchur, Schippmann, Switzer, & Roth, 1998). Another construct in the motivational realm that is highly relevant to performance is self-efficacy, an individual's belief in executing an action well (Bandura, 1996). Self-efficacy is related to both contextual performance (Speier & Frese, 1997) and task performance (Baum, Locke, & Smith, 2001).

Maslow's (1949) seminal study found that managers rated their satisfaction with needs similar to those identified by employees - security, social esteem, autonomy and self-actualisation. Maslow's (1949; 1950; 1968; 1970) concept of 'self actualisation' is particularly relevant to managers' aspirations. Managers are likely to aspire to 'self-actualise.' Efforts to move towards persons' full potential ('becoming or being') are an important aspect of a psychologically healthy person. Moderately high motivation in problematic environments tends to indicate positive affective wellbeing more than does extreme (too high or too low) goals. Unrealistic aspirations can create tension and anxiety. Happy managers tend to exhibit openness to experience, psychological resilience and the belief that they can control events. These are characteristics that Maslow (1970) associated with self-actualisation, the highest level of mental health (Heylighten & Bernheim, 2000). Managers' need for achievement (McClelland, 1985) is exhibited as the disposition required to effectively manage large organisations (Miner, 1978; O'Reilly & Pfeffer, 2000). Aspects of affective wellbeing, such as enthusiasm, indicate the level and intensity of individual motivation.

People with positive mental health are likely to have the requisite resources for goal attainment. Goal relevance is seen by some theorists as being essential to emotional reactions, such that the intensity of emotions is related with the perceived importance or desirability of a goal. Aspirations relate to managers' engagement with, and interest in, the environment. Raised aspiration levels and efforts are considered healthy when they are personally significant. While ambition may cause a degree of anxiety, active striving towards goals that are personally valued is congruent with developed countries' value systems.

Goal setting is an established way of increasing self-confidence and reducing performance anxiety (Locke & Latham, 1990). Highly satisfied needs were found by Vroom (1964) to be relatively unimportant with the exception of self-actualisation, which remained constant, a finding partly confirmed in this book. This supports Locke and Latham's (1990) Value theory, where rewards which satisfy individual values are likely to result in performance. Several theories of motivation and expectancy, goal setting theory and attribution theories indicate that employees with PA are likely to be more motivated (Wright & Staw, 1999a; 1999b). PA was positively associated with both dimensions of performance including non programmable (Influencing) and programmable (Motivating and Following tasks.

As predicted, managers reported elevated levels of Anxiety in relation to their performance. However, only modest levels of Anxiety (equating with eustress) were unlikely to have an adverse impact on accomplishing goals and ultimately performance. Thus, moderate levels of anxiety are likely to motivate managers' performance but excessive amounts are likely to be counterproductive, a finding consistent with the literature.

Work environments that encourage and foster these positive affective states are likely to enhance the motivation of managers to perform on these dimensions. This is likely to reduce feelings of strain in managers. Integrative approaches to motivation theory have provided new ways to approach organisational issues. Identifying which aspects of affective wellbeing and intrinsic job satisfaction predict managers' performance helps to indicate which motivational interventions are likely to be effective for desired performance outcomes. The personality trait conscientiousness affects motivational states by stimulating goal setting and commitment. Conscientiousness functions are an established motivator of job performance (Schmidt & Hunter, 2004). Performance is essentially a function of motivation. Thus, managers who are self-motivated to attain and retain a managerial job, by satisfactory performance, are likely to have high motivation and be conscious of their sense of self-worth (Klemp & McClelland, 1986).

Performance and job performance theory

Performance theory compares the difference between the desired behaviour with the actual behaviour a person exhibits on the job that is determined by a person's contribution to achieving organisational goals (Quinn et al., 1996). Two broad approaches to job performance are presented in the literature (Campbell et al., 1996). First, dimensions of the performance domain are identified which define categories of job performance that apply to all jobs. Second, the causal patterns of relations between the various dimensions and antecedents of job performance explain the variability and the causal sequences of job performance.

Performance has been suggested as a multi-dimensional and multilevel construct regarding criterion measures (Borman et al., 1993; Campbell et al., 1993). In addition, job performance is behavioural, episodic, and multi-dimensional (Motowidlo et al., 1997). Managers' rated performance was confirmed here to be multi-dimensional, consisting of eight distinct dimensions. Moreover, the effectiveness of performance may not be linear (Pritchard & Roth, 1991). As such, behavioural episodes that contribute to organisational goals form an important aspect of the job performance domain. Managerial effectiveness is a function of the evaluation of outcomes considered in relation to managers' performance.

Management performance may be considered to be synonymous with behaviour, as 'actions or behaviours that are relevant to the organisation's goals ... can be scaled (measured) in terms of each individual's proficiency (that is, level of contribution)' (Campbell et al., 1990: 40). Rating individual performance as one aspect of performance is potentially misleading, since various individual behaviours contribute to organisational goals. Behaviour is what a person does in a job and should not be confused with results that help or hinder an organisation to reach pre-determined goals, and which may be affected by factors outside a person's control. Managers' PA, NA, Enthusiasm, Anxiety, Relaxation and Intrinsic Job Satisfaction were also found in this study to be predictors of specific aspects of managers' job performance.

Volition and predisposition are known to determine the main source of variation in contextual performance (Borman & Motowidlo, 1993). Results from a meta-analysis by Judge et al., (2001) supported George and Brief's (1996) argument that positive affects (one of the indicators of extraversion) are related to distal and proximal measures of motivation. A person's disposition can be a significant determinant of job attitudes (Staw & Ross, 1985; George & Brief, 1992; Judge & Locke, 1993; Watson & Slack, 1993). As anticipated, dispositional affect, was also confirmed to be a strong predictor of performance, supporting Miner's (1978) finding that disposition (contextual performance) is linked with effective management in large organisations.

Expectancy theory

Vroom (1964) related expectancy theory to employee performance by predicting that employees will not perform a particular activity unless certain conditions are satisfied (Luthans, 1976). For motivation to be high, expectancy (an estimation made of the effort required by employees to achieve the target and the likelihood of a target being reached), instrumentality (the expectation the employee has of what will occur if they try) and valence (the employee's emotional response to anticipated outcomes), must also be high (Vroom, 1964). Motivation is predicted to be commensurately low, if expectancy, instrumentality or valence is low. Expectancy-based theories of motivation are founded on the assumption that job satisfaction results from the rewards that flow from performance. This supports Warr's (1987) view that affective wellbeing and job performance are linked by a reciprocal causality between these factors across time.

The data provided in this book provided general support for Vroom's expectancy theory. Managers with PA may have developed an expectancy that their efforts lead to high performance and that this performance will lead to positive outcomes (Wright, Cropanzano et al., 2002). Fit between goals and culture are better predictors of job motivation than either experience or technical skills (Pfeffer, 1994; O'Reilly & Pfeffer, 2000; Collins, 2001; Collins & Porras, 2004). However, more specific measures of expectancy, instrumentality and valence are needed to fully support the predictive power of expectancy theory.

Self-efficacy and social cognition theory

Wood and Bandura (1989: 409) conceptualised self-efficacy as the 'belief in one's capabilities to mobilize the motivation, cognitive resources, and courses of action needed to meet situational demands.' Self-efficacy theory is derived from social cognitive theory which determines a person's belief in their capacity to successfully perform a task (Bandura, 1996). Self-efficacy encompasses a wide range of predictors of performance levels for a specific task (Gist & Mitchell, 1992) that have been associated with job performance (Barling & Beattie, 1983; Gist, 1989). Self-efficacy influences performance through behavioural choices, such as goal level and effort. Such generative capabilities may influence performance (Bandura, 1986; Bandura, 1996).

From a performance perspective, self-efficacy is 'empowered feelings of possessing the capability and competence to perform' (Whetton & Cameron, 1991: 663). Gist and Mitchel (1992: 183) refined this definition to be 'a person's estimate of his or her capacity to orchestrate performance on a specific task.' Thus, self-efficacy is able to influence affective reactions to tasks and motivation. Positive feelings about oneself resulting from job achievement may lead to improved motivation and performance. Bandura (1988: 49) argued that 'human accomplishments and positive affective wellbeing require an optimistic and resilient sense of personal efficacy.' PA was hypothesised by George and Brief (1996) to potentially facilitate employees' achievement or performance. In the study reported here, PA was found to be a significant predictor of aspects of task and contextual performance.

George and Brief's (1996) position that PA may enhance a person's expectations of achieving effective performance, lends support to the existence of a path from affective wellbeing and intrinsic job satisfaction to performance. This causal path is thought to originate from PA, which in turn may lead to improved performance. These predictions were based on findings that indicate PA leads to enhanced self-efficacy (Forgas, 1992), and optimistic attitudes about future circumstances (Wright & Bower, 1992). Managers who are high in NA were likely to be less optimistic that their endeavours would result in success or that positive outcomes were imminent (Wright & Staw, 1999a; 1999b). In this case, a downward spiralling of performance creates an 'exacerbation cycle' that can be difficult to reverse (Storms & Missal, 1976).

Self-efficacy has been found to arrest decrements in performance by intervening in the attribution process (Fosterling, 1985). Enhancing affective wellbeing may be another way of arresting the exacerbation cycle. Bandura (1996: 80) has argued that 'Successes build a robust belief in one's personal efficacy.' This indicated that managers who believe in their capacity to perform a job will be more satisfied or happier. Allocating managers and tasks they can succeed with is one way to arrest the negative consequences of this cycle.

Theory of individual differences

There has been a major resurgence of interest in the psychology of individual differences, particularly General Mental Ability (GMA) and personality traits (Lubinski, 2000). GMA has been found to predict performance within jobs and occupations as well as learning about a job (Schmidt & Hunter, 2004). Managers' jobs are argued to consist of a complex array of activities, with a number of performance dimensions. The theory of individual differences predicts that the type of knowledge, skills, and work habits associated with task performance will be different from those associated with contextual performance. Motowidlo, Borman and Schmit (1997) and Borman and Motowidlo (1997) argued that the theory of individual differences should include contextual work activities in a conceptualisation of performance, a position supported in this book.

Motowidlo's (1997) extension of the theory of individual differences into contextual and task performance predicted that the frequency and value of the attribution of behavioural episodes in performance are determined by an individual's application of knowledge, skills and work habits. From the data in this study it was not possible to fully test Motowidlo et al.'s (1997) extension of the theory into individual differences. However, the type of knowledge, skills, and work habits associated with task performance were clearly different from those associated with contextual performance. The performance construct was found to consist of four contextual dimensions (Endorsing, Helping, Persisting, Following) and four task dimensions (Monitoring, Technical, Influencing, Delegating).

Another perspective from the theory of individual differences is provided by Warr (1997: 71) 'individual differences in personality and cognitive ability variables, in combination with learning experiences, lead to variability in knowledge, skills and work habits that mediate effects of personality and cognitive ability on job performance.' The theory of individual differences is congruent with employees who have a high level of intrinsic motivation and seek growth (McClelland, 1985).

Attribution theory

Attribution error is the propensity to over-attribute behaviour to internal causes in preference to external causes (Heider, 1958; George & Jones, 1996). This manifests as the 'tendency to attribute the behaviour of others to internal causes and to attribute one's own behaviour to external causes' (George & Jones, 1997: 118). Attribution theory indicates that self-ratings attribute good performance to their own behaviour and poor performance to environmental factors (Jones & Nisbett, 1972; De Vader et al., 1986). Attribution theory predicts that managers will tend to inflate their performance and not give themselves negative ratings. According to attribution theory, managers' self-report of their performance is not expected to be congruent with the assessments of those to whom they report.

Managers' contextual performance might elude the notice of superiors, the usual source of other ratings of contextual performance, and therefore be known only to the individual. Since ratings of contextual performance are inherently subjective, self-ratings of managers' contextual performance are likely to be a poor substitute for independent judgements. In order to counter the problem of attribution error, both superiors' and managers' ratings were used in this study to establish the structure of managers performance.

Informing managers that their performance would also be rated by their superiors was intended to moderate self-report attribution error. Rather than overestimating their own performance levels, managers may possibly have reacted to the knowledge that their self-report on performance was going to be compared to that of the person to whom they report. This expectancy may have encouraged managers to more accurately report on their own performance, and to be less inclined to overestimate their performance. Saul (1989: 80) found in a study of managers that 'descriptions of behaviour given by target managers' superiors were significantly correlated with the performance ratings of target managers'. This finding was confirmed in this study due to the high correlation (68%) between managers' and their superiors' performance ratings (see Table 6.17). This could in part be attributed to managers being made aware that their superiors would be rating their performance, possibly resulting in more realistic self-appraisals.

According to the Social Cognitive School, people vary in their capacity and desire to make accurate appraisal judgements, but formats with a clear purpose and accountability are likely to result in more accurate performance appraisals (Ilgen et al., 1993). Embedding accountability into performance management systems is likely to assist managers to rate their performance more accurately. Performance rating instruments with clear, behaviourally anchored items, also have the potential to improve the veracity of performance appraisals. The instruments used here were designed and implemented to meet these requirements (refer to Appendix 5).

In this study there was agreement between managers and their superiors on what were perceived to be the most important elements of performance. However, superiors' ratings were found to be the more valid measures of managers' performance, although managers and their superiors were found to perceive the same dimensions of performance, in terms of pattern relationships, loadings, and covariance.

The 8–dimensions and 32–indicators identified in the EFA were replicated in the CFA to represent all the relevant aspects of performance. Managers' performance was found to be generalizable and therefore provided a reliable measure of performance. In this case, superiors' ratings of managers' performance were clearly found to be the most reliable for appraising managers' performance.

Different levels of negative and positive outcomes result from the attribution process (i.e., over-attributing behaviour to internal or external causes). Attribution biases also affect upward appraisal and, possibly, sideways (peer) appraisal. Given the first-hand experience with external constraints, managers' peers are potentially in a better position to judge managers' performance, compared to their superiors. According to Beittenhausen and Fedor (1997) managers are more likely to prefer peer review to upward appraisal, which may be viewed as threatening to their authority. With upward reviews, a lack of familiarity with the constraints experienced by managers does not consistently result in empathetic or accurate appraisals. There is likely to be a serious problem of attribution error when relaying solely on self or peer evaluation.

Attitudes of managers towards multisource appraisal, in particular the accuracy and utility of the information gathered, will have an important influence on managers' acceptance of this method. Multisource feedback on performance is most effective when used for development purposes, rather than purely for performance appraisal, and when the measures are linked to an organisation's strategic goals. Multisource feedback is also particularly effective when superiors are accountable for developing managers (HayGroup, 1999). However, organisational dynamics must be conducive to the use of this form of appraisal.

Work adjustment theory

Work adjustment theory (Dawis & Lofquist, 1984) conceived of work as a continuous challenge by which individuals achieve and maintain congruence with their work environment (Dawis & Lofquist, 1984). Work adjustment theory suggested that aspects of personality, such as PA and NA, may predict performance (Hesketh & Adams, 1991). In certain circumstances, job performance will be more strongly associated with one axis of wellbeing (Warr, 1991). The work adjustment theory prediction was confirmed, as represented by one axis of affective wellbeing namely PA that was found to be associated with superiors' reports on contextual performance (Following) and task performance (Monitoring with negative Technical).

Contingency theory

According to contingency theory, an organisation should design its internal structure to fit the organisational environment in which it operates, in order to maximise the responsiveness to its external environment (Pfeffer, 1982; Jones, 1995). Critics of contingency theory argue that there was an overemphasis on the environment as a determinant of organisational structure. Instead they argued that tailoring the fit between structure and the environment was not a unidirectional process but was actually an interactive two-way process. Smircich and Stubbart (1985: 724) argued that 'environments are enacted through the social constructions and interactions of organised actors.' Managers are considered to inhabit an 'enacted environment', where they actively determine which elements of the organisation's environment to respond to (Weick, 1979). When human potential is expertly integrated with organisational strategies, it has the potential to liberate a powerful additive force.

From contingency theory it is known that managers inhabit environments that are largely a function of their perceptions. This may explain why managers from different organisations respond differently to identical environmental challenges (Jones, 1995; Allred, Snow, & Miles,

1996). Mintzberg (1973) developed a contingency of managerial work based on these differences that are incorporated into the evaluation of managers' performance (see Figure 3.1). However, this study confirmed there are considerable degrees of similarity in the perception of managers' jobs as well as important differences (McKenna, 1994). These similarities and differences need to be incorporated into the work roles managers are expected to undertake and their performance evaluated accordingly.

Different contextual performance may be more appropriate for different types of organisations, contingent upon the employment environment within which managers' work. For example, service industries may emphasise dimensions related to dealing with customers and representing the organisation to outsiders. Conservative organisations may value following orders and regulations and respecting authority, whereas team oriented organisations may find the altruistic behaviours of helping, cooperating and displaying courtesy to team members more important. Contextual performance dimensions such as conscientiousness are likely to be generic to all work organisations.

Competence

As Woodruffe (1992: 1) noted, 'competency often seems to be used as an umbrella term to cover almost anything that might either directly or indirectly affect job performance.' Earlier research about managerial competencies has tended to be organisationally specific in scope (Kanungo & Misra, 1992; Sandwith, 1993). For example, Spencer and Spencer (1993: 3) defined competency as 'an underlying characteristic of an individual that is causally related to criterion referenced and/or superior performance in a job situation.' Guion (1991: 335) refined this line of reasoning, describing competencies as consisting of underlying characteristics of people which indicate 'ways of behaviour or thinking, across situations, and enduring for a reasonably long period of time'. A competency represents a person's potential competencies that must be activated to ensure performance. Goleman (1998: 16) viewed a competency as 'a personal trait or set of habits that leads to more effective or superior performance ... an ability that adds clear economic value to the efforts of a person on the job'.

There is continuing debate about the utility of competencies, the generalisability of competencies, and the extent to which superior managers possess certain 'core competencies', regardless of organisation or industry. Researchers invariably refer to 'competency' in the literature for what is essentially 'domains of performance'. Competencies underpin tasks, which refer to actions that are normally qualified by time, function or location. Furthermore, tasks can change, whereas the underlying competencies slowly evolve over time and are therefore more static. Competencies are the associated abilities or inputs of job skills and personal attributes that determine performance. Competencies are represented by actions or behaviours that are relevant to the measured level of contribution to an organisation's goals, whereas competence refers to job performance and focuses on organisational outcomes. Competences are a set of deliverable outputs of job behaviour, or thinking, across situations. A competency refers to the potential to perform in a job, an enduring trait, a dimension of ability and the behaviour required for competent performance. Competency only represents a person's potential, which must be activated to become performance. Thus, managers' use of their competencies represents performance.

Findings from this book provide a more sophisticated identification of managers' competencies. Managers with high PA are more likely to perform contextual roles well. In work settings managers who exhibit positive emotions may be able to mobilize more social support from colleagues and thus facilitate better performance (Staw & Barsade, 1993). Effective managers undertake both contextual and task roles, so these dimensions should be included in appraisals of managerial competence. Equitable performance appraisals can be used to motivate performance if managers expect that appropriate effort will correspond to positive outcomes (Vroom, 1964; Campbell et al., 1970; Forster, 2005).

Contextual performance dimensions represent important generic competencies that apply across the range of situations encountered in organisations. Goleman (1996; 1998) extended the notion of what constitutes personal competency in relation to emotions. A wider conception incorporating contextual dimensions of individual performance is therefore justified for inclusion in appraisals of managers' performance. Devising a common metric for measuring managers' contextual and task performance goes some way to identifying the competencies required by managers to be effective in the global economy.

THEORETICAL IMPLICATIONS FOR AFFECTIVE WELLBEING

Revisiting the 'happy-productive worker' thesis

Chapter 2 began by attempting to define the concept 'happiness' in general and, specifically, in relation to work as the ultimate goal of human existence. The nature of happiness has challenged philosophers since the beginning of recorded history. Happiness is fundamental to human existence, but is elusive to define and difficult to measure, especially in relation to managers' job performance As documented in the Preface, a plethora of books (Argyle, 2001; Bruni, 2005; Layard, 2005; Martin, 2005) has appeared espousing the 'new science' of happiness during the period 2001–5. Sadly, for every book or article on happiness, there are literally hundreds more on depression and anxiety (Bagnall, 2004).

Wright and Staw (1991) claimed that a person's disposition towards happiness, not organisational conditions, was associated with performance. Ledford (1999: 30) extended this reasoning by concluding that if 'only trait-based happiness leads to performance, it was pointless to try to make employees happier as a way of improving performance'. This position assumes that employees are either born happy or unhappy, and that such a demeanour would not change, notwithstanding the design and experience of a job. However, a vast literature exists to indicate that trait affect is not solely determined by hereditary disposition, as approximately 50% is determined by other factors (1975; Hackman & Oldham, 1980; Clegg, 1984; Broadbent, 1985; Gerhart, 1987; Gardner & Cummings, 1988; Ilgen & Hollenbrook, 1991; Hesketh, 1993).This implies that 50% of personality traits has a genetic basis, as twin studies have shown (Benjamin, Ebstein, & Belmaker, 2001).

Trait based personality characteristics are a general propensity to apply or perceive situations from the trait, for example, happy or introverted. Thus, changing a trait based NA or PA, including 'happiness' can be difficult as this is an integral part of a person's outlook, personality or perception of life events. For example, a person with a trait high in 'suspicion' will perceive events via this 'lens'. Conversely, a person with a high optimism trait will perceive events via this 'lens'.

Changing traits is therefore not easy as they develop in the milieu of genetic, psychological and social factors such as emotions, behavioural and cognitive processes, all interacting in a complex environment, including culture, which results in complex human behaviour. Traits tend to be stable over the life span of the individual. All this points to the need for human resource policies and practices to determine which traits are most applicable to an organisation's culture and the required contextual and task performance. This study indicates the type of factors that can be used to help select managers who fit the organisation's performance requirements.

PA was the only variable in this study to be significantly associated with both task and performance dimensions. As such, managers with high PA were likely to perform well when Influencing, and when undertaking Monitoring and Following roles, supporting the argument that managers with dispositional PA will outperform those who are unhappy (negative PA). This is consistent with Wright and Staw's (1999a; 1999b) claim that a person's basic disposition is associated with performance. However, this a person's basic disposition is associated with performance. However, this position should not also be taken as evidence to support Wright and Staw's contention that organisational conditions do not influence the happiness of managers. A person's genetic makeup, socialisation and life experiences all contribute to happiness.

'Enthusiastic-naivety' or 'depressive-realism'?

In Chapter 1, Staw and Barsade's (1993) 'happier-and-smarter' ('enthusiasm-naivety') and the 'sadder-but-wiser' ('depressive-realism') hypotheses were reviewed. There is a substantial literature supporting a 'depressive-realism' view of performance, also called the 'sadder-but-wiser' effect by Staw and Barsade (1993). A positive relationship was found in this study between dispositional affect and performance. However, Weiss and Cropanzano (1996) made the countervailing argument by contending that emotional responses tend to produce decrements in performance. Activities resulting from a negative state are reasoned by Weiss and Cropanzano (1996) to be more extensive and constantly disruptive than those resulting from a positive state.

This position is consistent with Taylor's (1991) view that reactions to negative events have been found to produce stronger reactions than positive events. Work by Sinclair and Mark (1992) found that people in a positive mood were more likely to engage in simplified heuristic processing when making judgements and decisions. In contrast, people in a negative mood were found to be more likely to employ systematic processing strategies. Individuals reporting NA have been found to focus attention to improve the quality of decisions made (Schwarz & Bless, 1991; Forgas, 2002).

Perhaps people with NA are more rooted to organisational reality. Several studies support the depressive realism effect which indicates that individuals with depressive tendencies tend to avoid a range of biases. These include optimism bias (Martin & Stang, 1978; Lichtenstein, Fischoff, & Phillips, 1982) and the illusion of control (Langer, 1975). Weiss and Cropanzano (1996) present evidence from the literature to suggest that individuals who are least positive in affect may exercise more accurate information processing. A person with depressive tendencies may be less likely to overestimate their capacity to deal with ambiguous task circumstances (Tabacknick, Crocker, & Alloy, 1983).

This counter-intuitive position is highly speculative regarding the possible decrements in performance resulting from the emotion-performance relationship. The predicted state emotion–performance relationship may possibly hold for emotionally charged situations. People experiencing volatile emotional states may have extreme performance measurement of 'performance' not really objective because supervisors are subject to the same biases as managers. The most obvious bias is that generally people respond positively to optimistic and happy people and negatively to those who are melancholic. In this case, a person's affective reaction is what is being rated. As for 'performance' this is different matter.

When induced by everyday events, PA has been shown to promote cognitive flexibility, innovation, problem solving, and creativity (Ganster, 2005). In negotiation settings PA is reported to lead people to use problem solving that is focused on generating integrative solutions (Isen & Labroo, 2003). Transitory PA has been consistently shown to have a beneficial impact on a variety of decision making processes in a broad range of settings, including organisations (Isen & Baron, 1991; Staw & Barsade, 1993; George & Brief, 1996). State affect occurs over and above stable dispositional affect, which can also influence behaviour (Weiss, Nicholas, & Dauss, 1999). Overall, PA seems to improve many aspects of the decision making process, particularly those aspects concerned with generating innovative alternatives.

From this finding it could also be inferred that managers with a positive disposition, who also experience some Anxiety and Relaxation, are likely to be successful when performing Monitoring and Following roles. Moreover, as Weiss and Cropanzano (1996) anticipated, a simple linear relationship between either positive or negative states for affect and performance was indeed 'overtly simple'. The affect–performance relationship is far more complex than anticipated, as illustrated in Figure 8.1. Interest in the 'happy-performing managers' proposition and the wider 'happier-and-smarter' ('enthusiasm-naivety') and the 'sadder-but-wiser' ('depressive-realism') hypotheses may be seen with the broader context of the movement to Positive Organisational Scholarship (POS).

Positive Organisational Scholarship

The scope of psychological research is expanding to include happiness, wellbeing, courage, citizenship, play and the satisfactions of healthy work and healthy relationships (Cameron et al., 2003; Keyes & Haidt, 2003). The last decade has seen a growing movement in psychology to abandon the exclusive focus on the dark side of human existence with a preference to explore a more positive view of the mind (Snyder & Lopez, 2002; Cameron & Caza, 2004). Seligman (www.edge.org) puts the case for POS, 'By working on mental illness we forgot about making the lives of relatively untroubled people happier, more productive and more fulfilling. We didn't develop interventions to make people happier; we developed interventions to make people less miserable'.

As Bagnall (2004) observed (along with Tolstoy), unhappiness may be more interesting, but happy people do better in almost every area of life. As noted on Chapter 2, Lyubomirsky and colleagues found that happy people tend to acquire favourable life circumstances which engender success. A link between happiness and success has been made across many studies that indicate that happy individuals are successful across multiple life domains, such as marriage, friendship, health and job performance (Lyubomirsky et al., 2005). Optimistic CEOs receive higher performance ratings from their boards and have a greater return on investment (Pritzker, 2002). Further, Bagnall (2004) concurs with the POS approach and extends this line of reasoning by arguing that there are sound social and economic reasons for promoting happiness. For example, recent attention to 'positive psychology' has focussed attention on the potential benefits of positive feelings in the workplace (Seligman & Csikszentmihalyi, 2000; Pressman & Cohen, 2005)

Leading American psychologist Ed Diener told a roundtable on happiness economics, convened by the Brookings Institution in 2004, that even 'slightly happy people have more self-confidence, are better workers and better creative problem solvers, they steal less, have stronger immune systems, they're more likely to get married, stay married and rate their marriage better' (cited in Bagnall, 2004). As mentioned in Chapter 1, research reported here may be seen as part of the emerging POS movement, as typified by this paraphrased explanation below of the movement from the work of Cameron, Dutton, Quinn and Spreitzer (2003):

POS is not dependent upon any particular theory or framework but utilises the full range of organisational theories to understand, explain and predict the occurrence, causes, and consequences of exceptional individual, group, and organisational performance. POS as a health model, based on the premise that understanding how to enable human excellence in organisations unlocks potential, reveals possibilities, and facilitates a positive path to human and organisational welfare. The focus is on understanding the dynamics that lead to developing human strength, producing resilience and restoration, fostering vitality, and cultivating extraordinary individuals, units and organisations.

POS is orientated to investigating and understanding 'positive deviance', to discover the ways in which organisations and their members flourish and prosper in extraordinary ways. POS seeks to understand exemplars of human condition in organisations by studying organisations and organisational contexts characterised by appreciation, collaboration and vitality. Fulfilment with the purpose of creating abundance and human wellbeing are seen as the key indicators of success in the workforce. As such, employee wellbeing is viewed from an intrinsic goal orientated perspective, rather than as being the end to which all participants in organisational work life should aspire. POS seeks to rigorously understand what represents the best of the human condition founded on scholarly research and theory.

Applied research into employee wellbeing so far has mainly emphasised the disease model, where the focus is primarily on fixing what is amiss with someone. The disease model focuses on minimising the disabling symptoms or manifestations of such attitudinal, mental or physical dysfunctional behaviour as job stress, job burnout, job dissatisfaction, negative affectivity and decreased productivity. Work-related research has mainly been concerned with the potentially negative consequences of worker distress and dissatisfaction. In contrast, POS has an affirmative bias towards the health model to establish and maintain ways that organisations can improve people's working lives. From this perspective, employee health and wellbeing are seen in terms of the presence of the potential for growth, optimism, contentment, kindness, humility and actualisation, not as the absence of dysfunctional behaviour.

The next section deals with issues worthy of further investigation and analysis, including specifying a more comprehensive *Model of Managers' Performance* for future testing.

FUTURE RESEARCH

The primary focus among these is the robust measurement of managers' contextual and task performance. Robust measures are the foundation of any rigorous model assessment of the relationship between managers' affective wellbeing, intrinsic job satisfaction and performance. In this book a scale was developed to measure managers' contextual and task performance. Future findings in this area may lead to important practical applications for human resource practices for selection, reward systems, retention, and appraisals.

Investigating all the potential factors impacting on managers' affective wellbeing and performance was beyond the boundaries and resources of this book. This investigation builds on existing research into endogenous factors of performance, such as satisfaction, personality and motivation. Context-free (life in general) and facet-specific (specific to a job) affective wellbeing were beyond the parameters of this book. Endogenous (internal) factors influencing managers' behaviour need to be investigated in conjunction with exogenous (external) factors.

There are many relationships which may impinge on managers' affective wellbeing in relation to their performance, including general mental ability (GMA), age and personality (particularly Conscientiousness). Known managerial stressors, such as role overload, role conflict and role ambiguity (Rizzo, House, & Lirtzman, 1970; Peterson et al., 1995), and work to home overlap (Frone, Russell, & Cooper, 1992; Williams & Alliger, 1994) could also be included in the analysis of such a study.

The next section suggests additional dimensions that could be incorporated into a future model for testing.

Model of Managers' Affective Wellbeing and Performance

A more complete model of the relationship between the constructs of managers' affective wellbeing, intrinsic job satisfaction and their performance is given in Figure 8.2. Job characteristics, role conflict, role overload, role ambiguity, organisational commitment and extrinsic job satisfaction are logical extensions to the Partial Model shown in Figure 8.2 and would be suitable for future testing, using Structural Equation Modelling. Curtin Business School, Curtin University of Technology, Perth, Western Australia and Lancaster University Management School, Lancaster University, UK and St Mary's College, USA are developing an online instrument for collecting data from international organisations. This will enable data be collected to test the proposed *Model of Managers' Performance* shown in Figure 8.2.

Figure 8.2   Model of Managers' Performance

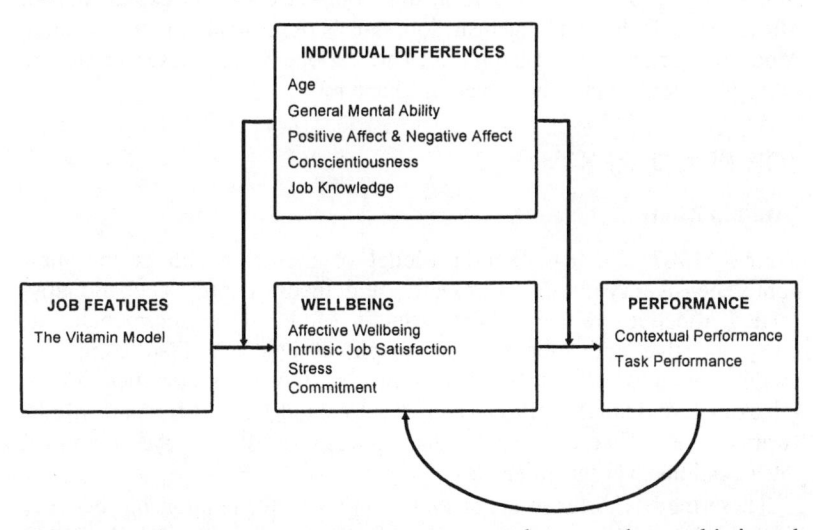

INDIVIDUAL DIFFERENCES
Age
General Mental Ability
Positive Affect & Negative Affect
Conscientiousness
Job Knowledge

JOB FEATURES
The Vitamin Model

WELLBEING
Affective Wellbeing
Intrinsic Job Satisfaction
Stress
Commitment

PERFORMANCE
Contextual Performance
Task Performance

This model represents a more complete and sophisticated conceptualisation of predictors of managers' performance than any currently available in the literature. By their very nature, all models are inadequate representations of reality, but some can be provide useful explanations. Many studies of social phenomena subscribe to a positivist perspective of organisations (Burrell & Morgan, 1979; Gioia & Pitre, 1990). By Warr's (1987: 2) admission 'conceptual frameworks of this kind are never entirely supported by empirical data because they are created relatively independently of published findings in order to shape perceptions and reach such activity' A more comprehensive explanation will be provided of the upward and downward spirals of managerial effectiveness, whereby positive or negative affective wellbeing and intrinsic job satisfaction lead to increased or reduced performance, which either enhances positive, or exacerbates negative affective wellbeing and intrinsic job satisfaction.

A causal variable set is used with moderator variables that suggest a complex set of relationships which are interactive rather than additive, as with the Partial Model. This may go some way towards establishing, for example if it is 'emotional intelligence abilities that matter more for superior performance' (McClelland cited in Goleman, 1998: 19). Empirical data will assist in demonstrating the causal link between certain individual differences and the level of managers' performance.

The following section provides background to the additional constructs that will be measured and incorporated into the Model of Managers' Performance. Table 8.2 provides a summary of concepts, constructs, dimensions, and measures used in this book. A complete explanation of affective wellbeing and intrinsic job satisfaction, including the Vitamin Model, is provided in Chapter 2. The various theory bases related to managers' performance are given in Chapter 3.

JOB FEATURES

Vitamin Model

Warr's (1987; 1994d) Vitamin Model of mental health is the most comprehensive synthesis of research and theories into occupationally-related affective wellbeing. The Vitamin Model is far more inclusive, comprehensive and supported by empirical evidence than competing models. Frameworks developed from the Job Characteristics Model (Hackman & Oldham, 1980) and the Demand-Control-Support Model (Karasek & Theorell, 1990) has guided most of the empirical investigations over three decades.

These models differ in scope and complexity for relationship between job characteristics and employee affective wellbeing (De Jonge & Schaufeli, 1998). Hackman and Oldham's Job Characteristics Model is essentially linear. Warr's Vitamin Model proposed a non-linear (quadratic) relationship between job characteristics and affective wellbeing. Karasesk and Theorell's, Demand-Control-Support Model is interactive and the most complex. Warr (1994d) recommended that future multivariate investigations should simultaneously measure several job characteristics.

Job characteristics

Organisation researchers have been studying the nature of jobs for nearly a century. In recent years this stream of research has focused on gaining a better understanding of the motivational and enriching aspects of jobs by indexing the existing characteristics of jobs. Enriched or complex jobs are assumed to be associated with favourable employees. Extensive research has been devoted to defining and understanding job dimensions (Dodd & Ganster, 1996). The psychological perceptions of job incumbents are used by researchers as the main basis for inferring the presence of job characteristics (Dodd & Ganster, 1996). Like all employees, managers have needs for psychological wellbeing and growth. There have been many attempts to develop conceptual models, perspectives and theories about job characteristics and wellbeing (Kahn & Byosiere, 1992).

Figure 8.3   Job Characteristics Model

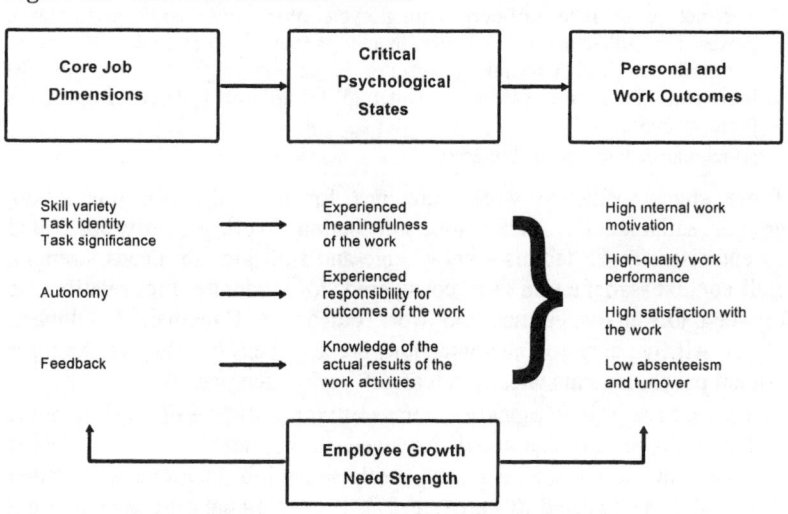

```
┌──────────────┐     ┌──────────────┐     ┌──────────────┐
│   Core Job   │ ──▶ │   Critical   │ ──▶ │ Personal and │
│  Dimensions  │     │ Psychological│     │Work Outcomes │
│              │     │    States    │     │              │
└──────────────┘     └──────────────┘     └──────────────┘
```

Skill variety
Task identity   ⟶   Experienced   ⎫   High internal work
Task significance   meaningfulness   ⎪   motivation
                             of the work   ⎪
                                                     ⎬   High-quality work
Autonomy   ⟶   Experienced   ⎪   performance
                             responsibility for   ⎪
                             outcomes of the work   ⎪   High satisfaction with
                                                     ⎪   the work
                             Knowledge of the   ⎪
Feedback   ⟶   actual results of the   ⎪   Low absenteeism
                             work activities   ⎭   and turnover

                         ┌──────────────────┐
                         │ Employee Growth │
                         │ Need Strength   │
                         └──────────────────┘

Source: From Hackman, J. Richard and Oldham, Greg R.: WORK REDESIGN ©
          (1980) by Addison-Wesley Publishing Co., inc. Adapted with the
          permission of Pearson Education, Inc., Upper Saddle River, NJ.

Numerous attempts have been made to develop conceptual models and theories that relate job characteristics to employee wellbeing (cf. Kahn &

Byosiere, 1992). Job characteristics assist in differentiating a person's psychological state from the external characteristics of a job. However, the Vitamin Model's 10 environmental job features are yet to be fully validated. There are considerable difficulties in operationalising such a wide array of job feature constructs. These features (characteristics) are essentially an extension of Hackman and Oldham's (1975) Job Characteristics Model (JCM) as depicted in Figure 8.3.

There is general agreement in the literature that the Job Diagnostic Survey (JDS) does measure the five core job dimensions of the JCM (e.g., Stone, 1975). As Cordery and Sevastos (1993: 34) noted 'job-design research has been dominated for nearly two decades by the Job Characteristics Model', which explains how enriched or complex jobs are associated with increased job satisfaction, motivation and job performance. Five core job characteristics - skill variety, task identity, task significance, autonomy, and feedback from the job - are considered to affect four critical psychological states - experience, meaningfulness of work, experienced responsibility for outcomes of work, and knowledge of the actual results of work activities (Hackman & Oldham, 1975; 1980). The JCM assists in differentiating a person's internal psychological states by describing the external characteristics of a job, such that:

> The net result is a self-perpetuating cycle of positive work performance powered by self-generated rewards that is predicted to continue until one or more of the three psychological states is no longer present, or until the individual no longer values the internal rewards that derive from good performance.

(Hackman & Oldham, 1980: 257).

These states influence work outcomes for internal work motivation, growth satisfaction, overall job satisfaction, work effectiveness, and absenteeism. Three factors - knowledge and skill growth, needs strength, and context satisfaction are considered to moderate the relationship between job characteristics and work outcomes (Hackman & Oldham, 1980). All five core job characteristics are assumed to influence the three critical psychological states which affect work outcomes.

To improve psychological outcomes at work, all five of Hackman and Oldham's core job characteristics need to be developed but specific outcomes are associated primarily with some job characteristics rather than with others (Fried & Ferris, 1987). Psychological outcomes and not directly measuredby the JCM. Reliable measures of affective wellbeing and intrinsic job satisfaction are needed to determine how these states are associated with job characteristics. Attributes of jobs are filtered through employees' perceptions and result in psychological states which determine a person's affective and behavioural responses (Dodd & Ganster, 1996).

There has been considerable research conducted into job characteristic perspectives of job design. A comprehensive meta-analysis of studies into Hackman and Oldham's (1980) JCM by Fried and Ferris (1987) supported the multi-dimensionality of job characteristics. Psychological and behavioural outcomes were both found to be related to job characteristics. While these results supported the intervening (i.e., mediating) role between job characteristics and outcomes, less support was found between jobs. Task identity has been shown to have a strong relationship with job performance (Fried & Ferris, 1987). Existing approaches to job redesign do not distinguish between contextual and task and performance. There is a need to identify the casual mechanism by which the changes to job design can enhance performance.

Table 8.1   Core Job Dimensions - Job Characteristics Model

Skill variety The degree to which a job requires a variety of different activities in carrying out the work, which involves the use of a number of different skills and talents of the person.
Task identity The degree to which the job requires completion of a whole and identifiable piece of work.
Task significance The degree to which the job has a substantial impact on the lives or work of other people, whether in the immediate organisation or in the external environment.
Autonomy The degree to which the job provides substantial freedom, independence and discretion to the individual in scheduling the work and in determining the procedures to be used in carrying it out.
Feedback The degree to which carrying out the work activities required by the job results in the individual obtaining direct and clear information about the effectiveness of their performance.

Source: Adapted from Hackman & Oldham (1975: 59).

Job characteristics and psychological states growth need were found to moderate the true variance found in the job characteristics and performance relationship. Campbell and Gingrich (1986) found participation to have a positive effect on performance involving complex tasks. This suggests that the effect of autonomy will be most noticeable for jobs involving complex tasks. For jobs with high task variety, increased autonomy contributed 16% of variance to performance. In addition, autonomy and feedback were found to interact with one another, with increased feedback and high autonomy again contributing 16% to performance' (Dodd & Ganster, 1996). A strong and consistent relationship is apparent between certain job characteristics and affective responses to job tasks, which are invariably linked to job and growth satisfaction. Neither perceived nor manipulated job characteristics impact on job performance, suggesting an additive and multiplicative effect.

Cognitions contribute to the additive and interactive effects of the core dimensions of JCM. In contrast to the established literature, Goleman (1998: 22) argued that workplace competences based on emotional intelligence play a far greater role in star performance than does intellectual or technical skill, so that the more 'complex the job, the more emotional intelligence matters'. Goleman's (1998; 1999; 2000; 2002) definitions and conceptualisation of emotional intelligence and emotional competence are much broader than the definition of affective wellbeing adopted in this study. Emotional intelligence may in some way be synergistic with managers' cognitions. Since managerial work involves complex tasks, it will be worth establishing whether emotions account for more variance in outstanding performance than is suggested by the JCM.

Job characteristics, affective wellbeing and intrinsic job satisfaction

Experimental and longitudinal findings suggest that job characteristics affect mental health (Warr, 1987; Martin & Wall, 1989) but this path is not reciprocal (e.g., Frese & Zapf, 1988). In a longitudinal study where mental health has been investigated as an outcome of job characteristics, significant improvements were confirmed in certain 'core' job characteristics (autonomy, feedback and task identification) resulting from job design (Wall & Clegg, 1981). The JCM assists in explaining how enriched or complex jobs increase job satisfaction, motivation and job performance (Hackman & Oldham, 1975; Hackman & Oldham, 1980). In a test of non-linear components, Warr found an association between opportunities for control, indicating an inverted U-shaped relationship between decision latitude and job satisfaction. However, using a cross-sectional analysis to test the Vitamin Model, Fletcher and Jones (1993) found little evidence to support this relationship. Warr's (1990a) findings highlighted the differential association between anxiety–contentment and work overload (i.e., job demands) on the one hand, and depression–enthusiasm and job complexity and skill use, on the other.

There is a paucity of studies using the JCM that are specifically concerned with the relationship between managers' job characteristics and their performance. Abdel-Halim (1978; 1979; 1981) studied managers' jobs using dimensions derived from the JCM. However, Abdel-Halim's findings were all based on the same dataset of 89 managers, making generalising from these studies problematic, since these findings have not been replicated. As managers invariably perform complex tasks it will be worth establishing the extent to which autonomy impacts on high variety (complex) tasks. This reasoning is predicated on the assumption that job characteristics meet individual managers' desire for growth, a proposition which can also be tested using a variation of Hackman and Oldham's Job Characteristics Survey (1975).

In general, there is support for the JCM's capacity to explain job satisfaction, but with some reservation about its value for measuring productivity (Umstsot, Bell, & Mitchell, 1976). As Moorhead and Griffin (1992: 659) noted, the 'JDS which is used to test the model is not always as valid and reliable as it should be'. A significant relationship has been found between affective disposition and the type of job a person undertakes. Individuals high on trait NA have been found to favour jobs that are lower in complexity (Spector, Fox, & Van Katwyk, 1999). People high in trait anxiety tend to have jobs that are low in autonomy, skill variety, and task identity. In contrast, individuals high in trait optimism favoured jobs with high levels of job characteristics and task significance (Spector, Jex, & Chen, 1995). Similarly, people with positive self-evaluations of themselves tended to work at complex tasks associated with increased job satisfaction (Srivastava, Locke, & Judge, 2002; Bono & Judge, 2003). These studies suggest that people, or organisations, self-select with an affective disposition into a particular type of job.

Role conflict, role overload and role ambiguity

Scholars have long assumed that individuals only possess finite resources to monitor their behaviour and environment (Cohen, 1988). Prolonged exposure to certain contextual stressors, such as role ambiguity and role conflict, are proposed to exhaust the cognitive resources necessary for effective job performance. Individuals are assumed to have a limited capacity to deal with and integrate stressors. A negative association is assumed between each role stressor and job performance. However, employees may find it difficult to function effectively in a work environment when multiple role stressors are present simultaneously. A negative relationship has been found between role ambiguity and performance in professional, technical and managerial jobs (Tubbs & Collins, 2000).

Where role conflict and role ambiguity simultaneously exceed a person's capacity to deal with stressors, job performance is likely to be impaired. Role conflict and role ambiguity were assumed to independently affect job performance. A less complex jobs are assumed to be less completely specified at higher organisational levels (Ilgen & Hollenbrook,

1991). High correlations between organisational level and role ambiguity are likely to be present when the level of responsibility is closely related to job complexity.

Role ambiguity is usually considered an unpleasant state that is associated with negative affective states. There may be an interactive effect between a person's job performance and the amount of role conflict and role ambiguity experienced. More research is justified into employees' responses to the joint presence of work stressors across a variety of job and types of organisations. Role ambiguity and role conflict have a joint interactive effect on job performance. If this proposition and assumption holds, then concurrent increases in both role ambiguity and role conflict will be associated with decrements in managers' job performance. The general proposition that role conflict and role ambiguity have a joint (interactive) effect on job performance ratings needs to be tested with managers.

Job characteristics, affective wellbeing and intrinsic job satisfaction

Following the recognition of the potential of intrinsic job satisfaction to improve motivation, some organisations reformed job designs to improve organisational effectiveness. Job-related affect is strongly related to work pressure on job demands and intrinsic job satisfaction. This is predicted to be more strongly related to superior support and task complexity than to job demands or work pressure. Job complexity may moderate the satisfaction–performance relationship for intrinsic work fulfilment. Therefore, it is important to consider investigating the relationships between job characteristics and other job features, affective wellbeing and intrinsic job satisfaction.

An interactive link between job characteristics, affective wellbeing and intrinsic job satisfaction is indicated in the literature. Managers' working environments are likely to influence their affective wellbeing and intrinsic job satisfaction. Generally, managers in jobs with high core dimensions are likely to be more satisfied, motivated and productive (Robbins, Millett, Cacioppe, & Waters-Marsh, 1998). If performance gives meaning to a job (making a person, for example, challenged and motivated or miserable and demotivated), then this may in turn affect intrinsic job factors. If performance is also intrinsic to a job, how managers feel may influence how they perform.

INDIVIDUAL DIFFERENCES

Age

Concerns about ageing workforces have become an important focus of developed economies. The ageing workforce is mainly a result of the post-World War II 'Baby Boom' generation. Many nations have found the Baby Boom phenomenon to be the main contributor to the large population increases in specific age groups in the workforce, such as managers. In the context of ageing populations there are important policy issues and concerns about encouraging older workers to continue to participate in the workplace. Continued participation in the workforce by older workers will depend on the individuals concerned finding the available jobs attractive. The capacity of older managers to undertake training in performing new roles is likely to become an important issue for the future. In particular, learning new competencies (and unlearning old habits) will be needed for older managers to cope with the explosion of information technology.

Older workers have been shown to learn more slowly about information technology (Czaja & Sharit, 1985; Elias, Elias, Robbins, & Gage, 1987). However, Warr (1994a) found no evidence that older workers forget new knowledge and skills at a faster rate than younger workers. Rate of acquisition of new technology competencies is arguably less important than the capacity to use the technology effectively. Therefore, older employees are likely to be able to learn new skills in information technology, if given conducive learning environments.

Retaining older workers in the workforce is likely to be increasingly used as a competitive strategy amongst organisations. Employees between 50 and 69 years of age will comprise 34% to 36% of the total workforce in developed economies by 2008 (Warr, 1994c). The implication of this occurrence on the social capital available to organisations and nation-states deserves consideration. Encouraging the expression of extra role (discretionary) behaviours from managers is important to generate social capital, the increased aging of the workforce will represent a major challenge for managers' and leaders. Drucker (2001) considers the most important issue regarding older workers is removing job rigidities to harness their competencies. Attracting and retaining older managers and employees is likely to depend upon more intrinsic motivators rather than extrinsic motivators, such as wages and hours of work. A strong and significant U-shape relationship has been found between intrinsic and extrinsic job satisfaction and age by Clark, Oswald and Warr (1996). Job satisfaction typically rises from the early thirties and reaches its peak at 36 years of age.

Meta-analyses by Waldman and Avolio (1986) and McEvoy and Cascio (1989) concluded that on average the correlation between age and job performance was close to zero. No difference between objective measures of performance was evident between older workers and younger workers

(Waldman & Avolio, 1986). Later work by Schmidt and Hunter (1998: 15) unambiguously asserted that the 'age of job applicants shows no validity for predicting job performance. Age is about as totally unrelated to job performance as any measure can be'. Job knowledge is a very important predictor of job performance. Job experience usually results in more job knowledge (Schmidt & Hunter, 2004). Older workers are likely to have accumulated considerable job knowledge by virtue of experience in the workplace. Learning plays a major role in job performance since training and performance is determined by GMA (Schmidt & Hunter, 1998). In addition, GMA predicts performance within jobs and occupations, including performance in learning.

GMA is stable over time and does not decrease for individuals (Deary, Whalley, Lemmon, Crawford, & Starr, 2000). Moreover, tasks which remain complex and cannot be automated, such as many aspects of managerial work that require controlled information processing continue to be correlated with GMA (Schmidt, Ones, & Hunter, 1992). A personality dimension of the Big-Five, Openness to Experience, is a long term dispositional trait that directly predicts job performance. Barrick and Mount (1991) argued that those who are open to experience desire to be involved in training and will consequently learn more. This indicates that older workers will be able to learn the job knowledge for longer than anticipated. Overall, there is a lack of specific empirical evidence on the relationship between individual age and performance, indicating that more research in this area needs to be undertaken.

General Mental Ability

Attention in personnel psychology is again focusing on the development of theories into the causes of job performance. Of particular interest is why general mental ability (GMA) is such a strong predictor of job performance. From a theoretical perspective the central determining variables in job performance are GMA, job experience (i.e., opportunity to learn), and the personality trait of conscientiousness. Considerable evidence exists to support the validity of GMA measures for predicting job performance compared to other existing methods (Schmidt & Hunter, 1981; Schmidt, Hunter, & Outerbridge, 1986; Ree & Earles, 1992; Schmidt & Hunter, 1998). The theoretical foundation for GMA is stronger than for any other personnel measure. For over 90 years theories of intelligence have been developed, tested, and the results widely published. An enormous research literature exists to contribute to a sophisticated understanding of the construct of intelligence when compared to interviews or assessment centres (Brody, 1992; Carroll, 1993; Jensen, 1998).

An enormous research literature exists to contribute to a sophisticated understanding of the construct of intelligence when compared to interviews or assessment centres (Brody, 1992; Carroll, 1993; Jensen, 1998).

Three combinations of GMA and job performance emerged from Schmidt and Hunter's (1998) meta-analytic of the highest multivariate validity and utility for job performance: GMA with a work sample test (mean validity of .63), GMA with an integrity test, which mainly measures conscientiousness (mean validity of .65), and GMA with a structured interview which partly measures conscientiousness and related personality traits, such as agreeableness and emotional stability (mean validity of .63). Both combinations are good predictors of performance in job training (.67 and .59, respectively), as well as performance on the job (Schmidt & Hunter, 1998). Up to 33% of managerial job performance was accounted by estimates of the manager's GMA. No other characteristic or combination of characteristics accounts for such a high proportion of managerial success. High correlations for validity were found for GMA as a predictor of job performance (.58), for professional-managerial jobs (.56), for high level complex technical jobs (.51), and for medium complexity jobs (Hunter, 1986). The highest determinants of the multivariate validity and utility for job performance were GMA plus a work sample test and GMA plus an integrity test, and GMA plus a structured interview.

In a rapidly changing and increasingly challenging world, the ability to learn and develop is a critical element in the formula for organisational success. The knowledge of how to perform on the job has been found to result in superior job performance (Hunter, 1989). Mental ability has been found to have a major direct causal impact on the acquisition of job knowledge. Thus, GMA has been found to be the best available predictor of job-related learning and the acquisition of job knowledge learned on the job (Schmidt, Hunter, & Outerbridge, 1986; Schmidt & Hunter, 1992) and of performance in job training programmes (Hunter, 1986; Ree & Earles, 1992). The reason more intelligent people have higher job performance is attributed to their capacity to quickly acquire larger amounts of job-related knowledge. GMA is an exceptionally good predictor of job-related learning with equivalent high predictive validity for performance in job training for all jobs at all levels. Mental ability therefore affects job performance indirectly through the application of job knowledge.

GMA can be measured using commercially available tests such as the Wonderlic Personnel Test which is considered equivalent to other known measures of GMA in the USA (Hunter, 1986) and Europe (Salgado & Anderson, 2002). The Wonderlic Personnel Test is the most widely used test of GMA which consists of 50 free-response items with equally represented verbal, quantitative and spacial material which can be administered in 10 minutes. Test-retest reliabilities (across test forms) of the Wonderlic Personnel Test range from .82 to .94 and alternative form reliabilities range from .73 to .95. Other measures of internal consistency (such as the KR-20) range from .88 to .94 (Saltzman, Strauss, Hunter, & Spellacy, 1998).

PANAS-Plus

Dispositional affect is an appropriate rating of individual managers' performance leading to a stronger operationalisation of the 'happy-productive worker' thesis (Wright & Staw, 1999a; 1999b). Depending on the time-frame instructions, these dimensions may also be measured as state or trait PA and NA. State affect represents a person's mood, while trait PA and NA represent enduring aspects of a person's personality. Refer to Chapters 2 and 6 for a description on PANAS (Watson & Clark, 1984) scale qualities and items.

Staw and Barsade (1993) argued that affect pleasantness descriptors denoting high positive affect or happiness ('happy', 'cheerfulness') and high negative affect or depression ('blue', 'gloomy') may be required to capture the construct of affective disposition. Wright and Staw (1999a: 11) also observed that 'Conspicuously missing from the PANAS scale are items such as 'happy', 'contented', 'pleased', 'unhappy' , arguing that these 'pleasantness items may be precisely the descriptors needed for predicting employee performance', as the items in the PANAS-Plus scale measure.

Conscientiousness

Only one of the Big-Five traits, conscientiousness, has been found to consistently predict job performance and career success in all job families (Barrick & Mount, 1991; Mount & Barrick, 1995). A meta-analytic estimate of .31 for conscientiousness for predicting job performance was reported by Mount and Barrick (1995). Conscientiousness was found to be higher for managers in high autonomy jobs than in low autonomy jobs. Conscientiousness was considered by Barrick, Mount and Strauss (1993) to affect motivational states, goal setting and goal commitment. They concluded that conscientiousness may act a motivational contributor to job performance. Conscientiousness also predicts performance in job training (Barrick & Mount, 1991; Schmidt & Hunter, 1998).

A meta-analytic estimate of the validity of conscientiousness for predicting performance in job training was .30 (Mount & Barrick, 1995). After controlling for GMA, employees who are higher in conscientiousness are likely to develop higher levels of job knowledge. This may be a result of highly conscientious individuals applying greater effort and spending more time focussing on job tasks. This job knowledge may result in higher levels of job performance (Schmidt & Hunter, 1998). Thus, there is a clear rationale for including a measure of conscientiousness in any consideration of managers' performance.

Although personality and non cognitive traits are important to job and training performance, they are less important compared to GMA. Intellectual ability has been found to be more important for predicting job performance than personality (Schmidt, Hunter, & Outerbridge, 1986; Ree & Earles, 1992; Schmidt & Hunter, 1992; Ree & Caretta, 1998; Ree & Carretta, 2002; Kuncel, Hezlett, & Ones, 2004). However, as indicated earlier in this section, Openness to Experience is a long term dispositional trait that has been shown to directly predict job performance (Barrick & Mount, 1991). From a broader perspective it is worthwhile to establish if there is a relationship between managers' contextual and task performance and trait personality factors.

Personality and performance

Personality measures are relevant for personnel selection (Robertson & Kinder, 1993; Anderson & Cunningham-Snell, 2000; Hermelin & Robertson, 2001; Salgado, Viswesvaran, & Ones, 2001; Anderson, Lievens, van Dam, & Ryan, 2004). Numerous meta-analyses of personality measures have confirmed that personality measures are valid predictors of job performance for a variety of occupational groups (Barrick & Mount, 1991; Ones & Viswesvaran, 1999; Barrick, Mount, & Judge, 2001; Borman, Penner, Allen, & Motowidlo, 2001; Salgado et al., 2001). These findings predominantly used the Five-Factor Model of personality as taxonomy for organising scales from inventories. Two of the Big-Five personality dimensions, conscientiousness and emotional stability, have shown in these meta-analyses to have generalised validity across criteria, occupations, organisations and countries. Conscientiousness and emotional stability have also been shown to have incremental validity over general mental ability (GMA) measures (Salgado & Anderson, 2002; Salgado et al., 2003).

This study only measured PA and NA, two of the five most widely recognised dimensions of personality (Mount & Barrick, 1995). Therefore, only limited conclusions were made about the influence of personality in terms of contextual performance, since only two dimensions (PA and NA) of personality disposition were measured that equate with extraversion and neuroticism respectively. In order to fully test the proposition that personality relates to managers' performance, it is necessary to test for at least five trait personality dimensions (Mount & Barrick, 1995).

An independent subsample is needed to guard against the possibility that individual level personality characteristics significantly influence the results. Contextual performance has been related to personality and motivation; whereas task performance is related to ability. Therefore, it is worth exploring further if aspects of personality are useful indicators of managers' contextual and task performance. Specifically, personality traits will be used to measure: job performance and job training (conscientiousness, extraversion, and neuroticism), age and job learning (openness to experience) and intrinsic job satisfaction (neuroticism, extraversion and conscientiousness).

The Big-Five

Personality traits may be defined as 'dimensions of individual differences in tendencies to show consistent patterns of thoughts, feelings, and actions' (McCrae & Costa, 1990: 23). A well-accepted theory of personality structure consisting of five factors has emerged from the personality literature (Digman, 1990; Barrick & Mount, 1991; Costa & McCrae, 1992). The Big-Five Factor taxonomy has been validated by a number of investigations using different theoretical frameworks. The Five-Factor structure remains stable over time (Costa & McCrae, 1988; Costa & McCrae, 1991), in a variety of cultures (Costa & McCrae, 1997), from ratings obtained from different sources and instruments (Goldberg, 1990; Ilies, Schmidt, & Yoon, 2002). The Big-Five personality dimensions are: openness to experience, conscientiousness, extraversion, agreeableness, and neuroticism (Barrick & Mount, 1991; Mount & Barrick, 1995). These five dimensions represent a complete description of personality.

Many instruments purport to measure the Big-Five personality traits. Of these, the NEO Five Factor Model (NEO PI-R™), developed by Costa and McCrae (1992; Costa & McCrae, 1996), is one of the most widely researched. A short version of the IPIP-NEO inventory, suitable for measuring the domain constructs of the Big-Five, is available free online (Buchanan, 2001). IPIP-NEO was designed to measures the same personality traits (5 broad domains and 30 subdomains of personality) as the original NEO PI-R™ but more efficiently (15–20 minutes), using fewer items (120 compared to 300) derived from the original inventory (Buchanan, Goldberg, & Johnson, 1999). However, while 20,000 persons have used the IPIP-NEO to ensure acceptable measurement reliability it is not equivalent to the NEO PI-R™.

Measuring emotional intelligence

A number of tests purport to assess emotional intelligence or emotional

Emotional Quotient Inventory (*EQ-i*), Multifactor Emotional Intelligence Scale (MEIS), Mayer–Salovey–Caruso Emotional Intelligence Test (MSCEIT V.2). Comparability of these measures was examined and conclusions and suggestions for future research on emotional intelligence measures were made (Conte, 2005; Daus & Ashkanasy, 2005).

Both Conte (2005) and Daus and Ashkanasy (2005) have noted that few independent, peer reviewed assessments of the reliability and validity of the Emotional Competence Inventory developed by Boyatzis, Goleman, and colleagues have been undertaken and published. In the absence of discriminant and predictive validity evidence 'the scale does not deserve serious consideration until peer-reviewed empirical studies using this measure are conducted' (Conte, 2005: 434).

Likewise, Conte (2005: 435) has also argued that the *EQ-i* was found to be 'lacking in discriminant validity evidence, and few studies have examined whether it provides incremental predictive validity above the contribution of established predictors such as cognitive ability and Big-Five personality dimensions'. *EQ-i* showed adequate reliability and some evidence of validity. Internal consistency reliability of the overall *EQ-i* was reported to be .76 (Bar-On, 2000). Adequate test-retest reliability of .85, after one month, and .75 after four months, has been exhibited (Bar-On, 2000). For convergent validity, the average correlation among *EQ-i* subscales was .50, similar to correlations among dimensions of traditional intelligence test (Gowing, 2001).

Discriminant validity studies showed *EQ-i* correlated .12 with the Wechsler Adult Intelligence Scale (Bar-On, 2000), and but an average correlation of approximately of .50 was found between the *EQ-i* and the Big-Five personality measures (Dawda & Hart, 2000). A study of retail managers by Slaski and Cartwright (2002) found criterion validity for the *EQ-i* was significantly correlated with morale (.55), stress (-.41), general health (-.50), and supervisor ratings of performance (.22). Supervisor ratings of performance are of particular interest for the proposed extension study of predictor of managers' performance. *EQ-i* demonstrates adequate reliability and some validity although there are concerns about its lack of discriminant validity (Conte, 2005; Daus & Ashkanasy, 2005).

The *EQ-i* is a 133–item self-report measure that takes approximately 30 minutes to complete. The measure yields an overall emotional quotient score as well as scores for five composite scales: (1) intrapersonal, (2) interpersonal, (3) adaptability, (4) general mood, and (5) stress management. *EQ-i* has a short form version (Bar-On EQ-i:S) (10–15 minutes to administer) and a 360° appraisal version (Bar-On EQ-360). The practical advantage for the *EQ-i* is its availability, time to complete and self-report response format.

Salovey and Mayer's conceptualisation of emotional intelligence is operationalised as an 'abilities measure' of emotional intelligence in the tradition of measures of intellectual intelligence called the MSCEIT V.2 (Mayer–Salovey–Caruso Emotional Intelligence Test; Mayer, Salovey, & Caruso, 2002). The MSCEIT has been normed with 5000 people, and has been stable for six years of psychometric investigation (Daus & Ashkanasy, 2005). MSCEIT exhibits strong internal consistency reliability (Conte, 2005). The MSCEIT's overall internal consistency reliability ranged from r¼0.90 to 0.96 (Mayer et al., 2004a), with reliabilities on the four branch scores ranging from 0.76 (facilitating branch) to 0.98 (understanding and perceiving branch) (Mayer, Salovey, & Caruso, 2002; 2004a; 2004b; Palmer, Gignac, Manocha, & Stough, 2005) A unitary, overall emotional intelligence factor has emerged when MSCEIT was subject to a Confirmatory Factor Analysis (Palmer et al., 2005). Also, a four-factor solution on each of the four branches provided an excellent fit to the data (Roberts, 2001; Day & Caroll, 2004; Palmer et al., 2005).

Evidence supporting the psychometric properties of MSCEIT, as operationalised by Mayer, Salovey and Caruso, strongly indicates that emotional intelligence is distinct from both cognitive ability and personality (Daus & Ashkanasy, 2005). The highest level of relationship between any emotional intelligence and cognitive ability is with the understanding emotions branch which correlates between 0.25 and 0.40, consequently sharing at most 16% of the variance when the range of correlations for overall emotional intelligence and cognitive ability ranges between 0.14–0.36 (Maycr et al., 2004a). This constitutes an acceptable level of discrimination from cognitive ability (Daus & Ashkanasy, 2005). Hierarchical model of emotional intelligence (cf. Gignac, 2005) are showing promising results for identifying the MSCEIT factor structure (Mayer, Panter, Salovey, Caruso, & Sitarenios, 2005). The MSCEIT consists of 141 items that yield a total emotional intelligence score, two area scores, and four branch scores. Eight task-level scores are reported for research and qualitative use only (Mayer, Caruso et al., 2000).

In all the data and evidence strongly support the claim that the ability model, as described and as operationalised by Mayer, Salovey and Caruso of emotional intelligence shows discriminant validity from the Big Five model of personality. However, it is worth bearing mind that as a construct the ability model of emotional intelligence is still requires further development (Jordan, Ashkanasy, & Hartel, 2003). As a predictor of managers' performance, *EQ-i* demonstrates adequate reliability and some validity but there are concerns about its lack of discriminant validity.

Emotional intelligence, Personality and GMA

Detractor of the emotional intelligence concepts argue that there is considerable overlap between some measures of and the Big-Five model of personality (Conte, 2005; Locke, 2005). A lack of discriminant validity is indeed evident between some emotional intelligence and the Big-Five personality dimensions. A meta-analysis by Van Rooy and Viswesvaran (2004) found that emotional intelligence and Big-Five personality dimensions had correlations (corrected for unreliability) that ranged from .23 to .34, suggesting that emotional intelligence measures are lacking in discriminant validity. However the 'ability model' of emotional intelligence does indicate discriminant validity from the Big-Five personality model (Daus & Ashkanasy, 2005).

In terms of criterion related and incremental validity the percentage of age of variance in performance explained by emotional intelligence was 5%, which is much lower than the claims of some emotional intelligence proponents (Van Rooy & Viswesvaran, 2004). Estimates of the percentage of variance of age in job performance that GMA accounts for range from 10%–26% (Hunter & Hunter, 1984; Schmidt & Hunter, 1998). Based on empirical research to date, broad claims that emotional intelligence is a better predictor than GMA are not supported.

Emotional intelligence as a concept and construct related to occupational success has not been subject to adequate scientific scrutiny. Data necessary for testing the unique association between emotional intelligence and work-related behaviour resides in proprietary databases. As a consequence researchers have been unable to conduct rigorous tests of the emotional intelligence measurement devices necessary to establish its unique predictive value (Conte, 2005; Daus & Ashkanasy, 2005; Landy, 2005). One solution is to ensure that more data about emotional intelligence is made available in the public domain and studies are published to ensure the construct validity is either established of refuted. Although construct validity of emotional intelligence is still underdeveloped there is enough support in the literature to justify measuring it in relation to managers' performance.

Work experience and job performance

Work experience is an aspect of job knowledge that depends on events experienced by an individual related to the performance of a job. Quinones and colleagues (Quinones, Ford, & Teachout, 1995: 888) have defined work experience as either the 'number of months spent in a particular job (job tenure), or the number of times a particular task has been performed'. However, a caveat to this definition is that individuals with the same amount of job tenure may differ considerably in the number and type of tasks performed (Schmitt & Cohen, 1989; Ford, Quinones, Sego, & Sorra, 1992). Experience is generally seen 'as events that occur in an individual's life that are perceived by the individual'(Quinones et al., 1995: 890). Like job performance, work experience is one of the most extensively researched concepts in organisations.

Work experience is often used to make inferences about an individual's future standard of job performance because of the central role it plays in human resource research and practice. Contemporary research has shown the work experience construct to be complex and multi-dimensional (Coovert & Craiger, 1991; Ford et al., 1992; DuBois & McKee, 1994). Ergo, recent work on the performance construct has suggested a multi-dimensional and multilevel perspective regarding criterion measures (Borman, White, Pulakos, & Oppler, 1991; Campbell et al., 1993). A considerable body of literature has linked work experience to a range of human resource functions, such as selection (Ash & Levine, 1985), training (Ford et al., 1992), career development (McCall, Lombardo, & Morrison, 1988; Campion, Cheraskin, & Stevens, 1994), and job performance (Quinones et al., 1995). An individual's life experiences are considered to be one of the most relevant ways of predicting job performance (Quinones et al., 1995).

A large amount of research has also been devoted to examining the relationship of work experience and job performance. A correlation of .18 between work experience and job performance was found in a meta-analysis by Hunter and Hunter (1984). A mean corrected correlation of .32 was found between work experience and job performance across a number of occupations reported in a meta-analysis undertaken by McDaniel, Schmidt and Hunter (1988). A meta-analysis of the existing literature by Quinones and colleagues (1995) revealed that the relationship between work experience and job performance was positive regardless of the work experience measure used. An estimated population correlation of .27 was found between experience and performance. Amount and task level measures of work experience had the highest correlations with measures of job performance.

Various measures of work experience capture different aspects of job-relevant experience. A stronger relationship was found using hard performance measures (i.e., work samples) compared to soft performance measures (i.e., supervisory ratings), a finding consistent with other investigations (Nathan & Alexander, 1988; Blakley, Quinones, Crawford, & Jago, 1994). Time on the job has consistently been shown to be an imperfect measure of what an individual actually does on the job (Ford et al., 1992). Time based and task level measures were seen as poor indicators of job experience. Variability in the relationship between experience and performance was seen as a function of level of specificity. Experience at the task level indicated the strongest relationship, with performance and organisational level showing the weakest.

Job knowledge

Job experience and job knowledge constructs although they are related but different. There are sound theoretical and practical reasons for differentiating between the constructs of job experience and job knowledge. Job experience and conscientiousness are antecedents of job knowledge. From a theoretical standpoint, the central variables determining job performance are GMA, job experience (i.e., opportunity to learn), and conscientiousness, a personality trait (Schmidt & Hunter, 1998) as shown in Figure 8.5.

Figure 8.4 Determinants of Job Performance

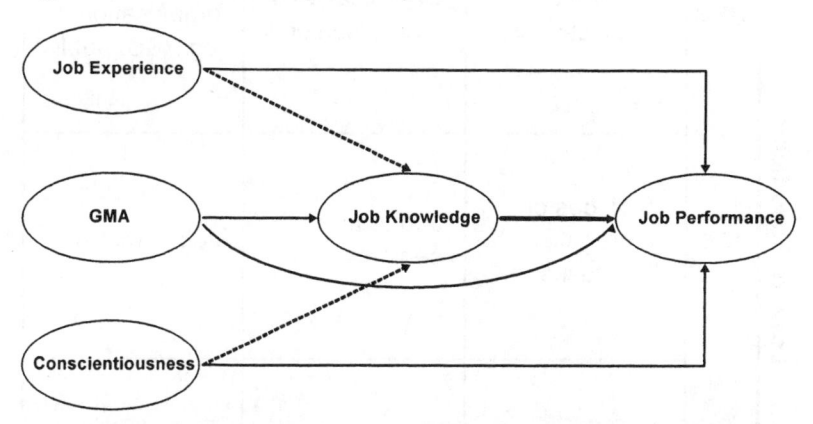

Source: Schmidt, F.L., Hunter, J.E. & Outerbridge A.N. (1986), Impact of job experience and ability on job knowledge, work sample performance, and supervisory ratings of job performance, Journal of Applied Psychology, 71, 432-439. American Psychological Association. Adapted with permission.

A number of measures can be used to represent an individual's level of work experience (Rowe, 1988; Hoffman, 1992). However, not all measures of work experience are identical. Empirical evidence exists to suggest that individuals with the equivalent amount of job tenure can vary considerably in the number and types of tasks they perform (Schmitt & Cohen, 1989; Ford et al., 1992). Time-based measures of experience (e.g., tenure) are usually adopted by most researchers, followed by amount of work experience and occasionally the type of work experience (Quinones et al., 1995). Further, as DuBois and McKee (1994) observed, experience is not equal to practice. Amount and task level measures appear to be a superior measure of what people actually do on the job. A range of contextual factors such as supervision, feedback, and ability to work in groups can have an impact on job performance.

A conceptual framework of measures of work experience (see Figure 8.6) was developed by Quinones and colleagues (1995) which specified the two general dimensions on which work experience measures can vary. The framework is formed into nine specific cells describing different measures of work experience with examples of measures within each cell.

Figure 8.5 Measures of work experience

Level of Specificity	AMOUNT	TIME	TYPE
ORG	Number of organisations	Organisational tenure/seniority	Type of organisation (eg R&D, public)
JOB	% of jobs or aggregate % of tasks	Job tenure seniority	Job complexity
TASK	% of times performing a task	Time on task	Task difficulty complexity criticality

Measurement Mode

Source: Adapted from: Quinones, Ford and Teachout (1995: 892)

From Figure 8.6 it will be apparent that individuals can vary in their level of experience performing specific tasks (Ford et al., 1992). Measurement mode and level of specificity were seen to capture the various measures of work experience. Dimensions of measurement mode (amount, time, type) and level of specificity (task, job, organisational) were used to form nine separate categories (3x3) of measures of work experience as shown in Figure 8.6.

Within this structure individuals can perform a particular task a given number of times (amount) and vary in the types of tasks that they have performed (type). For example, some may perform simple, routine tasks whereas others may perform more difficult, complex, and critical tasks. The amount of time spent working on a given task can vary (time) is most familiar measure used by researchers. Each of these measurement modes can be operationalised at three levels of specificity, either: task, job, or organisational. Each measure of task level experience captures a unique portion of an individual's overall level of work experience. For example, different people can perform a task the same number of times but the task may have different levels of difficulty. Thus, each measure of task level experience in this framework captures a somewhat unique portion of an individual's overall level of work experience.

This framework provides a well founded conceptualisation of the broad dimensions that characterise the various measures of work experience at the different levels of specificity within each dimension. The framework permits future work to focus on individual level issues of work experience and to expand our understanding so that there can be congruency across conceptualisation, operationalisation, and interpretation of various work experience measures.

Future research could further examine the relationship between various measures of work experience as a moderator of job knowledge. Since life events are clearly not discrete, an individual's work context needs to be considered when attempting to systematically investigate the experience construct. A lack of consistency in the definition and measurement of work experience has led to a call for further research to be undertaken to establish the true nature of the work experience construct (Rowe, 1988; Lance, Hedge, & Alley, 1989; Ford, Sego, Quinones, & Speer, 1991; Teachout, 1991; Hofmann, Jacobs, & Gerras, 1992; DuBois & McKee, 1994). Work experience is a complex and multi-dimensional construct which needs to be closely defined to ensure congruency between the conceptualisation, operationalisation, and interpretation of results (Ostroff & Ford, 1989).

As with job performance, future research is needed to confirm the multi-dimensional perspective of the work experience construct. Specifically, it is worth testing if the measurement mode and level of specificity will moderate the relationship between work experience and job performance. Measures of work experience may be predicted to be associated with job performance because they focus on what managers are actually doing rather than simply on how long they have been doing it. Work experience is effectively a measure of practice on the job and as such is a precursor of the opportunity and capacity to learn. As is the case for mental ability, the major direct causal effect of job experience is knowledge accumulated on the job. Until around five years on the job, increasing job experience leads to increasing job knowledge which in turn results in improved job performance (Schmidt & Hunter, 1981; Schmidt, Hunter, & Outerbridge, 1986; Ree & Earles, 1992; Schmidt & Hunter, 1998).

WELLBEING

Affective Wellbeing

Evidence supporting a monopolar model of affective wellbeing structure is theoretically and empirically robust. A monopolar construction is more stable over time and is appropriate for measuring state affect. The Four Factor Model of Affective Wellbeing (Sevastos, 1996) complemented and extended the constructs measured by PANAS-Plus. Refer to Chapters 2 and 6 for a description on The Four Factor Model of Affective Wellbeing scale qualities and items. Questionnaire items will be derived from established affective wellbeing and job satisfaction scales that provide psychometrically robust measures of dispositional and state affect that are suitable for predicting managers' performance.

Karasek's (1979; 1989; 1990) research highlighted an intriguing proposition worth further examination in relation to managers' affective wellbeing and performance: are managers who are experiencing high work pressure likely to report positive job satisfaction and high anxiety but low depression or do managers with less enriched jobs experience low pressure, dissatisfaction and low anxiety but increased depression?

Intrinsic Job Satisfaction

A meta-analysis by Judge, Heller and Mount (2002) found the Big-Five traits had a multiple correlation of .41 with job satisfaction, indicating support for the validity of the dispositional source of job satisfaction. The estimated true score correlations with job satisfaction were -.29 for Neuroticism, .25 for Extraversion, .02 for Openness to Experience, .17 for Agreeableness, and .26 for Conscientiousness. Three personality traits - Neuroticism, Extraversion, and Conscientiousness - displayed appreciable correlations with dispositional job satisfaction. Neuroticism emerged as the strongest and most consistent correlate of job satisfaction.

Conscientiousness displayed the second strongest correlation with job satisfaction. Neuroticism and Extraversion related to job satisfaction generalised across studies. Agreeableness and Openness to Experience displayed relatively weak correlations with job satisfaction. Extraversion showed a nonzero relationship with job satisfaction. Judge et al.'s findings supported a qualitative review by Tokar and Subich (1997) found 'Greater job satisfaction is related to lower neuroticism and its variants, as well as to higher extraversion and related traits'.

While the results linking the Big-Five traits to job satisfaction are striking, other frameworks could also explain the dispositional source of job satisfaction. A study by Connolly and Viswesvaran (Levi, 2002) showed that PA and NA display moderately stronger correlations with job satisfaction than those found in the meta-analysis by Judge et al. As noted in Chapter 2, research has suggested PA represents Extraversion and NA Neuroticism in the Five-Factor model, indicating that PA and NA are subsumed within the Five-Factor model (Watson & Clark, 1992a; Brief, 1998).

In Chapter 2 it was argued that PA and NA are temperaments which are linked to the hemispheric brain function. However, Judge et al have speculated, the Five-Factor model may contains an additional trait, Conscientiousness, which is potentially a better predictor of job satisfaction than the PA–NA typology (Organ & Lingl, 1995). PA and NA could be supplemented with Conscientiousness to obtain the maximum prediction of job satisfaction. Also, PA and NA are quasi-dispositional in that they also assess mood or 'affective traits' (Watson, 2000) and are possibly less stable than other dispositional measures (Judge & Bretz, 1993), and may to some degree be confounded with life satisfaction (Judge et al., 1998). The empirical validity of both frameworks and similarity between them warrants further integrative research into the personality-satisfaction relationship.

The Big-Five traits may influence job satisfaction through the categorization of attitudes from the cognitive, affective, and behavioural tripartite (Eagly & Chaiken, 1993). These traits may cognitively influence how individuals interpret the characteristics of their jobs. Individuals with positive core self-belief tend to interpret intrinsic job characteristics more positively (Judge et al., 2001). Affectively, these traits may influence job satisfaction through mood at work (Brief, 1998). From a behaviour standpoint, employees who are emotionally stable, extraverted, and conscientious are possibly happier at work as a result of achieving satisfying job outcomes.

Perhaps conscientious employees perform better and are more satisfied with their work because of the intrinsic rewards resulting from high performance. This effect may to a degree be attributed to situation selection. Possibly extraverted employees are more liable to create social interactions that make people happier (Magnus, Diener, & Fujita, 1993). Links have been established between personality and job performance (Barrick & Mount, 1991) and personality and job satisfaction (Judge et al., 2002).

As Judge et al. (2002) advised, 'perhaps the time has come for a framework that takes the linkages among personality, job performance, and job satisfaction into account'. A case has been established for integrating diverse frameworks of the dispositional source of job satisfaction in order to capture the psychological processes involved in explaining the relationships of the personality traits to job satisfaction. Researchers should be cautious when using affective wellbeing, intrinsic job satisfaction and performance instruments conceived of in developed cultures to conduct research in different cultures.

Affective organisational commitment

Organisational commitment and intrinsic job satisfaction have been found to be correlated with superiors' ratings of managers' performance and promotability (Meyer et al., 1989). Both Meyer, Allen and Smith (1993) and Meyer et al. (1989) have reported that affective commitment is positively related to employee performance. Affective commitment has been found to be correlated negatively with superiors' evaluations of managers' performance (Meyer et al., 1989; Meyer et al., 1993). The uncertainty of the relationship between commitment and superior performance also extends to the relationship between commitment and performance data.

Using a well worn equation, Purcell (2004: 3) argued that job commitment and satisfaction are triggered by (P)erformance, (A)bility, (M)otivation and (O)pportunity, or $P = f(A, M, O)$. People are predicted to perform well when they (Purcell, 2004):

- are able to do so (they can do the job because they possess the necessary knowledge and skills);
- have the motivation to do so (they will do the job because they are adequately incentivised); and
- work environment provides the necessary support and avenues for expression (e.g. functioning technology and the opportunity to be heard when problems occur).

Both Mayer and Schoorman (1992) and DeCotiis and Summers (1987) found support for the argument that commitment was positively associated with job performance. But Summers and Hendrix (1991) found no support for this proposition. Meyer and Shack (1989) found that first-level (front-line) managers' affective commitment correlated with their superiors' performance ratings. However, no significant correlation was found to exist between job satisfaction and the performance ratings. Employed administrators with the highest organisational commitment have reported fewer stressors and greater job satisfaction (Leong, 1996). Job satisfaction has been found to be more strongly aligned with organisational commitment, than with superiors' ratings of performance (Shore & Martin, 1989). Thus, it is worth testing if managers' affective organisational commitment may be associated with their contextual or task performance.

Stress

As noted in Chapters 1 and 3, workplace difficulties are often attributed to stress yet may actually be symptoms of depression and anxiety. Job-related depression and anxiety are aspects of affective wellbeing. Intrinsic and extrinsic stimuli resulting in emotional reactions, determine a person's reactions to stressful situations. Therefore, research on the construct of stress informs the study of the construct of affective wellbeing, and vice versa. Aspects of job satisfaction have been strongly linked with mental and psychological health problems in the workplace. Also mental illness and affective wellbeing in the workplace may be identified in measures of stress. The ASSET instrument is validated and suitable for the measurement of managers' workplace stress, mental health and affective wellbeing (Johnson & Cooper, 2003).

PERFORMANCE

Managers' task and contextual performance

To recap, evidence emerged from the literature and in this book to suggest that managers' job performance comprises contextual and task performance domains. Activities associated with contextual performance are relatively similar across jobs, whereas activities associated with task performance will vary between jobs. Contextual performance is linked with personality and motivation; while task performance is linked with ability. Contextual performance is discretionary and extra role, while task performance is prescribed and comprises in-role behaviour.

Chapters 3 and 6 provide a description on task and contextual performance literature. Appendix 5 provides the scales and items. Managers' contextual performance scales were from Borman and Motowidlo's (1997) 5–dimension taxonomy. Borman and Brush's (1993) 18–dimension taxonomy of managerial performance was used to develop and test the task performance scales.

Despite important recent advances, research into contextual

performance is still underdeveloped. Additional research is needed to stabilise the conceptualisation and measurement of contextual performance specifically for managers. Also, it needs to be further clarified whether the antecedents and impact of contextual performance, or other personality domains, are valid predictors of performance.

Contextual performance is not part of the formal in-role obligations of the job, but consists of behaviours that are classified as extra-role. Such behaviours are not an explicit requirement of the job. Also, extra-role behaviours are not usually directly or formally rewarded by organisations. Continuing controversy exists over whether employees classify such behaviours as extra-role, or in-role (Wolfe-Morrison, 1994; Pond et al., 1997).

Work conducted on contextual performance is predicated on the assumption that employees are clear on the boundary between in-role and extra-role behaviour (Organ, 1988; Podsakoff, 1990; Williams & Anderson, 1991). This assumption perception was challenged by Wolfe-Morrison (1994) who observed that role requirements evolve over time and that roles in organisations are now rarely fixed. Variations exist between how broadly employees define their job and specifically where they make the distinction between in-role and extra-role behaviour. While this in-role versus extra-role issue has revealed limitations in the interpretations by previous researchers, there is likely to be agreement that these behaviours are invariably not prescribed by the job, and that the omission of them is not punishable.

These behaviours, like all contextual activities, contribute to organisational effectiveness if displayed over time and across individuals. Little is known about the mechanisms linking individual performance to broader organisational outcomes. Improvements in individual task performance are considered to result in improvements in organisational effectiveness (Schmidt, Hunter, Outerbridge, & Trattner, 1986). This issue impacts on the validity of previous findings and so needs to be clarified before delving deeper into the research related to contextual performance.

Boyatzis's (1982) research identified which personal characteristics correlated with effective managerial performance. Many of the competencies identified for an effective manager are similar to those required for an effective leader. There is much conjecture in the literature about whether managers perform leadership roles (Kotter, 1986), suggesting that relevant leadership dimensions need to be integrated into an instrument developed to measure managers' performance. Boyatzis's Model of Effective Performance characterised the 'art of influencing' as the demonstrated behaviour resulting from the interaction between managers and their environments. This interpretation of decision making accounted for the central influence of critical skills and values of managers' performance. Managers certainly have to make decisions but far more importantly they need to enhance the decision making capabilities of those they work with (Mintzberg, 2004).

Validating the contextual and task performance scales would be particularly worthwhile. The CFA of the results, similar to the approach used to further develop the Measurement Model, will be undertaken with large international and independent samples. Recalibration and validation of the managers' contextual and task performance instrument would be especially worthwhile. This would involve replicating and extending the study in other organisations and countries.

Longitudinal data collection is necessary to determine whether managers' contextual and task performance can be replicated in independent samples. Post hoc modifications conducted on samples of 100 to 400 should be replicated in an independent sample before they can be accepted (Hoyle & Panter, 1995). The literature suggests that post hoc modifications conducted on small samples require validation by independent samples (Tabachnick & Fidell, 2001). Respecification of the Partial Model based on post hoc criteria has the potential to rectify these idiosyncrasies (Hoyle & Panter, 1995) and provides an opportunity that is particularly valuable for small samples (MacCallum, 1995). However, replication studies should not exclusively focus on model fit when examining parameter estimates for interpretability and meaningfulness because as MacCallum (1995: 35) advised, 'a model that fits well but yields nonsensical parameter estimates is of little value'.

Questions in this study provided by managers may have been too cognitively complex, especially for the superiors who were requested to rate the performance of several managers. One way of making the managers' performance scale more accessible to practitioners, without compromising its integrity, is to make it more parsimonious. Either shortening each item or changing each dimension into a one item paragraph for rating could achieve this. Simplifying ratings scales would result in less time required to complete the ratings.

There has been a call to expand the limited amount of research that has been conducted in non-English speaking countries (Meyer & Allen, 1997). This process would be substantially aided by the development of the managers' performance instrument for use in different cultures. The managers' performance instrument needs to be further tested in other cultures to provide validation for its use beyond Australia.

Summary on managers' task and contextual performance

Further research needs to be conducted to determine if there is a causal relationship between affective wellbeing, intrinsic job satisfaction and managers' performance. This would require a sophisticated longitudinal causal model. The finding that certain aspects of managers' affective wellbeing and job satisfaction predict aspects of their contextual and task performance suggests that a more comprehensive model could be devised to determine what other relationships may exist.

The 8–Dimensional Measurement Model of managers' contextual and task performance is suitable for replication. Opportunities for further research also include: a refinement and extension of the Partial Model, with the addition of other relevant personal and context variables, such as, growth needs strength, opportunities to perform, job challenge and rewards, career stages, job characteristics, role conflict, role overload and ambiguity, affective commitment and extrinsic job satisfaction. Macro factors, such as culture, also need to be included.

SUMMARY AND CONCLUSION

Despite the absence of equivocal empirical support, there has long been an adherence to the intuitively appealing notion that 'a happy worker is a good worker'. A resurgence of interest of the age-old 'happy-productive worker' thesis is evident despite the lack of evidence supporting such a relationship. The authors intended to further re-invigorate the debate on the 'happy-productive worker' thesis through a thorough investigation of the 'happy-performing manager' proposition. Research undertaken and articulated in this book established which indicators of managers' affective wellbeing and intrinsic job satisfaction were reliable predictors of performance. Certain trait and state indicators of affective wellbeing and intrinsic job satisfaction were found to predict dimensions of managers' contextual and task performance. This finding is in large part attributable to the more robust conceptualisation and measurement of the constructs involved in determining the relationship between happiness and performance in the workplace.

A more sophisticated understanding of how affective wellbeing and intrinsic job satisfaction interacts with managers' performance, contributes to a better comprehension of the nature of the relationships underlying these constructs. In the process, substantial progress towards establishing the veracity of the 'happy-performing manager' proposition was found which informs the broader 'happy-productive worker' thesis. These findings also inform a wider understanding of what underpins human performance at work. One of the outcomes of these findings is capacity to improve organisational effectiveness by changing individual behaviour. Ultimately, the strength of this relationship will determine important aspects of an organisation's competitive position.

As predicted in Chapter 1, performance was posited to account for some of the remaining 75% of affective wellbeing and intrinsic job satisfaction. This study found that a considerable amount of the variance of performance was caused by affective wellbeing and intrinsic job satisfaction, and vice versa.

The first canonical variate explained 31.25% of the variance of performance and the second canonical variate explained a further 21.16% of the variance of performance. Explaining such a large amount of this variance made it possible to develop a Partial Model with enhanced predictive power. Using two independent sources of information, one for the DVs (i.e., one-to-one congruence of superiors' ratings of managers' performance) and the other for the IVs (i.e. managers' self-report measures of affective wellbeing and intrinsic job satisfaction) eliminated unnecessary noise in the data caused by common method variance.

Managers' self-report of affective wellbeing and intrinsic job satisfaction were related to superiors' ratings of managers' performance to ensure the independence of the measures. As predicted, positive affective wellbeing and intrinsic job satisfaction were related to enhanced managerial performance, and poor affective wellbeing indicated reduced performance. Affective wellbeing self-report (PA, Intrinsic Job Satisfaction) was found to be positively associated with a dimension of superiors' report on task performance (Influencing). Positive associations for dimensions of affective wellbeing self-report (PA, Anxiety and Relaxation) were found to be positively associated with dimensions of superiors' report on contextual performance (Following) and task performance (Monitoring). These wellbeing variables were also negatively associated with a task performance dimension (Technical).

Of particular importance was the development and testing of the Measurement Model of managers' job performance. This permitted the construct of job performance to be measured to a standard previously unachievable. The methodology used ensured there was agreement between managers and their superiors on what were perceived to be the most important elements of performance. Consistent with the literature, self-report was found to be a less reliable measure of managers' performance because method ('halo effect') obscured the true nature of managers' ratings.

Superiors' ratings were found to be the more reliable measures of managers' performance and were independent of affective wellbeing and intrinsic job satisfaction. Until now, there has been no explicit and simultaneous measurement of both managers' contextual and task performance in the field. Measurements of contextual and task performance constructs were specifically identified as deserving of further development. Rated performance of managers was previously conceived of as a unidimensional construct. Cross-validation of self and superiors' ratings found managers' performance to be a multivariate construct consisting of both contextual and task performance.

The performance construct was found to consist of four contextual dimensions (Endorsing, Helping, Persisting, Following) and four task dimensions (Monitoring, Technical, Influencing, Delegating). These dimensions were confirmed through the latest multi-sample analysis and cross-validation techniques of managers' and superiors' ratings. An 8-Dimensional Measurement Model of managers' performance, derived from the survey data, was tested by Exploratory and Confirmatory Factor Analysis to differentiate the structure of managers' contextual and task performance.

The analysis described in this book does not provide evidence of causation. As Ashkanasy et al. (1998: 4) stated, 'Performance is another likely concomitant of affect at work, though whether it is a cause or a consequence is unclear'. However, the analysis does provide for certain inferences to be made about the relationships between aspects of managers' affective wellbeing, intrinsic job satisfaction and performance suggesting that happiness may have contributed to self-motivation. Performance is a barometric of the feeling that managers are effective. Well performing managers could also be happy as a consequence of their effective performance and the resulting rewards.

A number of implications for human resource practices emerged from this book. The main recommendation was that organisations should consider initiating ways to improve managers' affective wellbeing, intrinsic job satisfaction and performance. Replication of the Partial Model and managers' contextual and task performance scales, in conjunction with an extension of the scope of a more complete Model of Managers' Job Scope, Affective Wellbeing and Performance, is recommended.

This book extended upon the existing theoretical base of managers' affective wellbeing, intrinsic job satisfaction and performance, by devising a Partial Model that included performance constructs that have not been comprehensively dealt with in previous theoretical and empirical work. In the process of refining these scales, consideration is given to devising a cross-cultural version of the instrument suitable for use in a range of organisations and countries.

The Partial Model tested is suitable for use by human resource practitioners to inform initiatives that organisations could, to some extent, take to improve managers' affective wellbeing, intrinsic job satisfaction and performance. The potential of workplace initiatives to improve the quality of managers' working lives and organisational effectiveness was discussed. In combination, these benefits may result in more effective organisational outcomes including increased productivity, reduced organisational costs, reduced staff turnover, and avoidance of protracted legal actions arising from claims of unfair dismissal, breach of contract or diminished affective wellbeing. Suggestions were made about how managers' jobs might be improved to enhance, or avoid decline in, managers' affective wellbeing, intrinsic job satisfaction and performance.

The implications derived from this book to the body of management theory and practice were discussed and opportunities for further research were identified. Base data gathered for this book is suitable for replication and verification in subsequent investigations, and ultimately validation in relation to other organisational outcomes. The Partial Model provides an opportunity for researchers to extend the theoretical development of affective wellbeing and intrinsic job satisfaction in relation to managers' performance. This will assist human resource practitioners to align human resource practices within the broader framework of organisational strategies. Human resource managers need to recognise, measure and reward the desired performance of managers in relation to an organisation's strategic goals as this will ultimately facilitate organisational effectiveness

At the macro level, support is re-emerging for the recognition and inclusion of happiness in economic indicators (Bruni, 2005; Layard, 2005; Martin, 2005). Ironically, massive increases in living standards in developed countries in the past 50 years have not made people any happier. Notably, the incidence of depression in the workforce is spreading at an alarming rate. In this scenario, managers' 'personal troubles' have most certainly become 'public concerns'.

An important result of this increased understanding of how managers' affective wellbeing and intrinsic job satisfaction influences their behaviour is the realisation that managers' personal predicament caused by 'squeezing the pips' in organisations is now a public issue. Perhaps the time has come for organisations and nation-states to revisit the seminal issues. Politicians and organisational leaders need to start to incorporate happiness into contemporary public policy initiatives. Social and economic policy makers would do well to follow Bentham's (1776) principle of the 'greatest happiness for the greatest number'.

Promoting managers' and employees' affective wellbeing in the workforce is an important aspect of potentially improving individual and aggregate happiness. Regardless of the link with performance the authors of this book agree with Wright et al.'s (2002: 149) belief that 'promoting happiness is an intrinsic good for which all should work'. In particular, the capacity of managers to engender a feeling of hope through an optimistic outlook is important for motivating employees. Once the realisation takes hold at all levels of an organisation as to the desirability of positive individual wellbeing impacting on performance in organisational context, it will be apparent that managers' 'personal troubles' are indeed 'public concerns'.

Empowerment translates into agility and flexibility at the point of the performance-action axis. As we cross the threshold of the 'happy-productive workers' into the 'happy-performing managers', we can realise this tremendous potential of enabling managers through positive affective wellbeing and intrinsic job satisfaction in every corner of organisations, by every person, by every employee regardless of status, role or position.

Appendices

Appendix 1 Prefixes for questionnaire and dimension abbreviations

Table 9.1   Prefixes for questionnaire and dimension abbreviations

Items	Scales	Rater
1–20	PANAS	Managers' self-report
21–32	Job-related affective wellbeing	Managers' self-report
33–39	Intrinsic job satisfaction	Managers' self-report
40–61	Contextual performance	Managers' self-report
62–137	Task performance	Managers' self-report

Table 9.2   Abbreviations for variables

Variables	Abbreviation
Positive Affect	PA
Negative Affect	NA
Enthusiasm	Enth
Depression	Dep
Anxiety	Anx
Relaxation	Relax
Intrinsic Job Satisfaction	InJS

Table 9.3 Item abbreviations for contextual and task performance

Contextual performance dimension	Abbreviation
Persisting with enthusiasm and extra effort to complete task activities successfully	Persisting (Pers)
Volunteering to carry out task activities that are not formally part of own job	Volunteering (Vol)
Helping and cooperating with others	Helping (Help)
Following organisational rules and procedures	Following (Foll)
Endorsing, supporting and defending organisational objectives	Endorsing (End)
Task performance dimension	**Abbreviation**
Planning and organising	Planning (Plan)
Guiding, directing and motivating staff and providing feedback	Guiding (Guide)
Training, coaching and developing staff	Training (Train)
Communicating effectively and keeping others informed	Communicating (Comm)
Representing the organisation to customers & the public	Representing (Rep)
Technical proficiency	Technical (Tech)
Administration	Administrating (Admin)
Maintaining good working relationships	Maintaining (Maint)
Coordinating staff and other resources to get the job done	Coordinating (Coord)
Decision-making/problem-solving	Deciding (Decide)
Staffing	Staffing (Staff)
Persisting to reach goals	Persisting (Pers)
Handling crises and stress	Stressing (Stress)
Organisational commitment	Committing (Commit)
Monitoring and controlling resources	Monitoring (Mon)
Delegating	Delegating (Del)
Influencing others	Influencing (Inf)
Collecting and Interpreting data	Interpreting (Int)
Contributing to organisational effectiveness	Effectiveness (Effect)

Appendix 2   Conceiving and measuring managers' competency and performance

Table 9.4   Managers' competency and performance

Study	Finding	Methodology & Methods
Akiran & Turner (1996)	5 clusters from 45 competencies of successful bank branch managers, as perceived by subordinates.	Questionnaire developed from Chataway's (1982) naturalistic inquiry. Verified by a panel of 6 experienced bankers & extensively pre-tested.
Australian Standard Classification of Occupations (ABS, 1996; Pithers et al., 1996)	Task & function descriptions of Australian managers. Ranked eight managerial qualities of Australian managers.	Existing literature, census surveys, industry, public sector & union consultation.
Borman & Brush (1993)	Taxonomy of 18 managerial performance 'mega-dimensions' with definitions & two dimensions factor loading highest on each dimension. Percentage of common variance of each mega-dimension accounted for.	Meta-analysis of empirical studies of managers' performance. Behaviourally-based critical incidents & job activity statements. Factor analysed a pooled matrix to derive an 18–factor solution using expert judgement.
Boyatzis (1982)	19 competencies critical to effective management performance & management jobs in all types of organisations. Integrated model of managerial competence.	Cross-sectional survey of 2,000 managers in 41 different managerial jobs in 12 organisations. Re-analysed data from Behavioural Event Interviews.

Cameron & Tschirhart (1988)	Identified four groups of managers' skills: 1. Human relations. 2. Competitiveness & control. 3. Innovations & entrepreneurship. 4. Maintaining order & rationality. Effective managers demonstrate paradoxical skills.	Meta-analysis of the literature reporting the skill assessments of 500 middle & upper level managers in 150 organisations. Used 25 most frequently mentioned management skills from the literature, which were statistically analysed to yield four groups - participative, hard driving, nurturing & competitive).
Cammock et al. (1995)	Lay Model of Managerial Effectiveness. A 17 scale, 2 factor (Most effective/Least effective).	Social constructivist perspective using an ipsative scale. Constructs developed from interviews using Repertory Grid Technique. Six expert judges sorted 300 constructs into discrete categories for 170-item questionnaire.
Deves & Yeow (1994)	5 clusters of competencies associated with general management for bank managers.	Refined managerial competency profiles developed by Saul (1989) for management education. Self-rated questionnaire used to confirm qualitative information.
Dulewicz (1996)	10 Generic International Competencies.	Identified competencies from the Job Competencies Survey which were ranked by international managers.
Fenwick & De Ciera (1995)	Management Excellence Inventory of 20 managerial competencies used to develop & model.	Critical Incidence Technique & unspecified data gathering techniques to analyse & model 20 managerial competencies responsible for success or failure in performing an important aspect of particular job in significant number of instances.

Generic Management Competency Standards for Frontline Management, ANTA (1996)	Competencies of 'Frontline' Australian managers.	Competencies validated by national survey & workshops with 2,000 enterprises, employer & employee organisations.
Kaplan & Norton (1992; 1993; 1996b; 1996a)	Balanced Scorecard. A limited number of measures to give a fast but comprehensive view of the business. Measures how customers perceive them, what they excel at, how can they continue & improve value & how they look to shareholders.	Uses four different perspectives to measure performance, brought together in a single report. All measures are considered together to ascertain if improvements in one area have been achieved at the expense of others.
Mount et al. (1997; 2003)	Management Skills Profile (MSP). Detailed analysis of 122 items representing 18 skill areas describing managers' jobs.	Managers' performance feedback programmes based on model of job performance. Incorporated into Borman & Brush's (1993) Taxonomy of managerial performance. Completed by 22,431 managers, 3 subordinates, 3 peers & a supervisor.
Quinn et al. (Quinn et al., 1996)	Identified 24 key managerial leadership role competencies.	Developed by an expert focus group, consistent with contemporary literature. Modified competencies from feedback in the field.
Rothman & Stewart-Weeks (1995)	Identified capabilities of typical managers in organisations.	Self-administered questionnaire rating managers' in 475 large & medium-sized companies. Surveyed 3,020 Human Resource Managers, Training Managers, Personnel Managers & Corporate Planners. Variables drawn from research literature & focus groups.

Saul (1989)	Management performance assessed by task & people management competencies for Westpac.	Observed behaviours of managers' judged as excellent, average or poor performers. 103 behavioural constructs generated reviewed by senior managers & pre-tested with target population. 93 behaviours rated by 503 managers, immediate superior & 3 subordinates.
Savery, Dawkins & Mazzarol (1995)	Ranking Australian managers' qualities.	8 managerial qualities derived from World Competitiveness Report (1993) validated against literature & interviews with senior Asian leaders. Rating telephone interview with 502 Asian business executives in 5 key customer countries.
Skillscope, Centre for Creative Leadership (1996)	Tasks undertaken by first-line & middle managers.	360° assessment of managerial strengths. 98-item, 15–skill cluster questionnaire. Report high test/retest reliability & internal reliability.
Spencer & Spencer (1993)	12 competencies identified & weighted for A Generic Model of Managers.	Examined 36 managerial models from range of levels & functions for Job Competence Assessment (JCA), drawn from Behavioural Event Interview data.
Wawn & Green (1995)	Defined characteristics of ideal managers considered generic across a range of situations.	Existing literature, an expert focus group & structured interviews.
Lombardo & McCauley (1994)	Benchmarks, Centre for Creative Leadership, Greensboro, North Carolina. 106 items with 16 scales.	Based on interview and survey research of executives, experiences in their careers.

Kaplan & Norton (1992; 1993; 1996b; 1996a)	Balanced Scorecard. Measures were made of customers' perceptions, areas where an organisation excels, how an organisation can continue to improve value & how the organisation appears to shareholders.	Uses a limited number of measures of managers' performance to give a fast but comprehensive view of a business's performance. Four different perspectives used to measure performance.
Warr (1987; 1994a)	Competence, Autonomy & Aspiration assumed to be components of affective wellbeing that were causally linked to performance.	Purportedly measured performance, using self-report questionnaires across all job levels but not specifically managers' performance.
Saville & Holdsworth (1993)	SHL Core Competency Model. Inventory of 16 management competencies.	Developed from literature & field tested for factor purity.
Whetton & Cameron (1991; 1995; 2001)	10 behavioural characteristics of effective managers identified.	Interviews with senior officers in business, healthcare, education & state government. Peers & supervisors identified 402 characteristics of most effective manager.

Appendix 3 Dimensions of managers contextual performance

Table 9.5   Managers' contextual performance

% of variance accounted for	Definitions of managerial mega-dimensions with elements of citizenship, prosocial or model of soldier effectiveness content
2	Organisational commitment: working effectively within the framework of organisational policies, procedures, rules, and so forth; carrying out orders and directives; supporting reasonable policies of higher authorities in organisations.
10	Representing the organisation to customers and the public: representing the organisation to those not in the organisation; maintaining good organisational image to customers, the public, stockholders, the government, and so on (as appropriate); dealing with customer/client problems.
5	Maintaining good working relationship: developing and maintaining smooth and effective working relationship with supervisors, peers and subordinates; displaying personal concern for subordinates; backing up and supporting subordinates as appropriate; encouraging and fostering cooperation between subordinates.
2	Persisting to reach goals: persisting with extra effort to attain objectives; overcoming obstacles to get the job done.
13	Training, coaching and developing subordinates: identifying staff training needs and developing responsive training programmes and materials; or ensuring that such programmes/materials get developed; training teaching and coaching, subordinates; assisting subordinates in improving their skills.
10	Communicating effectively and keeping others informed: communicating orally and in written form; keeping subordinates, supervisors, and others informed; obtaining and then passing on information to those who should know.

Source: Adapted from Borman & Motowidlo (1993: 86).

Table 9.6   Source of items for contextual performance scales

Dimension	Source
1. Persisting with enthusiasm and extra effort to complete task activities successfully.	
1.1 Perseverance and conscientiousness.	Borman & Motowidlo (1993), Borman White, Gast, & Pulakos (1985)
1.2 Extra effort on the job.	Brief & Motowidlo (1986), Katz & Kahn (1978)
2. Volunteering to carry out task activities that are not formally part of own job.	
2.1 Suggesting organisational improvements.	Brief & Motowidlo (1986), Katz & Kahn (1978)
2.2 Initiative and taking on extra responsibility.	Borman et al. (1985), Brief & Motowidlo (1986), Katz & Kahn (1978)
2.3 Making constructive suggestions.	George & Brief (1992)
2.4 Developing oneself.	George & Brief (1992)
3. Helping and cooperating with others.	
3.1 Assisting/helping co-workers.	Borman et al. (1985), Brief & Motowidlo (1986), Katz & Kahn (1978)
3.2 Assisting/helping customers.	Borman et al. (1983), Brief & Motowidlo (1986)
3.3 Organisational courtesy.	Organ (1988)
3.4 Sportsmanship.	Organ (1988)
3.5 Altruism.	Smith, Organ & Near (1983)
3.6 Helping co-workers.	George & Brief (1992)
4. Following organisational rules and procedures	
4.1 Following orders and regulations and respect for authority.	Borman et al. (1983), Borman et al. (1985)
4.2 Complying with organisational values and policies.	Brief & Motowidlo (1986)
4.3 Conscientiousness.	Smith et al. (1983)
4.4 Meeting deadlines.	Katz & Kahn (1978)
4.5 Civic virtue.	Graham (1986)
5. Endorsing, supporting and defending organisational objectives	
5.1 Organisational loyalty.	Graham (1986)
5.2 Concern for unit objectives.	Borman et al. (1985)
5.3 Staying with the organisation during hard times and representing the organisation favourably to outsiders.	Brief & Motowidlo (1986)
5.4 Protecting the organisation.	George & Brief (1992)

Source: Adapted from Borman & Motowidlo (1997: 102).

Appendix 4 Dimensions of managers' task performance

Table 9.7 Mega-dimensions of task performance

% of variance accounted for	Mega-dimensions names, definitions, and the two dimensions loading highest on each mega-dimension
15	1. Planning and organising: formulating short and long term goals and objectives, forecasting possible problems for the unit/organisation and developing strategies for addressing these problems, organising and prioritising work, planning and organising own work, and time management. 1.1 Planning and allocating - planning/forming goals and allocating resources to meet them. 1.2 Strategic planning - developing and formulating long range plans in response to anticipate economic, technological, or marketing trends.
13	2. Guiding, directing, and motivating subordinates and providing feedback; providing guidance and direction to subordinates; motivating subordinates by providing them with recognition, encouragement, constructive criticism, and other feedback as appropriate; helping to set goals and maintaining performance standards for subordinates; and monitoring subordinate performance. 2.1 Supervision - evaluating the quality of subordinate job performance and providing recognition, encouragement, or criticisms of the subordinate. 2.2 Performance review - meeting periodically with subordinates to review performance against standards, including discussion of performance results, recommended salary increases, and counselling on strengths and weaknesses.
13	3. Training, coaching, and developing subordinates: identifying staff training needs and developing responsive training programmes and materials or ensuring that such programmes/materials get developed; training, teaching, and coaching subordinates; and assisting subordinates in improving their job skills. 3.1 Training - responsibility for formal and/or informal instruction for the purpose of teaching skills, including staff development and responsibility for orienting new employees. 3.2 Training of staff members - identifying staff training needs, developing training programmes and materials, participating in formal and informal training programmes, and monitoring training results.

10	4. Communicating effectively and keeping others informed: communicating orally and in written form; keeping subordinates, supervisors, and others informed; and obtaining and then passing on information to those who should know. 4.1 Communication - communicating effectively, thoroughly, and accurately. 4.2 Communication - effective and appropriate oral and written communication.
10	5. Representing the organisation to customers and the public: maintaining good organisational image to customers, the public, stockholders, the government, and so on (as appropriate); and dealing with customer/client problems. 5.1 Representing - representing the organisation to customers and the public. 5.2 Public relations and community service - responsibility for maintaining an appropriate organisation image, which may involve contributing professional expertise in response to community needs.
8	6. Technical proficiency: keeping up-to-date technically, solving technical problems, possessing sufficient technical job knowledge to perform effectively in own specialty, and providing technical advice to others in the organisation. 6.1 Know-how - keeping up-to-date technically. 6.2 Technical management - applying technical (as opposed to managerial) expertise on the job and providing current technical information to subordinates and others.
6	7. Administration and paperwork: handling paperwork requirements; performing day-to-day administrative tasks such as reviewing reports, going through mail, approving routine requests, and so on; keeping accurate records; and administering policies, as appropriate. 7.1 Administration - keeping accurate records and documenting actions. 7.2 Performing administrative duties - comprehending and interpreting paperwork, implementing practices/procedures, and record keeping.
5	8. Maintaining good working relationships: developing and maintaining smooth and effective working relationships with supervisors, peers, and subordinates; displaying personal concern for subordinates; backing up and supporting subordinates as appropriate; and encouraging and fostering cooperation between the subordinates. 8.1 Consideration - showing respect for others and maintaining smooth working relationship. 8.2 Interpersonal relations - maintaining a smooth running work unit that functions with minimal conflict and disruption.

3	9. Coordinating subordinates and other resources to get the job done: properly utilising personnel and other resources to increase unit and organisational effectiveness; coordinating the work in own unit; and balancing interests of own unit and those of the whole organisation, if necessary. 9.1 Coordination - negotiation with others to accomplish optimal utilisation of organisational resources. 9.2 Coordinating the unit - coordinating functional work groups within the larger unit, including developing personnel practices for the unit.
3	10. Decision-making/problem-solving: making sound and timely decisions, paying attention to and taking into account all relevant information in making decisions, and developing effective solutions to organisational problems. 10.1 Decision-making/business judgement - making sound and timely decisions based on available information. 10.2 Problem-solving - anticipating and responding to change by innovative problem-solving.
2	11. Staffing: maintaining staff and workforce; recruiting, interviewing, selecting, hiring, transferring, and promoting persons in the organisation; and maintaining an effective career development system. 11.1 Staffing - deciding on criteria for positions; interviewing, selecting, hiring, transferring, or promoting individuals. 11.2 Staffing/organisation development-building and maintaining a cohesive management team and identifying and developing replacements for employees.
2	12. Persisting to reach goals: persisting with extra effort to attain objectives and overcoming obstacles to get the job done. 12.1 Urgency/persistence/effort - persisting with special effort to reach goals and overcoming difficult obstacles to perform effectively.
2	13. Handling crises and stress: recognising and responding effectively to unexpected situations, handling crises and stress calmly and effectively, responding well to tight time deadlines, and addressing conflict appropriately. 13.1 Crisis action - recognising and responding to unexpected situations. 13.2 Crisis management - problem-solving and troubleshooting for urgent, unexpected situations.

2	14. Organisational commitment: working effectively within the framework of organisation policies, procedures, rules, and so on; carrying out orders and directives; and supporting reasonable policies of higher authorities in organisations. 14.1 Organisational commitment - acceptance of criticisms and/or loyal constructive criticisms of organisational goals, policies, and practices. 14.2 Compliance/effectiveness - application of policies, procedures, rules and regulations to meet organisation standards and objectives; and carrying out orders.
2	15. Monitoring and controlling resource: controlling costs and personnel resources and monitoring and overseeing utilisation of funds. 15.1 Budget control - responsibility for allocating funds internally and for monitoring and overseeing appropriate use of funds within existing constraints and guidelines. 15.2 Control - emphasising the meeting of deadlines and seeing to it that standards are met and that costs are controlled.
1	16. Delegating: assigning subordinates duties and responsibilities in line with their interests and abilities as well as the needs of the organisation, and delegating authority and responsibility to aid in subordinate growth. 16.1 Delegation - assigning subordinates duties and responsibilities in line with their abilities. 16.2 Delegation - effectively delegating responsibility and authority and avoiding trespassing on responsibility areas delegated.
1	17. Selling/influencing: persuading others in the organisation to accept own good ideas, presenting own positions clearly and decisively, and arguing effectively for position when appropriate. 17.1 Personal impact - successfully influencing others inside and outside of the organisation, convincing those holding opposing or neutral opinions, and pushing forward own positions or ideas. 17.2 Influencing and controlling - imposing own wishes on others from the managerial base of recognised organisational authority.
1	18. Collecting and interpreting data: knowing what data are relevant to address a problem or issue; properly interpreting numerical data and other information, thus facilitating correct inferences and effectively organising data to help solve problems and make decisions. 18.1 Data collecting - responsibility for obtaining, collecting, and organising information or data. 18.2 Data collection, analysis, and interpretation - compiling and/or coordinating the collection and analysis of data and making recommendations for future actions from analysis of data.

Source: Adapted from Borman & Brush (1993: 11-14).

Appendix 5 Managers' Wellbeing and Performance Questionnaire ©

HOW DO YOU FILL IN THE QUESTIONNAIRE?

Please answer each question and respond to each statement as frankly and objectively as possible without conferring with anyone else. Answer each question even if you are not certain of your response. There are no right or wrong answers, or any trick questions. If some questions appear repetitive, this is to ensure that we have accurately obtained your views.

Please read the instructions at the start of each section carefully before answering the questions. Preferably, answer all the questions in one session, which should take about 30 minutes. Try to do this when you are not likely to be interrupted.

Thank you for taking the time to help us.

POSITIVE AND NEGATIVE AFFECT

This part consists of words that describe different feelings and emotions. Read each item and then give a rating for each statement using the scale:

1 = Not At All or Slightly
2 = A Little
3 = Moderately
4 = Quite a Bit
5 = Extremely

Circle the response that best indicates to what extent you generally feel:

1)	Interested	1	2	3	4	5
2)	Distressed	1	2	3	4	5
3)	Excited	1	2	3	4	5
4)	Upset	1	2	3	4	5
5)	Strong	1	2	3	4	5
6)	Guilty	1	2	3	4	5
7)	Scared	1	2	3	4	5
8)	Hostile	1	2	3	4	5
9)	Enthusiastic	1	2	3	4	5
10)	Proud	1	2	3	4	5
11)	Irritable	1	2	3	4	5
12)	Alert	1	2	3	4	5
13)	Ashamed	1	2	3	4	5
14)	Inspired	1	2	3	4	5
15)	Nervous	1	2	3	4	5
16)	Determined	1	2	3	4	5
17)	Attentive	1	2	3	4	5
18)	Jittery	1	2	3	4	5
19)	Active	1	2	3	4	5
20)	Afraid	1	2	3	4	5

HOW YOUR JOB AFFECTS YOU

This section is concerned with how your job has been making you feel over the past few weeks. Give a rating for each statement using the scale:

    1 = Never
    2 = Occasionally
    3 = Some of the time
    4 = Much of the time
    5 = Most of the time
    6 = All of the time

Over the past few weeks, how much of the time has your job made you feel each of the following? Please circle the response that best describes how you felt.

21)	Gloomy	1	2	3	4	5	6
22)	Calm	1	2	3	4	5	6
23)	Anxious	1	2	3	4	5	6
24)	Enthusiastic	1	2	3	4	5	6
25)	Motivated	1	2	3	4	5	6
26)	Worried	1	2	3	4	5	6
27)	Restful	1	2	3	4	5	6
28)	Tense	1	2	3	4	5	6
29)	Depressed	1	2	3	4	5	6
30)	Optimistic	1	2	3	4	5	6
31)	Relaxed	1	2	3	4	5	6
32)	Miserable	1	2	3	4	5	6

HOW SATISFIED ARE YOU WITH YOUR JOB?

The following set of items deal with various aspects of your job. Please circle the appropriate number to indicate how satisfied or dissatisfied you feel with each of these features of your present job. Give a rating for each statement using the scale:

 1 = Very Dissatisfied
 2 = Moderately Dissatisfied
 3 = I'm Not Sure
 4 = Moderately Satisfied
 5 = Very Satisfied

Overall, how dissatisfied or satisfied are you with:

33)	The amount of variety in your job?	1	2	3	4	5
34)	The recognition you get for good work?	1	2	3	4	5
35)	Your chances of promotion?	1	2	3	4	5
36)	The opportunity to use your abilities?	1	2	3	4	5
37)	The attention paid to suggestions you make?	1	2	3	4	5
38)	The amount of responsibility you are given?	1	2	3	4	5
39)	The freedom to choose your own method of working?	1	2	3	4	5

MANAGERS' PERFORMANCE

The following questions are designed to assist in rating your achievements and behaviours on a range of job tasks. There are two parts.

In Part 1 you are asked how accurately the various statements describe your behaviour at work that is beyond job specific task performance. This is called 'Contextual Performance'. In Part 2, you are asked to consider how well you perform your job tasks, or 'Task Performance'.

Select the option that best describes each behaviour or task described in the following statements using the scale below:

        1 = Poor
        2 = Acceptable
        3 = Very Good
        4 = Excellent
        5 = Outstanding
       NA = Not Applicable

Then, circle the alternative (1–5) you have chosen, or NA if appropriate.

Please avoid giving generalised high or low ratings. Focus on the specific behaviours or characteristics described by the statement. Managers are unlikely to score uniformly Poor ('1') or Outstanding ('5') on all aspects of their job.

For any questions that do not apply to you don't guess, circle the 'Not Applicable' (NA) response.

MANAGERS' CONTEXTUAL PERFORMANCE

The following questions are designed to rate your contextual performance (i.e., general work behaviour beyond your formal job tasks). How accurately does each statement describe your behaviour at work?

Please circle the alternative (1–5) you have chosen, or NA if appropriate.

	Persisting with enthusiasm and extra effort to complete task activities successfully						
40)	Demonstrating perseverance and conscientiousness.	1	2	3	4	5	NA
41)	Persisting with effort to complete work successfully despite difficult conditions and setbacks.	1	2	3	4	5	NA
42)	Putting extra effort into your job.	1	2	3	4	5	NA
43)	Trying to make the best of the situation, even when there are problems.	1	2	3	4	5	NA
	Volunteering to carry out task activities that are not formally part of own job						
44)	Suggesting organisational improvements.	1	2	3	4	5	NA
45)	Assisting others with work-related problems.	1	2	3	4	5	NA
46)	Attending functions that are not mandatory but are important to the organisation.	1	2	3	4	5	NA
47)	Taking initiative and extra responsibility.	1	2	3	4	5	NA
	Helping and cooperating with others						
48)	Helping others with heavy work-loads.	1	2	3	4	5	NA
49)	Helping others who have been absent.	1	2	3	4	5	NA
50)	Maintaining effective working relationships with co-workers.	1	2	3	4	5	NA
51)	Consulting with those who might be affected by decisions.	1	2	3	4	5	NA
52)	Informing others before taking any important actions.	1	2	3	4	5	NA

Following organisational rules and procedures

53)	Adhering to organisational values and policies.	1	2	3	4	5	NA
54)	Obeying the rules and regulations of the organisation.	1	2	3	4	5	NA
55)	Treating organisational property with care.	1	2	3	4	5	NA
56)	Paying attention to announcements, messages, or printed material about the organisation.	1	2	3	4	5	NA

Endorsing, supporting and defending organisational objectives

57)	Showing loyalty to the organisation.	1	2	3	4	5	NA
58)	Exhibiting concern for organisational objectives.	1	2	3	4	5	NA
59)	Working within the organisation to effect change.	1	2	3	4	5	NA
60)	Representing the organisation favourably to outsiders.	1	2	3	4	5	NA
61)	Demonstrating concern about the image of the organisation.	1	2	3	4	5	NA

MANAGERS' TASK PERFORMANCE

The following questions are designed to rate your task performance.

How well do you consider you perform the following tasks:

Please circle the alternative (1–5) you have chosen, or NA if appropriate.

	Planning and organising						
62)	Planning and forming goals.	1	2	3	4	5	NA
63)	Allocating resources to meet goals.	1	2	3	4	5	NA
64)	Formulating strategies in response to anticipated challenges.	1	2	3	4	5	NA
65)	Planning and organising own time.	1	2	3	4	5	NA
66)	Organising and prioritising others' work.	1	2	3	4	5	NA
	Guiding, directing, and motivating staff and providing feedback						
67)	Reviewing staff performance against standards.	1	2	3	4	5	NA
68)	Providing guidance and direction to staff.	1	2	3	4	5	NA
69)	Motivating staff with recognition, encouragement, constructive criticism and feedback.	1	2	3	4	5	NA
	Training, coaching, and developing staff						
70)	Training, teaching, and coaching subordinates.	1	2	3	4	5	NA
71)	Identifying staff training needs.	1	2	3	4	5	NA
72)	Monitoring training results.	1	2	3	4	5	NA
73)	Ensuring training programmes and materials are developed.	1	2	3	4	5	NA

Communicating effectively and keeping others informed

74)	Communicating effectively, thoroughly, and accurately.	1 2 3 4 5 NA
75)	Keeping staff, superiors, and others informed.	1 2 3 4 5 NA
76)	Communicating orally.	1 2 3 4 5 NA
77)	Communicating in writing.	1 2 3 4 5 NA

Representing the organisation to customers and the public

78)	Representing organisation to customers and public.	1 2 3 4 5 NA
79)	Communicating in written form.	1 2 3 4 5 NA
80)	Contributing professional expertise in response to community needs.	1 2 3 4 5 NA
81)	Dealing with customer and client problems.	1 2 3 4 5 NA

Technical proficiency

82)	Keeping technically up-to-date.	1 2 3 4 5 NA
83)	Providing technical advice to others in organisation.	1 2 3 4 5 NA
84)	Solving technical problems.	1 2 3 4 5 NA
85)	Applying technical expertise.	1 2 3 4 5 NA

Administration

86)	Ensuring accurate records are kept and important actions are documented.	1 2 3 4 5 NA
87)	Performing administrative duties, such as comprehending and interpreting paperwork, reviewing reports and approving routine requests.	1 2 3 4 5 NA
88)	Implementing and administering policies, practices and procedures.	1 2 3 4 5 NA

Maintaining good working relationships

89)	Maintaining a work unit that functions with minimal conflict and disruption.	1 2 3 4 5 NA
90)	Backing up and supporting staff as appropriate.	1 2 3 4 5 NA
91)	Displaying personal concern for staff.	1 2 3 4 5 NA
92)	Fostering effective working relationships with co-workers.	1 2 3 4 5 NA

Coordinating staff and other resources to get the job done

93)	Negotiating to achieve optimal utilisation of organisational resources.	1 2 3 4 5 NA
94)	Coordinating the work in own area.	1 2 3 4 5 NA
95)	Coordinating functional work groups within a larger system.	1 2 3 4 5 NA
96)	Balancing interests of own unit with those of the whole organisation.	1 2 3 4 5 NA

Decision making/problem solving

97)	Making sound judgements based on all relevant available information.	1 2 3 4 5 NA
98)	Anticipating and responding to change by innovative problem solving.	1 2 3 4 5 NA
99)	Developing effective solutions to organisational challenges.	1 2 3 4 5 NA
100)	Anticipating the consequences of decisions.	1 2 3 4 5 NA
101)	Backing own judgement when making difficult decisions.	1 2 3 4 5 NA

Staffing

102)	Deciding on criteria for positions; interviewing, selecting, hiring, transferring, or promoting individuals.	1 2 3 4 5 NA
103)	Building and maintaining a cohesive management team.	1 2 3 4 5 NA
104)	Developing personnel practices in work area.	1 2 3 4 5 NA
105)	Maintaining an effective career development system.	1 2 3 4 5 NA

Persisting to reach goals

106)	Persisting with special effort to reach goals.	1 2 3 4 5 NA
107)	Overcoming obstacles to get the job done.	1 2 3 4 5 NA
108)	Acting with urgency when necessary.	1 2 3 4 5 NA

Handling crises and stress

109)	Responding to urgent unexpected situations.	1 2 3 4 5 NA
110)	Problem solving and troubleshooting in urgent, unexpected situations.	1 2 3 4 5 NA
111)	Responding to tight deadlines.	1 2 3 4 5 NA
112)	Handling crises effectively.	1 2 3 4 5 NA

Organisational commitment

113)	Applying policies, procedures, rules and regulations to meet organisational standards and objectives.	1 2 3 4 5 NA
114)	Producing constructive criticism of organisational goals, policies, and practices.	1 2 3 4 5 NA
115)	Accepting reasonable criticism from higher authorities in the organisation.	1 2 3 4 5 NA
116)	Working effectively within the framework of organisation policies, procedures and rules.	1 2 3 4 5 NA

Monitoring and controlling resources

117)	Controlling budgets by allocating funds internally.	1 2 3 4 5 NA
118)	Monitoring and overseeing appropriate use of funds within existing constraints and guidelines.	1 2 3 4 5 NA
119)	Monitoring and overseeing utilisation of funds.	1 2 3 4 5 NA
120)	Controlling personnel resources.	1 2 3 4 5 NA

Delegating

121) Assigning staff duties and responsibilities consistent with their abilities as well as the organisation's needs. 1 2 3 4 5 NA

122) Effectively delegating responsibility and authority. 1 2 3 4 5 NA

123) Avoiding interfering with areas of responsibility delegated to others. 1 2 3 4 5 NA

124) Delegating authority and responsibility to assist staff's professional development. 1 2 3 4 5 NA

Influencing others

125) Influencing others inside and outside of the organisation. 1 2 3 4 5 NA

126) Persuading others in the organisation to accept your ideas and position. 1 2 3 4 5 NA

127) Convincing those holding opposing or neutral opinions and promoting own positions or ideas. 1 2 3 4 5 NA

128) Presenting own position clearly and decisively. 1 2 3 4 5 NA

Collecting and interpreting data

129) Collecting, analysing, interpreting, compiling data to help solve problems and make decisions. 1 2 3 4 5 NA

130) Knowing what data are relevant to address a problem or issue. 1 2 3 4 5 NA

131) Drawing correct inferences from information. 1 2 3 4 5 NA

132) Making recommendations for future actions from analysis of data. 1 2 3 4 5 NA

Contributing to organisational effectiveness

133) Aligning and contributing to the organisation's purpose and goals. 1 2 3 4 5 NA

134) Contributing to organisational productivity. 1 2 3 4 5 NA

135) Contributing to organisational stability, continuity and cohesion. 1 2 3 4 5 NA

136) Enhancing organisational morale. 1 2 3 4 5 NA

137) Contributing to organisational adaptability. 1 2 3 4 5 NA

References

Abdel-Halim, A. A. (1978). Employee affective responses to organisational stress: Moderating effects of job characteristics. *Personnel Psychology, 31*, 561-579.

Abdel-Halim, A. A. (1979). Individual and interpersonal moderators of employee reactions to job characteristics: A re-examination. *Personnel Psychology, 32*, 121-137.

Abdel-Halim, A. A. (1981). Effects of role stress-job design-technology interaction on employee work satisfaction. *Academy of Management Journal, 24, June*, 260-273.

ABS. (1996). *ASCO - Australian Statistical Classification of Occupations* Canberra, Australian Government Printing Office: Australian Bureau of Statistics.

Ackrill, J. L. (1963). *Aristotle's Categories and De Interpretatione* (J. L. Ackrill, Trans.). Oxford, United Kingdom: Oxford University Press.

Adolphs, R., Tranel, D., Damasio, H., & Damasio, A. R. (1995). Fear and the human amygdala. *Journal of Neuroscience, 15*, 5879-5891.

Agho, A., Price, J. L., & Mueller, C. W. (1992). Discriminant validity of measures of job satisfaction, positive affectivity and negative affectivity. *Journal of Occupational and Organizational Psychology, 65*(12), 185-196.

Agho, A. O., Mueller, C. W., & Price, J. L. (1993). Determinants of employee job satisfaction: An empirical test of a causal model. *Human Relations, 46*(8), 1007-1027.

Akiran, N. K., & Turner, L. (1996). Upward elevation of bank branch managers competence: How to develop a measure in-house. *Asia Pacific Journal of Human Resources, 34*(3), 36-47.

Allport, G. W. (1961). *Pattern and growth in personality.* New York: Holt, Rinehart & Winston.

Allred, B. B., Snow, C. C., & Miles, R. E. (1996). Characteristics of managerial careers in the 21st Century. *Academy of Management Executive, 10*(4), 17-27.

Anderson, J. C., & Gerbing, D. W. (1984). The effect of sampling error on convergence, improper solutions and goodness-of-fit indices for maximum likelihood confirmatory factor analysis. *Psychometrika, 49*(2), 155-173.

Anderson, J. C., & Gerbing, D. W. (1988). Structural equation modelling in practice: A review and recommended two-step approach. *Psychological Bulletin, 103*(3), 411-423.

Anderson, N., & Cunningham-Snell, N. (Eds). (2000). *Personnel selection*. Malden, MA: Blackwell Publishing.

Anderson, N., Lievens, F., van Dam, K., & Ryan, A. M. (2004). Key directions for future research and practice. In International Association for Applied Psychology (Ed), *Applied Psychology: An International review* (Vol. 53, pp. 487-501): Blackwell Publishing.

Antonioni, D. (1996). Designing an effective 360-degree appraisal feedback process. *Organizational Dynamics, 25*(2), 24-38.

Appelbaum, E., Bailey, T., Berg, P., & Kalleberg, A. L. (2000). *Manufacturing advantage: Why high performance work systems pay off*. Ithica, NY: Cornell University Press.

Argyle, M. (2001). *The psychology of happiness*: Taylor & Francis Books Ltd.

Argyle, M., & Martin, M. (1991). The psychological causes of happiness. In F. Stack, M. Argyle & N. Schwarz (Eds), *Subjective well-being: An interdisciplinary perspective* (pp. 119-139). New York: Pergamon Press.

Argyris, C. (1992). *On organizational learning*. Cambridge, Massachusetts: Blackwell Publishers.

Argyris, C., & Schon, D. (1978). *Organisational learning: A theory of action perspective*. Reading, Massachusetts: Addison Wesley.

Armstrong, J. S., & Overton, T. S. (1977). Estimating nonresponse bias in mail surveys. *Journal of Marketing Research, 14*(3), 396-402.

Arvey, R. D., Bouchard, T. J., Segal, N. L., & Abraham, L. M. (1989). Job satisfaction: Environmental and genetic components. *Journal of Applied Psychology, 74*(2), 187-192.

Arvey, R. D., & Murphy, K. R. (1998). Performance evaluation in work settings. *Annual Review of Psychology, 49*, 141-168.

Ash, R. A., & Levine, E. L. (1985). Job applicant training and work experience evaluation: An empirical comparison of four methods. *Journal of Applied Psychology, 70*, 527-576.

Asher, H. B. (1983). *Causal modeling* (2nd ed). Beverly Hills, California: Sage Publications.

Ashkanasy, N. M. (2004). Emotions and performance. *Human Performance, 17*(2), 137-144.

Ashkanasy, N. M., Hartel, C. E., Fischer, C., & Ashforth, B. (1998). *A research program to investigate the causes and consequences of emotional experience at work*, Paper presented at the Annual Meeting of the Australasian Society of Psychologists, Christchurch, New Zealand, April, 1998.

Ashkanasy, N. N., & Daus, C. S. (2005). Rumors of the death of emotional intelligence in organizational behavior are vastly exaggerated. *Journal of Organizational Behavior, 26*(4), 441-452.

Atwater, L. E., & Yammarino, F. J. (1997). Self-other rating agreement: A review and model. *Research in Personnel and Human Resources Management, 15*, 121-174.

Australian Bureau of Statistics. (1996a). *ASCO - Australian Statistical Classification of Occupations* Canberra, Australian Government Printing Office: Australian Bureau of Statistics.

Australian Bureau of Statistics. (1996b). *Census of population and housing* Canberra, Australian Capital Territory: Australian Bureau of Statistics.

Australian National Training Authority, A. (1996). *Generic management competency standards for frontline management* Canberra, Australian Capital Territory: Australian Government Printing Service.

Avolio, B. J., & Sosik, J. J. (1999). A life-span framework for assessing the impact of work on white-collar workers. In S. L. Willis & J. D. Reid (Eds), *Life in the middle: Psychological and social development in middle age* (pp. 251-274). San Diego: Academic Press.

Bagnall, D. (2004, December 15). Science of happiness: The secret of happiness is the holy grail of the new millennium. *The Bulletin, Features, Summer Reading*, A6.

Bagozzi, R. P., & Heatherton, T. F. (1994). A general approach for representing multifaceted personality constructs: Application to state self-esteem. *Structural Equation Modeling*, 35-67.

Bandura, A. (1977). *Social learning theory*. Englewood-Cliffs, New Jersey: Prentice-Hall.

Bandura, A. (1986). *The social foundations of thought and action*.

Englewood Cliffs, New Jersey: Prentice-Hall.

Bandura, A. (1988). Reflection on nonability determinants of competence. In R. G. Sternberg & J. Kolligian, Jr. (Eds), *Competence considered: perceptions of competence and incompetence across the lifespan* (pp. 315-362). New Haven, Connecticut: Yale University Press.

Bandura, A. (1996). *Self-efficacy: The exercise of control*. New York: Freeman.

Bar-On, R. (2000). Emotional and social intelligence: insights from the Emotional Quotient Inventory (EQ-i). In R. Bar-On & J. D. A. Parker (Eds), *Handbook of emotional intelligence* (pp. 363-388). San Francisco, CA: Jossey-Bass.

Bar-On, R., Handley, R., & Fund, S. (2005). *The impact of emotional intelligence on performance*. Mahwah, NJ: Lawrence Erlbaum Associates.

Barker, C., & Coy, R. (Eds). (2005). *Understanding influence for leaders at all levels*. Sydney, NSW: Australian Institute of Management, McGraw-Hill.

Barling, J., & Beattie, R. (1983). Self-efficacy beliefs and sales performance. *Journal of Organizational Behavior Management, 5*, 41-51.

Barnard, C. (1938). *The functions of the executive*. Cambridge, Massachusetts: Harvard University Press.

Barney, J. B. (1986). Organizational culture: Can it be a source of competitive advantage? *Academy of Management Review, 11*(3), 566-665.

Barrick, M. R., & Mount, M. K. (1991). The big five personality dimensions and job performance: A meta-analysis. *Personnel Psychology, 44*(1), 1-26.

Barrick, M. R., Mount, M. K., & Judge, T. A. (2001). Personality and job performance at the beginning of the new millennium: What do we know and where do we go next? *International Journal of Selection and Assessment, 9*, 9-30.

Barrick, M. R., Mount, M. K., & Strauss, J. P. (1993). Conscientiousness and performance of sales representatives: Test of the mediating effects of goal setting. *Journal of Applied Psychology, 78*(5), 715-722.

Barsade, S. G., Brief, A. P., & Spataro, S. E. (2003). The affective revolution in organizational behavior: The emergence of a paradigm. In J. Greenberg (Ed), *Organizational behavior: The state of the science* (pp. 3-52). Hillsdale, New Jersey: Lawrence Erlbaum Associates, Inc.

Bartlett, M. (1950). Tests of significance in factor analysis. *British Journal of Psychology, 3*(Statistical Section), 77-85.

Bartz, D. E., Schwandt, D. R., & Hillman, L. W. (1989). Differences between T and D. *Personnel Administrator, 34*(6), 169-170.

Bateman, T. S., & Organ, D. W. (1983). Job satisfaction and the good soldier: The relationship between affect and employee citizenship. *Academy of Management Journal, 35, December,* 587-595.

Baum, J. R., Locke, E. A., & Smith, K. G. (2001). A multidimensional model of venture growth. *Academy of Management Journal, 44*(2), 292-303.

Becker, B., & Gerhart, B. (1996). The impact of human resource management on organizational performance: Progress and prospects. *Academy of Management Journal, 39,* 779-801.

Beer, M., Spector, B., Lawrence, P., Mills, D., & Walton, R. (1985). *Human Resource Management: A General Manager's Perspective.* New York: The Free Press.

Beer, M., Spector, B., Lawrence, P., Quinn Mills, D., & Walton, R. (1985). *Human resource management: A general manager's perspective.* Illinois: Free Press.

Beer, M., Spector, B., Lawrence, P. R., Mills, D. Q., & Walton, R. E. (1984). *Managing Human Assets: The Groundbreaking Harvard Business School Program.* New York: Free Press.

Befort, N., & Kattrup, K. (2003). Valuing task and contextual performance: Experience, job roles, and ratings of the importance of job behaviours. *Human Resource Management Research, 8*(1), 17-32.

Beittenhausen, K. L., & Fedor, D. B. (1997). Peer and upward appraisals: A comparison of their benefits and problems. *Group & Organization Management, 22*(2), 236-263.

Bellarosa, C., & Chen, P. Y. (1997). The effectiveness and practicality of occupational stress management interventions: a survey of subject matter expert opinions. *Journal Occupational Health Psychology, 12*(3), 247-262.

Benjamin, J., Ebstein, R. P., & Belmaker, R. H. (2001). Genes for human personality traits: "Endophenotypes" of psychiatric disorders?

World Journal of Biological Psychiatry, 54(2), 54-57.

Bennett, E. (2004, May 6th). Corporate initiatives to deal with depression has benefits for all. *The Australian Financial Review*, p. 17.

Bennis, W. (1997). Leaders of leaders. *Executive Excellence, 14*(9), 3-4.

Bennis, W., & Nanus, B. (1985). *Leaders: The strategies for taking charge*. New York: Harper & Row.

Bennis, W., & O'Toole, J. (2005). How business schools lost their way. *Harvard Business Review, 83,* 96-104, 154.

Bentham, J. (1776). *A fragment on government: being an examination of what is delivered, on the subject of government in general in the introduction of Sir William Blackstone's Commentarie*. London: Printed for J. Sheppard, W. Whitestone, J. Hoey [etc.], Dublin, 1776.

Bentler, P., & Chou, C. (1987). Practical issues in structural modelling. *Sociological Methods and Research, 16,* 78-117.

Bentler, P. M. (1990). Comparative fit indexes in structural models. *Psychological Bulletin, 107*(2), 238-246.

Bentler, P. M., & Bonett, D. G. (1980). Significance tests and goodness-of-fit in the analysis of covariance structures. *Psychological Bulletin, 88*(3), 588-606.

Bentler, P. M., & Dijkstra, T. (Eds). (1985). *Efficient estimation via linearization in structural models*. Amsterdam: North-Holland.

Bentler, P. M., & Wu, E. J. C. (1995). *EQS for Windows user's guide*. Encino, California: Multivariate Software.

Bernardin, H. J., & Beatty, R. (1984). *Performance appraisal: Assessing human behaviour at work*. Boston, Massachusetts: Kent Publishing Company.

Berry, W. D., & Feldman, S. (1985). *Multiple regression in practice*. London, United Kingdom: Sage Publications.

Birdi, K., Warr, P. B., & Oswald, A. (1995). Age differences in three components of employee well-being. *Applied Psychology: An International Review, 44,* 345-373.

Birren, J. E., & Renner, V. J. (1980). Concepts and issues of mental health and aging. In J. E. Birren & R. B. Sloane (Eds), *Handbook of mental health and aging* (pp. 3-33). Englewood Cliffs, New Jersey: Prentice Hall.

Blakley, B. R., Quinones, M. A., Crawford, M. S., & Jago, I. A. (1994). The validity of isometric strength tests. *Personnel Psychology, 47,* 247-274.

Bobko, P. (1990). Multivariate correlational analysis. In M. D. Dunnette & L. M. Hugh (Eds), *Handbook of industrial and organizational psychology* (2nd ed, pp. 637-686). Palo Alto, California: Consulting Psychologists Press.

Bollen, K. A. (1989a). A new incremental fit index for general structural equation models. *Sociological Methods and Research, 17*, 303-316.

Bollen, K. A. (1989b). *Structural equations with latent variables*. New York: Wiley.

Bollen, K. A., & Long, J. S. (1993). *Testing structural equation models*. Newbury Park, California: Sage Publications.

Bommer, W. H., Johnson, J. L., Rich, G. A., Podsakoff, P. M., & McKenzie, S. B. (1995). On the interchangeability of objective and subjective measures of employee performance: A meta-analysis. *Personnel Psychology, 48*(3), 587-605.

Bono, J. E., & Judge, T. A. (2003). Core self-evaluations: A review of the trait and its role in job satisfaction and job performance. *European Journal of Personality, 17*, 5-18.

Boomsma, D. I., & Molenaar, P. C. M. (1986). Using Lisrel to analyze genetic and environmental covariance structure. *Behavior Genetics, 16*(2), 237-250.

Borman, W. C., & Brush, D. H. (1993). More progress towards taxonomy of managerial performance requirements. *Human Performance, 6*(1), 1-21.

Borman, W. C., Hanson, M. A., Oppler, S. H., Pulakos, E. D., & White, L. A. (1993). Role of early supervisory experience in supervisor performance. *Journal of Applied Psychology, 78*.

Borman, W. C., & Motowidlo, S. J. (1993). Expanding the criterion domain to include elements of contextual performance. In N. Schmitt, W. C. Borman & Associates (Eds), *Personnel selection in organizations* (Vol. 71-98). San Francisco, California: Jossey-Bass.

Borman, W. C., & Motowidlo, S. J. (1997). Task performance and contextual performance: The meaning for personnel selection research. *Human Performance, 10*(2), 99-109.

Borman, W. C., Motowidlo, S. J., & Hanser, L. M. (1983). *A model of individual performance effectiveness: Thoughts about expanding the criterion space*. Paper presented at the Integrated Criterion Measurement for Large Scale Computerized Selection and Classification, 91st Annual American Psychological Association

Convention.

Borman, W. C., Penner, L. A., Allen, T. D., & Motowidlo, S. J. (2001). Personality predictors of citizenship performance. *International Journal of Selection and Assessment, 9*, 52-69.

Borman, W. C., White, L. A., & Dorsey, D. W. (1995). Effects of ratee task performance and interpersonal factors on supervisor and peer ratings. *Journal of Applied Psychology, 80*(1), 168-177.

Borman, W. C., White, L. A., Gast, I. F., & Pulakos, E. D. (1985). *Evaluating factors influencing job performance ratings: A causal modeling approach.* Paper presented at the 93rd Annual American Psychological Association Convention.

Borman, W. C., White, L. A., Pulakos, E. D., & Oppler, S. H. (1991). Models of supervisory job performance ratings. *Journal of Applied Psychology, 76*, 863-872.

Boyatzis, R. E. (1982). *The competent manager: A model for effective performance.* New York: Wiley.

Boyatzis, R. E., Goleman, D., & Rhee, K. (2000). Clustering competence in emotional intelligence: Insights from the Emotional Competence Inventory. In R. Bar-On & J. D. A. Parker (Eds), *Handbook of emotional intelligence* (pp. 343-362). San Francisco: California: Jossey-Bass.

Boyatzis, R. E., & McKee, A. (2005). *Resonant leadership: Renewing yourself and connecting with others through mindfulness, hope, and compassion.* Boston: Harvard Business School Press.

Boyatzis, R. E., & Sala, F. (2004). *Assessing emotional intelligence competencies* (Glenn Gehr ed). NY, NY: Nova Science Publishers.

Bradburn, N. M. (1969). *The structure of psychological well-being.* Chicago, Illinois: Aldine.

Bradburn, N. M., & Caplovitz, D. (1965). *Reports on happiness.* Chicago, Illinois: Aldine.

Brammall, B. (1999, March 17th). Ambition a big stress. *Herald Sun,* p. 11.

Brayfield, A. H., & Crockett, W. H. (1955). Employee attitudes and employee performance. *Psychological Bulletin, 52*(5), 396-424.

Brayfield, A. H., & Rothe, H. F. (1951). An index of job satisfaction. *Journal of Applied Psychology, 35*(5), 307-311.

Breusch, J. (2000, Sept 25th). Public service has lost expertise. *The Australian Financial Review,* p. 6.

Brewer, J., & Hunter, A. (1989). *Multi-method research: A synthesis of styles*. Thousand Oaks, California: Sage Publications.

Brief, A., & Motowidlo, S. J. (1986). Prosocial organizational behaviour. *Academy of Management Review, 11*(4), 720-725.

Brief, A. P. (1998). *Attitudes in and around organizations*. Thousand Oaks, CA: Sage.

Brief, A. P., Burke, M. J., George, J., Robinson, B. S., & Webster, J. (1988). Should negative affectivity remain an unmeasured variable in the study of job stress? *Journal of Applied Psychology, 73*(2), 193-198.

Brief, A. P., & Roberson, L. (1989). Job attitude organization: An exploratory study. *Journal of Applied Social Psychology, 19*, 717-727.

Brief, A. P., & Weiss, H. M. (2002). Organizational behavior: Affect at work. *Annual Review of Psychology, 53*, 29-307.

Broadbent, D. E. (1985). The clinical impact of job design. *British Journal of Clinical Psychology, 24*(1), 33-44.

Brody, N. (1992). *Intelligence*. New York: Academic Press.

Brogden, H. E. (1949). When testing pays off. *Personnel Psychology*, 271-183.

Brooks, R., & Faff, R. W. (1997). Financial deregulation and relative risk of Australian industry. *Australian Economic Papers, 36*(69), 308-320.

Brown, B. (2005). Test the waters before you jump in the deep end. *The Australian, April 20th*, 3.

Brown, K. A., & Mitchell, T. R. (1993). Organisational obstacles: Links with financial performance, customer satisfaction and job satisfaction in a service environment. *Human Relations, 46*(6), 725-757.

Brown, S. P., & Leigh, T. W. (1996). A new look at psychological climate and its relationship to job involvement, effort, and performance. *Journal of Applied Psychology, 81*(4), 358-368.

Browne, M. W., & Cudeck, R. (1993). Alternative ways of assessing model fit. In K. A. Bollen & J. S. Long (Eds), *Testing structural equation models* (pp. 136-162). Newbury Park, California: Sage Publishing.

Bruni, L. (2005). *A history of happiness in economics*. London, United Kingdom: Routledge.

Bryman, A., & Cramer, D. (1994). *Quantitative data analysis for social scientists* (revised ed). London, United Kingdom: Routledge.

Buchanan, T. (2001). *Online Implementation of an IPIP Five Factor Personality Inventory. Version 1,* from http://users.wmin.ac.uk/~buchant/wwwffi/introduction.html.

Buchanan, T., Goldberg, L. R., & Johnson, J. A. (1999). *Evaluation of an online Five Factor Inventory.* Paper presented at the 1999 Society for Computers in Psychology Conference.

Buckingham, M., & Coffman, C. (2005). *First, break all the rules: What the world's greatest managers do differently.* New York: Simon & Schuster.

Burke, M. J., Brief, A. P., & George, J. M. (1993). The role of negative affectivity in understanding relations between self-reports of stressors and strains: A comment on the applied psychology literature. *Journal of Applied Psychology, 78*(3), 402-412.

Burke, M. J., Brief, A. P., George, J. M., Roberson, L., & Webster, J. (1989). Measuring affect at work: Confirmatory analyses of competing mood structures with conceptual linkages to cortical regulatory systems. *Journal of Personality and Social Psychology, 57*(6), 1091-1102.

Burke, R. J., & Cooper, C. L. (2006). *The human resources revolution.* London: Elsevier.

Burns, N., & Grove, S. K. (1997). *The practice of nursing research: Conduct, critique, and utilization,* (3 ed). Philadelphia: W B Saunders.

Burrell, G., & Morgan, G. (1979). *Sociological paradigms and organizational analysis.* London, United Kingdom: Heinemann.

Byrne, B., Goffin, R. D., & Jackson, D. N. (1993). Modelling MTMM data from additive and multiplicative covariance structures: An audit of construct validity concordance. *Multivariate Behavioral Research, 28*(1), 67-96.

Byrne, B. M. (1994a). *Structural equation modelling with EQS and EQS/Windows: Basic concepts, applications and programming.* Newbury Park, California: Sage Publications.

Byrne, B. M. (1994b). Testing for factorial validity, replication and invariance of a measurement instrument: A paradigmatic application based on the Maslach Burnout Inventory. *Multivariate Behavioral Research, 29*(3), 489-507.

Byrne, B. M. (1995). One application of structural equation modelling from two perspectives: Exploring the EQS and LISREL strategies. In R. H. Hoyle (Ed), *Structural equation modelling: Concepts, issues and applications* (pp. 138-157). Thousand Oaks, California: Sage Publications.

Byrne, B. M. (1996). *Measuring self-concept across the life span: Issues and instrumentation.* Washington, DC: American Psychological Association.

Byrne, B. M., Shavelson, R. J., & Muthen, B. (1989). Testing the equivalence of factor covariance and mean structures: The issues of partial measurement invariance. *Psychological Bulletin, 105*(3), 456-466.

Cacioppo, J. T., & Berntson, G. G. (1994). Relationship between attitudes and evaluative space: A critical review, with emphasis on the separability of positive and negative substrates. *Psychological Bulletin, 115*, 401-423.

Cacioppo, J. T., Gardner, W. L., & Berntson, G. G. (1999). The affect system has parallel and integrative processing components: Form follows function. *Journal of Personality and Social Psychology, 76*, 839-855.

Cage, T., Daus, C. S., & Saul, K. (2004). *An examination of emotional skill, job satisfaction, and retail performance.* Paper presented at the 19th Annual Society for Industrial/Organizational Psychology, as part of the symposium.

Cameron, K. S., & Caza, A. (2004). Contributions to the discipline of positive organisational scholarship. *American Behavioral Scientist, 47*(6), 731.

Cameron, K. S., Dutton, J. E., & Quinn, R. E. (Eds). (2003). *Positive organizational scholarship: Foundations of a new discipline.* San Francisco, California: Berrett-Koehler Publishers.

Cameron, K. S., & Tschirhart, M. (1988). *Managerial competencies and organizational effectiveness* Detroit, Michigan: Business Administration, University of Michigan.

Cammock, P., Nilakant, V., & Dakin, S. (1995). Developing a lay model of managerial effectiveness: A social constructionist perspective. *Journal of Management Studies, 32*(4), 443-474.

Campbell, C. H., Ford, P., Rumsey, M. G., Pulakos, E. D., Borman, W. C., Felkder, D. B., de Vera, M. V., et al. (1990). Development of multiple job performance measures in a representative sample of jobs. *Personnel Psychology, 43*(2), 277-300.

Campbell, D. J., & Gingrich, K. F. (1986). The interactive effects of task complexity and participation on task performance: A field experiment. *Organizational Behavior and Human Decision Processes, 37*, 162-180.

Campbell, D. T., & Fiske, D. W. (1959). Convergent and discriminant validation by the multitrait-multimethod matrix. *Psychological Bulletin, 56*(2), 81-105.

Campbell, J. P. (1991). The role of theory in industrial and organizational psychology. In M. D. Dunnette & L. M. Hough (Eds), *Handbook of Industrial and Organizational Psychology* (2nd ed, Vol. 1, pp. 180-186). Palo Alto, California: Consulting Psychologists Press.

Campbell, J. P. (1996). Group differences and personnel decisions: Validity, fairness, and affirmative action. *Journal of Vocational Behavior, 49*(2), 122-158.

Campbell, J. P. (1998). The definition and measurement of performance in the New Age. In D. R. Ilgen & E. D. Pulakos (Eds), *The changing nature of performance: Implications for staffing, motivation and development* (pp. 399-429). San Francisco, California: JAI Press.

Campbell, J. P. (Ed). (1990). *Modeling the performance prediction problem in Industrial and organizational psychology* (2 ed, Vol. 1). Palo Alto, CA: Consulting Psychologists.

Campbell, J. P., Dunnette, M. D., Lawler, E. E., III., & Weick, K. E., Jr. (1970). *Managerial behavior, performance and effectiveness.* New York: McGraw-Hill.

Campbell, J. P., Gasser, M., & Oswald, F. (1996). The substantive nature of job performance variability. In K. Murphy (Ed), *Individual differences and behavior in organizations* (pp. 258-299). Hillsdale, New Jersey: Erlbaum.

Campbell, J. P., McCloy, R. A., Oppler, S. H., & Sager, C. E. (1993). A theory of performance. In N. Schmitt, W. C. Borman & Associates (Eds), *Personnel selection in organizations.* San Francisco, CA: Jossey-Bass.

Campbell, J. P., & Pritchard, R. D. (1976). Motivation theory in industrial and organizational psychology. In M. D. Dunnette (Ed), *Handbook of Industrial and Organizational Psychology* (pp. 63-103). Chicago, Illinois: Rand McNally.

Campion, M. A., Cheraskin, L., & Stevens, M. J. (1994). Career-related antecedents and outcomes of job rotation. *Academy of Management Journal, 37*, 1518-1542.

Caplan, R. D., Cobb, S., French, J. P., Jr, Harrison, R. V., & Pinneau, S. R., Jr. (1975). *Job demands and worker health.* Ann Arbor,

Michigan: The Institute for Social Research, The University of Michigan.

Caplan, R. D., Cobb, S., French, J. R. P., Jr., Harrison, R. V., & Pinneau, S. R., Jr. (1980). *Job demands and worker health: Main effects and occupational differences.*

Cardy, R. L., & Dobbins, G. H. (1986). Affect and appraisal accuracy: Liking as an integral dimension in evaluating performance. *Journal of Applied Psychology, 71*(4), 672-678.

Carlopio, J., Andrewartha, G., & Armstrong, H. (2005). *Developing management skills.* Frenchs Forest, New South Wales: Prentice-Hall.

Carlopio, J., & Gardner, D. (1995). Perception of work and workplace: Mediators of the relationship between job level and employee reactions. *Journal of Occupational and Organizational Psychology, 68*(4), 321-326.

Carlson, M., Charlin, V., & Miller, N. (1988). Positive mood and helping behaviour: A test of six hypotheses. *Journal of Personality and Social Psychology, 55*(2), 211-229.

Carnevale, A. P., Gainer, L. J., & Meltzer, A. S. (1988). Workplace basics: The skills employers want. *Training and Development Journal, 42,* 22-26.

Carroll, J. B. (1993). *Human cognitive abilities: A survey of factor analytic studies.* New York: Cambridge University Press.

Carroll, J. M., Yik, M. S., Russell, J. A., & Barrett, L. F. (1999). On the psychometric principles of affect. *Review of General Psychology, 3*(1), 14-22.

Carruthers, F. (2005, June 10). A point or two on motivation. *The Australian Financial Review,* p. 3.

Cartwright, S., & Cooper, C. L. (1997). *Managing workplace stress.* Thousand Oaks, California: Sage Publications.

Caruso, D. R., & Salovey, P. (2004). *The emotionally intelligent manager: How to develop and use the four key emotional skills of leadership.* San Francisco: Jossey-Bass.

Cascio, W. (1993). Downsizing: What do we know? What have we learned? *Academy of Management Executive, 7*(1), 95-104.

Cattell, R. B. (1966). The scree test for the number of factors. *Multivariate Behavioral Research, 1,* 245-276.

Cattell, R. B. (1978). *The scientific use of factor analysis in behavioral and life sciences.* New York: Plenum Press.

Centre for Creative Leadership. (1996). *Skillscope*. Greensboro, North Carolina: Centre for Creative Leadership.

Champoux, J. (1980). A three sample test of some extensions to the Job Characteristics Model of work motivation. *Academy of Management Journal, 23*, 466-478.

Chataway, J. G. (1982). Bank work: A study of the everyday bank activities of four suburban branch managers [PhD Thesis]. (Monash University).

Chen, P. Y., & Spector, P. E. (1991). Negative affectivity as the underlying cause of correlations between stressors and strains. *Journal of Applied Psychology, 76*(3), 398-407.

Chernis, C., & Goleman, D. (Eds). (2001). *The emotionally intelligent workplace: How to select for, measure, and improve emotional intelligence in individuals, groups, and organizations*. San Francisco, California: Jossey-Bass.

Child, D. (1990). *The essentials of factor analysis* (2nd ed). London, United Kingdom: Cassell.

Chou, C. P., Bentler, P. M., & Satorra, A. (1991). Scaled test statistics and robust standard errors for nonnormal data in covariance structure analysis. *British Journal of Mathematical and Statistical Psychology, 44*(2), 347-357.

Christensen, C. R., Andrews, K. R., & Porter, M. E. (1982). *Business policy: Texts and cases* (5th ed). Homewood, Illinois: Irwin.

Church, A. H., & Bracken, D. W. (1997). Advancing the state of the art of 360-degree feedback: Guest editors comments on the research and practice of multi-rater assessment methods. *Group & Organization Management, 22*(2), 149-161.

Chynoweth, C. (1998, October 17th). Motivational fit helps job search. *The Australian*, p. 33.

Cialdini, R. B. (1993). *Influence: The psychology of persuasion*. New York: Morrow.

Clark, A., Oswald, A., & Warr, P. B. (1996). Is job satisfaction U-shaped in age? *Journal of Occupational and Organizational Psychology, 69*(1), 57-81.

Clark, D. A., Beck, A. T., & Stewart, B. (1990). Cognitive specificity and positive-negative affectivity: Complimentary or contradictory views of anxiety and depression? *Journal of Abnormal Psychology, 99*(2), 148-155.

Clark, L. A., & Watson, D. (1991). Theoretical and empirical issues in differentiating depression from anxiety. In J. Becker & A. Kleinman (Eds), *Psychosocial aspects of depression* (pp. 39-65). New York: Lawrence Erlbaum Associates.

Clegg, C., Wall, T., & Kemp, N. (1987). Women on the assembly line: A comparison of the main interactive and explanations of job satisfaction, absence and mental health. *Journal of Occupational Psychology, 60*(4), 273-287.

Clegg, C. W. (1984). The derivation of job designs. *Journal of Occupational Behaviour, 5*(4), 131.

Cliff, N. (1987). *Analyzing multivariate data.* New York: Harcourt Brace Jovanovich.

Coetzee, C., & Schaap, P. (2004). *The relationship between leadership styles and emotional intelligence.* Paper presented at the 6th Annual Conference for the Society of Industrial and Organizational Psychology, Sandton, South Africa.

Cohen, D. (2005, 16 November). In pursuit of happiness. *The Australia,* p. 44.

Cohen, J. (1988). *Statistical power analysis for the behavioral sciences.* Hillsdale, New Jersey: Erlbaum.

Collins, J. (2001). *Good to great: Why some companies make the leap . . . and others don't.* New York: Harper Collins.

Collins, J., & Porras, J. I. (2004). *Built to last: Successful habits of visionary companies.* New York: HarperCollins.

Collins, R. R. (1988). *The strategic contribution of the personnel function, Australian personnel management: A reader.* Melbourne, Victoria: Macmillan.

Compton, R. (2005). Performance management: Panacea or corporate outcast? *Research and Practice in Human Resource Management, 13*(1), 46-54.

Comrey, A. L. (1978). Common methodological problems in factor analytic studies. *Journal of Consulting and Clinical Psychology, 46*(4), 648-659.

Comrey, A. L., & Lee, H. B. (1992). *A first course in factor analysis* (2nd ed). Hillsdale, New Jersey: Erlbaum.

Conger, J. (1998). *Charismatic leadership in organisations.* Thousand Oaks, California: Sage Publications.

Connolly, J. J., & Viswesvaran, C. (2000). The role of affectivity in job satisfaction: A meta-analysis. *Personality and Individual Differences, 29,* 265-281.

Conte, J. M. (2005). A review and critique of emotional intelligence measures. *Journal of Organisational Behaviour, 26*, 433-440.

Converse, J., & Presser, S. (1986). *Survey questions: Handcrafting the standardized questionnaire.* Thousand Oaks, California: Sage Publications.

Conway, J. M. (1996). Analysis and design of multitrait-mulitrater performance appraisal studies. *Journal of Management, 22*(1), 139-162.

Cook, J., Hepworth, S. J., Wall, T. D., & Warr, P. B. (1981). *A compendium and review of 249 work review measures and their use.* London, United Kingdom: Academic Press.

Cook, K. W., Vance, C. A., & Spector, P. E. (2000). The relation of candidate personality with selection interview outcomes. *Journal of Applied Social Psychology, 30*, 867-885.

Cooksey, R. W., & Gates, G. R. (1996). HRM: A management science in need of discipline. *Asia Pacific Journal of Human Resources, 33*(3), 15-38.

Cooper, C. L. (1996). *Handbook of stress, medicine and health.* London, United Kingdom: CRC Press.

Cooper, C. L. (2005). *Handbook of stress medicine and stress* (2nd ed). Boca Raton, Florida: CRC Press.

Cooper, C. L., & Cartwright, S. (1994). Healthy mind, healthy organization: A proactive approach to occupational stress. *Human Relations, 47*(4), 455-471.

Cooper, C. L., & Marshall, J. (1978). Sources of managerial and white collar stress. In C. L. Cooper & R. Payne (Eds), *Stress at work* (pp. 81-105). New York: Wiley.

Cooper, C. L., & Payne, R. (Eds). (1988). *Causes, coping and consequences of stress at work.* Chichester, New York: Wiley.

Coovert, M. D., & Craiger, J. D. (1991, April, 1991). *Determining the dimensionality of work experience and the prediction of job performance.* Paper presented at the Understanding the work experience construct in Personnel Research and Practice (Symposium).

Cordery, J. L., & Sevastos, P. P. (1993). Responses to the original and revised job diagnostic survey: Is education a factor in response to negatively worded items? *Journal of Applied Psychology, 78*(1), 141-143.

Costa, P. T., & McCrae, R. R. (1980). Influence of extraversion and neuroticism on subjective well-being: Happy and unhappy people. *Journal of Personality and Social Psychology, 38*(4), 668-678.

Costa, P. T., & McCrae, R. R. (1987). Validation of the five-factor model of personality across instruments and observers. *Journal of Personality and Social Psychology, 52*(1), 81-90.

Costa, P. T., & McCrae, R. R. (1988). Personality and adulthood: A six-year longitudinal study of self-reports and spouse ratings on the Neo Personality Inventory. *Journal of Personality and Social Psychology, 54*(5), 853-863.

Costa, P. T., & McCrae, R. R. (1997). *Longitudinal stability of adult personality* (Vol. 1). New York: Academic Press.

Costa, P. T., & McCrae, R. R. (Eds). (1991). *NEO Five-Factor Inventory (NEO-FFI) professional manual.* FL: Odessa.

Costa, P. T., & McCrae, R. R. (Eds). (1996). *Mood and personality in adulthood.* San Diego, CA: Academic Press.

Costa, P. T., Zonderman, A. B., McCrae, R. R., Cornoni-Huntley, J., Locke. B.Z., & Barbano, H. E. (1987). Longitudinal analyses of psychological well-being in a national sample: stability of mean levels. *Journal of Gerontology*, 42:50-45.

Costa, P. T. J., & McCrae, R. R. (1992). *Revised NEO Personality Inventory (NEO-PI-R) and NEO Five-Factor Inventory (NEO-FFI): Professional Manual.* FL.

Côté, S. (1999). Affect and performance in organizational settings. *Current Directions in Psychological Science, 8*(2), 65-68.

Cox, T., Griffiths, A., & Rial-Gonzalez, E. (2000). *Research on work related stress.* Ghent, Belgium: European Agency for Safety at Work.

Coyle-Shapiro, J., Kessler, I., & Purcell, J. (2004). Reciprocity or "it's my job": Exploring organizationally directed citizenship behavior in a National Health Service Setting. *Journal of Management Studies, 41*(1), 85-106.

Crabtree, S. (2004). Getting personal in the workplace: Are negative relationships squelching productivity in your company? *Gallup Management Journal,* June 10, http://gmj.gallup.com/content/default.asp?ci=11956.

Crampton, S. M., & Wagner, J. A. (1994). Percept-percept inflation in microorganizational research: An investigation of prevalence and effect. *Journal of Applied Psychology, 79*(1), 6-76.

Cranny, C., Smith, P., & Stone, E. A. (1992). *Job satisfaction: How people feel about their jobs*. New York: Lexington Books.

Cronbach, L. J. (1984). *Essentials of psychological testing* (4th ed). New York: Harper & Row.

Cropanzano, R., James, K., & Konovsky, M. A. (1993). Dispositional affectivity as a predictor of work attitudes and job performance. *Journal of Organizational Behavior, 14*(6), 595-606.

Cropanzano, R., & Wright, T. A. (1999). A five-year study of the relationship between well-being and performance. *Journal of Consulting Psychology, 51*, 252-265.

Cropanzano, R., & Wright, T. A. (2001). When a 'happy' worker is really a 'productive' worker: A review and further refinements of the happy-productive worker thesis. *Consulting Psychology Journal, 53*(3), 182-199.

Csikszentmihalyi, M. (1990). *Flow: The psychology of optimal experience*. New York: Harper & Row.

Cummings, T., & Huse, E. (1989). *Organisation development and change* (4th ed). New York: West Publishing Company.

Czaja, S. J., & Sharit, J. (1985). Age differences in attitudes toward computers. *Journals of Gerontology Series B: Psychological Sciences and Social Sciences, 53*, 329-340.

Dalai Lama, & Cutler, H. C. (1999). *The art of happiness: A handbook for living*. Adelaide, South Australia: Griffin Press.

Damasio, A. R. (1994). *Descartes' error: Emotion, reason, and the human brain*. New York: Grosset/Putnam.

Daniel, W. (1990). *Applied nonparametric statistics*. Boston: PWS-Kent Publishing Company.

Danner, D. D., Snowdon, D. A., & Friesen, W. V. (2001). Positive emotions in early life and longevity: Findings from the nun study. *Journal of Personality and Social Psychology, 80*, 804-813.

Daus, C. S., & Ashkanasy, N. N. (2005). The case for the ability-based model of emotional intelligence in organizational behavior. *Journal of Organizational Behavior, 26*(4), 453-466.

Daus, C. S., & Harris, A. (2003). *Emotional intelligence and transformational leadership in groups*. Paper presented at the Symposium Multilevel perspectives on emotions in organizations at the 18th Annual Meeting of the Society for Industrial and Organizational Psychologists, Orlando, FL.

Daus, C. S., Rubin, R. S., Smith, R. K., & Cage, T. (2004). *Police performance: do emotional skills matter?* Paper presented at the 19th Annual Meeting of the Society for Industrial and Organizational Psychologists, as part of the symposium Book 'em Danno!: New developments in law enforcement performance prediction.

Davidson, R. J. (1998). Affective styles and affective disorders: Perspectives from affective neuroscience. *Cognition and Emotion, 12*, 307-330.

Davidson, R. J., Ekman, P., Saron, C. D., Senulis, J. A., & Friesen, W. V. (1990). Approach-withdrawal and cerebral asymmetry: Emotional expression and brain physiology. *Journal of Personality and Social Psychology, 58*, 330-341.

Davis-Blake, A., & Pfeffer, J. (1989). Just a mirage: The search for dispositional effects in organizational research. *Academy of Management Review, 14*(2), 385-400.

Dawda, D., & Hart, S. D. (2000). Assessing emotional intelligence: reliability and validity of the Bar-On Emotional Quotient Inventory (EQ-i) in university students. *Personality and Individual Differences, 28*, 797-812.

Dawis, R. V., & Lofquist, L. H. (1984). *A psychological theory of work adjustment.* Minneapolis, Minnesota: University of Minnesota Press.

Dawis, R. V., & Lofquist, L. H. (1993). From TWA to PEC. *Journal of Vocational Behavior, 43*(1), 113-121.

Day, A. L., & Caroll, S. A. (2004). Using an ability-based measure of emotional intelligence to predict individual performance, group performance, and group citizenship behaviours. *Personality and Individual Differences,, 36*, 1443-1458.

De Jonge, J., Landeweerd, J. A., & Van Breukelen, G. J. (1994). The Masstricht Autonomy Questionnaire: Background, construction, and validation. *Gedrag En Organisatie, 7*(1), 27-41.

De Jonge, J. E., & Schaufeli, W. B. (1998). Job characteristics and employee well-being: A test of Warr's vitamin model in health care workers using structural equation modelling. *Journal of Organizational Behavior, 19*(4), 387-407.

De Nisi, A. S., & , & Mitchell, J. L. (1978). An analysis of peer ratings as predictors and criterion measures and a proposed new application. *Academy of Management Review*.

De Vader, C. L., Bateson, A. G., & Lord, R. G. (1986). Attribution theory: A meta-analysis of attributional hypotheses. In E. A. Locke (Ed),

Generalizing from laboratory to field settings (pp. 63-81). Lexington, Massachusetts: Lexington Books.

De Vries, D. L., Morrison, A. M., Shullman, S. L., & Gerlach, M. L. (1986). *Performance appraisal on the line.* Greensboro, North Carolina: Center for Creative Leadership.

Deary, I. J., Whalley, L. J., Lemmon, H., Crawford, J. R., & Starr, J. M. (2000). The stability of individual differences in mental ability from childhood to old age: Follow-up of the 1932 Scottish Mental Survey. *Intelligence, 28*, 49-55.

DeCotiis, T. A., & Summers, T. P. (1987). A path analysis of a model of the antecedents and consequences of organizational commitment. *Human Relations, 40*(7), 445-470.

DeFrank, R. S., & Cooper, C. L. (1987). Worksite stress management interventions: Their effectiveness and conceptualisation. *Journal of Managerial Psychology, 2*, 4-10.

Delaney, J. T., & Huselid, M. A. (1996). The impact of human resource management practices on perceptions of organizational performance. *Academy of Management Journal, 39*(4), 949-969.

Delbridge, A., Bernard, J. R. L., Blair, D., Peters, P., & Butler, S. (Eds). (1996). *The Macquarie dictionary* (Revised, 3rd ed). Sydney, New South Wales: The Macquarie Library.

Deluga, R. (1994). Supervisor trust building, leader-member exchange and organisational citizenship behaviour. *Journal of Occupational and Organizational Psychology, 67*(4), 315-326.

Deves, L., & Yeow, L. (1994). Educating bank managers: An evaluation of the Westpac management diploma. *Asia Pacific Journal of Human Resources, 31*(3), 92-102.

Diener, E. (1984). Subjective well-being. *Psychological Bulletin, 95*(3), 542-575.

Diener, E., & Biswas-Diener, R. (2003). Will money increase subjective well-being? *Social Indicators Research, 57*, 119-169.

Diener, E., Colvin, R. C., Pavot, W. G., & Allman, A. (1991). The psychic costs of intense positive affect. *Journal of Personality and Social Psychology, 61*(3), 492-503.

Diener, E., Fujita, F., & Smith, H. (1995). The personality structure of affect. *Journal of Personality and Social Psychology, 69*(1), 130-141.

Diener, E., & Iran-Nejad, A. (1986). The relationship in experience between different types of affect. *Journal of Personality and*

Social Psychology, 50, 1031-1038.

Diener, E., Larsen, R. J., Levine, S., & Emmons, R. A. (1985). Intensity and frequency: Dimensions underlying positive and negative affect. *Journal of Personality and Social Psychology, 48*(5), 1253-1265.

Diener, E., Sandvik, E., & Pavot, W. G. (1991). Happiness is the frequency, not the intensity, of positive versus negative affect. In F. Stack, M. Argyle & N. Schwarz (Eds), *Subjective well-being: An interdisciplinary perspective* (pp. 119-139). New York: Pergamon Press.

Digman, J. M. (1990). Personality structure: Emergence of the five-factor model. *Annual Review of Psychology, 41*, 417-440.

Dillon, W. R., & Goldstein, M. (1984). *Multivariate analysis: Methods and applications*. New York: Wiley.

Dipboye, R. L., & Flanagan, M. F. (1979). Research settings in industrial and organizational psychology: Are findings in the field more generalizable than in the laboratory? *American Psychologist, 34*, 141-150.

Dive, B. (2002). *The healthy organization*. London, United Kingdom: Kogan.

Dodd, N. G., & Ganster, D. C. (1996). The interactive effects of variety, autonomy, and feedback on attitudes and performance. *Journal of Organizational Behavior, 17*(4), 329-347.

Domeyko, M. (1996). *Absolute happiness: The way to a life of complete fulfilment*. Alexandria, New South Wales: Hay House.

Donaldson, G. (2005, May 18th). Employee management cost $31.5 billion. *Human Resources*, http://www.humanresourcesmagazine.com.au/articles/DA/0C02EBDA.asp?Type=59&Category=917.

Dreyfuss, J. (1990). Get ready for the new work force. *Fortune* (23 April), 166-181.

Drucker, P. (2001). *The Essential Drucker*. Oxford, UK: Butterworh-Heinemann.

DuBois, D., & McKee, A. S. (1994, May 1994). *Facets of work experience*. Paper presented at the Ninth Annual Conference of the Society for Industrial and Organizational Psychology, Nashville, TN.

Dulewicz, V. P. (1989). Performance appraisal and counselling. In P. Herriot (Ed), *Assessment and selection in organizations: Methods and practices for recruitment and appraisal* (pp. 645-649). New York: Wiley.

Dulewicz, V. P. (1996). *Personality, competencies, leadership style and managerial effectiveness*: Henley College, United Kingdom: Working Paper (HWP9214).

Dunham, R. B., Grube, J. A., & Castaneda, M. B. (1994). Organizational commitment: The utility of an integrative definition. *Journal of Applied Psychology, 79*(3), 370-380.

Dunnette, M. D., & Hough, L. M. (Eds). (1991). *Handbook of Industrial and Organizational Psychology* (2nd ed, Vol. 1). Palto Alto, California: Consulting Psychologists Press.

Dunnette, M. D., & Hough, L. M. (Eds). (1994). *Handbook of Industrial Psychology and Organizational Psychology* (2nd ed). Palo Alto, California: Consulting Psychologists Press.

Dunphy, D., & Stace, D. (1990). *Under new management: Australian organisations in transition.* Roseville, New South Wales: McGraw-Hill.

Eagly, A. H., & Chaiken, S. (1993). *The psychology of attitudes.* Fort Worth, TX: Harcourt Brace Jovanovich.

Eales, J., & Spence, L. (2005). Influencing behaviour in organisations. In C. Barker & R. Coy (Eds), *Understanding influence for leaders at all levels.* Sydney, NSW: Australian Institute of Management. McGraw-Hil.

Earnshaw, J., & Cooper, C. L. (2003). *Stress and employer liability.* London, United Kingdom: CIPD Books.

Easterbrook, G. (2005). The real truth about money. *Time, 165,* A32-A38.

Edwards, H. (2004). *Stress in the workplace: How to cause it.* London, United Kingdom: New Holland.

Edwards, J. R., Caplan, R. D., & Van Harrison, R. (1998). Person-environment fit theory: Conceptual foundations, empirical evidence and directions for future research. In C. L. Cooper (Ed), *Theories of organizational stress* (pp. 26-67). New York: Oxford University Press.

Elfenbein, H., & Ambady, N. (2003). Predicting workplace outcomes from the ability to eavesdrop on feelings. *Journal of Applied Psychology, 87*(5), 963-975.

Elias, P. K., Elias, M. F., Robbins, M. A., & Gage, P. (1987). Acquisition of wordprocessing skills by younger, middle-aged, and older adults. *Psychology and Aging,* 340-348.

Emerson, R. W. (1965). *Selected essays, lectures, and poems*. New York: Bantam. Emerson, RW.

Emmons, R. A., & Diener, E. (1985). Personality correlates of subjective well-being. *Personality and Social Psychology, 11*, 89-97.

Erikson, E. (1959). Identity and the life cycle. *Psychological Issues, 1*, 18-164.

European Union. (2001, November). Combating stress and depression-related problems. In *Official Journal C 6 of 09.01.2002*.

Evans, P. (1986). The strategic outcomes of human resource management. *Human Resource Management, 25*(1), 146-167.

Eysenck, H. J., & Eysenck, M. W. (1985). *Personality and individual differences: A natural science approach*. New York: Plenum Press.

Fabrigar, L. R., Wegener, D. T., MacCallum, R. C., & Strahan, E. J. (1999). Evaluating the use of exploratory factor analysis in psychological research. *Psychological Methods, 4*, 282.

Faragher, E. B., Cass, M., & Cooper, C. L. (2005). The relationship between job satisfaction and health: a meta-analysis. *Occupational and Environmental Medicine, 62*, 105-112.

Fay, D., & Sonnentag, S. (2002). Rethinking the effects of stressors: A longitudinal study on personal initiative. *Journal of Occupational Health Psychology, 7*, 221-234.

Fayol, H. (1916). *Administration Industrielle et Generale*. Paris, France: Dunod.

Feldman Barrett, L., & Russell, J. A. (1998). Independence and bipolarity in the structure of affect. *Journal of Personality and Social Psychology, 74*(4), 967-984.

Fenwick, M., & De Cieri, H. (1995). Building an integrated approach to performance management using critical incident technique. *Asia Pacific Journal of Human Resources, 33*(3), 76-91.

Fiedler, F. E. (1967). *A theory of leadership effectiveness*. New York: McGraw-Hill.

Fisher, C. D. (1980). On the dubious wisdom of expecting job satisfaction to correlate with performance. *Academy of Management Executive, 6*, 607-612.

Fisher, C. D. (2002). Antecedents and consequences of real-time affective reactions at work. *Motivation and Emotion, 26*(3), 30.

Fisher, C. D. (2003). Why do lay people believe that satisfaction and performance are correlated? Possible sources of a commonsense theory. *Journal of Organizational Behavior, 24*, 753-777.

Fisher, C. D., & Ashkanasy, N. M. (2000). The emerging role of emotions in work life: An introduction. *Journal of Organizational Behavior, 21*(2), 123-129.

Fisher, V. E., & Hanna, J. V. (1931). *The dissatisfied worker*. New York: Macmillan.

Fiske, D. W. (1982). Convergent-discriminant validation in measurements and research strategies. In A. Brinberg & L. Kidder (Eds), *New directions for methodology of social and behavioral science: Forms of validity in research* (Vol. 12, pp. 77-92). San Francisco, California: Jossey-Bass.

Flanagan, J. C. (1951). Defining the requirements of the executive's job. *Personnel, 28*(28), 3.

Flanagan, J. C. (1954). The critical incident technique. *Psychological Bulletin, 51*(4), 327-358.

Fletcher, B. (1991). *Work, stress, disease and life expectancy*. New York: Wiley.

Fletcher, B., & Jones, F. (1993). A refutation of Karasek's demand-discretion model of occupational stress with a range of dependent variables. *Journal of Organizational Behavior, 14*(4), 319-330.

Florida, R. (2003). *The rise of the creative class*. North Melbourne, Victoria: Pluto Press.

Fombrun, C., Tichy, N. M., & Devanna, M. A. (Eds). (1984). *Strategic human resource management*. New York: Wiley.

Ford, J. K., Quinones, M. A., Sego, D. J., & Sorra, J. (1992). Factors affecting the opportunity to perform trained tasks on the job. *Personnel Psychology, 45*, 511-527.

Ford, J. K., Sego, D. J., Quinones, M. A., & Speer, J. (1991, April 1991). *The construct of experience: A review of the literature and needed research directions*. Paper presented at the Sixth Annual Conference of the Society for Industrial and Organizational Psychology, St. Louis, MO.

Forgas, J. P. (1992). Affect in social judgments and decisions: A multi process model. In M. Zanna (Ed), *Advances in experimental social psychology* (pp. 227-275). New York: Academic Press.

Forgas, J. P. (2002). Towards understanding the role of affect in social thinking and behavior. *Psychological Inquiry, 13* (1), 90-102.

Forgas, J. P., Bower, G. H., & Moylan, S. J. (1990). Praise or blame? Affective influences on attributions for achievement. *Journal of*

Personality and Social Psychology, 59(4), 809-819.

Forster, N. (2005). *Maximum performance: A practical guide to leading and managing people at work.* Cheltenham, United Kingdom: Edward Elgar.

Forster, N., & Still, L. (2001). *A report on the effects of occupational stress on managers and professionals in Western Australia.* Perth, Western Australia: Centre for Women and Business, Graduate School of Management, The University of Western Australia and the Australian Institute of Management.

Fosterling, F. (1985). Attributional retraining: A review. *Psychological Bulletin, 98*, 495-512.

Foucault, M. (Ed). (1980). *Power/knowledge: Selected interviews and other writings, 1972-77.* New York: Pantheon.

French, J. R. P., Jr., Caplan, R. D., & Van Harrison, R. (1982). *The mechanism of job stress and strain.* New York: Wiley.

Frese, M., & Zapf, D. (1988). Methodological issues in the study of work stress: Objective vs subjective measurement of work stress and the question of longitudinal studies. In C. L. Cooper & R. Payne (Eds), *Causes, coping and consequences of stress at work* (pp. 375-411). New York: Wiley.

Fried, Y., & Ferris, G. (1987). The validity of the job characteristics model: A review and meta-analysis. *Personnel Psychology, 40*(2), 287-322.

Frone, M. R., Russell, M., & Cooper, L. M. (1992). Antecedents and outcomes of work-family conflict: Testing a model of the work-family interface. *Journal of Applied Psychology, 77*(1), 65-78.

Gabriel, P., & Liimatainen, M. R. (2000). *Mental health in the workplace: Introduction.* Geneva, Switzerland: International Labour Office. Retrieved October 1, 2004, from http://www.ilo.org/public/english/bureau/inf/pr/2000/37.html

Ganster, D. (2005). Executive job demands: Suggestions from a stress and decision-making perspective. *Academy of Management Review, 30*(3).

Ganster, D. C. (1989). Worker control and well-being: A review of research in the workplace. In S. L. Sauter, J. J. Hurrell & C. L. Cooper (Eds), *Job control and worker health* (pp. 3-23). New York: Wiley.

Ganster, D. C., & Schaubroeck, J. (1991). Work stress and employee health. *Journal of Management, 17*(2), 235-272.

Gardner, D. G., & Cummings, L. L. (1988). Activation theory and job design: Review and reconceptualization. *Research in Organizational Behavior, 10*, 81-122.

Gardner, P., & Koslowski, S. W. J. (1993). Learning the ropes: Co-ops do it faster. *Journal of Cooperative Behavior, 28*(3), 30-41.

Gebhardt, D., & Crump, C. E. (1990). Employee fitness and wellness programs in the workplace. *American Psychologist, 45*(2), 262-272.

George, J. M. (1991). State or trait: Effects of positive mood on prosocial behavior at work. *Journal of Applied Psychology, 76*(2), 299-307.

George, J. M. (1992). The role of personality in organizational life: Issues and evidence. *Journal of Management, 2*, 85-213.

George, J. M. (2000). Emotions and leadership: The role of emotional intelligence. *Human Relations, 53*, 1027-1055.

George, J. M., & Brief, A. P. (1992). Feeling good - doing good: A conceptual analysis of the mood at work-organizational spontaneity relationship. *Psychological Bulletin, 112*(2), 310-329.

George, J. M., & Brief, A. P. (1996). Motivational agendas in the workplace: The effects of feelings on focus of attention and work motivation. *Research in Organizational Behavior, 18*, 75-109.

George, J. M., & Jones, G. R. (1996). *Understanding and managing organizational behavior*. Reading, Massachusetts: Addison-Wesley.

George, J. M., & Jones, G. R. (1997). Organizational spontaneity in context. *Human Performance, 10*(2), 153-170.

George, J. M., & Zhou, J. (2002). Understanding when bad moods foster creativity and good ones don't: The role of context and clarity of feelings. *Journal of Applied Psychology, 87*, 687-697.

Gerbing, D. W., & Hamilton, J. G. (1996). Viability of exploratory factor analysis as a precursor to confirmatory factor analysis. *Structural Equation Modelling, 3*, 62-72.

Gerhart, B. (1987). How important are dispositional factors as determinants of job satisfaction? Implications for job design and other personnel programs. *Journal of Applied Psychology, 72*(3), 366-373.

Gervais, R., & Merchant, S. (1995). *The office*: Currency Press Pty Ltd.

Giga, S. I. (2001). *The implied employment relationship: Investigating the effects of psychological contract violations on employee well-being.* Unpublished doctoral dissertation Thesis. University of

Manchester.

Giga, S. I., Cooper, C. L., & Faragher, B. (2003). The development of a framework for a comprehensive approach to stress management interventions at work. *International Journal of Stress Management, 10*(4), 280-279.

Gignac, G. E. (2005). Evaluating the MSCEIT V2.0 via CFA: Corrections to Mayer et al. (2003). *Emotion, 5*(2), 233-235.

Gioia, D. A., & Longnecker, C. O. (1994). Delving into the dark side: The politics of performance appraisal. *Organizational Dynamics, 22*(3), 47-58.

Gioia, D. A., & Pitre, E. (1990). Multiparadigm perspectives on theory building. *Academy of Management Review, 15*(4), 584-602.

Gist, M. E. (1989). The influence of training method on self-efficacy and idea generation among managers. *Personnel Psychology, 42*(4), 787-805.

Gist, M. E., & Mitchell, T. R. (1992). Self-efficacy: A theoretical analysis of its determinants and malleability. *Academy of Management Review, 17*(2), 183-211.

Glendenning, P. M. (2002). Performance management: Pariah or messiah? *Public Personnel Management,* 161-178.

Goffin, R. D., & Jackson, D. N. (1992). Analysis of multitrait-multirater appraisal data: Composite direct product moment method versus confirmatory factor analysis. *Multivariate Behavioral Research, 27,* 363-417.

Goldberg, L. R. (1990). An alternative "Description of Personality": The Big-Five Factor Structure. *Journal of Personality and Social Psychology, 59*(1216-1229).

Goleman, D. (1995). *Emotional intelligence: Why it can matter more than IQ.* New York: Bantam Books.

Goleman, D. (1996). *Emotional intelligence.* London, United Kingdom: Bloomsbury.

Goleman, D. (1998). What makes a leader? *Harvard Business Review, 76*(November- December), 93-115.

Goleman, D. (1999). *Working with emotional intelligence.* London, United Kingdom: Bantam Books.

Goleman, D. (2000). Leadership that gets results. *Harvard Business Review, 78*(2), 78-89.

Goleman, D., Boyatzis, R., & McKee, A. (2002). *Primal leadership: Realizing the power of emotional intelligence.* Boston,

Massachusetts: Harvard Business School Press.

Gowing, M. K. (Ed). (2001). *Measurement of individual emotional Competence. The emotionally intelligent workplace*. San Francisco: Jossey-Bass.

Graen, G. (1976). Role-making processes within complex organizations. In M. D. Dunnette (Ed), *Handbook of Industrial and Organizational Psychology* (pp. 1201-1245). Chicago, Illinois: Rand-McNally.

Graen, G. B., & Uhl-Bien, M. (1995). Relationship-based approach to leadership: Development of leader*member exchange (LMX) theory of leadership over 25 years: Applying a multi-level multi-domain perspective. *Leadership Quarterly, 6*(Special Issue: Leadership: The multiple-level approaches Part I), 219-247.

Graham, J. W. (1986). *Organizational citizenship behavior informed by political theory*. Paper presented at the Annual meeting of the Academy of Management, Chicago, IL.

Green, D. P., Goldman, S. L., & Salovey, P. (1993). Measurement error masks bipolarity in affect ratings. *Journal of Personality and Social Psychology, 64*(6), 1029-1041.

Griffin, M. A., & Mathieu, J. E. (1997). Modelling organizational processes across hierarchical levels: Climate, leadership and group process in work groups. *Journal of Organizational Behaviour, 18*, 731-744.

Guadagnoli, E., & Velicer, W. F. (1988). Relation of sample size to the stability of component patterns. *Psychological Bulletin, 103*(2), 265-275.

Guehenno, J. M. (1995). *The end of the nation-state*. Minneapolis, Minnesota: University of Minnesota.

Guest, D. (2002). Human resource management, corporate performance and employee well-being: Building the worker into HRM. *The Journal of Industrial Relations, 44*(3), 335-358.

Guest, D. E. (1987). Human resource management and industrial relations. *Journal of Management Studies, 24*(5), 503-521.

Guest, D. E. (1990). Human resource management and the American dream. *Journal of Management Studies, 27*(4), 377-397.

Guest, D. E., Conway, N., & Dewe, P. (2004). Using sequential tree analysis to search for 'Bundles' of HR practices. *Human Resource Management Journal,, 14*(1), 79-96.

Guest, D. E., Michie, J., Conway, N., & Sheehan, M. (2003). Human resource management and corporate performance in the UK. *British Journal of Industrial Relations, 2*(41), 291-314.

Guion, R. M. (1991). Personnel assessment, selection and placement. In M. D. Dunnette & L. M. Hough (Eds), *Handbook of Industrial and Organizational Psychology* (2nd ed, pp. 327-398). Palto-Alto, California: Consulting Psychologists Press.

Gupta, N., & Beehr, T. A. (1982). A test of the correspondence between self-reports and alternative data sources about work organizations. *Journal of Vocational Behavior, 20*(1), 1-13.

Hackett, R. D., Bycio, P., & Hausdorf, P. A. (1994). Further assessments of Meyer and Allen's (1991) Three-component Model of Organizational Commitment. *Journal of Applied Psychology, 79*(1), 15-23.

Hackman, J., & Oldham, G. (1980). *Work redesign.* Reading, Massachusetts: Addison-Wesley.

Hackman, J. R., & Oldham, G. R. (1975). Development of the job diagnostic survey. *Journal of Applied Psychology, 60,* 159-170.

Hackman, J. R., Oldham, G. R., Jansen, J., & Purdy, K. (1975). A new strategy for job enrichment. *California Management Review, 17*(4), 57-71.

Hair, J. F., Anderson, R. E., Tatham, R. L., & Black, W. C. (1995). *Multivariate data analysis with readings.* New York: Maxwell Macmillan International.

Hakstian, A. R., Rogers, W. T., & Cattell, R. B. (1982). The behavior of number-of-factor rules with simulated data. *Multivariate Behavioral Research, 17,* 193-219.

Hales, C. P. (1986). What do managers do? A critical review of the evidence. *Journal of Management Studies, 23*(1), 88-115.

Hall, D. T. (1995). Executive careers and learning: Aligning selection, strategy and development. *Human Resource Planning, 18*(2), 14-23.

Hamel, G. (1996). Strategy as revolution. *Harvard Business Review, July-August,* 69-82.

Hamel, G., & Prahalad, C. (1994). Competing for the future. *Harvard Business Review, July-August,* 122-128.

Hamel, G., & Prahalad, C. K. (1989). Strategic intent. *Harvard Business Review, 67*(3), 63-76.

Hammer, M., & Champy, J. (1993). *Re-engineering the corporation.* New York: Harper Business.

Hampson, I. L., & Morgan, D. E. (1997). The world according to Karpin: A critique of Enterprising Nation. *Journal of Industrial Relations, 39*(4), 457-477.

Handy, C. B. (1996). *Beyond certainty: The changing worlds of organizations*. Boston, Massachusetts: Harvard Business School Press.

Hanson, P. G. (1986). *The joy of stress*. Islington, Ontario, Canada, Columbia, Canada: Island Scholastic Press.

Harris, M. M., & Bladen, A. (1994). Wording effects in the measurement of role conflict and role ambiguity: A multitrait-multimethod analysis. *Journal of Management, 20*(4), 887-901.

Harris, M. M., & Schaubroeck, J. (1988). A meta-analysis of self-supervisor, self-peer, and peer-supervisor ratings. *Personnel Psychology, 41*, 43-59.

Hart, S. L., & Quinn, R. E. (1993). Roles executives play: CEO's, behavioral complexity and firm performance. *Human Relations, 46*(5), 543-574.

Harter, J. K., Schmidt, F. L., & Hays, T. L. (2002). Business-unit-level relationship between employee satisfaction, employee engagement, and business outcomes: A meta-analysis. *Journal of Applied Psychology, 87*(2), 268-279.

Harter, J. K., Schmidt, F. L., & Keyes, C. L. M. (2002). Well-being in the workplace and its relationship to business outcomes: A review of the Gallup Studies. In C. L. M. Keyes & J. Haidt (Eds), *Flourishing: The positive person and the good life* (pp. 205-224). Washington, D.C: American Psychological Association.

Harter, S. (1990). Issues in the assessment of the self-concept of children and adolescents. In A. M. La Greca (Ed), *Through the eyes of the child: Obtaining self-reports from children and adolescents* (pp. 292-325). Boston, Massachusetts: Allyn & Bacon.

Haslam, N. (1995a). The discreteness of emotion concepts: Categorical structure in the affective circumplex. *Personality and Social Psychology Bulletin, 21*, 1012-1019.

Haslam, N. (1995b). Four grammars for primate social relations. In J. Simpson & D. Kenrick (Eds), *Evolutionary social psychology*: Lawrence Erlbaum, in press.

Hatcher, C. (2005). Influencing behaviour in organisations. In C. Barker & R. Coy (Eds). Sydney, NSW: Australian Institute of Management. McGraw-Hill.

Haybron, D. M. (2003). What do we want from a theory of happiness? *Metaphilosophy, 34*(3), 305-329.

HayGroup (1999). *What makes great leaders: Rethinking the route to effective leadership*: Findings from Fortune Magazine/Hay Group 1999 Executive Survey of Leadership Effectiveness. Retrieved December 1. 2004, from http://ei.haygroup.com/downloads/pdf/Leadership%20White%20Paper.pdf

Health and Safety Executive. (1995). *Stress at Work: A guide for employers*. Sudbury.

Health and Safety Executive. (2001). *Tackling work-related stress: A manager's guide to improving and maintaining employee health and well-being*. Sudbury, United Kingdom: Health and Safety Executive.

Heider, F. (1958). *The psychology of interpersonal relations*. New York: Wiley.

Heller, W., & Nitschke, J. B. (1998). The puzzle of regional brain activity in depression and anxiety: The importance of subtypes and comorbidity. *Cognition and Emotion, 12*, 421-447.

Hemphill, J. K. (1959). Job description for executives. *Harvard Business Review, 37*(5), 55-67.

Hendry, C., & Pettigrew, A. (1986). The practice of strategic human resource management. *Personnel Review, 15*(5), 3-8.

Heneman, R. L. (1986). The relationship between supervisory ratings and results-oriented measures performance: A meta-analysis. *Personnel Psychology, 39*, 811-826.

Hermelin, E., & Robertson, I. T. (2001). A critique and standardization of metaanalytic validity coefficients in personnel selection. *Journal of Occupational and Organizational Psychology, 74*(253-278).

Hersey, R. (1932). *Worker's emotions in the shop and home: A study of individual workers from the psychological and physiological standpoint*: University of Pennsylvania Press.

Herzberg, F. (1966). *The work and the nature of man*. Cleveland, Ohio: The World Publishing Company.

Herzberg, F., Mausner, B., & Snyderman, B. (1959). *The motivation to work*. New York: Wiley.

Hesketh, B. (1993). Toward a better adjusted theory of work adjustment. *Journal of Vocational Behavior, 43*(1), Special issue on the Theory of Work Adjustment. Academic Press.

Hesketh, B. (1997). Dilemmas in training for transfer and retention. *Applied Psychology: An International Review, 46*(4).

Hesketh, B., & Adams, A. (Eds). (1991). *Psychological perspectives on occupational health and rehabilitation.* Sydney, New South Wales: Harcourt Brace Jovanovich.

Heylighten, F., & Bernheim, J. (2000). Global progress 1: Empirical evidence for ongoing increase in quality-of-life. *Journal of Happiness Studies, 1*(3), 323-349.

Hill, L. A. (1992). *Becoming a manager: Mastery of a new identity.* Boston, Massachusetts: Harvard Business Press.

Hilton, M. (2006, 10-12 April). *Assessing the financial Return on Investment of good management strategies and the WORC Project,* Sydney.

Hinkin, T. R. (1995). A review of scale development practices in the study of organizations. *Journal of Management, 12*(5), 967-988.

Hippocrates translated by Jones, W. H. S. (1923, 1981). Volume II London. In: Harvard University Press.

Hoebel, B. G., Rada, P. V., Mark, G. P., & Pothos, E. N. (1999). Neural systems for reinforcement and inhibition of eating: Relevance to eating, addiction, and depression. In D. Kahneman, E. Diener & N. Schwarz (Eds), *Well-being: The foundations of hedonic psychology.* New York: Cambridge University Press.

Hoetler, J. W. (1983). The analysis of covariance structures: Goodness-of-fit indices. *Sociological Methods and Research, 11*, 325-344.

Hoffman, R. R. (1992). *The psychology of expertise: cognitive research and empirical AI.* New York: Springer-Verlag.

Hofmann, D. A., Jacobs, R., & Gerras, S. J. (1992). Mapping individual performance over time. *Journal of Applied Psychology, 77*, 185-195.

Hogan, J., & Roberts, B. (1996). Issues and non-issues in the fidelity/bandwidth tradeoff. *Journal of Organizational Behavior, 17*, 627-637.

Hogan, R., Hogan, J., & Roberts, B. (1996). Personality measurement and employment decisions: Questions and answers. *American Psychologist, 51*, 469-477.

Holmes-Smith, P. (1998). *Introduction to structural equation modelling using LISREL and AMOS.* Brisbane, Queensland: School Research, Evaluation, and Measurement Services.

Hooijberg, R., & Quinn, R. E. (1992). *Behavioural complexity and the development of effective managers.* Westport, Connecticut: Quorum Books/Greenwood Publishing Group.

Hoppock, R. (1935). *Job satisfaction.* New York: Harper.

Hosie, P. (1994). The mental health implications of work. *Singapore Management Review, 16*(11), 49-68.

Hosie, P. (2000). *Interim industry report on the job scope, psychological wellbeing and performance of managers.*

Hosie, P. (2003). *Study of the relationships between managers' job-related affective wellbeing, intrinsic job satisfaction and performance.* Unpublished PhD Thesis. The University of Western Australia. http://theses.library.uwa.edu.au/adt-WU2005.0001/.

Hosie, P. J., Smith, R. C., & Gunningham, C. J. (2003). Organisational behaviour: "Back to the future". *Journal of Doing Business Across Borders, 2*(2), 4-18.

Hoyle, R. H., & Panter, A. T. (1995). Writing about structural equation modelling. In R. H. Hoyle (Ed), *Structural equation modelling: Concepts, issues and applications* (pp. 158-176). Thousand Oaks, California: Sage.

Hu, L., & Bentler, P. M. (1999). Cutoff criteria for fit indexes in covariance structure analysis: Conventional criteria versus new alternatives. *Structural Equation Modeling, 6,* 1-55.

Hu, L., Bentler, P. M., & Kano, Y. (1992). Can test statistics in covariance structure analysis be trusted? *Psychological Bulletin, 112*(2), 351-362.

Huelsman, T. J., Furr, M. R., & Nemanick Jr., R. C. (2003). Measurement of dispositional affect: Construct validity and convergence with a circumplex model of affect. *Educational and Psychological Measurement, 63,* 655-673.

Hunter, J. E. (1986). Cognitive ability, cognitive aptitudes, job knowledge, and job performance. *Journal of Vocational Behavior, 29,* 340-362.

Hunter, J. E. (1989). *The Wonderlic Personnel Test as a predictor of training success and job performance.* Michigan: E. F. Wonderlic Personnel Test, Inc.

Hunter, J. E., & Hunter, R. E. (1984). Validity and utility of alternative predictors of job performance. *Psychological Bulletin, 96,* 798.

Hunter, J. E., & Schmidt, F. L. (1983). Quantifying the effects of psychological interventions on employee job performance and work-force productivity. *American Psychologist, 38,* 473-478.

Hunter, J. E., & Schmidt, F. L. (1990). *Methods of meta-analysis: Correcting error and bias in research findings.* Beverly Hills, CA: Sage.

Hunter, J. E., Schmidt, F. L., & Judiesch, M. K. (1990). Individual differences in output variability as a function of job complexity. *Journal of Applied Psychology,* 28-42.

Hurley, A. E., Scandura, T. A., Schriesheim, C. A., Brannick, M. T., Seers, A., Vandenberg, R. J., et al. (1997). Exploratory and confirmatory factor analysis: Guidelines, issues and alternatives. *Journal of Organizational Behavior, 18*(6), 667-683.

Hurrell, J. J., & McLaney, M. A. (1989). Control, job demands, and job satisfaction. In S. L. Sauter, J. J. Hurrell & C. L. Cooper (Eds), *Job control and worker health* (pp. 97-103). Chichester, United Kingdom: Wiley.

Huselid, M. A. (1995). The impact of human resource management practices on turnover, productivity, and corporate financial performance *Academy of Management Journal, 38*(3), 635-672.

Huselid, M. A., & Becker, B. E. (1997). *The impact high performance work systems, implementation effectiveness, and alignment with strategy on shareholder wealth.* Paper presented at the Academy of Management Proceedings.

Huselid, M. A., Jackson, S. E., & Randall, R. S. (1997). Technical and strategic human resource management effectiveness as determinants of firm performance. *Academy of Management Journal, 40*(1), 171-188.

Hutchins, R. M. (Ed). (1952). *Pascal's 'the provincial letters,' 'pensees,' and 'scientific treatises'* (Vol. 34). Chicago, Illinois: Britannica Inc.

Huy, Q. N. (2003). Emotional capability, emotional intelligence, and radical change. *Academy of Management Executive, 24,* 235-345.

IAER. (1998). Job security in the 1990s: How much is job security worth to employees? *Australian Social Monitor, Institute of Applied Economic Research, 1,* 1-7.

Iaffaldano, M. T., & Muchinsky, P. M. (1985). Job satisfaction and job performance: A meta-analysis. *Psychological Bulletin, 97*(2), 251-273.

Ichniowski, C. (1990). *Human resource management systems and the performance of US manufacturing businesses* Cambridge, Mass: National Bureau of Economic Research, Working paper No, 3349, 1990.

Ichniowski, C., Shaw, K., & Prennushi, G. (1997). The effects of human resource management practices on productivity: A study of steel finishing lines. *The American Economic Review, 87*(3), 291-313.

Ilgen, D. R., Barnes-Farrell, J. L., & McKellin, D. B. (1993). Performance appraisal: A process focus. *Research in Organizational Behavior, 15*, 141-197.

Ilgen, D. R., Fisher, C. D., & Taylor, F. W. (1979). Consequences of individual feedback on behavior in organizations. *Journal of Applied Psychology, 64*, 349-371.

Ilgen, D. R., & Hollenbrook, J. R. (1991). The structure of work: Job design and roles. In M. D. Dunnette & L. M. Hough (Eds), *Handbook of Industrial and Organizational Psychology* (2nd ed, pp. 165-207). Palo Alto, California: Consulting Psychologists Press.

Ilgen, D. R., Major, D.A., & Tower, S.L. (1994). The cognitive revolution in organizational behavior. In J. Greenberg (Ed), *Organizational behavior: The state of the science* (pp. 1-22). Hillsdale, New Jersey: Lawrence Erlbaum Associates, Inc.

Ilies, R., & Judge, T. A. (2003). On the heritability of job satisfaction: The mediating role of personality. *Journal of Applied Psychology, 88*, 750-759.

Ilies, R., Schmidt, F. L., & Yoon, K. (2002). Cross-cultural validity of the Five Factor Model of personality among Korean employees. *Journal of Cross Cultural Psychology, 33*, 215 - 233.

International Labor Organization (2004). *Review: International Labor Organization*: ILO, from http://www.ingentaconnect.com/content/ilo/ilr/2004/00000143/00000004;jsessionid=1e9pwrc6nw3fr.victoria

Irwin, D. A., Rebert, C. S., McAdam, D. W., & Knott, J. R. (1966). Slow potential change (CNV) in the human EEG as a function of motivational variables. *Electroencephalogy Clinical Neurophysiology, 21*, 412-413.

Isen, A. M. (1987). Positive affect, cognitive processes and social behavior. In L. Berkowitz (Ed), *Advances in experimental social psychology* (Vol. 20, pp. 203-253). San Diego, California: Academic Press.

Isen, A. M., & Baron, R. A. (1991). Positive affect as a factor in organisational behaviour. *Research in Organizational Behavior, 13*, 1-53.

Isen, A. M., & Labroo, A. A. (2003). Some ways in which positive affect facilitates decision making and judgment. In S. L. Schneider & J. Shanteau (Eds), *Emerging perspectives on judgment and decision research* (pp. 365-393). New York: Cambridge University Press.

Iverson, G., Stampfer, H. G., & Gaetz, M. (2002). Reliability of circadian heart pattern analysis in psychiatry. *Psychiatry Quarterly, 73*(3), 195-203.

Iverson, R. D., & Erwin, P. J. (1997). Predicting occupational injury: The role of affectivity. *Journal of Occupational and Organizational Psychology, 70*(2), 113-128.

Izard, C. (2002). Translating emotional theory and research into preventative interventions. *Psychological Bulletin, 128*(5), 796-824.

Jamal, M. (1997a). Job stress and employee affective well-being: A cross-cultural empirical study. *Stress Medicine, 15*(3), 153-158.

Jamal, M. (1997b). Job stress, satisfaction and mental health: An empirical examination of self-employed and non self-employed Canadians. *Journal of Small Business Management, 35*(4), 48-57.

James, L. R., Mulaik, S. A., & Brett, J. M. (1982). *Causal analysis: Assumptions, models, and data.* Beverly Hills, California: Sage.

James, R., Milton, J., & Gibb, R. (2000). Emotion in learning: A neglected dynamic. *Research and Development in Higher Education, 22*, 87.

Jansen, P., & Stoop, B. (1997). What successful managers really do?: Manager's self-descriptions instead of observation. *Gedrag En Organisatie, 10*(2), 78-94.

Jensen, A. R. (1998). *The g factor: The science of mental ability.* Westport, CT: Praeger.

Johnson, J. V. (1991). Collective control: Strategies for survival in the workplace. In J. V. Johnson & G. Johansson (Eds), *The psychosocial work environment: Work organizations, democratization and health* (pp. 121-132). Baywood, New York.

Johnson, S., & Cooper, C. (2003). The construct validity of the ASSET stress measure. *Stress and Health, 19*, 181-185.

Johnston, R. (1979). *Work and industrial relations* (Vol. 20). Perth, Western Australia: Finn and Collins.

Jones, E. E., & Nisbett, R. E. (1972). The actor and the observer: Divergent perceptions of the causes of behavior. In E. E. Jones, D. W. Kanouse, H. H. Kelly, R. E. Nisbett, S. Valins & B. Weiner (Eds), *Attribution: Perceiving the causes of behavior.*

Morristown, New Jersey: General Learning Press.

Jones, G. R. (1995). *Organizational theory: Text and cases*. Reading, Massachusetts: Addison-Wesley.

Jordan, P. J., Ashkanasy, N. M., & Hartel, C. E. J. (2003). The case for emotional intelligence in organizational research. *Academy of Management Review, 28*, 195-197.

Jordan, P. J., & Troth, A. C. (2004). Managing emotions during team problem solving: emotional intelligence and conflict resolution. *Human Performance, 17*, 195-218.

Jöreskog, K. G., & Sorbom, D. (1993). *LISREL 8: Structural equation modelling with the Simplis Command language*. Hillsdale, New Jersey: Lawrence Erlbaum Associates.

Jöreskog, K. G., & Wold, H. (1982). The ML and PLS techniques for modelling with latent variables: Historical and comparative aspects. In K. G. Jöreskog & H. Wold (Eds), *Systems under indirect observation: Causality, structure, prediction. Part 1* (pp. 263-270). Amsterdam, Holland: Sociometric Research Foundation.

Judge, T. A. (1993). Does affective disposition moderate the relationship between job satisfaction and voluntary turnover? *Journal of Applied Psychology, 78*(3), 395-401.

Judge, T. A., & Bretz, R. D. (1993). Report on an alternative measure of affective disposition. *Educational and Psychological Measurement, 53*, 1095-1104.

Judge, T. A., Heller, D., & Mount, M. K. (2002). Five-factor model of personality and job satisfaction A meta-analysis. *Journal of Applied Psychology, 87*(3), 530-541.

Judge, T. A., & Hulin, C. L. (1993). Job satisfaction as a reflection of disposition: A multiple source causal analysis. *Organizational Behavior and Human Decision Processes, 56*, 388-421.

Judge, T. A., & Locke, E. A. (1993). Effect of dysfunctional thought processes on subjective well-being and job satisfaction. *Journal of Applied Psychology, 78*, 475-490.

Judge, T. A., Locke, E. A., Durham, C. C., & Kluger, A. N. (1998). Dispositional effects on job and life satisfaction: The role of core evaluations. *Journal of Applied Psychology, 83*, 17-34.

Judge, T. A., Thoresen, C. J., Bono, J. E., & Patton, G. K. (2001). The job satisfaction-job performance relationship: A qualitative and quantitative review. *Psychological Bulletin, 127*(3), 376-407.

Judge, T. A., & Watanabe, S. (1993). Another look at the job satisfaction-life satisfaction relationship. *Journal of Applied Psychology, 78*(6), 939-948.

Jung, C. G. (1933). *Modern man in search of a soul.* London, United Kingdom: Routledge & Kegan.

Kahn, H., & Cooper, C. L. (1993). *Stress in the dealing room: High performers under stress* (1st ed). London, United Kingdom: Routledge.

Kahn, R. L., & Byosiere, P. (1992). Stress in organizations. In M. D. Dunnette & L. M. Hough (Eds), *Handbook of Industrial and Organizational Psychology* (2nd ed, pp. 571-650). Palo Alto, California: Consulting Psychologists Press.

Kahneman, D., Diener, E., & Schwarz, N. (Eds). (1999). *Well-being: The foundations of hedonic psychology.* New York: Russell Sage Foundation.

Kane, J. S., & Lawler, E. E. (1978). Methods of peer assessment. *Psychological Bulletin, 85,* 555-586.

Kanner, A. D., Coyne, J. C., Schaefer, C., & Lazarus, R. S. (1981). Comparison of two models of stress management: Daily hassles and uplifts versus major life events. *Journal of Behavioral Medicine, 4,* 1-39.

Kanungo, R., & Misra, S. (1992). Managerial resourcefulness: A reconceptualization of management skills. *Human Relations, 45*(12), 1311-1332.

Kaplan, R. S., & Norton, D. P. (1992). The balanced scorecard - Measures that drive performance. *Harvard Business Review, January-February,* 71-79.

Kaplan, R. S., & Norton, D. P. (1993). Putting the balanced scorecard to work. *Harvard Business Review, September-October,* 134-147.

Kaplan, R. S., & Norton, D. P. (1996a). *The balanced scorecard: Translating strategy into action.* Boston, Massachusetts: Harvard business School Press.

Kaplan, R. S., & Norton, D. P. (1996b). Using the balanced scorecard as a strategic management system. *Harvard Business Review, January-February,* 75-85.

Karambayya, R. (1989). *Organizational citizenship behavior: Contextual predictors and organizational consequences.* PhD Dissertation Thesis. Northwestern University.

Karambayya, R. (1990). *Contexts for organization citizenship behavior:*

Do high performing and satisfying units have better 'citizens'.Unpublished manuscript, Toronto, Ontario.

Karasek, R. A. (1979). Job demands, job decision latitude, and mental strain: Implications for job redesign. *Administrative Science Quarterly, 24*(2), 285-308.

Karasek, R. A. (1989). Control in the workplace and its health-related aspects. In S. L. Sauter, J. J. Hurrell & C. L. Cooper (Eds), *Job control and worker health* (pp. 129-159). Chichester, New York: Wiley.

Karasek, R. A., & Theorell, T. (1990). *Healthy work: Stress reconstruction of working life*. New York: Basic Books.

Karpin, D. (1995a). *Enterprising nation: Renewing Australia's managers to meet the challenges of the Asia-Pacific century* (Vol. 1, April). Canberra, Australian Capital Territory: Industry Task Force on Leadership and Management Skills: Australian Government Printing Service.

Karpin, D. (1995b). In search of leaders. *HR Monthly, June*, 11.

Kasl, S. V. (1989). An epidemiological perspective on the role of control in health. In S. L. Sauter, J. J. Hurrell & C. L. Cooper (Eds), *Job control and worker health* (pp. 161-190). Chichester, New York: Wiley.

Katz, D., & Kahn, R. L. (1978). *The social psychology of organisations* (2nd ed). New York: Wiley.

Katz, R. L. (1974). Skills of an effective administrator. *Harvard Business Review, 52*(5), 90-102.

Katzell, R. A., & Thompson, D. E. (1995). Work motivation: Theory and practice. In D. A. Kolb, J. S. Osland & I. M. Rubin (Eds), *The organizational behavior reader* (6th ed, pp. 110-124). Englewood Cliffs, New Jersey: Prentice-Hall.

Kauppinen-Toropainen, K., Kandolin, I., & Mutamen, P. (1983). Job dissatisfaction and work related exhaustion in male and female workers. *Journal of Occupational Behaviour, 4*, 193-207.

Keating, M. (1988). Change and the challenge ahead. *Directions in Government, July*.

Kelloway, K. E. (1995). Structural equation modeling in perspective. *Journal of Organizational Behavior, 16*, 215-224.

Kelloway, K. E., & Barling, J. (1991). Job characteristics, role stress and mental health. *Journal of Occupational Psychology, 64*, 291-304.

Kenny, D. T., & Cooper, C. L. (2003). Introduction: Occupational stress and management. *International Journal of Stress Management, 10*(4), 275-280.

Kenny, D. T., & McIntyre, D. (2004a). Constructions of occupational stress: Nuance or novelty? In A. G. Antoniou & C. L. Cooper (Eds), *Research companion to organizational health psychology*. Cheltenham, United Kingdom: Edward Elgar Publishing.

Kenny, D. T., & McIntyre, D. (2004b). Occupational stress, personality and social processes: Paradigms or permutations? In A.-S. Antoniou & C. Cooper (Eds), *New perspectives in occupational health*: Greek University Publishing.

Keyes, C. L. M., & Haidt, J. (Eds). (2003). *Flourishing: Positive psychology and the life well-lived* (1st ed). Washington, D.C: American Psychological Association.

Kim, J., & Mueller, C. W. (1978a). *Factor analysis: Statistical methods and practical issues*. Beverly Hills, California: Sage Publications.

Kim, J., & Mueller, C. W. (1978b). *Introduction to factor analysis: What it is and how to do it*. Beverly Hills, California: Sage Publications.

King, S. P., & Peter, L. (Eds). (1993). *Economic rationalism: Dead end or way forward?* St Leonards, New South Wales: Allen & Unwin.

Kinicki, A. J., McKee, F. M., & Wade, K. J. (1996). Annual Review, 1991-1995: Occupational health. *Journal of Vocational Behavior, 49*(2), 190-220.

Kitney, G. (1996, 12 April). Axe falls on easy targets. *Sydney Morning Herald,* p. 13.

Klemp, G., & McClelland, D. (1986). What characterises intelligent functioning among senior managers? In R. Sternberg & R. Wagner (Eds), *Practical intelligence: Nature and origins of competence in the every day world*. Cambridge, United Kingdom: Cambridge University Press.

Kline, P. (Ed). (1994). *An easy guide to factor analysis*. New York.

Kluger, A. N., & De Nisi, A. (1996). The effects of feedback interventions on performance: A historical review, a meta-analysis, and a preliminary feedback intervention theory. *Psychological Bulletin, 119*(2), 254-284.

Kluger, A. N., & Tikochinsky, J. (2001). The error of accepting the 'theoretical' null hypothesis: The rise, fall, and resurrection of commonsense hypotheses in psychology. *Psychological Bulletin, 127*(3), 101-114.

Koestner, R., Zuckerman, M., & Koestner, J. (1987). Praise, involvement, and intrinsic motivation. *Journal of Personality and Social Psychology, 53*(2), 383-390.

Koh, W. L., Steers, R. M., & Terborg, J. R. (1995). The effects of transformational leadership on teacher attitudes and student performance in Singapore. *Journal of Organizational Behavior, 16*, 319-333.

Koivumaa-Honkanen, H., Koskenvuo, M., Honkanen, R. J., Viinamaki, H., Heikkilae, K., & Kaprio, J. (2004). Life dissatisfaction and subsequent work disability in an 11-year follow-up. *Psychological Medicine, 34*, 221-228.

Konovsky, M. A., & Organ, D. W. (1996). Dispositional and contextual determinants of organisational citizenship behaviour. *Journal of Organizational Behavior, 17*(3), 253-266.

Konovsky, M. A., & Pugh, S. D. (1994). Citizenship behaviour and social exchange. *Academy of Management Journal, 37*(3), 656-669.

Kornhauser, A. W., & Sharp, A. A. (1932). Employee attitudes: Suggestions from a study in a factory. *Personnel Journal, 10*, 393-404.

Kotter, J. (1986). *The general managers*. New York: Free Press.

Krzystofiak, F., Cardy, R. L., & Newman, J. (1988). Implicit personality and performance appraisal: the influence of trait inferences on evaluations of behavior. *Journal of Applied Psychology, 73*, 515-521.

Kuncel, N. R., Hezlett, S. A., & Ones, D. S. (2004). Academic performance, career potential, creativity, and job performance: Can one construct predict them all? *Journal of Personality and Social Psychology, 86*(1), 148-161.

Lado, A. A., & Wilson, M. C. (1994). Human resource systems and sustained competitive advantage: A competency-based perspective. *The Academy of Management Review, 19*(4), 699-727.

Lance, C. E., Hedge, J. W., & Alley, W. E. (1989). Joint relationships of task proficiency with aptitude, experience, and task difficulty: A cross-level interactional study. *Human Performance, 2*, 249-272.

Landsbergis, P. A. (1988). Occupational stress among health care workers: A test of the job demands-control model. *Journal of Organizational Behavior, 9*(3), 217-239.

Landy, F. J. (2005). Some historical and scientific issues related to research on emotional intelligence. *Journal of Organizational Behavior, 26*(4), 411-424.

Landy, F. J., & Farr, J. L. (1980). Performance rating. *Psychological Bulletin, 87,* 72-107.

Lane, R. (2000). Neural correlates of conscious emotional experience. In R. Lane, L. Nadel, G. Ahern, J. Allen, A. Kasniak, S. Rapesak & G. Schwarz (Eds), *Cognitive Neuroscience of Emotion* (pp. 345-370). New York: Oxford University Press.

Lange, J. (1984, May 24/25). *12 issues in Australian tertiary telecommunications.* Paper presented at the Satellite communications in Australian tertiary education, Melbourne.

Langer, E. (1975). The illusion of control. *Journal of Personality and Social Psychology, 32,* 311-328.

Larsen, J. T., McGraw, P. A., & Cacioppo, J. T. (2001). Can people feel happy and sad at the same time? *Journal of Personality and Social Psychology, 81,* 684-696.

Larsen, R. J., & Ketelaar, T. (1989). Extraversion, neuroticism and susceptibility to positive and negative mood induction procedures. *Personality and Individual Differences, 10*(12), 1221-1228.

Larzelere, R., & Muliak, S. (1977). Single-sample tests for many correlations. *Psychological Bulletin, 84,* 557-569.

Latham, G. P., & Skarlicki, D. P. (1997). Leadership training in organizational justice to increase citizenship behavior within a labor union: A replication. *Personnel Psychology, 50*(3), 617-633.

Latham, G. P., & Wexley, K. N. (1994). *Increasing productivity through performance appraisal* (2nd ed). Reading, Massachusetts: Addison-Wesley.

Lawler, E. E. (2003). *Treat people right.* San Francisco: Jossey-Bass.

Lawler, E. E., Mohrman, S. A., & Ledford, G. E. (1995). *Creating high performance organizations.* San Francisco: Jossey-Bass.

Lawler, E. E., Mohrman, S. A., & Ledford, G. E. (1998). *Strategies for high performance organizations.* San Francisco: Jossey-Bass.

Lawler, E. E., & Porter, L. W. (1967). The effects of performance on job satisfaction. *Industrial Relations, 7,* 20-28.

Layard, R. (2005). *Happiness: Lessons from a new science.* York, United Kingdom: Allen Lane.

Lebel, P. (2005, May 25th-28th). *Address to conference.* Paper presented at the 9th International Conference on Global Business and Economic Development Management Challenges in Times of Global Change and Uncertainty, Seoul, Korea.

Ledford, G. E., Jr. (1999). Happiness and productivity revisited. *Journal of Organizational Behavior, 20*(1), 31-34.

LeDoux, J. E. (1995). In search of an emotional system in the brain: leaping from fear to emotion and consciousness. In M. S. Gazzaniga (Ed), *The cognitive neurosciences* (pp. 1049-1061). Cambridge, MA: MIT Press.

Lee, C. (1989). Can leadership be taught? *Training, 26*(7), 19-24.

Lee, T., & Ashforth, B. E. (1996). A meta-analytic examination of the correlates of the three dimensions of job burnout. *Journal of Applied Psychology, 81*(2), 123-133.

Legge, K. (1995). *Human resource management: Rhetoric and realities.* Basingstoke: MacMillan.

Leong, F. (1996). Toward an integrative model for cross-cultural counselling and psychotherapy. *Applied and Preventive Psychology, 5*(4), 189-209.

Levi, L. (1990). Occupational stress: Spice of life or kiss of death? *American Psychologist, 45*(10), 1142-1145.

Levi, L. (2002). More jobs, better jobs, and health. In M. F. Dollard, A. H. Winefield & H. R. Winefield (Eds), *Occupational stress in the service professions* (pp. ix-xii). London, United Kingdom: Taylor & Francis.

Lewinsohn, P. M., & Amenson, C. S. (1978). Some relations between pleasant and unpleasant events and depression. *Journal of Abnormal Psychology, 87*(6), 644-654.

Lichtenstein, S., Fischoff, B., & Phillips, L. D. (1982). Calibration of probabilities: The state of the art in 1980. In D. Kahneman, P. Slovic & A. Tversky (Eds), *Judgment under uncertainty: Heuristics and biases* (pp. 306-334). New York: Cambridge University Press.

Limerick, D., & Cunnington, B. (1993). *Managing the new ego.* Chatswood, New South Wales: Business & Professional Publishing.

Livingston, J. S. (1971). Myth of the well-educated manager. *Harvard Business Review, January-February,* 79-89.

Locke, E. A. (1976). The nature and causes of job satisfaction. In M. D. Dunnette (Ed), *Handbook of Industrial and Organizational*

Psychology (pp. 1297-1349). Chicago, Illinois: Rand McNally.

Locke, E. A. (2005). Why emotional intelligence is an invalid concept. *Journal of Organisational Behaviour, 26,* 425.

Locke, E. A., & Latham, G. P. (1990). *A theory of goal setting and task performance.* Englewood Cliffs, New Jersey: Prentice Hall.

Lombardo, M. M., & McCauley, C. D. (1994). *Benchmarks®: Developmental reference points - A manual and trainer's guide.* Greensboro. North Carolina: Center for Creative Leadership.

London, M., Smither, J. W., & Adsit, D. J. (1997). Accountability: The Achilles heel of multisource feedback. *Group & Organization Management, 22*(2), 162-184.

Lopes, P. N., Côté, S., & Salovey, P. (2005). An ability model of emotional intelligence: Implications for assessment and training. In V. Druskat, F. Sala & G. G. Mount (Eds), *Linking emotional intelligence and performance at work: Current research evidence* (pp. 53-80): Erlbaum,.

Lubinski, D. (2000). Scientific and social significance of assessing individual differences: Sinking shafts at a few critical points. In *Annual Review of Psychology* (Vol. 51, pp. 405-444).

Luthans, F. (1976). *Introduction to management: A contingency approach.* New York: McGraw-Hill.

Luthans, F. (2002). The need for and meaning of positive organizational behavior. *Journal of Organizational Behavior, 26*(6), 695-706.

Luthans, F., Rosenkrantz, S. A., & Hennessey, H. W. (1985). What do successful managers really do? An observation of managerial activities. *The Journal of Applied Behavioral Science, 21*(3), 255-270.

Luthans, F., Welsh, D. H., & Lewis, A. T. (1988). A descriptive study of managerial effectiveness. *Group & Organization Studies, 13*(2), 148-162.

Lyubomirsky, S., King, L., & Diener, E. (2005). The benefits of frequent positive affect: Does happiness lead to success? *Psychological Bulletin 131*(6), 803-855.

MacCallum, R. C. (1995). Model specification: Procedures, strategies, and related issues. In R. H. Hoyle (Ed), *Structural equation modeling: Concepts, issues and applications* (pp. 16-36). Thousand Oaks, California: Sage.

MacCallum, R. C., Browne, M. W., & Sugawara, H. M. (1996). Power analysis and determination of sample size for covariance structure modeling. *Psychological Methods, 1*(2), 130-149.

Mackay, C. J., Cox, T., Burrows, G. C., & Lazzarini, A. J. (1978). An inventory for the measurement of self-reported stress and arousal. *British Journal of Social and Clinical Psychology, 17*(3), 283-284.

Mackay, H. (1993). *Reinventing Australia: The mind and mood of Australia in the 90's*. Sydney, New South Wales: Angus & Robertson.

MacKenzie, S. B., Podsakoff, P. M., & Fetter, R. (1991). Organisational citizenship behaviour and objective productivity as determinants of managerial evaluations of salespersons' performance. *Organizational Behavior and Human Decision Processes*, 123-150.

Magnus, K., Diener, E., & Fujita, F. (1993). Extraversion and neuroticism as predictors of objective life events, a longitudinal study. *Journal of Personality and Social Psychology, 65*, 1046-1053.

Mahoney, T. A. (Ed). (1988). *Productivity defined. The relativity of efficiency, effectiveness and change*. San Francisco: Jossey-Bass.

Maier, N. R. F. (1958). *The appraisal interview: Objectives, methods and skills*. New York: Wiley.

Maister, H. (2001). *Practice what you preach: What managers must do to achieve a high performance culture*. New York: Free Press.

Maney, K. (2002). *Google's HQ provides blast from Silicon Valley past*: USA Today. Retrieved June 16. 2005, from http://www.usatoday.com/tech/columnist/2002/01/09/maney.htm

Manion, J. (2005). *Create a positive workplace! Practical strategies to retain today's workforce and find tomorrow's*. Chicago: Health Forum /AHA.

Mardia, K. V. (1974). Applications for some measures of multivariate skewness and kurtosis in testing normality and robustness studies. *Sankhva: The Indian Journal of Statistics, Series B, 36*, 115-128.

Marsh, H. W. (1989). Confirmatory factor analysis of multitrait-multimethod data: Many problems and a few solutions. *Applied Psychological Measurement, 13*, 335-361.

Martin, M., & Stang, D. (1978). *The Pollyanna Principle*. Cambridge, MA: Schenkman.

Martin, P. (2005). *Making happy people: The nature of happiness and its origins in childhood*. London, United Kingdom: Fourth Estate.

Martin, R., & Wall, T. D. (1989). Attentional demand and cost responsibility as stressors in shopfloor jobs. *Academy of Management Journal, 32,* March, 69-86.

Martinko, M. J., & Gardner, W. L. (1985). Beyond structured observation: Methodological issues and new directions. *Academy of Management Review, 10*(4), 676.

Martinko, M. J., & Gardner, W. L. (1990). Structured observation of managerial work: A replication and synthesis. *Journal of Management Studies, 27*(3), 329-357.

Maslow, A. H. (1949). The expressive component of behavior. *Psychological Review, 56,* 261-272.

Maslow, A. H. (1950). *Self-actualising people: A study of psychological health.* Paper presented at the Personality Symposium.

Maslow, A. H. (1968). *Towards a psychology of being* (2nd ed). New York: Van Nostrand.

Maslow, A. H. (1970). *Motivation and personality* (2nd ed). New York: Harper and Row.

Mastekaasa, A. (1994). Marital status, distress, and well-being: An international comparison. *Journal of Comparative Family Studies, 25,* 183-205.

Mathieu, J. E., & Zajac, D. M. (1990). A review and meta-analysis of the antecedents, correlates, and consequences of organizational commitment. *Psychological Bulletin, 108*(2), 171-194.

Matthews, G., Davies, D. R., Westerman, S. J., & Stammers, R. B. (2000). *Human performance, cognition, stress, and individual differences.* London, United Kingdom: Routledge.

Mayer, J., Caruso, D. R., & Salovey, P. (2000). Selecting a measure of emotional intelligence: The case for ability scales. In R. R. Bar-On & J. D. A. Parker (Eds), *The handbook of emotional intelligence* (pp. 320-342). San Francisco: Jossey-Bass.

Mayer, J. D. (1999). Emotional intelligence: popular or scientific psychology? *APA Monitor, 30,* 50.

Mayer, J. D., Panter, A. T., Salovey, P., Caruso, D. R., & Sitarenios, G. (2005). A Discrepancy in Analyses of the MSCEIT-Resolving the Mystery and Understanding Its Implications: A Reply to Gignac. *Emotion, 5*(2), 236-237.

Mayer, J. D., & Salovey, P. (1993). The intelligence of emotional intelligence. *Intelligence, 17*(4), 433-442.

Mayer, J. D., & Salovey, P. (1997). What is emotional intelligence? In P. S. D. Sluyter (Ed), *Emotional development and emotional intelligence: Implications for educators* (pp. pp. 3-31). New York: Basic Books.

Mayer, J. D., Salovey, P., & Caruso, D. R. (2000). Models of emotional intelligence. In R. J. Sternberg (Ed), *Handbook of Human Intelligence* (2 ed). New York: Cambridge.

Mayer, J. D., Salovey, P., & Caruso, D. R. (2002). *Mayer–Salovey–Caruso Emotional Intelligence Test (MSCEIT) users manual*. Toronto, Canada: MHS.

Mayer, J. D., Salovey, P., & Caruso, D. R. (2004a). Emotional intelligence: theory, findings, and implications. *Psychological Inquiry, 60*, 197-215.

Mayer, J. D., Salovey, P., & Caruso, D. R. (2004b). A further consideration of issues of emotional intelligence. *Psychological Inquiry, 60*, 249-255.

Mayer, R. C., & Schoorman, F. D. (1992). Predicting participation and production outcomes through a two-dimensional model of organizational commitment. *Academy of Management Journal, 35*(3), 671-684.

Mayo, E. (1933). *The human problems of an industrial civilization*. London, United Kingdom: Macmillan.

McCall, M. W., Lombardo, M. M., & Morrison, A. M. (1988). *The lessons of experience*. New York: Lexington.

McClelland, D. (1985). *Human motivation*. Glenview, Illinois: Scott Foresman Publishers.

McClelland, D. C. (1973). Testing for competence rather than for intelligence. *American Psychologist, 28*(1), 1-14.

McCoy, R. A., Campbell, J. P., & Cudeck, R. (1994). A confirmatory test of a model of performance determinants. *Journal of Applied Psychology, 79*(4), 493-504.

McCrae, R. R., & Costa, P. T. (1990). *Personality in adulthood*. New York: Guilford.

McDaniel, M. A., Schmidt, F. L., & Hunter, J. E. (1988). Job experience correlates of job performance. *Journal of Applied Psychology, 73*, 327-330.

McDonald, D., & Smith, A. (1995). A proven connection: Performance management and business results. *Compensation and Benefits Review, 27*(1), 59-62.

McDougal, W. (1905). *Physiological psychology*. London, United Kingdom: Aldine House.

McEvoy, G. M., & Cascio, W. F. (1989). Cumulative evidence of the relationship between employee age and job performance. *Journal of Applied Psychology, 74*, 11-17.

McGovern, T. V., Jones, B. W., & , & Morris, S. E. (1978). Comparison of professional versus student ratings of job interviewee behavior. *Journal of Counseling Psychology, 26*(176-179).

McKenna, E. F. (1994). *Business psychology and organisational behaviour*. Mahwah, New Jersey: Lawrence Erlbaum Associates.

McKnight, M. R. (1991). Management skill development: What it is. What it is not. In J. D. Bigelow (Ed), *Managerial skills: Explorations in practical knowledge* (pp. 204-218). Newbury Park, California: Sage.

McLennan, W. (1997). *Australian Standard Classification of Occupations*. Canberra: Commonwealth of Australia.

Meyer, G. J., & Shack, J. R. (1989). Structural convergence of mood and personality: Evidence for old and new directions. *Journal of Personality and Social Psychology, 57*(4), 691-706.

Meyer, J. P., & Allen, N. J. (1997). *Commitment in the workplace: Theory, research and application*. Thousand Oaks, California: Sage.

Meyer, J. P., Allen, N. J., & Smith, C. A. (1993). Commitment to organizations and occupations: Extension and test of a three-component conceptualization. *Journal of Applied Psychology, 78*, 538-551.

Meyer, J. P., Paunonen, S. V., Gellatly, I. R., Goffin, R. D., & Jackson, D. N. (1989). Organizational commitment and job performance: It's the nature of the commitment that counts. *Journal of Applied Psychology, 74*(1), 152-156.

Micceri, T. (1989). The unicorn, the normal curve, and other improbable creatures. *Psychological Bulletin, 105*(1), 156-166.

Millar, D. J. (1990). Mental health and the workplace. An interchangeable partnership. *American Psychologist, 45*(10), 1165-1166.

Mineka, S., Watson, D., & Clark, L. A. (1998). Comorbidity of anxiety and unipolar mood disorders. *Annual Review of Psychology, 49*, 377-412.

Miner, J. B. (1978). Twenty years of research on role motivation theory of managerial effectiveness. *Personnel Psychology, 31*, 739-760.

Mintzberg, H. (1973). *The nature of managerial work*: Harper Row.

Mintzberg, H. (1980). *The nature of managerial work*. Englewood Cliffs, New Jersey: Prentice-Hall.

Mintzberg, H. (2004). *Managers not MBAs: A hard look at the soft practice of managing and management development.* San Francisco. California: Berrett-Koehler.

Mitchell, T. R. (1979). Organizational behaviour. *Annual Review of Psychology, 30*, 243-281.

Mitchell, T. R. (1985). An evaluation of the validity of correlation research conducted in organizations. *Academy of Management Review, 10*(2), 192-205.

Mitchell, T. R., Green, S. G., & , & Wood, R. E. (Eds). (1981). *An attributional model of leadership and the poor performing subordinate.* Greenwich, CT: JAI Press.

Moorhead, G., & Griffin, R. W. (1992). Organizational behavior. In *Organization change and development.* Boston, Massachusetts.

Moorman, R. H. (1993). The influence of cognitive and effective based job satisfaction measures on the relationship between satisfaction and organizational citizenship behavior. *Human Relations, 46*(6), 759-776.

Moorman, R. H., & Podsakoff, P. M. (1982). A meta-analytic review and empirical test of the potential confounding effects of social desirability response sets in organizational behaviour research. *Journal of Occupational and Organizational Psychology, 65, June,* 131-149.

Morgan, G., & Smircich, L. (1980). The case of qualitative research. *Academy of Management Review, 5*(4), 491-500.

Morrison, E. W. (1996). OCB as a critical link between HR practices and service quality. *Human Resource Management, 35*(4), 493-512.

Morse, J. J., & Wagner, F. R. (1978). Measuring the process of managerial effectiveness. *Academy of Management Journal, 21*(1), 23-35.

Motowidlo, S. J., Borman, W. C., & Schmit, M. J. (1997). A theory of individual differences in task and contextual performance. *Human Performance, 10*(2), 71-83.

Motowidlo, S. J., Packard, J. S., & Manning, M. R. (1986). Occupational stress: It's causes and consequences for job performance. *Journal of Applied Psychology, 17*(4), 618-629.

Motowidlo, S. J., & Schmit, M. J. (1999). Performance assessment in unique jobs. In D. R. Llgen & E. D. Pulakos (Eds), *The changing nature of performance.* San Francisco: Jossey-Bass.

Motowidlo, S. J., & Van Scotter, J. R. (1994). Evidence that task performance should be distinguished from contextual performance. *Journal of Applied Psychology, 79*(4), 475-480.

Mount, M. K., & Barrick, M. R. (Eds). (1995). *The big five personality dimensions: Implications for research and practice in human resources management*: JAI Press, Inc.

Mount, M. K., Sytsma, M. R., Hazucha, J. F., & Holt, K. E. (1997). Rater-ratee race effects in developmental performance ratings of managers. *Personnel Psychology, 50*(1), 51-69.

Münsterberg, H. (1913). *Psychology and Industrial Efficiency*: Houghton Mifflin Company, The Riverside Press Cambridge.

Murphy, K., & Balzer, W. (1986). Systematic distortions in memory-based behavior ratings and performance evaluations: Consequences for rating accuracy. *Journal of Applied Psychology, 71*(1), 39-44.

Murphy, K. R. (1990). Job performance and productivity. In K. R. Murphy, & F. E. Saal (Ed), *Psychology in organizations: Integrating science and practice*. Hillside, New Jersey: Lawrence Erlbaum Associates.

Murphy, K. R. (1994). Potential effects of banding as a function of test reliability,. *Personnel Psychology, 47*, 477-495.

Murphy, K. R., & Cleveland, J. N. (1991). *Performance appraisal: An organizational perspective*. Needham Heights, Massachusetts: Allyn & Bacon.

Murphy, K. R., & Cleveland, J. N. (1995). *Understanding performance Appraisal: Social, Organizational. and goal based perspectives*. Thousand Oaks, CA: Sage.

Murphy, R. J. L. (1982). Sex differences in objective test performance. *British Journal of Educational Psychology, 52*, 213-219.

Nankervis, A., Compton, R., & McCarthy, T. (1996). *Strategic Human Resource Management*. Victoria: Thomson.

Nankervis, A. R., Compton, R. L., & McCarthy, T. E. (2004). *Strategic human resource management: Strategies and processes in strategic human resource management* (5th ed). South Melbourne, Victoria: Nelson.

Nathan, B. R., & Alexander, R. A. (1988). A comparison of criteria for test validation: A meta-analytic investigation. *Personnel Psychology, 41*, 517-535.

Neal, A., & Griffin, M. A. (1999). Developing a model of individual performance for human resource management. *Asia Pacific Journal of Human Resources, 37*(2), 244-259.

Nicholson, N. (2000). *Managing the human animal*. New York: Crown

Publishers.

Nickols, F. (2000). *Don't redesign your company's performance appraisal system, scrap it! A look at the costs and benefits of performance appraisal systems*: Distance Consulting.

Nie, N., Hull, H., Jenkins, J., Steinbrenner, K., & Bent, D. (1975). *Statistical package for the social sciences* (2nd ed). New York: McGraw-Hill.

Niehoff, B. P., & Moorman, R. H. (1993). Justice as a mediator of the relationship between methods of monitoring and organizational citizenship behavior. *Academy of Management Journal, 36*(3), 527-556.

Noe, R. A., Hollenbeck, J. R., Gerhart, B., & Wright, P. M. (1994). *Human resource management: Gaining a competitive advantage* (1st ed). Chicago, Illinois: Irwin.

Nunnally, J. C. (1978). *Psychometric theory* (2nd ed). New York: McGraw-Hill.

Nytrö, K., Saksvik, P. Ø., Mikkelsen, A., Bohle, P., & Quinlan, M. (2000). An appraisal of key factors in the implementation of occupational stress interventions. *Work and Stress, 13*, 213-225.

O'Reilly, C. A., & Pfeffer, J. (2000). *Hidden value: How great companies achieve extraordinary results with ordinary people*. Boston, Massachusetts: Harvard University Press.

Offermann, L. R., Bailey, J. R., Vasilopoulos, N. L., Seal, C., & Sass, M. (2004). The relative contribution of emotional competence and cognitive ability to individual and team performance. *Human Performance, 17*, 219-243.

Ohmae, K. (1995). *The end of the nation state*. New York: Harper Collins.

Ones, D. S., & Viswesvaran, C. (1999). Relative importance of personality dimensions for expatriate selection: A policy capturing study. *Human Performance, 12*, 275-294.

Organ, D. W. (1977). A reappraisal and reinterpretation of the satisfaction-causes-performance hypothesis. *Academy of Management Review, 2*(1), 46-53.

Organ, D. W. (1988). *Organizational citizenship behavior: The good soldier syndrome*. Lexington, Massachusetts: Lexington Books.

Organ, D. W. (1990). The motivational basis of organizational citizenship behavior. *Research in Organizational Behavior, 12*, 43-72.

Organ, D. W. (1994a). Organizational citizenship behavior and the good soldier. In M. G. Rumsey, C. B. Walker. & J. H. Harris (Eds),

Personnel selection and classification (pp. 53-68). Hillsdale, New Jersey: Lawrence Erlbaum Associates.

Organ, D. W. (1994b). Personality and organisational citizenship behavior. *Journal of Management, 20*(2), 465-478.

Organ, D. W. (1997). Organizational citizenship behavior: It's construct clean-up time. *Human Performance, 10*(2), 85-97.

Organ, D. W., & Konovsky, M. A. (1989). Cognitive versus affective determinants of organisational citizenship behaviour. *Journal of Applied Psychology, 74*(1), 157-164.

Organ, D. W., & Lingl, A. (1995). Personality, satisfaction, and organisational citizenship behaviour. *Journal of Social Psychology, 135*(3), 339-350.

Organ, D. W., & Moorman, R. H. (1993). Fairness and organizational citizenship behavior: What are the connections? *Social Justice Research, 6,* 5-18.

Organ, D. W., & Near, J. P. (1985). Cognitions vs affect in measures of job satisfaction. *International Journal of Psychology, 20,* 241-253.

Organ, D. W., & Paine, J. (1999). A new kind of performance for industrial and organizational psychology: Recent contributions to the study of organizational citizenship behavior. In C. L. Cooper & I. T. Robertson (Eds), *International review of industrial and organizational psychology* (pp. 338-368). Chichester, New York: Wiley.

Organ, D. W., & Ryan, K. (1995). A meta-analytic review of attitudinal and dispositional predictors of organizational citizenship behavior. *Personnel Psychology, 48*(4), 775-802.

Oshagbemi, T. (1991). Overall job satisfaction: How good are single vs. multiple item measures? *Journal of Managerial Psychology, 14,* 388-403.

Osipow, S. H., & Davis, A. S. (1988). The relationship of coping resources to occupational stress and strain. *Journal of Vocational Behavior, 32*(1), 1-15.

Ostroff, C., & Ford, J. K. (1989). Assessing training needs: Critical levels of analysis. In G. I. Associates (Ed), *Training and Development in organizations* (pp. 25-62). San Francisco: Jossey-Bass.

Page, C., Wilson, M., & Kolb, D. (1994). *Management competencies in New Zealand.* Wellington, Otago: Ministry of Commerce.

Palmer, B. R., Gignac, G. E., Manocha, R., & Stough, C. (2005). A psychometric evaluation of the Mayer-Salovey-Caruso Emotional Intelligence Test Version 2.0. *Intelligence, 33*, 285-305.

Palmer, I., & Dunford, R. (1996). Interrogating reframing: Evaluating metaphor-based analyses of organizations. In S. R. Clegg & G. Palmer (Eds), *The politics of Management Knowledge*. London: Thousand Oaks.

Park, A. (2005, January 17th). How full is that glass, really? *Time, 165*, A54-A61.

Parkes, K. R. (1990). Coping, negative affectivity and the work environment: Additive and interactive predictors of mental health. *Journal of Applied Psychology, 75*(4), 399-409.

Parkes, K. R. (1991). Locus of control as moderator: An explanation for additive versus interactive findings in the demand-discretion model for work stress. *British Journal of Psychology, 82*(3), 291-312.

Parkes, K. R., Mendham, C. A., & Von Rabenau, C. (1994). Social support and the demand-discretion model of job stress: Tests of additive and interactive effects in two samples. *Journal of Vocational Behavior, 44*(1), 99-113.

Parks, J. M., & Kidder, D. L. (1994). Til death us do part ... Changing work relationships in the 1990s. In C. L. Cooper & D. M. Rousseau (Eds), *Trends in organisational behaviour* (Vol. 1, pp. 111-136). Chichester, England: Wiley.

Patterson, M., West, M. A., Lawthom, R., & Nickell, S. (1997). Impact of people management practices on business performance. *Issues in People Management, 22*, 1-28.

Payne, R. L., & Fletcher, B. (1983). Job demands, supports and constraints as predictors of psychological strain among schoolteachers. *Journal of Vocational Behavior, 22*(2), 136-147.

Payne, W. L. (1986). A study of emotion, developing emotional intelligence: self-integration; relating to fear, pain, and desire. *Dissertation Abstracts International, 62(12-B), 6008. (UMI No. AAI3035464), 47*, 203A.

Pearsall, P. (1988). *Super immunity: Master your emotions and improve your health*. New York: McGraw-Hill.

Peck, M. S. (1978). *The road less travelled: A new psychology of love, traditional values and spiritual growth*. New York: Simon & Schuster.

Pedhazur, E. J. (1982). *Multiple regression in behavioral research:*

Explanation and prediction (2nd ed). Fort Worth, Texas: Holt, Rhinehart and Winston.

Penner, L. A., Midili, A. R., & Kegelmeyer, J. (1997). Beyond job attitudes: A personality and social psychology perspective on the causes of organizational citizenship behavior. *Human Performance, 10*(2), 111-131.

Perrow, C. (1986). *Complex organizations: A critical essay* (3rd ed). New York: Random House.

Peterson, M. F., Smith, P. B., Akande, A., Ayestaran, S., Bochner, S., Callan, V., et al. (1995). Role conflict, ambiguity, and overload: A 21-nation study. *Academy of Management Journal, 38*(2), 429-445.

Pettigrew, A., & Whipp, R. (1991). *Managing change for competitive success*. Oxford, United Kingdom: Blackwell.

Pfeffer, J. (1982). *Organizations and organization theory*. Boston, Massachusetts: Pitman.

Pfeffer, J. (1994). *Competitive advantage through people: Unleashing the power of the work force*. Boston, Massachusetts: Harvard Business School Press.

Pithers, R. T., Athanasou, J. A., & Cornford, I. R. (1996). Development of a set of Australian occupational descriptors. *Asia Pacific Journal of Human Resources, 33*(3), 140-146.

Ployhart, R. E., Wiechmann, D., Schmitt, N., Sacco, J. M., & Rogg, K. (2003). The cross-cultural equivalence of job performance ratings. *Human Performance, 16*(1), 49-79.

Podsakoff, P. M., Ahearne, M., & MacKenzie, S. B. (1997). Organizational citizenship behavior and the quantity and quality of work group performance. *Journal of Applied Psychology, 82*(2), 262-270.

Podsakoff, P. M., & MacKenzie, S. B. (1994). Organizational citizenship behavior and sales unit effectiveness. *Journal of Marketing Research, 31*(3), 351-363.

Podsakoff, P. M., & MacKenzie, S. B. (1997). Impact of organizational citizenship behavior on organizational performance: A review and suggestions for future research. *Human Performance, 10*(2), 133-151.

Podsakoff, P. M., MacKenzie, S. B., Morman, R. H., & Fetter, R. (1990). Transformational leader behaviors and their effects on followers trust in leader, satisfaction, and organizational citizenship behavior. *The Leadership Quarterly, 1*(2), 107-142.

Podsakoff, P. M., & Organ, D. W. (1986). Self-reports in organizational research: Problems and prospects. *Journal of Management, 12*(4), 531-544.

Pond, S. B., Nacoste, R. W., Mohr, M. F., & Rodriguez, C. M. (1997). The measurement of organizational citizenship behavior: Are we assuming too much? *Journal of Applied Social Psychology, 27*(17), 1527-1544.

Porter, L. W. (1963). Where is the organization man? *Harvard Business Review, 41*(6), 53-61.

Porter, M. E. (1990). *The competitive advantage of nations.* London, United Kingdom: Macmillan.

Prati, L., Douglas, C., Ferris, G. R., Ammeter, A. P., & Buckley, M. R. (2003). Emotional intelligence, leadership effectiveness, and team outcomes. *International Journal of Organizational Analysis*(11), 21-40.

Pressman, S. D., & Cohen, S. (2005). Does positive affect influence health? *Psychological Bulletin, 131*(6), 925-971.

Price, J. L., & Mueller, C. W. (1986). *Handbook of organizational measurement.* Marshfield, Massachusetts: Pitman.

Pritchard, R. D., & Roth, P. J. (1991). Accounting for non-linear utility functions in composite measures of productivity and performance. *Organizational Behavior and Human Decision Processes, 50*(2), 341-359.

Pritzker, M. A. (2002). The relationship among CEO dispositional attributes, transformational leadership behaviors and performance effectiveness. *Dissertation Abstracts International, 62(12-B), 6008. (UMI No. AAI3035464).*

Purcell, J. (2004). *The HRM-Performance link: Why, how and when does people management impact on organisational performance?* : University of Limerick.

Quinn, J. B. (1992). *Intelligent enterprise.* New York: Free Press.

Quinn, R. E. (1988). *Beyond rational management.* San Francisco, California: Jossey-Bass.

Quinn, R. E., Faerman, S. R., Thompson, M. P., & McGrath, M. R. (1996). *Becoming a master manager: A competency framework* (2 ed). New York: Wiley.

Quinn, R. E., Kahn, J. A., & Mandl, M. J. (1994). Perspectives on organizational change: Exploring movement at the interface. In J.

Greenberg (Ed), *Organizational behavior: The state of the science* (pp. 109-133). Hillsdale, New Jersey: Lawrence Erlbaum Associates.

Quinn, R. E., Spreitzer, G. M., & Hart, S. (1992). Integrating the extremes: Crucial skills for managerial effectiveness. In S. Srivastva, R. E. Fry & Associates (Eds), *Executive and organizational continuity: Managing the paradoxes of stability and change* (pp. 92-109). San Francisco, California: Jossey-Bass.

Quinones, M. A., Ford, J. K., & Teachout, M. S. (1995). The relationship between work experience and job performance: A conceptual and meta-analytic review. *Personnel Psychology, 48*, 887-910.

Raghunathan, T. R. (1995). A review of scale development practices in the study of organizations. *Journal of Management, 21*(5), 967-988.

Randall, D. M. (1990). The consequences of organizational commitment: Methodological investigation. *Journal of Organizational Behavior, 11*(5), 361-378.

Rao, M. V. H., & Pasmore, W. A. (1989). Knowledge and interests in organizational studies: A conflict of interpretations. *Organization Studies, 10*(2), 225-239.

Rasmussen, K. G. (1984). Nonverbal behavior, verbal behavior, resume credentials, and selection interview outcomes. *Journal of Applied Psychology, 69*, 551-556.

Ree, M. J., & Caretta, T. R. (1998). General cognitive ability and occupational performance. *International Review of Industrial and Organizational Psychology and Aging, 13*, 159-184.

Ree, M. J., & Carretta, T. R. (2002). g2K. *Human Performance, 15*(1/2), 3-23.

Ree, M. J., & Earles, J. A. (1992). Intelligence is the best predictor of job performance. *Current Directions in Psychological Science, 1*, 86—89.

Reichers, A. E. (1986). Conflict and organizational commitment. *Journal of Applied Psychology, 71*(3), 508-514.

Reinhold, B. R. (1997). *Toxic work: How to overcome stress, overload and burnout and revitalize your career.* New York: Plume Publishers.

Revesz, P. (1979). On the nonparametric estimation of the regression function. *Problems of Control and Confirmation Theory, 8*, 297-302.

Rheem, H. (1996). Performance management programs - Do they make any difference? *Harvard Business Review*, 3-4.

Rindskopf, D. (1984). Structural equation models: Empirical identification, heywood cases, and related problems. *Sociological Methods Research, 13*(August), 109-119.

Rizzo, J. R., House, R. J., & Lirtzman, S. I. (1970). Role conflict and ambiguity in complex organizations. *Administrative Science Quarterly, 15*(4), 150-163.

Robbins, S. P., Millett, B., Cacioppe, R., & Waters-Marsh, T. (1998). *Organisational behaviour: Leading and managing in Australia and New Zealand* (2nd ed). Sydney, New South Wales: Prentice Hall.

Robbins, S. P., Millett, B., Cacioppe, R., & Waters-Marsh, T. (2001). *Leading and Managing in Australia and New Zealand* (3rd ed): Prentice Hall Australia Ltd.

Roberts, R. D., Zeidner, M., & Matthews, G. (2001). Does emotional intelligence meet traditional standards for an intelligence? Some new data and conclusions. *Emotion, 1*, 196-231.

Robertson, I. T., & Kinder, A. (1993). Personality and job competencies: The criterion-related validity on some personality variables. *Journal of Occupational and Organizational Psychology, 66*(3), 225-244.

Robinson, S. L., & Wolfe-Morrison, E. (1995). Psychological contracts and OCB: The effect of unfulfilled obligations on civic virtue behaviour. *Journal of Organizational Behavior, 16*(3), 289-298.

Roethlisberger, F. J., & Dickson, W. J. (1939). *Management and the worker*. Cambridge, Massachusetts: Harvard University Press.

Rogers, C. R. (1961). *On becoming a person*. Boston, Massachusetts: Houghton Mifflin.

Rosenberg, S., & Sedlak, A. (1972). *Structural representations of implicit personality theory* (Vol. 6). New York: Academic Press.

Ross, P. (1989). Work, unemployment and mental health. *Journal of Occupational Psychology, 87*.

Rothman, J., & Stewart-Weeks, M. (1995). *Enterprising nation: Renewing Australia's managers to meet the challenges of the Asia-Pacific century. Industry task force on leadership and management skills* (Vol. 1). Canberra, Australian Capital Territory: Australian Government Printing Service.

Rowe, P. M. (1988). The nature of work experience. *Canadian Psychology, 29*, 109-115.

Rozell, E. J., Pettijohn, C. E., & Parker, R. S. (2002). An empirical evaluation of emotional intelligence: The Impact on management development. *The Journal of Management Development, 21*(4), 272-289.

Russell, B. (1930). *The Conquest of Happiness.* London, United Kingdom: Allen & Unwin.

Russell, J. A. (1980). A circumplex model of affect. *Journal of Personality and Social Psychology, 39,* 1161-1178.

Russell, J. A., & Barrett, L. F. (1999). Core affect, prototypical emotional episodes, and other things called emotion: Dissecting the elephant. *Journal of Personality and Social Psychology, 76*(5), 805-819.

Russell, J. A., & Carroll, J. M. (1999). On the bipolarity of positive and negative affect. *Psychological Bulletin, 125*(1), 3-30.

Russell, J. A., & Feldman Barrett, L. (1999). Core affect, prototypical emotional episodes, and other things called emotion: Dissecting the elephant. *Journal of Personality and Social Psychology, 76,* 805-819.

Ryff, C. D., & Keyes, C. L. M. (1995). The structure of psychological well-being revisited. *Journal of Personality and Social Psychology, 69*(4), 719-727.

Sackett, P. R., & Larson, J. R. (1991). Research strategies and tactics in industrial and organizational psychology. In M. D. Dunnette & L. M. Hough (Eds), *Handbook of Industrial and Organizational Psychology* (2nd ed, pp. 419-428). Palo Alto, California: Consulting Psychologists Press.

Saks, A. M. (1996). The relationship between the amount and helpfulness of entry training and work outcomes. *Human Relations, 49*(4), 429-451.

Salgado, J., & Anderson, N. (2002). Cognitive and GMA Testing in the European Community: Issues and Evidence. *Human Performance, 15*(1/2), 75-96.

Salgado, J. F., Anderson, N., Moscoso, S., Bertua, C., de Fruyt, F., Rolland, J. P., et al. (2003). A meta-analytic study of general mental ability validity for different occupations in the European Community. *Journal of Applied Psychology, 88*(6), 1068-1081.

Salgado, J. F., Viswesvaran, C., & Ones, D. S. (Eds). (2001). *Predictors used for personnel selection: An overview of constructs, methods and techniques.* London: Sage.

Salovey, P., Hsee, C. K., & Mayer, J. D. (1993). Emotional intelligence and the self-regulation of affect. In D.M. Wegney & J.W. Pennebaker (Ed), *Handbook of mental control* (pp. 258-277). Englewood Cliffs, NJ: Prentice Hall.

Salovey, P., & Mayer, J. D. (1990). Emotional intelligence. *Imagination, Cognition and Personality, 9*(3), 185-211.

Salovey, P., Rothman, A. J., Detweller, J. B., & Steward, W. T. (2000). Emotional states and physical health. *American psychologist, 55*, 110-121.

Saltzman, J., Strauss, E., Hunter, M., & Spellacy, F. (1998). Validity of the Wonderlic Personnel Test. *Archives of Clinical Neuropsychology, 13*, 611-616.

Sanchez, R., & Heane, A. (1996). *Reinventing strategic management: New theory and practice for competence-based competition.* Discussion paper Thesis. The University of Western Australia.

Sandwith, P. (1993). A hierarchy of management training requirements: The competency domain model. *Public Personnel Management, 22*(1), 43-62.

Satorra, A., & Bentler, P. M. (1988). *Scaling corrections for chi-square statistics in covariance structure analysis.* Alexandria, Virginia: American Statistical Association.

Saul, P. (1989). Using management competencies to improve management performance and stimulate self development. *Asia Pacific Resource Management*(August), 74-85.

Sauter, S. L., & Murphy, L. R. (2003). *Monitoring the changing organization at work: International practices and new developments in the United States.*Cincinnati, Ohio: National Institute for Occupational Safety and Health, Organizational Science and Human Factors Branch. Retrieved December 1. 2004, from http://www.ncbi.nlm.nih.gov/entrez/query.fcgi?cmd=Retrieve&db=PubMed&list_uids=14758746&dopt=Abstract

Savery, L., Dawkins, P., & Mazzarol, T. (1995). *Enterprising nation: Renewing Australia's managers to meet the challenges of the Asia-Pacific Century. Industry Task Force on leadership and management skills* (Vol. 1, Chapter 14). Deakin, Canberra: Australian Government Publishing Service.

Saville, S., & Holdsworth, S. (1993). *SHL Core Competency model: The inventory of management competencies.* Sydney, New South Wales: Saville & Holdsworth.

Schaubroeck, J., Ganster, D. C., & Fox, M. L. (1992). Dispositional affect and work-related stress. *Journal of Applied Psychology, 77*(3), 322-335.

Schimmack, U. (2001). Please, displeasure, and mixed feelings: Are semantic opposites mutually exclusive? *Cognition and Emotion, 15*(1), 81-97.

Schmidt, F. L. (Ed). (1993). *Personnel psychology at the cutting edge.* San Francisco: Jossey Bass.

Schmidt, F. L., & Hunter, J. E. (1981). Employment testing: Old theories and new research findings. *American Psychologist,* 1128—1137.

Schmidt, F. L., & Hunter, J. E. (1983). Individual differences in productivity: An empirical test of estimates derived from studies of selection procedure utility. *Journal of Applied Psychology,* 407-415.

Schmidt, F. L., & Hunter, J. E. (1992). Development of causal models of processes determining job performance. *Current Directions in Psychological Science, 1*(89—92).

Schmidt, F. L., & Hunter, J. E. (1998). The validity and utility of selection methods in personnel psychology: Practical and theoretical implications of 85 years of research findings. *Psychological Bulletin, 124,* 262-274.

Schmidt, F. L., & Hunter, J. E. (2004). General mental ability in the world of work: Occupational attainment and job performance. *Journal of Personality and Social Psychology*(86), 162-173.

Schmidt, F. L., Hunter, J. E., McKenzie, R. C., & Muldrow, T. W. (1979). The impact of valid selection procedures on work-force productivity. *Journal of Applied Psychology, 64,* 609-626.

Schmidt, F. L., Hunter, J. E., Outerbridge, A. M., & Trattner, M. H. (1986). The economic impact of job selection methods on the size, productivity, and payroll costs of the federal work-force: An empirical demonstration. *Personnel Psychology, 39,* 1-29.

Schmidt, F. L., Hunter, J. E., & Outerbridge, A. N. (1986). The impact of job experience and ability on job knowledge, work sample performance, and supervisory ratings of job performance. *Journal of Applied Psychology, 71,* 432—439.

Schmidt, F. L., Ones, D. S., & Hunter, J. E. (1992). Personnel selection. *Annual review of Psychology, 43,* 627—670.

Schmitt, N. (1994). Method bias: The importance of theory and measurement. *Journal of Organizational Behavior, 15*(5), 393-

398.

Schmitt, N., & Cohen, S. (1989). Internal analyses of task ratings by job incumbents. *Journal of Applied Psychology, 74*(96-104).

Schmitt, N., & Stults, D. M. (1986). Methodology review: Analysis of multitrait-multimethod matrices. *Applied Psychological Measurement, 10*, 1-22.

Schnake, M., Dumler, M. P., & Cochran, D. S. (1993). The relationship between traditional leadership, super leadership and organizational citizenship behavior. *Group & Organization Management, 18*(3), 352-365.

Schuler, R. S., & Jackson, S. E. (1987). Organizational strategy and organizational level as determinants of human resource management. *Human Resource Planning, 10*(3), 125-141.

Schuler, R. S., & Macmillan, I. (1984). Gaining competition advantage through human resource management practices. *Human Resource Management, 23*(3), 241-255.

Schwarz, N., & Bless, H. (1991). Happy and mindless, but sad and smart? The impact of effective states on analytic reasoning. In J. P. Forgas (Ed), *Emotion and social judgement*. Oxford, United Kingdom: Pergamon Press.

Schweiger, D. M., & De Nisi, A. S. (1991). Communications with workers following a merger: A longitudinal experiment. *Academy of Management Journal, 34*(1), 110-135.

Schweizer, K. (1992). A correlation-based decision-rule for determining the number of clusters and its efficiency in uni-and multi-level data. *Multivariate Behavioral Research, 27*, 77-94.

Scott, W. R. (1992). *Organizations: Rationale, natural, and open systems* (3rd ed). NJ: Simon & Schuster.

Scullen, S. E., Mount, M. K., & Judge, T. A. (2003). Evidence of the construct validity of developmental ratings of managerial performance. *Journal of Applied Psychology, 88*(1), 50-66.

Seligman, M. (2002). *Using the new positive psychology to realize your potential for lasting fulfillment*. New York: Free Press.

Seligman, M. E. P., & Csikszentmihalyi, M. (2000). Positive psychology: An introduction. *American Psychologist, 55*, 5-14.

Seltzer, J., & Bass, B. M. (1990). Transformational leadership: Beyond initiation and consideration. *Journal of Management, 16*, 693-703.

Selye, H. (1974). *The stress of life*. New York: McGraw-Hill.

Senge, P. M. (1990). *The fifth discipline: The art and practice of the learning organization*. New York: Doubleday - Currency.

Sevastos, P., Smith, L., & Cordery, J. L. (1992). Evidence on the reliability and construct validity of Warr's (1990) well-being and mental health measures. *Journal of Occupational and Organizational Psychology, 65*(1), 33-49.

Sevastos, P. P. (1996). *Job-related affective well-being and its relation to intrinsic job satisfaction.* Unpublished PhD Thesis. Curtin University.

Shore, L. M., & Martin, H. J. (1989). Job satisfaction and organizational commitment in relation to work performance and turnover intentions. *Human Relations, 42*(7), 625-638.

Simmons, B. L., Nelson, D. L., & Quick, J. C. (2003). Health for the hopefuls: A study of attachments behavior in home health care nurses. *International Journal of Stress Management, 10*(4), 361-375.

Simons, F. (1998, March, 27th). Finding a balance. *The Australian Financial Review*, pp. 23-26.

Sims, H. P., Jr. (1979). Limitations and extensions to questionnaires in leadership research. In J. G. Hunt & L. L. Larson (Eds), *Crosscurrents in leadership research* (pp. 202-221). Carbondale, Illinois: Southern Illinois University Press.

Sinclair, R. C., & Mark, M. M. (1992). The influence of mood state on judgement and actions: Effects on persuasion, categorization, social justice, person perception and judgemental accuracy. In L. L. M. Tesser (Ed), *The construction of social judgements* (pp. 1165-1193). Hillsdale, New Jersey: Lawrence Erbaum.

Skarlicki, D. P., & Latham, G. P. (1996). Increasing citizenship behavior within a labor union: A test of organizational justice theory. *Journal of Applied Psychology, 81*(2), 161-169.

Slaski, M., & Cartwright, S. (2002). Health, performance and emotional intelligence: an exploratory study of retail managers. *Stress and Health, 18*, 63-68.

Smircich, L., & Stubbart, C. (1985). Strategic management in an enacted environment. *Academy of Management Review, 10*(4), 724.

Smith, C. A., Haynes, K. N., Lazarus, R. S., & Pope, L. K. (1993). In search of the 'hot' cognitions: Attributions, appraisals, and their relation to emotion. *Journal of Personality and Social Psychology, 65*(5), 916-929.

Smith, C. A., Organ, D. W., & Near, J. P. (1983). Organizational citizenship behavior: Its nature and antecedents. *Journal of Applied Psychology, 68*(4), 653-663.

Smith, P. M. (1998, July). *Emotional competence and job performance: Job analysis and individual assessment.* Paper presented at the International Work Psychology Conference, Sheffield, United Kingdom.

Smithson, M. L. (1999). *If not significance testing, what should we teach in introductory statistics courses for psychology and the social sciences?* Canberra, Australian Capital Territory: Australian Consortium for Political and Social Research Incorporated. Retrieved September 15. 1999, from http://www.acspri.org.au/

Snell, S. A., & Youndt, M. A. (1995). Human resource management and firm performance: Testing a contingency model of executive controls. *Journal of Management, 21*(4), 711-737.

Snyder, C. R., & Lopez, S. J. (Eds). (2002). *Handbook of positive psychology.* New York: Oxford University Press.

Snyder, C. R., Sympson, S. C., Ybasco, F. C., Borders, T. E., Babyak, M. A., & Higgins, R. L. (1996). Development and validation of the State Hope Scale. *Journal of Personality and Social Psychology, 70*(2), 321-335.

Sonnentag, S., & Frese, M. (Eds). (2002). *Performance concepts and performance theory*: Chichester: Wiley.

Spector, P. E. (1987). Method variance as an artifact in self-reported affect and perceptions at work: Myth or significant problem?. *Journal of Applied Psychology, 72*(3), 438-443.

Spector, P. E. (1997). *Job satisfaction: Application, assessment, cause and consequences.* Thousand Oaks, California: Sage.

Spector, P. E. (2005). Introduction: emotional intelligence. *Journal of Organisational Behaviour, 26*, 409-410.

Spector, P. E., Dwyer, D. J., & Jex, S. M. (1988). The relationship of job stressors to affective, health, and performance outcomes: A comparison of multiple data sources. *Journal of Applied Psychology, 73*, 11-19.

Spector, P. E., Fox, S., & Van Katwyk, P. T. (1999). The role of negative affectivity in employee reactions to job characteristics: bias effect or substantive effect? *Journal of Occupational and Organizational Psychology, 72*, 205-218.

Spector, P. E., Jex, S. M., & Chen, P. Y. (1995). Relations of incumbent affect-related personality traits with incumbent and objective measures of characteristics of jobs. *Journal of Organizational Behavior, 16,* 59-65.

Speier, C., & Frese, M. (1997). Generalized self-efficacy as a mediator and moderator between control and complexity at work and personal initiative: A longitudinal field study in East Germany. *Human Performance, 10*(2), 171-192.

Spencer, L. M., Jr., & Spencer, S. M. (1993). *Competence at work: Models for superior performance.* New York: Wiley.

Spencer, L. M., McClelland, D. C., & Keiner, S. (1997). *Competency assessment methods history and state of the art.* Boston, Massachusetts: Hay McBer Research Press.

Srivastava, A., Locke, E. A., & Judge, T. A. (2002). *Dispositional causes of task Satisfaction: The mediating role of chosen level of task complexity.* Paper presented at the Core self-evaluations: New developments and research findings. Symposium presentation at the Society for Industrial and Organizational Psychology Annual Meetings, Toronto.

Stacey, C. A., & Gatz, M. (1991). Cross-sectional age differences and longitudinal change on the Bradburn affect-balance scale. *Journal of Gerontology, 46*(2), 76-78.

Stampfer, H. G. (1998). The relationship between psychiatric illness and circadian pattern of heart rate. *Australian and New Zealand Journal of Psychiatry, 33*(2), 187-198.

Stampfer, H. G. (2005). *Diagnostic applications of 24-hour monitored heart rate in psychiatry.*Unpublished manuscript, Department of Psychiatry, The University of Western Australia: Perth, Western Australia.

Stansfield, S., Head, J., & Marmont, M. (2000). *Work related factors and ill health: The Whitehall II Study.*Sudbury, United Kingdom: HSE Books. Retrieved Dec 1. 2000, from http://www.hse.gov.uk/research/crr_pdf/2000/crr00266.pdf

Staw, B. M. (1984). Organizational behavior: A review and reformulation of the Field's outcome variables. *Annual Review of Psychology, 35,* 627-666.

Staw, B. M. (1986). Organizational psychology and the pursuit of the happy/productive worker. *California Management Review, 28*(4), 40-53.

Staw, B. M., & Barsade, S. G. (1993). Affect and managerial performance: A test of the sadder-but-wiser vs. happier-and-smarter hypotheses. *Administrative Science Quarterly, 38*, 304-331.

Staw, B. M., Bell, N. E., & Clausen, J. A. (1986). The dispositional approach to job attitudes: A lifetime longitudinal test. *Administrative Science Quarterly, 31*(1), 56-77.

Staw, B. M., & Cohen-Charash, Y. (2005). The dispositional approach to job satisfaction: more than a mirage, but not yet an oasis. *Journal of Organizational Behavior, 26*, 59-78.

Staw, B. M., & Ross, J. (1985). Stability in the midst of change: A dispositional approach to job attitudes. *Journal of Applied Psychology, 70*(3), 469-480.

Steers, R. M. (1975). Problems in the measurement of organizational effectiveness. *Administrative Science Quarterly, 20*(4), 546-558.

Steiger, J. H. (1989). *EzPath causal modeling: A supplementary module for SYSTAT and SYGRAPH*. Evaston, Illinois: SYSTAT Inc.

Steiger, J. H. (1990). Structural model evaluation and modification: An interval estimation approach. *Multivariate Behavioral Research, 25*, 173-180.

Stewart, R. (1989). Studies of managerial jobs and behaviour: The ways forward. *Journal of Management Studies, 26*(1), 1-10.

Stone, E. A. (1975). Stress and catecholamines. In A. Friedhoff (Ed), *Catecholamines and behavior - 2: Neuropsychopharmacology* (Vol. 2, pp. 31-72). New York: Plenum.

Stone, R. (2002). *Human resource management* (5th ed). Brisbane, Queensland: Wiley.

Storey, J. (1989). *New Perspectives on Human Resource Management*. London: Routledge.

Storey, J. (1992). *Developments in the management of human resources*. Oxford: Blackwell.

Storms, M. D., & Missal, K. D. (1976). Attribution processes and emotional exacerbation of dysfunctional behavior. In J. Harvey, W. Ickes & R. F. Kidd (Eds), *New directions in attribution research* (Vol. 1, pp. 143-164). Hillsdale, New Jersey: Erlbaum.

Strauss, G. (1968). Relations - 1968 style. *Industrial Relations, 7, May*, 262-276.

Suh, E., Diener, E., & Fujita, F. (1996). Events and subjective well-being: Only recent events matter. *Journal of Personality and Social Psychology, 70*, 1091-1102.

Summers, T. P., & Hendrix, W. H. (1991). Modeling the role of pay equity perceptions: A field study. *Journal of Occupational Psychology,*

64, 145-157.

Sweeney, P. D., Schaeffer, D. E., & Golin, S. (1982). Pleasant events, unpleasant events, and depression. *Journal of Personality and Social Psychology, 43*(1), 136-144.

Tabachnick, B. G., & Fidell, L. S. (1996). *Using multivariate statistics* (3rd ed). New York: HarperCollins.

Tabachnick, B. G., & Fidell, L. S. (2001). *Using multivariate statistics* (4th ed). New York: Allyn & Bacon.

Tabacknick, N., Crocker, J., & Alloy, L. B. (1983). Depression, social comparison and the false consensus effect. *Journal of Personality and Social Psychology, 45*(3), 688-699.

Tatsuoka, M. M. (1970). *Discriminant analysis: The study of group differences*. Champaign, Illinois: Institute of Personality and Ability Testing.

Taylor, F. W. (1947). *Scientific management*. New York: Harper & Row.

Taylor, S. E. (1991). The asymmetrical impact of positive and negative events: The mobilization-minimization hypothesis. *Psychological Bulletin, 110,* 68-85.

Teachout, M. S. (1991). *Understanding the work experience construct in personnel research and practice*. Paper presented at the Sixth Annual Conference of the Society for Industrial and Organizational Psychology Symposium, St. Louis, MO.

Tellegen, A. (1985). Structures of mood and personality and their relevance to assessing anxiety with an emphasis on self-report. In A. H. Tuma & J. Maser (Eds), *Anxiety and the anxiety disorders* (pp. 681-706). Hillsdale, New Jersey: Erlbaum.

Terpstra, D. E., & Rozell, E. J. (1993). The relationship of staffing practices to organizational level measures of performance. *Personnel Psychology, 46,* 27-48.

Teuchmann, K., Totterdell, P., & Parker, S. K. (1999). Rushed, unhappy, and drained: An experience sampling study of relations between time pressure, perceived control, mood, and emotional exhaustion in a group of accountants. *Journal of Occupational Health Psychology, 4,* 37-54.

Thayer, R. E. (1978). Towards a theory of multidimensional activation (arousal). *Motivation and Emotion, 2,* 1-33.

Thayer, R. E. (1989). *The Biopsychology of Mood and Arousal.* New York.

The Gallup Organisation (2005). *The Gallup Organisation*. Retrieved 11

/11/05. 2005, from http://www.gallup.com/

The Institute for Employment Studies. (2001). *A critical review of psychosocial hazard measures* [E113:01]. UK Health and Safety Executive.

The US National Institute of Occupational Safety (2005). *Workplace safety and health topics*: The US National Institute of Occupational Safety. 2005, from http://www.cdc.gov/niosh/homepage.html

The West Australian. (2001, May 15). ACTU launches push for cut in work hours. *The West Australian*, p. 8.

Theorell, T. (1993). Influence exercised on the surrounding field in psychosomatic projects. *Psychotherapie Psychosomatik Medizinische Psychologie, 43*(5), 183-187.

Thomas, G. (2004). Identity crisis. *Air Transport World Cleveland, 14*(19), 38.

Thorndike, E. L. (1921). Intelligence and its measurement: a symposium. *Journal of Educational Psychology, 12*(3), 124-127.

Thorndike, R. L. (1949). *Personnel selection: Test and measurement techniques*. New York: Wiley.

Tichy, N., Fombrun, C., & Devanna, M. A. (1982). Strategic human resource management. *Sloan Management Review, 23*(2), 47-61.

Tokar, D. M., & Subich, L. M. (1997). Relative contributions of congruence and personality dimensions to job satisfaction. *Journal of Vocational Behavior, 50*(3), 482-491.

Tomarken, A. J., & Keener, A. D. (1998). Frontal brain asymmetry and depression: A self-regulatory perspective. *Cognition and Emotion, 12*, 387-420.

Tornow, W. W., & Pinto, P. R. (1976). The development of a managerial job taxonomy: A system for describing, classifying and evaluating executive positions. *Journal of Applied Psychology, 61*, 410-418.

Tracey, B. (1993). *Maximum achievement*. New York: Simon & Schuster.

Travaglione, A. (1998). *The determinants and outcomes of organisational commitment*. PhD Thesis. The University of Western Australia.

Truman, H. S. (1976). Leadership: The biggest issue. *Time*.

Truss, C., Gratton, L., Hope-Hailey, V., McGovern, P., & Stiles, P. (1997). Soft and hard models of human resource management: a reappraisal. *Journal of Management Studies, 34*(1), 53-73.

Tsui, A. S., & Ohlott, P. (1988). Multiple assessment of managerial effectiveness: Inter-rater agreement and consensus in effectiveness models. *Personnel Psychology, 41*(4), 779-803.

Tubbs, T. C., & Collins, J. M. (2000). Jackson and Schuler (1985) revisited: A meta-analysis of the relationships between role ambiguity, role conflict, and job performance [1]. *Journal of Management, 26*(1), 155-169.

Tucker, D. M., & Williamson, P. A. (1984). Asymmetric neural control systems of human self-regulation. *Psychological Review, 91*(2), 185-215.

Tucker, L. R., Koopman, R. F., & Linn, R. L. (1969). Evaluation of factor analytic research procedures by means of simulated correlation matrices. *Psychometrika, 34*(4), 421-459.

Turnball, S. (1999). Emotional labour in corporate change programmes: The effects of organisational feeling rules on middle managers. *Human Resource Development International, 2*(2), 125-146.

U.S. Department of Labor. (1991). *What work requires of schools.* Washington, DC: Secretary's Commission on Achieving Necessary Skills (SCANS).

Ullman, J. B. (1996). Structural equation modeling. In B. G. Tabachnick & L. S. Fidell (Eds), *Using multivariate statistics* (3rd ed, pp. 709-819). New York: Harper Collins.

Ulrich, D. (1997). *Human resource champions.* Boston, Massachusetts: Harvard University Press.

Umstsot, D. D., Bell, C. H., & Mitchell, T. R. (1976). Effects of job enrichment and task goals on satisfaction and productivity: Implications for job design. *Journal of Applied Psychology, 61*, 379-394.

Van de Snepscheut, J. L. A. (1993). *Springer texts and monographs in computer science.* New York: Springer-Verlage New York, Inc.

Van der Klink, J. J. L., Blonk, R. W. B., Schene, A. H., & Van Dijk, F. J. H. (2001). The benefits of interventions for work related stress. *American Journal of Public Health, 91*(2), 270-276.

Van Dyne, L., Cummings, L. L., & McLean-Parks, J. (1995). Extra-role behaviours: In pursuit of construct and definitional clarity (A bridge over muddied waters). *Research in Organizational Behavior, 17*, 215-285.

Van Dyne, L., & LePine, J. A. (1998). Helping and voice extra-role behaviors: Evidence of construct and predictive validity.

Academy of Management Journal(41), 108-119.

Van Rooy, D. L., & Viswesvaran, C. (2004). Emotional intelligence: A meta-analytic investigation of predictive validity and nomological net. *Journal of Vocational Behavior, 65*, 81-95.

Varghese, S. A. (2004). Transforming language into business influence: A tutorial on persuasion. *Education Review of Business Communication, 1*(1), 57-68.

Veenhoven, R. (1995a). Developments in satisfaction research. *Social Indicators Research, 37*, 1-46.

Veenhoven, R. (1995b). World database of happiness. *Social Indicators Research, 34*, 299-313.

Vickers, G. (1965). *The art of judgement: A study of policy making* (Vol. 3). London: Harper & Row Publishers.

Vinchur, A. J., Schippmann, J. S., Switzer, F. S., & Roth, P. L. (1998). A meta-analytic review of the predictors of job performance for salespeople. *Journal of Applied Psychology, 83*(4), 586-597.

Viswesvaran, C., Ones, D. S., & Schmidt, F. L. (1996). Comparative analysis of the reliability of job performance ratings. *Journal of Applied Psychology, 81*(5), 557-560.

Vroom, V. H. (1964). *Work and motivation.* New York: Wiley.

Waldman, D. A., & Avolio, B. J. (1986). A meta-analysis of age differences in job performance. *Journal of Applied Psychology,* 33-38.

Wall, T., & Clegg, C. (1981). A longitudinal field study of group work redesign. *Journal of Occupational Behaviour, 2*, 31-49.

Wall, T. D., Kemp, N. J., Jackson, P. R., & Clegg, C. W. (1986). Outcomes of autonomous work groups: A long-term field experiment. *Academy of Management Journal, 29*(2), 280-304.

Wall, T. D., & Wood, S. J. (2005). The romance of human resource management and business performance, and the case for big science *Human Relations, 48*(4), 429-462.

Wallis, C. (2005, January 17th). The new science of happiness: What makes the human heart sing? Researchers are taking a close look. What they've found may surprise you. *Time: Online Edition, 165(3),* A2.

Walz, S. M. (1995). *Organizational citizenship behaviors: Their effect on organizational effectiveness in limited-menu restaurants.* PhD Dissertation Thesis. Kansas State University.

Walz, S. M., & Niehoff, B. P. (1996). Organizational citizenship behaviors and their effects on organizational effectiveness in limited-menu restaurants. In J. B. Keys & L. N. Dosier (Eds), *Academy of Management best paper proceedings* (pp. 307-311). Columbia, South Carolina: Academy of Management.

Warr, P. B. (1986). A vitamin model of jobs and mental health. In H. W. Debus & H. W. Schroiff (Eds), *The psychology of work and organisation: Current trends and issues* (pp. 157-164). Amsterdam, Holland: Elsevier Science.

Warr, P. B. (1987). *Work, unemployment and mental health.* Oxford, United Kingdom: Clarendon Press.

Warr, P. B. (1990a). Decision latitude job demands and employee well-being. *Work & Stress,* 4(4), 284-294.

Warr, P. B. (1990b). The measurement of well-being and other aspects of mental health. *Journal of Occupational Psychology,* 63(3), 193-210.

Warr, P. B. (1991). Mental health, well-being and job satisfaction. In B. Hesketh & A. Adams (Eds), *Psychological perspectives on occupational health and rehabilitation.* Marrickville, New South Wales: Harcourt Brace Jovanovich.

Warr, P. B. (1992). Age and occupational well-being. *Psychology and Aging,* 7(1), 37-45.

Warr, P. B. (1994a). Age and job performance. In J. Snel & R. Cremer (Eds), *Work and aging in Europe* (pp. 309-322). London: Taylor and Francis.

Warr, P. B. (1994b). Age and work. In P. Collett, & A Furnham (Ed), *Social psychology at work* (pp. 236-253). London: Routledge.

Warr, P. B. (1994c). *Aging and employment*: Palo Alto, CA: Consulting Psychologists Press.

Warr, P. B. (1994d). A conceptual framework for the study of work and mental health: A healthier work environment. *Work & Stress,* 8(2), 84-97.

Warr, P. B. (1996a). Employee well-being. In P. B. Warr (Ed), *Psychology at work* (4th ed). London,, United Kingdom: Penguin.

Warr, P. B. (1999). Well-being and the workplace. In D. Kahneman, E. Diener & N. Schwarz (Eds), *Well-being: The foundations of hedonic psychology* (pp. 392-412). New York: Russell Sage Foundation.

Warr, P. B. (Ed). (1996b). *Psychology at work* (4th ed). London, United Kingdom: Penguin.

Warr, P. B., Barter, J., & Brownbridge, G. (1983). On the independence of positive and negative affect. *Journal of Personality and Social Psychology, 44*, 644-651.

Warr, P. B., Cook, J., & Wall, T. D. (1979). Scales for the measurement of some work attitudes and aspects of psychological well-being. *Journal of Occupational Psychology, 52*, 129-148.

Waterfield, R. (1993). *Letter on happiness*. London, United Kingdom: Elbury Press.

Watson, D. (1988). Intra-individual and inter-individual analyses of positive and negative affect: Their relation to health complaints, perceived stress and daily activities. *Journal of Personality and Social Psychology, 54*, 1020-1030.

Watson, D. (2000). *Mood and temperament*. New York: Guilford Press.

Watson, D., & Clark, L. A. (1984). Negative affectivity: The disposition to experience aversive emotional states. *Psychological Bulletin, 96*(3), 465-490.

Watson, D., & Clark, L. A. (1992a). Affects separable and inseparable: On the hierarchical arrangement of the negative affects. *Journal of Personality and Social Psychology, 62*(3), 489.

Watson, D., & Clark, L. A. (1992b). On traits and temperament: General and specific factors of emotional experience and their relation to the Five-Factor model. *Journal of Personality, 60*, 441-476.

Watson, D., Clark, L. A., & Carey, G. (1988). Positive and negative affectivity and their relation to anxiety and depressive disorders. *Journal of Abnormal Psychology, 97*(3), 346-353.

Watson, D., Clark, L. A., & Tellegen, A. (1988). Development and validation of brief measures of positive and negative affect: The PANAS Scales. *Journal of Personality and Social Psychology, 54*, 1063-1070.

Watson, D., & Pennebaker, J. W. (1989). Health complaints, stress, and distress: Exploring the central role of negative affectivity. *Psychological Review, 96*(2), 234-254.

Watson, D., Pennebaker, J. W., & Folger, R. (1987). Beyond negative affectivity: Measuring stress and satisfaction in the workplace. In J. M. Ivancevich & D. C. Ganster (Eds), *Job stress: From theory to suggestion* (pp. 141-157). New York: Haworth Press.

Watson, D., & Slack, A. K. (1993). General factors of affective temperament and their relation to job satisfaction over time. *Organizational Behavior and Human Decision Processes, 54*,

181-202.

Watson, D., & Tellegen, A. (1985). Towards a consensual structure of mood. *Psychological Bulletin, 98*(2), 219-235.

Watson, D., Vaidya, W. D. J., & Tellegen, A. (1999). The two general activation systems of affect: Structural findings, evolutionary considerations, and psychobiological evidence. *Journal of Personality and Social Psychology, 76*, 820-838.

Wawn, T., & Green, J. (1995). *Experienced insights: Opinions of Australian managers, ideals, strengths and weaknesses.* Canberra: AGPS.

Way, S. A. (2002). High performance work systems and intermediate indicators of firm performance within the US small business sector. *Journal of Management Studies, 28*, 765-785.

Wayne, S. J., & Green, S. A. (1993). The effects of leader-member exchange on employee citizenship and impression management behavior. *Human Relations, 46*(12), 1431-1440.

Weick, K. E. (1979). *The social psychology of organisations.* Reading, Massachusetts: Addison-Wesley.

Weiner, B. (1974). *Achievement motivation and attribution theory.* Morristown, New Jersey: General Learning Press.

Weiner, B. (1985). An attributional theory of achievement, motivation, and emotion. *Psychological Review, 92*(4), 548-573.

Weiss, H. M., & Cropanzano, R. (1996). Affective events theory: A theoretical discussion of the structure, causes and consequences of affective experiences at work. In B. M. Staw & L. L. Cummings (Eds), *Research in organizational behavior: An annual series of analytical essays and critical reviews* (Vol. 18, pp. 1-74). Greenwich, CT: JAI Press, Inc.

Weiss, H. M., Nicholas, J. P., & Dauss, C. S. (1999). An examination of the joint effects of affective experiences and job beliefs on job satisfaction and variations in affective experiences over time. *Organizational Behavior and Human Decision Processes, 78*, 1-25.

Wernefelt, B. (1984). Resource-based view of the firm. *Strategic Management Journal, 5*, 171-180.

Werner, J. M. (1994). Dimensions that make a difference: Examining the impact of in-role and extra-role behaviors on supervisory ratings. *Journal of Applied Psychology, 79*, 98-107.

West, M., Arnold, J., Corbett, M., & Fletcher, B. (1992). Editorial:

Advancing understanding about behavior at work. *Journal of Occupational and Organizational Psychology,* 65(1), 1-3. Editorial.

Westerman, J. W., & Rosse, J. G. (1997). Reducing the threat of rater non participation in 360-degree feedback systems: An exploratory examination of antecedents to participation in upward ratings. *Group & Organization Management,* 22(2), 288-309.

Westwood, R. I., & Posner, B. Z. (1997). Managerial values across cultures: Australia, Hong Kong and the United States. *Asia Pacific Journal of Management,* 14, 31-66.

Whetton, D. A., & Cameron, K. S. (1991). *Developing management skills in Australia.* South Melbourne, Victoria: Longman.

Whetton, D. A., & Cameron, K. S. (1995). *Developing Management Skills.* New York: Harper Collins.

Whetton, D. A., & Cameron, K. S. (2001). *Developing management skills* (5th ed): Prentice Hall.

Wheway, J., Mackay, C. R., Newton, R. A., Sainsbury, A., Boey, D., Herzog, H., et al. (2005). A fundamental bimodal role for neuropeptide Y1 receptor in the immune system. *Journal of Experimental Medicine,* 202, 1527-1538.

Whittle, S., Allen, N. B., Lubman, D. I., & Yucel, M. (2005). The neurobiological basis of temperament: Towards a better understanding of psychopathology. *Neuroscience and Biobehavioral Reviews, 1-15.*

Widaman, K. F. (1985). Hierarchically nested covariance models for multi-trait-multimethod data. *Applied Psychological Measurement,* 9(1), 1-26.

Wiener, Y., & Vardi, Y. (1980). Relationships between job, organization and career commitments and work outcomes - An integrative approach. *Organizational Behavior and Human Performance,* 26, 81-96.

Williams, D. G. (1989). Neuroticism and extraversion in different factors of the affect intensity measure. *Personality and Individual Differences,* 10(10), 1095-1100.

Williams, K. J., & Alliger, G. M. (1994). Role stressors, mood spillover and perceptions of work-family conflict in employed parents. *Academy of Management Journal,* 37(4), 837-868.

Williams, L. G., & Podsakoff, P. M. (1989). Longitudinal field methods for studying reciprocal relationships in organizational behavior research: Toward improved causal analysis. *Research in Organizational Behavior, 11*, 247-292.

Williams, L. J. (1995). Covariance structure modeling in organizational research: Problems with the method versus applications of method. *Journal of Organizational Behavior, 16*(3), 225-234.

Williams, L. J., & Anderson, S. E. (1991). Job satisfaction and organizational commitment as predictors of organizational citizenship and in-role behaviors. *Journal of Management, 17*(3), 601-617.

Williams, L. J., & Anderson, S. E. (1994). An alternative approach to method effects by using latent-variable models: Applications in organizational behavior research. *Journal of Applied Psychology, 79*(3), 323-331.

Williams, R. (1991). Transformation or chaos? Human resources in the 1990s. *HR Monthly, November*, 1-10.

Williams, R. E. (1956). *A description of some executive abilities by means of the critical incident technique.* Doctoral Dissertation Thesis. Columbia University.

Williamson, D. (2005). *Wiliamson's play Influence/Operator.* Sydney: Strawberry Hills, Currency Press.

Wise, R. A. (1996). Addictive drugs and brain stimulation reward. *Annual Review of Neuroscience, 19*, 319-340.

Witt, L. A. (1991). Exchange ideology as a moderator of job-attitudes-organizational citizenship behavior relationships. *Journal of Applied Social Psychology, 21*(18), 1490-1501.

Wolfe-Morrison, E. (1994). Role definitions and organizational citizenship behavior: The importance of the employee's perspective. *Academy of Management Journal, 37*(6), 1543-1567.

Wood, R., & Marshall, V. (1993). *Performance appraisal: Practice problems and issues,* Paris, France: Puma, OECD.

Wood, R. E., & Bandura, A. (1989). Impact of conceptions of ability on self-regulatory mechanisms and complex decision-making. *Journal of Personality and Social Psychology, 56*, 407-415.

Woodruffe, C. (1992). What is meant by a competency? In R. Boam & P. Sparrow (Eds), *Designing and achieving competency* (pp. 16-30). London, United Kingdom: McGraw-Hill.

World Health Organization (2005a). *Mental health and working life: Impact, issues and good practices.* Helsinki, Finland, from http://www.euro.who.int/document/mnh/ebrief06.pdf

World Health Organization (2005b, 7 May 2005). *WHO European Ministerial Conference on Mental Health: Facing the Challenges, Building Solutions*.Helsinki: WHO. Retrieved 1 Sep 2005. 2005, from http://www.euro.who.int/mentalhealth2005

Wright Mills, C. (1959). *The sociological imagination*. New York: Oxford University Press.

Wright, P. M., Gardner, T. M., Moynihan, L. M., & Allen, M. R. (2005). The relationship between HR practices and firm performance: Examining causal order. *Personnel Psychology, 58*(2), 404-447.

Wright, T. A., & Cropanzano, R. (1997). Well-being, satisfaction and job performance: another look at the happy/productive worker thesis. *Academy of Management Proceedings*, 364-371.

Wright, T. A., & Cropanzano, R. (2000). Psychological well-being and job satisfaction as predictors of job performance. *Journal of Occupational and Health Psychology, 5*(1), 84-94.

Wright, T. A., Cropanzano, R., Denney, P. J., & Moline, G. L. (2002). When a happy worker is a productive worker: A preliminary examination of three models. *Canadian Journal of Behavioural Science, 34*(3), 146-150.

Wright, T. A., Larwood, L., & Denney, P. J. (2002). The different 'faces' of happiness-unhappiness in organizational research: Emotional exhaustion, positive affectivity, negative affectivity, and psychological wellbeing as correlates of job performance. *Journal of Business and Management, 8*(2), 109-126.

Wright, T. A., & Staw, B. M. (1999a). Affect and favorable work outcomes: Two longitudinal tests of the happy-productive worker thesis. *Journal of Organizational Behavior, 20*(1), 1-23.

Wright, T. A., & Staw, B. M. (1999b). Further thoughts on the happy-productive worker. *Journal of Organizational Behavior, 20*(1), 31-34.

Wright, W. F., & Bower, G. H. (1992). Mood effects on subjective probability assessment. *Organizational Behavior and Human Decision Processes, 52*, 276-291.

Youndt, M. A., Snell, S. A., Dean, J. W., & Lepak, D. P. (1996). Human resource management, manufacturing strategy, and firm performance. *Academy of Management Journal, 39*(4), 836-866.

Yukl, G. (2002). *Leadership in organizations*. Delhi, India: Pearson Education.

Yukl, G. A. (1998). *Leadership in organizations* (4th ed). Upper Saddle

River, NJ: Prentice Hall.

Zikmund, W. G. (2002). *Business research methods* (7th ed). Mason, Ohio: Thompson Learning South-Western.

Zohar, D. (1999). When things go wrong: The effects of daily work hassles on effort, exertion and negative mood. *Journal of Occupational and Organizational Psychology, 72*, 265-283.

Index

8-Dimensional Model xx, 192–4, 198–200, 262, 324

abbreviations 329–30
Abdel-Halim, A.A. 302
Abraham, L.M. 46
Ackrill, J.L. 30
activation theory 53–4
activity theories 53–9
Adams, A. 289
Adolphs, R. 30, 42
Adsit, D.J. 152
AET (Affective Events Theory) 47–8
affective organisational commitment 320–21
affective wellbeing
  forms/typologies 27–9, 50
  measurement 32–3
  and performance 110–12
  as predictor of work outcomes 7
  principal axes 35
  promoting 274–6
  and questionnaire construction 318
  research conclusions 230–31
  research origins 29–32
  theories 51–3, 53–9, 60–66
age differences 305–6
Agho, A.O. 48–9, 116, 240
Ahearne, M. 94
Akande, A. 134
Akiran, N.K. 331
Alexander, R.A. 315
Allen, M.R. 12
Allen, N.B. 44
Allen, N.J. 150, 320, 323
Allen, T.D. 309
Alley, W.E. 317
Alliger, G.M. 297
Allman, A. 36
Alloy, L.B. 293

Allport, G.W. 65
Allred, B.B. 290
Ambady, N. 68
Amenson, C.S. 51
Ammeter, A.P. 248
Anderson, J.C. 143, 145, 190
Anderson, N. 308–9
Anderson, S.E. 98, 227, 322
Andrewartha, G. 73
Andrews, K.R. 7
Antonioni, D. 152
anxiety
  and motivation 283
  and PA/NA 52–3
  and stress xxv, 19
Appelbaum, E. 12
Appraisal Interview School 79, 82
Argyle, M. 32, 72, 292
Argyris, C. 76, 78
Aristotle 30, 53
Armstrong, H. 73
Armstrong, J.S. 230
Arnold, J. 7
Arvey, R.D. 46, 53, 176, 201
Ash, R.A. 314
Asher, H.B. 189
Ashforth, B.E. 20
Ashkanasy, N.M. 4, 17, 66–7, 311–13, 326
ASSET (An Organizational Stress Screening Tool) 19, 247
Athanasou, J.A. 134
attribution theory 287–9
Atwater, L.E. 253
Avolio, B.J. 267, 306
Ayestaran, S. 134

Bagnall, D. xvi, 30, 292, 295
Bagozzi, R.P. 188
Bailey, J.R. 68

Bailey, T. 12
Balzer, W. 83
Bandura, A. 80, 282, 285–6
Bar-On, R. 67, 311–12
Barbano, H.E. 52
Barker, C. 271
Barling, J. 17, 60, 134, 151, 285
Barnard, C. 99, 243
Barnes-Farrell, J.L. 83
Barney, J.B. 272
Baron, R.A. 24, 113, 254, 294
Barrett, L.F. 82
Barrick, M.R. 6, 177, 306, 308–10, 320
Barsade, S.G. 4, 6, 16, 47, 67, 109, 113–14, 155, 291, 293–4, 308
Barter, J. 37
Bartlett, M. 179
Bartz, D.E. 83
Bass, B.M. 248
Bateman, T.S. 99, 114
Bateson, A.G. 80
Baum, J.R. 282
Beattie, R. 285
Beatty, R. 82, 274
Beck, A.T. 59
Becker, B.E. 11–12
Beehr, T.A. 153
Beer, M. 10, 124, 242
Befort, N. 23
behavioural guidelines 254
Beittenhausen, K.L. 14, 288
Bell, C.H. 303
Bell, N.E. 46
Bellarosa, C. 275
Belmaker, R.H. 292
Benjamin, J. 292
Bennett, E. 276
Bennis, W. 81, 248, 270
Bent, D. 213
Bentham, J. xvi, 327
Bentham, Jeremy xvi–xvii
Bentler, P.M. 142–5, 160, 188–91
Berg, P. 12
Bernard, J.R.L. 29
Bernardin, H.J. 82, 274
Bernheim, J. 48, 282
Berntson, G.G. 42
Berry, W.D. 189

BES (behavioural engagement system) 41–2
Birdi, K. 55, 113–14
Birren, J.E. 65
BIS (Behavioural Inhibition System) 41–2
Biswas-Diener, R. 4
Bladen, A. 144
Blair, D. 29
Blakley, B.R. 315
Bless, H. 293
Blonk, R.W.B. 275
Bobko, P. 147, 227
Bochner, S. 134
Bohle, P. 272
Bollen, K.A. 145, 179, 190, 197
Bommer, W.H. 73, 159, 176–7, 211
Bonett, D.G. 190
Bono, J.E. 6, 303
Boomsma, D.I. 143
Borman, W.C. 13, 24, 74, 78, 80, 89, 93–106, 111, 116, 126, 132, 153, 175–6, 180–81, 183, 186, 269, 284, 286, 309, 314, 321, 331, 333, 336–7, 341
Bouchard, T.J. 46
Bower, G.H. 110, 286
Boyatzis, R.E. x, 74, 78, 86–8, 90, 92, 103, 243, 248, 253, 271, 311, 322, 331
Bracken, D.W. 152
Bradburn, N.M. 32–3, 37, 39, 69
Brammall, B. 14
Brayfield, A.H. 5, 46, 49, 109, 131
Brett, J.M. 133
Bretz, R.D. 319
Breusch, J. 15
Brewer, J. 122
Brief, A.P. 4, 10, 24, 31, 33–4, 49, 51, 69, 98, 100, 110, 113, 130, 227, 241, 254–5, 284–6, 294, 319, 337
Broadbent, D.E. 292
Brody, N. 307
Brogden, H.E. 258
Brooks, R. 13–14
Brown, B. 267
Brown, K.A. 48, 51

Brown, S.P. 248, 276
Brownbridge, G. 37
Browne, M.W. 190
Bruni, L. xvii, 72, 292, 327
Brush, D.H. 24, 78, 94, 96, 99, 103–6,
    111, 126, 132, 183, 186, 321, 331,
    333, 341
Bryman, A. 189
Buchanan, T. 310
Buckingham, M. 252, 268
Buckley, M.R. 248
Burke, M.J. 33–4, 49, 51, 110, 130,
    184, 227
Burke, R.J. xi
burnout *see* mental health problems
Burns, N. 129
Burrell, G. 79, 298
Burrows, G.C. 34
Butler, S. 29
Bycio, P. 189
Byosiere, P. 299–300
Byrne, B.M. 124, 144–6, 177–8,
    186–8, 190–91, 197–8, 201–2,
    204–5, 207

Cacioppe, R. 76, 304
Cacioppo, J.T. 42
Cage, T. 68
Callan, V. 134
Cameron, K.S. x–xi, 75, 78, 90, 285,
    294–5, 332, 335
Cammock, P. 75–6, 79, 89–92, 133,
    332
Campbell, C.H. 284
Campbell, D.J. 301
Campbell, D.T. 153, 178, 205
Campbell, J.P. 23, 73–5, 80, 82, 86,
    105, 112, 153, 251, 281–4, 291,
    314
Campbell, J.P. 104
Campion, M.A. 314
Canonical Correlation 147–8, 211–16,
    227–8
Caplan, R.D. 20, 54, 113
Caplovitz, D. 39
Cardy, R.L. 113
Caretta, T.R. 309
Carey, G. 40, 52

Carlopio, J. 48, 73, 76, 248, 261
Carlson, M. 255
Carnevale, A.P. 243
Caroll, S.A. 312
Carretta, T.R. 309
Carroll, J.B. 307
Carroll, J.M. 42, 82, 129
Carruthers, F. 268
Cartwright, S. 15–16, 21, 275, 311
Caruso, D.R. 17, 67–9, 311–12
Cascio, W.F. 13–14, 306
Cass, M. 19, 50, 108
Castaneda, M.B. 190
Cattell, R.B. 139, 141
Caza, A. 294
CFA (Confirmatory Factor Analysis)
    41, 143–5, 209
CFI (Comparative Fit Index) 190
Chaiken, S. 319
Champoux, J. 56
Champy, J. 14
Charlin, V. 255
Chen, P.Y. 46, 52–3, 227, 275, 303
Cheraskin, L. 314
Chernis, C. 266
Child, D. 174
Chou, C.P. 142–3, 160, 189
Christensen, C.R. 7
Church, A.H. 152
Chynoweth, C. 267
Cialdini, R.B. 126, 133, 271
Clark, A. 46, 305
Clark, D.A. 59
Clark, L.A. 33, 39–42, 46, 51–3, 111,
    116, 126, 130–31, 169, 172, 210,
    212, 246, 308, 319
Clausen, J.A. 46
Clegg, C.W. 20, 46, 49, 292, 302
Cleveland, J.N. 82–3, 153
Cliff, N. 148, 213
Cobb, S. 54, 113
Cochran, D.S. 99
Coetzee, C. 249
Coffman, C. 252, 268
Cohen-Charash, Y. 47
Cohen, D. 243
Cohen, J. 303
Cohen, S. 15, 19, 295, 314, 316

Collins, J. 15, 257, 259–61, 276, 285, 303
Collins, R.R. 276
Colvin, R.C. 36, 59
competence 290–91
Competing Values Framework 80, 84–5
competitive advantage 10, 276–7
Compton, R.L. 59, 84
Comrey, A.L. 139, 142–3, 183
Conger, J. 81, 253
Connolly, J.J. 46
conscientiousness 308–9
Conte, J.M. 67, 311–13
context-free affective wellbeing 27–9
contextual performance
 antecedents 98
 conception 101
 EFA analysis 180–83
 extra-role behaviour 98
 importance 254–5
 and managers tasks 321–4
 measuring 102, 337
 mega-dimensions definitions 336
 and organisational effectiveness 95
 and task performance 93–5, 95–6
contingency theory 289–90
Converse, J. 123
Conway, J.M. 175
Conway, N. 10
Cook, J. 28, 49, 111, 126, 131, 210, 212
Cook, K.W. 259
Cooksey, R.W. 128
Cooper, C.L. xi–xii, 15–17, 19, 21, 29, 50–51, 54, 108, 151, 247, 275, 321
Cooper, L.M. 297
Coovert, M.D. 314
Corbett, M. 7
Cordery, J.L. 130–31, 134, 141, 300
core affect 32
Cornford, I.R. 134
Cornoni-Huntley, J. 52
Costa, P.T. 37, 40–41, 51–2, 129, 246, 310
Côté, S. 67, 112
Cox, T. 34, 247

Coy, R. 271
Coyle-Shapiro, J. 3–4, 98–9, 253, 276
Coyne, J.C. 44
Crabtree, S. 272
Craiger, J.D. 314
Cramer, D. 189
Crampton, S.M. 177
Cranny, C. 48
Crawford, J.R. 306
Crawford, M.S. 315
Crocker, J. 293
Crockett, W.H. 5, 46, 109
Cronbach, L.J. 127, 133, 142
Cropanzano, R. 3–5, 7, 16, 46–7, 67, 69, 107, 109–10, 113, 115, 208, 221, 285, 293–4
Crump, C.E. 16
Csikszentmihalyi, M. 58, 295
Cudeck, R. 190, 251
Cummings, L.L. 53–4, 69, 98, 292
Cummings, T. 244–5
Cunningham-Snell, N. 309
Cunnington, B. 14
Cutler, H. 72
Czaja, S.J. 305

Dakin, S. 75, 91
Dalai Lama 31
Damasio, A.R. 16, 30–31, 53, 66
Damasio, H. 30
Daniel, W. 188
Danner, D.D. 4
data analysis techniques
 calibration 145–6
 Canonical Correlation 147–8, 211–16, 227–8
 CFA 41, 143–5, 209
 EFA 139–40
 factor loadings 142–3
 factor rotation 141
 MLE 140
 MTMM 146–7, 201–2, 204–9
 overview 139, 149
 scree tests 141
 Standard Multiple Regression analysis 148–9, 217–22
data sample
 characteristics 159–68

collection of 137–9
constraints 150
cross-sectional data 136–7
demographics 135–6, 162–3
educational qualifications 164
experience 163
multisample 160, 197–9
nominal information 161–2
recruitment 136
representativeness 160–61
responsibility levels 166–8
sector 163
seniority 165
tenure 163
work areas 166
Daus, C.S. 66–8, 249, 294, 311–13
David Brent (*The Office*) xvii–xviii
Davidson, R.J. 41–2, 129
Davies, D.R. 39
Davis, A.S. 247
Davis-Blake, A. 46
Dawda, D. 311
Dawis, R.V. 80, 289
Dawkins, P. 334
Day, A.L. 312
De Cieri, H. 89, 332
De Jonge, J. 130
De Jonge, J.E. 299
De Nisi, A.S. 152, 257
De Vader, C.L. 80, 177, 287
De Vries, D.L. 81
Dean, J.W. 11
Deary, I.J. 306
decision making 14
DeCotiis, T.A. 320
DeFrank, R.S. 275
Delaney, J.T. 11
Delbridge, A. 29, 73
Deluga, R. 99, 256
Demand Control Model 55–6, 59
demographics of data sample 135–6
Denney, P.J. 4–5, 113
depression xviii, 18, 52–3
depressive-realism 6–8, 293–4
Detweller, J.B. 253
Devanna, M.A. 242
Deves, L. 332
Dewe, P. 10

Dickson, W.J. 3
Diener, E. xix–xx, 34–8, 40, 43, 47–8, 50–51, 59–60, 65, 111, 295, 320
Digman, J.M. 310
Dijkstra, T. 189
Dillon, W.R. 213–14, 216
Dipboye, R.L. 150, 153
discretionary effort, rewarding 268–9
disengaged employees xv–xvi, 272–3
disposition 51
dispositional affect 47–8
dispositional theories 51–3
distress 19, 59
Dive, B. 13
Dobbins, G.H. 113
Dodd, N.G. 299, 301–2
Domeyko, M. 30
Donaldson, G. 272
Dorsey, D.W. 101
Douglas, C. 248
downsizing 13, 14
Dreyfuss, J. 251
Drucker, P. 305
DuBois, D. 314, 316–17
Dulewicz, V.P. 92
Dumler, M.P. 99
Dunford, R. 14
Dunham, R.B. 190
Dunnette, M.D. 23, 98, 154
Dunphy, D. 244
Durham, C.C. 48
Dutton, J.E. x, 295
Dwyer, D.J. 36

Eagly, A.H. 319
Eales, J. 271
Earles, J.A. 306–7, 309, 318
Earnshaw, J. 21
Easterbrook, G. 268
Ebstein, R.P. 292
ECI (Emotional Competence Inventory) 311
Edwards, H. xvii
Edwards, J.R. 20
EFA (Exploratory Factor Analysis) 139–40
effectiveness of managers 89–93
Ekman, P. 41

Elfenbein, H. 68
Elias, M.F. 305
Elias, P.K. 305
Emerson, R.W. 252
Emmons, R.A. 34–5, 37, 51
emotion 31–2, 41–5
emotional competences 266
emotional intelligence 17, 66–70, 249–52, 311–13
emotional responses 7, 16
employee disengagement xv–xvi, 272–3
employee respect 256–7
End State theories 60–66
enthusiastic-naivety 6–8, 293–4
environment changes xiv–xv
Epicurus 30, 31
EQ-i (Bar-On Emotional Quotient Inventory) 311–13
EQS computer program 144–5
Erikson, E. 65
Erwin, P.J. 59
ESM (Evaluative Space Model) 42–3
ethical considerations 155–6
eustress 19, 59
Evans, P. 49
expectancy theory 284–5
experience 313–15
extrinsic job satisfaction 46
Eysenck, H.J. 41
Eysenck, M.W. 41

Fabrigar, L.R. 140–41
facet-specific affective wellbeing 27–9
factor loadings 142–3
factor rotation 141
Faerman, S.R. 13, 80, 85
Faff, R.W. 13–14
Faragher, B. 19
Faragher, E.B. 19, 45, 50, 108, 268
Farr, J.L. 82
Fay, D. 20
Fayol, H. 75
Fedor, D.B. 14, 288
feedback to managers 263–5
Feldman Barrett, L. 31–2, 38, 42, 129
Feldman, S. 189
Fenwick, M. 89, 332

Ferris, G.R. 154, 248, 300–301
Fetter, R. 94
Fidell, L.S. 140–42, 148–9, 179–80, 188, 213–14, 227–8, 323
Fidell, L.S. 179
Fiedler, F.E. 81
financial incentives 268
findings of this book xx–xxii
Fischoff, B. 293
Fisher, C.D. 3, 5–6, 9, 17, 82, 153
Fisher, V.E. 3
Fiske, D.W. 153, 178, 205
Flanagan, J.C. 103
Flanagan, M.F. 150, 153
flatter structures 14
Fletcher, B. 7, 56, 64, 302
Florida, R. 245
Folger, R. 37
Fombrun, C. 242
Ford, J.K. 128, 314–17
Forgas, J.P. 110, 286, 293
Forster, N. 15, 19–21, 257, 260, 262, 271, 275, 291
Fosterling, F. 286
Foucault, M. 122
Four Factor Model of Affective Wellbeing 130–31, 168–74
Fox, M.L. 52
Fox, S. 303
French, J.R.P., Jr. 20, 54, 113
Frese, M. 150–51, 281–2, 302
Fried, Y. 154, 300–301
Friesen, W.V. 4, 41
Frone, M.R. 297
Fujita, F. 38, 47–8, 320
functionalist research 78–9
Fund, S. 67
Furr, M.R. 34

Gabriel, P. 17–18
Gaetz, M. 45
Gage, P. 305
Galgay Roth, P. 284
Ganster, D.C. 16, 52, 57, 294, 299, 301–2
Gardner, D. 48
Gardner, D.G. 53–4, 69, 292
Gardner, P. 6

Gardner, T.M. 12
Gardner, W.L. 42, 78, 90
Gasser, M. 74
Gast, I.F. 337
Gates, G.R. 128
Gatz, M. 52
Gebhardt, D. 16
Gellatly, I.R. 51
George, J.M. 5, 24, 31, 33–4, 36, 49, 51, 98, 110, 113, 177, 227, 241, 248–9, 254–5, 284–7, 294, 337
Gerbing, D.W. 143–5, 190
Gerhart, B. 11, 292
Gerlach, M.L. 81
Gerras, S.J. 317
Gervais, R. xvii
Gibb, R. 16
Giga, S.I. 19–20, 272, 274–5
Gignac, G.E. 312
Gingrich, K.F. 301
Gioia, D.A. 79, 83, 298
Gist, M.E. 285
Glendenning, P.M. 83
globalisation 13, 13–16, 273–4
GMA (General Mental Ability) 258–9, 306, 306–8
Goffin, R.D. 51, 146, 202, 205
Goldberg, L.R. 310
Goldman, S.L. 37
Goldman, S.L. 34
Goldstein, M. 213–14, 216
Goleman, D. 17, 67, 69, 80–81, 248, 250–52, 257, 266–7, 290–91, 302
Golin, S. 51
Good Soldier Effectiveness Model 101
Googleplex 245
Gowing, M.K. 311
Graen, G.B. 113, 246
Graham, J.W. 337
Gratton, L. 243
Green, D.P. 34, 37–8
Green, J. 334
Green, S.A. 99, 256
Green, S.G. 229
Griffin, M.A. 78, 96–8, 128, 248, 255
Griffin, R.W. 303
Griffiths, A. 247
Grove, S.K. 129

Grube, J.A. 190
Guadagnoli, E. 142
Guehenno, J.M. 14
Guest, D.E. 10, 15, 242
Guion, R.M. 80, 290
Gunningham, C.J. 270
Gupta, N. 153

Hackett, R.D. 189
Hackman, J.R. 54, 292, 298–303
Haidt, J. 294
Hair, J.F. 140–42, 145, 147–9, 179–80, 188, 191, 213–14, 216, 228
Hakstian, A.R. 141
Hales, C.P. 90, 95
Hall, D.T. 265
Hamel, G. 10, 12, 128
Hamilton, J.G. 143–4
Hammer, M. 14
Hampson, I.L. 276
Handley, R. 67
Handy, C.B. xiii, 12, 20
Hanna, J.V. 3
Hanson, P.G. 10
happier-and-smarter 6–8, 293–4
happiness xvi–xvii, 29–32, 70–72
  see also job-related affective wellbeing
'happy-performing managers' proposition xiv
'happy-productive worker' thesis
  commonsense theory xiii, 9
  and contemporary managerial issues 13–16
  evidence 5–6
  history xiii, 3–5
  and mental health 16–18
  overview 25–6, 107–9
  revisited 291–3
  significance 10–13
'hard' forces, v 'soft' 242–4
Harris, A. 249
Harris, M.M. 144
Harrison, R.V. 54, 113
Hart, S.D. 311
Hart, S.L. 75, 77–8
Hartel, C.E.J. 313
Harter, J.K. 6, 11–12, 47, 109

Harter, S. 121
Haslam, N. 38
hassles 48
Hatcher, C. 249, 271
Hausdorf, P.A. 189
Hawthorne studies 3
Haybron, D.M. 29–30
Haynes, K.N. 250
Hays, T.L. 6, 11–12, 109
Head, J. 277
Heatherton, T.F. 188
Hedge, J.W. 317
hedonic treadmill xvi
Heene, A. 276
Heider, F. 177, 287
Heller, D. 240, 318
Heller, W. 58
Hemphill, J.K. 103
Hendrix, W.H. 321
Hendry, C. 242
Heneman, R.L. 73
Hennessey, H.W. 78
Hermelin, E. 309
Hersey, R. 3
Herzberg, F. 3, 46, 268
Hesketh, B. 86, 289, 292
Heylighten, F. 48, 282
Hezlett, S.A. 309
Hill, L.A. 270
Hillman, L.W. 83
Hilton, M. 276
Hinkin, T.R. 142
Hippocrates 41
History of Happiness in Economics (Bruni) xvii
Hoebel, B.G. 42
Hoetler, J.W. 143
Hoffman, R.R. 315
Hofmann, D.A. 317
Hogan, J. 133
Holdsworth, S. 335
Hollenbrook, J.R. 292, 304
Holmes-Smith, P. 141, 180
home life 29
Hooijberg, R. 77
hope, generating 249–50
Hope-Hailey, V. 243
Hoppock, R. 3, 45

Hosie, P.J. xiv, 63, 156, 270
Hough, L.M. 98, 154
House, R.J. 297
Hoyle, R.H. 323
Hsee, C.K. 69
Hu, L. 189–90
Huelsman, T.J. 34
Hulin, C.L. 116
Hull, H. 213
Human Behaviour School 3
Human Relations Movement x, 3–4
human resource practices 10–12, 255–73
Hunter, A. 122
Hunter, J.E. 73, 258–9, 283, 286, 306–9, 313–15, 318, 322
Hunter, M. 308
Hunter, R.E. 259, 313–14
Hurley, A.E. 144
Hurrell, J.J. 56
Huse, E. 244–5
Huselid, M.A. 11–12
Huy, O.N. 249
hyperstress 19
hypostress 19
hypotheses, Measurement Model
  (1) 175–6, 200
  (2.1) 176, 200
  (2.2) 176–7, 201
  (3) 177, 177–8, 208–9
hypotheses, research
  (1) 112–13, 221, 224
  (2) 113–14, 224
  (3) 114, 224
  (4) 115, 224
  (5) 115, 225
  (6) 115–16, 225
  (7) 116–17, 225
  (8) 117, 225–6
hypotheses, results 222–6

Iaffaldano, M.T. 5, 49, 109
Ichniowski, C. 11–12, 16
Ilgen, D.R. 4, 82–3, 288, 292, 304
Ilies, R. 46–7, 310
individual differences
  age 305–6
  Big-Five personality traits 310

conscientiousness 308–9
GMA 258–9, 306, 306–8
job knowledge 315–18
personality 309–10
theory of 286–7
work experience 313–15
see also emotional intelligence
Influence: The Psychology of Persuasion (book, Cialdini) 271
Influence (play, Williamson) xvii
influencing 271–2
internal reliability 141–2
Internet, exacerbating 24/7 demand 13
intrinsic job satisfaction 45–6, 49–50, 131, 318–20
Iran-Nejad, A. 43
Irwin, D.A. 41
Isen, A.M. 24, 108, 113, 254, 294
Iverson, G. 45
Iverson, R.D. 59
Izard, C. 17

Jackson, D.N. 51, 146, 202, 205
Jackson, P.R. 20
Jackson, S.E. 11, 23
Jacobs, R. 317
Jago, I.A. 315
Jamal, M. 131
James, K. 5, 46
James, L.R. 133
James, R. 16
Jansen, P. 89, 176
JCM (Job Characteristics Model) 299–303
Jenkins, J. 213
Jensen, A.R. 307
Jex, S.M. 36, 303
job, terminology 28
Job Affect Scale 33
job categorisation 134–5
job design 244–5
job features 298–304
job knowledge 315–18
job-related affective wellbeing 27–9, 31, 39–41
job satisfaction
  and affective wellbeing 110–12
  and performance 6

recent research 45–7
as synonym for affective wellbeing 5
varying with age 305
and workplace mental health xxv
see also intrinsic job satisfaction
job stress 278–9
Johnson, J.A. 310
Johnson, J.L. 73
Johnson, J.V. 57
Johnson, S. 19, 247, 321
Johnston, R. 80
Jones, B.W. 113
Jones, E.E. 177, 287
Jones, F. 302
Jones, G.R. 10, 80, 84, 95, 98, 177, 287, 289–90
Jordan, P.J. 68, 313
Jöreskog, K.G. 144, 193–4
Judge, T.A. 6, 9, 23, 46–9, 107–9, 111, 116, 177, 239–40, 284, 303, 309, 318–20
Judiesch, M.K. 258
Jung, C.G. 31, 65

Kahn, H. 17
Kahn, J.A. 84
Kahn, R.L. 98–9, 175, 299–300, 337
Kahneman, D. xvi–xvii, 237, 268
Kalleberg, A.L. 12
Kane, J.S. 152
Kanner, A.D. 44, 47
Kano, Y. 189
Kanungo, R. 290
Kaplan, R.S. 92, 333, 335
Karambayya, R. 24, 100
Karasek, R.A. 20, 50, 54–7, 59, 64–5, 69–70, 298, 318
Karpin, D. 10, 14, 74, 89, 135, 248
Kasl, S.V. 56
Kattrup, K. 23
Katz, D. 98–9, 175, 337
Katz, R.L. 88, 98
Katzell, R.A. 108–9
Keating, M. 14
Keener, A.D. 41–2
Kegelmeyer, J. 116
Keiner, S. 68
Kelloway, K.E. 17, 60, 134, 144, 151

Kemp, N. 46
Kemp, N.J. 20
Kenny, D.T. 13, 247, 274–5
Ketelaar, T. 41, 51
Keyes, C.L.M. 12, 60, 65–6, 69, 294
Kidder, D.L. 98
Kim, J. 180, 184
Kinder, A. 309
King, L. xix
King, S. P. 4
Kinicki, A.J. 273
Kitney, G. 14
Klemp, G. 283
Kline, P. 180
Kluger, A.N. 9, 48, 152
Knott, J.R. 41
Koestner, J. 46
Koestner, R. 46
Koh, W.L. 254
Koivumaa-Honkanen, H. 4
Kolb, D. 92
Konovsky, M.A. 5, 36, 46, 99–100, 102, 114, 126, 132, 254, 256
Koopman, R.F. 141
Kornhauser, A.W. 3
Koslowski, S.W.J. 6
Kotter, J. 322
Krzystofiak, F. 113
Kuncel, N.R. 309

Labroo, A.A. 294
Lado, A.A. 23
Lance, C.E. 317
Landsbergis, P.A. 54, 56, 64
Landy, F.J. 67–8, 82, 313
Lane, R. 16
Lange, J. 229
Langer, E. 293
Larsen, J.T. 42
Larsen, R.J. 35, 41, 51
Larson, J.R. 123, 150, 153
Larwood, L. 113
Larzelere, R. 147
Latham, G.P. 83–4, 99, 110, 254, 256, 283
Lawler, E.E. xi–xii, 12, 23, 116, 152
Lawrence, P.R. 10, 124, 242
Lawthom, R. 11

Lay Model of Least and Most Effective Managers 90–92
Layard, R. xvi–xvii, 292, 327
Lazarus, R.S. 44, 250
Lazzarini, A.J. 34
leaders 74
leadership 248–9
Lebel, P. 13
Ledford, G.E., Jr. 4, 12, 51, 127, 292
LeDoux, J.E. 42
Lee, C. 253
Lee, H.B. 142–3, 183
Lee, T. 20
Legge, K. 242
legislation applicable to stress 279
Leigh, T.W. 248, 276
Lemmon, H. 306
Leong, F. 321
Lepak, D.P. 11
LePine, J.A. 94
Levi, L. 16, 247, 319
Levine, E.L. 314
Levine, S. 35
Lewinsohn, P.M. 51
Lewis, A.T. 78
Lichtenstein, S. 293
Lievens, F. 309
Liimatainen, M.R. 17–18
Limerick, D. 14
Lingl, A. 99, 114, 126, 319
Linn, R.L. 141
Lirtzman, S.I. 297
litigation, and stress 20–21
Livingston, J.S. 14, 248
Locke, B.Z. 52
Locke, E.A. 5, 45, 48, 67, 84, 109–10, 116, 282–4, 303, 313
Lofquist, L.H. 80, 289
Lombardo, M.M. 314, 334
London, M. 152
Long, J.S. 145
Longnecker, C.O. 83
Lopes, P.N. 67
Lopez, S.J. 294
Lord, R.G. 80
low energetic arousal 34
low strain jobs 55
Lubinski, D. 286

Lubman, D.I. 44
Luthans, F. 78, 89–90, 176, 250, 284
Lyubomirsky, S. xix–xx, 237, 295

MacCallum, R.C. 140, 143, 190, 323
Mackay, C.J. 34, 39
Mackay, H. 21
MacKenzie, S.B. 94–6, 98, 100, 110, 153, 262, 269
Macmillan, I. 15
Magnus, K. 320
Mahoney, T.A. 92
Maier, N.R.F. 82
Maister, H. 12, 256–7, 268
Major, D.A. 4
managerial theory 21–3
managers
  compared to workers xiv
  competency and performance measures 331–5
  competitive advantage through 10
  definitions 73–5
  implications for 241–55
  performance research 23–4
  roles 75–8, 277–8, 303–4
Managers not MBAs (Mintzberg) 269–71
Mandl, M. 84
Maney, K. 245
Manion, J. 264
Manning, M.R. 45
Manocha, R. 312
Mardia, K.V. 188
Mark, G.P. 42
Mark, M.M. 293
Marmont, M. 277
Marsh, H.W. 190
Marshall, J. 54
Marshall, V. 81–3, 85–6, 261
Martin, H.J. 321
Martin, M. 32, 293
Martin, P. xvi, 262, 268, 292, 327
Martin, R. 136, 302
Martinko, M.J. 78, 90
Maslow, A.H. 65, 282
Mastekaasa, A. 4
matched pairs 159
Mathieu, J.E. 150, 248

Matthews, G. 39
Mausner, B. 3
Mayer, J.D. 17, 66–9, 80, 252, 312
Mayer, R.C. 320
Mayer–Salovey–Caruso Emotional Intelligence Test (MSCEIT V.2) 311–12
Mayo, E. 39
Mazzarol, T. 334
MBAs (USA, full-time) 269–71
MBO (Management by Objectives) 82
  see also Performance Management School
McAdam, D.W. 41
McCall, M.W. 314
McCarthy, T.E. 59
McCauley, C.D. 334
McClelland, D.C. 68, 80, 253, 281–3, 287
McCoy, R.A. 75, 251
McCrae, R.R. 37, 40–41, 51–2, 129, 246, 310
McDaniel, M.A. 258, 314
McDonald, D. 84
McDougal, W. 43
McEvoy, G.M. 306
McGovern, P. 243
McGovern, T.V. 113
McGrath, M.R. 13, 80, 85
McGraw, P.A. 42
McIntyre, D. 274
McKee, A. x, 67, 248, 253
McKee, A. S. 314, 316–17
McKee, F.M. 273
McKellin, D.B. 83
McKenna, E.F. 279, 290
McKenzie, R.C. 258
McKenzie, S.B. 73
McKnight, M.R. 253
McLaney, M.A. 56
McLean-Parks, J. 98
McLennan, W. 134, 164
Measurement School 79, 81–2
MEIS (Multifactor Emotional Intelligence Scale) 311
Mendham, C.A. 57
mental health xxv, 60–63

mental health problems xviii–xix,
  16–19
Merchant, S. xvii
methodology employed
  affective wellbeing measures 128–31
  choice of 121–2, 150
  concepts, constructs, dimensions and
    measures 126–7
  constraints and limitations 150–56,
    226–30
  expert review and pilot 123–4
  intrinsic job satisfaction measures
    131
  measurement instrument
    development 132–4, 174–5
  methods 124–5
  overview xxii, 24, 137, 156–7
  sample characteristics 134–7
  unit of analysis 127–8
  see also model testing strategy
Meyer, G.J. 36, 41, 51, 320–21
Meyer, J.P. 51, 150, 320, 323
Micceri, T. 150
Michie, J. 10
Midili, A.R. 116
Mikkelsen, A. 272
Miles, R.E. 290
Millar, D.J. 16
Miller, N. 255
Millett, B. 76, 304
Mills, D.Q. 10, 124
Milton, J. 16
Mineka, S. 42
Miner, J.B. 282, 284
Mintzberg, H. 14, 74, 76–7, 113, 126,
  132–3, 243, 248, 252–3, 269–70,
  290, 323
Misra, S. 290
Missal, K.D. 286
Mitchell, J.L. 152
Mitchell, T.R. 48, 51, 153, 229, 244,
  285, 303
ML/MLE (Maximum
  Likelihood/Estimation) 140
Model for Effective Performance
  (Boyatzis) 86–8, 323
Model of Good Soldier Effectiveness
  101

Model of Managers' Affective
  Wellbeing and Performance 297–8
Model of Performance (Neal & Griffin)
  96–8
model testing results 192–4, 199–201
model testing strategy 187–91
Mohr, M.F. 98
Mohrman, S.A. 12
Molenaar, P.C.M. 143
Moline, G.L. 4–5
Moorhead, G. 303
Moorman, R.H. 99, 109, 154, 256
Morgan, D.E. 276
Morgan, G. 79, 298
Morris, S.E. 113
Morrison, A.M. 81, 314
Morrison, E.W. 99
Morse, J.J. 78
motivating people 261
motivation theory 281–3
Motowidlo, S.J. 13, 24, 45, 74, 80, 89,
  93–104, 106, 110–11, 114, 116,
  126, 132, 153, 175–6, 180–81,
  186, 269, 282, 284, 286, 309, 321,
  336–7
Mount, M.K. 6, 23, 177, 240, 306,
  308–10, 318, 320, 333
Moylan, S.J. 110
Moynihan, L.M. 12
MTMM (Multitrait–Multimethod
  Method) 146–7, 201–2, 204–9
Muchinsky, P.M. 5, 49, 109
Mueller, C.W. 48–9, 127, 142, 180,
  184
Mulaik, S.A. 133
Muldrow, T.W. 258
Muliak, S. 147
multirater/multisource assessment
  151–3, 195–7
multisample 160, 197–9
Münsterberg, H. 47, 68
Murphy, K.R. 74, 82–3, 95, 103, 133,
  153, 176, 201
Murphy, L.R. 14
Murphy, R.J.L. 228
Muthen, B. 197

NA (Negative Affect) 33

Nacoste, R.W. 98
Nankervis, A. 12, 19, 59, 75, 242
Nanus, B. 248
Nathan, B.R. 315
Neal, A. 78, 96–8, 128, 255
Near, J.P. 45, 53, 98–100, 337
Nelson, D.L. 249
Nemanick, R.C., Jr. 34
Newman, J. 113
Nicholas, J.P. 294
Nicholson, N. 17
Nickell, S. 11
Nickols, F. 264–5
Nie, N. 213
Niehoff, B.P. 99, 256
Nilakant, V. 75, 91
Nisbett, R.E. 177, 287
Nitschke, J.B. 58
NNFI (Non-Normed Fit Index) 190
Noe, R.A. 154
Norton, D.P. 92, 333, 335
Nunnally, J.C. 169, 178
Nytrö, K. 272

OCB (Organisational Citizenship Behaviour) 24, 95, 98–100, 253
Offermann, L.R. 68
Ohlott, P. 152
Ohmae, K. 14
older workers 305–6
Oldham, G.R. 54, 292, 298–303
Ones, D.S. 105, 306, 309
Oppler, S.H. 75, 314
O'Reilly, C.A. 11, 15, 260, 276, 282, 285
Organ, D.W. 3, 7, 24, 36, 45, 53, 78, 93–5, 98–102, 109–10, 114, 116, 126, 132, 151, 154, 177, 243, 250, 254–6, 261, 263, 269, 319, 322, 337
organisational effectiveness of managers 92–3
organisations, implications for 273–9
Oshagbemi, T. 45
Osipow, S.H. 247
Ostroff, C. 128, 317
Oswald, A. 46, 55, 114, 305
Oswald, F. 74

O'Toole, J. 270
Outerbridge, A.N. 306–7, 309, 315, 318, 322
Overton, T.S. 230

PA (Positive Affect) xxi–xxii, 6–8, 33, 259, 261, 285–6
Packard, J.S. 45
Page, C. 92
Paine, J. 3, 78, 93–5, 99–101, 109–10, 151, 243, 250, 255, 261, 263
pair congruence 159
Palmer, B.R. 312
Palmer, I. 14
PANAS (Positive Affect and Negative Affect Schedule) 33–7, 37–9, 129–30, 168–74
PANAS-Plus 308
Panter, A.T. 312, 323
Park, A. 235, 259
Parker, R.S. 257
Parker, S.K. 48
Parkes, K.R. 56–7, 229
Parks, J.M. 98
Partial Model (of Managers' Affective Wellbeing, Intrinsic Job Satisfaction and Performance) 8, 111–12, 237–9
Pascal, Blaise 30
Pasmore, W.A. 79
Patterson, M. 11, 16, 273
Patton, G.K. 6
Paunonen, S.V. 51
Pavot, W.G. 35–6
Payne, R. 51, 151
Payne, R.L. 56, 64
Payne, W.L. 67
Pearsall, P. 27
Peck, M.S. 255
Pedhazur, E.J. 189
Pennebaker, J.W. 36–7, 40, 129
Penner, L.A. 116, 309
performance 47–8, 96–8, 110–12
performance appraisal 78–80, 80–81, 85–6, 261–3
see also feedback to managers
Performance Management School 79, 83–4

performance measurement xxv, 78–80,
    105–6, 132–4
performance mega-dimensions 103–4
performance rating errors 154–5
performance theory 283–4
Perrow, C. 4
personality 309–10
Peter, L. 4
Peters, P. 29
Peterson, M.F. 134, 297
Pettigrew, A. 95, 242
Pettijohn, C.E. 257
Pfeffer, J. 11, 15, 46, 80, 128, 260, 276,
    282, 285, 289
Phillips, L.D. 293
physical health 29
Pinneau, S.R., Jr. 54, 113
Pinto, P.R. 103
Pithers, R.T. 134, 331
Pitre, E. 79, 298
Plato 30
Ployhart, R.E. 13, 105
Podsakoff, P.M. 51, 73, 94–6, 98, 100,
    102, 110, 126, 132, 151, 154, 262,
    269, 322
Pond, S.B. 98, 322
Pope, L.K. 250
Porras, J.I. 260, 276, 285
Porter, L.W. 4–5, 109, 116
Porter, M.E. 7, 14, 128
POS (Positive Organisational
    Scholarship) xix, 23, 294–6
Posner, B.Z. 260
Pothos, E.N. 42
Prahalad, C.K. 10, 128
Prati, L. 248
Prennushi, G. 11, 16
Presser, S. 123
Pressman, S.D. 15, 19, 295
Price, J.L. 48–9, 127, 142
Pritchard, R.D. 86, 281, 284
Pritzker, M.A. 295
Prosocial Organisational Behaviour
    100
prototypical emotional episodes 32
Proust, Marcel 31
psychological disorders *see* mental
    health problems

Pugh, S.D. 99, 254, 256
Pulakos, E.D. 314, 337
Purcell, J. 11, 253, 276, 320

questionnaires
    administration 137–9
    development 132–4, 174–5
    Managers' Wellbeing and
        Performance Questionnaire
        342–53
Quick, J.C. 249
Quinlan, M. 272
Quinn, J.B. 74, 132
Quinn Mills, D. 10, 242
Quinn, R.E. x–xi, 75–8, 80, 84–5,
    89–90, 92, 95, 105, 126, 283, 295,
    333
Quinones, M.A. 313–17

Rada, P.V. 42
Raghunathan, T.R. 178
Randall, D.M. 150, 154
Randall, R.S. 11
Rao, M.V.H. 79
Rasmussen, K.G. 113
RCFI (Robust Comparative Fit Index)
    190
Rebert, C.S. 41
recruitment, of managers 257–61
recruitment, research participants 136
Ree, M.J. 306–7, 309, 318
Reichers, A.E. 162–3
Reinhold, B.R. 13
Renner, V.J. 65
research needed 17, 296–8
research questions 112, 239–41
retention, of key employees 267–8
retention, of managers 257
Revesz, P. 188
Rhee, K. 67
Rheem, H. 83
Rial-Gonzalez, E. 247
Rich, G.A. 73
Rindskopf, D. 144
Rizzo, J.R. 297
RMSEA (Root Mean Square Error of
    Approximation) 143, 190
Robbins, M.A. 305

Robbins, S.P. 76, 304
Roberson, L. 34, 49
Roberts, B. 133
Roberts, R.D. 312
Robertson, I.T. 309
Robinson, B.S. 33, 49, 51
Robinson, S.L. 99, 254, 256
Rodriguez, C.M. 98
Roethlisberger, F.J. 3
Rogers, C.R. 65
Rogers, W.T. 141
Rogg, K. 13
Rosenberg, S. 104
Rosenkrantz, S.A. 78
Ross, J. 50, 69–70, 284
Ross, P. 60
Rosse, J.G. 152
Roth, P.L. 282
Rothe, H.F. 46, 49, 131
Rothman, A.J. 253
Rothman, J. 333
Rowe, P.M. 315, 317
Rozell, E.J. 11, 257
Rubin, R.S. 68
Russell, B. 72
Russell, J.A. 31–3, 35, 38–9, 42, 82, 129
Russell, M. 297
rust out 19
Ryan, A.M. 309
Ryan, K. 99, 132, 177
Ryff, C.D. 60, 65–6, 69

S-Bχ^2 (Satorra-Bentler chi-square) 144–5
Sacco, J.M. 13
Sackett, P.R. 123, 150, 153
sadder-but-wiser 6–8, 293–4
Sager, C.E. 75
Saks, A.M. 6
Saksvik, P.Ø. 272
Sala, F. 67
Salgado, J.F. 308–9
Salovey, P. 17, 34, 37, 67–9, 80, 252–3, 311–12
Saltzman, J. 308
Sanchez, R. 276
Sandvik, E. 35–6

Sandwith, P. 290
Saron, C.D. 41
Sass, M. 68
Satorra, A. 144–5, 188–9, 191
Saul, K. 68
Saul, P. 288, 332, 334
Sauter, S.L. 14
Savery, L. 334
Saville, S. 335
Schaap, P. 249
Schaefer, C. 44
Schaeffer, D.E. 51
Schaubroeck, J. 16, 52–3, 144
Schaufeli, W.B. 299
Schene, A.H. 275
Schimmack, U. 43
Schippmann, J.S. 282
Schmidt, F.L. 6, 11–12, 50, 73, 105, 109, 258, 283, 286, 306–10, 313–15, 318, 322
Schmit, M.J. 24, 74, 93, 95–7, 102–3, 116, 286
Schmitt, N. 13, 146, 246, 314, 316
Schnake, M. 99, 256
Schon, D. 76
Schoorman, F.D. 320
Schuler, R.S. 15, 23
Schwandt, D.R. 83
Schwarz, N. 111, 293
Schweiger, D.M. 257
Schweizer, K. 139
Scott, W.R. 76, 81, 254
scree tests 141
Scullen, S.E. 23
Seal, C. 68
Sedlak, A. 104
Segal, N.L. 46
Sego, D.J. 314, 317
selection of high-performing managers 257–61
self-assessment 151–3, 195–7
self-efficacy 285–6
self-image 29
self-knowledge 252–3
self-report 153–4, 195, 228–30
Seligman, M.E. P. 295
Seligman, M.E.P. 72, 294–5
Seltzer, J. 248

Selye, H. 19, 59–60
Senge, P.M. 78
Senulis, J.A. 41
Sevastos, P.P. 6, 8, 35, 38, 44, 49,
    57–9, 69–70, 111, 114–15, 117,
    126–7, 130–31, 134, 141, 169,
    210, 212, 228, 247, 300, 318
Shack, J.R. 36, 41, 51, 321
Sharit, J. 305
Sharp, A.A. 3
Shavelson, R.J. 197
Shaw, K. 11, 16
Sheehan, M. 10
Shore, L.M. 321
Shullman, S.L. 81
Simmons, B.L. 249–50
Simons, F. 14
Sims, H.P., Jr. 153
Sinclair, R.C. 293
Sitarenios, G. 312
Skarlicki, D.P. 99, 254, 256
Slack, A.K. 240, 284
Slaski, M. 311
Smircich, L. 79, 289
Smith, A. 84
Smith, C.A. 98–100, 250, 254, 320,
    337
Smith, H. 38
Smith, K.G. 282
Smith, L. 130–31, 134
Smith, P. 48
Smith, P.M. 20
Smith, P.B. 134
Smith, R.C. 270
Smith, R.K. 68
Smither, J.W. 152
Smithson, M.L. 214
Snell, S.A. 11
Snow, C.C. 290
Snowdon, D.A. 4
Snyder, C.R. 249, 294
Snyderman, B. 3
social cognition theory 285–6
Social Cognitive Process School 79, 83
social desirability, in responses 154
social life 29
'soft', v 'hard' forces 242–4
Sonnentag, S. 20, 281

Sorbom, D. 193–4
Sorra, J. 314
Sosik, J.J. 267
Southwest Airlines 245–6
Spataro, S.E. 4
Spector, B. 10, 124, 242
Spector, P.E. 11, 36, 46, 52–3, 56, 64,
    66, 227, 259, 303
Speer, J. 317
Speier, C. 282
Spellacy, F. 308
Spence, L. 271
Spencer, L.M., Jr. 68, 80, 135, 243,
    290, 334
Spencer, S.M. 80, 135, 290, 334
Spreitzer, G.M. 77, 295
squeezing the pips xiii, 12–13, 327
Srivastava, A. 303
Stace, D. 244
Stacey, C.A. 52
Stammers, R.B. 39
Stampfer, H.G. 44–5
Standard Multiple Regression analysis
    148–9, 217–22
Stang, D. 293
Stansfield, S. 277
Starr, J.M. 306
state, distinction from trait 36
Staw, B.M. 4–7, 16, 22, 46–7, 50–51,
    53, 67, 69–70, 108–9, 113–15,
    127, 131, 137, 150, 154–5, 283–4,
    286, 291–4, 308
Steers, R.M. 103, 254
Steiger, J.H. 190
Steinbrenner, K. 213
Stevens, M.J. 314
Steward, W.T. 253
Stewart, B. 59
Stewart, R. 78, 89–90, 95
Stewart-Weeks, M. 333
Stiles, P. 243
Still, L. 20–21
Stone, E.A. 48, 300
Stone, R. 13
Stoop, B. 89, 176
Storey, J. 242–3
Storms, M.D. 286
Stough, C. 312

Strahan, E.J. 140
Strauss, E. 308
Strauss, G. 3
Strauss, J.P. 308
stress
　causing physical illness 278–9
　definitions 18
　and the law 20–21
　public recognition of xvii–xviii
　as symptom of depression and anxiety xxv, 19
　terminology xxv, 19
　and wellbeing 321
　in the workplace 18–20
Stress in the Workplace: How to Cause it (Edwards) xvii
stressors, in the workplace 247–8
Stubbart, C. 289
Stults, D.M. 146
Subich, L.M. 319
Sugawara, H.M. 190
Suh, E. 47–8
Summers, T.P. 320–21
Super Factor (Second-Order Level) Model 65–6
Sweeney, P.D. 51
Switzer, F.S. 282

Tabachnick, B.G. 140–42, 148–9, 179–80, 188, 213–14, 227–8, 323
Tabacknick, N. 293
Tackling work-related stress (HSE) 275
task performance 93–6, 183–6, 338–41
Tatsuoka, M.M. 213
taxes, and happiness xvi
Taylor, F.W. 81–2
Taylor, S.E. 293
Teachout, M.S. 314, 316–17
Telic theories 60–66
Tellegen, A. 33–5, 37–9, 41–3, 52, 116, 130, 172, 212
tenure, lack of 13
Terborg, J.R. 254
Terpstra, D.E. 11
test strategy 187–91
Teuchmann, K. 48
Thayer, R.E. 34, 39

Theorell, T. 16, 50, 54–5, 69–70, 298–9
Thomas, G. 246
Thompson, D.E. 108–9
Thompson, M.P. 13, 80, 85
Thoresen, C.J. 6
Thorndike, E.L. 67
Thorndike, R.L. 81
Tichy, N.M. 242
Tikochinsky, J. 9
Time magazine xvi
Tokar, D.M. 319
Tomarken, A. J. 41–2
Tornow, W.W. 103
Totterdell, P. 48
Tower, S.L. 4
Tracey, B. 3, 29, 31, 66
training of managers 265–7
trait affect 36, 51
Tranel, D. 30
Trattner, M.H. 322
Travaglione, A. 101
Troth, A.C. 68
Truss, C. 243
Tschirhart, M. 78, 332
Tsui, A.S. 152
Tubbs, T.C. 303
Tucker, D.M. 69
Tucker, L.R. 141
Turnball, S. 17
Turner, L. 331
Twain, Mark 31
Two Factor Bipolar Model 130–31

Uhl-Bien, M. 246
Ullman, J.B. 160, 189–90
Ulrich, D. 244
Umstsot, D.D. 303
Understanding Influence for Leaders at all Levels (Barker & Coy) 271
unitarist research 78, 80–81
unmatched pairs 160
uplifts 48

Vaidya, W.D.J. 33
van Dam, K. 309
Van de Snepscheut, J.L.A. 241
Van der Klink, J.J.L. 275

Van Dijk, F.J.H. 275
Van Dyne, L. 94, 98
Van Harrison, R. 20
Van Katwyk, P.T. 303
Van Rooy, D.L. 313
Van Scotter, J.R. 94–6, 114, 153, 176
Vance, C.A. 259
Vardi, Y. 101
Varghese, S.A. 271
Vasilopoulos, N.L. 68
Veenhoven, R. 30, 72
Velicer, W.F. 142
Vickers, G. 133
Vinchur, A.J. 282
Viswesvaran, C. 46, 105, 309, 313
Vitamin Model 60–61, 64–5, 298–9
von Rabenau, C. 57
Vroom, V.H. 5, 80, 109–10, 283–5, 291

Wade, K.J. 273
Wagner, F.R. 78
Wagner, J.A. 177
Waldman, D.A. 306
Wall, T.D. 12, 20, 28, 46, 136, 302
Walton, R.E. 10, 124
Walz, S.M. 99
Warr, P.B. 8, 17, 27–9, 33–5, 37,
    39–40, 44, 46, 48–50, 52–6, 58,
    60–66, 69–70, 108, 111–16,
    126–8, 130–32, 134, 177, 236–7,
    240, 246–7, 268, 285, 287, 289,
    298–9, 302, 305, 335
Watanabe, S. 46
Waterfield, R. 30
Waters-Marsh, T. 76, 304
Watson, D. 33–43, 46, 51–3, 111, 116,
    126, 129–31, 169, 172, 210, 212,
    227, 240, 246, 284, 308, 319
Wawn, T. 334
Way, S.A. 11
Wayne, S.J. 99, 256
Webster, J. 33–4, 49, 51
Wegener, D.T. 140
Weick, K.E. 16, 23, 289
Weiner, B. 86, 110
Weiss, H.M. 3–4, 7, 47, 107, 115,
    293–4
Welsh, D.H. 78

Wernefelt, B. 10
Werner, J.M. 269
West, M. 7, 121, 280
West, M.A. 11
Westerman, J.W. 152
Westerman, S.J. 39
Westwood, R.I. 260
Wexley, K.N. 83
Whalley, L.J. 306
Whetton, D.A. 75, 90, 285, 335
Wheway, 278
Whipp, R. 95
White, L.A. 101, 314, 337
Whittle, S. 44
*WHO Mental Health Action Plan for
    Europe* 18, 279–80
Widaman, K.F. 143
Wiechmann, D. 13
Wiener, Y. 101
Williams, D.G. 41
Williams, K.J. 297
Williams, L.G. 51, 151
Williams, L.J. 98, 144, 227, 322
Williams, R. 10
Williams, R.E. 103
Williamson, David xvii
Williamson, P.A. 69
Wilson, M. 92
Wilson, M.C. 23
Wise, R.A. 42
Witt, L.A. 254
Wold, H. 144
Wolfe-Morrison, E. 98–9, 254, 256, 322
Wonderlic Personnel Test 307–8
Wood, R. 81–3, 85–6, 229, 261, 285
Wood, S.J. 12
Woodruffe, C. 290
WORC (Work Outcomes and Cost
    Benefits) project 276
work adjustment theory 289
work environments 245–7
work, terminology 28
Wright Mills, C. 274
Wright, P.M. 12
Wright, T.A. 4–7, 12, 16, 47, 51, 67,
    69, 108–10, 113, 115, 127, 131,
    137, 150, 154–5, 208, 221, 240,
    283, 285–6, 292, 308, 328

Wright, W.F. 110, 286
Wu, E.J.C. 144, 189–90

Yammarino, F.J. 253
Yeow, L. 332
Yik, M.S. 82
Yoon, K. 310
Youndt, M.A. 11
Yucel, M. 44

Yukl, G.A. 78, 81, 103

Zajac, D.M. 150
Zapf, D. 150–51, 302
Zhou, J. 5
Zikmund, W.G. 122–3, 135–7, 162, 228
Zohar, D. 48
Zuckerman, M. 46